"Mike Barnett and the diverse team provided readers with an outstanding ~~~ ~~~ engaging with biblical, historical and contemporary understandings of and approaches to the mission of God. Comprehensive in its scope, insightful and up-to-date in its approach, kingdom-oriented in its focus, this important work fills a gap for missiologists, missionaries, pastors and students alike. *Discovering the Mission of God* will be a significant reference work to keep on hand for years to come."

DAVID S. DOCKERY, president, Union University

"Mike Barnett has pulled together a stellar group of Baptist and other Christian contributors to explore the mission of God as it has unfolded in the Scriptures, in history and throughout the world today. These compelling essays will offer solid guidance to a new generation of Great Commission Christians from many Protestant denominations."

TODD JOHNSON, associate professor of global Christianity, Gordon-Conwell Theological Seminary

"This book represents a clear voice in a muddled church world. In these rapidly changing days when we are prone to chasing the latest trends, *Discovering the Mission of God* provides a needed anchor. God has a mission. It includes the church. We need to discover it. We need to accomplish it. Few books enable God's people to do so like this one. May it cause the church to regain its focus on God's mission!"

J. PAUL NYQUIST, PH.D., president, Moody Bible Institute

"I commend to you Mike Barnett's new work, *Discovering the Mission of God*. I do believe it will become a standard work in the field of missiology. In this powerful copy, he combines the work of a multitude of scholars and practitioners in a thorough study of history, practice, and varying philosophies about God's mission. Scholarly, yet not pedantic, this new work is bound to find a unique place for those who seek a biblical and theologically correct understanding of God's plan for the ages. I commend it to you without hesitation."

FRANK S. PAGE, PH.D., President and Chief Executive Officer, SBC Executive Committee

"*Discovering the Mission of God* is a massive project of 38 chapters with almost as many authors. And the ebook supplement adds an additional 16 chapters! A book of this magnitude and authorship demands attention. Indeed it will serve as a missiological feast for years to come. Some of the articles will move you to stand up and shout 'amen!' Others will prove provocative and raise serious question marks in your mind. Good! Let's have a healthy Christian conversation and let the debate begin."

DANIEL L. AKIN, president, Southeastern Baptist Theological Seminary

"Barnett has pulled together a great team of authors who have clearly communicated the glorious mission of God powerfully advancing through the centuries."

DR. BILL JONES, president, Columbia International University

Best Missional Practices for the 21st Century

DISCOVERING
THE MISSION OF
GOD

Mike Barnett, Editor
Robin Martin, Associate Editor

IVP Academic
An imprint of InterVarsity Press
Downers Grove, Illinois

InterVarsity Press
P.O. Box 1400, Downers Grove, IL 60515-1426
World Wide Web: www.ivpress.com
E-mail: email@ivpress.com

InterVarsity Press® is the book-publishing division of InterVarsity Christian Fellowship/USA®, a movement of students and faculty active on campus at hundreds of universities, colleges and schools of nursing in the United States of America, and a member movement of the International Fellowship of Evangelical Students. For information about local and regional activities, write Public Relations Dept., InterVarsity Christian Fellowship/USA, 6400 Schroeder Rd., P.O. Box 7895, Madison, WI 53707-7895, or visit the IVCF website at <www.intervarsity.org>.

All Scripture quotations, unless otherwise indicated, are taken from the THE HOLY BIBLE, NEW INTERNATIONAL VERSION®, NIV® *Copyright © 1973, 1978, 1984, 2011 by Biblica, Inc.™ Used by permission. All rights reserved worldwide.*

Chapter 3 is excerpted from John Piper, Let the Nations Be Glad! *Baker Academic, a division of Baker Publishing Group, 2003. Used with permission.*

While all stories in this book are true, some names and identifying information in this book have been changed to protect the privacy of the individuals involved.

Interior design: Beth Hagenberg

ISBN 978-0-8308-5635-0

Printed in the United States of America ∞

 InterVarsity Press is committed to protecting the environment and to the responsible use of natural resources. As a member of Green Press Initiative we use recycled paper whenever possible. To learn more about the Green Press Initiative, visit <www.greenpressinitiative.org>.

Library of Congress Cataloging-in-Publication Data

Discovering the mission of God : best missional practices for the 21st century / Mike Barnett, editor ; Robin Martin, associate editor.
   p. cm.
   Includes bibliographical references.
   ISBN 978-0-8308-5635-0 (pbk. : alk. paper)
   1. Missions. I. Barnett, Mike. II. Martin, Robin.

BV2070.D57 2012
266—dc23

2012018666

P	20	19	18	17	16	15	14	13	12	11	10	9	8	7	6	5	4	3	2
Y	29	28	27	26	25	24	23	22	21	20	19	18	17	16	15	14	13	12

CONTENTS

Preface. 11
    Jerry Rankin

Acknowledgments. 15
    Mike Barnett

Introduction: Discovering the Mission of God 17
    Mike Barnett

PART ONE: THE MISSION OF GOD IN THE BIBLE. . . 31

GOD'S MISSION

1. Word of God and Mission of God. 33
    Christopher J. H. Wright

2. The Missionary Message of the New Testament 49
    Joel F. Williams

3. The Supremacy of God in Missions Through Worship 68
    John Piper

4. The Kingdom of God and His Mission 85
    Alex Luc

5. God's Great Commissions for the Nations 99
    Jeff Lewis

GOD'S METHOD

6. Jesus Christ—the Living Word—and the Mission of God . . 114
    Bryan E. Beyer

7. The Heart of the Task 130
    Zane Pratt

8. The Church in the Mission of God 144
    Preben Vang

GOD'S POWER

9. The Power of the Gospel 158
   Robert L. Plummer

10. The Passion of Christ and the Martyrs. 171
    Jerry Rankin

PART TWO: THE MISSION OF GOD IN HISTORY . . . 187

ANCIENT ERAS

11. The First Decades of the Mission of God 189
    William J. Larkin Jr.

12. The Ante-Nicene Church on Mission 205
    John Mark Terry

13. The Gospel Goes East 220
    Zane Pratt

MISSIONARIES AND MOVEMENTS

14. Monastics on Mission. 235
    Karen O'Dell Bullock

15. Post-Reformation Missions Pioneers 250
    R. Alton James

16. The Great Century 267
    Howard Norrish

17. The Global Century 287
    Mike Barnett

PART THREE: THE MISSION OF GOD TODAY 307

THE TASK

18. The State of the Spread of the Gospel 309
    Jim Haney

19. Finishing the Task 323
    J. Scott Holste

20. Spiritual Warfare and the Mission of God 340
   Jerry Rankin

21. Apostles Even Now 355
   Don Dent

22. Strategic Prayer for God's Mission 370
   Mike Barnett

COMMUNICATING THE GOSPEL ACROSS CULTURES

23. Cultures and Worldviews 377
   Stan May

24. Tell His Story So That All Might Worship 391
   LaNette W. Thompson

25. Comprehensive Contextualization 406
   A. Scott Moreau

26. Effective Bridging and Contextualization 420
   Kevin Greeson

27. Back to Basics 435
   William R. Yount

THROUGH THE CHURCH

28. Church-Planting Movements 451
   David Garrison

29. Measuring Progress in the Mission of God 466
   Gary R. Corwin

30. Breaking Bad Missiological Habits 481
   Christopher R. Little

31. Multiplying Leaders on Mission with God 498
   R. Bruce Carlton

32. Creative-Access Platforms 517
   Tom Steffen

33. Biblical Lessons from the Persecuted Church 535
   Nik Ripken and Kurt Nelson

34. Women on Mission with God 554
      Meg Page

35. Caring for God's Missionaries 569
      Robert Edwards and Nathan Evans

36. The Trouble with Our Jerusalems 585
      Ed Stetzer

37. The Local Church and the Mission of God 600
      H. Al Gilbert

38. Where Do You Fit in the Mission of God? 610
      Clyde Meador

About the Contributors 623

Subject Index 631

Scripture Index 636

The following additional chapters are available in the *Discovering the Mission of God Supplement* original e-book:

1. Israel's Mission to All Peoples
      Timothy M. Pierce

2. The Love of God
      Gordon Fort

3. The Power and Presence of the Holy Spirit
      James M. Hamilton Jr.

4. Letter from the Field
      Brother John

5. The Business of Building Bridges
      Patrick Lai

6. God's Mission Today Through Prayer
      Natalie Shepherd and Peter Hawkins

7. Equippers for God's Mission
      Marty Glickman

8. Jesus Christ: The Way, the Truth, and the Life?
   Brad Roderick

9. The Left Side of the Graph
   Clyde Meador

10. Breaking Old Habits
    Rebekah A. Naylor

11. Principles and Practices
    Mike Barnett

12. Measuring Church Planting Progress at Avant
    Scott Harris

13. Human Needs Ministries for God's Mission
    J. Jeffrey Palmer

14. Preach and Heal
    Charles Fielding

15. Church and Agency Co-Laboring
    Jerry Rankin and Mike Edens

16. Eleven Implications for the North American Church
    J. D. Payne

PREFACE

Ignoring or misunderstanding the mission of God has resulted in a church that has lost its spiritual vitality and ability to impact culture and a contemporary world with a life-transforming message. We seldom think in terms of a sovereign God who is actively "on mission," for to do so would compel his people with the priority of being aligned with his divine activity. Pressed on the issue, one might define the mission of God as his eternal plan to redeem a lost world. Yet we often relegate that mission to the time-defined event of Jesus coming to earth to die to bear the sins of a lost world and be raised again.

The mission of God is not an afterthought when Jesus, having completed his earthly ministry, gathered with his followers on a hillside in Galilee and decided to send them out to make disciples of all nations. It was not in a moment of spontaneous inspiration that he decided the good news of the kingdom should break out of a narrow Jewish context and be declared to the whole world. No, this is something that was born in the heart of God before the foundation of the world. Certainly, it centered in the redemptive act of Christ dying on the cross and the glorious resurrection morning that followed, when sin and death were conquered once for all. But it was not just that moment that split time and opened the door to eternal life that defined the mission of God.

From the creation of the world the mission began to take shape. A glimpse of where it was going was given in the call to Abraham to leave his home and family so that all the families of nations would receive the blessing of being reconciled to God. The mission gained intensity as

God raised up a special people, Israel, to declare his glory and to tell of his salvation. But once salvation had been assured by the cross and an empty tomb, the mission was empowered by the coming of the Holy Spirit, and the born-again people of God became the instruments through which the mission was to be fulfilled.

To miss the overview of a big-picture perspective is to reduce the mission of God to whatever we choose to do in ministry and witness on his behalf. Classical mission scholars have defined "missions" as the activities of the church to fulfill God's mission, but the "mission" belongs to God. We need to rediscover the scope and vision of what God is doing and where he is going as he moves at an accelerated pace to reach every tribe, people, language, and nation with the gospel.

Discovering the mission of God helps bring all of our programs and activities into perspective. Too much of what we do has become ingrown and self-centered, feeding the fellowship of the redeemed, occasionally bringing an outsider into the kingdom, but seldom focused on the task of impacting a lost world to the ends of the earth.

There is a great deal of literature on the mission of God, but most of it is rather dated; written in a different era, applications are irrelevant to a contemporary world and God's activity today. Even the innovative challenges of more recent missiologists such as Donald McGavran and Ralph Winter are several decades removed from the dizzying global changes and visionary advances seen in the twenty-first century. Most historians would agree that there was greater advance toward global evangelization in the last decade of the twentieth century than in all two hundred years of modern missions since William Carey went to India in 1793. However, it appears that even that era has been superseded by the first decade of the new millennium as God moves through wars and ethnic violence, political upheaval, social chaos, economic instability, and natural disasters to turn the hearts of a people to search for spiritual answers that can be found only in Jesus Christ.

Discovering the Mission of God is an exciting compilation of writing and reflections by contemporary actors who are involved in the divine activity that is moving toward that elusive objective when all peoples have the opportunity to hear, understand, and respond to the gospel in their own cultural context. Modern-day missionaries are undeterred by closed doors, government restrictions, antagonistic religious world-views, and hostility toward a Christian witness. They are discovering creative access to resistant people, identifying with a hurting world, and offering hope in spite of personal risk and danger.

With the assistance of the International Mission Board, Dr. Mike Barnett has compiled and edited a comprehensive array of essays and insights, primarily from the perspective of a younger generation of scholars and mission leaders. The reader will find fresh insights into traditional biblical passages as doctrinal and theological positions reinforce the mission message. What happened to the mission of God from the New Testament for more than a millennium? How did it gain momentum from the Reformation and finally grow to prominence in the nineteenth and twentieth centuries? A reading of the historical section will serve to prepare one for the exciting insights into contemporary practices that reflect a God moving in providence and power to fulfill his mission.

A subtle impression emerges out of the multiplicity of writers contributing from diverse backgrounds and experiences to this volume from a biblical, historical, and contemporary perspective—it is an understanding that the mission accrues to the glory of God himself who alone is worthy of all praise, worship, honor, and glory. *Discovering the Mission of God* will challenge the church and motivate God's people to adjust priorities and personal agendas to become aligned with what God is doing to fulfill his mission today.

JERRY RANKIN, President Emeritus
International Mission Board, Southern Baptist Convention

Acknowledgments

This project would have been impossible without the support and endorsement of the International Mission Board. For years now, IMB has actively encouraged strategic partnerships with like-minded "Great Commission Christians" for the purpose of finishing the task of the mission of God to reach all nations with the gospel. It was with this end in mind that IMB encouraged and endorsed this volume. Special thanks go to Jerry Rankin and Clyde Meador for their vision, leadership, and advocacy throughout the project.

Thank you, authors! To the experienced writers and missiologists who carved out time to write a chapter, thank you. May God continue to use you to teach and write in order to equip the next generation of missionaries and champions for the mission of God. To the young, field-based, often inexperienced writer-missionaries, well done! You brought a freshness and "cutting edge" ethos to the work.

Appreciation also goes to my graduate students and others who handled a variety of administrative and editorial services. Thank you, Matthew Rennells, Joanna Schiestl, Allison Cox, Christy Herman, David Mauger, and Zach Hoffman. We would not have crossed the finish line without you. Special thanks to Joanne Lu and Nathan Poole who did some heavy lifting as proofreaders throughout the project. Keep using your literary gifts for the Lord, Joanne!

Thanks to my associate editor, Robin Martin. I volunteered you without your permission, Robin. Thanks for persevering to the end. You are a special lady. Your professional writing background and years of field experience say it all.

Finally, those who know me know that God's greatest gift to me has been Cindy. Without my beautiful, godly, servant-hearted wife, none of this would have been possible. Thank you.

MIKE BARNETT

INTRODUCTION

DISCOVERING THE MISSION OF GOD

Mike Barnett

What is the mission of God? You might think this is a simple question that requires no answer. After all, most of us know about the mission of God. Or do we?

Most readers of this book already have an interest in missions. You have read the Great Commission that Jesus gave the disciples (Matthew 28:18–20). You have prayed for God's missionaries. You have written checks for mission projects or programs of the church. Perhaps you have been on one or more mission trips in your homeland or even abroad. You are mission-minded lay people.

Others sensed a call to serve in the mission of God. You attended seminary, studied missiology, signed up as a candidate with a mission-sending agency, and are preparing for your first term of service.

And yes, some of you already serve faithfully as long-term career missionaries.

Some readers consider themselves barely novices in this mission of God stuff. You are a Christian—a follower of Christ—but you don't know much about God's mission. A friend encouraged you to attend a meeting or sign up for an overseas trip. You are just a normal person working in the marketplace of the world—a school teacher, accountant, businessperson, or technology consultant—certainly not a missionary. Sure you are interested, curious about God's mission; but you really don't have too much time to spend on this missions stuff. In fact, how did you get yourself into reading this book anyway? Hold that thought.

Perhaps a handful of you are not even sure you believe in the mission of God. Maybe you're not really sure you believe in God. For you this is another test, an examination of God and what he is about. Reading this book might be a life-changing experience for you.

All of us, regardless of our specific circumstances, are on a journey: a journey of discovery—discovering the mission of God. For me, it is a familiar journey. I keep coming back for more. But I recall the first time I really dug into the meaning of missions. On my first serious trek into the mission of God, I was already one of those career missionaries, thoroughly equipped and engaged in God's mission work. Or was I? My first journey was almost an accident. It began as a reading assignment—John Piper's book *Let the Nations Be Glad*—given by my field leader. It ended with my shock and embarrassment that I knew so little about the real mission of God.

The purpose of this book is to take you on *your* journey into the mission of God. We will set the agenda and keep you on track, but you are free to experience this mission of God in the way he intended for you. Follow his Spirit as you journey.

The Briefing

Before we begin the journey, we need some basic orientation and answers to a few foundational questions about the mission of God.

Whose mission is it? The phrase "mission of God" answers this question quite literally. But do we usually think of the mission as God's? As early as the 1930s, theologians like Karl Barth began to speak of mission as "an activity of God himself."[1] In 1952, at a missions conference in Willingen, Germany, the phrase "mission of God," or *missio Dei*, became the term of preference. Mission was being seen less as an activity of the church and more as "an attribute of God." The mission to preach and teach salvation to the world wasn't the church's idea—it came from God. As one theologian put it, "It is not the church that has a mission of salvation to fulfill in the world; it is the mission of the Son

---

[1]David J. Bosch, *Transforming Mission: Paradigm Shifts in Theology of Mission* (Maryknoll, NY: Orbis, 1991), 389.

and the Spirit through the Father that includes the church. . . . Mission is thereby seen as a movement from God to the world; the church is viewed as an instrument for that mission. There is church because there is mission, not vice versa."[2]

So it is not really the church's mission. Neither is it primarily the missionary's mission, nor just the mission agency's mission. It is God's mission. As John Stott writes, "The living God of the Bible is a sending God. . . . [He is] a missionary God!"[3] God ultimately accomplishes his mission. He has chosen followers of Christ as his instruments. But the mission of God does not exist because of the church; the church exists because of the mission of God. This reality is both comforting and disturbing. We should take comfort in the fact that the redemption of all nations does not depend on us because it is God's job, God's mission. On the other hand, we should be both humbled and disturbed by the fact that God has chosen the church as his instrument, his agent, in accomplishing his mission.

The apostle Paul wrote about this mysterious strategy of proclaiming "to the Gentiles the boundless riches of Christ" (Ephesians 3:8). "[God's] intent was that now, *through the church*, the manifold wisdom of God should be made known to the rulers and authorities in the heavenly realms" (Ephesians 3:10, emphasis added). This mission of God is a big mission. In fact, it not only impacts all nations on earth but it affects and transforms the heavens, the universe, and the entire creation of God. And the church is a key player in this cosmic drama. Though it is God's mission, followers of Christ must take seriously this design and God's call upon the church to be agents of his redemptive plan. This is serious business, this mission of God.

What is the mission of God? We acknowledged that it is God's mission, but what exactly is it? The Latin word *missio* means a "sending" of someone

---

[2]Ibid., 391. Bosch quotes Jürgen Moltmann, *The Church in the Power of the Spirit* (London: SCM Press, 1975), 64; Johannes Aagaard, "Trends in Missiological Thinking During the Sixties," *International Review of Mission*, vol. 62 (1973): 11–15; and Anna Marie Aagaard, "Missio Dei in Katholischer Sicht," *Evangelische Theologie*, vol. 34 (1974): 420–33.

[3]John R. W. Stott, *Christian Mission in the Modern World* (Downers Grove, IL: InterVarsity, 1975), 21; and "The Living God Is a Missionary God," in *Perspectives on the World Christian Movement*, 3rd ed. (Pasadena, CA: William Carey Library, 1999), 9.

with a purpose or duty to perform. It was often used to describe the task of a soldier sent out to perform a military function. So what is God's task? God describes his mission throughout the Bible, from Genesis to Revelation. In fact, the subject of his mission pervades Scripture. That makes the fact that we so often miss it that much more perplexing.

Though it is mentioned earlier in Genesis, God clearly reveals his mission in chapter 12 in a conversation with Abram, soon to be known as Abraham: "The Lord had said to Abram, 'Go from your country, your people and your father's household to the land I will show you. I will make you into a great nation, and I will bless you; I will make your name great, and you will be a blessing. I will bless those who bless you, and whoever curses you I will curse; and all peoples on earth will be blessed through you'" (Genesis 12:1–3).

This is the mission of God: "All peoples on earth will be blessed." A theme that flows throughout Scripture, it begins here with a promise to Abraham. And it ends in Revelation, as the heavenly hosts sing to the Lamb, "You are worthy to take the scroll and to open its seals, because you were slain, and with your blood you purchased for God persons from every tribe and language and people and nation. You have made them to be a kingdom and priests to serve our God, and they will reign on the earth" (Revelation 5:9–10). Everything between Genesis and Revelation is directly related to this mission of God, this sending of himself and his people to bless all the peoples on earth.

Why this mission? This is a fair question. If followers of Jesus Christ—the church—are to be, by design, agents of the mission of God, then surely we have the right to know why. Why is God so focused, so preoccupied as it were, on a blessing for all the peoples? This is the part that embarrassed me fifteen years ago when I first realized what God's mission was all about. It is an overused expression, but this mission of God is *about God.* The answer to "Why this mission?" is, simply put, God's glory. Again, this theme oozes out of Scripture. How can we miss it? Time after time God reveals to us how serious he is about his glory.

We teach and preach that the exodus event is all about God saving Israel from Pharaoh. But a closer look reveals the greater purpose, or mission, of God in that event. God tells Moses time after time to instruct Pharaoh to let his people go. This is the popular message of the book of Exodus. "Tell Pharaoh, 'Let my people go!'" But why? So they might worship him (Exodus 9:13). It is true that God is rescuing Israel—but not for Israel's sake. God desires that Israel worship him. That is the "why" behind the exodus event. That is the "why" behind the mission of God.

Listen to God as he instructs Moses what to tell Pharaoh:

> This is what the LORD, the God of the Hebrews, says: Let my people go, so that they may worship me, or this time I will send the full force of my plagues against you and against your officials and your people, so you may know that there is no one like me in all the earth. For by now I could have stretched out my hand and struck you and your people with a plague that would have wiped you off the earth. But I have raised you up for this very purpose, that I might show you my power and that my name might be proclaimed in all the earth. (Exodus 9:13–16)

God saved the Israelites so they would know he was still their God and so they would worship and serve him. God saved the Israelites so Pharaoh and all the nations would know that he was the one, true, living, and all-powerful God. His plan worked. He saved the Israelites from Pharaoh, and the nations shuddered and trembled (Exodus 15:14–16). He saved the Israelites from Pharaoh, and hundreds of years later the Messiah sprang from this seed of Abraham. He saved the Israelites from Pharaoh, and we are still reading and telling his glorious story to the nations today. This is the reason for the mission: God's glory.

God reveals this purpose throughout Scripture. One of my favorite examples is in Isaiah 48. Once again God reveals the reason for the mission. He patiently deals with the Israelites' short memory, and their lack of faith and obedience seems to have pushed God into a kind of strategic corner. Should he rescue them once again? The prophet projects God's voice in a kind of first-person soliloquy: "For my own name's sake I delay my wrath; for the sake of my praise I hold it back from you, so as not to destroy you completely. See, I have refined you, though not as silver; I have tested you in the furnace of affliction. For my own sake, for my own sake, I do this.

How can I let myself be defamed? I will not yield my glory to another" (Isaiah 48:9–11).

God's mission is that all families on earth would be blessed. The substance of this blessing is that they would know, worship, and serve God. The effect of this blessing is a full and meaningful life for them today and eternally. The ultimate result of this blessing is the lifting up of God's name, reputation, honor, and glory before the entire universe. This is the reason for the mission.

Where do we see it? As God goes about accomplishing his mission, shouldn't we be learning from him? How can we do that? Where do we look to learn about the mission of God?

The Bible. The first place to look for the mission of God is in the Scriptures. We look to the Bible not just as a proof text for missions—i.e., simply to justify our programs, trips, budgets, and agendas. God's mission is bigger than that. In recent years biblical scholars and teachers have rediscovered the missional basis of the Bible. Where we once searched the Bible for reasons for mission, today we understand that the mission is the reason for the Bible!

Christopher J. H. Wright captured this transforming concept in his book *The Mission of God: Unlocking the Bible's Grand Narrative.* For years Wright taught a course titled "The Biblical Basis of Mission." The more he studied God's mission, the more he realized a better title would be "The Missional Basis of the Bible." Wright concluded that the Bible did not merely include references, endorsements, and mandates for God's mission, but indeed "the writings that now comprise our Bible are themselves the product of and witness to the ultimate mission of God."[4] Wright summarizes his view in chapter 1 of this volume.

But we're getting ahead of ourselves. Back to the briefing.

This concept that the Bible itself exists because of God's mission is truly transformational. If the Bible exists because of the mission, the same must be said about the church. If this is true, then all that we do as Christ-followers must point toward the mission of God. Everything the church (and parachurch organizations) does should connect with the

---

[4]Christopher J. H. Wright, *The Mission of God: Unlocking the Bible's Grand Narrative* (Downers Grove, IL: IVP Academic, 2006), 22.

mission of God. This concept is not merely the product of the missionary zeal of a few Bible scholars. It is the testimony of the Bible itself. We trust that readers of this book who embrace the missional basis of Scripture will thrive in this journey of discovery. We hope those readers who doubt it today will find evidence to support it tomorrow.

A word of caution. This renaissance of "missional" awareness sometimes results in the co-opting of God's specific mission into a kind of vague, generic, and all-encompassing definition of church, ministry, and mission. In other words, once we are faced with the reality that the Bible is missional and we should all be about this mission of God in all that we do, there is a temptation or tendency to justify whatever we are doing today as definitively missional. The result is the claim that every ministry of the church is missional and every member a missionary. Indeed, this may or may not be so. Beware of this assimilation and potential watering down of the mission of God. Look to the Bible first and foremost for the definition and delineation of the mission of God.

To summarize, first we learn about the mission of God from the Bible. It is our record of God accomplishing his mission yesterday, today, and tomorrow. It begins with God's vision, records how he goes about his mission, and concludes with the mission accomplished. It tells us whose mission it is, and why. It includes his mandate for us to be engaged in his mission. It reveals that God uses us, the church, as his instruments. It displays his power as he works throughout history among all the peoples on earth. It motivates and empowers us to boldly serve and worship him. It inspires us to be on mission with God—to know where we fit in his mission.

History. Second, we learn about the mission of God by studying history. God continued to fulfill his mission after biblical times. According to his mission plan, he used Christ-followers working through the church among the nations. As we study how God worked in the past through peoples, politics, societies, economies, nations, and churches around the world, we learn lessons for tomorrow. Sometimes these lessons teach us *how* to be on mission with God. They highlight historic best practices for discipling all nations. They affirm our best strategies or redirect our worst ones. They inspire us as we celebrate through history the successes of God's people and the church on mission with him. Sometimes, however, these lessons teach us how to *not* be on mission with God. Our study of the history of God's mission is frequently messy and heart-sickening. It includes "the good, the bad, and the ugly" aspects of disciplers and the church. It teaches us—if we will listen and learn—not to repeat the mistakes of those who have gone before us.

When students of God's mission struggle with the reality that many of the great moments and personalities in the history of God's mission are characterized by frailty and failure, it is time to go back to the Bible. We find these same messy and sometimes ugly moments in the biblical accounts as well. We shake our heads and wonder why God continued to use people as his primary instruments. We wonder how he employed such a corrupt and sometimes even evil church as the vehicle. And then we remember that the glory of God is the reason for the mission. As God uses people working through the church, in spite of their failures and imperfections, he transforms them and their world. Then he receives the glory. The nations see that only he could have made it happen. He is the ultimate missionary. He is the one who accomplishes the miraculous, the supernatural.

The mission of God today. Finally, we learn about God's mission by studying how he is accomplishing it today. We listen to testimonies from missionaries, mission agencies, and new believers from around the world; and we learn more about God's mission. We analyze the challenges and trends of twenty-first century missions, and we learn more about where we fit. We celebrate the progress of God's mission, and it inspires us to serve him. God teaches us all about his mission through the Bible, history, and his mission today.

How does God do it? How does God accomplish his mission? We know to look to the Bible, history, and missions today. But what do we learn when we look there? What principles dominate these accounts of the mission of God? What plans do we see God and his followers making? How do they serve his mission? What practices can we learn?

God's love. God blesses all peoples through his love. God loves us into his blessing and his kingdom. "For God so loved the world that he gave his one and only Son, that whoever believes in him shall not perish but have eternal life" (John 3:16). But this method of God's mission, this love of God, isn't one-sided—i.e., just him to us. Jesus taught, "Love the Lord your God with all your heart and with all your soul and with all your mind" (Matthew 22:37). And it doesn't stop there. This love of God flows throughout the mission of God: from him to us; from us to him; and, yes, from us to each other. "Love your neighbor as yourself" (Matthew 22:39). God's method begins with his love. As you read the following chapters, look for the love of God in the mission of God. It is everywhere.

People-to-people. God extends his mission *to* people *through* people. I tell my students that if God had contracted me as a strategy consultant when he was drawing up his plan, I would have advised against depending on people to accomplish his mission. Think about it. With the universe at his disposal, God could have used so many other resources. Indeed, he could have *spoken* into being the blessing for all the peoples. He could have marshaled heavenly powers and beings to complete his mission. But he chose to work through people. Remember the promise to Abraham: "All peoples on earth will be blessed through you" (Genesis 12:3). Through Abraham and his descendants (those who are his spiritual descendants, whether Jews or Gentiles), God reaches the nations. He connects with, transforms, and empowers people to reach people with the good news of his mission through his Son, Jesus Christ. As you study the Bible, history, and God's mission today, look for the people-to-people dynamic. Learn from God.

Discipling all peoples. Though we misuse and abuse the word *disciple*, it remains a foundational, biblical, and missional word to describe the method of God. It was Jesus' word. Many younger followers of Christ have abandoned the term "discipleship" because of its confused meaning. The academic community divided it into at least three distinct categories: evangelism, discipleship, and church planting. Seminaries offer degrees and faculties in each specialty. Publishers carefully categorize their titles, and practitioners become specialists in one field or the other. Consequentially, churches call leaders who specialize in one of these "ministries." No wonder our "twenty-something" church leaders are giving up on the term "disciple." If only we could recapture Jesus' simple yet powerful meaning when he commanded his followers to disciple all nations (Matthew 28:18–20).

The "Great Commission" of Christ to his disciples was as much instruction as commandment. He told them to go into the world and "disciple all nations."[5] Then he told them how to do it. We disciple by baptizing new believers in the name of the three-in-one God and teaching them to obey all that Jesus commanded. The genius of this job assignment is subtle. By teaching each other how to *obey* all that Jesus commanded, we insure our continued involvement in the mission of God. By mentoring each other to do more than *know* the words of Christ—indeed, to *live* them—our lives are transformed and we recognize our call to be a part of God's mission.[6] We learn how to work in his mission by observing how he accomplishes it. We rely on his power ("And surely I am with you always"), we ultimately discover where we fit, and we go for it. This is discipling all nations. This is how God does it, this mission of his.

Equipping the saints. Paul briefs us on training in his letter to believers in Ephesus. We regularly teach and preach these "equipping" verses (Ephesians 4:9–13), but seem to struggle with their application. Could it be that what has been missing in our thinking is the mission of God? Paul says that Jesus intends some of us to be equippers of the ones who do the bulk of the work of the church. Some are to be apostles—sent ones, going to those who have yet to hear. We think of our missionaries. Some are to be prophets—gifted proclaimers or "forth-tellers" of the gospel truths. We think of our preachers. Some are to be evangelists—those most effective defenders of the faith whom God uses to attract others. We think of our most active outreachers in church and parachurch ministries. (All believers are to be witnesses, per Acts 1:8, but some are especially gifted to share the good news of Christ with those who have never heard.) Some are to be pastors or

---

[5]Steven Hawthorne, "The Story of God's Glory," in *Perspectives on the World Christian Movement*, Ralph Winter, ed. (Pasadena, CA: William Carey Library, 1999), 110, 112n3. See also Robert Coleman, *The Master Plan of Discipleship* (Grand Rapids: Revell, 1987).

[6]William R. Yount and Mike Barnett, *Called to Reach: Equipping Cross-Cultural Disciplers* (Nashville: Broadman & Holman, 2007), 37.

shepherds who protect and lead our churches. We think of our church staff pastors and their associates. And some are to be teachers—who clearly communicate the Word of God. We think of Bible teachers, teaching pastors, and educational leaders.

But here is the key to these equippers: they are to coach all disciples to do the work and ministries of the church and its assignment in the mission of God. Most Westerners (and Western-influenced churches) have turned this best practice of God on its head. We employ "equippers" to teach and lead us, but we also expect them to do the bulk of the work and ministry of the church as well. When we think of this tactical approach outside the context of God's mission, it seems possible to get it wrong. After all, a good-sized staff of professionally trained ministers can handle all the tasks of a church—preaching, teaching, hospital visits, Christian education, worship, weddings, funerals, and community service. They lead the way and we lay people passively plug in if and when we are able. But if the context for this assignment of "equippers" is the mission of God to reach all peoples on earth, then it becomes obvious that we cannot train and hire enough professional "equippers" to do the work. Indeed, everyone must do the work. The church must be indigenous, or home-grown, and dependent upon grassroots workers rather than elite equippers. Thus, the genius of God's method— equippers coaching "the saints" to get the job done—makes perfect sense. Look for the equippers and the workers in God's mission.

Through the church. One last practice of God on mission clarifies the role of the church. I came to Christ through the Jesus movement of the early 1970s, an antiestablishment movement of young believers. We were passionate about the Bible and a personal relationship with Jesus, but we weren't so excited about the church. Many of us avoided the organized church and sought authentic Christian community in student groups or informal Bible studies. We were "Lone Ranger" followers of Christ. We were twentieth-century versions of a "churchless Christianity."[7] How ironic that many significant organized churches

---

[7]This refers to recent discussions led by Ralph Winter on movements of Christ-followers who do not associate with a commonly understood community of believers or "church." See Herbert E. Hoefer, *Churchless Christianity* (Pasadena, CA: William Carey Publishing, 2001).

and parachurch organizations today are led by those same recalcitrants who met Jesus through the nonconforming Jesus movement. God does have a sense of humor!

The bottom line is that we cannot be long-term Lone Rangers or churchless Christians and be on mission with God. It simply is not his plan. Sure, he can use an individual and disconnected believer as a witness and catalyst for his mission. But ultimately we are to be catalysts for the multiplication of his church—the primary and nonnegotiable instrument of his mission. The teachings of Christ and the letters of the apostles clearly define this vital role of the church. As Paul summarizes it, "Now to him who is able to do immeasurably more than all we ask or imagine, according to his power that is at work within us, to him be glory in the church and in Christ Jesus throughout all generations, for ever and ever! Amen" (Ephesians 3:20–21).

By what power? In the text above, Paul uses the phrase "according to his power." Where does this power of God to accomplish his mission come from? This may be the most profound but least understood aspect of his mission. It comes from the gospel. Paul says more than once that the gospel is powerful (Romans 1:16; Colossians 1:6). If you have ever shared the good news of Jesus with one who had never heard it, you probably know about this power. Are we so accustomed to the gospel that we've lost our sense of its power? I hope not. Of course, the power to understand God's Word and act accordingly comes from the Holy Spirit, our coach along the journey of God's mission (Matthew 28:20; Acts 1:8). The power also comes from the passion, or suffering, of Christ. Mel Gibson's film *The Passion of the Christ* demonstrated this. Hollywood's rendition of the last days of Jesus' life and his death on a cross profoundly impacted unbelievers and believers alike around the world. Do you sense this power? This is the power for God's mission. Read about it in the chapters that follow.

Where do we fit? The last question in our briefing asks where we fit in the mission of God. Clyde Meador's chapter will focus on this question, but the entire volume seeks to inform and challenge us on this point. After discovering the mission of God, we no longer can say that we do not fit. We are unable to pass the responsibility to missionaries or mission pastors. We are all called by God to participate in his mission of blessing all the peoples.

The Layout

This discovery journey follows three major themes: "The Mission of God in the Bible," "The Mission of God in History," and "The Mission of God Today." Each theme builds on itself in order to lay a foundation of understanding about God's mission and where we fit. We do not apologize for the directness of this approach. This volume of discovery intends to challenge each reader to make a personal and prayerful assessment of where he or she best fits in God's mission and to commit wholeheartedly to that task.

We've enlisted a mix of highly acclaimed authors and younger, emerging writers in the field of missions. Readers will notice that almost all our authors are experienced in living and working cross-culturally, and about half are still field-based. We seek reports and observations from the leading edges of the mission of God. There is risk in this approach, but we hope for fresh thinking from field strategists and practitioners without sacrificing well-reasoned and well-developed principles and strategies. Our authors come from a variety of church and missions backgrounds, all of which are "Great Commissional" in nature. The message of this volume is intended for the broader community of Great Commission Christian workers and their constituencies.

In addition, the *Discovering the Mission of God Supplement* e-book includes sixteen extra chapters that supplement the content of the printed book. The *Supplement* is intended as a companion to this main book to provide even more resources for going deeper into God's mission. See www.ivpress.com for more information.

Our greatest regret is that we do not have more authors from the non-Western world. With this in mind, many of our sidebar case studies highlight their lives and work.

Bon Voyage

This is a journey of discovery of the mission of God. As you begin this literary trek, remember God's mission of a blessing to all the peoples on earth. This is a survey of its past, a briefing on its present, and a glimpse into its future. God's mission dominated his relationship with Israel. It came to a climax with the birth of Emmanuel ("God with us")—Jesus Christ's life, work, crucifixion, and resurrection. It is completely and finally fulfilled in Revelation. Mission accomplished. May this journey of discovery be life-changing and work-changing! May God's Spirit lead you every step of the way for the sake of his mission and glory forever!

Discussion Points

1. What do we mean when we say this is God's mission?

2. What category of reader are you—missionary, student, missional lay person, seeker? What do you expect to get out of this discovery journey?

3. Which question in the briefing spoke to you? Share your insights.

4. Do you know where you fit in God's mission? What is your role today? What do you see on the horizon?

Further Reading

Bosch, David J. *Transforming Mission: Paradigm Shifts in Theology of Mission.* Maryknoll, NY: Orbis, 1991.

Winter, Ralph D., and Steven C. Hawthorne. *Perspectives on the World Christian Movement*, 3rd ed. Pasadena, CA: William Carey Library, 1999.

Wright, Christopher J. H. *The Mission of God: Unlocking the Bible's Grand Narrative.* Downers Grove, IL: InterVarsity, 2006.

PART ONE

THE MISSION OF GOD
IN THE BIBLE

In the beginning was the Word. . . . The Word became flesh and made his dwelling among us" (John 1:1,14). The mission of God is as basic as this—God sent his Son, the Word, to reveal himself to his creation. He outlines this mission throughout his written revelation: from beginning to end, from Genesis to Revelation. Why do we so often miss this primary message of the Bible? How can we overlook this preoccupation of God to be on mission to reach all peoples on earth? Perhaps, at its core, this is a function of our self-centeredness. Like the Israelites before us, we pilfer the mission of God and make it our own.

As you read these chapters on the mission of God in the Bible, remember that this is God's mission, not ours. He is the one on mission. Learn from him. What is his mission? How does he accomplish it? What patterns repeat themselves throughout this mission of God? Where does the power for the mission come from? And how do these lessons from the Bible inform our role in God's mission today? The Bible is our best textbook, our primary training manual for the mission of God. Learn your mission lessons well in this first part of your discovery journey.

See also the following e-chapters in the *Discovering the Mission of God Supplement* e-book:

- Israel's Mission to All Peoples—Timothy M. Pierce
- The Love of God—Gordon Fort
- The Power and Presence of the Holy Spirit—James M. Hamilton Jr.
- Letter from the Field—Brother John

1

WORD OF GOD AND
MISSION OF GOD

READING THE WHOLE BIBLE FOR MISSION

Christopher J. H. Wright

A Short Personal Journey

I remember them so vividly from my childhood—the great banner texts around the walls of the missionary conventions in Northern Ireland where I would help my father at the stall of the Unevangelized Fields Mission, of which he was Irish Secretary after spending twenty years in Brazil. "Go ye into all the world and preach the Gospel to every creature," they urged me, along with other similar imperatives in glowing Gothic calligraphy. By the age of twelve I could have quoted all the key ones: "Go ye therefore and make disciples . . ." "How shall they hear . . . ?" "You shall be my witnesses . . . to the ends of the earth." "Whom shall we send? . . . Here am I, send me." I knew my missionary Bible verses. I had responded to many a rousing sermon on most of them.

By the age of twenty-one I had a degree in theology from Cambridge, where the same texts had been curiously lacking. At least it is curious to me now. At the time there seemed to be little connection at all between theology and mission in the minds of the lecturers, or of myself, or, for all I knew, in the mind of God. "Theology" was all about God—what God was like, what God had said and done, and what mostly dead people had speculated on such questions. "Mission" was about us, the living, and what we've been doing since Carey (who, of course, was the first missionary, we so erroneously thought). Or more precisely, mission is what we evangelicals do since we're the ones who know the Bible told us (or some of us, at least) to go and be missionaries. "The Bible" was somewhere in the middle—the object of critical study by theologians and the source of motivational texts for missionaries.

"Mission is what *we* do." That was the assumption—supported, of course, by clear biblical commands that were taken seriously by at least some people in the church. Mission was a task that some specially called folks got involved with. I had little concept at that time that mission should have been the very heartbeat of theology and the key to knowing how to interpret the Bible (hermeneutics).

Many years later, including years when I was teaching theology as a missionary in India, I found myself teaching a module called "The Biblical Basis of Mission" at All Nations Christian College, an international mission-training institution in England. The module title itself embodies the same assumption. *Mission* is the noun, the given reality. It is something *we* do, and we basically know what it is. And the reason why we know we should be doing it—the basis, foundation, or grounds on which we justify it—must be found in the Bible. As good evangelicals we need a biblical basis for everything we do. What, then, is the biblical basis for mission? Roll out the texts. Add some that nobody else has thought of. Do some joined-up theology. Add some motivational fervor. And the class is heartwarmingly appreciative. Now they have even more biblical support for what they already believed anyway, for these are All Nations students after all. They only came because they are committed to doing mission.

There is the task (mission). Here are some folks who are going to do it (the missionaries). And here are the bits of the Bible that might encourage them (the missionary texts). That is what everybody seemed to mean by the biblical basis of mission.

This mild caricature is not in the least derogatory in intent. I believe passionately that mission is what we should be doing, and I believe the Bible endorses and mandates it. However, the more I taught that course, the more I used to introduce it by telling the students that I would like to change its name from "The Biblical Basis of Mission" to "The Missional Basis of the Bible." I wanted them to see not just that the Bible contains a number of texts which happen to provide a rationale for missionary endeavor, but that the whole Bible is itself a "missional" phenomenon.

The Bible as the Product of God's Mission

A missional understanding of the Bible begins with the Bible's very existence.[1] For those who affirm some relationship (however articulated) between these texts and the self-revelation of our creator God, the whole canon of Scripture is a missional phenomenon in the sense that it witnesses to the self-giving movement of this God toward his creation and toward us, human beings who have been made in God's own image but who are wayward and wanton. The writings which now comprise our Bible are themselves the product of, and witness to, the ultimate mission of God.

> The very existence of the Bible is incontrovertible evidence of the God who refused to forsake his rebellious creation, who refused to give up, who was and is determined to redeem and restore fallen creation to his original design for it. . . . The very existence of such a collection of writings testifies to a God who breaks through to human beings, who disclosed himself to them, who will not leave them unilluminated in their darkness . . . who takes the initiative in re-establishing broken relationships with us.[2]

Furthermore, the processes by which these texts came to be written were often profoundly missional in nature. Many of the biblical texts emerged out of events, struggles, crises, or conflicts in which the people of God engaged with the constantly changing and challenging task of articulating and living out their understanding of God's revelation and redemptive action in the world. Sometimes these were struggles internal to the people of God themselves; sometimes they were highly

---

[1]Inevitably, writing the opening chapter for a project that bears a similar title as my own book, *The Mission of God: Unlocking the Bible's Grand Narrative* (Downers Grove, IL: InterVarsity, 2006), means that I cannot avoid thinking along the same lines as I developed in that book. What follows includes some extracts from the introduction and part one of that work. But readers will need to consult the rest of the book for in-depth wrestling with what a missional hermeneutic means, along with my attempts to work it through the whole biblical canon.
[2]Charles R. Taber, "Missiology and the Bible," *Missiology* 11 (1983): 229–45.

argumentative (polemical) struggles with the competing religious claims and worldviews that surrounded them. So a missional reading of such texts is definitely not a matter of first finding the "real" meaning by objective interpretation (exegesis), and then cranking up some "missiological implications" as a sermon (homiletic) supplement to the text itself. Rather, a missional reading will observe how a text often has its *origin* in some issue, need, controversy, or threat that the people of God needed to address in the context of their mission. The text in itself is a *product* of mission in action.

This is easily demonstrated in the case of the New Testament.[3] Most of Paul's letters were written in the heat of his missionary efforts: wrestling with the theological basis of the inclusion of the Gentiles, affirming the need for Jew and Gentile to accept one another in Christ and in the church, tackling the baffling range of new problems that assailed young churches as the gospel took root in the world of Greek polytheism, confronting incipient heresies with clear affirmations of the supremacy and sufficiency of Jesus Christ, and so on. And why were the Gospels so called? Because they were written to explain the significance of the *evangel*—the good news about Jesus of Nazareth, especially his death and resurrection. Confidence in these things was essential to the missionary task of the expanding church. And the person to whom we owe the largest portion of the New Testament, Luke, shapes his two volumes in such a way that the missionary mandate to the disciples to be Christ's witnesses to the nations comes as the climax to volume one and the introduction to volume two.

But we can also see in the Old Testament that many texts emerged out of the engagement of the Israelites with the surrounding world in the light of the God they knew in their history and in covenantal rela-

---

[3]Marion Soards comments, "Mission studies should remind biblical scholars that many of the writings that we study (often in painstaking and even painful detail) came to be because of the reality of mission. An awareness of, and a concern with, the key issues of mission studies may well help biblical studies find foci that will bring deeper appreciation of the meaning of the Bible." Marion L. Soards, "Key Issues in Biblical Studies and Their Bearing on Mission Studies," *Missiology* 24 (1996): 107. With this I fully agree. See also Andreas J. Köstenberger, "The Place of Mission in New Testament Theology: An Attempt to Determine the Significance of Mission within the Scope of the New Testament's Message as a Whole," *Missiology* 27 (1999): 347–62, and the works referred to there.

tionship. People produced texts in relation to what they believed God had done, was doing, or would do in their world. Genesis presents a theology of creation that stands in sharp contrast to the polytheistic creation myths of Mesopotamia. Exodus records the exodus as an act of Yahweh that comprehensively confronted and defeated the power of Pharaoh and all his rival claims to deity and allegiance. The historical narratives portray the long and sorrowful story of Israel's struggle with the culture and religion of Canaan. Texts from the time of the Babylonian exile of Israel, as well as postexilic texts, emerge out of the task that the small remnant community of Israel faced to define their continuing identity as a community of faith in successive empires of varying hostility or tolerance. Wisdom texts interact with international wisdom traditions in the surrounding cultures, but do so with staunch monotheistic disinfectant. And in worship and prophecy, Israelites reflect on the relationship between their God, Yahweh, and the rest of the nations—sometimes negatively, sometimes positively—and on the nature of their own role as Yahweh's elect priesthood in their midst. All of these are themes and conflicts that are highly relevant to missional engagement between God's people and the world of nations.

The Bible, then, is a missional phenomenon in itself. The writings which now comprise our Bible are themselves the product of, and witness to, the ultimate mission of God. The individual texts within it often reflect the struggles of being a people with a mission in a world of competing cultural and religious claims. And the canon eventually consolidates the recognition that it is through these texts that the people whom God has called to be his own (in both Testaments) have been shaped as a community of memory and hope, a community of mission, a community of failure and striving.

In short, a missional hermeneutic proceeds from the assumption that the whole Bible renders to us the story of God's mission through God's people in their engagement with God's world for the sake of God's purpose for the whole of God's creation. Mission is not just one of a list of things that the Bible happens to talk about, only a bit more urgently than some. Mission is, in that much-abused phrase, what it's all about.

Reading the Scriptures with the Risen Jesus and the Apostle Paul

The Risen Jesus. Now to say, "Mission is what the Bible is all about," is a bold claim. I would not expect to be able to turn any phrase that began, "The Biblical Basis of . . ." around the other way. There is, for example, a biblical basis for marriage; but there is not, I presume, "a marital basis for the Bible." There is a biblical basis for work, but work is not "what the Bible is all about." However, I take some encouragement for my claim from an impeccable authority: it seems to me that Jesus comes very close to saying, "This is what the Bible is all about," when he gave his disciples their final lecture in Old Testament hermeneutics. "This is what is written: The Messiah will suffer and rise from the dead on the third day, and repentance for the forgiveness of sins will be preached in his name to all nations, beginning at Jerusalem" (Luke 24:46–47). Now Jesus is not quoting a specific text here, though we would love to have been able to ask which Scriptures he particularly had in mind (doubtless the two from Emmaus could have filled in the gaps). The point is that he includes the whole of this sentence under the heading "This is what is written."

Jesus seems to be saying that the whole of the Scripture (which we now know as the Old Testament) finds its focus and fulfillment *both* in the life, death, and resurrection of Israel's Messiah *and* in the mission to all nations which flows out from that event. Luke tells us that with these words Jesus "opened their minds so they could understand the Scriptures." Or, as we might put it, he was setting their interpretive (hermeneutical) orientation and agenda. The proper way for disciples of the crucified and risen Jesus to read their Scriptures is *messianically* and *missiologically*.

> *The proper way for disciples of the crucified and risen Jesus to read their Scriptures is* messianically *and* missiologically.

For Jesus, then, the Old Testament was as much about mission as it was about himself. Or rather, the two are inseparable parts of the same fundamental reality: the saving mission of God. If you know who Jesus is from the Scriptures (that he is the Messiah of Israel who embodied their identity and their mission); and if you know what Israel is from the Scriptures (called into existence to be a "light to the nations"); then to confess Jesus as Messiah is to commit yourself to his mission to the nations. You can't have one without the other—not if you believe the Scriptures and read them as Jesus taught his disciples to. The necessity of mission is as rooted in the Bible as the identity of the Messiah.

The apostle Paul. When we turn to Paul, we find the same integration of mission and the [Old Testament] Scriptures. As I said above, if we inquired about the biblical basis for Christian mission, traditionally we would be pointed to the familiar words of the Great Commission (Matthew 28:16–20) and related New Testament texts. But for Paul the scriptural basis for mission went much further back. And of course, in any case, the "Great Commission" in its present form in the text of the canonical Gospels did not yet exist in the early decades of Paul's mission.

Paul had to justify both his mission practice and his mission theology on the basis of the Scriptures we now call the Old Testament. But that was no problem, for throughout those Scriptures he found a rich and deep theology of the mission of God for the world and the nations, and he built his own mission theology on that foundation. Here are just a few examples:

Paul goes back to creation—and sees the mission of God as bringing the whole of the created order to liberation along with the children of God (Romans 8:18–27). Thus Paul proclaims the resurrection of the Messiah as the firstfruits of that new creation, and can affirm that when any person is "in Christ" that new creation has already begun (2 Corinthians 5:17).

Paul goes back to Abraham—and sees the mission of Israel as the people called into existence as the covenant people of God with the express purpose of being the agent of God blessing all nations (Galatians 3:6–8). So crucial is this foundation block of Paul's theology that he speaks of God announcing the gospel "in advance" to Abraham—that is, the good news that God intends to bless the nations (and always had, from the very call of Abraham).

Paul goes back to the prophets—and sees God's purpose for the gathering in of the nations to become part of Israel and of Israel itself coming to renewed faith and restoration, so that by this means all Israel will be saved, as Torah, Prophets, and Psalms all declared (Romans 9–11).

So for Paul, then, the clear message of the whole of the Scriptures was the salvation of the nations and the renewal of creation through the mission of God through Israel and Israel's Messiah. His own personal mission as "apostle to the nations" was thus grounded in the Bible. For Paul, biblical theology was mission theology—the mission of God.

Though he was not present for Jesus' Old Testament hermeneutics lecture on the day of resurrection, Paul clearly had his own way of reading the Scriptures radically transformed with the same double focus. Testifying before Festus, he declared that he was saying "nothing beyond what the prophets and Moses said would happen—that the Messiah would suffer and, as the first to rise from the dead, would bring the message of light *to his own people and to the Gentiles*" (Acts 26:22–23, emphasis added). It was this dual understanding of the Scriptures that shaped Paul's life and work as the apostle of the Messiah, Jesus, to the Gentiles.

However, even if we accept that Jesus and Paul offer us a Messiah-focused and mission-generating hermeneutic of the Scriptures, we may still question the claim that somehow there is a missional hermeneutic of the whole Bible such that "mission is what it's all about." This uneasiness stems from the persistent, almost subconscious, paradigm that mission is fundamentally "something we do." This is especially so if we fall into the evangelical reductionist habit of using the word *mission* or *missions* as more or less synonymous with evangelism. Quite clearly, the whole Bible is not just "about evangelism," even though evangelism is certainly a fundamental part of biblical mission as entrusted to us. The appropriateness of speaking of "a missional basis of the Bible" becomes apparent only when we shift our paradigm of mission from *our* human agency to the ultimate purposes of *God* himself. For clearly the Bible is, in some sense, "all about God." What, then, does it mean to talk of the mission of God?

Whose Mission Is It Anyway?

God with a mission. The God revealed in the Scriptures is personal, purposeful, and goal-orientated. The opening account of creation portrays God working toward a goal, completing it with satisfaction, and resting—content with the result. And from the great promise of God to Abraham in Genesis 12:1–3 we know this God to be totally, covenantally, and eternally committed to the mission of blessing the nations through the agency of the people of Abraham. From that point on, the mission of God could be summed up in the words of the hymn, "God is working his purpose out as year succeeds to year," and as generations come and go.

The Bible presents itself to us fundamentally as a narrative—an historical narrative at one level but a grand, metanarrative at another. It begins with a God of purpose in creation. It moves on to the conflict and problem generated by human rebellion against that purpose. It spends most of its narrative journey in the story of God's redemptive purposes being worked out on the stage of human history. And it finishes beyond the horizon of its own history with the eschatological hope of a new creation.

This has often been presented as a four-point narrative: creation, fall, redemption, and future hope. This whole worldview is predicated on teleological monotheism—i.e., there is one God at work in the universe and in human history, and that God has a goal, a purpose, a mission, which will ultimately be accomplished by the power of his word and for the glory of his name. This is the mission of the biblical God.

To read the whole Bible in the light of this great overarching perspective of the mission of God is to read "with the grain" of this whole collection of Scriptures that constitute our canon. This foundational point is a key assumption of a "missiological hermeneutic" of the Bible. It is nothing more than to accept that the biblical worldview locates us in the midst of a narrative of the universe behind which stands the mission of the living God. All creation will render "glory to the Father and to the Son and to the Holy Spirit, as it was in the beginning, is now, and ever shall be." That is a missional perspective.

Humanity with a mission. When we read in Genesis 1 that God made human beings in God's own image, the very least we could infer from that is that they will be like the God we have just been reading about in the same chapter. Humans will be purposeful creatures with a goal to accomplish. But this is not left to inference alone. Human beings were given a very explicit mission: the mandate to fill the earth and subdue it and to rule over the rest of creation (Genesis 1:28). This delegated authority within the created order is moderated by the parallel commands in the complementary account: to work the Garden of Eden and take care of it (Genesis 2:15).

The care and keeping of creation is our human mission. We are on the planet with a purpose that flows from the creative purpose of God himself. Out of this teleological understanding of our humanity flows our ecological responsibility; our economic activity involving work, productivity, exchange, and trade; the ethic of social and economic justice; and the whole cultural mandate. To be human is to have a purposeful role in God's creation. This multidimensional mission flows not only from past reality (the fact of creation) but also from our future hope. The biblical (eschatological) vision assures us of a new creation, of which Christ is the heir and in which all our work in this creation will be purged and redeemed for the glory of God.

Israel with a mission. Once again, let's be clear. I am not talking about the Israelites sending out foreign missionaries (or their failure to do so, with the rather ambiguous exception of Jonah). My point is not to see what bits of the Old Testament can support our agenda of sending missionaries, but rather what the Old Testament contributes to our understanding of the mission of God in history for the nations and for all creation. From that angle we can see enormous missiological implications in the four major pillars of Old Testament faith: monotheism, election, ethics, and eschatology.[4]

The uniqueness and universality of Yahweh. Old Testament monotheism means that Yahweh alone is God and there is no other (e.g., Deuteronomy 4:35,39). This ultimately means the radical displacement of all other rival gods and that Yahweh is God over the whole earth and all nations (e.g. Psalm 96; Jeremiah 10:1–16; Isaiah 43:9–13; 44:6–20). Thus the New Testament affirms the uniqueness and universality of Jesus (cf. Philippians 2:9–11, based on Isaiah 45:23; and 1 Corinthians 8:5–6, based on Deuteronomy 6:4). This uniqueness and universality of

---

[4]Each of these vast themes receives one or more chapters in *The Mission of God*.

Jesus Christ stands at the front lines of a missiological response to global relativism and religious pluralism found at the heart of some forms of postmodernist philosophy.

Yahweh's election of Israel for the purpose of blessing the nations. After Genesis 10 and 11, what could God do about the scattered and rebellious world of nations? Genesis 12:1–3 gives the answer: God chose and called Abraham for the explicit purpose of bringing them blessing. So fundamental is this divine agenda that Paul describes the Genesis declaration as announcing "the gospel in advance" (Galatians 3:8). And the concluding vision of the whole Bible signifies the fulfilment of the Abrahamic promise, as people from every nation, tribe, people, and language (echoing the same words in Genesis 10) are gathered among the redeemed in the new creation (Revelation 7:9). The election of Israel is one of the most fundamental pillars of the biblical worldview and of Israel's historical sense of identity.[5] Israel's election did not result in a rejection of the nations, but was explicitly for their ultimate benefit. If we might paraphrase John, in a way he probably would have accepted, "God so loved the world that he chose Israel." Thus, rather than asking them to go somewhere, God's mission for them was to be something— a light—in the sight of the nations.

The ethical dimension of Israel's "visibility" among the nations. This raises the missiological dimension of Israel's holiness. Israel was called to be distinctive from the surrounding world in ways that were not merely religious but also ethical. This very purpose is expressed in Genesis 18:19. In the context of, and in stark contrast to, the world of Sodom and Gomorrah, Yahweh says of Abraham, "For I have chosen him, so that he will direct his children and his household after him to keep the way of the LORD by doing what is right and just, *so that* [emphasis added] the LORD will bring about for Abraham what he has promised him." This verse, in a remarkably tight syntax, binds together election, ethics, and mission as three interlocking aspects of God's

---

[5]This has been shown clearly, and in a way that underlines its importance for the whole mission of the biblical God through the people of God for the world, in the works of N. T. Wright, especially his *New Testament and the People of God* (Minneapolis: Fortress, 1992), 244-79, and *Jesus and the Victory of God* (Minneapolis: Fortress, 1996).

purpose. His choice of Abraham is for the sake of his promise (to bless the nations), but the accomplishment of that demands the ethical obedience of his community—the fulcrum in the middle of the verse. A similar dynamic relationship between ethics and mission can be seen elsewhere (e.g., Exodus 19:4–6; Deuteronomy 4:6–8; Jeremiah 4:1–2).

Eschatological vision; ingathering of nations. Israel saw the nations as witnesses of all that God was doing in Israel and, eventually, as the beneficiaries of all that history. The nations could thus be invited to rejoice, applaud, and praise Yahweh, the God of Israel (Psalm 47; 1 Kings 8:41–43; Psalm 67). Beyond that was the eschatological vision that there would be those of the nations who would not merely be joined to Israel but would come to be *identified* as Israel, with the same names, privileges, and responsibilities before God (Psalm 47:9; Isaiah 19:19–25; 56:2–8; 66:19–21; Zechariah 2:10–11; Amos 9:11–12; Acts 15:16–18; Ephesians 2:11—3:6). This is the breathtaking dimension of Israel's prophetic heritage that most profoundly influenced the theological explanation of the Gentile mission in the New Testament. It certainly underlies James's interpretation of the Christ event and the success of the Gentile mission in Acts 15 (quoting Amos 9:12). And it likewise inspired Paul's efforts as a practitioner and theologian of mission (e.g., Romans 15:7–16).

Jesus with a mission. Jesus did not just arrive. He had a very clear conviction that he was sent. But even before Jesus was old enough to have clear convictions about anything, his double significance for Israel *and* for the world was recognized by Simeon as he cradled the infant Jesus and spoke words rarely recognized for the missiological significance of their double messianic claim: "Sovereign Lord, as you have promised, you may now dismiss your servant in peace. For my eyes have seen your salvation, which you have prepared in the sight of *all nations*, a light for revelation to *the Gentiles*, and the glory of your people *Israel*" (Luke 2:29–32, emphasis added).

At his baptism Jesus received the affirmation of his true identity and mission. The voice of his Father combined the identity of the Servant figure in Isaiah (echoing the phraseology of Isaiah 42:1) and that of the Davidic messianic king (echoing the affirmation of Psalm 2:7). Both of these dimensions of his identity and role were energized with a sense of mission. The mission of the Servant was both to restore Israel to Yahweh and also to be the agent of God's salvation reaching to the ends of the earth (Isaiah 49:6). The mission of the Davidic messianic king was both to rule over a redeemed Israel according to the agenda of many prophetic texts and also to receive the nations and the ends of the earth as his inheritance (Psalm 2:8).

Jesus' sense of mission—the aims, motivation, and self-understanding behind his recorded words and actions—has been a matter of intense scholarly discussion. What seems very clear is that Jesus built his own agenda on what he perceived to be the agenda of his Father. His will was to do his Father's will. God's mission determined his mission. In the obedience of Jesus, even to death, the mission of God reached its climax. And, of course, in his resurrection glory he passed on that mission to his disciples, now mandated to replicate communities of obedient discipleship among all nations (Matthew 28:18–20).

The church with a mission. In Luke 24:45–48 Jesus entrusted to the church a mission rooted in his own identity, passion, and victory as the crucified and risen Messiah. "You are *witnesses*," he said—a mandate repeated in Acts 1:8: "You will be my witnesses." It is almost certain that Luke intends us to hear in this an echo of the same words spoken by Yahweh to Israel in Isaiah 43:10–12.

> "You are my witnesses," declares the LORD, "and my servant whom I have chosen, so that you may know and believe me and understand that I am he. Before me no god was formed, nor will there be one after me. I, even I, am the LORD, and apart from me there is no savior. I have revealed and saved and proclaimed—I, and not some foreign god among you. You are my witnesses," declares the LORD, "that I am God."

The Israelites knew the identity of the true and living God; therefore they were entrusted with bearing witness to that in a world of nations and their gods. The disciples knew the true identity of the crucified and risen Jesus; therefore they were entrusted with bearing witness to that to the ends of the earth. Mission flows from the identity of God and his Christ.

Paul goes further and identifies the mission of his own small band of church planters with the international mission of the Servant, quoting Isaiah 49:6 in Acts 13:47 and saying quite bluntly, "For this is what the Lord has commanded us: 'I have made you a light for the Gentiles, that you may bring salvation to the ends of the earth.'" This is a missiological hermeneutic of the Old Testament if ever there was one. As the NIV footnote shows, Paul has no problem applying the singular "you"—which was spoken to the Servant—to the plural "us."

So again, the mission of the church flows from the mission of God and the fulfillment of his purposes and his Word. It is not so much, as someone has said, that God has a mission for his church in the world as that God has a church for his mission in the world. Mission is not just something we do, though it certainly includes that. Mission, from the point of view of our human endeavor, means the committed participation of God's people in the

> It is not so much, as someone has said, that God has a mission for his church in the world as that God has a church for his mission in the world.

purposes of God for the redemption of the whole creation. Mission, like salvation, belongs to our God and to the Lamb. We are those who are called to share in its accomplishment.

Conclusion

Putting these perspectives together, a missiological hermeneutic of Scripture means that we seek to read any part of the Bible:

In the light of God's purpose for his whole creation, including the redemption of humanity and the creation of the new heavens and new earth;

In the light of God's purpose for human life in general on the planet and of all the Bible teaches about human culture, relationships, ethics, and behavior;

In the light of God's historical election of Israel, its identity and role in relation to the nations, and the demands God made on the Israelites' worship, social ethics, and total value system;

In the light of the centrality of Jesus of Nazareth, his messianic identity and mission in relation to Israel and the nations, his cross and resurrection;

In the light of God's calling of the church, the community of believing Jews and Gentiles who constitute the extended people of the Abraham covenant, to be the agent of God's blessing to the nations in the name of, and for the glory of, the Lord Jesus Christ.

Such a commitment to reading the whole Word of God in the light of the whole mission of God opens up enormous vistas for theological, ethical, and missional reflection. It is the purpose of the rest of this book and the project it launches to explore these frontiers for all they are worth.

Discussion Points

1. What does Wright mean when he says the Bible is usually "somewhere in the middle" between theology and mission?

2. What does he mean by the "missional basis of the Bible"?

3. How would a missional understanding of the Bible change who we are as disciplers?

4. How might it change who we are as the church?

5. What else did you learn from this chapter that you want to remember and apply?

Further Reading

Bauckham, Richard. *Bible and Mission: Christian Witness in a Postmodern World.* Carlisle and Grand Rapids: Paternoster and Baker Academic, 2003.

Blauw, Johannes. *The Missionary Nature of the Church.* New York: McGraw Hill, 1962.

De Ridder, Richard R. *Discipling the Nations.* Grand Rapids: Baker, 1975.

Hedlund, Roger. *The Mission of the Church in the World.* Grand Rapids: Baker, 1991.

Kaiser, Walter C., Jr. *Mission in the Old Testament: Israel as a Light to the Nations.* Grand Rapids: Baker, 2000.

Köstenberger, A. J., and P. T. O'Brien. *Salvation to the Ends of the Earth: A Biblical Theology of Mission.* Downers Grove, IL: InterVarsity, 2001.

Schnabel, Eckhard J. *Early Christian Mission.* Two volumes. Downers Grove, IL: InterVarsity, 2004.

Senior, Donald, and Carroll Stuhlmueller. *The Biblical Foundations for Mission.* London: SCM, 1983.

Wright, Christopher J. H. *The Mission of God: Unlocking the Bible's Grand Narrative.* Downers Grove, IL: InterVarsity, 2006.

————. *The Mission of God's People: A Biblical Theology of the Church's Mission.* Grand Rapids: Zondervan, 2010.

Wright, N. T. *Jesus and the Victory of God.* Minneapolis: Fortress, 1996.

2

THE MISSIONARY MESSAGE
OF THE NEW TESTAMENT

Joel F. Williams

The New Testament is a missionary book. The writers of the New Testament were actively involved in the missionary work of the church, and the various books within the New Testament were written for people who had only recently believed in Jesus through the efforts of missionaries. In other words, the New Testament came into existence within a missionary context.[1] Apart from God's heart for the world and apart from the efforts of God's people to spread the message of God's love, the New Testament would not exist.

The purpose of this chapter is to examine what the New Testament teaches about the theme of mission, especially the mission that God has given to the church.[2] The focus of the chapter is not so much on demonstrating the importance of the mission theme in the New Testament, as the importance of that theme is assumed by the very existence of the New Testament itself. The goal is to clarify the nature of the missionary task given to God's people. We need to listen carefully to the teaching of the New Testament as to what the mission is and how we are to accomplish it. The term "mission" communicates that those who receive the mission are sent to accomplish a task. Being sent on a mission also necessarily involves movement, at least on the part of

---

[1]Christopher J. H. Wright, *The Mission of God: Unlocking the Bible's Grand Narrative* (Downers Grove, IL: InterVarsity, 2006), 49–50.

[2]For more on the mission theme in the New Testament, see "Further Reading" at the end of this chapter.

some: going from one place to another, from one ethnic group to another. Therefore, to understand the missionary work of the church according to the New Testament, it is important to examine what God's people are sent to do. What does God want believers to accomplish as they go to the ends of the earth, as they move from working with one ethnic group to another?

This chapter walks through the missionary message of the New Testament, first by looking at the Gospels, then at Acts and the Epistles, and finally at the book of Revelation. This three-part division makes it possible to present: (1) the background to the mission of the church in the life, saving work, and teaching of Jesus; (2) the example and practice of the early church in seeking to fulfill its mission; and (3) the end result of God's work through the church. It is clear, in each of these three sections in the New Testament, that God is actively involved in the mission he has given to his people to reach the world with the good news about Jesus.

The Gospels

The Gospels are not missionary training handbooks; instead they present the story of the life, death, and resurrection of Jesus. Nevertheless, the theme of mission is important to the story, because Jesus himself is on a mission and because the story ends with Jesus sending his followers on a mission to the nations. The final commissioning scene at the end of the story is foreshadowed in the Gospels through the faith response of exemplary Gentiles toward Jesus, the training of Jesus' disciples for mission, and the teaching of Jesus that looks ahead to the worldwide scope of God's work.

Jesus was on a mission during his work on earth. In the Synoptic Gospels (Matthew, Mark, and Luke), the nature of this mission is clarified through statements about what Jesus *came* to do, about what he *was sent* to do, and about what he *must* do. In this way, the Gospel writers showed that Jesus' mission involved proclaiming a message and providing salvation. Jesus came to preach a message about the kingdom of God (Mark 1:38-39; Luke 4:43). Mark's Gospel summarizes Jesus' proclamation as "the good news of God" (Mark 1:14), in which he called for repentance and faith in light of the nearness of God's kingdom (Mark 1:15; cf. Matthew 4:23). Jesus made it clear that his message of good news was particularly directed toward the poor and oppressed (Luke 4:16–21; cf. Matthew 11:2–6; Luke 7:18–23).[3] Jesus also came to provide salvation, "to seek and to save the lost" (Luke 19:10). To accomplish his mission of bringing salvation, Jesus must suffer, die on the cross, and rise again (Matthew 16:21; Mark 8:31).[4] Jesus "did not come to be served, but to serve, and to give his life as a ransom" (Mark 10:45; cf. Matthew 20:28). Jesus taught that his work of salvation was particularly directed toward those who recognized their own sinfulness and lost condition (Matthew 9:12–13; Mark 2:17; Luke 5:31–32; 19:10). By announcing and initiating God's kingdom on earth and by establishing the way of salvation, Jesus laid the foundation for the continuing missionary work of his followers.

The mission of Jesus is a particularly prominent theme in John's Gospel.[5] Approximately forty times in John's Gospel, Jesus is identified as the one who is *sent* by the Father (e.g., 3:17; 5:30; 7:28–29; 8:26; 12:44–45; 14:24; 17:3). In addition, John's Gospel speaks repeatedly of Jesus as the one who *comes* from the Father (e.g., 5:43; 8:42; 10:10; 12:46; 13:3; 16:28; 18:37) and the one who is *given* by the Father (e.g., 3:16; 6:32). Several implications follow from the fact that Jesus is the sent-one from God. In this role, Jesus was determined to accomplish not his own will but the will of the one who sent him (4:34; 5:30; 6:38; 8:29; 9:4). He spoke not his own message but the words of the one who sent him (3:34; 7:16; 8:26; 12:49; 14:10,24). He sought not his own honor but the glory of the one who sent him (7:18). These implications will also follow for those who are commissioned by Jesus (17:18; 20:21).

---

[3] On Jesus' description of his mission in Luke 4:16–21, see especially William J. Larkin Jr., "Mission in Luke," in *Mission in the New Testament: An Evangelical Approach*, ed. William J. Larkin Jr. and Joel F. Williams (Maryknoll, NY: Orbis, 1998), 158–63.

[4] The necessity of Jesus' death—that it *must* happen—is a repeated theme in Luke's Gospel (Luke 9:22; 13:33; 17:25; 22:37; 24:6–7,26,44–46).

[5] On the mission theme in John's Gospel, see especially Andreas J. Köstenberger, *The Missions of Jesus and the Disciples According to the Fourth Gospel: With Implications for the Fourth Gospel's Purpose and the Mission of the Contemporary Church* (Grand Rapids: Eerdmans, 1998). See also Andreas Köstenberger and P. T. O'Brien, *Salvation to the Ends of the Earth: A Biblical Theology of Mission* (Downers Grove, IL: InterVarsity, 2001), 203–26.

Jesus' task, what he was sent to accomplish, involved both revelation and redemption. Jesus, as the divine Word (1:1) and the Word become flesh (1:14)—as, therefore, both God and man—is the perfect revelation of God (1:18). Jesus is also the Lamb of God who takes away the sin of the world (1:29) so that whoever believes in him may have eternal life (3:14–16).

The story of the Gospels drives toward the Great Commission at the end, but it is not a surprise ending. The final commissioning scene is foreshadowed in several ways. First, the Gospels give examples of Gentiles who responded with faith toward Jesus: the Magi from the East who came to worship the king of the Jews (Matthew 2:1–12); the centurion who sought healing for his servant (Matthew 8:5–13; Luke 7:1–10); the demon-possessed man in the region of the Gerasenes who was delivered by Jesus (Mark 5:1–20; cf. Matthew 8:28–34); the Syrophoenician woman who asked for help for her daughter (Mark 7:24–30; cf. Matthew 15:21–28); the deaf and mute man in the Decapolis (Mark 7:31–37); the Greeks who wanted to see Jesus (John 12:20–22); the centurion at the cross (Matthew 27:54; Mark 15:39; Luke 23:47). Jesus did not target his outreach toward Gentiles during his time on earth, since he was sent "to the lost sheep of Israel" (Matthew 15:24; compare also the similar limitation of the disciples' ministry before the resurrection, Matthew 10:5–6,23). However, Jesus did respond positively toward Gentiles who came to him in faith, as a foreshadowing of what was to come.

Second, Jesus called his disciples and trained them in missionary work with a view toward sending them out as his apostles ("sent ones"). When Jesus called disciples, he promised that he would send them out to "fish for people" (Mark 1:17; Matthew 4:19; Luke 5:10). Jesus chose twelve disciples in particular as his apostles so that he might send them out to proclaim his message and to have authority over demonic beings (Mark 3:13–19; Luke 6:12–16). Jesus sent out the Twelve on a "short-term mission trip" (Matthew 10:1–42; Mark 6:7–13; Luke 9:1–6), and then later a larger group of seventy-two (Luke 10:1–16). Jesus was preparing his followers for a future mission that extended beyond his own ministry to the people of Israel, one that moved out toward the ends of the earth.

Third, Jesus foreshadowed the coming Great Commission by teaching about the future worldwide impact of the gospel message. Already at the beginning of his ministry, Jesus angered the crowd in his hometown synagogue by suggesting that God had a concern for widows and lepers beyond those who lived in the land of Israel (Luke 4:22–30). Jesus wanted the temple to be a house of prayer for all nations (Mark 11:17). He promised that the gospel would be preached to all nations before the end of the age (Matthew 24:14; Mark 13:10; cf. Matthew 26:13; Mark 14:9). Jesus was concerned for the "other sheep" (John 10:16) who were "the scattered children of God" beyond the nation of Israel (John 11:52).[6] Jesus looked ahead and saw a new stage in God's plan in which the message of salvation would go out to all the nations of the world.

The Gospel story then ends with the Great Commission. Perhaps the most well-known description of it is in Matthew 28:18–20.[7] The key word "all" pervades Jesus' teaching throughout this passage.[8] Because Jesus has *all* authority, his followers can accept the mission given to them with hope and confidence. The task is to make disciples of *all* nations, teaching them to obey *all* the things commanded by Jesus. Jesus concludes with a promise to be with his people *all* the days to the very end of the age.

Although it may not be completely clear in English translations, the main command in the passage is not "go" but "make disciples." The emphasis of Jesus' commission is on making disciples of all nations, and going

[6]For other previews of a worldwide mission, see Matthew 5:13–16; 12:15–21; 24:31; 25:32; Mark 13:27; Luke 13:28–30.

[7]Mark's Gospel apparently followed a somewhat different pattern than the other canonical Gospels. Mark seems to have ended his Gospel abruptly without narrating the postresurrection meeting between Jesus and his disciples that was predicted by Jesus (Mark 14:28) and announced by the angel at the empty tomb (16:7). As a result, the clearest description of the present mission for Jesus' followers in Mark's Gospel appears in Jesus' eschatological discourse, where the mission involves the proclamation of the gospel to all nations in the midst of persecution (13:9–13). For more on the interpretive problems related to the end of Mark's Gospel, see Joel F. Williams, "Literary Approaches to the End of Mark's Gospel," *Journal of the Evangelical Theological Society* 42 (1999): 21–35. On the mission theme in Mark's Gospel, see Joel F. Williams, "Mission in Mark," in *Mission in the New Testament,* 137–51.

[8]D. A. Carson, "Matthew," in *The Expositor's Bible Commentary*, ed. Frank E. Gaebelein (Grand Rapids: Zondervan, 1984), 8:594.

becomes imperative in the sense that it is the necessary prerequisite for accomplishing that task.[9] People become disciples by identifying with the lordship of Jesus Christ through baptism and by learning to obey all that Jesus taught (cf. Matthew 11:28–30). Disciples set aside a life of self-interest and make a commitment to follow the pattern of Jesus' life and teaching (Matthew 16:24; cf. Matthew 10:24–25). The task, according to the Great Commission in Matthew's Gospel, is more than just bringing people to an initial conversion experience, as important as that is. Believers must also acknowledge Jesus' authority over their lives and grow in their understanding of Jesus' commands and in their obedience to them.

In contrast to Matthew's Gospel, Luke presents Jesus' final commission more as a statement of fact and a promise than as a command or mandate (Luke 24:45–49). The mission to the nations fulfills Scripture, Jesus' disciples are witnesses, and the promised Spirit will come. Just as the Old Testament looked ahead to the death and resurrection of the Messiah, so also it pointed to the message of salvation being proclaimed among all the nations of the world, the message that forgiveness of sins is now available to all who repent (24:46–47). The role of Jesus' disciples in the mission is to serve as witnesses (24:48). A witness is someone who has had a firsthand experience and is willing to talk about it. Followers of Jesus function as witnesses for Christ as they recognize what Jesus has accomplished for them through his death and resurrection and as they freely tell others about their experience with Jesus. However, the essential precondition for an effective witness is the empowerment of the Holy Spirit. Jesus therefore indicated that the disciples should wait for the coming of the Spirit, so that they might be clothed with power from on high (24:49). The book of Acts, Luke's second volume, starts with a commissioning scene similar to the one found at the end of Luke's Gospel, his first volume. In Acts 1:8, the

---

[9]In more technical language, "make disciples" is an imperative and also the main verb of the sentence—that is, the main action emphasized by Jesus. "Go" is a preceding participle of attendant circumstance, which expresses an additional action that serves as a prerequisite for the action of the main verb to occur. It is necessary to go in order to make disciples of all nations. I take the following participles, "baptizing" and "teaching," to be participles of means, expressing the way that disciples are made. For more on the use of the participles in Matthew 28:19–20, see Daniel B. Wallace, *Greek Grammar Beyond the Basics: An Exegetical Syntax of the New Testament* (Grand Rapids: Zondervan, 1996), 640–45.

themes of a worldwide mission, the role of Jesus' followers as witnesses, and the empowerment of the Holy Spirit will appear once again.

In John's Gospel, Jesus commissions the disciples after his resurrection with the words "As the Father has sent me, I am sending you" (John 20:21). Jesus compares the mission of his disciples with his own mission. The disciples' mission is similar to that of Jesus, since like Jesus they must accomplish the will, speak the words, and live for the glory of the one who sent them. Yet John's Gospel presents the actual task of the disciples in somewhat different terms than that of Jesus, which was accomplished through his incarnation and atonement. Their task does not repeat Jesus' work but builds on it. John's Gospel speaks about the task of the disciples in terms of harvesting (4:38), bearing fruit (15:16), and bearing witness to Jesus (15:26–27). In addition, John's Gospel indicates that believers confirm the truth of their witness concerning Jesus by loving one another. When believers love one another and live in unity, the world comes to know the truth of their message (13:34–35; 17:21).

The Gospels help us to see the extent to which the mission is the work of God. The Father sent his Son, Jesus, as the perfect revelation of God and as the Savior of the world. Without him, we have no hope. Having accomplished our salvation through his death and resurrection, Jesus commissioned his followers to take the message of salvation to the ends of the earth. Yet this mission is not accomplished in our own strength. Jesus promised to be present with his people to the end of the age, and he promised that he would send the Spirit of God, who would empower his people to be effective witnesses. God provides salvation and enables his people to bring the message of salvation to the world.

Acts and the Epistles

Both the book of Acts and the Epistles portray the early church as actively involved in accomplishing the mission given by Jesus after his resurrection. The Gospels end with the Great Commission; the book of Acts begins with it in 1:8.[10] Once again, Jesus identifies his followers

---

[10]A study of the mission theme in Acts may also be found in Robert L. Gallagher and Paul Hertig, eds. *Mission in Acts: Ancient Narratives in Contemporary Context*, American Society of Missiology Series 34 (Maryknoll, NY: Orbis, 2004).

as witnesses who will declare what they know to be true about him to the whole world—that is, in Jerusalem, in Judea and Samaria, and to the ends of the earth. All of this will take place through the power of the Holy Spirit. The rest of the book is not a constant repetition of Jesus' commission but rather a description of what the early church did to accomplish the task. Luke recounts the spread of the gospel within Jerusalem (chapters 1–7), then out to Judea and Samaria (chapters 8–12), and then toward the ends of the earth (chapters 13–28).

Luke gives repeated summary statements concerning the growth and spread of the church, as believers, filled with the Spirit, boldly share the message about Jesus (e.g., Acts 2:47; 5:14; 6:7; 9:31; 11:24; 12:24; 16:5; 19:20). The book offers a picture of the ever-expanding sphere of gospel availability, with the gospel moving out geographically but also crossing ethnic boundaries to the Samaritans and to the Gentiles. Persecution was not able to stop the spread of the message. In fact, it had the opposite effect in that it caused followers of Jesus to move to other places, taking the gospel with them (e.g., 8:1–4).

Internal conflicts within the community of believers didn't stop the spread of the message. This was because individuals who were filled with the Spirit and wisdom and faith showed leadership in solving the conflicts through faithful and humble service to the church (e.g., 6:1–7). The book ends somewhat abruptly with Paul under house arrest in Rome, boldly and freely teaching about the Lord Jesus Christ. In a sense, the book is over but the story is not, since the gospel has not reached the ends of the earth. The point is that everyone who participates in bringing the message to the ends of the earth has a part to play in the story.

The book of Acts emphasizes God's involvement in the continuing mission of the church. In order to empower his people to serve him effectively, God pours out his Spirit on them (1:4; 2:17,33; 10:44–47; 11:15–16). As a result, the Spirit enables believers to speak the word of God with boldness (4:31), bears witness to the truth about Jesus (5:32), grants guidance to God's servants (8:29; 16:6), provides leaders for the church (20:28), and sets some apart for special tasks (13:2,4). God is actively involved every step along the way in bringing people to salvation. He is the one who appoints them to eternal life (13:48), grants them repentance (11:18), opens their hearts to respond to the gospel with faith (14:27; 16:14), and saves them by his grace (15:11).

Luke begins Acts in an intriguing way by referring to his former book, his Gospel, in which he wrote "about all that Jesus began to do and teach" (1:1). The implication is that Luke's second volume, the book of Acts, will report all that Jesus continued to do and teach. Indeed, Jesus is active in the missionary work of the church, sometimes quite directly, as when he confronted Paul on the road to Damascus and sent him to take the gospel to the Gentiles (9:3–6,15; 22:8,21; 26:15–18). Yet Jesus is active throughout the mission of the church, since miracles and healing come through the power of his name (3:6,16; 4:10,30; 16:18) and salvation is found in his name (10:43; 13:38–39; 16:31)—and in his name alone (4:12). God is so completely involved in the mission of the church that when Paul reports on the success of his missionary journeys he does so by explaining what God did (14:27; 15:4; 21:19). Paul recognized that everything done through his ministry was ultimately the work of God.

> *Indeed, Jesus is active in the missionary work of the church.*

When the book of Acts describes the movement of the gospel out toward the ends of the earth, beyond Judea and Samaria, it does so by reporting the missionary journeys of Paul. Paul's letters also stand out within the collection of epistles in the New Testament because of their number and length. The result is that both within the book of Acts and within the New Testament epistles the apostle Paul functions as the exemplary missionary. In a real sense, Paul is the canonical standard for missionary work.[11] Since he stands as the model missionary in the New

---

[11]For an extended argument in support of this point, see Christopher R. Little, *Mission in the Way of Paul: Biblical Mission for the Church in the Twenty-First Century*, Studies in Bible and Literature vol. 80 (New York: Peter Lang, 2005), 75–130. For other studies concerning Paul's missionary work, see Roland Allen, *Missionary Methods: St. Paul's or Ours?* reprint ed. (Grand Rapids: Eerdmans, 1962); Dean S. Gilliland, *Pauline Theology and Mission Practice* (Grand Rapids: Eerdmans, 1983); W. P. Bowers, "Mission," in *Dictionary of Paul and His Letters*, ed. Gerald F. Hawthorne and Ralph P. Martin (Downers Grove, IL: InterVarsity, 1993), 608–19; P. T. O'Brien, *Gospel and Mission in the Writings of Paul: An Exegetical and Theological Analysis* (Grand Rapids: Baker, 1995); Peter Bolt and Mark Thompson, eds., *The Gospel to the Nations: Perspectives on Paul's Mission* (Downers Grove, IL: InterVarsity, 2000).

Testament, it is important to look closely at the nature of his ministry. Descriptions of Paul's mission in Acts and in his own letters provide insights into the following: Paul's *goal* in his missionary work, his *character*, his *sphere of activity*, his *strategy*, and his *confidence*.

Paul's *goal* was to proclaim the good news concerning Jesus Christ where it was not known and to gather those who responded with faith in Jesus into local churches where together they could grow in their faith and love. In other words, "Paul was a pioneering, church-planting evangelist."[12] Paul understood that he was called by God to preach the gospel, especially among the Gentiles (Acts 13:47; 20:24; 26:17–18; Romans 1:1–5; 15:15–16; 1 Corinthians 9:16; Galatians 1:15–16; Ephesians 3:7–12). The gospel is the message about God's Son, Jesus Christ, who through his death and resurrection brings salvation, the forgiveness of sins, and a right standing before God to all who put their faith in him (Romans 1:1–5; 3:21–26; 10:9–10; 1 Corinthians 15:1–8; Ephesians 2:8–10). Since salvation comes by faith in Jesus and not through works of the law, everyone—both Jews and Gentiles—can live by faith (Galatians 2:14–21; Romans 3:21–30). Therefore, Gentiles are fellow heirs, fellow members of the body, and fellow partakers of the promise through the gospel (Ephesians 3:1–6).

As part of his missionary work, Paul sought to start churches in the cities where he proclaimed the gospel, gathering his converts into local congregations. These churches (normally meeting in a home; e.g., Romans 16:3–5; 1 Corinthians 16:19; Colossians 4:15; Philemon 1–2) were places where believers could regularly come together for worship and mutual edification, the building up of one another in faith and love (1 Corinthians 14:26; Ephesians 4:11–16). Paul referred to this aspect of his mission work as "planting" (1 Corinthians 3:5–9) and as "laying a foundation" upon which others may build (1 Corinthians 3:10–15). Paul's hope in all his work was that he might bring every believer to maturity in Christ (Colossians 1:28–29). Therefore, the apostle felt the daily pressure of his concern for all the churches that he started (2 Corinthians 11:28); and he sought to nurture these newly formed congre-

---

[12]Don N. Howell Jr., "Mission in Paul's Epistles: Genesis, Pattern, and Dynamics," in *Mission in the New Testament*, 70.

gations through his letters and through follow-up visits, not only by himself but also by his co-workers.

In Romans 15:19, Paul wrote that he had fully proclaimed the gospel of Christ over the entire eastern Mediterranean area ("from Jerusalem all the way around to Illyricum"), so that he was now looking to move on to Spain in order to bring the gospel where it was not known. Paul obviously had not finished the whole task of evangelism and discipleship throughout the entire eastern Mediterranean area. Yet he felt free to move on to a new region because his goal was to plant churches in major cities, leaving behind believing communities that would continue to grow and to spread the message about Jesus (cf. Acts 13:49; 19:10).

Paul considered the ministry of the gospel a treasure (2 Corinthians 4:1–6), but it was not a treasure that he hoarded for himself. Others could join in the struggle for the cause of the gospel (Philippians 4:3). In his letters, Paul did not repeatedly exhort his churches to join in the task of sharing the gospel and continuing the mission. The apostle did, however, commend believers for their participation in the work of the gospel (Philippians 1:3–5,27; 2:16; 4:3; 1 Thessalonians 1:8), and he found encouragement in the progress of the gospel through the work of others (Philippians 1:12–18). Paul assumed that God would call some to be evangelists (Ephesians 4:11) and that every believer would be prepared to share the gospel in the struggle against the forces of evil (Ephesians 6:15). Paul also asked his churches to pray for him in his missionary work in order that he might have an opportunity to speak the message of God with boldness (Ephesians 6:19–20; Colossians 4:2–4; 2 Thessalonians 3:1–2). For Paul, the gospel ministry did not demand repeated exhortations for support, because the gospel itself is powerful. It is the power and wisdom of God (Romans 1:16; 1 Corinthians 1:23–25), able to spread rapidly (2 Thessalonians 3:1) and to grow and bear fruit all over the world (Colossians 1:3–8).[13]

---

[13]On the role of Paul's churches in the spread of the gospel, see O'Brien, *Gospel and Mission*, 109–31; Eckhard J. Schnabel, *Early Christian Mission*, 2 vols., Downers Grove, IL: InterVarsity, 2004, 2:1451–75; Robert L. Plummer, *Paul's Understanding of the Church's Mission: Did the Apostle Paul Expect the Early Christian Communities to Evangelize?* (Milton Keynes, UK: Paternoster, 2006).

Paul's *character*, and therefore his mission, was marked by integrity and by love for people. First Thessalonians 2:1–12 describes Paul's initial missionary work in the city of Thessalonica, an endeavor that lasted for only a brief time, perhaps just a few weeks (Acts 17:1–10). Paul spoke the gospel in the midst of strong opposition (1 Thessalonians 2:2), and those who believed turned away from their devotion to idols in order to serve the living and true God (1:9). Throughout his work among the Thessalonians, the apostle showed complete integrity (2:10). He never in any way sought to deceive them. He never pretended to be someone he was not in order to receive honor from them or to take their money (2:3,5; cf. 2 Corinthians 2:17). Instead, he worked diligently to provide for himself and to keep from being a burden to them (1 Thessalonians 2:9). Paul loved these people, so that he came to share with them not only the gospel but his whole life as well (2:8). He was gentle among them, like a mother caring for her children (2:7–8), and deeply concerned for their well-being, like a father (2:11–12). Undoubtedly, part of Paul's impact as a missionary grew out of his sincere love for people.

Paul's targeted *sphere of activity* was anywhere that the gospel had not yet been proclaimed. His ambition was to bring the gospel to the places where Christ was not known (Romans 15:20–21), to the regions beyond the established church (2 Corinthians 10:16). He didn't want to build on someone else's foundation; his desire instead was to go where people had not heard about Jesus and to be the one to lay the foundation (Romans 15:20; 1 Corinthians 3:10). Paul recognized the value of others building on the foundation that he had laid (1 Corinthians 3:10–15), of others watering what he had planted (1 Corinthians 3:5–9). Both those who start churches and those who continue to build them up are co-workers with God (1 Corinthians 3:7–9). However, while Paul recognized the value of those who served the Lord in places where the church was already established, he himself felt an obligation to the unreached. That was one reason why Paul felt hindered in coming to minister in the city of Rome (Romans 15:22). Yet he was eager to preach the gospel there as well (Romans 1:15), and from there to go on to Spain, hopefully with the help of the believers in Rome (Romans

15:23–33). What he anticipated in working with an already established church, like the one in Rome, was a relationship of mutual benefit, in which both Paul and the Roman believers would be mutually encouraged by one another's faith (Romans 1:11–12). Paul's role as a pioneer missionary did not free him to bypass an already established church on his way to unreached people, nor did it place him in a position of superiority over such a church.

Paul's missionary *strategy* was flexible. He followed general patterns, but his plans were subject to change in light of the guidance of the Spirit and also in light of practical considerations. He typically targeted cities that were centers of trade and commerce (e.g., Thessalonica, Corinth, Ephesus), assuming that the message would then spread to the surrounding region. Paul also normally went to cities where there was a Jewish synagogue (e.g., Pisidian Antioch, Berea, Corinth), although that was not always the case (e.g., Lystra, Philippi). Paul's practice had the practical advantage of putting him in contact with Jewish people and Gentile God-fearers, who already had an understanding of the Scriptures. Yet it was also reflective of a theological conviction concerning the salvation-historical priority of the people of Israel (cf. Romans 1:16).

Paul seems to have decided to move from east to west in his missionary work, moving from one region to the next adjoining region. His travel plans, however, were open to change—as happened, for example, when he passed by the Roman province of Asia and went on to Macedonia. The guidance of the Holy Spirit and the direction of a divinely given vision moved the apostle in a new direction (Acts 16:6–10). Paul could also change his travel plans for practical reasons—as happened, for example, when he delayed his arrival in Corinth with the hope of avoiding another painful visit (2 Corinthians 1:15—2:1).

Paul generally worked and traveled as part of a team. Indeed, it would be difficult to understand the scope and impact of his mission without taking into consideration the contribution of his many coworkers. Yet he also found it necessary on occasion to press on by himself (Acts 17:14–16). Paul often supported his missionary work through his own manual labor, using his training as a tentmaker (Acts

18:1–5; cf. Acts 20:33–35; 1 Thessalonians 2:9). Sometimes he accepted gifts in support of his mission from one of the churches he started (Philippians 4:10–20), and sometimes he did not (1 Corinthians 9:1–18). The advantage of Paul's flexibility was that he could follow whatever means best served the progress of the gospel. He could become all things to all people so that by all possible means he might save some (1 Corinthians 9:22).

Paul's *confidence* grew out of his conviction that God was at work through the power of the Spirit in the lives of believers and in the newly formed churches, as well as in his own life and ministry.[14] At the end of his first missionary journey, the apostle stopped briefly at the churches he had started, encouraged the new believers, appointed leaders, prayed for them, and committed them to the Lord (Acts 14:21–23; cf. Acts 20:32). Paul could leave these churches and give them the freedom to stand on their own because he knew that, whether he was present with them or absent from them, God was at work in their midst (Philippians 1:27; 2:13). This confidence in the work of God runs as an underlying theme throughout Paul's teaching and interactions with his churches. For Paul, believers began their new life not through human wisdom or effort but through the power of God and the work of the Spirit (1 Corinthians 2:4–5; Galatians 3:1–5,14). Having begun by the Spirit, they could press on, living in obedience to God's will and developing a Christlike character, all through dependence on the Spirit's empowerment (Romans 8:3–4; Galatians 5:16–25). Paul was confident that just as God had begun a good work within them he would also bring it to completion (Philippians 1:6).

Paul's interactions with the churches he started make sense within the context of his trust in God's involvement in the mission. He quickly established leaders in the congregations (Acts 14:23). For example, Paul was able to spend only a brief time planting the church in Thessalonica, but when he wrote 1 Thessalonians he was already encouraging the church to show respect and love for the leaders in their

---

[14]For a sustained development of this point, along with an exploration of its implications for mission work, see Roland Allen's *The Spontaneous Expansion of the Church*, reprint ed. (Grand Rapids: Eerdmans, 1962).

congregation (1 Thessalonians 5:12–13). Paul could establish local leaders within the churches because he believed that in reality the Holy Spirit was the one who appointed them (Acts 20:28). All the finances of the churches were under the authority of the churches themselves, and Paul was careful not to have access to any of these funds (1 Corinthians 16:1–4; 2 Corinthians 8:18–20). He encouraged churches to give to the poor believers in Jerusalem, but their participation in this gift was by their own generosity and not by an imposed obligation (2 Corinthians 8:1–15; 9:7).

Paul's letters are not filled with detailed directions about how to live in every possible situation in life; rather his moral instructions were normally communicated through general principles, with the assumption that the Holy Spirit would guide believers in making specific choices (Romans 8:12–14). Paul entrusted congregations with the task of church discipline; if someone in the church was not living according to the ways of God, the believers in the church were responsible for the tasks of confronting and disciplining (1 Corinthians 5:1–13; 6:1–6; 2 Corinthians 2:5–11). Of course, Paul had convictions about how congregations should think and act, but he pressed for godly responses by means of persuasion, not by taking away their independence and responsibility and setting up an organizational structure that gave continuing control to an outsider.

Paul wanted believers to follow his teaching out of their own free will, not by compulsion (Philemon 12–14). Because of his confidence in the work of the Spirit, the apostle could expect believers to submit their own interests to the interests of others within the congregation (Philippians 2:1–4). Such mutual submission grows out of the work of the Spirit and out of an attitude of respect for what Christ is doing in the lives of others (Ephesians 5:18–21). In all these various ways, Paul showed an astonishing confidence in new believers and newly formed churches because he sincerely believed that God was at work in their midst.

Paul's attitude of confidence in God also extended to the way in which he viewed himself and his ministry. He had a sense of his own inadequacy—a recognition that in his own strength he was insufficient to spread the knowledge of God (2 Corinthians 2:14–16; cf. 1 Timothy

1:12–16). Paul saw himself as a clay pot: fragile and of little worth in itself; but within this clay pot was a treasure, the ministry of the gospel (2 Corinthians 4:1–7). So as God used him in all of his weakness, what became obvious was the power of Christ rather than the sufficiency of the servant (2 Corinthians 12:7–10). Therefore, when Paul reported on his missionary work, he did not boast in his accomplishments but rather spoke only about what Christ had done (Romans 15:18). Paul had confidence, not because he trusted in his own strength but because he knew that the mission was God's work and that God took pleasure in using inadequate servants to accomplish his will.

Revelation

The book of Revelation is well known as a description of God's final judgment on a rebellious world. The inhabitants of the earth whose names have not been written in the book of life follow the beast and join in his fight against the Lord and his anointed one. God sends judgments on the earth, a taste of his wrath as a final call to repentance, but the people curse God and refuse to repent. Then Jesus, the King of kings and Lord of lords, comes and strikes down the nations assembled against him with the sword from his mouth.

Although this aspect of the book of Revelation—God's conflict with the nations—is well known, what is often overlooked is the extent to which Revelation emphasizes the turning of the nations to the true worship of God.[15] Revelation envisions not only a mass rebellion against God but also a mass conversion of the nations, an uncountable multitude from every nation, tribe, people, and language worshiping before the throne of God and before the Lamb (Revelation 7:9–10; 15:4). Jesus Christ, the Lamb of God, will be their shepherd, and God himself will dwell with them and wipe every tear from their eyes (7:15–17). The eternal gospel will be proclaimed to all the people of the world, in order to call on them to fear God and to give glory to the one who made the heavens and the earth (14:6–7; cf. 11:13). Some from all

---

[15]Grant R. Osborne surveys what the book of Revelation conveys about mission and the witness of God's people in *Revelation*, Baker Exegetical Commentary on the New Testament (Grand Rapids: Baker Academic, 2002), 41–43.

the tribes of the earth will recognize their part in the death of Jesus and will respond with repentant sorrow (1:7). Jesus, the ruler of the kings of the earth, will take those who repent from every tribe, language, people, and nation and make them into a kingdom and into priests to serve God, because he loves them and has released them from their sins by his blood (1:5–7; 5:9).

Some from all the tribes of the earth will recognize their part in the death of Jesus and will respond with repentant sorrow (1:7).

When God restores all things, making a new heaven and a new earth, the nations will be there—no longer rebellious but healed, cleansed from their devotion to falsehood and oppression (21:24–27; 22:2). The nations will bring into this new world their glory and honor, the best of all their treasures, to give them to the Lord God Almighty and to the Lamb (21:24,26). Although God will judge those who steadfastly refuse to repent, he also wants to pour out his love upon people from every nation who will turn to him for salvation.

In the book of Revelation, the role that God's people play in bringing the nations to God is that of faithful witnesses to the truth, faithful even to the point of death. God's people will overcome through the blood of the Lamb and through the word of their testimony (12:11). Yet faithfulness to the message about Christ means putting devotion to Jesus before life itself, because the powerful of the world stand opposed to the truth (11:7; 12:11,17; 17:6; cf. 2:13; 6:9–11; 20:4). In this, Jesus serves as the perfect example, as the faithful and true witness who gave his life (1:5; 3:14).

The book of Revelation helps us to see the end of the story, the end result of God's work in human history and, therefore, the end of the mission. At the end of the story, Christ rules over all the earth and God dwells with his people, a vast multitude from every nation, tribe, people, and language. This conclusion is never in doubt, because the mission is God's work, and he will accomplish his plan.

Conclusion

God's involvement in the church's mission is an overarching theme in the New Testament. The Gospels present the mission of Jesus, God's

Son, who came to provide salvation through his death and resurrection. After his resurrection, Jesus sent his followers out on a mission to make disciples of all nations. The book of Acts and the Epistles make clear that this mission is possible because God pours out his Spirit upon his people, empowering them to speak the message with boldness and opening the hearts of others to receive it. Paul's great confidence came from his recognition that God would complete what he had started in the lives of his people. The book of Revelation confirms that the mission will in fact be accomplished.

Without question, God will accomplish his will and draw to himself people from all the nations of the world, so that he might shower his grace and love upon them for all eternity. Therefore, the crucial question focuses not on God's involvement but on ours. Will we be a part of what God is doing in the world? Will we participate in the mission of God?

Discussion Points

1. The Gospels cover the life, ministry, death, and resurrection of Jesus before he sent the apostles on a mission to all nations. What can we learn about God's mission from the Gospels?

2. Was the Great Commission at the end of the Gospels a "surprise ending"? Why or why not?

3. How was Jesus still active in carrying out the mission of the church in Acts after he ascended to the Father?

4. Based on the New Testament, write in one sentence a clear statement of the mission of God.

Further Reading

Bosch, David J. *Transforming Mission: Paradigm Shifts in Theology of Mission*, American Society of Missiology Series 16. Maryknoll, NY: Orbis, 1991, 15–178.

Green, Michael. *Evangelism in the Early Church*, 2nd ed. Grand Rapids: Eerdmans, 2003.

Hahn, Ferdinand. *Mission in the New Testament*, Studies in Biblical Theology 47. Naperville, IL: Alec R. Allenson, 1965.

Köstenberger, Andreas J., and Peter T. O'Brien. *Salvation to the Ends of the Earth: A Biblical Theology of Mission*, New Studies in Biblical Theology. Downers Grove, IL: InterVarsity, 2001.

Larkin, William J., Jr., and Joel F. Williams, eds. *Mission in the New Testament: An Evangelical Approach*, American Society of Missiology Series 27. Maryknoll, NY: Orbis, 1998.

Little, Christopher R. *Mission in the Way of Paul: Biblical Mission for the Church in the Twenty-First Century*, Studies in Bible and Literature 80. New York: Peter Lang, 2005.

Moreau, A. Scott, Gary R. Corwin, and Gary B. McGee. *Introducing World Missions: A Biblical, Historical, and Practical Survey.* Grand Rapids: Baker Academic, 2004, 40–70.

Schnabel, Eckhard J. *Early Christian Mission*, 2 vols. Downers Grove, IL: InterVarsity, 2004.

Senior, Donald, and Carroll Stuhlmueller. *The Biblical Foundations for Mission.* Maryknoll, NY: Orbis, 1983.

Wright, Christopher J. H. *The Mission of God: Unlocking the Bible's Grand Narrative.* Downers Grove, IL: InterVarsity, 2006, 501–30.

3

THE SUPREMACY OF GOD IN MISSIONS THROUGH WORSHIP

John Piper

[More than any other contemporary writer or theologian, the writings of Dr. John Piper have revolutionized thinking regarding missions. As with others, my own perspective, after many years in mission leadership, was radically changed by his book *Let the Nations Be Glad! The Supremacy of God in Missions.* The call to missions and global strategies will never be adequate if motivated by the need of a lost world or from a sense of obligation. The only compelling motivation for missions is for the glory of God and his worship among all peoples. With the permission of Dr. Piper, Desiring God Ministries, and Baker Books of Grand Rapids, Michigan, we are privileged to include in this volume an abridged copy of chapter 1 of his book.—Jerry Rankin, International Mission Board president emeritus]

Missions is not the ultimate goal of the church. Worship is. Missions exists because worship doesn't. Worship is ultimate, not missions, because God is ultimate, not man. When this age is over, and the countless millions of the redeemed fall on their faces before the throne of God, missions will be no more. It is a temporary necessity. But worship abides forever.

Worship, therefore, is the fuel and goal in missions. It's the goal of missions because in missions we simply aim to bring the nations into the white-hot enjoyment of God's glory. The goal of missions is the gladness of the peoples in the greatness of God. "The Lord reigns; let the earth *rejoice*; let the many coastlands *be glad*!" (Psalm 97:1).[1] "Let the peoples praise thee, O God; let all the peoples praise thee! Let the nations *be glad and sing for joy*!" (Psalm 67:3–4).

But worship is also the fuel of missions. Passion for God in worship precedes the offer of God in preaching. You can't commend what you don't cherish. Missionaries will never call out, "Let the nations *be glad*!" who cannot say from the heart, "I *rejoice* in the Lord. . . . *I will be glad and exult in thee*, I will sing praise to thy name, O Most High" (Psalm 104:34; 9:2). Missions begins and ends in worship.

If the pursuit of *God's* glory is not ordered above the pursuit of *man's* good in the affections of the heart and the priorities of the church, *man* will not be well served and *God* will not be duly honored. I am not pleading for a diminishing of missions but for a magnifying of God. When the flame of worship burns with the heat of God's true worth, the light of missions will shine to the most remote peoples on earth. And I long for that day to come!

Where passion for God is weak, zeal for missions will be weak. Churches that are not centered on the exaltation of the majesty and beauty of God will scarcely kindle a fervent desire to "declare *his glory* among the nations" (Psalm 96:3). Even outsiders feel the disparity between the boldness of our claim upon the nations and the blandness of our engagement with God.

Albert Einstein's Indictment

For example, Charles Misner, a scientific specialist in general relative theory, expressed Albert Einstein's skepticism over the church with words that should waken us to the shallowness of our experience with God in worship:

> The design of the universe . . . is very magnificent and shouldn't be taken for granted. In fact, I believe that is why Einstein had so little use for organized religion, although he strikes me as a basically very religious man. *He must have looked at what the preachers said about God and felt that they were blaspheming. He had seen much more majesty than they*

---

[1] Scripture quotations, some of which may be John Piper's own translations, are reproduced as found in Piper, *Let the Nations Be Glad! The Supremacy of God in Missions*, 2nd ed. (Grand Rapids: Baker, 2003). Italics in Scripture quotations indicate emphasis added by Piper.

had ever imagined, and they were just not talking about the real thing. My guess is that he simply felt that religions he'd run across did not have proper respect . . . for the author of the universe.[2]

The charge of blasphemy is loaded. The point is to pack a wallop behind the charge that in our worship services God simply doesn't come through for who he is. He is unwittingly belittled. For those who are stunned by the indescribable magnitude of what God has made, not to mention the infinite greatness of the One who made it, the steady diet on Sunday morning of practical "how to's" and psychological soothing and relational therapy and tactical planning seem dramatically out of touch with Reality—the God of overwhelming greatness.

It is possible to be distracted from God in trying to serve God. Martha-like, we neglect the one thing needful, and soon begin to present God as busy and fretful. A. W. Tozer warned us about this: "We commonly represent God as a busy, eager, somewhat frustrated Father hurrying about seeking help to carry out His benevolent plan to bring peace and salvation to the world. . . . Too many missionary appeals are based upon this fancied frustration of Almighty God."[3]

Scientists know that light travels at the speed of 5.87 trillion miles a year. They also know that the galaxy of which our solar system is a part is about 100,000 light-years in diameter—about five hundred eighty seven thousand trillion miles. It is one of about a million such galaxies in the optical range of our most powerful telescopes. In our galaxies there are about 100 billion stars. The sun is one of them, a modest star burning at about 6,000 degrees Centigrade on the surface, and traveling in an orbit at 155 miles per second, which means it will take about 200 million years to complete a revolution around the galaxy.

Scientists know these things and are awed by them. And they say, "If there is a personal God, as the Christians say, who spoke this universe into being, then there is a certain respect and reverence and wonder and dread that would have to come through when we talk about him and when we worship him."

---

[2]Quoted in *First Things*, Dec. 1991, no. 18, 63 (italics added).
[3]Quoted in Tom Wells, *A Vision for Missions* (Carlisle, PA: Banner of Truth Trust, 1985), 35.

We who believe the Bible know this even better than the scientists because we have heard something even more amazing:

> "To whom then will you compare me, that I should be like him?" says the Holy One. Lift up your eyes on high and see: who created these [stars]? He who brings out their host by number, calling them all by name; by the greatness of his might, and because he is strong in power not one is missing. (Isaiah 40:25–26)

Every one of the billions of stars in the universe is there by God's specific appointment. He knows their number. And, most astonishing of all, he knows them by name. They do his bidding as his personal agents. When we feel the weight of this grandeur in the heavens, we have only touched the hem of his garment. "Lo, these are but the outskirts of his ways! And how small a whisper do we hear of him" (Job 26:14). That is why we cry "Be exalted, O God, *above* the heavens!" (Psalm 57:5). God is the absolute reality that everyone in the universe must come to terms with. Everything depends utterly on his will. All other realities compare to him like a raindrop compares to the ocean, or like an anthill compares to Mount Everest. To ignore him or belittle him is unintelligible and suicidal folly. How shall one ever be the emissary of this great God who has not trembled before him with joyful wonder?

The Second Greatest Activity in the World

The most crucial issue in missions is the centrality of God in the life of the church. Where people are not stunned by the greatness of God, how can they be sent with the ringing message, "*Great* is the Lord and *greatly* to be praised; he is to be feared above all gods!" (Psalm 96:4)? Missions is not first and ultimate; God is. And these are not just words. This truth is the lifeblood of missionary inspiration and endurance. William Carey, the father of modern missions, who set sail for India from England in 1793, expressed the connection:

> When I left England, my hope of India's conversion was very strong; but amongst so many obstacles, it would die, unless upheld by God. Well, I have God, and His Word is true. Though the superstitions of

the heathen were a thousand times stronger than they are, and the example of the Europeans a thousand times worse; though I were deserted by all and persecuted by all, yet my faith, fixed on the sure Word, would rise above all obstructions and overcome every trial. God's cause will triumph.[4]

Carey and thousands like him have been moved by the vision of a great and triumphant God. That vision must come first. Savoring it in worship precedes spreading it in missions. All of history is moving toward one great goal, the white-hot worship of God and his Son among all the peoples of the earth. Missions is not that goal. It is the means. And for that reason it is the second greatest human activity in the world.

God's Passion for God Is the Foundation for Ours

One of the things God uses to make this truth take hold of a person and a church is the stunning realization that it is also true for God himself. Missions is not *God's* ultimate goal, worship is. And when this sinks into a person's heart everything changes. The world is often turned on its head. And everything looks different—including the missionary enterprise.

The ultimate foundation for our passion to see God glorified is his own passion to be glorified. God is central and supreme in his own affections. There are no rivals for the supremacy of God's glory in his own heart. God is not an idolater. He does not disobey the first and great commandment. With all his heart and soul and strength and mind he delights in the glory of his manifold perfections.[5] The most passionate heart for God in all the universe is God's heart.

This truth, more than any other I know, seals the conviction that worship is the fuel and goal of missions. The deepest reason why our passion for God should *fuel* missions is that God's passion for God fuels missions. Missions is the overflow of our delight in God because missions is the overflow of God's delight in being God. And the deepest reason why worship is the *goal* in missions is that worship

---

[4]Quoted in Iain Murray, *The Puritan Hope* (Edinburgh: Banner of Truth Trust, 1971), 140.
[5]I have tried to unfold this wonderful truth of the Father's delight in himself, that is, his Son, in *The Pleasures of God: Meditations on God's Delight in Being God* (Portland, OR: Multnomah Press, 1991), chapter one, "The Pleasure of God in His Son."

is God's goal. We are confirmed in this goal by the Biblical record of God's relentless pursuit of praise among the nations. "Praise the Lord, all nations! Extol him, all peoples!" (Psalm 117:1). If it is God's goal it must be our goal.

The Chief End of God Is to Glorify God and Enjoy Himself Forever

God chose his people for his glory:

> He chose us in him before the foundation of the world that we should be holy and blameless before him. He destined us in love to be his sons through Jesus Christ according to the purpose of his will *upon the praise of the glory of his grace.* (Ephesians 1:4–6; cf. vv. 12, 14)

God created us for his glory:

> Bring my sons from afar and my daughters from the end of the earth, every one who is called by my name, *whom I created for my glory.* (Isaiah 43:6–7)

God called Israel for his glory:

> You are my servant Israel in whom *I will be glorified.* (Isaiah 49:3)

> I made the whole house of Israel and the whole house of Judah cling to me, says the Lord, *that they might be for me a people, a name, a praise, and a glory.* (Jeremiah 13:11)

God spared Israel in the wilderness for the glory of his name:

> *I acted for the sake of my name, that it should not be profaned* in the sight of the nations in whose sight I had brought them out. (Ezekiel 20:14)

God gave Israel victory in Canaan for the glory of his name:

> What other nation on earth is like Thy people Israel, whom God went to redeem to be His people, *making Himself a name,* and doing for them great and terrible things, by driving out before His people a nation and its gods? (2 Samuel 7:23)

God did not cast away his people for the glory of his name:

> Fear not, you have done all this evil, yet do not turn aside from following the Lord. . . . For the Lord will not cast away his people *for his great name's sake.* (1 Samuel 12:20–22)

Jesus sought the glory of his Father in all he did:

> He who speaks on his own authority seeks his own glory; but *he who seeks the glory of him who sent him* is true, and in him there is no falsehood. (John 7:18)

Jesus told us to do good works so that God gets glory:

> Let your light so shine before men, that they may see your good works and *give glory to your Father who is in heaven.* (Matthew 5:15; cf. 1 Peter 2:12)

Jesus endured his final hours of suffering for God's glory:

> "Now is my soul troubled. And what shall I say? 'Father, save me from this hour?' No, *for this purpose I have come to this hour. Father, glorify Thy name."* Then a voice came from heaven, *"I have glorified it, and I will glorify it again."* (John 12:27–28)

> Father, the hour has come; *glorify thy Son that the Son may glorify thee.* (John 17:1; cf. 13:31–32)

The ministry of the Holy Spirit is to glorify the Son of God:

> *He will glorify me,* for he will take what is mine and declare it to you. (John 16:14)

God instructs us to do everything for his glory:

> So whether you eat or drink, or whatever you do, *do all to the glory of God.* (1 Corinthians 10:31; cf. 6:20)

God tells us to serve in a way that will glorify him:

> Whoever renders service [let him do it] as one who renders it by the strength which God supplies; *in order that in everything God may be glorified* through Jesus Christ. To him belong glory and dominion forever and ever. Amen. (1 Peter 4:11)

God's plan is to fill the earth with the knowledge of his glory:

> For the earth will be filled with *the knowledge of the glory of the Lord* as the waters cover the sea. (Habakkuk 2:14)

Everything that happens will redound to God's glory:

> From him, to him and through him are all things. *To him be glory for ever.* Amen. (Romans 11:36)

In the New Jerusalem the glory of God replaces the sun:

> And the city has no need of sun or moon to shine upon it, for *the glory of God is its light*, and its lamp is the Lamb. (Revelation 21:23)

God's passion for God is unmistakable. God struck me with this most powerfully when I first read Jonathan Edwards' book entitled *The Dissertation Concerning the End for Which God Created the World*. There he piles reason upon reason and scripture on scripture to show this truth: "The great end of God's works, which is so variously expressed in Scripture, is indeed but ONE; and this *one* end is most properly and comprehensively called, THE GLORY OF GOD."[6] In other words, the chief end of God is to glorify God, and enjoy himself for ever.

The Belittling of God's Glory and the Horrors of Hell

The condition of the human heart throws God's God-centeredness into stark relief. Man by nature does not have a heart to glorify God. "All have sinned and *fall short of God's glory*" (Romans 3:23). In our wickedness we suppress the truth that God is our Sovereign and worthy of all our allegiance and affection. By nature we exchange the glory of the immortal God for dim images of it in creation (Romans 1:18,23). We forsake the fountain of living waters and hew out for ourselves broken cisterns that can hold no water (Jeremiah 2:13).

The nations "are darkened in their understanding, alienated from the life of God because of the ignorance that is in them, due to their hardness of heart" (Ephesians 4:18). By nature we were all once dead in trespasses and sins following the slave master Satan, and therefore children of wrath (Ephesians 2:1–3). Our end was "eternal punishment" (Matthew 25:46), and "exclusion from the presence of the Lord's glory" (2 Thessalonians 1:9), and endless torments in "the second death which is the lake of fire" (Revelation 14:11; 20:10; 21:8).[7]

The infinite horrors of hell are intended by God to be a vivid demonstration of the infinite value of the glory of God. The Biblical assumption

---

[6] Jonathan Edwards, *A Dissertation Concerning the End for Which God Created the World, The Works of Jonathan Edwards*, Vol. 1, ed. by Sereno Dwight (Edinburgh: Banner of Truth Trust, 1974), 119.
[7] In defense of the reality of eternal conscious torment in hell for those who reject the truth of God see *Let the Nations Be Glad! The Supremacy of God in Missions* (Grand Rapids: Baker, 1993), 120–28.

of the justice of Hell is a clear testimony to the infiniteness of the sin of failing to glorify God. All of us have failed. All the nations have failed. Therefore the weight of infinite guilt rests on every human head because of our failure to cherish the glory of God. The Biblical vision of God then is that he is supremely committed, with infinite passion, to uphold and display the glory of his name. And the Biblical vision of man without grace is that he suppresses this truth and by nature finds more joy in his own glory than he does in God's. God exists to be worshipped, but man worships the work of his own hands. This two-fold reality creates the critical need for missions. And the very God-centeredness of God, which creates the crisis, also creates the solution.

God Is Most Glorified in Us when We Are Most Satisfied in Him

But is it loving for God to exalt his own glory? Yes it is. And there are several ways to see this truth clearly. One way is to ponder this sentence: *God is most glorified in us when we are most satisfied in him.* This is perhaps the most important sentence in my theology. If it is true, then it becomes plain why God is loving when he seeks to exalt his glory in my life. For that would mean that he would seek to maximize my satisfaction in him, since he is most glorified in me when I am most satisfied in him. Therefore God's pursuit of his own glory is not at odds with my joy, and that means it is not unkind or unmerciful or unloving of him to seek his glory. In fact it means that the more passionate God is for his own glory the more passionate he is for my satisfaction in that glory. And therefore God's God-centeredness and God's love soar together.

Duty or Delight in a Hospital Room?

To illustrate the truth that God is most glorified in us when we are most satisfied in him, consider what I might say on a pastoral visit when entering the hospital room of one of my people. They look up from their bed with a smile and say, "O, Pastor John, how good of you to come. What an encouragement." And suppose I lift my hand, as if to deflect the words, and say matter-of-factly, "Don't mention it. It's my duty as a pastor." Now what is wrong here? Why do we cringe at such a thoughtless pastoral statement? It *is* my duty. And duty is a good thing.

So why does that statement do so much damage?

It damages because it does not honor the sick person. Why? Because delight confers more honor than duty does. Doing hospital visitation out of mere duty honors duty. Doing it out of delight honors the patients. And they feel that. The right pastoral response to the patient's greeting would have been: "It's a pleasure to be here. I'm glad I could come." Do you see the paradox here? Those two sentences would show that I am "seeking my own." "It's *my* pleasure to be here. *I'm* glad I could come." And yet the reason these statements are not selfish is that they confer honor on the patient, not on the pastor. When someone delights in you, you feel honored. When someone finds happiness in being around you, you feel treasured, appreciated, glorified. It is a loving thing to visit the sick because it makes you glad to be there.

This then is the answer to why God is not unloving to magnify his glory. God is glorified precisely when we are satisfied in him—when we delight in his presence, when we like to be around him, when we treasure his fellowship. This is an utterly life-changing discovery. It frees us to pursue our joy in God and God to pursue his glory in us. Because they are not two different pursuits. God is most glorified in us when we are most satisfied in him.

God Exalts Himself in Mercy

There is another way to see how God's passion for his own glory is loving. And here the connection between the supremacy of God and the cause of missions becomes explicit. The connection between missions and the supremacy of God is found in this sentence: The glory God seeks to magnify is supremely the glory of his mercy. The key text is Romans 15:8–9:

> I tell you that Christ became a servant to the circumcised [Jewish people] to show God's truthfulness, in order to confirm the promises given to the patriarchs, and *in order that the nations might glorify God for his mercy.*

Notice the interlocking truths in these great missionary verses.

1. *Zeal for the glory of God motivates world missions.* Paul gives three reasons that Christ humbled himself as a servant and came into the world on that first great missionary journey from heaven to earth. First,

"Christ became a servant . . . *to show God's truthfulness.*" Second, he came "in order *to confirm [God's] promises.*" Third, he came "in order that the nations *might glorify God* for his mercy."

In other words Christ was on a mission to magnify God. He came to show that *God* is truthful. He came to show that *God* is a promise-keeper. And he came to show that *God* is glorious. Jesus came into the world *for God's sake*—to certify *God's* integrity; to vindicate *God's* work; to magnify *God's* glory. Since God sent his Son to do all this, it is plain that the primary motive of the first great mission to unreached peoples—the mission of Jesus from heaven—was God's zeal for the glory of God. That's the first truth from Romans 15:8–9: Zeal for the glory of God motivates world missions.

2. *A servant spirit and a heart of mercy motivate world missions.* "Christ became a *servant* . . . in order that the nations might glorify God for his *mercy.*" Christ became a servant . . . and Christ brought mercy. He was a servant not only in that he humbled himself to do what the Father wanted him to do at great cost to himself. He was also a servant in that he lived his life for the sake of extending mercy to the nations. During his lifetime he showed the connection between compassion and missions. We see this, for example, in Matthew 9:36–38:

> When Jesus saw the crowds, he had compassion for them, because they were harassed and helpless, like sheep without a shepherd. Then he said to his disciples, "The harvest is plentiful, but the laborers are few; pray therefore the Lord of the harvest to send out laborers into his harvest."

Jesus' compassion came to expression in the call to pray for more missionaries. From first to last mercy was moving missions in the life of Jesus.

And not only in his life, but also in his death. "You were *slain* and by your *blood* you ransomed men for God from every tribe and tongue and people and nation" (Revelation 5:9). Mercy was the very heart of Jesus' mission. No one deserved his mission. It was all mercy and all servanthood. That's the second truth from Romans 15:8–9: a servant spirit and a heart of mercy motivate world missions.

A heart for the glory of God and a heart of mercy for the nations make a Christ-like missionary. These must be kept together. If we have no zeal for the glory of God, our mercy becomes superficial, man-centered human improvement with no eternal significance. And if our zeal for the glory of God is not a revelling in his mercy, then our so-called zeal, in spite of all its protests, is out of touch with God and hypocritical (cf. Matthew 9:13).

In Summary: The Power of Missions Is Worship

What we have been showing is that God's supremacy in his own heart is not unloving. It is, in fact, the fountain of love. God's full delight in his own perfections overflows in his merciful will to share that delight with the nations. We may reaffirm then the earlier truth that worship is the fuel and goal that drives us in missions, because it is the fuel and goal that drives God in missions. Missions flows from the fullness of God's passion for God and it aims at the participation of the nations in the very passion that he has for himself (cf. John 15:11; 17:13,26; Matthew 25:21,23). The power of the missionary enterprise is to be caught up into God's fuel and God's goal. And that means being caught up in worship.

Only One God Works for People Who Wait for Him

This remarkable vision of God as one who "exalts himself to show mercy" (Isaiah 30:18) impels world missions in more ways than one. One way we have not pondered is the sheer uniqueness of this God among all the gods of the nations. Isaiah realizes this and says, "From of old no one has heard or perceived by the ear, no eye has seen a God besides thee, who works for those who wait for him" (Isaiah 64:4). In other words, Isaiah is stunned that the greatness of God has the paradoxical effect that he does not need people to work for him, but rather magnifies himself by working for them, if they will renounce self-reliance and "wait for him."

Isaiah anticipated the words of Paul in Acts 17:25, "God is not served by human hands as though he needed anything, since he himself gives to all men life and breath and everything." The uniqueness at the heart of Christianity is the glory of God manifest in the freedom of grace. God is glorious because he does not need the nations to work for him. He is free to work for them. "The Son of man came not to be served but to serve and to give his life a ransom for many" (Mark 10:45). Missions is not a recruitment project for God's labor force. It is a liberation project from the heavy burdens and hard yokes of other gods (Matthew 11:28–30).

Isaiah says that such a God has not been seen or heard anywhere in the world. "From of old no one has heard or perceived by the ear, no eye has seen a God besides thee." What Isaiah sees everywhere he looks are gods who have to *be served* rather than serve.

The Most Shareable Message in the World

There is yet another way that such a God motivates the missionary enterprise. The gospel demand that flows from such a God to the nations is an eminently shareable, doable demand, namely to rejoice and be glad in God. "The Lord reigns; let the earth *rejoice*; let the many coastlands *be glad!*" (Psalm 97:1). "Let the peoples praise thee, O God; let all the peoples praise thee! Let the nations *be glad and sing for joy!*" (Psalm 67:3–4). "Let the oppressed see it and *be glad*; you who seek God, *let your hearts revive!*" (Psalm 69:32). "Let all who seek thee *rejoice and be glad in thee! May those who love thy salvation say evermore, God is great!*" (Psalm 70:4). What message would missionaries rather take than the message: Be glad in God! Rejoice in God! Sing for joy in God! For God is most glorified in you when you are most satisfied in him! God loves to exalt himself by showing mercy to sinners.

The liberating fact is that the message we take to the frontiers is that people everywhere should seek their own best interest. We are summoning people to God. And those who come say, "In your presence is fullness of joy and at your right hand are pleasures for evermore" (Psalm 16:11). God glorifies himself among the nations with the command, "Delight yourself in the Lord!" (Psalm 37:4). His first and great requirement of all men everywhere is that they repent from seeking their joy in other things and begin to seek it only in him. A God who cannot be served[8] is a God who can only be enjoyed. The great sin of the world is not that the human race has failed to work for God so as to *increase* his glory, but that

---

[8]I am aware that the Bible is replete with pictures of God's people serving him. I have dealt in some detail with the way service can be conceived biblically so as not to put God in the category of an employer who depends on wage earners. See *Desiring God: Meditations of a Christian Hedonist* (Portland, OR: Multnomah, 1986), 138–43.

we have failed to delight in God so as to *reflect* his glory. For God's glory is most reflected in us when we are most delighted in him.

Leaving Family and Possessions for the Sake of the Name

When Jesus turned the rich young ruler away because he was not willing to leave his wealth to follow Jesus, the Lord said, "It will be hard for a rich man to enter the kingdom of heaven" (Matthew 19:23). The apostles were amazed and said, "Who then can be saved?" (v. 25). Jesus answered, "With men this is impossible, but with God all things are possible" (v. 26). Then Peter, speaking as a kind of missionary who had left his home and business to follow Jesus, said, "Lo, we have left everything and followed you. What shall we have?" (v. 27). Jesus answered with a mild rebuke of Peter's sense of sacrifice: "Everyone who has left houses or brothers or sisters or father or mother or children or lands, *for my name's sake*, will receive a hundredfold and inherit eternal life" (v. 29).

The one point of focus for us here is the phrase, "for my name's sake." The motive that Jesus virtually takes for granted when a missionary leaves home and family and possessions is that it is *for the sake of the name of Jesus*. That means for the sake of Jesus' reputation. God's goal is that his Son's name be exalted and honored among all the peoples of the world. For when the Son is honored, the Father is honored (Mark 9:37). When every knee bows at the name of Jesus, it will be "to the glory of God the Father" (Philippians 2:10–11). Therefore God-centered missions exists for the sake of the name of Jesus.

"For the Sake of His Name Among All the Nations"

Paul makes crystal clear in Romans 1:5 that his mission and calling are for the name of Christ among all the nations: "We have received grace and apostleship to bring about the obedience of faith *for the sake of his name among all the nations*."

The apostle John described the motive of early Christian missionaries in the same way. He wrote to tell one of his churches that they should send out Christian brothers in manner "worthy of God." And the reason he gives is that "they have gone out *for the sake of the name*, taking nothing from the Gentiles" (3 John 6–7).

John Stott comments on these two texts (Romans 1:5; 3 John 7): "They knew that God had superexalted Jesus, enthroning him at his right hand and bestowing upon him the highest rank, in order that every tongue should confess his lordship. They longed that Jesus should receive the honor due to his name."[9] This longing is not a dream but a certainty. At the bottom of all our hope, when everything else has given way, we stand on this great reality: the everlasting, all-sufficient God is infinitely, unwaveringly, and eternally committed to the glory of his great and holy name. For the sake of his fame among the nations he will act. His name will not be profaned for ever. The mission of the church will be victorious. He will vindicate his people and his cause in all the earth.

The zeal of the church for the glory of her King will not rise until pastors and mission leaders and seminary teachers make much more of the King. When the glory of God himself saturates our preaching and teaching and conversation and writings, and when he predominates above our talk of methods and strategies and psychological buzz words and cultural trends, then the people might begin to feel that he is the central reality of their lives and that the spread of his glory is more important than all their possessions and all their plans.

The Call of God

God is calling us above all else to be the kind of people whose theme and passion is the supremacy of God in all of life. No one will be able to rise to the magnificence of the missionary cause who does not feel the magnificence of Christ. There will be no big world vision without a big God. There will be no passion to draw others into our world where there is no passion for worship.

God is pursuing with omnipotent passion a worldwide purpose of gathering joyful worshipers for himself from every tribe and tongue and people and nation. He has an inexhaustible enthusiasm for the supremacy of his name among the nations. Therefore let us bring our affections into line with his, and, for the sake of his name, let us re-

---

[9]John Stott, "The Bible in World Evangelization," in Ralph D. Winter and Steven C. Hawthorne, eds., *Perspectives on the World Christian Movement* (Pasadena, CA: William Carey Library, 1981), 4.

nounce the quest for worldly comforts, and join his global purpose. If we do this, God's omnipotent commitment to his name will be over us like a banner, and we will not lose, in spite of many tribulations (Acts 9:16; Romans 8:35–39). Missions is not the ultimate goal of the church. Worship is. Missions exists because worship doesn't. The Great Commission is first to delight yourself in the Lord (Psalm 37:4). And then to declare, "Let the nations *be glad and sing for joy!*" (Psalm 67:4). In this way God will be glorified from beginning to end and worship will empower the missionary enterprise till the coming of the Lord.

> Great and wonderful are your deeds,
> O Lord God the Almighty!
> Just and true are your ways,
> O King of the ages!
> Who shall not fear and glorify your name, O Lord?
> For you alone are holy.
> All nations shall come and worship you,
> For your judgments have been revealed. (Revelation 15:3–4)

Discussion Points

1. Piper says that missions is not the ultimate goal of the church. What does he say is ultimate? What does he mean by that?

2. Piper says the most crucial issue in missions is the centrality of God in the life of the church. Why is this so?

3. Discuss what Piper calls "God's passion for God." Why is this a difficult concept for some to embrace? How does God's passion for God affect the mission of God?

4. What is the "most shareable message in the world"? What difference should this make in our lives as followers of Christ?

Further Reading

Hawthorne, Steven C. "The Story of His Glory." In *Perspectives on the World Christian Movement*, 4th ed., edited by Ralph D. Winter and Steven C. Hawthorne. Pasadena, CA: William Carey Library, 2009.

Kaiser, Walter C., Jr. *Mission in the Old Testament: Israel as a Light to the Nations.* Grand Rapids: Baker, 2000.

Larkin, William J., and Joel F. Williams, eds. *Mission in the New Testament: An Evangelical Approach.* Maryknoll, NY: Orbis Books, 2000.

Piper, John. *Let the Nations Be Glad! The Supremacy of God in Missions.* 2nd ed. Grand Rapids: Baker, 2003.

4

THE KINGDOM OF GOD
AND HIS MISSION

Alex Luc

The Bible begins and ends with the kingdom (reign) of God. It begins in Genesis with God as the ruler of the universe commanding the creation into existence, and it ends in Revelation with God sitting on his throne and reigning over the new heaven and new earth with his people. Though his lordship has been challenged by the rebellion of satanic powers and by the rejection of humankind, God is on mission to realize his reign over his creation according to his purpose and design. The kingdom of God transcends human barriers and corrects our narrow vision about God's work in this world.

Terminology of the Kingdom of God

The exact phrase "the kingdom of God" is not used in the Old Testament, but the idea is taught throughout its writings. In connection with the teaching of the kingdom of God, the term "kingdom" (*malkut*, e.g., Psalm 145:11) occurs much less frequently than the term "King" (*melek*, e.g., Psalm 24:7) or the related verb "be King/reign" (*malak*) for God.[1] The Old Testament terminological usage reveals that the kingdom of God refers primarily to the dynamic reign of God, and that

---

[1] In reference to God being "King," the Hebrew noun *melek* occurs forty-one times and its verb *malak* thirteen times, for a total of fifty-four times. The common noun "kingdom" (*malkut*) occurs only eight times, and its Aramaic parallel occurs only three times. See "Melek" in *Theological Dictionary of the Old Testament*, Vol. VIII, ed. G. Botterweck, H. Ringgren, and H. Fabry (Grand Rapids: Eerdmans, 1997), 365–66.

the idea of realm (a territorial kingdom) is only secondary, unlike human kingdoms. In other words, our understanding of the kingdom of God depends on our understanding of its King. The kingdom is a transcendent and righteous kingdom, because its King is holy. The kingdom is eternal because its King is eternal.

This focus on the person of the King rather than the realm of the kingdom continues in the New Testament, where the kingdom of God is present in the person of Jesus. The New Testament concept of the "kingdom" (*basileia*) or "reign" of God reflects what is in the Old Testament. In the Gospels, the expressions "the kingdom of God" and "the kingdom of heaven" are used synonymously, as shown by their context and interchangeability. The use of "heaven" instead of "God" is primarily due to Jewish reverence.[2]

Kingdom and Mission in the Old Testament

God is the ruler of all because he is the creator of all. God's kingdom transcends time, space, ethnicity, and culture, because God is transcendent. God's kingdom is not to be identified with human kingdoms. On the other hand, the kingdom points to God's sovereign rule and intimate involvement within history. He rules over the history of the universe, the world, and Israel.[3] The Old Testament presents to us such a wide scope of the kingdom of God and at the same time the challenges it is confronting. Because of the fallen world, God is on mission for his redemptive purpose. Mission is the means by which God's sovereign power moves history toward the complete realization of his sovereign will for his creation. In other words, God's mission is for his kingdom.

Creator and ruler of all. From the beginning, the Bible introduces God as Creator and King. God's Word in Genesis 1:3, "God said, 'Let there be light,' and there was light," may be compared to a royal command, as commented in Psalm 33:9: "For he spoke, and it came to

---

[2]C.C. Caragounis, "Kingdom of God/Kingdom of Heaven," in *Dictionary of Jesus and the Gospels*, ed. J. B. Green, S. McKnight, and I. H. Marshall (Downers Grove, IL: InterVarsity, 1992), 417,426.

[3]Much has been written on the subject of the kingdom of God in the Old Testament, including Bruce K. Waltke, with Charles Yu, *An Old Testament Theology: An Exegetical, Canonical, and Thematic Approach* (Grand Rapids: Zondervan, 2007).

be; he commanded, and it stood firm." God the Creator is at the same time the Ruler.[4]

However, the kingship of God is more evident in his delegating human beings to rule on earth. God created them in his image and "blessed" them, saying, "Be fruitful . . . and subdue . . . rule" all that was on the earth and in the sky (Genesis 1:26–28). This pronouncement, commonly called the cultural mandate, is a blessing and a commission from God. God has created all that is in the world, and for his purpose he "placed" (in a way, "sent") humankind to govern in his place (Genesis 2:8).[5]

From the beginning, God's desire has been to have humankind take part in his rule over his creation (cf. Revelation 22:5). In Psalm 8, the psalmist comments on this reality with amazement: "You have made them a little lower than the angels and crowned them with glory and honor. You made them rulers over the works of your hands" (vv. 5–6). The delegating (or sharing) of his rule has given us a glimpse of his love for humanity, which becomes most explicit in the coming of the Son of God. When humankind has fallen in sin, the King of all comes to the garden and seeks them, and promises them sovereignty over the subsequent conflict and triumph for the offspring of the woman (Genesis 3:15):

A   I will put enmity
B   between you [the serpent] and the woman,
C   between your offspring and the woman's offspring,
D   and he will crush your head, and you will strike his heel.

What is clear in this announcement is God's sovereignty. In A, we see that it is God who initiates the spiritual conflict in human history, the nature of the conflict; and it is God who determines how, and consequently when, the conflict will end. Here "enmity" is the first biblical term for spiritual warfare. B and C show the nature of the conflict, and the idea of Satan being the chief over a host of demonic forces is first noted here. Unlike the dualistic belief of some ancient religions, the

---

[4]Examples of the Hebrew jussive form "Let . . . be" *(yĕhi)* used in a king's command: 2 Kings 18:29 and Ezra 1:3.
[5]The verb "put" *(śim,* Genesis 2:8) is used idiomatically for the idea of "appointing" to a task in Genesis 45:9, and as a parallel term to God's "sending" of Joseph to Egypt, where God for his purpose "put" *(śim)* him in service to Pharaoh (Genesis 45:7–8).

conflict is not a power match between God the Creator and the serpent, a creature. Rather, as reflected in C and D, the warfare is between the serpent/his offspring and humankind, whose ultimate victory comes only through the incarnate Son of God.[6]

The announcement also signals a new dimension of God's mission. As subsequent history shows, the cultural mandate is now accompanied by the evangelistic mandate, a mandate that sinners need to be brought back to submission to the lordship of God in accordance with his plan of salvation.

Sovereignty over a fallen world. God's sovereignty does not nullify human freedom or exempt humans from responsibility, even in a fallen world where human beings by nature will sin and demonic forces will tempt and control. God's encounter with Cain in Genesis 4 reminds us of this fact. Here we encounter the first use of the word "sin" in the Bible. God warns Cain not to give in to his anger, which eventually leads to murder, because "sin is crouching at your door," and he "must rule over it" (v. 7). It is a call to seek help from the one who warns him (cf. Eve's implicit reference to God's help in v. 1). The warning shows that Cain's heart is still responsible for resisting sin, which is like a beast ready to devour. The human heart is the battlefield where spiritual warfare takes place, where satanic powers attempt to win. The story also reflects the needy human condition. God's call to "rule" over sin must now follow his earlier call to rule over the earth. It is a call to turn from self-reliance to dependence on God.

God's calling of Noah and later of Abraham tells us that the Lord of history continues to involve people in his mission. Following the flood, the tower of Babel shows people's rebellious attempt to reach high, while God has to come "down" to confront their sin (Genesis 11:7). But for the consequently divided humankind, God calls Abraham. God's promise to Abraham, in light of Near Eastern parallels, suggests that God is the sovereign in the relationship. Here Abraham is sent by his King on a mission not just to become a blessed people, but to be a channel through which all the families of the earth will be blessed (Genesis 12:1–3).

---

[6]The complexity is due partly to the Hebrew pronoun for "he" (*hûʾ*). When used to refer to the collective noun "offspring," the pronoun sometimes functions as "they": e.g., "I know what they (*hûʾ*) are . . . " (Deuteronomy 31:21).

The faith of Abraham is a contrast to the doubt of Adam and Eve. The subsequent content of Genesis devotes major sections to the lives of Abraham, Isaac, Jacob, and Joseph, illustrating how God, in his sovereign rule of history, preserves his people and blesses others through them. For example, Abraham saves the Sodomites but rejects their king's reward, because he refuses to be known as one who, instead of being blessed by God and blessing others, is "made rich" by a Gentile king (Genesis 14:23). Isaac's life may not seem as colorful, but God blesses him and through him blesses other people with Isaac's repeated chances of discovering and recovering water sources (Genesis 26:18–22).

As for Jacob, even his deceiver, Laban, admits that God "has blessed me because of you" (Genesis 30:27). Later, we are told that God has "blessed the household of the Egyptian because of Joseph" (Genesis 39:5). Through Joseph, both Egypt and neighboring peoples are saved from starvation and see the power of God. Joseph's assurance to his brothers at the end of Genesis provides a fitting conclusion to God's sovereignty and his blessing others through the seed of Abraham: "You intended to harm me, but God intended it for good to accomplish what is now being done, the saving of many lives" (Genesis 50:20).

Guiding a nation for all nations. As Israel's history continues to unfold, we encounter God's calling of Moses for his redemptive mission. God has "come down to rescue" his people (Exodus 3:8). Moses' mission is summarized in the "sign" God gives him: "This will be the sign to you that it is I who have sent you: When you have brought the people out of Egypt, you will worship God on this mountain" (Exodus 3:12). It is a sign that requires faith in God's sovereignty over the coming events, long before Moses brings the people out.

It appears to some that God's hardening of Pharaoh's heart is an unreasonable act, but the three stages of hardening in the narrative of Exodus 4–12 suggest that Pharaoh's freedom and responsibility are not denied:

A   God predicted divine hardening (before the plagues, 4:21; 7:3)

B   Pharaoh hardened his own heart (during the first five plagues)

A'   God hardened Pharaoh's heart (beginning with the sixth plague, 9:12)

God's hardening starts with the sixth plague. Here human freedom in B is balanced and enclosed by the sovereign control of God in A and A'.[7]

For Moses, God's prediction of his hardening is an assurance of his sovereignty over his mission. It is after God's prediction that Moses leaves for Egypt (Exodus 4:21). Growing up in the Egyptian palace, Moses knows well the spiritual challenge posed by Pharaoh and the Egyptian religious system. The Egyptians consider Pharaoh, whose life and heart are protected and empowered by his god, as divine. The episode demonstrates God's reign over the powers of darkness, including punishing "all the gods of Egypt" (Exodus 12:12).

After leaving Egypt, Moses and the people sang, "The LORD reigns for ever and ever" (Exodus 15:18). Israel is called to be the King's people, his "treasured possession" out of all nations, and "a kingdom of priests and a holy nation" (Exodus 19:5–6). That Israel is a people for all peoples remains clear in this call. But they can succeed in this mission only by dependence on God, who has carried them "on eagles' wings" (v. 4).

Though the kingdom of Israel is not to be identical to the kingdom of God, their kingdom is expected to reflect the holy character of God's kingdom among the nations (cf. Leviticus 19:2; Deuteronomy 32:8). Continuing the heritage of Abraham, Israel is to be a people of faith in their Lord and a blessing to others. This is a people through whom the nations will witness the glory of God's reign, a people living righteously by God's grace.

Israel's entrance and survival in Canaan, as narrated in the historical and prophetic books of the Old Testament, also display God's lordship. God, being the owner of the earth, has the right to remove the Canaanites from Canaan because of their sins, and later to exile Israel to Assyria and Babylon when his people turn away from him. When the people of Israel determine to have a king "such as all the other nations have," it is considered a rebellious act because "they have rejected me [God] as their king" (1 Samuel 8:5,7). The rejection, however, does not hinder God's plan to bless humanity by bringing about an everlasting kingdom through the ideal Son of David (2 Samuel 7:12–16; 1 Chronicles 17:14).

---

[7]Alex Luc, "Leb, Heart," *The New International Dictionary of Old Testament Theology and Exegesis*, vol. 2 (Grand Rapids: Zondervan, 1997), 750.

Serving the King of all. Despite human rebellion and satanic control, the earth continues to be the Lord's, and God remains its King (Psalm 24:1–10). In the Psalms, the Lord is acknowledged as the King of the universe, the earth, and Israel. The psalmists reflect an understanding of their mission for the world as the people of God, even if it sometimes means that the nations first need to undergo God's judgment. The nations, just like Israel, can have the joy of salvation in his kingdom: "The LORD reigns, let the earth be glad" (Psalm 97:1). The prayer in Psalm 67:1–2 clearly echoes God's promise to Abraham in Genesis: "May God . . . bless us . . . so that your ways may be known on earth, your salvation among all nations."

Psalm 47 points to the fulfillment of the Abrahamic promise with the nations becoming the people of God: "God reigns over the nations; . . . the nobles of the nations assemble as the people of the God of Abraham" (vv. 8–9). Psalm 22 begins with the well-known words, "My God, my God, why have you forsaken me?" (quoted by Jesus on the cross), and concludes with the "turning" of the nations to God, because "dominion belongs to the LORD" (Psalm 22:1,27–28). Israel is exhorted to "say among the nations, 'The LORD reigns'" (Psalm 96:10). The kingdom of God provides both the goal and the message for Israel's mission.

> *The kingdom of God provides both the goal and the message for Israel's mission.*

The narrative of Job (a Gentile) affirms God's sovereignty over the nations and over satanic powers, reminding us also of the "enmity" mentioned in Genesis 3:15. Job's story shows that the victory of spiritual warfare does not depend on exemption from sufferings or protection from satanic attacks, but on the gaining of the human heart. Satan's goal is to prove that human faith in God is ultimately utilitarian, including the faith of a best saint of God (Job 1:8–9). The implication is that every faith is bribed and God's plan is a failure. But Satan is wrong. Job has shown that there is such a thing as genuine faith, a faith not in what God gives but in who God is. It is a faith that brings glory to the lordship of God.

Hope in the coming King. By the time of Isaiah, the people of God have lived through many kings and uncertainties. But the prophet's vision of God sitting on the throne changes his life. It is in witnessing this vision of the King, whose glory fills the "whole earth," that Isaiah is called and sent (Isaiah 6:1–8). Though Isaiah spends his life in Judah, the impact of his mission goes beyond his people to the nations, beyond his time to the era of the coming of the Messiah.

For Isaiah, the reign of the Messiah will result in breaking all human barriers, and "of the greatness of his government and peace there will be no end" (Isaiah 9:7). There will not only be peace for humankind but harmony for nature (Isaiah 11:6–9). This vision of peace is accomplished not by coercion but first by atonement of human sin through his death (Isaiah 53). In the Messiah, both the cultural and the evangelistic mandates will be fulfilled. In his coming, even the evil Egypt and Assyria of his time can one day be called by God as "my people" and "my handiwork" on the same level with Israel (Isaiah 19:25). One day, all evil powers on earth and in the heavens will be eliminated (Isaiah 24:21), when God moves history toward consummation, including the coming of "new heavens and a new earth" (65:17).

It is in light of this grand vision that Isaiah, along with other prophets, calls God's people to dedication and action, to be "a light for the Gentiles, that [God's] salvation may reach to the ends of the earth," following the steps of the ideal Servant (Isaiah 49:3,6). The story of Jonah's mission to the people of Nineveh is an example of God's reign over nature and his concern for the Gentile world. Daniel is also a light to the Gentiles of his time. By his witness, even King Nebuchadnezzar of Babylon acknowledges that God's kingdom is an "eternal" kingdom (Daniel 4:3). In Malachi, while the glory of Israel seems to have faded during the postexilic era, God reminds his people that he is still "a great king" and that his name is "to be feared among the nations" (Malachi 1:14).

Kingdom and Mission in the New Testament

If our understanding of the kingdom depends on our understanding of its King, as we have seen in the Old Testament, it is in the person of Jesus that we understand the kingdom in the New Testament. It is in Jesus that we understand the kingdom of God as both an "already" and a "not yet" reality. Jesus has come and is coming again. It is in this

Christ-centered reality that we witness the reign of God at work, and the fulfillment of the Old Testament hope.

Jesus, the kingdom hope fulfilled. Jesus began his ministry with the preaching of the kingdom of God (Matthew 4:17; Mark 1:15). His message is "the message about the kingdom" (Matthew 13:19), and his gospel is the "gospel of the kingdom" (Matthew 24:14). Early in his ministry, Jesus, quoting Isaiah 61:1–2, shows that he is God's anointed Servant fulfilling the Old Testament hope: He has come to proclaim the good news (Luke 4:18). Later in the same chapter, in association with physical healing and casting out demons, Jesus makes it clear that he "must proclaim the good news of the kingdom of God to the other towns also, because that is why I was sent" (Luke 4:43). His claim suggests that while his mission is holistic, it remains spiritually focused—i.e., on people's essential need to have a relationship with God through committing their lives to his lordship.

Both social and evangelistic concerns have an important place in the kingdom of God, because the King cares about both; and prioritizing one over the other is difficult and at times may seem overly simplistic. Given the context of a fallen world, however, if priority is determined by what human beings ultimately need, the evangelistic concern deserves greater attention. In responding to Nicodemus, who admits seeing the power of God in Jesus' work, Jesus points him to the need to be born again by the Spirit to enter the kingdom of God (John 3:1–8).

The kingdom is a present reality that people must respond to with urgency. In showing his power "by the Spirit of God" over the demonic, Jesus announces that "the kingdom of God has come upon you" (Matthew 12:28; Luke 11:20). On another occasion, when asked of the timing of the kingdom's arrival, Jesus answers that "the kingdom of God is in your midst" (Luke 17:21). All who hear Jesus must now decide either to submit to or reject his lordship. But the "already" is inseparable from the "not yet," because the Son of Man will come "in his kingdom" and "in his Father's glory with his angels" (Matthew 16:27–28). The parables of Jesus play an important part in helping the disciples to understand both the present and future aspects of the kingdom. It is in Jesus that the present and the future reside. To live for the kingdom is to live for the King.

Jesus is not only the light of Israel but also "the light of the world" (John 8:12). Both ideas are rooted in the messianic hope of the Old Testament (e.g., Isaiah 9:1–2; 49:6). Israel is a people for all peoples. In the Sermon on the Mount, Jesus reminds his disciples that they are also "the light of the world" (Matthew 5:14). Unlike the nationalistic ideal of his contemporaries, Jesus points his disciples back to the kingdom vision of the Old Testament, a vision of the Messiah for all peoples. In a postresurrection appearance, Jesus tells his disciples, "As the Father has sent me, I am sending you" (John 20:21). The disciples must follow the steps of their Lord.

In the steps of the King. Through his death and resurrection, Jesus has demonstrated decisively the victory of God's reign over history. As the Lord of the universe, Jesus sends forth his disciples: "All authority in heaven and on earth has been given to me. Therefore go and make disciples of all nations" (Matthew 28:18–19). The Great Commission is accompanied by his great promise: "I am with you always, to the very end of the age" (v. 20). This last verse of Matthew echoes the beginning of the book, where the angel announces Jesus as Immanuel, "God with us" (Matthew 1:23). The presence of the Son will be with his people as they follow his steps in the mission of God.

The book of Acts begins with Christ speaking about the kingdom of God (1:3) and ends with Paul proclaiming the kingdom of God (28:31). In response to the disciples' concern for the kingdom of Israel (1:6), Jesus lifts their vision to the greater work of God: "You will receive power when the Holy Spirit comes on you; and you will be my witnesses in Jerusalem, and in all Judea and Samaria, and to the ends of the earth" (Acts 1:8, cf. John 20:21–23). While tracing the steps of the disciples in mission, Acts testifies to the irresistible power of God the Holy Spirit in shattering the powers of darkness. Miraculous signs and healing accompany Philip when he preaches "the good news of the kingdom of God" in Samaria, baptizing many (Acts 8:5–12).

The power of God's reign is manifest not just in signs and wonders, but in lives being transformed. It is manifest not just in strengths, but in sufferings. In encouraging the disciples to continue to stand firm,

Paul says, "We must go through many hardships to enter the kingdom of God" (Acts 14:22; see also 2 Thessalonians 1:4–5). While miracles are important for the preaching of the gospel in some contexts, they are not an essential component of effective missionary witness. The miraculous is at God's initiative according to his purpose.[8]

When Paul and Barnabas made a decisive turn to the Gentiles after being rejected by their countrymen, they quoted Isaiah 49:6, saying, "For this is what the Lord has commanded us: 'I have made you a light for the Gentiles'" (Acts 13:47). Here they follow the steps of the ideal Servant to be a light for the world. Later, as if paraphrasing Jesus' words in John 20:21 ("As the Father has sent me, I am sending you"), Paul says, "God was reconciling the world to himself in Christ. . . . And he has committed to us the message of reconciliation. We are therefore Christ's ambassadors" (2 Corinthians 5:19–20). As an ambassador for the King, Paul sees his ministry to the world as an extension of Jesus' mission that God has initiated.

While the term "kingdom" occurs infrequently in Paul's writings, the concept of the kingdom of God is evident. The tension in the Gospels between "already" and "not yet" is also seen in Paul's teaching. But given the Christological focus in his message, the kingdom of God (or Christ) is sometimes seen as synonymous to life in the Spirit or in the body of Christ.[9] In addressing the issue of the weak and the strong, Paul warns that "the kingdom of God is not a matter of eating and drinking, but of righteousness, peace and joy in the Holy Spirit" (Romans 14:17). Unlike earthly kingdoms, the kingdom of God is characterized by the fruit of the Spirit.

As for the "not yet," Paul is confident that God is in control of the final outcome of history. The end will come when Christ "hands over the kingdom" to the Father after destroying all rebellious dominions (1 Corinthians 15:24). Paul reminds believers that it is just a matter of time before God will "crush Satan under your feet" (Romans 16:20; cf. Genesis 3:15).

---

[8]William J. Larkin, "Mission in Acts," in *Mission in the New Testament: An Evangelical Approach*, ed. W. J. Larkin and J. F. Williams (Maryknoll, NY: Orbis, 1998), 178–79.

[9]L. J. Kreitzer, "The Kingdom of God/Christ," in *Dictionary of Paul and His Letters*, ed. G. F. Hawthorne, R. P. Martin, and D. G. Reid (Downers Grove, IL: InterVarsity, 1993), 524–25.

Reigning with the King forever. God's kingdom is progressing toward its victorious end, a process no power can stop. It is in keeping with this vision that God's people are called to be his witnesses in this world. Jesus says, "This gospel of the kingdom will be preached in the whole world as a testimony to all nations, and then the end will come" (Matthew 24:14). Jesus' words call for a sense of urgency and responsibility. The end will certainly come.

The last book of the Bible keeps this future vision in front of God's people. It is a vision of the glory of God's reign and the testimony of God's redeemed "from every tribe and language and people and nation" (Revelation 5:9–10). It is a vision of victory to honor the "King of kings" (Revelation 17:14; 19:16), and a vision of eternal peace because "the kingdom of the world has become the kingdom of our Lord and of his Messiah" (Revelation 11:15). The last chapter of Revelation echoes and brings to a climax God's original plan for people to take part in his rule. Here the people are God's grateful servants, who have been redeemed by the blood of the Lamb, and they will reign with him forever (Revelation 22:3–5).

Revelation's future vision is also a vision of the inevitable judgment of the rebellious. A voice in heaven proclaims, "Now have come the salvation and the power and the kingdom of our God, and the authority of his Messiah. For the accuser of our brothers and sisters . . . has been hurled down" (Revelation 12:10). The devil and his company, all the powerful forces that rebel against God's reign, will be punished forever (Revelation 20:10). The scene of the eternal destiny of the lost, in Revelation 20:13–15, undoubtedly leaves Christian readers of Revelation with a sense of urgency for evangelization—an urgency heightened by the words of Jesus at the end of the book, "Yes, I am coming soon" (Revelation 22:20).

Conclusion

As we have seen, God is on mission from the beginning to establish his reign on earth according to his purpose for his creation. Despite the fact that the lordship of God in the present world is challenged by satanic powers and by human rebellion, history will testify that God's purpose will be done on earth as in heaven. The people of God, redeemed by the blood of Christ, will reign with their King forever.

The kingdom of God broadens our vision. It helps us not only see current issues in mission more holistically, but also appreciate that our own mission is part of a journey that former servants of God have traveled. We see a journey continuously guided by the sovereign power of God to its glorious end. In pursuing the mission of God, the church is promised the presence of Jesus and the empowerment of the Holy Spirit.

When all is done and gone in our present world, the kingdom of God continues, because God's kingdom is an eternal kingdom. As Christians, to live for what is eternally significant is to submit to and to take part in God's eternal rule in a universe greater than ourselves, our family, our church, our society, and our world.

Discussion Points

1. Luc says our understanding of the King most influences our understanding of the kingdom. Why, then, do we so often focus on the *realm* more than the King himself?

2. What mandate is accompanied by the cultural mandate? As God's people, what is our role in both of these mandates? How does this impact our involvement in God's mission?

3. How does our understanding of Jesus clarify the "already" but "not yet" concept of the kingdom of God?

4. How does this chapter answer the question, "Why is your mission to bless all peoples, Lord?"

Further Reading

Dyrness, William A. *Let the Earth Rejoice! A Biblical Theology of Holistic Mission.* Westchester, IL: Crossway, 1983.

Glasser, Arthur F. *Announcing the Kingdom: The Story of God's Mission in the Bible.* Grand Rapids: Baker, 2003.

Kaiser, Walter C., Jr. *Mission in the Old Testament: Israel as a Light to the Nations.* Grand Rapids: Baker, 2000.

Köstenberger, A. J., and P. T. O'Brien. *Salvation to the Ends of the Earth: A Biblical Theology of Mission.* Downers Grove, IL: InterVarsity, 2001.

Larkin, William J., and Joel F. Williams, eds. *Mission in the New Testament: An Evangelical Approach.* Maryknoll, NY: Orbis, 1998.

Terry, J. M., E. Smith, and J. Anderson, eds. *Missiology.* Nashville: Broadman & Holman, 1998.

Wright, Christopher J. H. *The Mission of God: Unlocking the Bible's Grand Narrative.* Downers Grove, IL: InterVarsity, 2006.

5

GOD'S GREAT COMMISSIONS
FOR THE NATIONS

Jeff Lewis

Steve Hawthorne says, "The story of God accomplishing His mission is the plot of the entire Bible. Therefore, God's mission is the backbone upon which the Bible is built and is best understood."[1] When missionaries or pastors are asked to support missions biblically or to explain the church's responsibility in missions, the answer usually comes from one of the mission imperatives found in the New Testament. The verses used most often are "Therefore go and make disciples of all nations" (Matthew 28:19) and "Go into all the world and preach the gospel to all creation" (Mark 16:15). Many Christians conclude that these mission imperatives are part of the smorgasbord of biblical commands that we can choose from. If Hawthorne is correct that God's mission is the plot and backbone of the entire Bible, then the commissioning imperatives of the metanarrative of Scripture become the foundation upon which all followers of Christ discern God's will for their lives. Those imperatives define our role in the mission of God today.

The majority of Jesus' mission imperatives were expressed during his last forty days on earth, the time between his resurrection and ascension. During this time he spoke about the kingdom of God (Acts 1:3) and opened the eyes of his disciples to what the Scriptures said about him and his mission (Luke 24:45–47). To grasp fully the weight

---

[1]Steven C. Hawthorne, *Perspectives on the World Christian Movement Study Guide* (Pasadena, CA: William Carey Library, 1997), 1–1.

of these imperatives, we must recognize the grand biblical narrative—the story of God's acts in history, his absolute authority, and the context of his mission. Before we examine the five commissioning imperatives of Christ, we need to review the genesis of God's story.

In the Beginning

As the introduction of the biblical narrative (Genesis 1–11) comes to a close, we are faced with the incessant, rebellious nature of man. Thousands of years have passed since the first heinous crime of Adam and Eve against the sovereign King, after which sin, Satan, and death began their provisional reign on earth. With the entrance of these enemies of God into the biblical account, first-time readers of Scripture might experience a sense of hopelessness toward the future of the human race and its relationship with God. But hope is providentially restored by the faithful, redemptive intervention of God in the major storylines: creation/fall, Cain and Abel, the flood, and the tower of Babel.

The final rebellious act in the introduction of Scripture is the story of mankind's defiance in regard to the tower of Babel. The peoples' blatant disobedience is revealed in their refusal to yield to God's commissioning to "be fruitful and increase in number; fill the earth and subdue it" (Genesis 1:28). Their response was, "Come, let us build ourselves a city, with a tower that reaches to the heavens, so that we may make a name for ourselves; otherwise we will be scattered over the face of the whole earth" (Genesis 11:4). God's judgment upon the people was to confuse their language and scatter them over the face of the whole earth. The result of God's judgment, as described in Genesis 10, was the creation of the nations, the families of the earth.

As the story of the tower of Babel concludes, and the genealogy of Shem is compiled, we are tempted to conclude that God has given up on humanity. Will he simply create his own nation so that he and Israel might live happily ever after, disengaged from the rest of the world? Will the general focus of the Old Testament be about the fortunes of the nation that evolves from Abram, or the hope for all nations? Should Israel be understood as the center of God's world, or the vehicle by which God will accomplish his mission? These questions are answered immediately in the covenant that God makes with Abram.

God's Covenant

As God calls Abram to become a sojourner in a land that he will disclose, he proclaims his purpose or mission in the covenant itself. He announces to Abram, "I will make you into a great nation, and I will bless you; I will make your name great, and you will be a blessing. I will bless those who bless you, and whoever curses you I will curse; and all peoples on earth will be blessed through you" (Genesis 12:2–3). This covenant is to be understood in the context of God's catastrophic judgment at Babel, which resulted in the creation of "all the peoples on earth." The covenant declares the redemptive hope for all the peoples of the earth. It is the genesis of the "good news" for all nations (Galatians 3:8).

Through Abraham. The hope for the nations is revealed through three stages of biblical history, beginning with the great nation that would evolve from Abraham. As God lavished his blessing upon Israel, he glorified his name among the nations (Psalm 67). As the people of Israel yielded to the sovereign rule and reign of God, following his laws and statutes, they became a living example of their redemptive God and King's goodness to the nations (Deuteronomy 4:5–8). God's purpose was accomplished in this stage by manifesting his greatness through the establishment of Israel (2 Samuel 7:23) and setting Jerusalem "in the center of the nations" (Ezekiel 5:5).

Through Jesus. Second, God's mission of blessing the nations reaches its zenith when Jesus is sent into the world, not to bring judgment but the hope of salvation (John 3:17). Jesus is the promised seed of Abraham (Galatians 3:16), "the radiance of God's glory" (Hebrews 1:3), made manifest to the nations (Isaiah 9:1–2), proclaimed to be the "Savior of the world" (John 4:42; 1 John 4:14). He is the promised Servant who has come to restore Israel and to be a light to the nations so that God's salvation might reach to the ends of the earth (Isaiah 49:6). God's promise of blessing the nations is accomplished through Jesus.

Through the body of Christ. The final stage of God's mission is accomplished through the body of Christ, the church, which has been sent into the world (John 17:13–18). The church is the extension of the mission of God through Jesus Christ, for the church is to be the living manifestation of Christ's rule on the earth (Colossians 1:13–18). "[God calls] . . . the church, the community of believing Jews and Gentiles who constitute the extended people of the Abraham covenant, to be the agent of God's blessing to the nations in the name and for the glory of the Lord Jesus Christ."[2] The church's mission in the world is to be understood in the context of the evolution of God's mission.

God's promise to bless the nations has not been fully accomplished, but its fulfillment is inevitable. God declares his faithfulness in fulfilling his promise: "My name will be great among the nations, from where the sun rises to where it sets" (Malachi 1:11). The psalmist proclaims, "All the ends of the earth will remember and turn to the Lord, and all the families of the nations will bow down before him" (Psalm 22:27). God grants us a glimpse of the fulfillment of his promise: "After this I looked, and there before me was a great multitude that no one could count, from every nation, tribe, people and language, standing before the throne and before the Lamb" (Revelation 7:9). God's promise to Abraham will be accomplished.

Five Great Commissions

The link between the promise to Abraham to be a blessing to the nations and the future fulfillment expressed in Revelation is a faithful God accomplishing his purpose through his people. This mission is plainly and emphatically proclaimed in the five commissioning imperatives found in the four Gospels and the book of Acts. Each imperative relates to the themes and purposes of its book and further defines for us the Great Commission that is discovered in the culmination of all five statements. Each statement adds a unique and essential component to our understanding and application of the Great Commission.

1. Make disciples of all nations—Matthew 28:18–20. The commissioning imperative found in Matthew's Gospel, normally referred to as the Great Commission, is the first of the five statements. Jesus declares, "All authority in heaven and on earth has been given to me.

---

[2]Christopher Wright, *The Mission of God: Unlocking the Bible's Grand Narrative* (Downers Grove, IL: InterVarsity, 2006), 67–68.

Therefore go and make disciples of all nations, baptizing them in the name of the Father and of the Son and of the Holy Spirit, and teaching them to obey everything I have commanded you. And surely I am with you always, to the very end of the age."

Matthew stresses that "the kingdom of heaven has come near" (Matthew 3:2; 4:17). Herein Jesus proclaims and describes the kingdom as it infiltrates this present evil age.[3] The King, who has been given all authority, has come—but not in glorious splendor to usher in catastrophic judgment, as the Jews anticipated. He has come as the sovereign ruler of all creation entering this present evil age to seek and save the lost, inviting them to enter his kingdom.

Throughout his Gospel, Matthew expresses the reality of Jesus' reign through his authority over disease, hunger, demons, sin, and death. Jesus' statement, "All authority in heaven and earth has been given to me" (Matthew 28:18), points to the central theme of Matthew's narrative. The commissioning statement that follows in verses 19 and 20 is based on this central authority theme. The King has come, proclaiming the good news of the kingdom; speaking life into the spiritual morgue of mankind; giving hope to the displaced, poor, sick, and disenfranchised of society; and revealing his authority over the enemies of God and people—sin, Satan, and death.

The grammatical structure of Christ's command in verses 19 and 20 informs us about the central theme of this mandate. Jesus uses four verbs to explain what his followers are to be about. "Make disciples of all nations" is the main verb expressed in the imperative. It is the anchor or foundation from which the other three verbal ideas flow. "Go," "baptizing," and "teaching" are participles, giving definition and clarity to the main action of Christ-followers. Donald Hagner states, "Participles when linked with the imperative verb themselves take on imperatival force and function as imperatives."[4] All four of these actions are to be seamlessly integrated in the life of every follower of

---

[3]G. E. Ladd describes "that the Kingdom of God is God's reign defeating His enemies, bringing men into the enjoyment of the blessings of the divine reign." *The Gospel of the Kingdom*, reprint (Grand Rapids: Eerdmans, 1994), 123.

[4]Donald A. Hagner, *Word Biblical Commentary: Matthew 14–28* (Dallas: Word, 1995), 882.

Christ; they shape our purpose and demand our full obedience.

The command to make disciples of all nations reveals that we are to be about the multiplication of other faithful followers of the King among the nations. Christ's call was not to make converts, but disciples. Throughout the Gospels, Jesus frankly defines what disciples look like. Disciples of Christ strive to be like their teacher (Matthew 10:25). They are to hate their father and mother, die to themselves, and renounce all that they have (Luke 14:26–33). The description continues in John's Gospel as Jesus declares that his followers are to hold to his teaching, love one another, and bear much fruit as they remain in the vine (John 8:31; 13:35; 15:5–8). These passages create the portrait of what Christ commissions us to nurture among the nations.

The process of making disciples is disclosed as God emptied himself, being made in human likeness, and became Immanuel—"God with us" (Philippians 2:7; Matthew 1:23). In doing so, Jesus became the living manifestation of what it looks like to live in relationship with the Father. He is the example of kingdom living. Discipleship involves the mentor being a living example of what new life in Christ looks like (1 Corinthians 11:1), living out the implications of the fact that God "has rescued us from the dominion of darkness and brought us into the kingdom of the Son he loves" (Colossians 1:13).

Go and live among them. Making disciples of all nations assumes that we go and live among them for an extended period of time. Nations must see the reality of Christ lived out in their culture. The first subordinate participle found in verse 19 clarifies this point. Jesus says, "Therefore go and make disciples of all nations." Unfortunately, this phrase has been interpreted out of context as though it only refers to the routine activities of life—as you go about your daily business. "Go" takes on imperatival force since it is linked to the imperative main verb. Jesus commands that we go to all nations. This going and living among the nations is seldom accomplished through short-term missions excursions.[5] It often demands kingdom living among the nations for decades.

---

[5]Nevertheless, short-term missions and ministry trips are important for the development of faithful followers of Christ and can also be effective for the development of vision and long-term strategies.

The nations we are to disciple are not geographical or political countries, like China or Turkey, but people or ethnic groups. We are to
disciple the more than 11,000 people groups in the world today. This
commissioning statement challenges the complacency of Western
Christians who think they can fulfill their responsibility to Christ
simply by increasing church membership and sending a few mission
teams among the nations.

Baptizing them. The next subordinate participle—"baptizing"—adds
clarification to the task of making disciples. This verb indicates that
making disciples includes evangelism, the verbal and visual witness of
the good news, and flows beyond conversion as we share our lives in
Christ with the disciple. We should never separate evangelism and discipleship. Evangelism is an early step to disciple-making.

Teaching them. The last subordinate participle, further clarifying
disciple-making among the nations, is "teaching them to obey everything I have commanded you." Before we interpret this phrase as it relates to the entire framework of Christ's teaching, it is essential to check
the context of Matthew's Gospel. Arthur F. Glasser explains, "Within
Matthew are five major messages that constitute the dominant thrust
of Jesus' instruction on discipleship in relation to the Kingdom of
God."[6] The disciples are instructed to observe the ethics of the kingdom
(Matthew 5–7), the mission of the kingdom (10), the commitment of
the kingdom (13), the community of the kingdom (18), and the stewardship of the kingdom (24–25). The ethics of the kingdom demand
more than knowledge of Christ's teachings; it requires obedience. As
kingdom citizens we nurture each other to be Christ-followers in more
than name. We learn to obey all he commanded, even this commission
to disciple all nations.

2. Preach the gospel to all creation (Mark 16:15). Mark's Gospel is a
book of rapid actions used to validate his premise that Jesus is the Son
of God. This Gospel has only one long discourse, since Mark's emphasis is on the deeds of Jesus. His desire is to convince his Roman
audience that the miraculous activity of Jesus reveals his authority over

---

[6]Arthur F. Glasser, Charles E. Van Eugen, and Dean S. Gilliland, *Announcing the Kingdom: The
Story of God's Mission in the Bible* (Grand Rapids: Baker, 2003), 236.

nature, demons, disease, and death. He is the Servant of the Lord (Isaiah 42:1) who demonstrates his sovereign power and authority through his life, suffers in death, and is triumphant through his resurrection. It is out of this context that we have the most active of all the commissioning statements: "Go into all the world and preach the gospel to all creation."[7]

The imperative found in Mark's commissioning statement is to preach the gospel to all of creation. The Greek word translated "preach" is *kērussō*, meaning "to herald, proclaim, or preach." The emphatic call of Christ to "preach the gospel" is not limited to today's context of vocational preachers and their homilies from pulpits. This command is for all followers of Jesus. Gerhard Friedrich states, "The messengers of Jesus are like sheep delivered to the wolves (Matthew 10:16). As the Lord was persecuted, so his servants will be persecuted (John 15:20). The servants of Christ are, as it were, dedicated to death (Revelation 12:11). But the message does not perish with the one who proclaims it. The message is irresistible (2 Timothy 3:1). It takes its victorious course through the world (2 Thessalonians 3:1)."[8]

The Son of God has emphatically directed his followers to proclaim his "good news" to all creation no matter the cost.

Mark's commissioning statement has one participle—"Go into all the world"—that supports the main verb. Like the similar statement in Matthew, the participle takes on imperatival force. Twice now, in Mathew and Mark, Jesus has commanded us to go. Yet we live as though this command is only for those who receive a missionary call like Paul's. Christians are ambassadors and sojourners in this life. Our home is not of this world. We are called to live life yielded to the Son's directives and mission, not determining our geographical location based on a place we call home, closeness to family, safety, or lifestyle preference. We are to determine location based on the dynamic will of God as he calls us to "go into all the world." So the critical question is not whether we should go, but whether we should stay where we are.

---

[7]Some of the earliest manuscripts do not include Mark 16:9–20.
[8]Gerhard Friedrich, *Theological Dictionary of the New Testament* (Grand Rapids: Eerdmans, 1965), 696.

3. Proclaim to all nations the message of repentance for the forgiveness of sins (Luke 24:46–49). The central theme of Luke's Gospel is that Jesus is the Savior of all peoples. This theme repeats itself throughout the text. Mary is instructed by the angel Gabriel to name her son Jesus (1:31), which means "the Lord saves." The angel of the Lord declares to the shepherds, "Today in the town of David a Savior has been born to you; he is the Messiah, the Lord" (2:11). While holding the baby Jesus, Simeon prophesies, "For my eyes have seen your salvation, which you have prepared in the sight of all nations: a light for revelation to the Gentiles, and the glory of your people Israel" (2:30–32). Luke quotes Isaiah: "All people will see God's salvation" (3:6). When Jesus proclaims that he is the promised Messiah, he clarifies for the people in his hometown synagogue that he has also come for the Gentiles (4:16–27). Jesus tells Zacchaeus, "The Son of Man came to seek and to save the lost" (19:10), which in Luke includes Jews, Samaritans, Gentiles, the poor, the rich, the sinners, and the outcast. The brushstrokes from these verses portray a Savior for all peoples.

Proclaim the cross and resurrection. In Luke's Gospel, the Savior of the world commissions his disciples when he opens their minds to the Scriptures and states, "This is what is written: The Messiah will suffer and rise from the dead on the third day, and repentance for the forgiveness of sins will be preached in his name to all nations, beginning at Jerusalem. You are witnesses of these things. I am going to send you what my Father has promised; but stay in the city until you have been clothed with power from on high" (24:46–49). The Old Testament not only predicted that the Christ should suffer and be crucified and that he should rise from the grave, but that repentance and the forgiveness of sins would be preached to all nations.

"It speaks volumes about the importance of the church's mission to the nations that these three themes—his cross, his resurrection, and worldwide gospel proclamation—are linked together so intimately and given equal scriptural endorsement."[9] The evangelical church aggressively proclaims the cross and resurrection of Christ, but in comparison

[9]Glasser, Van Eugen, and Gilliland, *Announcing the Kingdom*, 231.

only gives lip service to the proclamation of repentance for the forgiveness of sins among the nations. These three statements define the church's relationship to Christ. Luke's commissioning statement challenges every believer toward a scriptural equilibrium wherein our involvement in Christ's purpose among the nations exists on the same level as our association with his death and resurrection.

Proclaim repentance and forgiveness. Luke teaches that Christ's followers are to proclaim to the nations the message of "repentance for the forgiveness of sins," and that they are to begin in Jerusalem and wait for power from on high. Repentance "signifies turning away from sin and rebellion against God. It is a reorientation, a change in thinking that results in turning to God in faith."[10] When the Pharisees complain about Jesus associating with sinners at Levi's house, Luke highlights Jesus' response: "I have not come to call the righteous, but sinners to repentance" (5:32). The portrait of repentance flows from Luke's pen: Peter falling at the feet of Jesus (5:8), the leper falling on his face and begging (5:12), the sinful woman anointing Jesus with tears and perfume (7:36–50), the woman touching the hem of his garment (8:44), heaven rejoicing over the one who repents (15:7,10), the prodigal son repenting (15:17–21), and the blind beggar calling out for mercy (18:35–39). Twice Jesus declares, "But unless you repent, you too will all perish" (13:3,5).

Our charge is to go among the nations as representatives of Christ, communicating his message of authentic repentance that leads to the blessings of salvation and the forgiveness of sins. The disciples were to begin this ministry to the nations in Jerusalem. The most prevalent application of this statement is that we should start at home. While it is essential that we are faithful to Christ's commissioning where we live, Jerusalem was not the disciples' home. They were Galileans. "Jerusalem," therefore, relates not only to the fulfillment of Isaiah's prophecy (Isaiah 2:3) but also to the strategy of God. Acts 2 reveals the strategic nature of the disciples beginning in Jerusalem, as God brought Jews "from every nation under heaven" (Acts 2:5) to the city for Pentecost. Ultimately, God's strategy—his mission and commissions—is to preach the gospel to all nations.

---

[10]Andreas J. Köstenberger and Peter T. O'Brien, *Salvation to the Ends of the Earth: A Biblical Theology of Mission* (Downers Grove, IL: InterVarsity, 2001), 125.

4. Receive the Holy Spirit and be sent like Christ (John 20:21–22).
John captures a unique element from the commissioning statements
spoken by Jesus Christ. The three commissioning statements found
in the Synoptic Gospels reflect a similar relationship between God
the Son and his followers: Jesus Christ giving marching orders to
his disciples. The commissioning statement found in John's Gospel,
however, takes us beyond the simple fact that he is God and we are
not—so "Just do it!" John captures the beauty of the intimacy and
unity between the triune God and his disciples as it relates to their
commissioning.

The Father and Son are one. John is explicit in stating why he wrote
his Gospel: "But these are written that you may believe that Jesus is the
Messiah, the Son of God, and that by believing you may have life in his
name" (20:31). John's first declaration—"In the beginning was the
Word, and the Word was with God, and the Word was God" (1:1)—
asserts that Jesus is God. Throughout his Gospel, John stresses the
unique relationship that the Son has with the Father:

> Very truly I tell you, the Son can do nothing by himself; he can do only
> what he sees his Father doing. (John 5:19)

> I and the Father are one. (John 10:30)

> Do not believe me unless I do the works of my Father. But if I do them,
> even though you do not believe me, believe the works, that you may know
> and understand that the Father is in me, and I in the Father. (John 10:38)

> Don't you believe that I am in the Father, and that the Father is in me?
> (John 14:10)

The Father sent the Son. From this oneness of the Father and the Son
flows another essential theme: the sending activity of the Father. Two
major words that develop this theme are *pempō* ("to send; to thrust")
and *apostellō* ("to go to a place appointed; to send away"). Of the
seventy-nine times that *pempō* is used in the New Testament, John uses
it thirty-one times. The first occurrence is when Jesus says, "My food
is to do the will of him who *sent* me and to finish his work" (4:34).
Other examples include:

Whoever does not honor the Son does not honor the Father, who *sent* him. Very truly I tell you, whoever hears my word and believes him who *sent* me has eternal life. (John 5:23–24)

I have come down from heaven not to do my will but to do the will of him who *sent* me. (John 6:38)

Whoever believes in me does not believe in me only, but in the one who *sent* me. The one who looks at me is seeing the one who *sent* me. (John 12:44–45)

John uses *apostellō* in his well-known declaration that "God did not *send* his Son into the world to condemn the world, but to save the world through him" (3:17). Other examples of Jesus' use of *apostellō* are found in the following passages:

The works that the Father has given me to finish—the very works that I am doing—testify that the Father has *sent* me. (John 5:36)

You have never heard his voice nor seen his form, nor does his word dwell in you, for you do not believe the one he *sent*. (John 5:38)

I know him because I am from him and he *sent* me. (John 7:29)

Jesus sends us as the Father sent him. The crescendo of Jesus' use of *apostellō* reaches its pinnacle in the high priestly prayer of John 17:

Now this is eternal life: that they know you, the only true God, and Jesus Christ, whom you have *sent*. (v. 3)

They knew with certainty that I came from you, and they believed that you *sent* me. (v. 8)

As you *sent* me into the world, I have *sent* them into the world. (v. 18)

May they also be in us so that the world may believe that you have *sent* me. I have given them the glory that you gave me, that they may be one as we are one—I in them and you in me—so that they may be brought to complete unity. Then the world will know that you *sent* me and have loved them even as you have loved me. (vv. 21–23)

Jesus connects the oneness of the Father and the Son, and the Father's sending of the Son, with his prayer for us that we would be sent into the world in the same way as the Son. In being sent as the Son, we experience intimate communion with God. This is a staggering thought.

We are empowered by the Holy Spirit. With these verses in mind, John invites us to observe the first evening after the resurrection. The disciples were cowering behind locked doors, for fear of the Jewish authorities, when Jesus appeared. After showing them his pierced hands and side, Jesus said, "Peace be with you! As the Father has sent me, I am sending you." And then he breathed on them and said, "Receive the Holy Spirit" (20:21–22).

We have been given the same commissioning that the Father gave the Son. Not only are we invited to share in the intimacy of the Father and the Son, but Jesus breaths on his disciples—telling them to receive the Holy Spirit, giving them a foretaste of the promise to come. It is through the Holy Spirit that we have fellowship with God (Father, Son, and Holy Spirit); and it is by the empowering of the Spirit that we accomplish Jesus' sending task.

5. *Be my witnesses in Jerusalem, and in all Judea and Samaria, and to the ends of the earth (Acts 1:8).* Jesus' last commissioning statement was spoken moments before he ascended to the right hand of the Father. Luke explains that Jesus, after his suffering and resurrection, spent forty days teaching his disciples about the kingdom, clarifying what he had taught them for almost three years. At the end of those forty days the disciples asked Jesus, "Lord, are you at this time going to restore the kingdom to Israel?" (Acts 1:6). The disciples were still looking for a kingdom that brought political restoration to Israel and liberation from the yoke of Roman bondage. Their ethnic longing blinded them to the truth that Jesus had been teaching them for years. They missed the fact that God's kingdom was redemptive in nature; it was to be realized in the hearts of those who became his followers, and proclaimed to the nations (Matthew 24:14). "It is spread by witnesses, not by soldiers, through a gospel of peace, not a declaration of war, and by the work of the Holy Spirit, not by the force of arms, political intrigue or revolutionary violence."[11]

Jesus quickly refocused his disciples on God's mission: "It is not for you to know the times or dates the Father has set by his own authority.

---

[11]John Stott, *The Message of Acts: The Spirit, the Church, and the World* (Downers Grove, IL: InterVarsity, 1994), 42.

But you will receive power when the Holy Spirit comes on you; and you will be my witnesses in Jerusalem, and in all Judea and Samaria, and to the ends of the earth" (Acts 1:7–8). Not only is our calling birthed in the context of the sovereign authority of Christ and accomplished in relationship with the ever-present Son (Matthew 28:18,20), but we are empowered to accomplish the mission of God through the promise of the Father (Luke 24:49)—the Holy Spirit, the Spirit of Christ living in us (Romans 8:9). God has not left us to our own imagination to accomplish his mission and our calling. He has given us his Spirit that we might imitate Jesus in the manner he accomplished the Father's will (John 17:4). We accomplish our calling as witnesses as we yield to the Father's will: not by formulating our own great ideas but by obeying the prompting of the Father as Jesus modeled (John 5:30; 6:38; 14:10).

The call to be witnesses moves us beyond communicating sterile facts about Jesus to expressing our personal experience in Christ. Paul's ministry under house arrest in Rome, in which he spent two years speaking about the kingdom of God and the Lord Jesus Christ (Acts 28:30–31), defines the focus of our witness. We are to bear witness of our passion for and knowledge of Christ and to articulate the gospel of the kingdom. We are to be living witnesses that God came to give life and to defeat the enemies of God and his people, inviting us into a life of blessings in his redemptive reign.

Jesus declares that his disciples will be his witnesses "in Jerusalem, and in all Judea and Samaria, and to the ends of the earth" (Acts 1:8). The standard application of this statement is that our witness is to be concentric in its movement. We first start with our local communities and progressively move toward the nations. The only concentric advancement of the disciples' witness, however, occurs in the first ten chapters of Acts. After the Holy Spirit descended on the household of Cornelius, the movement of the gospel became simultaneous: both local and international. That simultaneous advancement must be reflected in our churches.

Conclusion

The Great Commission that Jesus Christ has given his followers emanates from the character of our King; was predicted by the prophets; is birthed in our intimate relationship with the triune God; is empowered and directed by the Holy Spirit; and is accomplished through the witness, nurture, and reproduction of Christ's disciples in community among all peoples. These five commissioning statements define the very essence of the church. Our greatest sin is rejecting our calling as described in these statements. But our greatest privilege and joy is found in embracing his sending—the mission of God.

Discussion Points

1. How does our understanding of the Great Commission change when we consider it as the collection of five commands?

2. What practical difference does our understanding of these five imperatives make in our involvement in the mission of God?

3. Consider the major points of each commissioning statement. How will you begin to apply these mandates in your daily walk with Jesus Christ?

4. Which commissioning statement made the greatest impact on you, and why?

5. Write a statement that captures the major point of each of these commissioning statements and memorize it.

Further Reading

Glasser, Arthur F., Charles E. Van Engen, and Dean S. Gilliland. *Announcing the Kingdom: The Story of God's Mission in the Bible.* Grand Rapids: Baker, 2003.

Köstenberger, Andreas J., and Peter T. O'Brien. *Salvation to the Ends of the Earth: A Biblical Theology of Mission.* Downers Grove, IL: InterVarsity, 2001.

Lewis, Jeffrey C. *God's Heart for the Nations.* Littleton, CO: Caleb Resources, 2002.

Stott, John. *The Message of Acts: The Spirit, the Church, and the World.* Downers Grove, IL: InterVarsity, 1994.

Wright, Christopher J. H. *The Mission of God: Unlocking the Bible's Grand Narrative.* Downers Grove, IL: InterVarsity, 2006.

6

JESUS CHRIST
—THE LIVING WORD—
AND THE MISSION OF GOD

Bryan E. Beyer

In the past God spoke to our ancestors through the prophets at many times and in various ways, but in these last days he has spoken to us by his Son, whom he appointed heir of all things, and through whom also he made the universe" (Hebrews 1:1–2). The writer of Hebrews penned these words to believers who apparently were considering whether they should remain Jesus-followers or revert to their pre-Messiah Jewish faith. He lovingly admonished them for their lack of spiritual growth and urged them to press on to maturity in Christ (Hebrews 5:11—6:2).

The writer of Hebrews stressed Jesus' superiority over everything his readers might find in their old ways. Jesus stood superior to the angels and to Moses (Hebrews 1:4–14; 3:1–6). His person and work were superior to Aaron and the Old Testament priesthood (Hebrews 4:14—5:10). Jesus offered a superior priesthood (Hebrews 7), a superior covenant (Hebrews 8), a superior sanctuary (Hebrews 9), and a superior sacrifice (Hebrews 10). How could these believers consider settling for what they had in Judaism when Jesus offered them the fulfillment of all they embraced as true?

To be sure, Jesus stood as one of many who shared God's truth with God's people. However, his person and work bore testimony to one of Scripture's central declarations. Jesus did not merely communicate God's

Word as prophets before him had done. Rather, he modeled through his life both a complete surrender to and an embodiment of God's kingdom purpose. He spoke the Word of God, but he also *was* the

> *Indeed, the writers of Scripture affirm that Jesus, the Word of God, is central to accomplishing the mission of God.*

Word of God (John 1:1).[1] Indeed, the writers of Scripture affirm that Jesus, the Word of God, is central to accomplishing the mission of God.

Jesus' Coming Announced in the Old Testament

The New Testament writers unanimously affirm Jesus as the ultimate fulfillment of the Old Testament revelation. Although the subject of the New Testament's use of the Old Testament comprises a study all its own,[2] scholars agree that the New Testament writers saw the Old Testament as unequivocally pointing to Jesus (Galatians 4:4–5). Some key examples illustrate the point.

Genesis 3:15. Even as God banished Adam and Eve from Eden, he affirmed that Satan, embodied in the serpent, would not have the last word. Satan "struck Christ's heel" in that sin's entry into the human race rendered the cross necessary. However, through his death and resurrection, Jesus—Eve's ultimate seed, or descendant—would strike the serpent's head, administering the deathblow to the forces of darkness as he fulfilled the mission of God.

Genesis 12:1–3. One cannot overstate the importance of these verses with respect to the mission of God. God affirmed he would make a great nation of Abram/Abraham, the father of the Hebrew faith and a man of faith. God tested Abraham's faith for twenty-five years until he gave him Isaac, the son of promise (Genesis 21:1–5). God reaffirmed the promise to Abraham (Genesis 15:1–6; 17:1–22; 18:1–15; 22:15–18), as well as to Abraham's son Isaac (Genesis 26:1–5,23–24) and Abraham's grandson Jacob (Genesis 28:12–15; 35:11–12). The New Testament writers are

---

[1]For a complete discussion of the mission of God, see Christopher J. H. Wright, *The Mission of God: Unlocking the Bible's Grand Narrative* (Downers Grove, IL: InterVarsity, 2006).

[2]See, for example, Walter C. Kaiser Jr., Darrell L. Bock, and Peter Enns, *Three Views on the New Testament Use of the Old Testament* (Grand Rapids: Zondervan, 2007).

quick to make the link between Abraham and Jesus (Matthew 1:1; Luke 3:34), and the apostle Paul also specifically ties the ultimate fulfillment of Genesis 12:3 to the Lord Jesus (Galatians 3:16). The mission Abraham experienced in its infancy came to full fruition in Christ.

Deuteronomy 18:15–19. Deuteronomy contains a series of "farewell speeches" that Moses delivered as God's people camped just east of the Jordan River. Around 1400 BC,[3] Moses told the Israelites that God would raise up another prophet to guide them into the future God had for them (Deuteronomy 18:15–19). Though many other prophets followed Moses, Peter clearly understood Jesus as the ultimate fulfillment of Moses' words (Acts 3:21–24).

2 Samuel 7. King David's early reign featured many military victories and the establishment of the fairly short-lived Israelite empire. He subdued the Philistines, King Saul's nemesis (2 Samuel 5:17–25), as well as the other surrounding nations (2 Samuel 8 and 10). But David's heart troubled him; he lived in a cedar palace, but the ark of God sat in a mere tent in Jerusalem (2 Samuel 7:2). Encouraged by Nathan the prophet, who assumed he did not have to seek God's counsel if the king wanted to build him a temple (2 Samuel 7:3), David determined to do something to rectify this gross inequity. The Lord, however, had other plans. He rejected David's request but rewarded David's attitude. He would build David a house—a house of people! God promised that David's descendant would build the temple (2 Samuel 7:12–13). Further, sin among members of the dynasty would bring God's discipline but not rejection, for God would establish David's throne forever (2 Samuel 7:14–16).

God's mission did indeed continue through Solomon (970–930 BC), who built the temple and continued David's dynasty. Generations later, exile threatened the continuation of David's line, but God's purposes continued through Zerubbabel, a descendant of David and an instrument of God's purpose in bringing his people home to Judah (Ezra 3:2; Haggai 2:20–23). And in the fullness of time, the angel Gabriel's announcement to Mary confirmed her son would one day

---

[3] I am following the earlier chronology and assuming a 1446 BC for the date of the exodus. Some evangelicals suggest a date of about 1290 BC.

assume David's throne forever (Luke 1:32–33). Through Jesus, the Davidic covenant would find its fullest and ultimate expression.

Isaiah 42:1–4; 52:13—53:12; 61:1–2. Isaiah 40–66 focuses especially on the return from Babylon and the grand dimension that God's mission would take at that time. Isaiah looked ahead to a time in the distant future when God's mission would move far beyond merely bringing his chosen people home. He would reach all nations with his saving love (Isaiah 45:22; 66:19).[4] Isaiah used the term "servant" to describe an individual who would play a primary and strategic role in accomplishing God's mission.

Isaiah 42:1–4 describes the Servant as God-chosen and Spirit-anointed. His rather unassuming approach nonetheless led to amazing results—results that ultimately would reach the ends of the earth. Matthew proclaimed Jesus as the fulfillment of Isaiah's words, as the Gospel writer saw the Lord do great works of healing while urging people not to tell others (Matthew 12:18–21).

Isaiah 52:13—53:12 comprises Isaiah's greatest expression of the Servant's role in accomplishing the mission of God. The Servant astounded even kings as they considered his great works in contrast to his humble appearance. The general population did not recognize his greatness, for his early life seemed fairly ordinary. As his ministry began, the Servant's life course included much suffering—suffering he endured for others as part of God's plan. He even died for the rebellion of others, his death brought on and endorsed by the very God who sent him. He died among wicked men, but was buried in a rich man's tomb. Paradoxically, the Servant's apparent defeat led to victory, not only for himself but for those for whom he interceded.

Five different New Testament writers cite Isaiah's prophecy, proclaiming Jesus as the clear fulfillment of Isaiah's words.[5] The significant number of appeals by the New Testament writers provides early

---

[4]For a complete discussion of the Great Commission implications of Isaiah's message, see Bryan E. Beyer, *Encountering the Book of Isaiah: A Historical and Theological Survey* (Grand Rapids: Baker, 2007), 263–75.

[5]The five New Testament writers who specifically cite Isaiah 52:13—53:12 are Matthew (Matthew 8:17); Luke (Luke 22:37; Acts 8:32–33); John (John 12:38), Paul (Romans 10:16; 15:21), and Peter (1 Peter 2:22).

testimony to the link the early church made between Isaiah's words and the life and ministry of Jesus in fulfilling God's mission.[6] Jesus' life also provides believers an example to follow; for the Christian, servanthood for the cause of Christ both aligns oneself with God's mission and provides the greatest freedom one can attain.[7]

Isaiah 61:1–2 again describes God's, Spirit-led anointed one. He would bring good news to the poor, heal the brokenhearted, proclaim freedom to captives and prisoners, and announce the year of God's favor. Luke 4:16–30 describes how Jesus announced himself as the fulfillment of Isaiah's words, though the citizens of his hometown of Nazareth found this difficult to believe, if not blasphemous. Nevertheless, Jesus' ministry featured the full extent of Isaiah's words and more.

Jeremiah 23:5–6; 33:15–18. Jeremiah's prophetic message included two closely parallel predictions of a "righteous Branch of David." This individual's wise and just reign would advance God's cause and bring security to God's people. In fact, Jeremiah announced that a great spirit of cooperation between kingship and priesthood was coming. Such words anticipate the New Testament's announcement that in Jesus we have both our great High Priest and the King of kings (Hebrews 7:22–25; Revelation 19:11–16). Thus, in prosecuting the mission of God, Jesus' work include both ruling the world and interceding for his people.

Daniel 7:13–14. The prophet Daniel lived through a period of world history marked by great upheaval, first as the Chaldean empire established itself under Nebuchadnezzar II (605–562 BC) in the wake of the crumbled Assyrian empire, and second as the Persians under Cyrus the Great (559–530 BC) defeated Babylon in 539 BC and established their own empire. Through visions, God gave Daniel insights into the future of human history. Daniel 7 describes four earthly kingdoms, the last of which in particular would become proud and bring great affliction to the earth. However, Daniel then saw "one like a son of man, coming with the clouds of heaven" (Daniel 7:13). This figure received authority and a kingdom to rule forever over people of every nation and language.

---

[6]Beyer, *Encountering the Book of Isaiah,* 210–12.
[7]For an excellent discussion of biblical servant leadership, see Don N. Howell, *Servants of the Servant: A Biblical Theology of Leadership* (Eugene, OR: Wipf and Stock, 2003).

At his trial before the Sanhedrin, Jesus cited this passage and said he would one day fulfill Daniel's words (Matthew 26:64). This declaration effectively gave the Council what it was seeking—a reason to condemn Jesus. In their eyes, he had incriminated himself and committed blasphemy. Little did they realize that the one they condemned really was the one whose second coming would fulfill the mission of God on earth.

Micah 5:2. Micah, a contemporary of Isaiah, foretold a great ruler who would come from Bethlehem, one of Judah's smallest clans. King David hailed from Bethlehem (1 Samuel 16:1–13), and so would this king. Micah stressed this king's importance by declaring, "(His) origins are from of old, from ancient times." That is, his appearance was no surprise in the mission of God.

The religious leaders of Herod's day well understood Micah's passage as messianic, for when Herod questioned them as to where the Messiah was to be born they immediately referenced Micah's words (Matthew 2:3–6). Tragically, apparently not one of those who knew Micah's words bothered to travel five miles south from Jerusalem to determine whether in fact Micah's words had been fulfilled. But indeed they had been fulfilled in Jesus' birth, as God's mission rolled onward.

Zechariah 3:8; 6:9–13. Zechariah's prophetic utterances highlight two aspects of Jesus' ministry. First, he announced the coming of God's servant, someone with the title of "the Branch" (Zechariah 3:8). In its context, the statement suggests the high priest Joshua fulfilled this title. However, the Old Testament's development of the Branch motif (Isaiah 4:2; Jeremiah 23:5; 33:15; Zechariah 6:12–13) suggests its highest fulfillment in Jesus, whose Hebrew name literally was Joshua.

Zechariah's second "Branch prophecy" (Zechariah 6:9–13) took the concept even farther. This special Branch would build the Lord's temple. He also would rule as both king and priest on his throne, bringing peace between two offices that sometimes vied for power in Old Testament times (2 Chronicles 26:16–21). Jesus fulfilled Zechariah's words as he took the temple concept to a whole new level, the term becoming a designation both for his own body (John 2:19–21) and for the church (1 Corinthians 3:16–17; Ephesians 2:19–21). And, as stated above, he also reigns as both King of kings and as our great High Priest.

Jesus' Titles and Roles

Jesus came to earth to do his Father's will, but that will comprised many facets. Those who anticipated his coming and saw his ministry described his fulfillment of the mission of God by highlighting his many titles and/or roles that aligned with that mission. The following terms comprise an illustrative, but not exhaustive, list.

Creator. Genesis 1:1—2:4 describes God's creation of the universe, but the apostle Paul specifically named Jesus Christ as the agent of creation: "All things have been created through him and for him. He is before all things, and in him all things hold together" (Colossians 1:16–17). The creation and sustaining of the universe form part of Christ's role in the grand mission of God.

Immanuel. This name, which means "God with us," stresses Jesus' heavenly origin. Around 735–734 BC, the prophet Isaiah challenged King Ahaz of Judah to trust God in the face of an imminent attack by an Israel-Syria coalition (Isaiah 7:1–9). He offered Ahaz the opportunity to name a sign for God to fulfill, so eager was the Lord to show himself faithful. Ahaz, however, refused, hiding his intent to appeal to Assyria for help behind his false piety (Isaiah 7:10–12). Isaiah responded, "Therefore the Lord himself will give you a sign: The virgin will conceive and give birth to a son, and will call him Immanuel" (Isaiah 7:14).

Evangelical scholars differ as to whether the sign of Immanuel had some sort of initial fulfillment in the days of Ahaz. All agree, however, that the Gospel writer Matthew saw in Jesus' conception and birth the ultimate fulfillment of Isaiah's words (Matthew 1:18–23). In Jesus, God came to humanity directly and immediately, in a manner unparalleled in human history. The Son of God actually took on a human nature to accomplish the mission (Philippians 2:5–8).

Wonderful Counselor. In Isaiah 9, the prophet described a day of spiritual light that would come to people who had walked in darkness (vv. 1–2). In verse 6, Isaiah described the birth of a special son that would be born to the nation and have four special names or titles.[8] The Hebrew word translated "wonderful" is a word that typically denotes

---

[8]For a fuller treatment of these four names see Beyer, *Encountering the Book of Isaiah*, 84-85.

marvelous, wonderful acts that only God can do.[9] Thus the name suggests that Christ is the source of heavenly wisdom and counsel.

Mighty God. This name is peculiar in that it appears to ascribe deity to its owner. The name appears nowhere else in Scripture other than in Isaiah 10:21, where it unambiguously designates the Lord God. Evangelicals, of course, recognize this as pointing to Christ's deity.

Everlasting Father. The title could also be rendered "Father of eternity" or "Father of the ages." It suggests the everlasting quality of its bearer and/ or his control over eternity and time itself. This child was born into time but also transcended it, for he had created all (Hebrews 1:10–12).

Prince of Peace. The word "prince," by its nature, emphasizes sonship. This also fits well the identity of its holder. The Hebrew word *shalom* has as its fundamental meaning the idea of completeness or wholeness. This Prince will bring to society a peace that transcends merely the absence of armed conflict. Rather, he will bring about a society whose every aspect aligns itself with God's purpose. *Shalom* is more than the absence of war; it describes life as it was meant to be. Jesus, as the Prince of Peace, rules as God's Son and brings peace both in this life (Romans 5:1) and in the age to come.

Root of Jesse/David. The expression "Root of Jesse" appears in Isaiah 11 (particularly in verses 1 and 10) and designates the Spirit-led leader whose wisdom, understanding, counsel, strength, knowledge, and fear of the Lord lead him to execute justice among his people. The Root of Jesse, as the Prince of Peace (Isaiah 9:6), brings harmony to his kingdom. He will also stand as a banner or signal flag for peoples of all nations who will seek him. The expression "Root of Jesse" makes an important point: although the prophets elsewhere link Jesus with the line of David, the title "Root of Jesse" indicates Isaiah was announcing the coming of another David rather than the coming of David's de-

---

[9]The word *pele'* occurs thirteen times in the Old Testament. The Holman Christian Standard Bible renders the word "wonders" (Exodus 15:11; Isaiah 25:1; Psalm 77:11,14; 78:12; 88:10,12; 89:5), "wonder" (Isaiah 29:14), "wonderful" (Isaiah 9:6; Psalm 129:92), and "extraordinary things" (Daniel 12:6). All apply to God's wonderful acts. The lone exception may be Lamentations 1:9, where the word is translated "astonishing" and describes Jerusalem's downfall. At the same time, Jerusalem's downfall did come about because of God's righteous judgment, which does qualify as an extraordinary act of God.

scendant.[10] Jesus' reign would prove to be even better than David's.

The expression "Root of David" and the related expression "Root and Offspring of David" occur twice in the book of Revelation (5:5 and 22:16, respectively). In 5:5, the term links the triumphant Jesus with Israel's past glory under David; Jesus' connection with David's line further confirmed his right to kingship. In 22:16, Jesus confirms to John the truth of all the apostle has seen and invites all who will to align themselves with the mission of God so that they might enjoy all the blessing such a relationship will bring (v. 17). As the Root and Offspring of David par excellence, Jesus embodies the ultimate fulfillment of the promise God made to Israel's king (2 Samuel 7:8–16).

Messiah/Christ. The term "Messiah" derives from the Hebrew *mashiach*, which means "anointed one." The Greek equivalent is *Christos*, a common designator for Jesus in the New Testament. The Old Testament term occurs thirty-eight times and the related verb *mashach* ("to anoint") occurs seventy times. Kings, priests, and prophets all received anointing, a public act that symbolically set them apart for service to God.[11] Psalm 105:15 uses the term in the plural, describing God's people in the early days of their history. John also applies the concept to Christians, who receive an anointing from the Holy Spirit (1 John 2:27).

God's anointing of individuals to participate in his grand mission was not ethnically limited. Isaiah described Cyrus the Great, Persia's first king, as God's anointed and God's shepherd, called to "rescue" God's people by decreeing they could return to their homeland (Isaiah 44:28; 45:1).

The Messiah is God's chosen instrument to bring about God's kingdom and fulfill the mission of God. Though this term does not commonly appear in the Old Testament prophets, the concept of the Messiah often appears in Isaiah even though the word "anointed" occurs only once related to the future Messiah (Isaiah 61:1).[12]

---

[10]J. Alec Motyer, *The Prophecy of Isaiah: An Introduction and Commentary* (Downers Grove, IL: InterVarsity, 1993), 121.

[11]"Anointed priest" in Leviticus 4:3 designates the high priest, whereas 1 Kings 19:15–16 describes the anointing of two kings (Hazael and Jehu) and a prophet (Elisha). Many other examples occur.

[12]See, for example, Isaiah 9:6–7; 11:1–10; 32:1–4; 42:1–4; 52:13—53:12. Early and even modern Jewish interpreters often understand one or more of these passages as messianic, though they do not believe they point to Jesus.

The Greek term *Christos* ("Christ") occurs more than five hundred times in the New Testament, the first time in Matthew 1:1 and the last time in Revelation 20:6. The term occurs more than fifty times in the Gospels. It commonly occurs with the name "Jesus"; indeed, the expressions "Jesus Christ" and "Christ Jesus" together appear 226 times! What the Old Testament proclaims in a somewhat

What the Old Testament proclaims in a somewhat veiled way, the New Testament boldly trumpets. Jesus, God's Son, is our ultimate Messiah who fulfills Old Testament prophecies, accomplishes God's redemptive purpose, and champions the mission of God.

veiled way, the New Testament trumpets boldly. Jesus, God's Son, is our ultimate Messiah, who fulfills Old Testament prophecies, accomplishes God's redemptive purpose, and champions the mission of God.[13]

Lion of the tribe of Judah. The designation of Jesus as "the Lion of the tribe of Judah" occurs only once in Scripture but is significant for the topic at hand. Revelation 4–5 describes John's grand vision of heaven's throne room and the majesty of the one who sat on heaven's throne.[14] As John looked closely, he saw in God's right hand a scroll with seven seals (Revelation 5:1). John desperately wanted to know what that scroll contained, but no one was found worthy to take it and open it, a tragedy that caused John to weep (Revelation 5:2–4). But one of the twenty-four elders intervened. "Do not weep! See, the Lion of the tribe of Judah, the Root of David, has triumphed. He is able to open the scroll and its seven seals" (Revelation 5:5).

John's description of this scene places the triumphant Jesus center stage (literally, center throne room!) in the accomplishment of the mission of God. Jesus' finished work on the cross resulted in the redemption of people "from every tribe and language and people and nation" and fitted them to reign as priests forever with their Lord (Revelation 5:9–10).

Lamb of God. The expression "Lamb of God" occurs twice in John's

---

[13]For a thorough discussion of the concept of Messiah, see Ralph P. Martin, "Messiah," in the *Holman Illustrated Bible Dictionary* (Nashville: Broadman & Holman, 2003), 1111–16.
[14]The vision has much in common with Daniel's vision in which he saw the majesty of God and the dominion of the Son of man (Daniel 7:9–14).

Gospel, both times spoken by John the Baptist in reference to Jesus as the one who takes away the world's sin (John 1:29,36). The proximity of Jesus' death to the Jewish feast of Passover and Jesus' connection to the Passover lamb no doubt relates to this usage, a connection others also recognized (1 Corinthians 5:7). Interpreters also have noted the link between John's words about the crucified Jesus in John 19:36 ("Not one of his bones will be broken") to instructions for the Passover lamb (Exodus 12:46).

The book of Revelation contains the shortened title "the Lamb" twenty-eight times in reference to Christ. The Lamb plays a central role in prosecuting God's final mission in the world, leading his saints triumphantly to realize God's ultimate kingdom and defeating his enemies (Revelation 7:17; 12:11; 14:1–4). He fulfills the role of both sacrificial lamb and shepherd of the sheep.

Lord. Jesus shares the title "Lord" with God the Father. This title occurs in the New Testament more than one hundred times in conjunction with Jesus' name. While the Greek word *kurios* can serve as a respectful designation of a superior ("sirs" in Acts 16:30), when the term describes Jesus it designates him as Lord of all, as supreme Master and King (Romans 10:9; Philippians 2:11). Thus, to confess Jesus as Lord means to surrender everything one is and has to his sovereign keeping and guidance. Jesus has received from his Father all authority to pursue, through his disciples, the mission of God (Matthew 28:18–20).

Savior. For the Old Testament writers, God's salvation had both physical and spiritual dimensions. God saved his people from enemies such as Egypt (Exodus 15:2) and Assyria (Isaiah 37:35–37), enabling them to live in security and safety. But God's salvation reached far beyond the physical. He desired an everlasting relationship with his people—one his own salvation would accomplish (Isaiah 45:17). In fact, he called all nations to experience it (Isaiah 45:22).

The New Testament exalts Jesus as Savior for all who place their faith in him. The angels who announced his birth so designated him (Luke 2:11); and Jesus, through his victory over death, showed the title to be more than fitting (Acts 5:31).

Jesus, the Word

The Bible stresses the role of words, the truth they express, and the importance of receiving God's words into our minds and allowing them to shape our lives (John 8:32; Romans 12:2). The New Testament highlights these same concepts regarding Jesus' words and the importance of receiving his teaching. The Synoptic Gospels and Acts affirm the primary role of God's Word as it came through Jesus and later through his apostles (Matthew 7:24–25; Mark 8:38; Luke 5:1; Acts 1:1; 4:4,29,31). However, the Johannine literature—particularly the Gospel of John and the book of Revelation—especially stresses the role of Jesus as the living, unequaled embodiment of the Word of God.

John begins his Gospel by describing how the Word of God existed in the beginning with God. Through him all creation came into existence (John 1:1–3). Finally, in God's perfect timing, "The Word became flesh and made his dwelling among us" (John 1:14). The Word thus becomes not only something John and the other disciples heard, but something they experienced and saw firsthand. They heard, they saw, they observed, and they even touched "the Word of life" that was revealed to them in Jesus Christ (1 John 1:1–3). This affirmation of their seeing and touching the Word further emphasizes John's understanding of Jesus as the living Word. John's Gospel also stresses the close link between God, his Word, and Jesus in numerous other places (e.g., John 3:34; 5:24,38; 8:40,47; 14:24; 17:8,14).

Revelation 19 describes the second coming of Jesus Christ, his defeat of sin's forces, and the establishment of his everlasting kingdom. Elsewhere in the book, John closely connected Jesus with the Word of God (Revelation 1:2,9; 20:4). In Revelation 19:11–16, he described Jesus' triumphant return. After keeping his readers in suspense as to the identity of the rider of the white horse, John revealed his identity by returning to the theme with which he began his Gospel: "His name is the Word of God" (Revelation 19:13). Jesus, the embodiment of God's Word and the living Word, plays

Jesus, the embodiment of God's Word and the living Word, plays the lead role in the mission of God as he brings human history as we know it to a dramatic close.

the lead role in the mission of God as he brings human history as we know it to a dramatic close.

Jesus, the Living Model for Accomplishing the Mission of God

The Bible calls everyone everywhere to participate in the mission of God. We have already seen how Jesus plays the central role in fulfilling this mission. Nonetheless, the Scriptures insist that the mission of God has a place for all who place their faith in Christ. Everyone who aligns with the mission has a role to play in fulfilling it. As we participate in the calling God has given us, the Bible encourages us to look to Jesus, "the pioneer and perfecter of faith" (Hebrews 12:2), as our example. Jesus especially models for his followers two important characteristics of one who is on mission with God: surrender to God's will and kingdom proclamation.

Surrender to God's will. The Scriptures call people to surrender their lives to God's will (Romans 12:1–2). Those who desire an example need only to look to Jesus, who despite his status as Son of God incarnate completely surrendered his life and will to his Father (John 4:34; 5:30; 17:4; Hebrews 10:7). He resolutely set his face toward Jerusalem, warning his disciples that suffering and death awaited him (Matthew 16:21). And in the Garden of Gethsemane Christ modeled for his followers submission, even to death, to the will of his Father (Luke 22:39–44). In his words, "Yet not my will, but yours be done" (Luke 22:42), he made his grand final choice, and the battle of the ages was won. The writer of Hebrews put it this way: "Son though he was, he learned obedience from what he suffered and, once made perfect, he became the source of eternal salvation for all who obey him" (Hebrews 5:8–9). Likewise, the apostle Paul could find no greater example of humility and self-denial for the sake of God's work than Jesus' incarnation and death (Philippians 2:5–8).

Kingdom proclamation. The kingdom motif plays a central role in the Bible and particularly in Jesus' public ministry.[15] The kingdom of

---

[15]For a thorough study of the kingdom of God, see the CD-ROM *The Kingdom of God in Time and Eternity* (Columbia, SC: Columbia International University Distance Education and Media Development, 2005); George Eldon Ladd, *Crucial Questions about the Kingdom of God*

God is God's dynamic reign or rule throughout history. When Jesus urged people, "Repent, for the kingdom of heaven has come near" (Matthew 4:17), he was calling them to submit their lives to God's rule. The consummation of God's kingdom, in which God would defeat his enemies and his children would know everlasting peace, was yet to come. Meanwhile, submission to God's kingdom meant submitting to God's rule in the present, serving him, and aligning oneself with his work and will, that the grand mission of God might be hastened.

During Jesus' earthly ministry, many Jews anticipated a glorious kingdom in which the Messiah would come, overthrow Roman tyranny, and establish Israel's prominence at a level beyond that of David's days (Isaiah 2:1–4; 11:1–10). Jesus' great miracles reinforced the messianic hope in the minds of many (John 6:15). However, Jesus' rejection of such a mission and his call to take up a cross discouraged many from following him. Many failed to see the Messiah's role of Suffering Servant in the Old Testament (Isaiah 52:13—53:12), perhaps because in a time of Roman domination they longed for freedom, not more suffering! At his arrest, even Jesus' disciples fled into the night (Matthew 26:56), unaware that the dawn of the resurrection lay just ahead.

After Jesus' resurrection, he continued speaking of the kingdom of God, though his disciples still sought a political kingdom (Acts 1:3,6). Instead, Jesus gave them the next step in the mission of God: "You will be my witnesses in Jerusalem, and in all Judea and Samaria, and to the ends of the earth" (Acts 1:8). It was a commission all four Gospel writers would affirm (Matthew 28:18–20; Mark 16:15; Luke 24:46–49; John 20:21).[16] As the early church continued the ministry of Jesus, they likewise proclaimed that kingdom (Acts 8:12; 14:22; 19:8; 20:25; 28:23,31). The proclamation of the kingdom today includes a call to people everywhere to join that kingdom through submitting their lives to God through faith in the Lord Jesus Christ.

(Grand Rapids: Eerdmans, 1954); Peter Gentry and Stan Norman, "Kingdom of God," in the *Holman Illustrated Bible Dictionary*, 987–89.

[16]Mark 16:9–20 is not found in all early Greek manuscripts. Nevertheless, Jesus' Great Commission is clearly established by the other accounts.

Conclusion

Jesus plays a central role, as the living Word, in prosecuting the mission of God in the world. His coming was repeatedly announced with anticipation by the Old Testament writers and repeatedly affirmed by the New Testament writers. Jesus' titles and roles from both Old and New Testaments likewise point to his central role. Jesus taught the Word of God with authority, but more than anyone else he embodied the Word of God by his life. Our challenge and calling as Jesus-followers is to lay hold of that Word, to lay hold of God's mission, and to align ourselves totally with his purpose. To know him is life itself (John 17:3), and to make him known is our only reasonable response (2 Corinthians 5:14–21).

Discussion Points

1. Read John 1:1–18. How does Jesus both stand in the line of God's messengers and stand distinct from them?

2. Regarding Genesis 12:1–3, Beyer asserts, "One cannot overstate the importance of these verses with respect to the mission of God." Why are these verses so important?

3. Recall the prophet Isaiah's many descriptions of God's kingdom and prophecies of Jesus. Why do you think God privileged Isaiah to see so many details about Jesus' life and ministry?

4. How did Jesus' life and ministry impact the apostle John's understanding of the mission of God?

5. Why does surrender to God's will play such an important role in accomplishing God's mission, and how did Jesus model this for us?

Further Reading

Bauckham, Richard. *Bible and Mission: Christian Witness in a Postmodern World*. Grand Rapids: Baker Academic; Carlisle, UK: Paternoster, 2003.

Beyer, Bryan E. *Encountering the Book of Isaiah: A Historical and Theological Survey*. Grand Rapids: Baker Academic, 2007.

Blauw, Johannes. *The Missionary Nature of the Church*. New York: McGraw Hill, 1962.

Gentry, Peter, and Stan Norman. "Kingdom of God," in the *Holman Illustrated Bible Dictionary*. Nashville: Broadman & Holman, 2003, 987–89.

The Kingdom of God in Time and Eternity. CD-ROM. Columbia, SC: Columbia International University Distance Education and Media Development, 2005.

Ladd, George Eldon. *Crucial Questions about the Kingdom of God*. Grand Rapids: Eerdmans, 1954.

Martin, Ralph P. "Messiah," in the *Holman Illustrated Bible Dictionary*. Nashville: Broadman & Holman, 2003, 1111–16.

Wright, Christopher J. H. *The Mission of God: Unlocking the Bible's Grand Narrative*. Downers Grove, IL: InterVarsity, 2006.

7

THE HEART OF THE TASK

Zane Pratt

Mention the word "missions," and a host of diverse images comes to the minds of the average churchgoers. Some will picture doing orphanage work in a teeming South Asian city. Others will picture volunteers building a church building somewhere in Latin America. Quite commonly, when people think of missions they envision middle-aged white men in pith helmets standing in the African jungle preaching to villagers, while snakes slither nearby and disease threatens to strike at any moment. Other images range from Scripture distribution at European ports, to camps for inner-city kids in America, to door-to-door evangelism in the suburbs. Medical care for the poor and food distribution to the hungry rank high on most people's lists.

For many Western Christians, missions has come to include anything that church members do in an organized way outside the walls of the church. It may be noble, it may be entertaining, or it may simply be fun, but anything done in an intentional way with non-Christians is thought of as missions. If asked to define the actual task of missions, most churchgoers would probably propose a combination of outreach (however defined) with meeting human needs. Most have a sense that missions involves going somewhere else, but in popular usage that can be almost anywhere. "Missions" has become a vague concept.

Only One Command

Jesus had a significantly clearer idea in mind when he sent his followers out on his mission. In the Great Commission, the Lord of the church defined the task of his church in unmistakable terms. In words known to every child growing up in an evangelical church, Jesus told his disciples,

> (18) All authority in heaven and on earth has been given to me. (19) Therefore go and make disciples of all nations, baptizing them in the name of the Father and of the Son and of the Holy Spirit, (20) and teaching them to obey everything I have commanded you. And surely I am with you always, to the very end of the age. (Matthew 28:18–20)

This passage contains only one verb in the imperative. There is one, and only one, command. That command is to make disciples. All the rest is commentary. Verse 18 gives the justification for missions, and the rest of the verbs in verse 19 are participles that explain where and how we are to carry out the imperative of disciple-making. Verse 20 gives the church its essential provision for carrying out Jesus' mission. However, at the heart of it all there is one command and one task. The heart of the mission of the church is to make disciples.

This does not mean that the rest of the passage is inconsequential. The context is crucial. Each component is essential if God's people are to fulfill their mission correctly. To begin at the beginning, Jesus prefaced the Great Commission with a very important declaration: "All authority in heaven and on earth has been given to me." The foundation for missions is the sovereign lordship of Jesus Christ. Without this understanding, missions becomes an enterprise that is difficult to justify.

The very concept of missions is unpopular in most of the world. It is unpopular in secular Western society, where highly intolerant voices of relativistic tolerance denounce anyone who claims to possess universal truth or who attempts to spread their understanding of absolute truth to others. If the news or entertainment media mention missions or missionaries at all, it is usually in a derogatory fashion. It is also unpopular with the majority of the governments of those countries that most need to hear the good news. Country after country has closed its doors to missionary activity and has made the proclamation of the gospel illegal. However, Jesus has all authority in heaven and on earth. He is the sovereign Lord of the universe. He is a higher authority than any government on earth and an enduring absolute in the face of any passing cultural prejudice. He has the right to send the gospel into every corner of this planet, and he has the power to break down every barrier that stands in the way of that happening. Because Jesus is Lord, the church has the right to make disciples from among all people groups, whatever the world may say.

The sovereign lordship of Jesus Christ, however, is a two-edged sword. It not only gives the church the *right* to fulfill the Great Commission—it also gives it the *obligation* to do so. Jesus not only has all authority in heaven and on earth over the nations. He also has that authority over his people. As Eric Liddell's father said, in the movie *Chariots of Fire*, "The kingdom of heaven is not a democracy!" God owns his people. It is true that God, as Creator, owns everyone, and as the rightful king of the universe has absolute authority over them. But for all who have been saved by the death and resurrection of Jesus, he owns them in a special way by redemption. "You are not your own; you were bought at a price" (1 Corinthians 6:19–20).

Jesus does not enter the lives of his followers as a helpful adjunct to make things better, more enjoyable, or more fulfilling. He enters to take full possession of that which is rightfully his. Jesus has the right to set the agenda for the lives of his followers. We live for him, not for ourselves. He has the right to send us away from comfort and convenience. He has the right to separate us from family and friends. He has the right to send us into danger. He has the right to ask us to lay down our lives for him—and he has, in fact, done so. The Great Commission is not an option, but a command from one who has full authority to command whatever he wants from us. Jesus is Lord, and his lordship lays the necessary foundation for missions, giving his people both the authorization and the obligation to fulfill his global task.

The Great Commission also defines the scope of missions. Jesus commanded his followers to make disciples of all nations. The phrase rendered in most English translations as "all nations" would be better translated "all people groups." The Greek word used here for nations is *ethne,* from which we derive our English term for ethnic groups.

Jesus followed the entire thrust of biblical revelation in making it clear that God's heart is global. God called Abraham to himself so that all families on earth might be blessed through Abraham (Genesis 12:1–3); he intends for the entire earth to be filled with the knowledge of his glory as the waters cover the sea (Habakkuk 2:14); he sent his Son to purchase, with his blood, people from every tribe, language, people, and nation (Revelation 5:9); and at the end of time he will be worshiped by a multitude no one can count from every nation, tribe, people, and language (Revelation 7:9–10).

God's redeeming purpose has always been global, and it has always had a specific people group focus. It is not enough to have believers and churches in every political country in the world. God sees the globe as a mosaic of people groups, far more numerous and complex than the political map of the world. Countries come and go, and borders shift. God's heart for all tribes and languages remains the same. The task of missions will not be fulfilled until there are disciples of Jesus Christ among every people group on earth.

What Is a Disciple?

This leaves us still with the nature of the task itself. What is a disciple? And how is one made? A disciple is more than just a convert. A disciple is also more than just a student, although this concept is closer. In the world of Jesus' day, education was not carried out in the impersonal classroom setting so familiar to us today. A teacher gathered around him learner-followers who entered into a full-time relationship with that teacher. They lived with him and went around with him in the normal affairs of life. He taught them his ideas and thoughts directly in a small group setting. They also heard those teachings expressed, often in formulaic fashion, as the teacher spoke in more general terms to larger audiences. They observed and embraced the teacher's character and way of life. The discipleship relationship was so all-encompassing that disciples even picked up the mannerisms of their teacher. They became, in effect, small reproductions of their teacher through the intimacy and constancy of their relationship with him.

That was precisely the kind of relationship Jesus had with his followers—to the greatest extent with the Twelve, but to a large extent also with a bigger group of at least seventy. This kind of relationship is what he envisioned when he gave the Great Commission. This is the goal of missions, as set by Jesus. Jesus commanded his disciples to make other disciples who would also be learner-followers, who would walk intimately with Jesus (now through his Spirit), who would imbibe not only the teaching of Jesus but also his character and way of life, and who would become so much like Jesus that they would remind people of him. This is what defines success in the mission enterprise. In the aftermath of nineteenth-century revivalism, the goal of evangelism and missions has all too often been reduced to seeking "decisions." Jesus, however, never commanded his followers to go after "decisions." He commanded them to make disciples.

This focus on disciple-making has significant consequences for how the gospel is proclaimed. If the goal is simply to get decisions, there is a strong temptation to water down the message and to skip the hard, unpleasant, unpopular parts until after the person has made some sort of (uninformed) commitment. Too much evangelistic preaching avoids the meaning and the cost of discipleship, and then people wonder why the attrition rate is so high in most churches. Biblical conversion is conversion to discipleship, not conversion to a fire insurance policy; and a "convert" with no commitment to a life of discipleship may very well not be born again at all.

If we are to see disciples as the fruit of our work, it is imperative that we include the rough edges of the gospel. We must make God the focus of the message. It is fundamentally the good news about God, and his character and deeds that should be the substance of our proclamation. In particular, his holiness, and his hatred of all sin and all evil, must be stressed before the message of his love can ever be understood as good news. The reality and awfulness of sin must also be stressed, along with the total inability of human beings to do anything at all to save them-selves or even to contribute to their own salvation.

Popular Western culture promotes self-esteem as the supreme value, and this idea has so infected Western evangelicalism that there is strong pressure to leave out any part of the message that might make people feel bad about themselves. In reality, one goal of the gospel is to shatter people's self-esteem and to drive home to them that they are guilty sinners. They need to know that they are dead in their trespasses and sins, that they are slaves to their sin, that they are spiritually blind and unable to understand the things of God unless he opens their eyes, and that they deserve only hell. The only way to heaven is through brokenness, humility, and repentance. That is also the only way to a life of discipleship. For that reason, it is imperative that we set the good news of salvation in the context of the bad news about lostness. We must proclaim the necessity of repentance as the flip side of the coin of faith, because the New Testament unites the two inseparably. The call to salvation is also, inseparably, a call to sanctification, to service, and to suffering for Jesus. Our message needs to make that clear, because our goal is disciples, not decisions.

How Do We Make Disciples?

What is involved in making disciples? Jesus gives us three subordinate participles in the Great Commission that help us to understand the task.

Going. The first of those explanatory words is "going." The people of God are not to wait for the nations to come to them. Indeed, given the natural inability of fallen humanity even to seek God (Romans 3:11), the nations never will come to know him unless we go to them. At this point we need to remember again the lordship of Jesus Christ over our lives. If the point of becoming a Christian is to make my life better, going where Christ is not yet known in order to make disciples for him makes little sense. If the point of becoming a Christian is to become a disciple of Jesus who lives under his gracious sovereign lordship, it makes all the sense in the world.

We will never make disciples unless we *are* disciples, because we will never embrace separation from family and the very real possibility of discomfort, danger, and suffering unless we have grasped that we are not our own and that we exist for his glory. One of the essential components of the Great Commission task of making disciples is that we must go where there aren't yet disciples. The default command for a believer in Jesus is to go where Christ is not yet known, and it takes a special call from God to stay with integrity where the gospel is already abundantly available.

Baptizing. The next subordinate participle is "baptizing." In the New Testament, clearly faith was expressed through baptism. In our evangelical culture, people who wish to follow Jesus are usually invited to pray the "Sinner's Prayer," often in conjunction with an evangelistic invitation at the close of a worship service or evangelistic crusade in which they are urged to walk the aisle to the front to meet the pastor, evangelist, or some duly trained counselor. There is certainly nothing wrong with any of these practices. They are entirely extrabiblical, however, and they do not actually save anyone. The Sinner's Prayer is nowhere to be found in the Bible, and the New Testament does not typically portray people as becoming Christians by praying. The invitational system in church services was not invented until the nineteenth century, yet millions of people were saved in the intervening eighteen centuries without it.

The default command for a believer in Jesus is to go where Christ is not yet known, and it takes a special call from God to stay with integrity where the gospel is already abundantly available.

In the New Testament, individuals became Christians by repenting and believing as a result of a radical, supernatural work of the Holy Spirit in their lives. This was an internal event. Believers then professed their faith publicly through baptism. Baptism was an emblem of the radical nature of conversion. It was compared, symbolically, to holding a funeral for the person one was before turning to Christ (Romans 6:3-7). The new birth brings death to sin, death to this world, and death to the dominion of Satan. New Testament believers were burying everything they had ever been and proclaiming that they had become a new creature in Christ.

The New Testament, therefore, presents baptism as a fitting emblem for the beginning of a life of discipleship. Jesus presented it as a component of making disciples because it represents the radical break with everything past that constitutes biblical conversion, and it represents the radical commitment to the lordship of Jesus Christ that constitutes biblical discipleship.

Teaching. The third subordinate participle is "teaching." This word is the verbal form of the same Greek root behind the word "disciple." It involves far more than a lecture in a classroom. Biblical teaching does, indeed, involve cognitive content. God doesn't waste words. Everything he has spoken to us in Scripture is worth knowing. That includes the theological parts as well as the ethical parts. In this anti-intellectual age, too many Christians make an absurd distinction between theology and "practical" teaching, with a strong preference for the latter over the former. In the Bible, there is nothing more practical than theology. All of Christian practice is rooted in the truth about who God is, what he has done, and what his world is like. This is the substance of theology, and it is the foundation of Christian discipleship.

The teaching component of discipleship must include the whole counsel of God. Believers need to know the Bible front to back. They need to understand the great themes of the Bible and the flow of biblical revelation. Their minds need to be saturated with Scripture, and their worldview needs to be reshaped by Scripture. They need to know how to interpret Scripture accurately in context. They need to understand how to apply Scripture to their lives in situations that may be quite different from anything actually found in the world of the Bible. There is a cognitive dimension to discipleship. There is a body of teaching that must be learned, absorbed, and understood; and that body of teaching is the content of the Word of God. Disciples of Jesus Christ need to learn all of it, and keep learning for the rest of their lives.

In addition to the cognitive dimension, however, there is also a character dimension. Jesus told his followers to teach new disciples, not just to know everything he had taught but specifically to obey everything he had commanded. Head knowledge without obedience is not enough. Discipleship changes your life. A real disciple of Jesus becomes like Jesus in character and way of life. Salvation must involve sanctification. This includes putting off the deeds of the flesh and, indeed, putting them to death by the power of the Holy Spirit (Romans 8:13; Ephesians 4:17–32; Colossians 3:5–11). It also involves putting on the compassion, kindness, humility, gentleness, patience, forbearance, forgiveness and love of Christ (Colossians 3:12–14). It involves cultivating the fruit of the Spirit (Galatians 5:22–23). Sanctification that is only negative is the legalism of the Pharisee, not the evidence of real grace that characterizes life in Christ.

Salvation also involves service. A true disciple gladly embraces the service of his or her Lord. Because we exist only by his grace and for his glory, and because we are no longer our own but entirely his, biblical disciples serve Jesus by working for the edification of his people and for the advancement of his gospel. A disciple must be more than simply a knowledge gatherer. In the process of making disciples we must indeed teach knowledge, but along with that knowledge we must also teach obedience to everything that Jesus commanded.

In the process of making disciples we must indeed teach knowledge, but along with that knowledge we must also teach obedience to everything that Jesus commanded.

Baptism and teaching are complementary components of the task. Baptism, like death and birth, happens only once. It represents the beginning of discipleship, and it clearly portrays just how radical that beginning really is. Teaching is a lifelong process. No Christian ever outgrows the need to grow as a disciple. No believer ever comes to the point where he or she has learned everything there is to know in the Bible. And certainly no believer ever reaches the point of complete and perfect obedience. Discipleship will only be complete when we see Jesus face to face in glory. Until then, every believer needs to engage the process of discipleship seriously. The teaching task of the Great Commission, then, is to lay a foundation of knowledge and obedience that will enable that lifelong pursuit.

What Resources Are Needed?

If the Great Commission is all about making disciples from among all people groups, and discipleship involves baptizing and teaching obedience to everything Jesus commanded, what resources are needed for the task?

God's Word. First and foremost, the work of the Great Commission requires access to the Word of God. It is very difficult to teach people the whole counsel of God if his words are not available to them. For this reason, the translation, printing, and distribution of the Bible are core components of biblical mission work. While English speakers have a multitude of Bible translations available to them, most unreached people groups don't yet have one translation of the Word of God in their heart language. Bible translation is one of the first priorities in any strategy to reach a people group.

Because many people groups are comprised of oral learners who may or may not even be able to read their heart language, Scriptures often need to be distributed in audio format to be accessible to the people who need them. In addition, Bible distribution in the heart languages of unreached people groups in restricted-access countries is often forbidden or tightly controlled, so creative methods of distribution may be necessary. Bible translation and distribution are tasks that all Great Commission Christian organizations can agree on, and these tasks are often carried out by partnerships between all evangelical agencies trying to reach a given people group. Making disciples requires access to the Word of God. Far too many lost people still have no such access. Getting the Bible into their hands in their heart language is an essential component of the Great Commission.

God's people. The second essential resource is people who will go wherever Christ is not yet known in order to make disciples. God's clear plan is to use his people to call more people to himself. Jesus told his followers that they would receive the power of the Holy Spirit specifically in order to be witnesses to him to the ends of the earth. In order to make disciples, however, you need to be a disciple yourself. You can't give away what you don't have. Jesus sent out disciples to make disciples, and the method still stands. It isn't possible to separate the message from its messengers. The credibility of the gospel depends on the character of the witnesses. If the lives of cross-cultural Christian workers are not conspicuously different, in a Christlike way, from the lives of others around them, lost people will see no need to pay any attention to them.

In much of the world, Christianity is tied in people's minds to Western culture as portrayed in the Western entertainment media. Because that media paints a very immoral picture of life in the West, and because the West is regarded as "Christian," the gospel message often has an uphill climb simply to be heard. Cross-cultural Christian workers need to go out of their way to contradict the slanderous impression left by our movies and television programs. Also, since evangelism is actually a call to discipleship, our effectiveness is closely tied to our ability to model what we proclaim. New believers will watch our lives to see what the life of a disciple really involves, and they will pattern their lives on what they observe in us. The work of the Great Commission requires witnesses who themselves are maturing disciples of Jesus Christ and who are willing to go to the ends of the earth to make disciples of those who have never heard.

God's church. There is a third resource necessary to fulfill the Great Commission, and it is one that often escapes the attention of individualistic Western Christians. That resource is the church. We tend to think of discipleship as something that happens on our own, or perhaps in a one-on-one relationship with an older Christian. The Bible makes it clear that discipleship happens in the body of Christ. In Ephesians, Paul says,

> He gave the apostles, the prophets, the evangelists, the shepherds and teachers, to equip the saints for the work of ministry, for building up the body of Christ, until we all attain to the unity of the faith and of the knowledge of the Son of God, to mature manhood, to the measure of the stature of the fullness of Christ, so that we may no longer be children, tossed to and fro by the waves and carried about by every wind of doctrine, by human cunning, by craftiness in deceitful schemes. Rather, speaking the truth in love, we are to grow up in every way into him who is the head, into Christ, from whom the whole body, joined and held together by every joint with which it is equipped, when each part is working properly, makes the body grow so that it builds itself up in love. (Ephesians 4:11–16 ESV)

We only grow to maturity in Christ in the context of the body of Christ, and the body of Christ only functions correctly when each part is working properly. We need more than our own private study or one older mentor to become mature disciples of Jesus. We need the entire body of Christ.

In his great discussion on spiritual gifts in 1 Corinthians 12—14, Paul tells us that God has made us intentionally dependent on each other. No believer can say that he or she is unnecessary, and no believer can say that he or she doesn't need any other believer. No one has all the spiritual gifts, so no one person has all that another believer needs to grow to maturity as a disciple. Discipleship only happens in the church. Making disciples, therefore, requires both that cross-cultural workers engage in church themselves as an essential component of their own discipleship and that they plant churches as the only context in which disciple-making can happen.

God, in his grace, sometimes calls people to himself through his Word alone, without a human witness being directly involved. Bless his name when he does! His normal pattern, however, is for his Holy Spirit to use both his Word and his people in the process of calling people out of darkness into his marvelous light. The content of the gospel is the biblical witness to the person and work of Jesus Christ and his gracious summons to undeserving sinners. The carriers of that message may include print, audio, and/or video media, but in the economy of God those media are best accompanied by living witnesses who both proclaim gospel content and model what it means to be a growing disciple of Jesus in the fellowship of the body of Christ. Both in the preconversion and postconversion stages of discipleship (for the process of discipleship begins in the very manner in which the gospel is shared, and the two stages are intimately connected) the work of the Great Commission is intensely relational. Disciples of Jesus who invest themselves in the lives of both unbelievers and young believers, while living and growing in the context of Christ's body, are the most effective means of fulfilling the global mission of God.

God's presence. When we understand the Great Commission as Jesus meant it, we can easily become overwhelmed. The task is way over our heads. If we have any sense of realism about ourselves at all, we realize that we are completely inadequate for the task. It is at this point that the closing statement of the Great Commission becomes really good news. "And surely I am with you always, to the very end of the age." Jesus promises his own presence to his people as they carry out his mission.

This has always been the very best gift God could give when he assigns a task to his servants.

When God met Moses at the burning bush to send him back to Egypt to rescue his people, Moses understandably felt too small to do the job (Exodus 3). "Who am I," he asked God, "that I should go to Pharaoh and bring the Israelites out of Egypt?" God didn't respond by giving Moses a pep talk about what a great guy he was. He didn't try to boost his self-esteem or restore his confidence in himself. In fact, God didn't say anything at all about Moses in his answer to Moses' question, because the abilities and resources of Moses were irrelevant. God simply said, "I will be with you." He was all that Moses would need.

When Jesus was born, he was given a name that means the same thing and sounds almost identical in Hebrew: Immanuel, "God with us" (Matthew 1:22). This name not only signified his essential deity but also revealed the graciously intimate and sufficient character of the God that he is. Now, at the end of his ministry on earth, Jesus promises to remain Immanuel—to remain the all-sufficient God with us. He didn't promise technique, technology, or money, which are the tools we usually depend on in our flesh. He didn't promise safety, comfort, or health, which are the conditions our flesh usually craves. He just promised himself. He reminded us at the beginning of this statement, however, that all authority in heaven and on earth has been given to him. He is the sovereign Lord of the universe. He is more than enough. In calling his people to a task that is humanly impossible, he ends the call by promising the one resource that can actually make it happen—his own presence to the very end.

Conclusion

The authority for missions lies in the sovereign lordship of Jesus Christ, who has all authority in heaven and on earth. The heart of the task is to make disciples who have been baptized as a symbol of their radical new commitment to Jesus and who are taught both to know and to obey everything Jesus commanded. The scope of the task is all people groups on earth. God's provision for the task is the all-sufficient presence of Jesus. That, and nothing less, is the missions mandate of the people of God. That is the heart of the task.

Discussion Points

1. What is the central task of missions? What is this based on? How can you use this to evaluate the opportunities your church has outside its own fellowship?

2. What is a disciple? How are disciples made?

3. What does baptism represent, and what role does it play in the life of discipleship?

4. What is the scope of the missions task? How much remains to be done?

5. What are the implications of the lordship of Jesus Christ for the missions endeavor?

Further Reading

Bavinck, J. H. *An Introduction to the Science of Missions.* Phillipsburg, NJ: Presbyterian & Reformed, 1960.

Dever, Mark. *The Gospel and Personal Evangelism.* Wheaton: Crossway, 2007.

———. *Nine Marks of a Healthy Church.* Wheaton: Crossway, 2000.

Hammett, John. *Biblical Foundations for Baptist Churches.* Grand Rapids: Kregel, 2005.

Piper, John. *Let the Nations Be Glad.* Grand Rapids: Baker, 2003.

Wells, David. *God the Evangelist.* Grand Rapids: Eerdmans, 1987.

8

THE CHURCH
IN THE MISSION OF GOD

Preben Vang

Most Christians who take Jesus' command in Matthew 28:19–20 seriously will agree that planting churches is a significant part of fulfilling the Great Commission. The evangelical "success" of the church-growth and church-planting movements during the last forty or so years has only strengthened these convictions. Yet when we stop to ask believers—even church planters—"What exactly is a church?" we often get a blank stare or some vague description that sounds mostly like an explanation of the church they grew up in (conveniently corrected for the things they didn't care much for). If the conversation probes further into how the church fits into God's plan for his kingdom, answers get truly muddy. The question begs itself, therefore: Do we run around the world starting churches without giving much thought to the most essential question—What is a church, and how does it fulfill God's purposes?

Do we run around the world starting churches without giving much thought to the most essential question— What is a church, and how does it fulfill God's purposes?

Most Christians involved with missions and ministry, and maybe especially church planters, are activists. They are eager to get things done and will gladly read whatever book, or attend whatever seminar, that can help them with the how-to of their task. The why, for some reason, seems less important.

Looking at Acts, we are struck by the amazing absence of practical questions and answers regarding the church. The book doesn't even give us a full description of how to conduct a worship service! Sure, there are hints here and there of how the early church tackled certain practical situations, but not many of us struggle with disputes between Greek- and Hebrew-speaking widows during church meals (Acts 6).

Certain patterns on the how-to for church planting seem to develop from Paul's ministry. Usually, he first went where faith was most likely to be found (the synagogue), then to the public square (e.g., a lecture hall in Ephesus, Acts 19:9). But even when he explains the Lord's Supper (1 Corinthians 11:20–34) or speaks about preaching (1 Corinthians 1:21), Paul gives us very little practical information. Throughout, he remains short on the how and long on the why. It seems the New Testament aims to emphasize that if we truly get the why, the how will have enough guidance to work itself out in any setting.

The Church and God's Grand Story

To arrive at a satisfying understanding of the church and its significance for God's mission on earth, we must consider the church in light of God's redemptive story. Isolated proof texts (even thorough exegesis of specific and seemingly significant biblical passages) will ultimately come up short. In fact, the Western world, with its extremely individualized understanding of life and of the divine/human encounter, has often fallen prey to interpretations that reduce ecclesiology (the doctrine of church) to a matter of creating theaters for spiritual inspiration. In the United States, churches even come in the drive-in variety—or in a multiplex format where attendees can choose their favorite individualized worship style on the same campus.

Seen in light of God's grand story, however, the church is nothing less than God's kingdom community. The purpose of this community is to be a light to the nations (Isaiah 42:6) in order that these nations will turn from their rebellion and begin to worship the triune God of heaven and earth (see Luke 1:78–79). Put differently, the church functions as God's kingdom-vehicle on earth, intended to be a community that exists to evidence God's story—a specific and tangible story of creation, fall, redemption, and restoration, revealed through God's historical actions among his people. In a very real sense, then, the church is a storyteller: a reminder to all creation that the God who promised to call people into a new covenant with himself, and to pour out his Spirit upon all flesh, spoke the truth (Acts 2:17; Romans 8:22). Indeed, the church's task is to evidence the power of the Light to conquer darkness.

Kingdom communities portray kingdom life through participation in a story that transforms life's priorities (Acts 2:42–47). Moreover, the book of Acts not only portrays the young church as the community that represents God's restoration of his people; it boldly proclaims a renewal that transforms the very results of Babel in Genesis 11:6–9. Opposite Babel, where people were scattered throughout the earth and cursed with language barriers that disabled community and communication, Pentecost parades a gathering of people from "every nation under heaven" (Acts 2:5) who all understood the same speech as if spoken in their own language (v. 6). It is not that God undid what he had done at Babel, but rather that he re-enabled what was possible before Babel: people of all languages could now again understand God's actions and become part of *his* covenant community.

That such emphasis on the international character of the church is foundational to a biblical ecclesiology proves even clearer from Luke's subtle references in his Pentecost account. In his description of the Spirit's coming with the "sound like the blowing of a violent wind" (Acts 2:2), Luke summons Old Testament images of scenes such as when God revealed himself to the prophet Elijah (1 Kings 19:11–12; 2 Kings 2:11) and when he gave the law at Sinai (Exodus 19:16–19). Moreover, the interpretation of the law-giving at Sinai given by the Hellenistic Jewish philosopher, Philo—an interpretation known to many of Luke's readers—reads like a direct parallel to the experience at Pentecost: "And a voice sounded forth from out of the midst of the fire which had flowed from heaven, a most marvelous and awful voice, the flame being endowed with articulate speech *in a language familiar to the hearers*, which expressed its words with such clearness and distinctness that the people seemed rather to be seeing than hearing it."[1]

---

[1]Philo, *Decalogue* 46, italics added.

Luke's explicit use in his Pentecost account of Philo's conjunction of fire and divine communication at Sinai enables him to suggest implicitly that the giving of the Spirit not only parallels but also fulfills the giving of the law.[2] The law (God's Word and covenantal revelation), which the Talmud taught was intended for all the nations of the world, claiming that it was given in the seventy languages that made up the nations of the world,[3] was now demonstratively fulfilling its goal. Pentecost was no longer a mere commemoration of past renewals,[4] but the establishment of a new international community promised by God, instituted by Christ, and constituted by the Spirit. The church was born as God's kingdom community and vehicle.

> *The church was born as God's kingdom community and vehicle.*

The Church and the Kingdom of God

The above conclusions should not be misconstrued to affirm the Augustinian notion that the church equals the kingdom, giving church leaders and church hierarchy the power to include or exclude individuals from that kingdom. Nor should it allow us to separate our talk of kingdom and church so strongly that we reduce the church to a mere human institution designed for inspirational and teaching purposes—a place for those who know a bit more than the rest to dispense biblical knowledge to the faithful and give spiritual guidance to seekers. In the end, a church that sees itself as a mere religious institution, a gathering of (or gathering place for) people with related religious convictions, remains irrelevant.

The kingdom of God is where God rules in glory. Unrelated to geographical areas and boundaries, the kingdom exists where God is King. This is not only an Old Testament notion of theocracy, but a *de facto* reality expressed throughout the New Testament as well. Surely God

---

[2]Luke T. Johnson sees Luke's use of Moses typology to be so strong that "it would be surprising if the use of sound and fire and languages here did not allude to the Sinai event." *The Acts of the Apostles*, Sacra Pagina, no. 5, ed. D. J. Harrington (Collegeville, MN: Liturgical Press, 1992), 46. See also the connection between wind and the future restoration of Israel in Ezekiel 37.
[3]*b. Shab.* 88b.
[4]The book of Jubilees explains Pentecost as a covenant-renewal feast; *Jubilees* 6:17–21.

rules *de jure* (by right) at all times in all places, but Jesus' message that the kingdom of God has come near expresses a spatial and evidential reality that refuses separation from human experience and devotion. When, for example, John the Baptist becomes confused in his prison cell about whether Jesus truly was the Christ or if he should wait for another, Jesus replied by pointing to kingdom evidences and affirming the listeners' need to recognize God's presence in their midst (Luke 7:18–22). Eschatological expectations were now experienced in history. The kingdom had arrived—it was here already, though not fully.

It is in this tension of the already/not fully that the biblical teaching on both kingdom and church should be understood. As mentioned above, the church is neither to be equated with God's kingdom nor should it be understood as completely distinct from the kingdom. Rather, we may say that the proclamation of the kingdom calls forth the church. The relationship between church and kingdom is such that when the gospel of the kingdom is proclaimed, the Holy Spirit calls forth a new community, a people characterized by God's presence and recognized by their obedience to their King. The kingdom is, in other words, expressed through the church. No place on earth will the "already" of the kingdom come to expression

> *The kingdom is, in other words, expressed through the church.*

stronger than in the community that recognizes God's kingship and gathers to celebrate his rule and glory. In that sense, the church is a genuine foretaste of what is to come in full at God's appointed time.

When the church falls short of this experience, the explanation is found in the already/not fully character of its existence. This tension doesn't only run between the church and the world; it runs through the community itself and its individual members. On the community level, this is recognized in Paul's exhortations throughout his epistles. On the individual level, Paul exclaims even for himself that "although I want to do good, evil is right there with me" (Romans 7:21). God's Spirit is poured out and has created the empowered and obedient kingdom community we call church. Yet, since Christ presently does not fill all in all, we recognize that the full, unadulterated experience of the kingdom remains tenuous and aloof.

The Church and Its Worship

It follows from the above paragraphs that "worship," in the Christian sense of the term, refuses reduction to a mere synonym for specifically designed church events called by that name. It is true, obviously, that from the beginning God set off a special day for worship and rest, but the biblical mandate to worship goes far beyond weekly events and speaks to the whole encounter between God and his creation. Even beyond the act of ascribing worth to God, Christian worship celebrates the awareness that all of life is granted by the God who let himself be known as the Almighty Father through his Son and by his Spirit. The experience of the truth of God's story, and the awareness of our participation in it, awakens a desire to express that story with adoration toward the King who made it happen. Put differently, worship occurs when people recognize that their fellowship with the Creator has been reestablished by his Son's redemptive death on the cross and his Spirit's re-creative work in their lives. It is for this purpose that God calls forth the community recognized as the church (Greek: *ekklēsia*). The church is a community of people who, because they themselves have experienced the power of God's actions, exist to tell about it, to express it through their lives, and to bring others into an experience of participation in God's story. The church is God's kingdom community filled with actors who participate in the drama of God's story.

> *It follows from the above paragraphs that "worship," in the Christian sense of the term, refuses reduction to a mere synonym for specifically designed church events called by that name.*

Considering the connection between church and worship even further, it quickly becomes obvious that Christian worship primarily directs its focus toward the triune God and only secondarily toward the worshiping community itself. By its very nature, a kingdom community cannot be self-serving. When it seems to become so, it ceases to be a kingdom community, or church (at least in the strict sense of the term), and worship turns into religious entertainment. In the Christian sense of the term, worship is not a means to some other end. Worship is itself the end! Worship is *the* purpose of the Christian life and of Christian communities. Christians and churches turn things upside down when they turn worship into an event that functions as a means to another end—even when that end is evangelism, religious education, moral correction, entertainment, motivation, fellowship, or even missions. Biblically speaking, evangelism, entertainment, fellowship, and various church programs are the means. They are the

The focus of a church that is recognizably Christian, then, is to call all of creation back into God-honoring, Christ-focused, and Spirit-directed kingdom communities.

means Christian communities use to bring people (even nations) from their rebellion against God (caused and characterized by the fall in Genesis 3) to the worship of God. Again, the ultimate goal of all Christian effort is to bring all of humanity back to the worship of God! That is, back into the kingdom where God rules in glory. The focus of a church that is recognizably Christian, then, is to call all of creation back into God-honoring, Christ-focused, and Spirit-directed kingdom communities.

The Church and Its Prophetic Call

The church began with three thousand people who recognized Christ's role in God's goal and purpose for his creation. They repented and were baptized in response to the call presented by Peter's Pentecost sermon. As they were baptized, they became part of a new community of believers who understood themselves to be the people to whom the fulfillment of God's eschatological promises had come. God had forgiven their sins and given them the empowering gift of his Holy Spirit to evidence and enable their participation in the promised new kingdom community.

Called forth by the Spirit, this new community proves to be the answer to the prophetic call—a reversal of the prophetic indictment, so to speak. What this means is that the church followed the call sounded by the Old Testament prophets. Summarizing the prophetic literature of the Old Testament, we notice how the prophets consistently brought three major charges or warnings against God's people. The first was the charge of idolatry. The people were breaking the first commandment; God did not reign supreme. The second charge against the people was that they had turned their worship of God into a formality—a lifeless, nontransforming, going-through-the-motions ritualism. There was an obvious disconnect between the people's external ceremony and the genuineness of their inner devotion. The third prophetic charge was that the people exercised, or had accepted, social injustice. They lacked a genuine concern for the poor. These are the three serious indictments that weave through all the Old Testament prophetic material—the very charges that later brought the judgment of the Babylonian exile.

In stark contrast, the community described in Acts 2 embodied the correction to these prophetic charges. Leaving no room for idolatry, Luke described the new church community as fully guided by God's Spirit and giving unyielding attention to the presence of God (Acts 2:42). The teaching, the fellowship, the breaking of bread, and the prayers together expressed the undeviating focus on God called for by the prophets. The "teaching" refers directly to a focus on God's will and purpose. The "fellowship" emphasizes the reality of the new kingdom community promised by the prophets and called forth by God's Spirit. The "breaking of bread" locks the gaze on God's pivotal action for his people—the Passover that symbolized God's power to bring his people out of darkness and into his promised land and its intended fulfillment in the cross and resurrection of Christ. The "prayer" brings devotion, intimacy, and thanksgiving to the forefront. Acts defines in this way the church as God's true community, a community whose focus, task, and reason for existence is anchored outside themselves in God's purpose for all nations—indeed for his whole creation.

Acts defines in this way the church as God's true community, a community whose focus, task, and reason for existence is anchored outside themselves in God's purpose for all nations—indeed for his whole creation.

Religious formalism has no room in this new community. Their devotion (v. 42) was much more than ritualism, or mere attendance to a system of activities. Rather, it was a genuine cry from the heart which, over and beyond participation in the services (v. 46a), came to expression every time and every place they met—even when they met in their private homes (v. 46b). They replaced the externality of mere participation with a sincerity of heart that resulted in constant praise of God (vv. 46c–47). When church members like Ananias and Sapphira tried to reduce their devotion to mere ritual expressions (hypocrisy), they were immediately exposed as unworthy of the kingdom (Acts 5:1–10).

Luke's emphases when he summarizes the life of the Christ-following community in the opening chapters of Acts bring a powerful crescendo to the purpose of the church as a kingdom vehicle. With no room for the church to be self-serving, this text answers even the prophetic charge that God's plan for his people included taking care of the poor (Acts 2:44–45). These verses defy relegation to a discussion of utopian visions of society as some commentators try to do. Rather, the emphasis is on *how* the new community answers the call given by the prophets of old and makes sure no one goes hungry and unclothed (v. 45b). The church, God's kingdom community, must understand itself as God's obedient people, sent to the world to express God's story through their life and word.

The Church and Its Mission

Several things follow from the above discussion. First, the church is not an add-on to the Christian life. Rather, individual Christians live their lives through the church as vital parts of a body. It simply violates the language of Scripture to speak of the church as an organization designed to be a filling station for individual Christians who have need of special encouragement and support. Scripture rarely, if ever, talks about the Christian faith in individual terms. The language remains plural and points to community. Paul's use of the body metaphor in 1 Corinthians 12 indicates that the very

The church is not an add-on to the Christian life. Rather, individual Christians live their lives through the church as vital parts of a body. It simply violates the language of Scripture to speak of the church as an organization designed to be a filling station for individual Christians who have need of special encouragement and support.

notion of solo Christians is an oxymoron. No limbs on a body can exist apart from the body; once they are disconnected from the body, they will invariably rot and die. Even when Paul reminds the Corinthians, "Don't you know that you yourselves are God's temple and that God's Spirit dwells in your midst?" (1 Corinthians 3:16), he uses plural language speaking about the community, not the individual.

The same holds true when Paul speaks of election and redemption in Ephesians 1; the language remains plural, pointing to the in-Christ community. He chose *us* in him (Ephesians 1:4,11); adopted *us* in Christ (v. 5); gave grace freely to *us* in him (v. 6); *we* have redemption through his blood (v. 7); and he made his will known to *us* in Christ (v. 9). Paul's language is church language. He speaks to the church body as a community who, because they together can be called "Christ's body," can trust that the promises of God will be fulfilled in and through them. There is no hint anywhere that Paul can even fathom a Christian disconnected from the church body. In fact, the worst thing that can happen when a church member proves not to be a Christ-follower, is that he or she is removed from the community (1 Corinthians 5:13). Removal from the kingdom community would also remove them from the promises of God.

From this, it becomes obvious that the extreme individualism that characterizes Western thinking and societies, and resultantly Western churches, can easily generate an understanding of church that misrepresents the biblical portrayal. Add to this a Western business model that equates success with numerical growth at all levels (number of customers, sales, traffic, input/output, etc.), and "church" stands in real danger of becoming self-serving and utilitarian. Individuals stop thinking of themselves as members of a body and begin to think in terms of places to attend. The church has become a service institution for its members. From the perspective of the "organization" itself, employees are hired and buildings erected to accommodate this quest for service. Since the church is now considered a gathering place for individuals, the focus is on attracting more revenue-generating attendees than are claimed by sister churches, which ultimately function as competitors. Buildings must therefore be larger, programs more extravagant, and worship more appealing. It is not much of an exaggeration (if even one at all) to say that many modern churches are more dependent—even for their worship services—on electrical power to run the service than on God's power to transform the people.

That this danger is real can be seen in what is now considered acceptable church language: "We exist to serve the needs of those who enter our doors." The biblical language seems to run in the exact opposite direction to such a statement:

The call is not to attend and be served, but to join and become a servant.

"The church exists to call those who live in the fallen world to become members of God's kingdom community, a community whose sole focus is on showing and telling God's story." The call is not to attend and be served, but to join and become a servant.

Theologians often use three Greek terms to describe the church: *martyria, koinonia,* and *diakonia. Martyria* speaks to the testimony: the community's witness to how God's story has affected them, and their preaching of what significance this has for their life and surroundings right now. To be a martyr is to be an unwavering witness, even in the face of death (e.g., 2 Corinthians 11:23–28).

Koinonia speaks to fellowship: not in the sense of a mere get-together with little programming except food, but rather in the sense of genuine sharing of life. The Greek word *koinonia* is used to express what happens in a marriage when two people are joined for life. It is used to describe business relationships when two people sell what they own individually in order to start as partners in a new joint venture. They are now bound together in *koinonia*. The flippant notion that church members have *koinonia* just because they meet in the "fellowship hall" is rather foreign to Scripture. Rather, *koinonia* happens when members of the same church body realize their total dependence upon each other.

Diakonia speaks to service. When the first deacons were elected in Acts 6, they were elected to serve at the tables. To be a deacon is to be a servant whose whole aim is to minister to others. Although the title of deacon is reserved for those elected to serve the church in a special capacity, the whole of God's kingdom community is characterized by the word *diakonia*. The Christ who came to save says about himself that he did not come to be served, but to serve (*diakonēsai*—Mark 10:45). For the church to reflect him, *diakonia* must be a fitting description of her.

Another aspect that flows from the above study is the international character of the church. Like God's kingdom, the church is an all-peoples proposition—it is for all peoples, to all peoples, and in all peoples. This was evident at Pentecost, as mentioned previously, and it has enormous missiological implications. Historically, churches from Western civilizations and countries have understood themselves as the sending arm of the kingdom. Part of the reason for that has obviously been that Christianity took firm root early in European soil and the civilization it created produced wealth, knowledge, technological expertise, and prominence. The American culture epitomized this even further. A resultant sense of priority is latent in Western societies that makes us consider ourselves "primary Christian countries." Unfortunately, a similar notion often drives Western churches to send missionaries to start churches in other countries. To accept that churches from the East and the Global South now send missionaries to the West to help us create genuine kingdom communities can still be difficult for some.

Things are changing fast, however, as Phil Jenkins' work so amply demonstrates.[5] The world has become missiologically flat.[6] Opposite the business world, where much of the "flatness" has been caused by outsourcing (businesses subcontracting and moving their manufacturing processes to cheaper labor markets), churches outside Western civilizations don't necessarily see themselves as expressions or extensions of "Western Christianity." They are kingdom communities in their own right. In fact, many of these churches see Western churches as weak and powerless and view themselves as a much clearer expression of the New Testament church.

As described in Acts, the New Testament church is multinational and multiethnic. It's a global-village church, so to speak. The days

---

[5]Philip Jenkins, *The Next Christendom: The Coming of Global Christianity* (New York: Oxford University Press, 2002), and *The New Faces of Christianity: Believing the Bible in the Global South* (Oxford: Oxford University Press, 2006).

[6]I use the word "flat" in a sense similar to its use by Thomas L. Friedman in his 2005 book, *The World Is Flat: A Brief History of the Twenty-First Century* (New York: Farrar, Straus and Giroux).

when some churches saw themselves as sending churches while others were receiving churches are gone. Now churches around the globe both send and receive. That many Western, especially American, churches remain wealthier than most churches in the East and Global South only means that they can afford to do more. It is a God-granted opportunity to expand their *diakonia*. On the level of *martyria* and *koinonia*, however, they are receivers as well as senders. As the global kingdom community experiences unusual and unprecedented growth in areas of the world where Christian churches traditionally have found little foothold, missionaries and church planters from everywhere will move in all directions. When at the same time cultural embodiments of "church" prove more and more suspect (and less and less powerful and meaningful), churches from around the globe will need to learn from each other what it means to be a true kingdom community. As they do, they will all experience that the tower of Babel has been replaced by the power of Pentecost. They speak the same language and have the same focus: to create communities— churches—that genuinely proclaim God's story of creation, fall, redemption, and restoration through life and words.

Conclusion

So what is a church, and how does it fulfill God's purposes? Since the beginning of God's grand story, God's kingdom community has been the vehicle for his mission to all nations. It is in and through this community that God's kingdom is both expressed and experienced on earth. The purpose of missions and evangelism is to bring all of God's creation into a true, life-encompassing worship of God. God's prophetic call upon the church is to call all people—from all people groups and nations—to establish communities whose life-focus is to worship the true, living, triune God. As a community, the church does not come together to decide its own agenda. That has already been established, and no convenient substitute can be given. If a church is to be Christian in the true sense of the term, it must be defined by its mission as God's kingdom vehicle.

Discussion Points

1. Why is the church *necessary* in the first place?

2. How would you define the relationship between the kingdom of God and the church?

3. When starting a church, what would be "Western" and what would be nonnegotiable?

4. What influence will a focus on *community* have on the presentation of the gospel—and why?

Further Reading

Friedman, Thomas. *The World Is Flat: A Brief History of the Twenty-First Century.* New York: Farrar, Straus and Giroux, 2005.

Glasser, Arthur. *Announcing the Kingdom: The Story of God's Mission in the Bible.* Grand Rapids: Baker, 2003.

Jenkins, Philip. *The Next Christendom: The Coming of Global Christianity.* New York: Oxford University Press, 2002.

———. *The New Faces of Christianity: Believing the Bible in the Global South.* Oxford: Oxford University Press, 2006.

Spencer, Aida Besancon, and William David Spencer. *The Global God: Multicultural Evangelical Views of God.* Grand Rapids: Baker, 1998.

Stone, Bryan. *Evangelism After Christendom: The Theology and Practice of Christian Witness.* Grand Rapids: Brazos Press, 2007.

9

THE POWER OF THE GOSPEL

Robert L. Plummer

Faithful missionaries hunger to see the power of God. They want spiritual renewal in their own lives. As God's emissaries, they desire to see the people around them repent of their sins, believe in Christ, and serve God anew in the power of the Holy Spirit. Missionaries long to see new churches started and entire people groups transformed into obedient disciples of Jesus Christ. In sum, missionaries desire to see an outpouring of God's power through their lives and labors.

As we look to the Bible for the source of power in missions, we are struck by the lack of suggested methods or techniques. When referring to the forceful advance of the gospel, the locus of that power frequently seems to be in the gospel *itself.* The apostle Paul writes, "For I am not ashamed of the gospel, for it is the power of God for salvation to everyone who believes" (Romans 1:16 ESV). What does Paul mean in saying that the gospel is "the power of God"? What does it look like for a missionary's life and work to demonstrate this power of the gospel?

Meaning of the Term "Gospel"

Before we describe the power of the gospel, we must clarify our terms. What, in fact, is "the gospel"? The English word "gospel" or "good news" is a translation of the Greek word *euangelion*. It has several meanings in the Greek New Testament.[1]

Euangelion can be a genre designation, referring to one of the four

---

[1]Outside the New Testament, *euangelion* can mean simply "good tidings," with no reference to the story of Jesus.

theological biographies about Jesus included in our New Testament—i.e., the Gospel of Matthew, the Gospel of Mark, etc. *Euangelion* can refer to the propositional statements of what God has done to save lost humanity by sending Christ as Savior. Essentially, the gospel can be boiled down to the confession "that Christ died for our sins in accordance with the Scriptures, that he was buried, [and] that he was raised on the third day in accordance with the Scriptures" (1 Corinthians 15:3–4).[2]

In close connection with the meaning above, *euangelion* can have further connotations of God's dynamic saving Word. In this sense, the gospel refers to the preaching, reception, and powerful advance of God's Word as it saves and transforms lost humanity. The gospel becomes more than repeatable propositions, though certainly not less. It is especially in this third sense that we see the authors of the New Testament employing the term *euangelion* (or near synonyms) in relation to power.

The Bible Speaks of the Gospel as a Power

Most readers of this book are accustomed to speaking of the gospel as a propositional summary of God's saving intervention in Christ (for example, in statements such as "I came to believe the gospel when I was thirteen years old," or "This little booklet explains the gospel"). Yet the Bible, as noted above, also frequently presents the gospel as a dynamic power. We will now survey a number of texts that touch on this theme in an attempt to better understand what the Bible means in describing the gospel as a power.

The Old Testament. The Old Testament provides an important conceptual background for understanding the gospel as a power. In the New Testament, the gospel of Christ is sometimes called "the word of the Lord" or simply "the word" (e.g., Acts 8:25; 10:36; 13:44; Philippians 1:14; 1 Thessalonians 1:6,8; 2 Thessalonians 3:1; 1 Peter 1:25 ESV). Underlying this usage is the rich background of "the word of the LORD" in the Old Testament. God creates the world by speaking words (Genesis 1:1–31). These words are effective—i.e., they accomplish exactly what God intends for them to do. When God says, "Let there be light" (Genesis 1:3), there is

---

[2]English Scripture quotations in this chapter are from the English Standard Version (ESV).

no question as to the result. Thus, in the Old Testament, God's word creates or brings into existence the very thing spoken (cf. Romans 4:17).

We find a similar use of God's word in the historical and prophetic books. The word of the Lord is nearly personified as it "comes upon" various persons (e.g., 1 Samuel 3:1; 15:10; 2 Samuel 7:14; 24:11; 1 Kings 13:1–9). The word so overpowers the recipients that they are helpless to resist its influence or demands (1 Samuel 10:10; 1 Kings 6:11). God's word is not a flimsy hope or appeal; it actually accomplishes the purposes he has for it, sometimes purposes that are counterintuitive or inscrutable to humans (Isaiah 6:9–13).

Isaiah 55:10–11 speaks very clearly of this effective, powerful nature of God's word: "As the rain and the snow come down from heaven, and do not return to it without watering the earth and making it bud and flourish, so that it yields seed for the sower and bread for the eater, so is my word that goes out from my mouth: It will not return to me empty, but will accomplish what I desire and achieve the purpose for which I sent it."

Throughout the entire Bible, the message of salvation in Christ is more than words on paper or sounds coming out of a preacher's mouth. The gospel is a God-empowered, creative, saving force, working in and through the speaker and hearers to transform people from all nations who reflect the glorious image of Christ.

Jeremiah records a similar statement, as the Lord himself testifies, "'Is not my word like fire,' declares the LORD, 'and like a hammer that breaks a rock in pieces?'" (Jeremiah 23:29).[3] Thus we see that God's word in the Old Testament is more than simply a repetition of statements, but actually an effective, powerful, creative, dynamic force. It should not surprise us, then, to find a similar use in the New Testament.

The Gospels. Throughout the entire Bible, the message of salvation in

[3]See also Genesis 15:1,4; Exodus 9:20–21; Numbers 3:16,51; 11:23; 15:31; 24:13; 36:5; Deuteronomy 5:5; 9:5; 18:22; 34:5; Joshua 8:27; Jeremiah 20:7–9. John L. McKenzie writes, "The word of Yahweh may be called sacramental in the sense that it effects what it signifies. When Yahweh posits the word-thing, nothing can prevent its emergence." "The Word of God in the Old Testament," *Theological Studies* 21 (1960): 196. See also Oskar Grether, *Name und Wort Gottes im Alten Testament*, Beihefte zur Zeitschrift für die altestamentliche Wissenschaft 64 (Giessen, Germany: Töpelmann, 1934), especially 59–185.

Christ is more than words on paper or sounds coming out of a preacher's mouth. The gospel is a God-empowered, creative, saving force, working in and through the speaker and hearers to transform people from all nations who reflect the glorious image of Christ (Romans 8:28–30).

One of Jesus' parables will suffice as a witness from the Gospels. The well-known "parable of the sower" (Mark 4:1–20; Matthew 13:1–23; Luke 8:4–15) illustrates this aspect of the gospel. The seed sown in the parable is "the word"—i.e., the gospel of Christ. We must be careful not to press the details of the parable beyond Jesus' intent, but the organic and fruitful nature inherent in the "word-seed" is hard to miss. Where the word is received, it produces a stunning crop: thirty, sixty, or even a hundred times what was sown (Mark 4:20). The hearers are responsible for what they have heard; they must not let worldly cares choke the word (Mark 4:19). Still, it is the word that lands on the "good soil" that grows into a flourishing plant.

What is truly enduring and potent and productive? Only the word of the Lord. As Jesus says, "Heaven and earth will pass away, but my words will never pass away" (Mark 13:31). Or, as he says elsewhere, "As for everyone who comes to me and hears my words and puts them into practice, I will show you what they are like. They are like a man building a house, who dug down deep and laid the foundation on rock. When a flood came, the torrent struck that house but could not shake it, because it was well built" (Luke 6:47–48). The "word of the Lord" provides the only secure foundation for evangelism, missions, discipleship, and church planting.

Acts. The book of Acts is punctuated with a motif that highlights the dynamic nature of the gospel. As the saving message spreads and more people come to faith in Jesus, Luke underscores the divine intentionality and the gospel's inherent empowerment with the strategic repeated phrase, "The word of God spread" (Acts 6:7; 12:24; 19:20).[4] How many of us would describe the success of our missionary work with these same words? If not, is our perspective somehow sub-biblical? Have we exalted human response or activity above the divine message we convey?

---

[4]See also Acts 2:41; 4:4,29,31; 6:2,4; 8:4,14,25; 10:36,37,44; 11:1,19; 13:5,7,44,46,48,49; 14:3,25; 15:7,35,36; 16:6,32; 17:11,13; 18:11; 19:10; 20:32.

When people come to faith, from the Lord's perspective his saving word is progressing triumphantly—the word of God is growing. Commentators of Acts have long noted the significant placement of this phrase ("The word of God spread") in the summary sections of Acts.[5] Strikingly, with each movement of growth the gospel not only includes more people but more diverse people groups—first Hebraic Jews, then Greek-speaking Jews, then Samaritans, then Gentiles.

The Epistles.[6] Due to limited space, we will focus only on Paul in this section. The apostle to the Gentiles possibly provides us with the most explicit and repeated reflection on the dynamic nature of the gospel. In speaking of Paul's understanding of the dynamic nature of the gospel, I mean that he viewed the gospel (or "the word of God") as an effective force which inevitably goes forth and accomplishes God's will. The same "word" that indwells apostles also indwells ordinary Christians in the church. In each case, the word cannot be contained. If God's word truly dwells in an individual or community, that individual or community will inevitably be characterized by the further spreading of that word.[7] From a missionary perspective, then, how important it is for Christians to grasp the gospel firmly, genuinely, and consistently!

Paul repeatedly described the gospel as a dynamic power:

(1) Romans 1:16: "For I am not ashamed of the gospel, *because it is the power of God that brings salvation* to everyone who believes: first to the Jew, then to the Gentile."[8] In this text the gospel is described not simply as the content of what Jesus has done to bring about salvation, but it is actually the effective "power" which applies that salvation to believing Jews and Gentiles.

[5] See Jerome Kodell, "'The Word of God Grew': The Ecclesial Tendency of Logos in Acts 6,7; 12,24; 19,20," *Biblica* 55 (1974): 505–19; Brian S. Rosner, "The Progress of the Word," in *Witness to the Gospel: The Theology of Acts*, ed. I. Howard Marshall and David Peterson (Grand Rapids: Eerdmans 1998), 215–33; Ernst Haenchen, *Die Apostelgeschichte*, 15th ed. (Göttingen, Germany: Vandenhoeck & Ruprecht, 1968), 217, 330, 502.
[6] In several places, the wording in this section on the Epistles is directly dependent on my book *Paul's Understanding of the Church's Mission* (Paternoster, 2006).
[7] So Peter T. O'Brien, *Gospel and Mission in the Writings of Paul: An Exegetical and Theological Analysis* (Grand Rapids: Baker; Carlisle: Paternoster, 1995), 96–97, 113–14, 127–28, 138; and "Thanksgiving and the Gospel in Paul," *New Testament Studies* 21 (1974–1975): 153–55. For a more extended study on this topic, the reader is referred to the second chapter of my book *Paul's Understanding of the Church's Mission* (Milton Keynes, UK: Paternoster, 2006).
[8] Here and following in this section, italics are added to Scripture texts for emphasis.

(2) 1 Corinthians 1:17–25: "For Christ did not send me to baptize, but to preach the gospel. . . . For the message of the cross is foolishness to those who are perishing, but to us who are being saved *it is the power of God.* . . . But we preach Christ crucified: . . . to those whom God has called, both Jews and Greeks, *Christ the power of God and the wisdom of God.*" The gospel is a dynamic power. Moreover, it is a power that is effective to the "called." In Pauline usage, the "called" refers to those persons effectually summoned to faith through the proclaimed message.[9] In other words, God, in his mysterious purposes, summons to faith through the proclaimed word. Because God's word is powerful, effective, and saving, those who are called through this gospel respond in belief and repentance. This is an effectual calling that results in justification. Or, in Paul's words, "Those [God] called, he also justified" (Romans 8:30).

(3) 1 Corinthians 14:36: "Was it from you that *the word of God* came? Or are you the only ones it has reached?" Here Paul portrays "the word of God" (i.e., the gospel) in the active role of "coming" (*exēlthen*) and "reaching" (*katēntēsen*). These verbs are frequently used in Acts to describe persons on a journey.[10] In this rhetorical question to the Corinthian Christian community, Paul almost personifies the gospel as a traveling missionary. The emphasis is not on the activity of the heralds of the gospel, but on the activity of the gospel itself.

(4) 1 Thessalonians 1:5: "Our gospel *came to you not simply with words but also with power*, with the Holy Spirit and deep conviction. You know how we lived among you for your sake." Though Paul could have written, "We came with the gospel" (cf. 2 Corinthians 10:14),[11] he chooses to depict the gospel as the powerful agent arriving in Thessalonica to accomplish God's will of saving persons.

---

[9]L. Coenen writes, "Paul understands calling as the process by which God calls those, whom he has already elected and appointed, out of their bondage to this world, so that he may justify and sanctify them (Romans 8:29f.), and bring them into his service. This means that the call is part of God's work of reconciliation and peace (1 Corinthians 7:15)." L. Coenen, "Call; καλέω," in *NIDNTT*, 1:275. K. L. Schmidt writes, "If God or Christ calls a man, this calling or naming is a *verbum efficax*." K. L. Schmidt, "καλέω," in *TDNT*, 3:489. Also note meaning number 4 of καλέω in BDAG: "choose for receipt of a special benefit or experience" (BDAG, 503).

[10]See the uses of ἐξέρχομαι in Acts 1:21; 7:3,4,7; 10:23; 11:25. See also the uses of καταντάω in Acts 16:1; 18:19,24; 20:15; 21:7; 25:13.

[11]Peter T. O'Brien notes this point. He adds, "Gospel is . . . regarded as a living force, almost personalized." O'Brien, "Thanksgiving and the Gospel in Paul," 153.

(5) 1 Corinthians 9:12: "If others have this right of support from you, shouldn't we have it all the more? But we did not use this right. On the contrary, we put up with anything rather than *hinder the gospel* of Christ." In this text Paul does not speak of himself as conveying the gospel to others; his concern is that he not stand in the way of God's word. The gospel is depicted as the active agent bringing salvation.

(6) 2 Timothy 2:8–9: "Remember Jesus Christ, raised from the dead, descended from David. This is my gospel, for which I am suffering even to the point of being chained like a criminal. But *God's word is not chained.*" Here we see the gospel described as both *content* (Jesus Christ raised from the dead) and *power* (the unchained word). While Paul can be put in prison and his ministry curtailed or stopped, no such thing is true for "God's word" (i.e., the gospel). It is effective and will continue to bring salvation to all whom God calls.

(7) Colossians 1:4–7: "We have heard of your faith . . . the faith and love that spring from the hope stored up for you in heaven and about which you have already heard in the true message of the gospel that has come to you. In the same way, *the gospel is bearing fruit and growing* throughout the whole world—just as it has been doing among you since the day you heard it and truly understood God's grace." The gospel not only "comes" to the Colossians, it "grows"[12] and "bears fruit" in the whole world. These agricultural metaphors speak to the inherent certainty of growth, which is present in the gospel because it is God's effective word.[13]

(8) 1 Corinthians 4:15: "Even if you had ten thousand guardians in Christ, you do not have many fathers, for in Christ Jesus I became your father [literally, "I begat you," or "I birthed you"] *through the gospel.*" Here the gospel is the means of bringing about the spiritual birth of Paul's converts. One gets the sense that Paul's various metaphorical references to the gospel are attempts to describe the dynamic nature of an entity which, in some sense, remains beyond human definition.

(9) 1 Thessalonians 2:13–16: "When you received the word of God, which you heard from us, you accepted it not as a human word, but as it actually is, the word of God, *which is indeed at work in you who believe.*

---

[12]See also Acts 6:7; 12:24; 19:20; 1 Corinthians 3:7.
[13]See also Romans 1:16; 1 Corinthians 1:17–25; 9:11–12.

For you, brothers and sisters, became imitators of God's churches in Judea, which are in Christ Jesus: You suffered from your own people the same things those churches suffered from the Jews." The Thessalonians' imitative missionary behavior of proclaiming and suffering are produced by "the word of God" which is "at work" in the Thessalonian believers. Not Paul's human instruction, but the divine message that he conveyed, is the source of life which determines the Thessalonians' present missionary position.

(10) 2 Thessalonians 3:1: "As for other matters, brothers and sisters, pray for us *that the message of the Lord may spread rapidly* [literally, "run"] and be honored, just as it was with you." Here again, Paul is not the agent of mission; the *word itself* is "running." Not only through Paul, but also through the Thessalonians, this word is running its inevitable God-ordained course.

(11) 1 Thessalonians 1:6–8: "You became imitators of us and of the Lord, for you welcomed the message in the midst of severe suffering with the joy given by the Holy Spirit. And so you became a model to all the believers in Macedonia and Achaia. *The Lord's message rang out from you* not only in Macedonia and Achaia—your faith in God has become known everywhere." The Thessalonian Christians were an example to others by virtue of their being a launching point for the gospel. The replication of the apostolic mission was complete in them.[14] As "the Lord's message" had progressed effectively through the apostle Paul, now it was advancing through the Thessalonian church (1 Thessalonians 1:8; 2:13–14; 2 Thessalonians 3:1).

(12) Colossians 3:16: "Let *the word of Christ dwell in you richly*, teaching and admonishing one another in all wisdom, singing psalms and hymns and spiritual songs, with thankfulness in your hearts to God." The gospel's "dwelling" in the Colossians will be manifested by their "teaching and admonishing one another" in the pattern of the apostle himself. As the gospel takes up residence in believers, they will be competent to teach and encourage each other.

---

[14] As the apostolic example fades into the background, the example of the churches themselves and their leaders comes to the foreground (e.g., 1 Corinthians 1:2; 11:16; 14:33; 2 Corinthians 8–9; Philippians 3:17; 1 Thessalonians 1:6; 2:14–16; 2 Thessalonians 3:7–9; 1 Peter 5:3). This process did not take long, as the book of Acts indicates that Paul and the other apostles rarely lingered with their new churches.

(13) 1 Corinthians 15:1–2: "Now, brothers and sisters, I want to remind you of the gospel I preached to you, which you received and on which you have taken your stand. *By this gospel you are saved,* if you hold firmly to the word I preached to you. Otherwise, you have believed in vain." To speak of the gospel metaphorically as a place in which one "stands" illustrates again that there is more to Paul's understanding of "the gospel" than content and the act of proclaiming that content. The gospel is a sphere in which the power of salvation is operative. The church is now within that sphere; and because of the gospel's dynamic quality, the church is caught up in the gospel and becomes an agent of its continuing advance.

The purpose of this brief survey of Pauline texts is to demonstrate that the apostle spoke of the gospel as more than a propositional summary. Paul consistently referred to the gospel as God's powerful, dynamic, effective word. And that powerful word was not only operative in Paul's apostolic mission but in all individuals and communities where the gospel was believed.

Unleashing the Power of the Gospel

C. H. Spurgeon is often quoted as saying, "Scripture is like a lion. Who ever heard of defending a lion? Just turn it loose; it will defend itself."[15] We might say the same thing about the gospel, the authoritative précis, or summary, of *all* Scripture. How, then, can we unleash this powerful gospel in our lives and ministries?

Keep the gospel of Christ central. Every year publishers pour out new books on evangelistic or missionary methods. It might be a good idea, in such an environment, to read the missionary training manuals from a previous generation. We need to realize that our current "cutting edge" books and blogs will sound just as dated to the next generation. Methods come and go, but the gospel must remain central.

As Titus considers choosing elders/pastors for Crete, Paul charges him, "[A pastor] must hold firmly to the trustworthy message as it has

---

[15]Paraphrase of Spurgeon's words from C. H. Spurgeon, *Speeches by C. H. Spurgeon at Home and Abroad,* ed. G. H. Pike (London: Passmore & Alabaster, 1878). 17. Thanks to Donnie Hale for locating this quote.

been taught, so that he can encourage others by sound doctrine and refute those who oppose it" (Titus 1:9).

Likewise, Paul lists a number of key moral qualifications for church elders/pastors:

> An elder must be blameless, faithful to his wife, a man whose children believe and are not open to the charge of being wild and disobedient. Since an overseer manages God's household, he must be blameless—not overbearing, not quick-tempered, not given to drunkenness, not violent, not pursuing dishonest gain. Rather, he must be hospitable, one who loves what is good, who is self-controlled, upright, holy and disciplined. (Titus 1:6–8)

If the gospel is God's word, then we must reverently and faithfully proclaim it, being careful not to distort it in any way or misrepresent God. Moreover, if God has ordained that his saving word will triumph as an unstoppable force, we must do everything possible to release that word and then stay out of its way. That is, we must not do anything that would distract from or compromise that word. Rather, our lives must faithfully show God's transformation of our hearts, words, and deeds. Similarly, as we work in the mission field our success isn't measured by the number of professions but by leaving behind persons who "hold firmly to the trustworthy message as it has been taught" (Titus 1:9). These are the kind of persons who can be entrusted to carry forward the gospel—in areas and ways that nonnative missionaries could never do.

Unfortunately, as the old hymn says, we are "prone to wander."[16] Yes, we are prone to roam away from the gospel, prone to believe the lie that the gospel is the entry ticket but then the Christian life is something in addition (fill in the blank: spiritual disciplines, moralism, dramatic spiritual gifts, mysticism, etc.). Or, as missionaries, we believe that accepting the gospel saves our converts but they need something else to motivate them to live in obedience or to reach others. No! All true Christian living and ministry must be in direct, organic relationship with the gospel of Jesus Christ.

What are some practical steps that missionaries can take to cling to the gospel? How can we be sure that our lives and ministries are rooted

---

[16]"Come, Thou Fount of Every Blessing," words by Robert Robinson.

in and growing out of the gospel? How can we be sure that our converts are holding on to Christ and the gospel, not to some program or pragmatics? Here are a few practical suggestions:

1. Memorize and prayerfully meditate on core gospel passages (e.g., Romans 3:21–31 and 1 Corinthians 15:3–11).

2. Listen to gospel-saturated sermons (e.g., the sermons of Tim Keller, John Piper, C. J. Mahaney, Mark Driscoll, or Daniel Montgomery).

3. Read gospel-focused books (e.g., writings by Martin Luther, Jerry Bridges, Richard F. Lovelace, or C. J. Mahaney).

4. Have a transparent ministry, speaking openly about the dangers you personally face from gospel substitutes (Galatians 1:8–10; Philippians 3:2–11).

5. Warn others repeatedly and passionately about the dangers of false gospels and gospel substitutes (Matthew 24:11,24; Acts 20:28–32).

6. Don't reward human performance. When the grace of God is demonstrated in someone's life, encourage them by publicly giving thanks to God (Philemon 4–6).

Assess your teaching and life in light of the gospel. We are exhorted in Scripture to examine ourselves to see if we are in the faith (2 Corinthians 13:5). We are to watch our life and doctrine closely (1 Timothy 4:16). One part of such self-examination is to assess our own thoughts, actions, relationships, and ministries in light of the gospel. Are we really trusting in and proclaiming the grace of Christ, or have we subtly come to rely upon our own efforts for acceptance before God? A private corruption of the gospel will spill over into our public teaching as well.

Tim Keller, senior pastor of Redeemer Presbyterian Church in New York, warns of the danger of beating up ourselves and our people with moralistic teaching and preaching ("Do this! Don't do that!"). Keller writes:

> At the heart of Redeemer's ministry and its philosophy of preaching to post-modern audiences is the conviction that "the gospel" is not just a way to be saved from the penalty of sin, but is the fundamental dynamic for living the whole Christian life—individually and corporately, privately and publicly. In other words, the gospel is not just for non-Christians, but

also for Christians. This means the gospel is not just the A-B-C's but the A to Z of the Christian life. It is not accurate to think "the gospel" is what saves non-Christians, and then, what matures Christians is trying hard to live according to Biblical principles. It is more accurate to say that we are saved by believing the gospel, and then we are transformed in every part of our mind, heart, and life by believing the gospel more and more deeply as our life goes on.[17]

We would do well to be reminded of the Lutheran injunction, "The law says, 'Do this and live.' The gospel says, 'It is done. Now live.'" How do our thoughts about our co-workers, our words toward our spouse and children, our teaching and actions in ministry, etc., line up with the fact of Christ's saving death for our sins? As we train and send out church planters, is the gospel of Jesus Christ the unchanging core and motivation for their ministry?[18]

Conclusion

As we seek to have ministries that center on and are empowered by the gospel of Christ, we must commit ourselves to this truth—that all evangelistic proclamation, all church planting, all missionary strategizing, all counseling, all marriage tips, all exhortations, all calls to holiness, must be informed by, rooted in, and never move beyond the cross of Christ. As the apostle Paul said to the Corinthians, "For I resolved to know nothing while I was with you except Jesus Christ and him crucified" (1 Corinthians 2:2).

A warning must be made here as well. There has been a buzz about the gospel in some recent theological literature. It is becoming more common for missionaries, theological authors, and churches to identify themselves as "gospel-centered" or "all about the gospel." This is a good trend, insofar as such persons or churches really are focused on the gospel of Jesus Christ. As with all trends, though, there is a danger of people jumping on the "gospel bandwagon" with little understanding of

---

[17]Tim Keller, "Keller on Preaching in a Post-Modern City," *The Movement*, E-Newsletter of the Redeemer Church Planting Center, June 2004.

[18]For more on applying God's word, see Robert Plummer, *40 Questions About Interpreting the Bible* (Grand Rapids: Kregel, 2010).

what they are actually affirming. Being "gospel-centered" can become little more than a slogan such as "I follow Paul" or "I follow Apollos" (1 Corinthians 1:12). Being gospel-centered means being centered on the person of Jesus and what he has done to save us. All of life, ministry, ethics, etc., must organically flow from the space-time historical intervention of God in the propitiatory death of his Son. When our lives and ministries are so focused, we can expect to see God's power displayed, for the gospel is his powerful, saving word.

Discussion Points

1. What do we mean when we say the word *gospel*?

2. What is a favorite text of yours that demonstrates the power of the gospel?

3. Why isn't Paul ashamed of the gospel?

4. Plummer says we are "prone to wander," prone to believe the lie that the gospel is the entry ticket but then the Christian life is something in addition. What else do we add to the gospel as a requirement for faith? Is this a good practice? Why or why not?

Further Reading

Köstenberger, Andreas J., and Peter T. O'Brien. *Salvation to the Ends of the Earth: A Biblical Theology of Mission*. New Studies in Biblical Theology 11. Downers Grove, IL: InterVarsity; Leicester, UK: Apollos, 2001.

Marshall, I. Howard. "Who Were the Evangelists?" In *The Mission of the Early Church to Jews and Gentiles*. Wissenschaftliche Untersuchun Genesis zum Neuen Testament 127, edited by Jostein Ådna and Hans Kvalbein. Tübingen, Germany: Mohr Siebeck, 2000, 251–63.

O'Brien, Peter T. *Gospel and Mission in the Writings of Paul: An Exegetical and Theological Analysis*. Grand Rapids: Baker; Carlisle, UK: Paternoster, 1995.

Plummer, Robert L. *Paul's Understanding of the Church's Mission: Did the Apostle Paul Expect the Early Christian Communities to Evangelize?* Paternoster Biblical Monographs. Milton Keynes, UK: Paternoster, 2006.

Ware, James Patrick. *The Mission of the Church in Paul's Letter to the Philippians in the Context of Ancient Judaism*. Supplements to Novum Testamentum 120. Leiden, Netherlands: Brill, 2005.

10

THE PASSION OF CHRIST AND THE MARTYRS

Jerry Rankin

Passion is a term that is generally understood as an intense desire for something.[1] It is often used as a sensual reference to sexual desires and the physical expression of one's love. It implies an obsessive interest that compels affection and behavior, often in a disproportionate balance in the context of life's realities and responsibilities. I would have to acknowledge a passion for certain foods, for my favorite sports teams, and for my grandchildren—talking about them constantly and assuming everyone should be as interested in them as I am.

But the passion of Christ stands alone in his suffering and death to redeem a lost world. This terminology merits exploring because the mission of God will be fulfilled only by those so passionate for God's glory and the winning of the lost that they are willing to suffer to make the gospel known and even to die for the sake of bringing the peoples of the world into the kingdom of God.

The Cross of Christ

A few years ago Mel Gibson produced and directed a widely acclaimed film entitled *The Passion of the Christ*. This detailed narrative of the final week of the life of Christ graphically portrayed in brutal detail his suffering and crucifixion. The agony in the Garden of Gethsemane,

---

[1]Material in this chapter is adapted from the introduction and epilogue written by the author in *Lives Given, Not Taken*, published by the International Mission Board in 2005.

his arrest, the mockery of a trial, collaboration of jealous Jewish religious leaders and arrogant Roman authorities simply set the stage for the cruel mob lynching. Beaten and bruised, his back was stripped of flesh in a merciless lashing. A crown of thorns pressed upon his brow added to the pain, only to be followed by having to bear a heavy, wooden cross, the implement of his execution. After being ridiculed and stripped naked, he was subjected to the ultimate cruelty of nails being driven through his hands and feet to precipitate a slow and painful death, which brought to a climax the suffering Jesus willingly bore that the mission of God might be fulfilled.

This was only the physical expression of a passionate love for God and for a lost world that supersedes our ability to comprehend. As the writer of Hebrews expressed it, "For the joy set before Him [Jesus] endured the cross, despising the shame" (Hebrews 12:2 NASB). He willingly poured out his life in a passionate commitment of obedience to the will of the Father that a lost world might be saved and God might be glorified among the nations.

The mission of God will not be fulfilled by humanly devised strategies of gospel proclamation and cross-cultural witness.

The mission of God will not be fulfilled by humanly devised strategies of gospel proclamation and cross-cultural witness. It will not result from a massive mobilization of God's people responding to the challenge to go as missionaries. We do not carry out the Great Commission to disciple the nations from a sense of obligation and obedience because someone has got to do it. The only motivation for the mission of God is a love for a lost world that will lead to a willingness to sacrifice one's own personal plans and desires and even die for the sake of the nations. The challenge and witness of Scripture tells us that we are called to this purpose. "To this you were called, because Christ suffered for you, leaving you an example, that you should follow in his steps" (1 Peter 2:21). In the second chapter of Philippians we are

The only motivation for the mission of God is a love for a lost world that will lead to a willingness to sacrifice one's own personal plans and desires and even die for the sake of the nations.

exhorted to have the same mind of Christ who "made himself nothing by taking the very nature of a servant. . . . He humbled himself by becoming obedient to death—even death on a cross!" (Philippians 2:7–8).

Paul's Passion

The apostle Paul is exemplified as the prototype of a cross-cultural missionary. When, in God's providence, the gospel began to spread beyond the narrow Jewish context of its beginnings, this unlikely rabbi was chosen to be an apostle to the Gentiles. He went to Cyprus, Asia, and Bithynia, proclaiming salvation in Jesus Christ. When the Holy Spirit closed the door and forced him to Troas, he responded to the Macedonian vision and swept across Europe planting churches. He wrote to those in Rome that he was coming to preach the gospel to them and on beyond them to Spain. He said in 2 Corinthians 10:16 that he had been called to the regions beyond!

What is it that drove Paul to see the gospel as relevant to all peoples and cultures, to persist in his missionary journeys in spite of being arrested, beaten, and stoned? Why would he suffer deprivation, hunger, exposure, persecution, and injustice without being deterred as Christ's witness? Was it only because of obedience to that personal encounter with his soon-to-be Lord on the road to Damascus? Or was he driven by a passion for the mission of God, to see the lost come into the kingdom of God?

That passion was expressed in terms of being a debtor, obligated to share the gospel with both Jew and Greek (Romans 1:14). He testified to being compelled by the love of Christ (2 Corinthians 5:14). The only thing that mattered was what Christ did through him to bring the nations to obedience to the faith. His desire and passion was that "those who were not told about him will see, and those who have not heard will understand" (Romans 15:21).

The Passion of Martyrs in Dangerous Places

We live in a world today that is increasingly hostile to the gospel. Missionaries are prohibited in an increasing number of countries. Some researchers contend that there were more Christian martyrs in the twentieth century than all the rest of Christian history combined. But this is the kind of world into which Jesus sent his disciples to be witnesses. He did not tell us to make disciples of all nations only where we are welcomed to proclaim the gospel, or in those places we can do so without danger. No, fulfilling the Great Commission was an unqualified mandate. The mission of God would be realized only by those who share the passion of Christ to do whatever it takes, whatever the cost.

We used to be able to identify the dangerous places in the world where our missionaries would be at risk, but no longer; everywhere one goes to proclaim the gospel he or she is vulnerable to danger. Our world changed after September 11, 2001, never to be the same again. International relations are strained, ethnic conflicts have escalated, Muslims and Hindus fight to retain traditional values threatened by global modernization. Political disruptions, social upheaval, economic uncertainty, and natural disasters create a hostile environment for the Christian message.

Yet, this is the world to which Jesus is calling us in the twenty-first century. God's purpose and desire to be exalted among the nations is unchanged. Yet reaching the ends of the earth will not be without sacrifice and suffering.

Rarely am I awakened by a phone call in the middle of the night. It was 1:30 in the morning of December 30, 2002, when the shrill ringing of the telephone startled me. It was the call I knew to be inevitable someday but that I hoped would never come. A missionary had been killed—not one, but three. Our associate regional leader for Northern Africa and the Middle East had just received word that Martha Myers, Bill Koehn, and Kathy Gariety had been murdered. The three had been shot at the Jibla Baptist Hospital in Yemen by an assailant as the clinic opened Monday morning, and a fourth victim—a missionary pharmacist—had been wounded.

Just two weeks earlier I had spoken at a conference sponsored by the Evangelical Fellowship of Mission Agencies for personnel staff from 120 member organizations. The topic was "Sending Missionaries into a Dangerous and Chaotic World," an issue relevant in the aftermath of the tragedy of September 11, 2001. These agency leaders, responsible for enlisting and training missionary personnel, were encountering a new dimension of reticence on the part of candidates to go into a dangerous world. The previous week Bonnie Witherall, an American missionary serving with Operation Mobilization, had been murdered in Lebanon.

A reporter attending the EFMA conference had already requested an interview following my presentation. Referencing the death of Witherall, she asked how this incident would affect our training and protection for our Southern Baptist missionaries. I elaborated on our training and the precautions our missionaries were taught to take, but in the course of my reply I was later quoted as saying, "It is not unlikely that we (the IMB) will experience such a tragedy, for no other organization has as many missionary personnel so extensively deployed and pushing to the edge of lostness." Little did I realize that two weeks later we would, indeed, experience such a tragedy.

Our staff had already been trained in risk management and crisis response. However, the hypothetical exercises in the workshops did not fully prepare us for the realities we were now facing. From time to time missionaries have died suddenly in traffic accidents or plane crashes; illness sometimes takes the life of beloved colleagues prematurely. But I recalled my first experience with this kind of tragedy as president of the International Mission Board. On March 28, 1995, Dr. Chu Hon Yi and his wife, Kei Wol, were found murdered in their apartment in Khabarovsk, Russia. These Korean-Americans from Virginia had established an effective ministry among the medical community in this far-eastern Russian city soon after the doors began to open to the former Soviet Union. I recalled the difficulty in trying to console and minister to their family and church fellowship. The answers were elusive as we tried to explain any rationale for their brutal murders.

Now, as I got dressed on the morning of December 30, 2002, CNN was already broadcasting news of unnamed American missionaries killed by assumed terrorists in Yemen. There was an outpouring of support and consolation, but it did not take long for the questions to come, initially from the media, but surprisingly from mission-minded churches as well. "Why do missionaries go to dangerous places?" "How can the

"Why do missionaries go to dangerous places?" "How can the IMB be so irresponsible to send missionaries to places where their lives will be endangered?"

IMB be so irresponsible to send missionaries to places where their lives will be endangered?" There were demands to bring the missionaries home. Others reflected that this loss of life was such a waste and could have been avoided. Apparently the top priority in the minds of many was the safety of missionaries.

The next month personnel with Frontiers were murdered on the Horn of Africa, and in March of 2003 Bill Hyde, a veteran missionary who had served in the Philippines for twenty years, was killed in a terrorist bombing at the airport in Davao City. Then on March 15, 2004, five IMB personnel in Iraq were assaulted by gunmen as they drove from the city of Mosul. David McDonnall, Karen Watson, and Larry and Jean Elliott were all killed; only Carrie McDonnall survived.

Those who give their lives in service for Christ overseas are readily recognized as martyrs, for the word itself means "witness"; those who shed their blood do so as a witness to their faith and as a testimony to their obedience and devotion to their Lord Jesus Christ. Some would argue with the qualifications of a martyr, insisting that only a violent and unnatural death would apply. Others would say that a martyr is only one who dies an untimely death as the direct consequence of preaching the gospel and sharing their faith, usually in a hostile environment.

Most of those who hold on to the safety, comforts, and security of their American lifestyle would readily acknowledge martyrs as those who die on foreign soil because they have given their lives as the ultimate sacrifice for the cause of Christ. However, these few missionaries who were victims of violence pale in comparison to the multitudes of believers who are persecuted and killed for their faith in their own communities, by government authorities, religious vigilantes, or even their own family. These missionaries died because of their willingness to be in a place where their life was vulnerable; their presence in a place of danger was due to a commitment to a higher calling than life itself. We would not quibble over the circumstances, the means of death, nor the motives of those who take their lives. I am confident a martyr's crown awaits those who "did not love their life, even when faced with death" (Revelation 12:11 NASB).

Why This Passion?

Why would these missionaries and others go to places where their lives would be endangered? Why would they go to a place such as Iraq during a war, where Muslim radicals and insurgents target Americans? Why would others go to places such as Afghanistan, Bosnia, Sudan, or Chechnya and serve among people who are at war and where Americans often are not appreciated no matter how valued and needed their humanitarian aid? The answer is simple. It is because of God's call and their decision to be obedient wherever he leads. That willingness to be obedient, even when it means risk and sacrifice, comes from the passionate conviction that Jesus is the answer for a hurting world. Mis-

Missionaries in the nineteenth century did not expect to return to enjoy retirement years at home. They carried their own caskets as a standard part of their shipment to the field.

sionaries in the nineteenth century did not expect to return to enjoy retirement years at home. They carried their own caskets as a standard part of their shipment to the field. Most of the missionaries going to West Africa died of violence, malaria, or other diseases within a few years of arrival, but they kept going. There was a passion for their calling to take Christ to a lost world.

It is strange that the media do not question journalists going into war zones, traveling with troops in the midst of mortar attacks, in order to get a story, gripping photos, or video footage to spread the news of tragedy and war. Yet they think it foolish for one to risk his or her own life to bring life to those whose very existence is threatened, to give hope to those in darkness and despair, to proclaim news of salvation to those in bondage to sin. An important aspect of military training is instilling into all soldiers absolute compliance and unquestioning obedience to their commanding officer. They don't have the option of obeying orders only if it is safe. How much more should those who claim to be followers of Christ be willing to obey the orders of our supreme Commander-in-Chief who told us to go into all the world and disciple all nations?

To insist that missionaries avoid the dangerous and risky places or that local believers should give priority to personal safety is to belittle the lostness of a world without Christ, to demean the responsibility of obedience to God's call, and to succumb to a convoluted system of values that says one's safety and comfort is a higher priority than sharing the gospel. Counting converts and adding notches to one's statistical belt do not motivate one to confront animosity and adversity for the cause of Christ. That comes only because of a conviction that Jesus Christ is the only hope of salvation and that those who fail to respond in repentance and faith in him are bound for an eternal destiny in hell.

This is not just the biased opinion of narrow-minded Christians. Jesus himself said in John 14:6, "I am the way and the truth and the life. No one comes to the Father except through me." His early followers reminded both Jews and Gentiles in their testimony in Acts 4:12, "Salvation is found in no one else, for there is no other name under heaven given to mankind by which we must be saved." Jesus is the only, exclusive, unique way of salvation. Just as Jesus was motivated by love to give his own life as a sacrifice for the sins of the world, those who go to share that good news in a lost world go, motivated by their love for God and for the people he died to save. They don't take risks out of foolish disregard for their own life or just to get people to change their religious affiliation, but by the passion of Christ.

A missionary strategy coordinator was training some new short-term personnel who were to be dispersed throughout a rather hostile area to witness and plant seeds of the gospel. He told them they could be arrested for preaching the gospel and added, "If that happens, just be sure it's true." He explained that they would probably get deported but that it was more important for the gospel to be there than for them. Their efforts would be futile if they neglected to plant the gospel in order to guarantee their own safety. This seems to be Paul's sentiments as expressed in 1 Corinthians 15:32, "If I fought wild beasts in Ephesus with no more than human hopes, what have I gained?" If one is going to get arrested and maybe die, it might as well be for sharing the gospel.

Lives Given, Not Taken

Those who go to places of danger do not do so reluctantly, heels dug in, conscripted into service contrary to their will. It is not a matter of a mission agency or church imposing an assignment they are obligated to fill. Their willingness to respond to the needs of others supersedes their own ambitions and desires. They are driven by a conviction that only by going and living out their faith through their presence—an incarnational witness—can the need be met among the people to whom God has called them. They have a personal relationship with God and commitment to his lordship that enables them to hear his call and feel the passion of his heart.

Most of those who endure kidnapping and threats or experience a violent death know the risks involved. Our personnel are thoroughly trained in matters related to security and safety. But there is something more important, more compelling, than self-preservation. Paul described it as the high calling of God. Obedience to God's call, the opportunity to minister to people who are hopeless and in despair, and sharing the love of Christ are worth the risk.

After Bill Koehn, Martha Myers, and Kathy Gariety were killed in Yemen, it was often said that the gunman didn't take their lives that morning, for he couldn't take from them what they had already given. Jesus made his call clear: "Jesus said to his disciples, 'Whoever wants to be my disciple must deny themselves and take up their cross and follow me'" (Matthew 16:24). The call to follow Christ was a call to die. The call to discipleship and obedience has always been to deny self—to die to one's own ambitions and even to self-preservation. So these and other martyrs didn't die when their lives were suddenly ended by an assassin's bullet or a terrorist's bomb; they had died to self when they trusted Jesus as their Savior years earlier. When they left promising business and medical careers in the United States to go as missionaries to Yemen, they gave their lives and died. Each day they served the Lord in Yemen—healing the sick, ministering to orphans, widows, and prisoners—they had to lay their lives on the altar and die. They knew the risks. As a hospital administrator, Bill had been threatened many times. Martha had been kidnapped. They knew they would probably not live to retirement and had already made arrangements to be buried in Yemen.

The ancient church father Tertullian said, "The blood of the martyrs is the seed of the church." Rather than a defeat for the kingdom, blood that is spilled as a life witness has the power to give authenticity to the gospel. Already there is evidence that many in the community who were benefactors of the compassionate medical care they found at Jibla Baptist Hospital have begun to consider the claims of Christ. Those who silently observed and evaluated the faith that motivated these American missionaries to come to such a remote location have begun to consider the validity of their witness. Once they saw it was something these missionaries considered worth giving their lives for, they too began to embrace the truth of the gospel.

Reaching all peoples and fulfilling the mission of God will not be accomplished without the blood of martyrs. That is not our strategy, and it is never intentional. We give high priority to providing security for missionary personnel and their families. But Jesus sent his disciples into a hostile environment to share the gospel and demonstrated the cost by giving his own life on the cross. We must not think that the call to take up our cross and die was only for those in the first century. It will always be the cost for reaching our world for Christ.

Passion for the Mission of God

In his final instructions to his disciples, Jesus reminded them that they would be hated and persecuted just as he had been. They were not to be of this world, and therefore the world would hate them. In fact, Jesus added, "The time is coming when anyone who kills you will think they are offering a service to God. They will do such things because they have not known the Father or me" (John 16:2–3). If we want to know why people are killed and missionaries are martyred, the answer is simple. It is not because of lack of security, flaws in international relations, or insensitivity to diverse and conflicting worldviews. It is because of a sinful and fallen world that does not know God. Rather than threats and dangers causing us to withdraw and cower in fear, they should compel us to go and confront a sinful world that does not know God with the life-changing power of the gospel.

We should not be surprised that governments place restrictions on a Christian witness. In the name of religion, missionaries who seek to feed, clothe, house, and minister to Afghan refugees are imprisoned and condemned. Persecution of those simply seeking to worship Jesus is rampant in China, Turkmenistan, Laos, and across Northern Africa. Those who dare go as missionaries are often branded as "the enemy" by those with distorted worldviews and perverted religious convictions.

We could list a litany of tragedies and disasters throughout these last few years. Did God know these things would happen? Did he know three missionaries would be killed in Yemen, four would be gunned down in Iraq, and every other tragedy that has occurred? Absolutely! He has not predestined such tragedies, but he has not relinquished his throne. What he has predestined is a way to use any and every event for his purpose, and his desire is to be glorified and exalted among the nations.

I don't know the implications of all that we are experiencing. It is hard to see and anticipate how God can use the current global environment of war, hatred, and violence; but there is no doubt in my mind that he who is sovereign over the nations is shaking the heavens and earth. Just as we have seen incomprehensible events bring the disintegration of the Soviet Union and open the doors of China to an unprecedented harvest, I believe that in the near future we will look back and see how God has used these events to break down the barriers of the Muslim world. Already missionaries throughout Northern Africa and the Middle East are reporting neighbors expressing disillusionment with a Muslim faith used to justify terrorist activity, asking questions that reflect a search for hope and security that only Jesus can provide. We must be confident that God can and will use the tragedies, dangers, and chaos of our world to create a spiritual hunger and enable his purpose to be fulfilled.

How should we approach the threats of a hostile culture that doesn't welcome our witness? In the fourth chapter of Acts, Peter and John were arrested and threatened. But notice how they responded: "Why do the nations rage and the peoples plot in vain? The kings of the earth rise up and the rulers band together against the Lord and against his anointed one" (Acts 4:25–26). Recognizing the providence of God, these New Testament believers didn't pray that God would remove these threats and dangers and restore their comfort zone. They prayed, rather, that God would take note of these threats and allow them to speak the truth confidently (v. 29). They recognized this was an unprecedented opportunity for witness. As he did then, God is using the current turmoil and threats in our world to share a message of hope, to proclaim that security is found not in cultural and religious traditions but only in our Lord Jesus Christ. Threats should simply compel us to speak the Word of God more boldly and with confidence. And when we do, we can expect God to extend his hand to demonstrate his power through signs and wonders through the mighty name of Jesus (v. 30).

Recently, in a volatile area of the world where a country was experiencing an attempt to overthrow the government, the US State Department issued an advisory that all nonessential American citizens should evacuate. There were demonstrations in the streets, and anarchy prevailed. Parents of missionaries serving in that country expected their children to come home in response to this notice. But the missionaries decided that they would not leave for three reasons. First, they considered themselves "essential" personnel. Second, God had called them to that country, and they could not be disobedient to his call out of regard for their own safety. Third, it is during times such as this that chaos and uncertainties create the greatest openness to spiritual answers; they could not abandon the people during what may be the greatest opportunity for witness.

An unwillingness to suffer or entail risk implies a conditional commitment that inhibits what God is able to do through us. Sometimes even missionaries draw a bottom line that is short of total surrender because they come out of the American culture of entitlement that views safety, health, and security as fundamental rights. One missionary, speaking to colleagues, reminded them that they were to view life through the lens of eternity in which they, like Paul, view suffering as "momentary light affliction," and that "suffering is not worthy to be compared with the glory that is to be revealed" (1 Peter 5:1). He challenged the assumption that we have a right to be comfortable. Acknowledging the dangers of life on the mission field, he reminded his audience that the call to ministry is not a call to comfort, safety, and self-indulgence, as our American culture would have us believe. Most of the world knows this, and we need to recognize that comfort and safety are blessings, not rights.

Americans were indignant when terrorists flew planes into the Pentagon and the World Trade Center on September 11, 2001; but in reality we were simply experiencing what most of the world has always experienced. It is right that we should grieve when missionaries are killed, but thousands of Christians die for their faith throughout the world every year. They don't have an American passport that allows them to escape their ongoing threats and dangers. No international agency stands poised to rush to their defense. So Christian believers are massacred in villages across Indonesia, arrested and imprisoned in China and Vietnam, and countless numbers disappear throughout the Muslim world. Is our faith not as valuable as the faith of national Christians who live every day with the possibility it may be their last?

First Peter 4:12–13 says, "Dear friends, do not be surprised at the fiery ordeal that has come on you to test you, as though something strange were happening to you. But rejoice inasmuch as you participate in the sufferings of Christ, so that you may be overjoyed when his glory is revealed." James 1:2 echoes the same theme: "Consider it pure joy, my brothers and sisters, whenever you face trials of many kinds." These words don't reflect the typical American mindset that would avoid suffering, eschew potential trials, and choose a comfortable lifestyle. Most of the world knows suffering and deprivation but would never know the hope eternity can offer if we were unwilling to risk our lives and identify with their suffering and the passion of Christ. Placing physical life ahead of everything else matches the thinking of an atheist or communist who embraces materialism and earthly existence as the ultimate good in life, but makes no sense whatsoever to a Christian committed to the kingdom of God and eternal values.

We readily forget that the sacrifice of one's life is one of the most powerful tools in God's spiritual armament for extending the kingdom to the ends of the earth. Why is the gospel flourishing in China? Before new believers are baptized they are asked if they will faithfully follow Christ even when the authorities drag them out of their homes, confiscate their belongings, threaten their families, and throw them in jail. They are taught to say, if sentenced to death, "You do not take my life from me, but I offer it freely to you as a testimony of faith in Jesus

Christ who loved me and gave his life for me." How can the witness of the church be deterred by threats and suffering in the face of that attitude? The possibility of death is inconsequential for believers who have already dealt with it.

Conclusion

We need to explode a prominent and oft-quoted myth that the safest place on earth is in the center of God's will. Would we conclude that these faithful servants who were victims of tragedies were not in the center of God's will? Why do some die while others do not? Does God, in his providence, sort out, like the wheat and the tares, those who are in his will, placing a hedge of protection around them, while others are left vulnerable to the forces of an evil and fallen world? Not at all. We are not exempt from danger, suffering, and possibly death just because we go in faithful obedience as missionaries or give our lives to God in full surrender. He doesn't put a hedge of protection and safety around us because we have answered his call. In fact, he doesn't even guarantee that we will see response and success in our witness. Our call is to obedience—period!

Karen Watson, from Bakersfield, California, was one of the workers killed in Iraq. She had resigned her job in America, sold her house and car, given away most of her possessions, and packed what was left in a duffle bag to go share Christ with those desperately in need of the hope only he can provide. She was fully aware of the risks involved. Karen had left a letter with her pastor to be read in the event she didn't return: a two-page, handwritten letter in which she had written in big capital letters across the top, "There are no regrets." She continued, "My calling is to obedience, suffering is expected, and His glory is my reward." That is the passion of Christ that will fulfill the mission of God.

Discussion Points

1. Does passion for the task always result in suffering or martyrdom?

2. Why is simple obedience not sufficient motivation for fulfilling the mission of God?

3. Why is suffering and martyrdom, driven by the passion of Christ, such an effective witness?

Further Reading

Bridges, Erich, and Jerry Rankin. *Lives Given, Not Taken: 21st Century Southern Baptist Martyrs.* Richmond, VA: International Mission Board, 2005.

PART TWO

THE MISSION OF GOD IN HISTORY

In part one we learned how foundational and comprehensive God's mission is to the entire Christian faith and church. We saw the beginning, middle, and end of the mission of God revealed in Scripture and for eternity.

Part two provides an opportunity to peek inside of this "middle" part of the mission of God. How has God worked throughout history to accomplish his mission to all nations? What lessons from the mission can we learn from the ancient church? How might the Holy Spirit inspire and even clarify our call through the stories and testimonies of missionaries from the past? What practices—"best" and "worst"—can we glean from the mission movements of recent history? What patterns repeat themselves in the role of God and people in his mission story? What does this mean for us who are on mission with God today?

Your discovery journey continues. Enjoy the tour!

11

THE FIRST DECADES OF
THE MISSION OF GOD

William J. Larkin Jr.

A survey of the early stages of the mission of God through the New Testament church is best conducted in terms of decades: the thirties, forties, fifties, and sixties, through AD 100.[1]

The obvious primary source is the Bible. Acts, though a selective history, does provide a basic framework for this history. It presents the early church's advance through recounting the mission of persecuted Hellenistic Jewish Christians and through the lives and work of Peter and Paul. But much else was happening. In fact, every so often in Acts Christians appear who come from various places about which Luke has told us nothing regarding the spread of the gospel. These too provide hints for how the gospel advanced in the first century. Other evidence will come from Paul's letters, the General Epistles, and Revelation. Ancient church historians also assist, particularly Eusebius, who published his *Ecclesiastical History* about AD 325.

The Thirties: Message and Spirit-Driven Mission

In the thirties, church advance is message-driven and Spirit-driven. This is a breakthrough decade from the start, from the day of Pentecost. In Acts 2, the Spirit is poured out and Peter preaches the heart

---

[1]For further background on the history of the early church's mission, see Eckhard J. Schnabel, *Early Christian Mission*, 2 vols. (Downers Grove, IL: InterVarsity, 2004). For further background on the church's mission in Acts, see William J. Larkin, "Acts," in *The Gospel of Luke, Acts*, Cornerstone Biblical Commentary 12 (Carol Stream, IL: Tyndale, 2006).

of a message-driven mission when he proclaims the promise, "Everyone who calls on the name of the Lord will be saved" (Acts 2:21). He presents that promise of salvation as "for you and your children and for all who are far off—for all whom the Lord our God will call" (v. 39). And people respond to this message—3,000 that first day (v. 41). Now that number is not an exaggeration to be understood "evangelistically speaking." It is a true number and fits with what we know about the population of Jerusalem. At that time Jerusalem's population was probably, at the low end, about 60,000. Some would place it at 110,000 to 120,000. At festival time, such as Pentecost, there may have been as many as a million people who would come to the city. So 3,000 responding is certainly a wonderful work of the Spirit, but not an incredible proportion of the population.

Now among the people responding were both visitors and resident foreigners (Acts 2:5–11). The outpouring of the Spirit enables the apostles to speak in their languages, even though they are Galileans and only know Aramaic and Greek. This miracle's missiological significance is that the gospel is intended to go to every people and tribe and tongue and nation.

> *This miracle's missiological significance is that the gospel is intended to go to every people and tribe and tongue and nation.*

Geographic expansion. The audience cries out and identifies themselves, "Parthians, Medes and Elamites; residents of Mesopotamia, Judea and Cappadocia, Pontus and Asia, Phrygia and Pamphylia, Egypt and the parts of Libya near Cyrene; visitors from Rome (both Jews and converts to Judaism); Cretans and Arabs—we hear them declaring the wonders of God in our own tongues" (Acts 2:9–11). Since these are Pentecost visitors, some of these pilgrims may have been the first evangelists who, in AD 30, took the gospel to these parts of the world. There is some evidence from elsewhere in the New Testament that this could well be the case.

The Roman province of Pontus in north-central Asia Minor was the home of Aquila, who encountered Paul in Corinth in AD 50–52 and was probably already a Christian (Acts 18:1–4). In the province of Asia (western Asia Minor), there were Christians at Ephesus before Paul arrived (Acts 18:24; 19:1). It is interesting that Luke's list only explicitly says "visitors" had arrived from Rome (Acts 2:10). Claudius's decree (Acts 18:2) in AD 41 was addressed to the Jews who were described as "increasing in Rome." This probably refers to the fruit of Christian evangelism among Jews, since the Romans didn't make a distinction between Jews and Christians. They were all Jews as far as the empire was concerned. Since there was a potential of disturbance between unbelieving Jews and Jewish Christian converts, Claudius issued a decree in AD 41 ordering them to continue their traditional mode of life and not hold meetings.[2] This was just eleven years after Pentecost. Apollos (Acts 18:24) was an Alexandrian from the province of Egypt. In fact, one early manuscript (D) says that Apollos learned in his own home country the way of the Lord.

So on the very day in which the Spirit is poured out upon the church, there is set in motion a Spirit-driven dynamic to the ends of the earth. In fact, the evidence indicates that across the Roman Empire (in five of the forty-some provinces) fruitful mission was already being carried out in the thirties. The early church's mission had already touched 13 percent of the empire during the first decade of witness.

Ethnic expansion. In the thirties, the church expanded ethnically as well as geographically. In a sense, this is the more important expansion since it takes the Jews out of their cultural comfort zones so that the goal of gospel witness across cultures to the ends of the earth could be achieved. In the early chapters of Acts, expanding ethnic outreach matches geographical advance.

Philip's mission to "the ends of the earth." In Jerusalem, Palestinian Hebrew-speaking Jewish Christians witness to Hellenistic Jews (Acts 2–5). Then, at Stephen's death, there is a scattering of Hellenistic Jewish Christians (8:1). Philip goes down to Samaria and crosses that cultural threshold, bearing witness to the gospel of Christ with a great response—much joy in Samaria (8:4–8). This was a very difficult move. The Jews had no dealings with the Samaritans (John 4:9). There was

---

[2]Cassius Dio Cocceianus, *Roman History* (Cambridge, MA: Harvard University Press; London: W. Heinemann, 1968–1970), 60.6.6.

real enmity between them, but God breaks through. In fact, there is uncertainty in the church in Jerusalem. They send down apostles to check it out, and the apostles lay hands on the Samaritans, saying, in essence, "Yes, they have received the gospel of Christ." And the Holy Spirit is present as an open witness (Acts 8:14–17).

As Luke presents it, the next one to experience this witness across cultural thresholds is a God-fearer Gentile, possibly a proselyte (Acts 8:26–40). Philip is told by an angel of the Lord to leave the great work that is going on in Samaria and take the wilderness road down toward Gaza. There he encounters an Ethiopian eunuch. "Ethiopia" refers to territory that is modern-day Sudan. It was actually the "ends of the earth" as far as first-century Mediterranean peoples were concerned.[3] In typical ethnocentric fashion, they viewed the Mediterranean basin as the very center of the earth. The earth's "four corners" were inhabited by the Indians to the east, the Ethiopians to the south, the Scythians (Russians) to the north, and the Celts (Scots) to the west.[4]

With this witness to the Ethiopian eunuch, already by Acts 8, God is making sure that the message gets to the ends of the earth (Acts 1:8).

With this witness to the Ethiopian eunuch, already by Acts 8, God is making sure that the message gets to the ends of the earth (Acts 1:8).

The cross-cultural conversion of Peter. But God is not done with this cross-cultural mission. He will also take the Palestinian Jews, particularly the apostles, and help them understand that the gospel needs to go directly to the Gentiles.

He begins with the cross-cultural conversion of Peter (Acts 10:1—11:18). An angel comes and stands in the house of Cornelius, a Roman centurion and God-fearer up in Caesarea, and says, "Send to Joppa for Simon who is called Peter. He will bring you a message through which you and all your household will be saved" (11:13–14). And God works on Peter, too, through a vision of clean and unclean food with the

---

[3]Strabo, *The Geography of Strabo* (London: W. Heinemann; Cambridge, MA: Harvard University Press, 1960–1969), 17.2.1–3.

[4]Ephorus, *Fragments*, in Felix Jacoby, G. Schepens, Charles W. Fornara, and Pierre Bonnechere, *Die Fragmenta der griechischen Historiker* (Leiden, Germany: Brill, 2005), vol. 2A sect. 70 frag. 30a l. 4.

command, "Get up, Peter. Kill and eat" (10:13). Peter refuses. While he is puzzling over this vision, men arrive from Cornelius to summon Peter according to the angel's word. The Holy Spirit confirms and guides, saying, "So get up and go downstairs. Do no hesitate to go with them, for I have sent them" (10:20).

So Peter, with the Spirit's help, puts all this divine guidance together and draws the conclusion, "God has shown me that I should not call anyone impure or unclean" (10:28). Thus, Peter begins his message to Cornelius, his household, and his friends: "I now realize how true it is that God does not show favoritism but accepts from every nation [culture] the one who fears him and does what is right" (10:34–35). Before Peter is finished with his sermon, the Holy Spirit falls on those who are there; and Peter says, "Surely no one can stand in the way of their being baptized with water. They have received the Holy Spirit just as we have" (10:47). As he will assert later, these Gentiles don't have to become Jews in order to become Christians, because God "purified their hearts by faith" (Acts 15:9).

Paul's mission to the Gentiles. Peter's "conversion" matches one in the preceding chapter (Acts 9:1–19): the conversion of a man whose primary mission will be to cross cultural thresholds to the Gentiles—Saul of Tarsus (later referred to as Paul). Interestingly, Luke has not told his readers that the gospel has gone to Damascus; but it must have, for Paul is headed there to persecute Christians when Jesus stops him in his tracks. "Saul, Saul, why do you persecute me?" (v. 4). Led blind into Damascus, he receives his commission through Ananias to bear witness before the Gentiles, the nations and their kings, and the people of Israel. Indeed, the risen Lord tells Ananias that God will show Saul "how much he must suffer for my name" (vv. 15–16). Then, after a brief time of witnessing in Damascus, Paul goes off and witnesses in Arabia, the territory east of the Jordan River, part of modern-day Jordan and Syria (Galatians 1:17; 2 Corinthians 11:32–33). He returns and then is sent off to Jerusalem and from there back to his home area of Tarsus in Cilicia. Finally, he is summoned back to Syria, this time to Antioch (Acts 9:26–30; 11:25–26). So over about a ten-year period (mid-30s to mid-40s), Paul is involved in witness in the eastern end of the Mediterranean basin.

Even though the gospel has gone to the "ends of the earth" representatively, in the witness to the Ethiopian eunuch, Luke has not yet presented a direct mission to pagan Gentiles. That is the last cultural threshold for Jewish Christian witnesses to cross. Acts 11 tells us that those Christians, scattered by the persecution that came at Stephen's martyrdom, traveled as far as Phoenicia, Cyprus, and Syrian Antioch, "spreading the word" (Acts 11:19). Evidently they have born witness beyond the hill country of Judea and Samaria (8:1) and down onto the coastal plain; and, yes, churches were being planted there: in Lydda, Joppa, Tyre, Sidon, and Ptolemais (9:32,36; 21:3–4,7; 27:3). And at Syrian Antioch they don't just speak to Jews, they speak directly to Gentiles. The hand of the Lord is with them and many turn to the Lord (11:20–21). Again, the church in Jerusalem has to come and check it out; they send Barnabas. He rejoices at the genuine advance of the gospel. Yes, the grace of God is at work here (11:22–23).

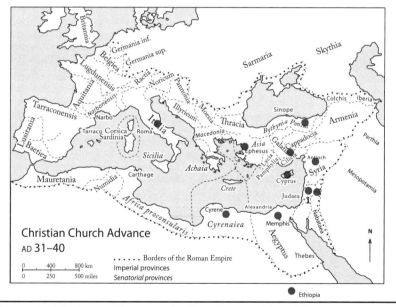

Figure 11.1. The Roman Empire in the First Century. Adapted from *Early Christian Mission*, vol. 2, by Eckhard J. Schnabel (Downers Grove, IL: InterVarsity, 2004), 1589.

So much has been happening in this breakout decade. At Pentecost, a witness is born that bears fruit not only in Jerusalem and Judea, but from the very beginning throughout the empire: north to Pontus, west to Rome, and south to Alexandria. Shortly thereafter, Hellenistic Jewish Christians, scattered by persecution in the wake of Stephen's martyrdom, extend the witness to Samaria, onto the coastal plain and north to Phoenicia, west to the island of Cyprus, and then on to Syrian Antioch. Philip's divinely orchestrated encounter with the Ethiopian eunuch assures that the gospel goes south to the "ends of the earth" in this first decade. Finally, Paul's witness in Arabia and his own home area, Cilicia, takes the gospel east and north. And this is just the first decade of the church's advance.

The Forties: Mandate-Driven Mission

The forties were a decade of the church engaged in a mandate-driven mission to the ends of the earth. Luke's selective presentation in Acts of the church's advance recounts, in the main, only the mission of two individuals: Peter, one of the Twelve, and Paul, the apostle who was "untimely," or "abnormally," born (1 Corinthians 15:8). What about the other eleven apostles?

Going to "another place." In Acts 12:17, we see this very curious statement. Peter has been imprisoned (12:3–4), probably about AD 41–42. He is miraculously released from prison and meets with the church that has been praying for him. He tells them to inform James (probably the brother of Jesus) and the brothers about his miraculous release. Then Luke says that Peter "left for another place." Where? Luke doesn't tell us where that other place is. What he does present after this verse is a change in leadership in the Jerusalem church. Actually, this verse may also point to it. Up to this time, the apostles have been the Jerusalem church's main leadership. Even at the point of persecution they stay in Jerusalem, holding together the church (8:1). Actually the persecution was probably directed primarily against Hellenistic Jewish Christians and not the apostles who were Hebrew-speaking Christians. But from now on in the book of Acts, elders are the ones who are leading the church. This is especially the case at the Jerusalem Council (Acts 15).

Why was there this transition from apostles to elders, from Peter to James, the brother of our Lord? First Corinthians refers to the apostles doing missionary work (1 Corinthians 9:5; 15:10). In Romans, Paul will say his aim in his missionary labors was not to build on anyone else's foundation (Romans 15:20).

It may be that the twelve apostles implement the command of our Lord, found in Acts 1:8, by staying in Jerusalem for twelve years. Then, in concert, they each venture out on their own missions to the ends of the earth. There is evidence for this, for example, from Eusebius in his *Ecclesiastical History*:

> Such was the condition of things among the Jews that the Holy Apostles and disciples of our Savior were scattered throughout the whole world. Thomas, as tradition relates, obtained by lot Parthia; Andrew, Scythia; John, Asia—and he stayed there and died in Ephesus; but Peter, it seems, preached to the Jews of the Dispersion in Pontus, Galatia, Bithynia, Cappadocia and Asia and, at the end, he came to Rome, was crucified head downward for so he demanded to suffer.[5]

So "another place" could well have been cities in the provinces of north-central Asia Minor: Pontus, Galatia, Cappadocia, Asia, and Bithynia (1 Peter 1:1). Eusebius says that Thomas went to Parthia, which in its eastern regions is modern-day Pakistan. But there is also tradition that Thomas went to India (*Acts of Thomas*, 1:1). Andrew, Eusebius says, went to Scythia, modern-day Ukraine, and even to Thrace, modern-day Bulgaria (*Acts of Andrew*, 9).[6] Eusebius also notes that John went to Asia, in western Asia Minor (modern-day Turkey); and Thaddaeus, a member of the group of seventy sent out by Jesus in Luke 10, was sent by the apostle Thomas to Edessa, in northwestern Mesopotamia (eastern modern-day Turkey).[7]

So during the first half of the forties the church is advancing further east, to Edessa, Parthia, and India; and further north, to territory around the Black Sea, Bithynia, Scythia, and Thrace—through the witness of Thaddaeus, Thomas, Peter, and Andrew. This is a mandate-

---

[5]Eusebius of Caesarea, *Eusebius' Ecclesiastical History* (Oxford: Clarendon Press, 1881), 3.1.1.
[6]For both *Acts of Thomas* and *Acts of Andrew*, see Edward Hennecke, *New Testament Apocrypha* vol. 2, ed. Wilhelm Schneemelcher (Philadelphia: Westminster Press, 1976).
[7]Eusebius, *Ecclesiastical History*, 1.13.4, 11; 2.1.6–8. Note: This Thaddaeus was likely not the same Thaddaeus (Judas) who was one of the twelve apostles.

driven church advance. In other words, the apostles received the Great Commission and acted on it.

Paul's first missionary journey. For Luke, Paul's first missionary journey (AD 45–47) is the key missions event of the second half of the forties. It is also mandate-driven. The Holy Spirit's command inaugurates it: "The two of them, sent on their way by the Holy Spirit, went down to Seleucia and sailed from there to Cyprus" (Acts 13:4). At his conversion, Paul was called to be an apostle to the Gentiles. So, now divinely sent out, he goes to Cyprus and then to central Asia Minor, speaking the gospel to both Jews and Gentiles (13:4—14:28). In fact, some cities on the journey, like Lystra, don't seem to have a Jewish population. Therefore Paul finds himself witnessing directly and only to Gentiles. At the end of this first missionary journey, he concludes that God had, indeed, opened a door of faith for the Gentiles (14:27).

The multiethnic church challenge. This particular decade climaxes, in AD 49, with an event decisive for church advance among all cultures: the Jerusalem Council (Acts 15). If God is breaking through to people of various cultures, how are they going to live together in the church? The Jews faced a particular multiethnic church challenge, both in terms of initiation and in terms of table fellowship: Do non-Jews have to become Jews in order to be Christians? Must they be circumcised and keep the Jewish law (15:5)? Do Gentile Christians have to keep the Jewish food laws in order to sit at table with Jewish Christians (cf. Galatians 2:11–14)? The council met and struggled with these matters, basically concluding three things:

(1) With regard to circumcision, they said, "No." Culture must not swallow up grace. You must not put a cultural requirement on those who are responding by faith to the gospel. Because the grace of God has come to them, Gentile Christians have believed the gospel to be saved. In fact, it is the same grace way that salvation came to the Jews (Acts 15:9–11).

(2) With regard to table fellowship, they said, "Freedom must not disregard cultural identity and sensibilities." Jewish Christians who are still keeping a kosher table do not need to stop keeping a kosher table. And Gentile Christians who would eat with them are asked to use their freedom in love. They should voluntarily give up their rights by respecting

their Jewish Christian brothers' and sisters' cultural sensibilities (Acts 15:28–29). That means that when having table fellowship with Jewish Christians, who are keeping a kosher table, they should not eat things offered to idols, blood, or things strangled (i.e., still containing blood)— things considered unclean by the Jew.

(3) And in all, love must preserve unity in diversity. "You, my brothers and sisters, were called to be free. But do not use your freedom to indulge the flesh; rather, serve one another humbly in love" (Galatians 5:13).

In reality, the Jerusalem Council did not settle once and for all the multiethnic church challenge. It was the beginning, not the end, of this ongoing tension between church and culture. However, it does reveal a church movement that was truly mandate-driven, even to the point of wrestling with such a controversial issue as this.

The Fifties: Master-Driven Mission

In the thirties there was a message- and Spirit-driven mission to the ends of the earth. In the forties the church pursued a mandate-driven mission. In the fifties came the Master-driven mission.

Paul's second missionary journey. The power of the risen Christ came to Europe, challenging and transforming cultures during Paul's second missionary journey (AD 50–52; Acts 15:40—18:22). Paul seems to be thinking of moving ahead almost in a contiguous fashion. He has worked in Galatia, in central Asia Minor; now he wants to work in western Asia Minor, but the Holy Spirit forbids him (16:6–7). Forced west to Troas on the Aegean, he receives the Macedonian vision (16:8–10). The Lord directs the mission with ever outward (here westward) momentum, so Paul follows him over into Greece—first to Macedonia and then down into Achaia.

In Macedonia, in one town after another, Paul proclaims that Jesus is Lord, challenging and relativizing earthly political claims. For instance, at Thessalonica the Jews charge Paul of upsetting the whole inhabited world by teaching people to follow and do things against the decrees of Caesar, by saying there is another king—namely Jesus (Acts 17:6–7). This particular Caesar, Claudius, was very uneasy about his power. He would issue decrees forbidding any prophet or soothsayer to declare, on threat of banishment, when the emperor's reign would be over.[8] So when Paul declared in the gospel message that King Jesus will return (1 Thessalonians 1:9–10), this was taken as a challenge to the earthly king. Ultimately this is true, for though Jesus' kingdom is not of this world, his coming will terminate the reigns of all earthly kings.

Paul's third missionary journey. In the third missionary journey (AD 54–57), which begins in Acts 18:23, Paul witnesses mainly in one place, Ephesus, but the church still advances in mission. First, the gospel spreads throughout the region of western Asia Minor. Luke tells us that Paul spends two years in Ephesus, but the result was "so that all the Jews and Greeks who lived in the province of Asia [in western Asia Minor] heard the word of the Lord" (19:10). Other New Testament books give evidence that indeed the gospel was going out from Ephesus to other places in the region without Paul's direct witness. In Colossians 1:7, Paul mentions Epaphras, "our dear fellow slave" from whom those in Colossae learned of the saving grace of God (cf. Philemon 23). In Colossians 4:16, Paul writes, "After this letter has been read to you, see that it is also read in the church of the Laodiceans." Laodicea is another city to which the gospel has come, though Paul does not personally minister there. In addition to the churches at Ephesus and Laodicea, could others of the seven churches of Revelation (Smyrna, Pergamum, Thyatira, Sardis, and Philadelphia) have been planted during this season of multiplied witness in a Master-driven mission?

Second, during the third missionary journey the church advances powerfully, effectively challenging the very heart of a culture: its worship (Acts 19:23–40). The goddess Artemis, a nurturing goddess, was worshiped in Ephesus and over the whole inhabited world (vv. 26–27). The silversmiths did not exaggerate with that claim. Archaeological evidence of the worship of Artemis has been uncovered as far away as Spain.[9] A yearly two-week festival gathered people from all over the world to worship Artemis in a temple that was one of the "seven wonders of the

---

[8]Cross-reference Cassius Dio Cocceianus, *Roman History*, 56.25.5–6; 57.15.8; and Tacitus, *Annals* (Cambridge, MA: Harvard University Press; London: W. Heinemann, 1937), 6.20; 12.52; 14.9.
[9]Cross-reference Strabo, *The Geography of Strabo*, 4.1.5.

ancient world." The temple of Artemis had sixty-foot pillars, only a few
of which stand today. The area covered by the temple's plaza extends
about a third-again the size of a football field. Paul comes to Ephesus
and preaches the gospel that Jesus is Lord, and that gods made by human
hands are no gods at all (v. 26). One prominent silversmith points out
that if the people believe, the trade in the trinkets of Artemis worship
will decline (v. 27). As Luke presents it, the climax of Paul's missionary
witness at Ephesus is the great contrast between the irrational response
of the pagan religionists and the effective proclamation of Paul. The
people gather and riot without even knowing why they have assembled.
At the least perceived provocation, they cry out for two hours, "Great is
Artemis of the Ephesians!" (vv. 28–34).

So in the fifties, the gospel has made further advances. It has gone to
Macedonia and to Achaia. It has probably gone farther west to Illyricum,
modern-day former Yugoslavia. Paul says he has fully preached the gospel
in a great circle from Jerusalem to as far as Illyricum (Romans 15:19).

The Sixties to AD 100: A Missional DNA-Driven Mission

A message- and Spirit-driven mission, a mandate-driven mission,
and a Master-driven mission. Now in the sixties to AD 100, the
church demonstrates that it is on a missional DNA-driven mission. These decades are marked by suffering, yet unstoppable witness, generational transfer, and the final vision for mission.

The Mission of God:

30s – Message- and Spirit-driven
40s – Mandate-driven
50s – Master-driven
60s – Missional DNA-driven

Figure 11.2.

In the midst of suffering.
From AD 57–63 Paul was a prisoner in chains, yet his witness was unstoppable. The latter part of the book of Acts (Acts 21–28) puts this
principle on display: the greater the difficulty, the greater the strength
from God and the more bold and unstoppable the witness. For example, Paul is accosted, arrested in the temple by the temple guard,
dragged out of the temple precincts, and beaten to within an inch of his
life (21:27–32). The Roman commander and a detachment of soldiers

come and rescue Paul (21:32–34). So angry is the crowd, trying to get a hold of Paul, that the soldiers literally have to lift him up out of their reach as they take him up the steps to the Antonia Fortress (21:35–36). When they are about to enter the barracks, Paul says to the commander, "Please let me speak to the people" (21:37–39). *What a great opportunity!* Paul is thinking. *I'll never have this many Jews before me with great acoustics in a great setting.* "Let me to speak to the people." And he preaches to the crowd. It doesn't have a great effect, but he does bear witness to them (22:1–22). And ever after that in Acts, prisoner Paul gives an unstoppable witness. Yes, suffering is present—even to the point of martyrdom, as Eusebius notes: Peter is crucified upside down and Paul is beheaded.[10] But still, the gospel message goes forward.

Consolidation and advance. But these decades, the sixties to AD 100, are also a time of consolidation and advance into the next generation. Paul goes to Rome and prison, but is apparently released after about two years (cf. Acts 28:30–31; 2 Timothy 4:16). He probably proceeds to Spain (Romans 15:24; *1 Clement* 5:5–7; *Muratorian Canon* 35–39),[11] and then returns to Rome. Based on the Pastoral Epistles, Paul bears witness in Crete and leaves Titus there (Titus 1:5). He then goes on to Nicopolis, capital of Epirus, a region in western Greece between Achaia and Illyricum, asking Titus to join him (3:12). He evidently heads through Macedonia (Philippians 2:24) and Troas (2 Timothy 4:13), back toward Ephesus (1 Timothy 1:3). He is arrested either at Ephesus or Miletus and possibly passes through Corinth in being conducted back to Rome (2 Timothy 4:20).

Handing on the truth of God. Paul's activities, recounted in the Pastoral Epistles, involve not only his further witness and his strengthening already planted churches, but his transfer of these tasks to the next generation. He counsels this pattern of transfer: "Be strong in the grace that is in Christ Jesus. And the things you have heard me say in the presence of many witnesses entrust to reliable people who will also be qualified to teach others"

---

[10]Eusebius, *Ecclesiastical History*, 3.1.1; 2.25.5.

[11]Irenaeus, *Adversus Haereses*, 1.10.2; *1 Clement* (Cambridge, MA: Harvard University Press; London: W. Heinemann, 1912); for *Muratorian Canon*, see Edward Hennecke, *New Testament Apocrypha* vol. 1, Wilhelm Schneemelcher, ed. (Philadelphia: Westminster, 1976), l. 35–39.

(2 Timothy 2:1–2). In other words, hand on the truth of God to faithful and competent individuals who will teach others also. Part of handing on that truth is the matter of further witness.

> "Be strong in the grace that is in Christ Jesus. And the things you have heard me say in the presence of many witnesses entrust to reliable people who will also be qualified to teach others" (2 Timothy 2:1–2).

It is fascinating to notice in 2 Timothy, the very last extant letter we have from Paul, his dispatch of this next generation to further witness: Titus to Dalmatia, modern-day Yugoslavia, and Crescens to Galatia (4:10). Early manuscripts vary on this last destination. The word is either "Galatia" (central Asia Minor) or "Gallia" ("Gaul," modern-day France). A case can be made that it could well be "Gallia." If so, this missional DNA-driven mission is being worked out in the next generation as it takes the church's mission even further: "Preach the word; be prepared in season and out of season. . . . Do the work of an evangelist, discharge all the duties of your ministry" (4:2,5).

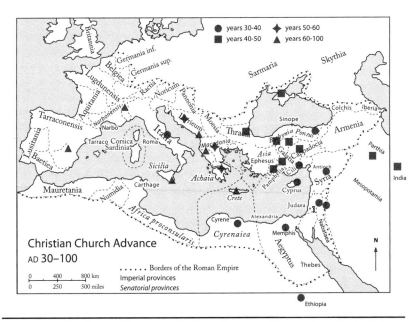

Figure 11.3. The Roman Empire in the First Century. Adapted from *Early Christian Mission*, vol. 2, by Eckhard J. Schnabel (Downers Grove, IL: InterVarsity, 2004), 1589.

By the mid-sixties and certainly by the end of the first century AD, the early church's gospel witness has ringed the Mediterranean basin from Syria to Spain, from Egypt to Rome and perhaps Gaul (France). It has moved outward beyond the boundaries of the Roman Empire: east to Parthia (Iran) and India; south to Ethiopia (Sudan); and north around the Black Sea in Scythia and Thrace (Ukraine, Bulgaria). According to the biblical and early church data, in a little less than three-quarters of a century the church has been planted in twenty-three of the forty-odd provinces of the Roman Empire (almost 60 percent of them).

Finally, the book of Revelation, written on the cusp of the second century AD, presents the final vision that powered this missional DNA. It addresses seven churches of western Asia Minor, many of which are not referred to elsewhere in the New Testament, such as Smyrna, Pergamum, Thyatira, Sardis, and Philadelphia (Revelation 1:11). Yet, obviously, the gospel has been planted in them too.

Conclusion

That final vision is captured in a word of praise to the Lord Jesus Christ. "You are worthy to take the scroll [probably a record of the events of the rest of history] and to open its seals [setting in motion those events], because you were slain, and with your blood you purchased for God persons from every tribe and language and people and nation [culture]. You made them to be a kingdom and priests to serve our God, and they will reign on the earth" (Revelation 5:9–10). With that end in view, the church advances with its witness to the ends of the earth and so populates that richly diverse throng around the throne at the last day.

Whether being message- and Spirit-driven, mandate-driven, Master-driven, or missional DNA-driven, the church in the twenty-first century has the same charge: take the good news to the ends of the earth. The first-century church excellently models the duty and the joy of the church in every age.

Discussion Points

1. How does the message of the gospel (Luke 24:46–48) still motivate for missions?

2. What principles of solving the multiethnic church challenge (Acts 15) are particularly applicable to the church today?

3. If engaged with the gospel, what cultural and religious power centers of today will produce, by God's grace, the same results as Paul's contesting Artemis worship in first-century Ephesus (Acts 19:23–40)?

4. How can missional DNA be developed in your church so that it transfers from generation to generation (2 Timothy 2:1–2; 4:9–22)?

Further Reading

Gallagher, Roger, and Paul Hertig, eds. *Mission in Acts: Ancient Narratives in Contemporary Context*. Maryknoll, NY: Orbis, 2004.

Gehring, Roger W. *House Church and Mission: The Importance of Household Structures in Early Christianity*. Peabody, MA: Hendrickson, 2004.

Larkin, William J. *Acts*. IVPNTC. Downers Grove, IL: InterVarsity, 1995.

———. "Acts." In *The Gospel of Luke, Acts*. Cornerstone Biblical Commentary 12. Carol Stream, IL: Tyndale, 2006.

Larkin, William J., and Joel F. Williams, eds. *Mission in the New Testament: An Evangelical Approach*. Maryknoll, NY: Orbis, 1998.

Plummer, Robert L. *Paul's Understanding of the Church's Mission: Did the Apostle Paul Expect the Early Christian Communities to Evangelize?* Eugene, OR: Wipf & Stock, 2006.

Schnabel, Eckhard J. *Early Christian Mission*, 2 vols. Downers Grove, IL: InterVarsity, 2004.

———. *Paul the Missionary: Realities, Strategies and Methods*. Downers Grove, IL: InterVarsity, 2008.

12

THE ANTE-NICENE CHURCH ON MISSION

John Mark Terry

This chapter will explain how the church grew from the small group that met in the "upper room" in Jerusalem to become the dominant religion in the Roman Empire by AD 325. Understanding the church's early growth can help us understand the church's contemporary growth. Martin Hengel said, "The history and the theology of early Christianity are mission-history and mission-theology."[1] He means that one cannot understand the history of the early church without considering the missionary activity of the church. Further, one can only understand the development of the church today by studying its past expansion. The successes and failures of Christianity's past should inform its future.

Historians usually divide this period of church history into two parts, separated by the Council of Nicaea in AD 325. The period before Nicaea is called the Ante-Nicene, and the period after is call the Post-Nicene. This chapter will focus primarily on the methods employed by the Ante-Nicene church. When you finish this chapter, hopefully you will understand how the church grew during this crucial period in its history.

The Post-Apostolic Context

The end of the apostolic era coincided with the death of John at Ephesus (AD 95–100). What was the state of the church at that time?

---

[1]William C. Weinrich, "Evangelism in the Early Church," *Concordia Theological Quarterly* (January–April 1981): 61.

Basic characteristics of the churches. Acts and the Epistles tell of clusters of house churches in Palestine, Asia Minor, Greece, Cyprus, Crete, and Rome. Paul and his associates planted most of these. Traditions of the early church hold that Thaddeus preached in Edessa; Mark founded the church at Alexandria; and Peter preached in Bithynia and Cappadocia. There are also ancient traditions that Paul went to Spain and Thomas went to India. Even if one accepts these traditions, it is clear the churches were few. Also, these churches were generally small in size. The churches at Jerusalem, Antioch, Ephesus, and Rome were exceptions. Rodney Stark estimates that the number of Christians in AD 100 was as low as about 7,500.[2] The New Testament indicates that most of the churches met in homes, such as the one that worshiped in Philemon's home (Philemon 2). This practice continued until the time of Constantine.[3] For the most part, they were urban churches. This was because Paul preached primarily in the cities of the empire. It's not clear if this was a conscious strategy on his part, but it certainly was his pattern.

In the beginning the church reflected a strong Jewish influence. However, as the number of Gentile churches increased, churches became more Hellenistic. This trend greatly accelerated when Jerusalem was destroyed in AD 70 and the Jewish Christians of Jerusalem were scattered. Thus, the New Testament was written in Greek, as were the majority of Christian documents during the second century. Therefore, at the end of the apostolic age one can say that the church was limited in size (perhaps no more than a hundred congregations or clusters of house churches), mainly urban, and primarily Greek-speaking.

General factors affecting church expansion. Most introductions to the New Testament list the factors that made 4 BC (or thereabouts) the right time for Jesus' birth. These same factors also positively affected the missionary activity of the early church. Perhaps the greatest general factor was the excellent Roman road system. Everywhere the Romans went they built fine roads. These roads improved commerce within the empire and also made it possible to dispatch Roman legions to trouble spots quickly. During this period, travel was safer than at any later time

---

[2]Rodney Stark, *The Rise of Christianity* (Princeton, NJ: Princeton University Press, 1996), 7.
[3]Laurie Guy, *Introducing Early Christianity* (Downers Grove, IL: InterVarsity, 2004), 24.

until the nineteenth century. The relative ease of travel was a great help to early missionaries.

Another reason for the safety of travel was the Pax Romana (Peace of Rome). The Romans brought and enforced peace in the Mediterranean world. Their legions and proconsuls ensured stability in the region. The Roman navy cleared the sea of pirates so that sea travel was less risky than before. All in all, the period under study was congenial to missionary travel.

The widespread use of the Greek language also aided the early missionaries. Whereas modern missionaries spend months or even years in language study, the evangelists of Ante-Nicene times could go almost anywhere in the empire and communicate through the Greek language.

Greek philosophy was widely taught and admired all over the empire. This helped the Christian mission in two ways. First, it imbued the educated classes with a love for truth. Secondly, it caused people to become dissatisfied with the superstitions of their traditional religions.

The presence of Jews and synagogues in the cities of the empire proved significant also. The Jews propagated a religion of strict monotheism. This was a novel concept to most citizens. The Jews also taught that God was personal and that people could have a personal relationship with him. The Jews proselytized actively, and in many cities there were a good number of "God-fearers" (Gentile inquirers) who attended the synagogues. These "God-fearers" proved a fertile ground for early church planters. In fact, opposition of the Jews to Christianity in Asia Minor and Greece was surely due in part to jealousy at the loss of their Gentile adherents. Paul wrote that "when the set time had fully come, God sent his Son" (Galatians 4:4). This was that "set time," God's special moment in history, not only for the incarnation but also for church expansion.

The Illegal Church

During its first years, Christianity was viewed by the Roman authorities as a sect of Judaism. Because Judaism was a *religio licitas* (legal religion), Christians enjoyed protection under Roman law. After AD 100 Christianity lost that status, and the Roman government considered Christianity a secret society and a danger to the stability of the empire.

Specifically, Roman officials persecuted Christians because they refused to bow down to statues of Caesar and say, "Caesar is lord." The authorities interpreted the believers' refusal as disloyalty or even treason. Beyond this, many pagans accused Christians of atheism, incest, and cannibalism. They accused Christians of atheism because they refused to worship idols, of incest because Christians practiced "the kiss of peace," and of cannibalism because visitors misunderstood the words of the Lord's Supper: "This is my body."[4]

Periods of persecution. Before AD 250 most persecutions of Christians were localized and brief in duration; however, in AD 250 Decius became emperor, and he targeted Christians in his campaign to return Rome to its classic culture and glory. He decreed that all the people should make an annual sacrifice to the Roman gods and to the emperor. Those who refused were subject to torture or death. The famous Christian theologian, Origen, refused to sacrifice and suffered terrible torture and imprisonment. Thankfully, this persecution only lasted about one year until the death of Decius.

A more intense empire-wide persecution began in 303. Emperor Diocletian ordered that Christian worship cease, churches be destroyed, the Scriptures be burned, and Christians who refused to recant be arrested and imprisoned. Christians found guilty were subject to exile, loss of property, torture, service in the salt mines, or execution. This persecution continued until Emperor Constantine issued the Edict of Milan in 313, which granted toleration to Christianity.[5] In spite of persecution, or perhaps because of it, the church grew steadily during the Ante-Nicene period.

Growth in the second century. Christianity spread naturally along the main roads and rivers of the empire. It spread eastward by way of Damascus and Edessa into Mesopotamia; southward through Bostra and Petra into Arabia; westward through Alexandria and Carthage into North Africa; and northward through Antioch into Armenia, Pontus, and Bithynia. Later it spread even farther to Spain, Gaul, and Britain.[6]

---

[4]Earle E. Cairns, *Christianity Through the Centuries* (Grand Rapids: Zondervan, 1996), 87.
[5]Ibid., 91–93.
[6]J. Herbert Kane, *A Global View of Christian Missions* (Grand Rapids: Baker, 1975), 10.

Egypt and North Africa became strongholds of Christianity during the second century. Tradition has it that Mark founded the church at Alexandria, but this is not certain. The early church in Egypt was originally limited to those who spoke Greek, though a strong Coptic church developed later. Christians from Egypt probably carried the gospel into North Africa.[7]

North Africa produced the first Latin-speaking churches. In the early years, these churches seem to have appealed more to the upper classes, the Latin-speaking people. Then again, churches were planted primarily in the cities and towns. During this period villages remained largely untouched.[8]

Paul, Peter, and John had all evangelized in Asia Minor, and that region contained many churches which grew steadily. Pliny, a Roman official, wrote to Emperor Trajan in AD 112 concerning the Christians in Bithynia. He complained that "there are so many people involved in the danger. . . . For the contagion of this superstition has spread not only through the free cities, but into the villages and rural districts." Pliny went on to say that "many persons of all ages and both sexes" were involved.[9] Obviously, the churches in Bithynia were growing and multiplying, and this seems to have been true in and around Ephesus as well.

Many scholars believe the church at Rome was founded by Jews and proselytes to Judaism who were converted on the day of Pentecost (Acts 2:10–11). While this is just a theory, it is a fact that the Roman church grew in size and prestige year by year. For the first hundred years of its existence, church members used common Greek in their services. This shows that the church drew its members from the poorer classes of society. There are no records of the size of the Roman congregation until the time of the Novatian controversy in AD 251. Eusebius quotes from a letter written by Bishop Cornelius of Rome in which he states there were 46 presbyters; 7 deacons; 7 subdeacons; 42 clerks; 52 exorcists, readers, and janitors; and 1,500 widows and needy in the church. Some

---

[7]Stephen Neill, *A History of Christian Missions* (New York: Penguin, 1986), 34.
[8]Ibid.
[9]B. J. Kidd, ed., *Documents Illustrative of the History of the Church* (London: Society for Promoting Christian Knowledge, 1920), 1:39.

scholars calculated the total church membership at that time at around 30,000. If that was true in AD 251, then the Roman church must have been large during the second century as well.[10]

Kenneth Scott Latourette estimates that by the end of the second century Christians were active in all the provinces of the Roman Empire as well as in Mesopotamia.[11] This seems to be a fair estimation in light of a passage from Tertullian. Writing about AD 200, he reported that many became Christians, including "different races of the Gaetuli, many tribes of the Mauri, all the confines of Spain, and various tribes of Gaul, with places in Britain, which, though inaccessible to Rome, have yielded to Christ. Add the Sarmatae, the Daci, the Germans, the Scythians, and many remote peoples, provinces, and islands unknown to us."[12]

In another book, Tertullian boasts to the pagans, "We have filled every place belonging to you, cities, islands, castles, towns, assemblies, your very camp, your tribes, companies, palace, senate, forum! We leave you your temples only."[13] Tertullian may have employed some hyperbole, but it does seem clear that the church had penetrated, at least to some extent, every part of Roman society by AD 200.

Growth in the third century. Christianity grew steadily but not dramatically from AD 200 until 260. Then, beginning about AD 260, the church grew very rapidly until Emperor Diocletian's edict of persecution in AD 303. Up until AD 260, the church remained a mainly urban institution, but the mass movement in the latter third century was primarily a rural phenomenon. Several factors affected this remarkable growth. First, this was a period of civil strife in the empire. This was the era of the "barrack emperors," when the Roman Empire was threatened externally with invasion by Germanic tribes and internally with chaos in Rome itself. Secondly, there was great economic dislocation. Inflation made survival very difficult for rural folk who found it

---

[10]Pamphilus Eusebius, *Ecclesiastical History*, trans. C. F. Cruse (Grand Rapids: Baker, 1984), 265.
[11]Kenneth Scott Latourette, *A History of the Expansion of Christianity* (New York: Harper & Brothers, 1937), 1:85.
[12]Alexander Roberts and James Donaldson, eds., *The Ante-Nicene Fathers* (Grand Rapids: Eerdmans, 1951), 3:44.
[13]Kidd, *Documents*, 1:143.

difficult to market their produce. Even the shipment of produce became risky as peace and order began to break down.[14]

As usually happens, the rural folk began to question their traditional cults as the hard times continued. In contrast, Christians presented a simple gospel that offered both social justice and assurance of power over demonic forces. Thousands, perhaps millions, rejected their old gods and accepted Christ. This was the greatest period of growth in the Ante-Nicene period.

Great growth was possible because the church was free of persecution during these forty years. The government was so preoccupied with other problems that it left the church alone. This respite from persecution continued during the early years of Diocletian's reign.

The era of peace and progress ended when Emperor Diocletian issued his edict of persecution in AD 303. This terrible period of persecution lasted until Constantine assumed control in AD 311. During the persecution, 1,500 Christians died as martyrs, and many more suffered lesser persecutions. Many Christians recanted under torture or the threat of it, including the bishop of Rome. Lasting peace came when Constantine issued his edict of toleration in AD 311 and his famous Edict of Milan in AD 313.[15]

The expansion of the church by AD 325. By AD 300, the gospel had been preached in every city and province of the empire. However, the distribution of churches was uneven. The church had grown more rapidly in Syria, Asia Minor, Egypt, and North Africa, including significant centers in Rome and Lyons. Growth in other areas—Gaul, for example—had been slow. Harnack believed that in one or two provinces at least half the people were Christians, and in several cities Christians were in the majority. He estimated the number of Christians in the empire at three or four million at the time of Constantine.[16] Under Constantine's rule the number of Christians increased rapidly because it became advantageous to be a Christian. When Christianity

---

[14]W. H. C. Frend, *The Early Church* (Philadelphia: Fortress, 1982), 110–11.

[15]Kane, *Global View*, 32.

[16]Adolf Harnack, *The Mission and Expansion of Christianity in the First Three Centuries* (New York: G. P. Putnam's Sons, 1908), 2:325.

became the favored religion, church memberships swelled, although the quality may have declined in proportion. Still, the Ante-Nicene church made remarkable progress and withstood tremendous onslaughts. The question remains: How did the church grow?

Who Did God Use?

Missionaries. From its inception, Christianity has been a missionary religion. The missionaries of the second and third centuries followed the example set by the apostles. Eusebius says of them: "The holy apostles and disciples of our Savior, being scattered over the whole world, Thomas, according to tradition, received Parthia as his allotted region; Andrew received Sythia, and John, Asia, where . . . he died at Ephesus." Peter appears to have preached through Pontus, Galatia, Bithynia, Cappadocia, and Asia, to the Jews . . . finally coming to Rome.[17] According to Eusebius, the twelve apostles took deliberate steps to evangelize the world they knew.

According to Eusebius, the twelve apostles took deliberate steps to evangelize the world they knew.

It seems that there were itinerant missionaries in the second century who followed the Pauline model in their ministry. Eusebius tells of their work in his church history. The *Didache*, from the second century, also speaks of itinerant "apostles and prophets" in need of hospitality.[18] So it seems there was a body of full-time missionaries in the second century. Origen testifies to their continuance in the third century: "Some of them have made it their business to itinerate, not only through cities, but even villages and country houses, that they might make converts to God."[19] In fact, Pantaenus, the predecessor of Clement and Origen, left Alexandria and went into Asia as a missionary; and Eusebius believed he traveled as far as India.[20] This brief review of the source material indicates that the office of missionary continued in the church after the first century.

---

[17]Eusebius, *Ecclesiastical History*, 82 [1.1.1–3].
[18]Henry Bettenson, ed., *The Early Christian Fathers* (New York: Oxford University Press, 1956), 71 [11–12].
[19]Roberts, *Ante-Nicene Fathers*, 4:468.
[20]Eusebius, *Ecclesiastical History*, 190 [5.10.1–3].

Missionary bishops. During the Ante-Nicene period bishops continued the missionary activity of the apostles. The bishops of large urban centers led in the evangelization of adjacent rural areas. Further, existing churches consecrated bishops and sent them into new areas to organize Christians into churches. Also, a bishop or bishops living near a group of Christians would gather and instruct believers until they could elect their own bishop.[21]

Irenaeus and Gregory Thaumaturgos exemplify missionary bishops. Irenaeus (AD 130–200) was bishop of Lyons. In one of his books he speaks of preaching in the Celtic language to the tribes around Lyon.[22] Gregory was won to Christ by Origen. About AD 240 he was chosen bishop of his hometown in Pontus. According to tradition, when he became bishop he had a congregation of seventeen; but when he died, there were only seventeen pagans left in the city. The numbers may be exaggerated, but clearly Gregory evangelized successfully. He exposed pagan miracles as frauds and performed so many wonders himself that he became known as Gregory Thaumaturgos (worker of wonders). He also replaced pagan feasts with festivals in honor of the martyrs. He thus sought to ease the transition from paganism to Christianity.[23]

Lay missionaries. Though missionaries and bishops set an example in evangelism, lay people spread the gospel for the most part. They shared the gospel while engaged in their daily activities. It's easy to imagine laymen conversing with their acquaintances in their homes, at the market, and on the street corners.[24]

In addition, Christians shared the gospel as they moved about. Christian traders evangelized as they traveled through the empire, much as did the Christians dispersed from Jerusalem (Acts 8:4). Christians serving in the Roman army, though relatively few in the early years, carried the gospel as well. They witnessed wherever they were stationed. Some scholars believe Roman soldiers first brought the gospel to Britain. Further, the government pensioned retiring soldiers

---

[21]R. Dwayne Conner, "The Hierarchy and the Church's Mission in the First Five Centuries" (ThD diss., The Southern Baptist Theological Seminary, 1971), 208.

[22]Neill, *History of Christian Missions*, 31.

[23]Latourette, *History of the Expansion of Christianity*, 1:89–90.

[24]Michael Green, *Evangelism in the Early Church* (Grand Rapids: Eerdmans, 1970), 173.

by giving them a plot of land in a new territory. These retired soldiers sometimes established churches in those remote places. This was definitely the case in southeastern Europe.[25]

Women played a major part in the expansion of the church. Harnack writes: "No one who reads the New Testament attentively, as well as those writings which immediately succeeded it, can fail to notice that in the apostolic and sub-apostolic age women played an important role in the propaganda of Christianity and throughout the Christian communities. The equalizing of men and women in grace and salvation (Galatians 3:28) produced a religious independence among women, which aided the Christian mission."[26] Because the early churches met in homes, many women were able to make their homes into house churches. Also, many women died bravely as martyrs, and thus gave a testimony for Christ.

The ancient church rightly regarded Perpetua as a great hero of the church. Vibia Perpetua and her slave, Felicitas, became Christians at the same time. Roman authorities in Carthage arrested both of them during the persecution of Christians decreed by Emperor Septimus Severus. Though her family pleaded with her to consider their feelings and the welfare of her infant child, Perpetua remained true to her faith. Before she was led into the arena to die, Perpetua shared her faith with the crowd. As she entered the arena, Perpetua encouraged the weeping Christians: "Give out the Word to the brothers and sisters; stand fast in the faith, love one another, and don't let our suffering become a stumbling block to you."[27]

How Did God Grow His Church?

Missionary methods. Paul and Peter often preached in public, and this practice continued in the second and third centuries when conditions permitted. Eusebius records that Thaddeus preached publicly at Edessa,

---

[25]W. O. Carver, *The Course of Christian Missions* (New York: Fleming H. Revell, 1932), 51.
[26]Harnack, *Mission and Expansion*, 2:64.
[27]Ruth Tucker, *From Jerusalem to Irian Jaya* (Grand Rapids: Zondervan, 2004), 33–34.

and reports Thaddeus saying, "Since I was sent to preach the word, summon for me tomorrow an assembly of all your citizens, and I will preach before them and sow in them the word of life."[28] Early evangelists were fervent in their preaching. J. G. Davies says that they preached so as to "bring the hearers to repentance and belief . . . [and] to force upon them the crisis of decision."[29] The steady growth of the church testifies to their efforts.

W. O. Carver believed that teaching was another important method. The early catechetical schools developed into training schools for presbyters (pastors) in Antioch, Alexandria, Edessa, Caesarea, and other places.[30] All of these schools sent people into missions. Sometimes teachers, like Pantaenus of Alexandria, set an example in this. These teachers worked as evangelists inside and outside of their schools. Pagans as well as catechumens attended their schools and heard their teaching. The great missionary bishop, Gregory Thaumaturgos, was won to Christ by Origen at the school in Alexandria.[31]

Early Christians often spread the gospel through the use of their homes. Because there were no church buildings until about AD 250, congregations met in one or several homes. The home setting provided a relaxed, nonthreatening atmosphere. The warm hospitality afforded by Christian homes surely influenced many. Whole households were sometimes converted, as was that of the Philippian jailer (Acts 16). The New Testament contains many references to house or home churches, and the Ante-Nicene church followed this model.[32]

Oral witness through preaching and personal testimony was the main method of evangelism, but literature also became an increasingly effective means of propagating the gospel. Literature evangelism included apologies, letters, polemics, and the distribution of the Scriptures. W. O. Carver says all the Ante-Nicene Fathers "were in varying degrees missionaries of the pen."[33]

---

[28]Eusebius, *Ecclesiastical History*, 47 [1.13.20].
[29]J. G. Davies, *The Early Christian Church* (Garden City, NY: Anchor Books, 1967), 19.
[30]Carver, *Course of Christian Missions*, 47–50.
[31]Harnack, *Mission and Expansion*, 2:362.
[32]Green, *Evangelism in the Early Church*, 207.
[33]Carver, *Course of Christian Missions*, 49.

The early church spread the gospel primarily through personal contact and example. This was much the same as in apostolic times.

The early church spread the gospel primarily through personal contact and example.

The church established no elaborate missionary societies or organizations; instead, Christians shared and demonstrated the gospel in their daily lives. Justin Martyr tells about this is his *Apology*: "He has urged us . . . to convert all . . . and this I can show to have taken place with many that have come in contact with us, who were overcome, and changed from violent and tyrannical characters, either from having watched the constancy of their neighbor's lives or from having observed the wonderful patience of fellow travelers under unjust exactions, or from the trial they made of those with whom they were concerned in business."[34]

Christians also maintained a public testimony by their conduct at their trials and martyrdoms. Though some recanted under pressure or torture, many gave wonderful testimonies for Christ. When threatened with death if he didn't recant, Polycarp of Smyrna said, "Eighty and six years have I served him, and he never did me wrong; and how can I now blaspheme my King that has saved me?"[35] Roman persecution didn't destroy Christianity; rather, it strengthened it. The blood of the martyrs really did prove to be the seed of the church. Many pagans accepted Christ because of the Christians' testimonies.

The early Christians won others through social service. Adolf Harnack lists ten different ministries performed by the Christians: alms in general, support of teachers and officials, support of widows and orphans, support of the sick and infirm, the care of prisoners and convicts in the mines, the burial of paupers, the care of slaves, providing disaster relief, furnishing employment, and extending hospitality.[36]

It seems that benevolent activities affected evangelism positively because the pagan emperor, Julian the Apostate (AD 332–363), complained about it: "Atheism [i.e., Christianity] has been especially advanced

---

[34]Kidd, *Documents*, 74.
[35]Eusebius, *Ecclesiastical History*, 147 [4.15.20].
[36]Harnack, *Mission and Expansion*, 1:153.

through the loving service rendered to strangers, and through their care for the burial of the dead . . . the godless Galileans care not only for their own poor but for ours as well."[37] Thus, in the early church there was no dichotomy between social service and evangelism. Both were natural activities integral to the church's mission.

Why Did the Church Grow?

So far this chapter has presented information about the expansion of the early church and especially the methods used by the church. This last section tries to answer the question of why the church grew. Six factors are noted.

1. The church grew because of divine blessing. It was God's will for the church to grow, and God blessed the efforts of the early Christians. The early church was the instrument of the Holy Spirit in fulfilling the mission of God to redeem all nations. Origen said, "Christianity . . . in spite of the small number of its teachers was preached everywhere in the world. . . . We cannot hesitate to say that the result is beyond any human power."[38]

2. The church grew because of the zeal of the Christians. They gave of themselves sacrificially for the faith. The early Christians possessed a burning conviction that expressed itself in missionary activity.

3. The appealing message of the church was another important factor. Latourette says that the uniqueness of Jesus was the key. The love of God and the offer of forgiveness and eternal life through Christ appealed to the people of the Roman Empire.[39]

4. The organization and discipline of the church aided its growth also. Walter Hyde believes that the organization of the church on the imperial pattern was a positive factor.[40] Certainly the faithfulness of the bishops enabled the church to persevere in the face of persecution. Also, the strict discipline of the church presented a marked contrast to the licentious pagan cults.

---

[37]Neill, *History of Christian Missions*, 37–38.
[38]Roberts, *Ante-Nicene Fathers*, 4:350.
[39]Latourette, *History of the Expansion of Christianity*, 1:168.
[40]Walter W. Hyde, *Paganism to Christianity in the Roman Empire* (Philadelphia: University of Pennsylvania Press, 1946), 187.

5. The church grew because of its inclusiveness. It attracted people of all classes and races. It became a universal religion. It burst the bonds of restrictive Judaism to become a religion for the world.

6. Christianity prospered because of the ethical standards of the early church. This is not to say that the churches or believers were perfect, but their lives were so different from their pagan neighbors' lives that they attracted notice. Their morality and works of charity commended the faith to many.

Conclusion

By AD 325 the church existed in every part of the Roman Empire. Stephen Neill has estimated the number of Christians to be at least five million, and Rodney Stark has suggested six million.[41] By AD 500 the vast majority of people in the empire called themselves Christians, and missionaries had carried the gospel to many lands outside the empire. The church did not employ secret formulas to achieve growth, but rather followed the example of the apostles in their preaching and teaching. The main innovation of the post-apostolic church was literature evangelism, particularly the apologies. Still, the key remained, as it does today, in the lives and witness of individual believers. The great missionary itinerants and bishops carried the banner of Christ, but it remained for the rank and file Christians to make most of the contacts and conversions.

Discussion Points

1. Will the persecution of Christians today lead to church growth as in the early church?

2. How can believers today practice holistic evangelism like the early Christians?

3. How can laypersons be mobilized to evangelize the world?

4. How could ethical living by believers contribute to world evangelization?

---

[41]Neill, *History of Christian Missions*, 39; Stark, *Rise of Christianity*, 7.

Further Reading

Cairns, Earle E. *Christianity Through the Centuries.* Grand Rapids: Zondervan, 1996.

Eusebius Pamphilus. *Ecclesiastical History.* Translated by C. F. Cruse. Grand Rapids: Baker, 1984.

Frend, W. H. C. *The Early Church.* Philadelphia: Fortress, 1982.

Green, Michael. *Evangelism in the Early Church.* Grand Rapids: Eerdmans, 1970.

Harnack, Adolf. *The Mission and Expansion of Christianity in the First Three Centuries*, 2 vols. Translated by James Moffatt. New York: G. P. Putnam's Sons, 1908.

Kidd, B. J., ed. *Documents Illustrative of the History of the Church*, 3 vols. London: Society for Promoting Christian Knowledge, 1920.

Latourette, Kenneth Scott. *A History of the Expansion of Christianity*, 7 vols. New York: Harper & Brothers, 1937.

Neill, Stephen. *A History of Christian Missions.* Baltimore: Penguin, 1986.

Stark, Rodney. *The Rise of Christianity.* Princeton, NJ: Princeton University Press, 1996.

13

THE GOSPEL GOES EAST

Zane Pratt

The gospel didn't just go west after Pentecost. It also went east. The book of Acts follows the apostolic careers of Peter and then Paul, and the flow of the narrative naturally leads the reader north and west from Palestine into Asia Minor, and from there over to Europe. From the point where the New Testament leaves off, church history as taught in the West generally concentrates on the advance of the gospel among the ancestors of those historians in the Mediterranean world and in Europe. From the way church history is taught in Europe and North America, one could be forgiven for thinking of Christianity as a Western religion that disappeared from the continent of Asia[1] in the early centuries of its existence, only to be reintroduced for real in the early days of the modern era. Such an understanding would be wrong.

The gospel went east as well as west after Pentecost, and it flourished on the continent of its birth for many centuries. However, Christian history in the East followed a very different track than in the West. Asia itself is a different environment, with its vast size and its variety of ancient civilizations and religions. Christianity in Asia never achieved majority status and never enjoyed the protection and

The story of the gospel in Asia is a story of perseverance and missionary advance in the face of overwhelming odds. There are serious lessons that evangelicals today can learn from the advance and decline of the ancient churches of Asia.

---

[1]Throughout this chapter "Asia" refers to the modern continent of Asia, not to the Roman province of Asia, located in western modern-day Turkey.

comfort of state sponsorship as it did in Europe. The story of the gospel in Asia is a story of perseverance and missionary advance in the face of overwhelming odds. There are serious lessons that evangelicals today can learn from the advance and decline of the ancient churches of Asia.

God's Global Diaspora

God had been preparing for the advance of the gospel among the nations for many centuries before Christ, and that preparation occurred in western Asia as well as in the Mediterranean world. When the Chaldeans under Nebuchadnezzar conquered Judah in the early sixth century BC, pockets of Jews were scattered all over the Babylonian Empire, carrying with them the knowledge of the God of Israel. The subsequent absorption of the Babylonian Empire by the Persians later that century simply expanded the area of the Jewish Diaspora in Asia. The existence of this international Jewish community meant that the text of the Hebrew Bible was widely available across western Asia at the time of Jesus. There were converts to Judaism in Roman and Persian Asia in the first century AD, and there were others who were attracted to the theology, ethics, and morality of biblical Judaism but were not quite prepared to take the radical step of conversion. These communities of Jews and God-fearing Gentiles spread from the eastern shore of the Mediterranean deep into Central Asia, and they provided a ready springboard for the gospel as it moved east after Pentecost.

The book of Acts records the foundations of the church in Asia. On the day of Pentecost, there were Jews and Jewish converts from all over the Diaspora gathered in Jerusalem, and many were drawn to the sound of the apostles speaking in their native languages.

> When they heard this sound, a crowd came together in bewilderment, because each one heard their own language being spoken. Utterly amazed they asked: "Aren't all these who are speaking Galileans? Then how is it that each of us hears them in our native language? Parthians, Medes and Elamites; residents of Mesopotamia, Judea and Cappadocia, Pontus and Asia, Phrygia and Pamphylia, Egypt and the parts of Libya near Cyrene; visitors from Rome (both Jews and converts to Judaism);

Cretans and Arabs—we hear them declaring the wonders of God in our own tongues!" (Acts 2:6–11)

Parthia, Media, Elam, and Mesopotamia were all in the Persian Empire. Cappadocia, Pontus, Asia, Phrygia, and Pamphylia were part of the Roman Empire, but were located in Asian Anatolia (modern-day Turkey). Parts of Arabia were under Roman control, and other parts were under Persian control, but all of it was in Asia. Judea itself is on the western edge of the Asian continent. At the end of the second chapter of Acts, there is no indication as to how many among the three thousand new believers were from which countries, but it seems plausible that many if not most were Asians. It is no surprise that churches were subsequently to be found in these areas in the early centuries of the Christian era. Those in Anatolia remained oriented toward the West. Those outside the Roman Empire, however, looked east; and that is the direction their missionary activities would take them.

The Marginalized East

One reason why Western church historians tend to treat the Church of the East with suspicion is that the Eastern church is generally regarded as unorthodox.[2] For the most part, the Eastern church was solidly Nicene in its theology. Arianism made far deeper inroads in the Roman West than in the Persian East. In the Christological controversies that followed Nicaea,[3] however, the East charted an independent course. In terms of official allegiances, Chalcedonian Christianity made little headway east of the Roman boundary with Persia. Part of the Eastern church was Monophysite (the Armenians and the Syrian Jacobites), but the largest Christian body in the East was known as Nestorian.

---

[2]Indeed, until recently Western church historians often ignored the development of the churches east of the Roman Empire. See Philip Jenkins, *The Lost History of Christianity* (New York: HarperOne, 2008), for a provocative overview. The "Church of the East" in this chapter generally refers to the denomination or body known by that name, also frequently called the Syrian church or the Nestorians.

[3]The Council of Nicaea, AD 325, held in Nicaea (modern-day Iznik, Turkey) was the first ecumenical council of the Christian church, called by Emperor Constantine I, to solve the problem created in the Eastern church by Arianism. Arianism was a heresy proposed by an Alexandrian presbyter, Arius, who suggested that Christ was a created being, not truly divine.

Christological controversies. Monophysites held that Jesus was one person, so he must have had one and only one nature (*mono*: one; *physis*: nature). The rest of the church held that Jesus, in order to be both fully divine and fully human, must have had two full natures—one divine and one human. Nestorius, nurtured by a school of biblical interpretation based in Antioch that was passionate about the two natures of Christ, became patriarch of Constantinople in the fifth century AD. In his zeal to safeguard the reality of the two natures, he used language to describe the unity of Christ's person that others regarded as dangerously weak. Nestorius and his followers were accused of teaching that the divine Jesus and the human Jesus were two completely separate persons, who just happened to occupy the same space at the same time. In response to the Monophysite and (supposed) Nestorian positions, the Western church defined itself at the Council of Chalcedon as believing in Jesus as one person with two complete natures: human and divine, without confusion, without change, without division, and without separation. Both the Nestorians and the Monophysites were declared to be heretical by the council.

The Chalcedonian definition of Christology remains the official theological position of most of the Western church, from the Greek Orthodox and Roman Catholics to Southern Baptists and the Assemblies of God. Most of the church in the East aligned itself with the theological tradition of Nestorius. However, before the Church of the East is dismissed as hopelessly heretical, several points need to be made.

First, it now seems clear that Nestorius himself was never a Nestorian as defined by Western theologians. He may have used incautious language, but his Christology was not substantially different from that of Chalcedon.

Second, Nestorius was not the founder of the church movement that would subsequently bear his name. The Church of the East existed long before Nestorius was born. That church was already drawn to the careful, nonallegorical school of Bible teaching based in Antioch before Nestorius was condemned by the Western church. The Eastern church's alignment with Nestorius was simply the culmination of processes already begun before the split with the West took place. Thus, it is ironically accurate to say that Nestorianism is the name of a heresy in which Nestorius did not believe, and of a church movement Nestorius did not start.

Third, it also seems fair to say that Nestorianism is the name of a heresy that the "Nestorian" church movement itself did not really believe. It is true that different Eastern theologians and Eastern church councils, in reaction especially to the Monophysites, expressed themselves in incautious ways. However, the caricature of Nestorian Christology, of two totally separate Persons who just happened to occupy the same space at the same time, seems to be more of an invention of Western polemicists than an actual reality.

Orthodoxy or heresy? In assessing the orthodoxy of the Church of the East, several things need to be kept in mind. First, the Christological controversy in the Mediterranean world was conducted largely in the Greek language, and much of the dispute was over shadings of differences between Greek words. The Church of the East functioned in Aramaic, and some of these subtle differences in Greek could not readily be reproduced in their language.

Second, as with Nestorius, the motivation behind the Christological formulations of the Church of the East was a fear that Monophysite theology produced a Jesus in which his humanity was swallowed up in the infinity of his divinity. Their point was simply that Jesus has a full, real humanity as well as full, real divinity.

Third, there was a political dimension to the split with Chalcedonian Christianity as well. As long as Christians were persecuted in the Roman Empire, Christians under Persian rule were not thought of as a Roman fifth column, even though Christianity originated in Roman territory. Once Rome embraced Christianity as its official religion, however, Christians in Persian territory were regarded as potential spies and traitors. Rome was Persia's greatest enemy. Christians had experienced persecution already in Persia before the time of Constantine, but once Rome went "Christian" their situation became ever more precarious. It was highly advantageous politically for the Christians in Persia to reject the official church of the Roman/ Byzantine emperors and to embrace an identity which was declared illegal in Rome.

Fourth, it is just as unlikely that the average "Nestorian" believer could have articulated an accurate expression of Nestorian Christology as it is that the average American evangelical today could articulate an accurate expression of Chalcedonian Christology. The fact that the Church of the East of today could reach and sign a common Christological declaration with the Vatican without any sense of betraying their own theological heritage shows how little difference of substance there really was.[4] The Church of the East did indeed develop theological problems by the time of its near-demise in the High Middle Ages. However, these problems do not seem directly connected with the Christological controversies of the fourth and fifth centuries.

The Gospel Goes East

The gospel spread eastward fairly rapidly. Antioch, where the followers of Jesus were first called Christians (Acts 11:26) stands at the crossroads between Syria and Anatolia, and is not far from Upper Mesopotamia. The good news took root early in Edessa (modern Urfa in eastern Turkey), and that city just to the east of the Euphrates River became the key center both for theological education and for deliberate missionary activity to the East. Upper Mesopotamia was a major battleground between Persia and Rome, and the border between them shifted many times in the centuries between the time of Christ and the eventual collapse of Persia to the forces of Islam in the seventh century. This area became the natural bridge for the Christian faith to move into Persia.

At first, most of the converts to Christianity in the Persian Empire were either Jews or Arameans. Over time, however, Persians started coming to Christ as well. Long before the conversion of Constantine, there were Christian communities as far east as Herat in what is now Afghanistan and Samarkand in modern Uzbekistan. The gospel had also been introduced to India early in the Christian era. Indian Christian tradition states that the apostle Thomas brought the good news to the subcontinent, and the ancient Christian community in

---

[4]"Common Christological Declaration Between the Catholic Church and the Assyrian Church of the East," November 11, 1994, Vatican website, www.vatican.va/roman_curia/pontifical_councils/chrstuni/documents/rc_pc_chrstuni_doc_11111994_assyrian-church_en.html.

South India bears his name to this day. History cannot substantiate this claim of apostolic foundation. Nevertheless, we can be certain that the church in India dates back very early. The churches of India and Persia linked up over time; and although this linkage has ebbed and flowed, it has persisted in some form to this day.

In the shadow of Zoroastrianism. Around AD 226 a revolution occurred in the Persian Empire that had far-reaching consequences for the Church of the East. The Sassanians overthrew the Parthians, who had ruled Persia up to that point, and they established a brilliant dynasty that lasted until Islam swallowed them up in the seventh century. The Sassanians instituted Zoroastrianism as the state religion of Persia. That, combined with the adoption of Christianity as the state religion of Rome the following century, changed the official attitude of the Persian state toward Christianity from one of toleration to suspicion and periodic persecution.[5]

However, it was during this time that the gospel spread more aggressively than ever. Even in the environment of persecution, Christianity became a major force in Persian society. This was the period when the churches of Persia and India established their ties. Christian communities could be found all the way from Mesopotamia to the Indian border, as well as in the south of India. Nestorian missionaries were already at work among the Turkic tribes that were penetrating through Central Asia into northern Afghanistan by the sixth century.

It was also toward the end of this time that the gospel first reached China. The famous Nestorian monument in Xian, erected in AD 781, tells of the arrival of a Nestorian missionary named Alopen in 635. During the time between the arrival of this pioneer missionary and the building of the monument, Nestorian Christianity seems to have flourished under the T'ang Dynasty in China. It never attained anything close to majority status, and it always stood in the shadows of Confucianism, Taoism, and Buddhism in Chinese society. Nevertheless, Christianity made respectable inroads into China during that period of history.

---

[5]Samuel Hugh Moffett, *A History of Christianity in Asia*, vol. 1 (Maryknoll, NY: Orbis, 1998), 106ff.

There is little clear historical evidence regarding what happened after the monument was set up. The T'ang Dynasty collapsed in AD 907, however, and by the end of that century Christianity had disappeared from China. By the seventh century, Christian missions had advanced all the way across Asia. Unfortunately, by the tenth century this first advance had been partially reversed, and the gospel was no longer heard in the Far East.

In the shadow of Islam. Meanwhile, back in the Persian and Mesopotamian heartland of the Church of the East, another radical change had taken place. Muhammad died in Medina in AD 632, and within ten years the Arabic armies of Islam completely conquered the Persian Empire.

The Christians of this new Islamic Empire had a profound impact on their new masters. In the early days of the Islamic conquest, the new Muslim rulers were essentially desert nomads who knew little about how to run an empire. Education, administration, and medicine were largely in Nestorian Christian hands in the early centuries of the Umayyad and Abbasid Caliphates. The cultural brilliance of early Islamic civilization owed an enormous debt to these Christians, who conveyed the riches of classical knowledge to this new empire. However, Islam was even less tolerant of conversion out of its ranks than Zoroastrianism had been. During the Sassanian period, Nestorian Christianity had made serious inroads at the expense of the state religion. Under Islam, in the old Nestorian heartlands of Mesopotamia, Persia, and northern Arabia, Nestorianism could do no more than hold its own. It certainly survived far better than Zoroastrianism, which virtually vanished. The history of the Middle East after AD 642, however, is one of steady Islamization, with no threat from Christianity to Islam's dominant status.

Nestorian Christianity

While Islam was consolidating its hold on the Middle East, Nestorian Christianity was quietly incubating in obscurity in northern Central Asia. During the period of Nestorian presence in China in the T'ang Dynasty, some of the Turko-Mongol tribes to the northwest of China were exposed to Nestorianism, and it had taken root. There were both

Christians and Manicheans among the Uighur tribes, and the Keraits became predominantly Nestorian.

Genghis Khan. As providence would have it, the Keraits were among the early supporters of a Mongol chieftain named Temujin—better known to the world as Genghis Khan. Genghis led a confederation of Turkic and Mongol tribes to devastate and conquer more of the Eurasian continent than anyone before in history. He himself was a shamanist, but Nestorian Christians had an honored place in his retinue; and under Mongol rule the fortunes of the Church of the East revived one last time. Mongol conquest was brutal, but Mongol rule was actually fairly tolerant; and the *Pax Mongolica* that followed the conquest brought widespread communication, safe trade, and religious toleration to Asia for virtually the only time in its history.

Through the Turko-Mongol conquest of China, Nestorianism once again spread from Mesopotamia to the Pacific, and it stretched north-south from the northern steppes of Central Asia to the Thomas Christians of South India. Even in the Persian heartland, Christians were favored for a time under Mongol rule; and there were several Nestorian queens among the Mongol rulers of Persia, raising hopes of a Christian king who would finally give the Church of the East the status of ruling religion. Such hopes, however, came to nothing.

Tamerlane. The empire of Genghis splintered among his sons after his death. The Mongol ruling families in China and in the Mongolian heartland became Buddhist, while those in Central Asia and Persia embraced Islam. From its second high water mark in the thirteenth century, the Church of the East rapidly declined to the point of near-extinction by the end of the fourteenth. Timur the Lame (Tamerlane), a petty Turkic chieftain in Samarkand who conquered most of Genghis' old empire in the last half of the fourteenth century, was a rabidly anti-Christian Muslim. He did his best to exterminate Christianity from the areas he ruled. After the collapse of the Mongol dynasty in China, Nestorianism once again disappeared from the Middle Kingdom. By the fifteenth century, Christianity in Asia was reduced to the Thomas Christians in South India and a few enclaves of Nestorians in Persia and Upper Mesopotamia. There would not be another renaissance for the ancient Church of the East. Christianity would come again to Asia. The next time, however, it would come from the west.

A faded remnant. There are still relics of the Nestorian past in Asia. The Nestorian monument in Xian, China, is one. There are Nestorian graveyards in Kyrgyzstan, in the heart of Central Asia. The Thomas Christians still live in South India, although they are now divided into several factions: one that maintains its old traditions, another that has submitted to the authority of the Roman pope, and another that has become Protestant. Small pockets of Assyrian Christians still live in Iran, Turkey, and Iraq, some of whom still maintain their Nestorian identity and others who have become a Uniate church under the authority of Rome.

Even in areas where the church has disappeared entirely, the evidence of the past is still present. An embroidered hat commonly worn in northern Afghanistan displays a pattern of three crosses repeated several times; and many oriental rugs of the type known as Bukharan (which are actually Turkmen rugs that were marketed by Persian-speaking merchants from the ancient city of Bukhara) also contain this pattern of three crosses, in some cases clearly visible and in others distorted from the passage of time. The Central Asians who wear these hats and weave these rugs have no idea where this pattern comes from or what it means. They continue the tradition simply because it is tradition. Despite these faint echoes of the past, however, it is clear that the once-vibrant and far-flung Church of the East has virtually disappeared. What happened?

Why the Decline in the East?

Several theories have been proposed to explain the disappearance of these early churches in the East.

A minority church. It is true that the Church of the East was always a minority religion. It never enjoyed state protection. Quite the opposite, in fact: through most of its history, the Nestorians faced official state hostility to one degree or another. The Asian church suffered centuries of persecution—not continuously, but in waves of intensity interspersed with periods of relative peace. The final persecution, under

Timur in the fourteenth century, seems to have dealt the final blow to Nestorian vitality. In Muslim areas, the political and economic attractions of conversion to the majority faith, and the fact that conversion could only be a one-way street, slowly sapped the strength from the Nestorian community.

A foreign religion. In China, Christianity was always regarded as a foreign religion, not truly at home in the Middle Kingdom. However, the Church of the East endured incredible persecution from the Zoroastrian Sassanians and came out stronger. Why did it succumb a thousand years later?

A lost gospel. L. E. Browne, in his famous work *The Eclipse of Christianity in Asia from the Time of Muhammad till the Fourteenth Century*,[6] reasoned that the Church of the East collapsed because it eventually lost its grip on the gospel. Love for God and faith in Christ were replaced by ritual practice. Western visitors to Central and East Asia during the Mongol period frequently commented negatively on the low moral standards of the Nestorians they encountered.[7] Living faith and living holiness will sustain a community of believers through discrimination and persecution. When that faith and holiness disappear, there is little to motivate perseverance through suffering, and the community disappears.

Lessons to Learn

There are significant lessons we can learn from the history of the Church of the East. The first is the church's zeal for missions, particularly in the early centuries. These people had nothing going for them, humanly speaking. They were never more than a persecuted minority. They had no expectations of safety or comfort. The continent they were attempting to evangelize was vast, and forbidding mountains and deserts covered the center of it. The Asian civilizations they were trying to penetrate were ancient and sophisticated, with well-established religious traditions intimately interwoven into the fabric of the culture.

---

[6]Laurence Edward Browne, *The Eclipse of Christianity in Asia from the Time of Muhammad till the Fourteenth Century* (Cambridge: Cambridge University Press, 1933).
[7]Christopher Dawson, ed., *Mission to Asia: Narratives and Letters of the Franciscan Missionaries in Mongolia and China in the Thirteenth and Fourteenth Centuries* (New York: Harper Torchbooks, 1966), 144–45.

Even so, their passion for the gospel, in the midst of persecution, propelled them from one end of Asia to the other. This kind of missionary zeal, and this kind of passion for the evangelization of Asia, should stand as both a rebuke and an encouragement to modern Christians in regard to undertaking the same task.

LESSONS LEARNED

- *Missionary zeal and passion for evangelism are vital.*
- *The gospel travels through the marketplaces.*
- *Always guard the gospel.*

Second, the manner in which the Church of the East did missions is instructive. While it is true that missionary priests and monks played a role in the evangelization of Asia, they were by no means the only ones involved. In an environment where missionary support was almost impossible and where the state was often opposed to institutional Christianity, Christian merchants played a key role in the spread of Christianity across the continent. In particular, the Turkic and Mongol tribes of Central Asia seem to have been impacted significantly by Nestorian merchants traveling along the Silk Road. Business as mission is not a new idea. Actually, it probably wasn't a conscious idea at all to those early Christian traders. They were genuine businesspeople, doing real business as they carried goods from East and South Asia to the Middle East and Europe. They were also committed to their faith, so it was only natural for them to share that faith as they did their business. The combination of business and evangelism was effective. It got the Christian message into places where traditional clergy-driven missions would have been hard-pressed to enter. The same is true today; and it is particularly true in Asia, most of which is still officially hostile to the gospel.

Third, and most important, the experience of the Church of the East illustrates the critical importance of guarding the gospel. When the ancient Asian church lost its grip on the biblical gospel, it ended up losing all the ground it had gained on the largest continent in the world. Human tradition and human practice crept into the church all too easily.

The Church of the East had its roots in a school of biblical interpretation, based out of Antioch, which prided itself in its careful exegesis and its rejection of the fanciful allegorizing so common in the rival school of Alexandria. Yet over the centuries the biblical gospel was lost, replaced by rituals and ascetic practices. At the same time, ironically, biblical holiness of life seems to have been replaced with moral laxity. With a message laced with man-made traditions and with lives that no longer adorned the message they were preaching, the Asian church lost its power to persuade and even its will to survive. Purity of doctrine and purity of life are nonnegotiable in the work of the gospel, and the fate of the ancient Asian church is clear testimony to this reality.

Conclusion

The gospel spread east as well as west following the day of Pentecost. Western Christians have largely forgotten this fact, but there was a day when there were probably more followers of Jesus in Asia than in Europe. At one time there were thriving centers of Christianity in portions of what is now Turkey, Iraq, Iran, India, Afghanistan, the Central Asian republics, and China. This church was a suffering church. It never enjoyed state sponsorship. It always existed as a minority within society. It went through periods of intense persecution. And yet for a millennium and a half it thrived. It was a missionary church. From the start, churches in western Asia sought to take the gospel east into places where Jesus was not yet known. Some of this missionary activity was the work of priests and monks, but much of it was done by merchants who shared their faith as they carried out their business. Despite its early vitality, however, the Church of the East virtually disappeared in the fourteenth and fifteenth centuries. Today, this once great church exists only in small pockets in Upper Mesopotamia and South India. Locked in survival mode and bound by tradition, the tiny Church of the East gives little evidence of its mighty heritage.

The history of Christianity in Asia has important lessons to teach believers today. First, these Christians were zealous for evangelism. They carried the gospel across the largest continent in the world, through deserts and the highest mountains on earth, on foot or on horseback, with no guarantee of safety. In sharing their faith, they didn't just face the mild discomfort of personal rejection—they faced persecution that often was severe. In the face of these difficulties, they persevered for centuries in their efforts to bring the knowledge of Jesus across their continent. Their commitment to the task of the Great Commission, regardless of the cost, stands as a challenge to Western Christianity with its obsession on comfort and personal safety. Second, the Church of the East didn't leave the task of evangelism to professional clergy. Businessmen on the Silk Road carried their faith with them, and these merchants were critical to the spread of the gospel in the early centuries of Asian Christianity. They demonstrated both the responsibility and the effectiveness of laypeople in evangelism, and they unconsciously modeled the success of business as mission. Third, the experience of the Church of the East shows that the church of every time and place must guard the gospel. When the gospel is lost, the church withers and dies. Finally, however, the history of the Church of the East shows that the gospel is not foreign to Asia. It thrived there in the past. It can thrive there again.

Discussion Points

1. What kinds of difficulties and obstacles did the Church of the East face as it sought to take the gospel across Asia? How did its members respond? What does their example have to teach the modern evangelical church in the West?

2. What role did business play in the spread of the gospel in Asia? What advantages did that role bring to the task?

3. Why did the Church of the East, once larger in population and geographical scope than European Christianity, shrink into near-oblivion? What lessons do we learn from its decline?

Further Reading

Dawson, Christopher, ed. *Mission to Asia: Narratives and Letters of the Franciscan Missionaries in Mongolia and China in the Thirteenth and Fourteenth Centuries*. New York: Harper Torchbooks, 1966.

Foltz, Richard C. *Religions of the Silk Road*. New York: St. Martin's Press, 1999.

Grousset, Rene. *The Empire of the Steppes: A History of Central Asia*. Translated by Naomi Walford. New Brunswick, NJ: Rutgers University Press, 1970.

Jenkins, Philip. *The Lost History of Christianity*. New York: HarperCollins, 2008.

Moffett, Samuel Hugh. *A History of Christianity in Asia, Volume I: Beginnings to 1500*. Maryknoll, NY: Orbis, 1998.

14

MONASTICS ON MISSION

Karen O'Dell Bullock

The first-century church exploded with the powerful preaching of the gospel of the risen Jesus Christ and the coming of the Holy Spirit. Beginning around AD 64 and culminating in the "Age of Martyrs" nearly 250 years later, persecution stalked believers, seeking to eradicate their teachings. It drove the public witness of believers underground into hidden house churches, caves, and even subterranean cemeteries, where tomb art from that period still speaks to visitors today of Christian faithfulness.

After Constantine's act of toleration of Christians (Edict of Milan, AD 313), persecution ceased. Christianity went from being the despised religion to the only acceptable religion of the empire. The Roman government returned property to believers and built churches. Emperors attended the services, bringing with them the pomp and splendor of their courts. Liturgical elements enhanced the simple worship patterns of former years. A priestly class arose and new emphasis was placed upon the priestly acts: baptism, ordination, observance of the Lord's Supper.

When the state wed the church, their union birthed political and militaristic ventures as well as spiritual. As heretics launched twisted truths, the church splintered into varied schools of response, each with its own leaders, training centers, and interpretations to defend. In some corners of the Christian landscape the church's vitality waned, and by the end of the fourth century many believers feared that the church itself was compromised. Recovery of its purity and devotion to Christ was essential for survival. The monastic movement of the Roman Catholic Church was a reaction to this compromise—an attempt to rediscover the true faith.

We tend to characterize monks and nuns as spiritual separatists who isolate themselves from the world in pursuit of experiencing God through solitude and simplicity. Space does not allow a summary of the variety of monastic orders and their contributions to society and humanity. However, history reveals that throughout the centuries certain monks and nuns have focused on spreading the gospel of Jesus Christ to the world. These monastics discovered the mission of God and became active participants. This chapter tells some of their stories.[1]

GOD'S MISSIONARY ARMY: THE JESUITS

Rigorous and lengthy spiritual and intellectual training prepared Jesuits for their mission. Ignatius Loyola (1495–1556), the founder of the new order in 1540, had been a soldier who, upon reading the life of Christ and biographies of the saints, devoted the remainder of his energies to reforming the church from within and preaching the gospel to the newly discovered pagan world. In its first 30 years the order grew to 1,000 members, until, after 70 years, the order's membership numbered more than 8,500. Relentless obedience to Christ characterized the group's focus. To their three traditional vows (poverty, chastity, and obedience) the Jesuits added another—to go without question, delay, or the provision of journey-funds wherever the Pope might order "for the salvation of souls." They lived on alms and relied solely on benefactions to maintain and expand their work. Soon Loyola had

---

[1]This chapter highlights the lives and work of monastics on mission from the sixth through the twentieth centuries. Although the theological variances of these representative expressions of Christianity are pronounced, the focus here is upon individual believers who offered their lives to God in vocational missional service within the cultural and ecclesial structures available to them. Themes of simplicity, sacrifice, and service are foundational scriptural elements characterizing mature believers across the ages; see Matthew 5–7 and 1 Peter.

founded grammar schools, two colleges in Rome, and missions in India, Malaysia, the Congo, Ethiopia, Brazil, Japan, and China.

In the latter seventeenth century, Vatican officials consolidated the church's missionary outreach by establishing the "Sacred Congregation for the Propagation of the Faith," or simply *Propaganda*, a board of clerics who were charged with the responsibility of spreading the faith. Using French missionaries almost exclusively, the *Propaganda* re-exerted its control over the missions in the New World which had been established by Spain and Portugal. At about the same time, the Jesuits came under harsh opposition when the order was accused of modifying some of the church's teachings to find better acceptance within the Chinese culture. Jesuits in Portugal, Spain, and France were charged with "accommodation" and expelled by papal decrees from 1759 to 1764. Nevertheless, Jesuits continued to teach Christ and his church, to find ways to disciple new converts, and to serve the people with whom they lived.

Portraits of Mission-Hearts

"By thy God-inspired life thou didst embody both the mission and the dispersion of the Church."—From a hymn written by Saint Columba, also known as Colum Cille (meaning "dove of the church")

Columba (c. 521–597)—Celtic "dove" to the Scots. The Irish monastic movement was one of the first missionary ventures to cross central Europe and on northward into Iceland. Celtic missionaries trekked into unknown lands and built small churches and schoolrooms, surrounded by simple huts for the monks. They then built dwellings for the students and their families who soon joined them. Sending pairs of missionary brothers ahead into neighboring regions to share the gospel, a few teachers remained in each settlement to study the language of the people, translate portions of the Scriptures and hymns into the local dialects, and disciple new converts in the faith. Celtic missionaries preached justification by faith in Jesus Christ, accepted the Holy Scriptures as the source of faith and life, refused to appeal to the state for help, and avoided politics. They chose to preach the truth simply rather than to attack indigenous religions and expose errors they found. They chose from among new converts promising young men to train for church leadership, and then discipled them to maturity. Baptism followed this lengthy process. One of the greatest Celtic missionaries was Columba, whose evangelistic faith centers, 1,500 years later, still thrive today.[2]

Columba was born into a noble Irish family in County Donegal. He joined the monastic life at Clonard Abbey as a young man, where he studied with Finian (c. 495–579), under whose leadership he became a deacon and a priest. His fervor for evangelism and church planting was pronounced; he founded several churches and at least twenty-seven monasteries in Ireland alone. When he was almost forty, Columba's outspoken behavior embroiled him in a series of confrontations with his superiors that ultimately led to a battle at Cooldrevny in the year 561, where almost three thousand men were killed. This event changed his life.

Columba left Ireland for Britain, tradition says, vowing to win to Christ a number equal to those who had been slain in battle. In 563 he settled in a small community off the western coast of Scotland on a tiny wind-swept island called Iona, where waves still pound the barren landscape. Here he and his team of twelve established the traditional life of prayer, meditation, Bible study, manual labor, and a training center for evangelism. From this isolated spot, dozens of church-planting monks were sent to preach the gospel, build churches, and establish other monasteries to do the same.

Columba was a hands-on missionary. For thirty-four years he took with him several others each time he traveled into Scotland and the neighboring islands to evangelize the people who lived there. In many ways, his theological understanding was grounded as much in miracles

---

[2]E. H. Broadbent, *The Pilgrim Church* (London: Pickering and Inglis, 1974), 34-35. Columba founded monasteries in Ireland at Derry, Durrow, and probably Kells. The Kells manuscript contains elaborately beautiful illustrations, some of which may be attributed to Columba.

as in theology, ethics, and formal creeds,[3] demonstrated by his repeated confrontations with the Druids. Columba was especially instrumental in winning to Christ the Picts in the Scottish Highlands, converting King Brude, who, from inside the walls of his city, watched Columba day after day stand outside to pray for his salvation.

The influence of Celtic missionaries like Columba cannot be overestimated in these early days of the Middle Ages. While the Roman model of missionary strategy ultimately prevailed over time, the warm-hearted influence of the Celtic missionaries flavored the Christian heritage of these regions where, many years later, the modern missionary movement recaptured and advanced that initial zeal for evangelism.

> "You seem to glow with the salvation-bringing fire which our Lord came to send upon the earth."—Pope Gregory II to Boniface[4]

Boniface (Wynfrith, 680–754)—Roman "apostle" to the Europeans.[5]

Another significant monk was Boniface, missionary to the Netherlands and Germany, for whom the importance of sowing God's Word was critical.[6] Born in the village of Crediton in Devonshire, England, Wynfrith entered a Benedictine monastery as a young lad. He grew up praying several hours daily, working with his hands, and studying. He

---

[3]Kenneth Scott Latourette, *The Thousand Years of Uncertainty*, in vol. 2 of *A History of the Expansion of Christianity* (Grand Rapids: Zondervan, 1970), 54. See also Lisa Bitel, *Isle of the Saints: Monastic Settlement and Christian Community in Early Ireland* (Ithaca, NY: Cornell University Press, 1994); and Thomas Owen Clancy and Gilbert Markus, *Iona: The Earliest Poetry of a Celtic Monastery* (Edinburgh: Edinburgh University Press, 1995). Legends surrounding Columba abound. In fact, he is credited with the first sighting of a monster in the River Ness (but not actually the Loch itself), which he supposedly confronted with a cross and forced to flee.
[4]Quoted in "Letter of Gregory II" [dated 719], in James Harvey Robinson, ed., *Readings in European History*, vol. 1 (Boston: Ginn and Co., 1904), 105.
[5]Bruce L. Shelley, *Church History in Plain Language* (Waco, TX: Word, 1982), 176. Shelley notes that while the emphasis upon individual conversion was "the method used by Protestant missions under the evangelical movements of the nineteenth century, with individual change of heart," it was "mass conversion" that expanded the church and converted Europe during the Middle Ages. During all of this period, however, there were individuals who were obsessed about Christian missions and whose lives focused upon reaching those who had never heard of Christ. Boniface was such a Christian brother.
[6]Stephen Neill, *A History of Christian Missions* (New York: Penguin, 1979), 74. While Neill called Boniface the "man who had a deeper influence on the history of Europe than any Englishman who has ever lived," Boniface's efforts to be missional meant, as he and his church understood his task, that he also delivered to Europe an emphasis upon "Church over Christ, and Sacrament more than Scripture." See V. Raymond Edman, *The Light in Dark Ages* (Wheaton: Van Kampen, 1949), 192.

produced the first Latin grammar in England, a number of poems, and a treatise on metrics. He was ordained into the priesthood at age thirty, but found little satisfaction in ministering within his region. Burdened for those who had never heard the gospel of Jesus Christ, he searched for ways to take this news to other lands—particularly the continent across the English Channel.

Wynfrith took action in the year 716 when he left his monastery to share the gospel with the Frisians in Holland, unfortunately to be met with opposition and indifference until he aborted the mission as unsuccessful. He returned home only to gird himself for another launch— this time to Rome, to garner the endorsement of Pope Gregory II for his plan to see Europe converted. With this support in hand, Wynfrith traveled back to Germany, to the Low Countries, and on to Bavaria and Thuringia, sharing with the inhabitants of hamlets and villages along the way. So many Hessians came to faith that in 723 Gregory summoned Wynfrith back to Rome to give account of his work, urging him to accept the position of monastery abbot, a powerful and influential administrative post. When Wynfrith declined, desiring instead to spend his life in missions, Gregory pledged his own resources to sustain Wynfrith, now called Boniface, and consecrated him a missionary bishop to Germany. His life then changed dramatically.

Immediately upon returning to Germany, Boniface observed the weak faith of the so-called believers. Some had mixed magical arts and pagan practices with Christianity, worshiping gods they believed to dwell in forests. Outraged at this sacrilege, Boniface performed an act of Old Testament proportions when he assembled the people before the sacred oak of Thor, which stood near the swamps of Geismar. With relentless strokes, his axe struck the trunk of the massive tree until it fell and broke into four pieces, causing the people to declare the superiority of the Christian God. He then used its timber to build a prayer chapel.

Soon Boniface abandoned his practice of smashing pagan sites, committing himself instead to dialoguing with the people. He asked questions about their so-called gods: their origins, their seemingly human attributes, their relationships with the beginning of the world. This method resulted in devout conversions, and Boniface and his team built churches and cloisters and discipled the new converts. Large numbers of women joined the missionary ranks.[7] Later, Boniface founded the famous monastery at Fulda, still today a center of Catholic Christianity in Germany, and served as the bishop of Mainz, calling five councils between 742 and 747 to deal with clerical reform and heresy. Although his vision of the church included a rigid uniformity to Roman practice that ultimately stifled other expressions of Christianity, his heart for missions prevailed at the end.

Boniface resigned his administrative posts in 753 to return to Holland, where, as a simple evangelist, he spent his last year devoted to the lost. In the still largely unevangelized Frisia, Boniface saw many people converted. He lived his last hours at Dorkum on the bank of the Borne River, where he and fifty assistants were erecting tents in which to celebrate the confirmation of a group of new believers. Before they finished, however, a horde of marauding thugs thundered through the clearing and slaughtered Boniface and all of his brothers. Boniface lived and died concerned for those who had never heard of Christ. To his last breath, his desire was to share the gospel with them.[8]

> "Death has no terrors for a sincere servant of Christ who is laboring to bring souls to a knowledge of the truth."[9]—Raymond Lull to his Muslim captors in 1307

Raymond Lull (1235–c. 1315)—Bridge-builder to the Muslims. The impact of the military conquests of the two hundred years between 1095 and 1291 stained the pages of church history and, perhaps like no

---

[7]Ruth Tucker, *From Jerusalem to Irian Jaya* (Grand Rapids: Zondervan, 1983), 48–49. Tucker includes Kenneth Scott Latourette's telling comment, "For the first time in a number of centuries, we find women taking an active part in missions. . . . Not until again in the nineteenth century—unless it may be in the Mennonite enterprise of the eighteenth century—do we find them so prominent as representatives of the faith among newly Christian peoples." Kenneth Scott Latourette, *The Thousand Years of Uncertainty*, in vol. 2 of *A History of the Expansion of Christianity* (Grand Rapids: Zondervan, 1970), 95.

[8]C. H. Talbot, *The Anglo-Saxon Missionaries in Germany* (Lanham, MD: Sheed and Ward, an imprint of Rowman & Littlefield Publishing Group, 1954), 23–149. When the new converts arrived on the scene, they found Boniface murdered, still clutching a copy of Ambrose's "The Advantage of Death," which bore two deep slashes. This volume is on display today at the Deanery Cathedral Museum, next to the Dom Cathedral, in Fulda, Germany.

[9]Quoted from Lull's *Vita Prima*, in Charles Hardwick, *A History of Missions During the Middle Ages* (Oxford: originally published by Oxford University Press; repr., Macmillan, 1863), 365.

other series of events, left a lingering callosity with which believers and Muslims still must deal in the twenty-first century. Called the Crusades and launched from Europe, these conquests attempted to wrest back from the Muslims the Holy Lands held sacred by both Jews and Christians. The Roman Catholic Church desired to regain and expand its territory, but demonstrated little care for the souls of the Saracens as they launched the offensives. This series of unholy wars cost thousands of lives on both sides, killing innocents from Britain to Jerusalem, and ended in little territorial change. The Crusades distanced factions of the eastern and western halves of the church and created bitter enmity between Muslims and Christians that would last for the next millennium. Not all professing Christians approved of the militaristic methods the church used to deal with the Muslims, however. Raymond Lull is a fine example of those who viewed Muslims as potential brothers and sisters in Christ; and despite the church's edicts, he spent his life trying to reach them.

Raymond Lull was born on the island of Majorca off the coast of Spain, a land that had been reclaimed from the Muslims not long before his birth. His wealthy father gave him a knight's education, even though Raymond chose wild living and decadence over study. As a young man, Raymond was appointed to court to supervise the King of Aragon's feast tables, where he won acclaim as a fine poet, possessing both intellectual and creative genius.

In July of 1266, at thirty years of age, Raymond experienced a radical conversion, complete with mystical visions and a fierce renunciation of all that he had previously squandered. He arranged financial provision for his wife and two children, gave the remainder of his wealth to the poor, and resigned his court position. Forsaking comfort and convinced that devotion to Christ dictated a reclusive life, Raymond moved to a cell where he spent his days fasting, praying, and meditating on Scripture. A second vision, however, which Lull later related in *The Tree of Love*, redirected him to invest the remainder of his life in missions—to win the Saracens for Christ.

Lull's first step was preparation. For nine years he studied Arabic with a Muslim slave; and when a tragic fight took the life of this slave, Raymond resolved more than ever to serve God. He wrote 321 books in Latin, Catalan, and Arabic, many of which were directed to Islam's challenges to Christianity. His book *Ars Major Generalis* (1275) wrestled with the Muslim philosophers Avicenna and Averroës on the grounds that Christianity was rational, a new method of cross-cultural and interfaith bridge-building. Further, his *Libre de Contemplacio en Deu* proclaimed that the Holy Land should be conquered "by love, prayers, and the shedding of tears and blood" rather than by force of arms.[10] Influenced by Francis of Assisi's courage in sharing Christ with Sultan Saladin's nephew, Sultan Malik al-Kamil, Lull was emboldened to follow in similar steps.

Lull founded schools to train missionaries to Muslims, teaching theology, philosophy, Arabic, and the geography of Muslim lands. He journeyed to North Africa, visiting at length with the Muslim intellectuals, or *ulema*. His words lacked season at times, enraging those for whom he cared most. At the same time, his evangelistic-philosophical bridge was not wholly embraced by the church. His forceful contrasts between Christianity and Islam seem insensitive to modern thinkers, yet his motive of love was unwavering. He suffered imprisonment, was banished twice, and lived for years in hiding. At eighty years of age, Lull traveled back to his beloved Tunis and Algiers to make a last attempt to share Christ. The next year, on June 30, 1315, he was set upon by a Muslim mob in Bugia, Algiers, and stoned to death.[11]

Despite his many failings, Lull's keen intellect, which discovered ways to build bridges of understanding, and his sharp perception that the "enemy" must first know the love of Christians, makes Raymond Lull a mission model for the kingdom today.

"The good odour of our faith began to be spread throughout China."[12]
—Written by Matteo Ricci upon the good reception of the 1584 Chinese translation of the Ten Commandments

---

[10]Samuel M. Zwemer, *Raymond Lull: First Missionary to the Moslems* (New York: Funk and Wagnalls, 1902), 53.

[11]Ibid., 142–43.

[12]Louis J. Gallagher, trans., *China in the Sixteenth Century: The Journals of Matthew Ricci, 1583–1610* (New York: Random House, 1953). This volume is an English translation of Nicola Trigault's Latin manuscript of Ricci's Italian diaries and other letters, published after Ricci's death in 1615.

Matteo Ricci (1552–1610)—Jesuit scientist-philosopher to the Chinese. Christian influence in China followed the Nestorian pattern from the sixth through the thirteenth centuries, after which time Friar John, a Catholic missionary, came to preach under the protection of the Mongols. The next century saw the suffocation of Christianity as the Ming Dynasty expelled all Christians. By the time Matteo Ricci came to Macao, almost two hundred years later, mission work was starting afresh. Ricci's influence upon the educated classes of China across the next twenty-seven years resulted in laying a permanent foundation of Christianity—the faith that today resides in the lives of countless millions.

Matteo Ricci was born the son of an Italian aristocrat in 1552 in Macerata, Italy. He studied in Rome, where he mastered law, mathematics, cosmology, astronomy, theology, and philosophy. Joining the Jesuit order when he was almost twenty, Ricci longed to be a missionary to Asia—like Francis Xavier, whose ministry in India and Japan was legendary. Ricci followed in his steps as he traveled first to Goa, where Xavier himself had established educational work among the children. After four years, and impatient to work at higher levels of intellectual discourse, Ricci received his orders to the Portuguese port city of Macao.

He arrived in the coastal city in 1582. Considered a foreign spy, Ricci determined that in order to gain the trust of the people he must present himself as a "Chinese among the Chinese." He learned the Chinese language and fell in love with the culture. He shaved his head and donned a Buddhist monk's robe. And after a number of years, Ricci saw people converted, a church planted, and the exchange of mutual respect. He changed his attire to that of a Confucian scholar so that even more doors would open for him, and soon found welcome in the inner circles of the literati.

The political and intellectual context of late Ming society held the potential for beneficial contact between Christianity and the educated Chinese. Since the intellectuals sought reform on a moral platform and were receptive to reading and discussing the merits of the Christian message, they became Ricci's target group for evangelism. He refuted the errors in Buddhism and Daoism while, at the same time, affirming what humanistic elements were congruent between Confucian philosophy and the moral teachings of Christianity. On a scientific level, Ricci satisfied the curiosity of the Chinese by demonstrating fascinating knowledge of large and small clocks; mathematical and astronomical instruments; prisms; musical instruments; oil paintings and prints; cosmographical, geographical, and architectural works with diagrams and maps of towns and buildings; and large volumes, magnificently printed and splendidly bound.[13] He became a scholar of scholars.

In 1601 Ricci moved to Beijing and became the emperor's protected clock-winder, and for the next decade ministered to the Chinese with opportunities afforded few other foreigners. His central passion was always to convince the Chinese of the universal value of Christianity. By mastering the language and presenting himself first in the manner of a Buddhist monk and then as a Confucian scholar, he demonstrated his view that Western customs were not essential to the universal claims of Christianity. Instead, Ricci's ministry was characterized by an exchange of ideas that enhanced respect on both sides for both cultures. He held out the possibility that any particular culture can be the receptacle of Christian truth.[14]

> "By blood, I am Albanian. By citizenship, an Indian. By faith, I am a Catholic nun. As to my calling, I belong to the world. As to my heart, I belong entirely to the Heart of Jesus."[15]—Mother Teresa

Agnes Gonxha Bojaxhiu (1910–1997)—Mother Teresa of Calcutta, Sister of Charity to the world. Tiny in form but colossal in faith, Mother Teresa's life mission was proclaiming God's love for humanity, especially for the poorest of the poor. Teresa was born as Agnes Bojaxiu on August 26, 1910, in Skopje, Macedonia, in the former Yugoslavia. She became an active member of her church youth group and, encouraged by her pastor, participated in missions. When just seventeen, she responded to God's call and became a missionary nun when she joined an

---

[13]Joseph Brucker, "Matteo Ricci," in *Catholic Encyclopedia*, New Advent website, www.newadvent.org/cathen/13034a.htm.

[14]See the excellent review of Ricci's work in Chung-Yan Joyce Chan, "Commands from Heaven: Matteo Ricci's Christianity in the Eyes of Ming Confucian Officials," *Missiology: An International Review*, vol. XXXI, no. 3 (July 2003): 269–87.

[15]"Mother Teresa of Calcutta (1910–1997)," Vatican website, www.vatican.va/news_services/liturgy/saints/ns_lit_doc_20031019_madre-teresa_en.html.

Irish order well known for its work among the poor in India. She taught geography in a convent school and soon became its principal. After a bout with tuberculosis, however, she stepped down from convent teaching and was sent away to recuperate.

On the train to Darjeeling, Teresa sensed that God was speaking to her heart. She moved to Calcutta, where she opened a school in the slums for the poorest children. She learned the basics of medicine and visited the homes of the sick. She also found men, women, and children dying on the streets who had been rejected by local hospitals as hopeless cases. Her heart broke over these "wounded ones" who became increasingly dear to her. These were her own people—gifts from God that no one else wanted. In 1949 several of her former pupils joined her work, renting a small room so they could care for those who were otherwise condemned to die helplessly in gutters. This caring group became known as the Missionaries of Charity.[16]

The City of Calcutta then provided the place where Teresa and twelve other helpers opened the first "Home for the Dying." Increasingly called "Mother Teresa" by those to whom she brought hope, this gentle, quiet woman continued to establish more homes for the dying and unwanted, lepers, and AIDS victims. In 1966 the Missionaries of Charity Brothers was founded, an organization of men also called to minister to the poor alongside of the sisters. Homes for the unwanted then opened in Rome, Tanzania, Australia, and South Bronx, New York.

Mother Teresa also gained worldwide acclaim for her tireless efforts on behalf of world peace. Her work earned numerous humanitarian awards, including the Nobel Peace Prize in 1979. In receiving this award, she revolutionized the ceremony itself, insisting on a departure from the ceremonial banquet and asking that the funds (six thousand dollars that year) be donated to the poor in Calcutta instead. She quietly said that earthly rewards were important only as they could help her provide for the world's needy people—and this sum would feed hundreds for a year. Beginning in 1980, homes began to spring up around the world for drug addicts, prostitutes, and battered women, along with

---

[16]"Mother Teresa: The Early Years," Global Catholic Network website, www.ewtn.com/
motherteresa/life.htm.

more orphanages and schools for poor children. In 1985 the first hospice for AIDS victims opened in New York, and later homes were added in San Francisco and Atlanta. The United States conferred upon Mother Teresa the Medal of Freedom, the highest US civilian award.

In 1991 Mother Teresa returned to her native Albania (now Serbia) and opened a home in Tirana. By this time there were also 168 homes established in India.[17] Despite severe health problems, during her final years of life Mother Teresa continued to respond to the needs of the destitute. By 1997 her sisters numbered more than 4,000 and, together with the brothers and one million co-workers, operated more than 450 centers in 40 countries around the world. Mother Teresa died on September 5, 1997, and was honored with a state funeral by the government of India. She would have preferred that such expense be better utilized by helping to feed or clothe or heal others.

Mother Teresa left a testament of unshakable faith, invincible hope, and extraordinary love. Jesus commended those who *in his name* feed the hungry, bring water, provide a home, clothe the poor, heal the sick, and care for those in prison. "Truly I tell you, whatever you did for one of the least of these brothers and sisters of mine, you did for me" (Matthew 25:40). Mother Teresa offered to the world a model of missionary simplicity, sacrifice, and service—a life so consumed by the sheer overflowing love of Christ that he spilled out onto everyone she met.

Conclusion

These stories represent radical Christians through the ages who have sought to live wholly unto God. Their lives have preached profound sermons about God's mission. What may be learned today from lessons like these? Among others, missional living requires an utter trust in God and the willingness to risk, for it may lead to stepping outside of traditional forms and exact a heavy price. Although age and maturity

---

[17]"Mother Teresa: A Vocation of Service," Global Catholic Network website, www.ewtn .com/motherteresa/vocation.htm. That webpage also recounts that on February 3, 1994, at a National Prayer Breakfast, sponsored by the US Senate and House of Representatives in Washington, DC, eighty-three-year-old Mother Teresa challenged the audience on such topics as family life and abortion. She said, "Please don't kill the child. I want the child. Give the child to me."

may be factors, the preparation of the soul is as essential as the training of the mind. Ultimately, God is the One who accomplishes his mission—not human beings apart from him. Today he is writing the present chapter; and the kingdom's prayer warriors, communicators of the gospel, evangelists, church planters, resource "networkers," and justice-seekers are still answering God's call to agitate for restoration in his world. Whether old or young, rich or poor, male or female, formally educated or untrained, God calls to kingdom assignments those he can trust with his eternal purposes.

Discussion Points

1. We tend to think of Christian monks and nuns as cloistered individuals who seldom engage with the outside world. Is this true? What was the preoccupation of the monastic missionaries of this chapter?

2. In what ways did the monastic missionaries defy their cultural norms to follow Christ and participate in God's mission? What are some cultural norms that you would have to consider to do the same?

3. How could the spiritual disciplines of poverty, chastity, and obedience be refocused and applied in your life? Your community of faith? Your denomination?

4. In what ways did the monastic missionaries in this chapter address issues of social justice in their contexts? Did this advance the cause of God's mission? How could you demonstrate your devotion to Christ with similar results?

Further Reading

Clancy, Thomas Owen, and Gilbert Markus. *Iona: The Earliest Poetry of a Celtic Monastery*. Edinburgh: Edinburgh University Press, 1995.

Gallagher, Louis J., trans. *China in the Sixteenth Century: The Journals of Matthew Ricci, 1583–1610*. New York: Random House, 1953.

Latourette, Kenneth Scott. *The Thousand Years of Uncertainty*. In vol. 2 of *A History of the Expansion of Christianity*. Grand Rapids: Zondervan, 1970.

Neill, Stephen. *A History of Christian Missions*. New York: Penguin, 1979.

Simons, Walter. *Cities of Ladies: Beguine Communities in the Medieval Low Countries, 1200–1565.* The Middle Ages Series. Philadelphia: University of Pennsylvania Press, 2001.

Tucker, Ruth. *From Jerusalem to Irian Jaya.* Grand Rapids: Zondervan, 1983.

Zwemer, Samuel M. *Raymond Lull: First Missionary to the Moslems.* New York: Funk and Wagnalls, 1902.

15

Post-Reformation
Missions Pioneers

R. Alton James

That goes together like RC Cola and a moon pie" was a phrase I heard as a child when someone wanted me to understand that two things naturally went together. For many twenty-first-century Christians the concepts of Christianity and missions are as natural as "an RC Cola and a moon pie." Why, of course, they go together. However, that has not always been the case. We will review the process that Protestant Christians after the Reformation went through to make a shift from thinking missions had been accomplished, to understanding that they were under the mandate as well.

In our contemporary world Christians are challenged to be "radical" in their approach to living for Christ and in taking the gospel to the unreached peoples of the world. This theme is really an old theme being played to new music. The Christian world has "discovered" cell groups and house churches as being new approaches, but in reality they are old approaches in a new setting. Denominations and individual Christians today struggle with how to engage a sinful world without becoming infected by the sin. In our efforts to give guidance we struggle with the issue of legalism. After the Reformation, which began in 1517, the church faced all these issues. Let's explore these topics to understand the story and ponder the implications for us today.

The Story to Understand: The Missionless Era

Ed Stetzer, missional strategist and researcher, maintains that one of the tragedies of the Reformation was the Protestant loss of a "missional focus," which the Catholic Church used as part of its argument that the Protestant churches were defective.[1] Between 1500 and 1700 the Catholic Church converted more people in the newly discovered world than it lost in Europe due to the Reformation. Why, generally, weren't the early Reformation leaders focused on missions?

Theology. The first reason would be the theology of the Reformers. In order to inform people of the great work God is doing today, I often start missions presentations by quoting Colossians 1:6, in which Paul declares the gospel "that has come to you. In the same way, the gospel is bearing fruit and growing throughout the whole world—just as it has been doing among you since the day you heard it and truly understood God's grace." The Reformers used the same verse to declare that, from their perspective, the Great Commission was intended for the original apostles and not their successors. Martin Luther, John Calvin, and many other early Reformers assumed that the apostles had completed the Great Commission, and the message had fallen on deaf ears. Since the message had been rejected, the sins of the fathers would be visited on their descendants. Their belief was that the church did not have the power or the responsibility to commission missionaries. Also, some Reformers' view of the sovereignty of God lessened the responsibility of humanity. The expansion of the church was the work of God alone. Couple this with the belief that the second coming of Christ was near, and the Reformers' theology had little or no room for missions activity.

Struggles and divisions. A second factor centered upon the struggles and divisions of the early Protestant churches in the sixteenth and seventeenth centuries. The poor economic status of many early churches prohibited, or at least inhibited, mission work. The Thirty Years War in Germany (1618–1648) produced economic and social hardships, and the church was basically in a survival mode. At the conclusion of the

---

[1]Ed Stetzer, *Planting New Churches in a Postmodern Age* (Nashville: Broadman & Holman, 2003), 23. See also Stephen Neill, *A History of Christian Missions*, 2nd ed. (New York: Penguin, 1986), 188.

war, the German Reformed religion was made a legal religion in the country. An additional problem was that the only thing the early Reformers were unanimous on was their hatred for Rome and the pope.

Isolation. The isolation of Protestant Europe from the newly discovered mission areas of the world also contributed to a lack of missionary zeal. Protestant countries had little access to or communication with the outside world. Protestant Europe was also more concerned with its economic interests than the spiritual welfare of people. As late as 1792, the British would not allow William Carey to travel on their ships because his role as missionary was seen as inconsequential at best, and a threat to developing commerce at worst. Carey had to travel on a Dutch vessel.

No Protestant missionary orders. The Roman Catholic Church utilized the religious orders, which included the Franciscans, Dominicans, and the Society of Jesus, or Jesuits, as their missionaries. These orders were under the control of the Catholic Church and could be deployed to accomplish the mission work of the church. The Protestants did not have any groups comparable to the Catholic orders. The Protestants appeared to be more concerned with winning the Catholics, while the Catholics were traveling to the newly discovered lands and converting the nationals.

Pause to Ponder

First, a faulty theology served as a hindrance to the early Protestant Church being involved in missions. A proper theology will result in the church doing missions. When the church fails to do missions, there is a failure in fulfilling the purpose that God desires. The church must remain faithful in teaching and following the missions mandate of the Lord. Are there issues of theology that may be hindering the church of the twenty-first century in doing missions?

Second, a lack of contact and information hindered the mission efforts of the Reformation Church. It is vital for Christians to be aware of the peoples of the world who still need to hear the gospel of Christ. As people become more aware of the needs, they will become more involved in praying, giving, and going for missions. How can we enable members of our churches to learn of the need of the people groups of the world to hear and respond to the message of salvation?

The Story to Understand: First Sparks

Even with these limiting factors there were still some brief flickers of the missionary flame from the early Reformation movement. Trading companies of European nations expanded their trading horizons as they sent ships around the world; and as these ships made their voyages, chaplains traveled with the crews. Though the crew was their primary focus, some chaplains sought to share the message of Christ with nationals in port cities. At various times, trading companies issued orders against this practice. Yet, in a limited way, the gospel was taken to the ends of the earth via the efforts of some chaplains.

Another early example of missions from the Reformation took place when John Calvin sent dozens of his followers to France, and in 1555 he also sent workers to establish a colony for the purpose of evangelizing nationals in Brazil. The success of both adventures was limited at best, and Jesuits eventually overtook the Brazilian colony.

The first Lutheran missionary was Justinian von Welz (1621–1668), the son of an Austrian nobleman. He penned four tracts (1663–1664) challenging Protestants to the task of world missions. In one instance he wrote:

> Is it right that we evangelical Christians keep the gospel to ourselves alone, and never seek to spread it? . . . that we have so many theological students everywhere and give them no opportunity . . . in the spiritual vineyard . . . but prefer to make them wait . . . for a parish . . . ? Is it right that we evangelical Christians spend so much money on all kinds of ostentatious dress, luxuries of food and drink, many unnecessary amusements and expensive habits, but until now have given no thought to . . . spreading the gospel?[2]

Justinian's passionate calls fell upon deaf ears and he was unable to gain the support of the Lutheran officials, but he still went as a missionary to the Dutch colony of Suriname, where he served until his death. His

---

[2]James A. Scherer, *Justinian Welz: Essays by an Early Prophet of Mission* (Grand Rapids: Eerdmans, 1969), 59. See also Gerald H. Anderson, ed., *Biographical Dictionary of Christian Missions* (Grand Rapids: Eerdmans, 1999), s.v. "Welz, Justinian von."

writings, and the commitment of his own life to the task of missions, would inspire others to be obedient.

Pause to Ponder

First, those Christians who either work in international settings or travel abroad can expand their purpose by using the opportunity to share the gospel, reflecting the role that some of the trading company chaplains filled.

Second, sometimes we can have good intentions, like Calvin, with our missions efforts, but the results do not develop the way we anticipated. "Failures" occur in missions, so expect some along the way. Learn from them and commit to remain faithful even after experiencing disappointments.

Third, the challenges from the pen of Welz are as biting today as when they were written. How can we not be stirred to action when we know of the lost condition of the world? As our college and seminary graduates and current ministers search for churches to serve, could it be that their search area needs to be global as they think about people groups that need to hear the gospel for the first time? Should greater consideration be given to planting churches that may not look like the churches of the past in terms of composition, buildings, worship styles, and structure? What does the way we spend our money as individuals, churches, and conventions say about our commitment to the Great Commission? Are we giving sacrificially?

The Story to Understand: Anabaptists

The missional outlook for Protestants at the time of the Reformation appeared to be dismal at best and needed a new paradigm in order to change course. Ed Stetzer asserts, "Church planting is done properly when leaders make a decision to engage an unchurched world in radical fashion."[3] One group that attempted to engage the world in this "radical fashion" was the Anabaptists (re-baptizers) of the Radical Reformation, who went beyond the reforms of Luther, Calvin, and Ulrich Zwingli

---

[3]Stetzer, *Planting New Churches*, 13.

when they practiced believer's baptism. They connected their belief regarding baptism with the concept of taking the gospel to the nations in the Great Commission, since both the going and baptizing were in the same passage. Hans Kasdorf notes that for Anabaptists, "The missionary mandate and radical obedience were considered to be inseparable ingredients for a life of discipleship under Christ's lordship."[4]

The Missionary Conference of Augsburg (August 20–24, 1527) resulted in a missions strategy. Prior to this meeting the Anabaptist strategy focused on finding people with similar backgrounds, using itinerant preachers, establishing house churches, emphasizing the authority of Scripture, including laity in evangelism and leadership, and accepting the reality of persecution (the names of two thousand martyrs are listed, and estimates range as high as five thousand).[5] These concepts were enlarged after the conference to focus on gathering people into local congregations and developing a systematic approach to sending out missionaries under the authority of the local church. The missionaries usually worked in teams of three.[6] George H. Williams was impressed with "the mobility, the purposefulness, and the testimonial missionary urgency of every convert, whether a commissioned elder or the steadfast wife of a weaver evangelist."[7]

Even though the Anabaptists didn't achieve their ambitious desire to expand the kingdom of God to "the Turks, Tartars, Greeks, Jews, and heathen,"[8] they did achieve a more important accolade—they were found faithful.

Pause to Ponder

Christians today should be challenged by the faithfulness of the Anabaptists. Like the Anabaptists, whose success could only be partially determined by their numbers, the church today must measure success by faithfulness. Numerical growth is important because numbers represent

---

[4]Hans Kasdorf, "The Anabaptist Approach to Mission," in *Anabaptism and Mission* (Scottdale, PA: Herald Press, 1984), 52.
[5]Ibid., 53–58.
[6]Ibid., 58–65.
[7]George H. Williams, *The Radical Reformation* (Philadelphia: Westminster, 1962), 845.
[8]Ibid., 246.

individuals trusting the Lord. Even in situations where great numbers are not trusting in Christ, however, the ultimate measure of success is the believer's faithfulness to be obedient to the calling of living a life marked by radical discipleship.

David Garrison identifies ten elements that are found in every church-planting movement: extraordinary prayer, abundant evangelism, intentional planting of reproducing churches, emphasis on the authority of God's Word, local leadership, lay leadership, house churches, churches planting churches, rapid reproduction, and healthy churches.[9] A comparison of this list with the strategies of the Anabaptists reveals remarkable similarities. The Anabaptists were basically following practices found in church-planting movements today, yet they didn't experience what would be considered a church-planting movement. Missionaries in the past and today have been faithful to their tasks without always seeing a resulting movement of multiplying churches. That's OK. There are steps missionaries can take to contribute to the development of a church-planting movement, but it must always be acknowledged that such movements of the gospel are the work and gift of God.

The Story to Understand: Pietists

A radical challenge to the traditional thinking of Protestantism came to the post-Reformation churches through Pietism. The roots of the modern mission movement are firmly planted in Pietism. Stephen Neill maintains, "The history of missions supported by churches on the European continent begins only with the emergence of the movement called Pietism."[10]

Philip Spener. The Pietists were orthodox in their theology, but stressed experience and the implications of the gospel beyond a narrow confessional interpretation. Philip Spener (1635–1705) became the major spokesman and preacher for Pietism in Germany. He was one of the first Lutherans to understand and apply Martin Luther's teaching of the priesthood of the believer. In fact, Spener perhaps understood

---

[9]David Garrison, *Church Planting Movements: How God Is Redeeming a Lost World* (Midlothian, VA: WIGTake Resources, 2004), 172.
[10]Stephen Neill, *A History of Christian Missions*, 2nd ed. (New York: Penguin, 1986), 194.

and implemented the conviction even more than Luther.

Spener had read some of the German mystics and English Puritans as well as traveled in several Protestant countries. In 1666 he settled in Frankfurt, Germany, as chief pastor in that area, and began to set in motion certain changes. He gathered small groups in his home for Bible reading, prayer, and religious discussions for the purpose of deepening the spiritual life. These groups were given the name *collegia pietatis* (Latin for "schools of piety").

In 1675 Spener wrote *Pia Desideria* ("Devout Wishes," or "Heart's Desires").[11] This work had three major parts. In the first section, Spener set forth the corrupt conditions in the church. In the second, he indicated the possibility of effecting change in order to improve these conditions. He looked back at the problems faced by the New Testament churches and the early church, and then showed that in light of Christian history change could come. Finally, Spener proposed a series of changes designed to meet the problems. These changes included more extensive use of Scripture; stress upon the priesthood of all believers; an emphasis upon practice versus knowledge in Christianity because the believer should not only know, but also do; personal conversion; holiness; close fellowship in the group; and responsibility for witness to others. In addition, Spener addressed the matter of religious controversies and encouraged that sermons be for edification rather than for controversial discourse. He called for changes in the schools and universities and in the training of ministers, including modifications in preaching and in preaching technique.

At first these proposals were well received, but gradually their implications became clear and opposition arose. This stress on inwardness and on morality was out of place in Lutheranism. When Pietists began to criticize dancing, playing cards, going to the theater, and other controversial issues, a great deal of opposition arose. Spener finally ended up in Berlin. With the support of the emperor, he continued to exert influence in breaking down scholasticism and in injecting new life into Lutheranism. The universities of Saxony closed their doors to the new

---

[11]Philip Jacob Spener, *Pia Desideria*, trans. and ed. Theodore G. Tappert (Philadelphia: Fortress, 1964).

sect, and the Pietists opened their own university at Halle in 1694. For ten years Spener built up the school.

A. H. Francke. The second major spokesman for Pietism was A. H. Francke (1663–1727). Francke was a professor at Leipzig, where, in 1687, he experienced what he described as "a divine new birth." Francke spent some time with Spener and fully adopted his outlook. Soon opposition arose, and eventually Francke was forced out of Leipzig. But he secured a professorship at the University of Halle, which was to become the major center of Pietism for the next several decades.

Francke not only stressed the matter of an inward experience and ethical concerns, but also began many benevolent enterprises. He set up homes for orphans and poor children, as well as a publishing agency to distribute the Bible. He aroused a zeal for missions in Halle, and soon missionaries were going out to many parts of the world. The Pietists comprised an evangelical wing within Lutheranism, not a separate church. The movement flourished until Francke's death in 1727, at which time it continued in influence, though not to the extent as under Spener and Francke.

Pause to Ponder

First, Pietism's commitment to the priesthood of the believer is interesting in light of contemporary discussions. Do we believe in the priesthood of the *believer* or the priesthood of the *believers*? The concept of the priesthood of the *believer* developed in reaction to restrictions of the Roman Catholic Church regarding who could read and interpret Scripture. Luther and the leaders of Pietism rejected the concept that this privilege should be limited to priests of the Catholic Church. The concept of the priesthood of the *believers* developed as a safeguard against relativism and letting each believer determine the tenets of the faith. This concept brings accountability that affirms essential doctrinal beliefs. In reality, both concepts are needed for evangelical believers today.

Second, though a complete overview and critique of Pietism is beyond the scope of this chapter,[12] it is clear that the movement's emphasis upon right behavior alongside right doctrine was a refreshing

---

[12]For more on this subject, see Dale W. Brown, *Understanding Pietism* (Grand Rapids: Eerdmans, 1978); and the entire issue of *Christian History* V, no. 2 (1986).

wind of renewal for the church. Right behavior included ministering to the needs of others and being a people of missions. Right belief without right behavior still left Christians short of what God desires. A vibrant expression of faith takes place when the two are interwoven.

Third, the use of small groups for studying the Word of God and for having accountability was a forerunner of what we call cell groups or even house churches. The concept was radical in the seventeenth and eighteenth centuries, and continues to be viewed that way by many today. Yet the number of cell groups and house churches is exploding around the world. The desire to control or institutionalize these communities deprives them of the impulse that gave them birth.

Fourth, Alan Hirsch identifies the following six elements of the DNA of the first-century church, which he calls its "apostolic genius": (1) recognition that Jesus is Lord of their personal lives and their corporate life; (2) disciple-making as reflected in Matthew 28:19; (3) missional-incarnational impulse of engaging lostness; (4) apostolic environment in which leadership impacts the social environment; (5) organic systems that are not blocked by centralized institutions; and (6) *communitas*, which are groups that look beyond themselves.[13] Pietism contained each of these fundamentals. Are these appropriate elements for the contemporary church? What would need to change in your personal life, the life of your church, and the life of your denomination in order to return to this DNA?

Fifth, Pietism unfortunately degenerated, in its worst expressions, to a legalistic approach with a list of dos and don'ts that determined one's faithfulness and commitment. The desire for holiness was commendable, but the resulting legalism was regrettable. Christians continue to struggle with measurements of holiness and legalism. Legalism stifles the church, though the lack of acceptable standards of living leads to anarchy.

The Story to Understand: Halle University

The cultivation of the missionary phase took place within the fertile soil of Halle University. The original impetus came when King

---

[13]Alan Hirsch, *The Forgotten Ways* (Grand Rapids: Brazos Press, 2006), 18–19.

Frederick IV of Denmark developed a concern for the Indians in the Danish colony of Tranquebar in southeast India. No one from Denmark was willing to undertake the task, so the king looked to Halle University for recruits. Francke recommended Bartholomäus Ziegenbalg and Heinrich Plütschau for this endeavor.

In 1706 these two men became the first Protestant missionaries to reach India, but they were not welcomed by either the Danish traders or the chaplains of the East India Company. Indians of the higher castes viewed them with disdain, and those from the lower castes showed no interest in their message. In Europe the mission received scathing remarks from Lutherans; encouragement both in words and finances came primarily from Halle University. Plütschau worked faithfully in Tranquebar until he returned to Europe in 1711 to respond to the critics of the mission. He never returned to India. Ziegenbalg became fluent in the Tamil language and translated the entire New Testament by 1714 and a significant portion of the Old Testament by the time of his death in 1719.

Five overarching principles developed from the Danish-Halle Mission in India.[14] The first principle came as the missionaries searched for an opportunity to gain acceptance by the Indians. In contemporary terminology, the schools they founded provided the missionaries with a legitimate platform that met a need for the nationals. The presence and the message of the missionaries were legitimized by the education they provided in their schools. The second principle grew out of the first: students in the schools learned to read and write, which naturally led to a need to have the Bible in their own heart language. The third principle was perhaps the most controversial for this period, but has stood the test of time. The missionaries advocated that the proclamation of the gospel had to be done within the context of understanding the religion and culture of the people. Harsh critics claimed this principle would lead to compromise, causing a demise of the focus upon conversion. The fourth principle kept a focus on evangelism, as the mission insisted upon genuine personal conversion in contrast to people be-

---

[14]Neill, *History of Christian Missions*, 195–97.

coming Christians for economic benefits, such as being given jobs and financial assistance. Finally, the missionaries saw the need for an indigenous Indian leadership base. Unfortunately, though, only fourteen Indian pastors were ordained in the first hundred years of the Tranquebar mission, and the first ordination didn't take place until 1733.

Pause to Ponder

First, the Danish-Halle Mission used a "felt need" to gain entrance into the community. Is it acceptable in contemporary missions to utilize felt needs as opportunities to gain access to people groups? If so, what would some of these be? What is the danger of utilizing this approach? What steps should be taken to avoid developing dependencies upon the missionaries?

Second, the Danish-Halle Mission emphasized education. What is the challenge in the twenty-first century in light of the fact that 70 percent of the world's people live in oral-based societies? Are people groups required to read and write before they can be converted and discipled? What role should Chronological Bible Storying have in our strategies today?[15] Is it possible that literacy has become a barrier that keeps people from salvation in Christ? If so, does this mean that Scripture translation is not needed? Or does it lead to the realization that multiple approaches are needed?

Third, the desire for indigenous leadership was a worthy goal that was largely unmet by the Danish-Halle Mission. This lack of development hindered the expansion of the work. There were concerns about the training, quality, and abilities of indigenous leadership. The desire was to meet European standards. One of the accepted principles of a church-planting movement is the need for indigenous leadership. Is it possible that missionaries continue to impose their cultural standards for leadership to the detriment of the expansion of the kingdom of God? How can biblical indigenous leadership be developed while avoiding foreign cultural trappings?

---

[15]Chronological Bible Storying (CBS) is communicating portions of the Bible orally in narrative form in the order they are recorded.

The Story to Understand: Moravian Brethren

Today's Moravian Brethren look to John Hus as their founder. Hus was a professor/priest/preacher/reformer in Prague who was burned at the stake by the Catholic Church in 1415 for his insistence on preaching and teaching the simple gospel from the Bible. In 1457, followers of Hus, along with other dissenter refugees living in Moravia, organized what became known as the "Unity of the Brethren." Martin Luther was inspired by these precursors to the Reformation. In the wake of the Reformation, they were persecuted at the hands of both Protestants and Catholics.

In 1722 a group of Moravians settled in Germany on the estate of Count Nicolaus Ludwig von Zinzendorf (1700–1760). On this estate they established a village that they called Herrnhut, "the Lord's watch." There, in 1727, they reorganized the Moravian Church and dated their beginnings from this point.[16]

Zinzendorf had been influenced by the Pietists, but he also saw some strengths in the older Lutheranism. Spener was his godfather, and he had studied at Francke's grammar school. His wealthy pietistic family wanted him to be more than a preacher, so he became a lawyer. Zinzendorf's life motto was "I have one passion; it is He, and He alone." In 1727 Zinzendorf, unhappy in law, was ordained by the Lutherans. He sought to influence the Moravians to become a part of Lutheranism. The Moravians, however, did not want to do this. Instead, Zinzendorf himself came more and more under their influence. A revival began at a prayer meeting. By 1727 Zinzendorf had become a spiritual superintendent of the Moravians at Herrnhut. The Moravians retained their identity separate from the Pietists, but they stressed many of the same teachings. They became very missionary-minded, and were soon sending out missionaries to many places.

Mission endeavors for the Moravians developed from an encounter Zinzendorf had while visiting Copenhagen for the coronation of King Christian VI in 1731. In 1722 Hans Egede had been sent to Greenland as a missionary from Denmark. The early work was feeble

---

[16]See the entire issue of *Christian History* I, no. 1 (1982).

and discouraging, though there were some converts. During his trip to Copenhagen, Zinzendorf met two Eskimos who had been baptized by Egede, as well as a baptized Negro servant from the Danish West Indies. August 21, 1732, is celebrated by the Moravians as the beginning of their missionary work, the first outreach being to the slaves of Saint Thomas in the Virgin Islands. When Zinzendorf learned that there was a strong possibility that the Greenland mission would be abandoned, he decided the Moravians would fill the gap. Moravian work in Greenland began in 1733—though, as it turned out, Egede was not ready to leave Greenland, and his greatest number of converts came after he demonstrated the love of Christ to the nationals during a smallpox outbreak in 1733. Egede and the Moravians, under the leadership of Christian David, labored simultaneously in Greenland.

Zinzendorf spent much of his fortune on missions and devoted time to promoting the missionary cause and mentoring missionaries. By the time of Zinzendorf's death in 1760, the Moravians had sent 226 missionaries to 10 countries. The Moravians only provided their missionaries with transportation to their destinations; upon arrival they were expected to work in their trade to support themselves. Some did work full-time doing evangelism and pastoral ministry, while being supported financially by the labors of other missionaries. Each person sent was considered a missionary whether their prior background had been clergy or laity. Each missionary had the common task of living a life in obedience to the gospel and, therefore, being able to commend it to those who had never heard the gospel.

Determined to "reach souls for the Lamb," the dedication of the Moravians to missions led to a commitment to support their missionaries in constant prayer. On August 27, 1727, 24 men and 24 women at Herrnhut made a covenant to spend an hour each day in a scheduled time of prayer, which ultimately developed into a 24/7 prayer meeting that lasted for 100 years.

The impact of Moravian missions goes beyond sheer numbers, as impressive as they were. The faithfulness and tenacity of the Moravian missionaries shined brightly as beacons for others to follow. John

Wesley, whose ministry led to the formation of the Methodist Church, experienced severe disappointment as a missionary in Georgia but was drawn to and encouraged by the faith and commitment of the Moravians. During a storm as he crossed the Atlantic, Moravians on board the ship impressed him with their joy and peace in the face of potential death. After his Aldersgate conversion experience in England, Wesley sought out Zinzendorf for guidance and doctrinal instruction. Wesley and others were used by God in the revival movement known as the Great Awakening, which changed England and the American colonies. This revival movement changed the spiritual climate of England and prepared the soil for the ministry of a Baptist shoe cobbler, William Carey, who served as the first Baptist missionary to India. Carey is commonly called the father of modern missions, but he was inspired by the work of the Moravians, as documented in his 1792 publication, *An Enquiry into the Obligation of Christians to Use Means for the Conversion of the Heathen*.

Pause to Ponder

The story of Moravian missions is almost breathtaking because of these believers' level of commitment. The commitment to prayer was unprecedented. The number of missionaries sent was unprecedented. Does it seem realistic to think that these two facts are related? Does it appear that a greater commitment to praying for missions will result in a greater commitment to involvement in missions?

Financial support was obviously different for Moravian missionaries in the eighteenth century compared to those serving with today's mission agencies. A term to describe the efforts of those working separate jobs to support their ministry efforts is "tentmaking," based on the apostle Paul's example of working as a tentmaker to support himself (Acts 18:3). Churches also supported Paul, so his approach varied according to the situation. What is the role of tentmaking in today's missions efforts? Do you have a skill that could be utilized in this way? What are the strengths and weaknesses of the tentmaking approach and of the model of being supported by others? Are both acceptable approaches?

Conclusion

The story for the post-Reformation missions pioneers is only partially told in this chapter. The remarkable expansion of the Roman Catholic Church, the fascinating story of missions in colonial America, the stories of John Eliot and David Brainerd, for example, are incredibly inspiring. Space does not permit an analysis of the good, bad, and ugly aspects of post-Reformational missions. Nevertheless, as we understand the story more completely, may we take time to pause to ponder the implications for our own lives. We are all called to a life of radical obedience to the Great Commission. Where do we fit in the mission of God? Where do you fit?

Discussion Points

1. What would need to change in your personal life, the life of your church, and the life of your denomination in order to return to the "apostolic genius" DNA of the first-century church?

2. Is it acceptable in contemporary missions to utilize "felt needs" as opportunities to gain access to people groups? If so, what would some of these be? What is the danger of using this approach? What steps should be taken to avoid developing dependency upon the missionaries?

3. "Unprecedented prayer and unprecedented numbers of missionaries." Does it seem realistic to think that these two facts are related? Does it appear that a greater commitment to praying for missions will result in a greater commitment to involvement in missions? So, what are the implications for our churches today?

Further Reading

Garrison, David. *Church Planting Movements: How God Is Redeeming a Lost World*. Midlothian, VA: WIGTake Resources, 2004.

Hirsch, Alan. *The Forgotten Ways*. Grand Rapids: Brazos Press, 2006.

Kasdorf, Hans. "The Anabaptist Approach to Mission." In *Anabaptism and Mission*. Scottdale, PA: Herald Press, 1984.

Neill, Stephen. *A History of Christian Missions*. New York: Penguin, 1986.

Scherer, James A. *Justinian Welz: Essays by an Early Prophet of Mission*. Grand
    Rapids: Eerdmans, 1969.
Spener, Philip Jacob. *Pia Desideria*. Translated and edited by Theodore G.
    Tappert. Philadelphia: Fortress, 1964.
Williams, George H. *The Radical Reformation*. Philadelphia: Westminster,
    1962.

16

THE GREAT CENTURY

Howard Norrish

In his classic multivolume work, *A History of the Expansion of Christianity*, Kenneth Scott Latourette coined the term "the great century" of missions. From his mid-twentieth-century view, "Christianity was now taken to more peoples than ever before and entered as a transforming agency into more cultures than all the preceding centuries."[1] This chapter provides a few biographical sketches from this extraordinary age.

The Roots of the Great Century

Effective mission is birthed out of revival and good theology. The Reformation in Europe represented a fundamental shift in the worldview of Christians: from the medieval tendency to abandon the social world and seek closer union

> *Effective mission is birthed out of revival and good theology.*

with God (monasticism) to a vision of world transformation in obedience to God. The gospel would have great consequences in all nations.

John Eliot, who arrived in Boston, Massachusetts, in 1631, grew concerned for the Algonquins of Massachusetts. The Puritan missionary learned their language, preached the gospel, and concentrated on their domestic, public, and personal welfare for about forty years (1646–1680). Eliot was the first apostle to the American Indians. David Brainerd followed. His diary reveals his desire that Jesus would

---

[1]Kenneth Scott Latourette, *The Great Century in Europe and the United States of America (A.D. 1800–A.D. 1914)*, vol. 4 of *A History of the Expansion of Christianity* (New York and London: Harper & Brothers Publishers, 1941), 7.

establish his kingdom among the Native Americans. He wrote, "I had no notion of joy from this world; I cared not where or how I lived or what hardships I went through so I could gain souls for Christ."[2] Brainerd preached God's love and saw the Holy Spirit's power break upon the Indians from 1745 until he died in 1747.

Brainerd's diary influenced future missionary pioneers such as William Carey of India and Robert Morrison of China. His account inspired the hearts of Samuel Mills, James Richards, Francis Robbins, Harvey Loomis, and Bryan Green, the five undergraduates at Williams College who met in August of 1806 to talk and pray. When a storm came, they sheltered by a haystack and continued praying. The result was a decision to dedicate their lives to preaching the gospel in all nations. This "haystack prayer meeting" is considered the birthplace of American foreign missions.

The changing spiritual backdrop of Europe also set the stage for the coming Great Century. Protestantism had become introverted and demoralized. Puritanism had lost the vision of world mission and world transformation. It treated conversion as an escape from the present. The emphasis was on correct doctrine—intellectual assent to the truth.

The Great Evangelical Awakening that began in Germany (the Moravian Revival in 1727) and spread through the English-speaking world was countercultural not just to the coldness of spiritual life in the church but as a reaction to the arid philosophies (rationalism and deism) of the Enlightenment. In this great revival, the individual experience of conversion and the blessing of fellowship with God sparked concern not just for friends and neighbors but for all people everywhere. These Christians believed that the gospel transformed people. Correct doctrine, yes—but supremely important was heart awareness of salvation in Jesus. Biblical faith lay in the heart of man rather than in his intellect. The emphasis was on the authority of Scripture, the fallen nature of humankind, conversion, and the walk of faith.

Revival broke out of the restrictive, monopolistic, ecclesiastical

---

[2]Phillip E. Howard Jr., *The Life and Diary of David Brainerd* (New York: Moody, 1949).

structures. Evangelism was innovative. Notables like John Wesley, George Whitfield, and Jonathan Edwards led the movement; many evangelists and preachers, however, were laypeople rather than professional clergy. Real and observed needs of the people took priority. The gospel met with astonishing results, while the current church had very little appeal. Revival brought a theology of hope and belief that world mission would lead to world transformation.

John Wesley died in 1791. William Carey delivered his great sermon in Nottingham in 1792: "Expect great things from God. Attempt great things for God."[3] This is considered the foundation point of the modern missionary movement.

Early Missionary Pioneers

William Carey (1761–1834)—Pioneer to the Hindu peoples.[4] William Carey was born in a village in central England. His father was a poor handloom weaver, but became the village schoolmaster when Carey was six. Carey's only formal education came through this school. He was an avid reader and loved to memorize. At fourteen he was apprenticed to a shoemaker. A friend persuaded Carey to join a small nonconformist church, where he was converted. In his employer's home he discovered a New Testament commentary containing Greek phrases. Greek fascinated Carey, so he began to learn it in his spare time. He also read about the explorations of Captain James Cook in the Southern Seas, kindling in his mind a passion for missions.

Ten years later Carey was pastoring a church and earning a living making and mending shoes. His passion was studying languages—Hebrew, Greek, French, Italian, and Dutch—and he had a genius for mastering them. In 1793 the newly formed Baptist Missionary Association chose him as their first missionary to India. Carey, his wife Dorothy, their four young children, and Dorothy's sister (to

---

[3]S. Pearce Carey, *William Carey: Father of Modern Missions*, ed.Peter Masters (London: Wakeman Trust, 1923). This was part of Carey's conclusion in his address to the Baptist Association Convention, May 30, 1793.

[4]Material in this section drawn from Vishal and Ruth Mangalwadi, *The Legacy of William Carey* (Wheaton: Crossway, 1993); and Kellsye Finnie, *William Carey* (Carlisle, UK: OM Publishing, 1992).

help with the children) arrived in Bengal, never to return to England. With almost no money and few to back him, Carey started to explore transforming India for his Master—the Lord Jesus. The breadth of influence he eventually came to have throughout Indian society was huge.[5]

Carey's greatest passion was the translation and distribution of the Bible. He saw this not just as the foundation of the church but as vital for the transformation of India. William Ward, a printer, joined Carey in 1799; and they established a printing press, as well as a college, in Serampore—a small Danish colony, because the British forbade evangelism among Hindus. Ward, Carey, and Joshua Marshman worked together there and were collectively known as the "Serampore Trio." This press produced twenty-four different language translations of the Bible. Carey realized India wouldn't be evangelized through missionaries but through Indian Christians. The purpose of Serampore College was to train them.

Carey realized India wouldn't be evangelized through missionaries but through Indian Christians. The purpose of Serampore College was to train them.

Carey believed in radical discipleship and was committed to a biblical worldview. He passionately believed in a personal, rational Creator. He believed in the inductive method of research. He modeled hard work and much of the time was a "tentmaker." He saw India in terms of intense spiritual warfare. But Carey taught that Satan's kingdom had been defeated in history by the death and resurrection of Jesus Christ. Jesus was already King over the kingdoms of this world. He understood that Jesus' command, "Make disciples of all nations," implied that all nations could and would be discipled before Jesus returned. Carey died in 1834, the same year Charles Spurgeon was born.

---

[5]Today in India Carey is remembered as a botanist (a plant is named after him), an industrialist (introducing the steam engine to India), an economist (introducing savings banks to India), a developer of humane treatments for leprosy, a builder of the largest printing press in India, a champion of agricultural reform, a leader in the study of astronomy in India, a champion of women's rights, the father of the Indian Renaissance of nineteenth-twentieth century India, professor of Oriental languages (at Fort William College, teaching Bengali, Sanskrit, and Marathi), an influence for a generation of the Indian Civil Service to respect the Indians they governed, founder of dozens of schools, and pioneer of the idea of lending libraries.

Henry Martyn (1781–1812)—Pioneer to the Muslim peoples.[6] Henry Martyn was born in Truro, in southwest England, to parents who were greatly influenced by John Wesley. His father, cashier to a local merchant, was self-taught. His mother died when he was two. Martyn excelled in school, especially in Latin and Greek. He went to Cambridge University at age seventeen. Though he was a brilliant mathematician, languages and grammar were his delight; he mastered seventeen of them!

On January 1, 1800, Martyn was stunned by news of his father's death. In his grief he turned to the Bible, starting to read in Acts. Gradually he realized Jesus was a living person, at which point his conversion soon followed.

Martyn learned much from Charles Simeon of Holy Trinity Church in Cambridge, who was a renowned preacher and teacher of the Evangelical Awakening. Martyn won high honors with prizes in mathematics, classics, and languages. He could have chosen any path, but Simeon challenged him about "the transcendent excellence of Christian ministry" and the need for servants of Christ in India. Martyn didn't want to be poor for Christ's sake. He aimed to study law, since it was lucrative. God began to speak to him, however. He spent more time alone with God and caught such glimpses of the love of Jesus and his majesty that he became more than willing to be poor for Jesus' sake. He was also deeply affected by reading David Brainerd's diary. To the shock of his friends, Martyn decided in 1802 that, God enabling him, he would go to India.

He prepared for India by becoming Charles Simeon's assistant for eighteen months. The East India Company forbade missionary efforts in India, so at Simeon's suggestion Martyn applied, and was accepted, as a chaplain to British troops in the East India Company. Upon arriving in Madras in April of 1806, he uttered the thrilling statement, "Now let me burn out for God."

"Now let me burn out for God."

Martyn moved to Calcutta, where he met William Carey and the others from the "Serampore Trio." Knowing of his language skills, they

[6]Material in this section drawn from Constance Evelyn Padwick, *Henry Martyn* (Chicago: Moody, 1980).

challenged him in regard to the Muslim languages of South and West Asia—Arabic, Persian (Farsi), and Urdu—and the need for Scriptures in those languages.

Martyn soon moved to Patna in Bihar to a British military compound. There he found the British as pagan as the Indians. The local British judge had married a Muslim woman, built a mosque, and openly renounced Christianity. Most in the expatriate community resented Martyn's ministry. Additionally, Indians distrusted him. Martyn wrote, "Here every native I meet is an enemy to me because I am an Englishman." He started schools for Indian children, staffed by Indians. He also began a serious study of Islam and developed sensitivity to the Muslim mind.

In April of 1809 Martyn moved to Kanpur. He was faithful as chaplain to the expatriates, but languages were his priority. His aim was to translate the New Testament first into Urdu and Sanskrit, followed by Arabic and Farsi. By 1810 the Urdu New Testament was ready. While his Urdu translation was excellent literature, it was also idiomatic and simple enough for the least educated. Today's Urdu New Testament is still based on that translation.

Martyn contracted tuberculosis in Kanpur. He still continued to preach in the open air, often while coughing blood. Only one convert is known from his preaching in Kanpur. A young Muslim attended one of his meetings and later declared himself a follower of Jesus and was baptized. He became the first Indian clergyman of the Church of England and a preacher of the gospel to Muslims.

Though Martyn completed Arabic and Farsi translations of the New Testament, they were substandard. He decided that an idiomatic translation required living in Iran and Arabia. This thought gripped his mind. And his tuberculosis was so serious that he thought a sea voyage might help. In October of 1810 he left to travel to Arabia.

Martyn's life represented a paradox. The weaker his body became, the stronger his spirit grew. His life flamed with one desire—to give Asia a Farsi New Testament before he died. During his travels and stops at various ports, Martyn discovered how deficient his Arabic New Testament was. He arrived in Persia in May of 1811. In Bushire he joined a caravan to Shiraz to find scholarly help to complete the Farsi New Testament. The next month Martyn arrived in Shiraz, where he found Muslim scholars to help him. He wrote, "Whether life or death be mine, may Christ be magnified in me. If He has a work for me to do, I cannot die."

Martyn's life represented a paradox. The weaker his body became, the stronger his spirit grew. His life flamed with one desire— to give Asia a Farsi New Testament before he died.

Martyn wore only Persian dress, lived in a room without furniture, and ate with his hands. He had no fellowship. Life held both encouragements and discouragements. Muslim boys stoned him. A Muslim scholar helping him translate the Gospels remarked, "There is something so awfully pure about Jesus." A stream of mullahs, poets, and others visited, eager to meet this "beardless boy" who knew so much about religion.

In February of 1812 he completed the Farsi New Testament and Psalms. He traveled to Tabriz to present a copy to the Shah of Persia. Before he left Shiraz, a young man who had bitterly opposed Martyn put his faith in Jesus. Martyn reached Tabriz, but was unsuccessful in seeking an audience with the Shah. Instead, the British ambassador took a New Testament to the Shah on his behalf and gained approval for distribution in the Shah's territories. The Shah was overjoyed at such excellent use of the Persian language.

Martyn decided to return to England by way of Istanbul. He made it to Tokat, in north-central Turkey, where plague was raging. It is thought that he collapsed in the street and died there. Armenian Christians buried the unknown Englishman "of whom the world was not worthy" (Hebrews 11:38).

Martyn left two of the most perfect and influential translations of the New Testament that West and South Asia have ever seen. He said, "Even if I never see a native converted, by my patience and continuation in the work, God may design to encourage future missionaries." Martyn left us an example not of a perfect man but of what God can do with an imperfect man who takes the call of God seriously.

William Burns (1815–1868)—Pioneer to the Chinese people.[7] I have chosen the Scottish missionary William Burns as the pioneer to the Chinese people because as an evangelist and church planter he had a wide itinerant ministry in China. At the time, his mission strategy was considered revolutionary.

Burns was the son of a Church of Scotland minister. At school he preferred sports to study. He rarely read anything except Bunyan's *Pilgrim's Progress* and a book about the Scottish hero William Wallace. Burns wanted to be a farmer, but his father sent him to Aberdeen Grammar School. He excelled academically there, leading to his eventually studying law at Aberdeen University. Burns was saved in 1832. Reflecting on that experience, he said, "An arrow from the quiver of the King of Zion was shot by his Almighty sovereign hand through my heart . . . and the Spirit of God shone with full light upon the glory of Jesus as Saviour for such as I was."

He switched from studying law to studying divinity at Glasgow University. He was a founding member of Glasgow University Students' Missionary Society. He later applied, unsuccessfully, to the India Committee to go to India.

Robert Murray McCheyne, a minister at Dundee, asked Burns to take his place while he traveled to Palestine. Before going to Dundee, Burns helped his father with preaching at Kilsyth, and revival broke out. He moved to St. Peter's Church in Dundee in 1839. His anointing to preach was obvious, and crowds flocked to the church. His life was steeped in prayer. Burns also read Brainerd's diaries during this time.

Revival continued in Kilsyth and Dundee. There were all-night prayer meetings. A report said, "People began to melt before the Lord." Many wanted to repent and get right with God. As the revival spread to other parts of Scotland, it was clear that this was an unusual outpouring of the Spirit of God.

Burns was ordained, and then in June of 1847 he sailed for China, arriving in Hong Kong in November of that year. The ports of Canton, Amoy, Foochow, Ning-po, and Shanghai were opened to foreigners due

---

[7]Material in this section drawn from Agnes Clarke, *China's Man of the Book: The Story of William Chalmers Burns, 1815–1868* (London: OMF, 1968).

to the 1842 Treaty of Nanking. Hong Kong was ceded to Britain. When Burns reached China, there were fifty missionaries in these six centers.

Burns gave himself to the study of Chinese. He moved from expatriate quarters to live among the Chinese. He had three prayer requests—fluency to preach in Chinese, access into inland China, and openness in people's hearts to the truth about the Lord Jesus.

In February of 1849 Burns crossed to the mainland with two Chinese assistants. He went from village to village, staying a few days in each. Every few months he returned briefly to Hong Kong. For sixteen months he worked in Canton. Burns seldom lacked hearers, but his message didn't reach hearts. Still, he sowed in hope. In June of 1851 he moved up the coast to Amoy. Though the dialect there was different, by February of 1852 he was preaching regularly in the open air in Amoy. Burns needed help. He sent his entire year's salary back to Scotland. The head of the mission remarked, "Surely that field is ripe unto harvest when the reaper sends home his own wages to fetch out another labourer!"

Burns also worked on *Pilgrim's Progress* in Chinese. He was fascinated that Bunyan's work was so effective in communicating to the Chinese mind. He also put together a Chinese hymnbook. His delight was open-air evangelism with a team of Chinese evangelists. In 1854 Burns began to see conversions. When he moved on, he left two Chinese Christians to disciple the new believers. In one place a church of twenty was birthed.

In 1854 Burns began to see conversions. When he moved on, he left two Chinese Christians to disciple the new believers. In one place a church of twenty was birthed.

In 1855 Burns made Shanghai his base. He preached and distributed Scriptures on the rivers and canals. In 1856 he met the newly arrived Hudson Taylor and took him preaching from village to village. Both dressed as the Chinese did and had a team of Chinese evangelists with them.

Burns ventured further inland. Once his team was arrested for selling books and preaching. The magistrate required them to kowtow and remain kneeling for questioning. Burns respectfully refused, saying he would go down on one knee to a sovereign, but would only go down on two knees and kowtow to the King of kings—the Lord Jesus. The magistrate had no idea Burns was a foreigner. With his hair shaved, except for a portion plaited in a queue, his speech, appearance, and actions were Chinese. He called himself Pin Wei Lin. He said he was a teacher of the religion of Jesus, and he exhorted people to good deeds. His Chinese colleagues were imprisoned and tortured, while Burns was sent to Canton with his Bibles and other books. It took a month to get there, and his Bibles were soon distributed.

Burns later returned to visit house churches that had emerged from earlier trips. These visits were filled with joy at how some had progressed and with sorrow when some needed discipline. Chinese Christians were suffering persecution in many ways: being robbed, having their rice fields destroyed, being banned from the village well, and even enduring physical violence. The missionaries decided Burns should go to Peking to secure a general and permanent settlement of the rights of Christians in China. He failed in this, but made an excellent case before the authorities, showing he would have made a brilliant lawyer.

In Peking he wrote fifty hymns in Mandarin and retranslated *Pilgrim's Progress* into Mandarin. He translated the Psalms directly from Hebrew into Mandarin to retain the poetic form and make it easier to memorize. In 1867 Burns began itinerant preaching tours from Peking. He traveled to Tientsin and up to Niew Chwang in Manchuria. It was bitterly cold that winter, and Burns fell ill. He died in April of 1868 while in Niew Chwang (now called Yingkou).

Burns was a gifted evangelist and was deeply convinced that believers received "the whole Christ," who was not only Savior but also Lord. He often used the phrase "No cross—no crown" while discipling new believers. Before going to China, he had been delayed in Scotland, where God used him in bringing revival. In China his main work was preparing a highway for our God—sowing by voice and by pen. Burns died in a frontier situation in which the gospel had not been preached. His greatest delight was blazing a trail over fresh horizons. He proclaimed the whole counsel of God. His trumpet gave no uncertain sound (1 Corinthians 14:8).

The Ebb and Flow of the Great Century

These three examples of early pioneers reflect the best of the early years of the Great Century of modern missions. What characterized this first era?

The First Wave (1790–1859).[8] Ralph Winter[9] described this "First Wave" of modern missions as driven by a love for the Lord Jesus and a passion (willingness to suffer) for the sake of those yet to know Christ. Indeed, missionaries were willing to give their lives for the mission of God; few in Africa during this era survived more than two years.

It was a European era, although Americans quickly joined the flow and made their mark. It was a time of rapid development of denominational missions agencies, although missionaries were relatively free from denominational supervision during this first wave, primarily due to slow transnational communications.

Winter points out that it was an era of good missiology. Many missionaries were lay tentmakers—a biblical and historical pattern regularly associated with the extension of God's kingdom and mission. There was a persistent passion to get the Scriptures into the vernacular language of the peoples being reached. This is when the indigenous "three-self principles" of Henry Venn and Rufus Anderson became the best practice of the day. Church planters sought to start movements that were self-supporting, self-governing, and self-propagating.

Finally, the first wave was characterized as a time when the coastlands and islands of the world were being reached. Penetrating inland areas was slow due to the lack of infrastructure in Africa and South America and government opposition in Asia. By the middle of the nineteenth century, we begin to see a decline in sending out missionaries from Europe.

---

[8]Material in this section drawn from Ralph D. Winter, "Four Men, Three Eras," in *Perspectives on the World Christian Movement*, 3rd ed., ed. Ralph D. Winter and Steven C. Hawthorne (Pasadena, CA: William Carey Library, 1999).

[9]Editor's note: On May 20, 2009, Dr. Ralph Winter went to be with the Lord. Ralph's legacy as one of the most influential missiologists of the twentieth century lives on through his teachings and writings, and most powerfully through the lives of those he challenged and coached. Though I knew him only casually as a senior colleague and professor, I recall his passion (even his obsession) as a pioneer for the mission of God. He always pushed us to the frontiers of lostness for the sake of the gospel of Jesus Christ. His academic "first love" was the history of God's mission.—Mike Barnett

The tide recedes (1790–1860). The 1790s saw the "routinization" of the Evangelical Awakening, as consolidation and order became paramount. Denominational divisions hardened. Political forces used evangelicals as a bulwark against the extreme political revolutionary movements (e.g., Jacobinism) flowing from France. Evangelicals became "respectable." The upper classes could be saved by faith in Jesus but not change their "station" in life. Universal sinfulness was rejected, as it was "socially leveling." The gospel became identified with an elite culture that was deeply conservative in its approach to domestic policies. Revival didn't just die out in early nineteenth-century England; it was deliberately suppressed by the elite leadership of the evangelical church. Evangelical faith was seen as the cement to hold a hierarchical society together.

> *The evangelical movement was drowning in a sweeping sectarian riptide. Rigid definitions of doctrine led to ecclesiastical separations. Evangelism was replaced by a desire to "protect" gains. This led to an erosion of confidence in the power of the gospel to transform cultures.*

The evangelical movement was drowning in a sweeping sectarian riptide. Rigid definitions of doctrine led to ecclesiastical separations. Evangelism was replaced by a desire to "protect" gains. This led to an erosion of confidence in the power of the gospel to transform cultures. Social and political endeavors were regarded as useless. Many saw the vision of a world where all human life was enriched by the progress of the kingdom of God as unbiblical, substituting that notion with a concern to maintain the purity of their subculture against the wider world. This had serious consequences for missions.

The gospel became confused with civilization, colonialism, and commerce. Colonial powers had certain objectives. Colonies were developed to meet the economic needs of the West. This led to limited production of raw materials with little diversification of agriculture and industry. Ghana produced cocoa, Malaysia produced rubber and tin, Egypt produced cotton, etc.

Colonial powers developed structures that gave them control. They maintained this imbalance of power because they had access to technology, systems, and ideas. They withheld much of this from all but an "elite." The perception was that the great Asian cultures were backward compared to a growing materialistic culture, and a sub-Christian ideology was imposed on them. Colonial powers created dependency on foreign resources, foreign experts, foreign institutions, and foreign religion.

At that time, even mission-based institutions determined programs through funding practices. For nationals, learning a foreign language (such as English) and a foreign cultural way of doing things became important. This perception of the superiority of the foreign culture was probably the greatest obstacle to faithful gospel proclamation.

Sadly, missionaries were often part of the colonizing force. There was a turning away from the tentmaking of the Moravians and people like William Carey and Henry Martyn because it was possible to be "fully supported" by the denominational missionary society since a banking system enabled money to be transferred from "home" to "the field." This caused a separation of the missionary from the ordinary life of the community.

The Second Wave (mid-nineteenth century). Revivals broke out in North America in the 1830s under Charles Finney and others. This continued up to the Great Revival of 1857, in which about one million people were added to evangelical churches. This is often called the Second Evangelical Awakening (Second Great Awakening). Americans became more involved in missions. D. L. Moody was at the heart of this.

Second-Era Pioneers

Of the thousands of missionary pioneers we could choose from to illustrate the second era of the Great Century, here are just three.

James Hudson Taylor (1832–1905).[10] Hudson Taylor was born in Yorkshire, Northern England. His father was a Methodist preacher who also ran a pharmacy. Nurtured by talk of overseas missions, when he was only six years old Taylor determined to be a missionary in China. After his conversion, in which he put himself completely at God's disposal, at age seventeen, Taylor sensed that the Lord said to him, "Then go for Me

---

[10]Material in this section drawn from Dr. and Mrs. Howard Taylor, *Hudson Taylor in Early Years: The Growth of a Soul* (London: CIM, 1911).

to China." He started to prepare himself. He read Dr. Medhurst's book on China and saw the value of medical work. He had worked in his father's pharmacy, and in 1851 he began work as a doctor's assistant.

Taylor lived frugally, following his father's advice: "See what you can do without." His rationale was simple: "When I get to China I will have no claim on anyone for anything. My only claim will be on God. How important to learn . . . to move man through God by prayer alone."

When he was twenty, Taylor moved to London to further his medical studies. In 1854, at the age of twenty-one, he landed in Shanghai under the auspices of the Chinese Evangelisation Society (CES). Priority was given to learning Mandarin, so he devoted several hours a day to doing that, in addition to continuing his medical studies. He travelled out of Shanghai, accompanying William Burns and others, preaching and attending to simple ailments. After three years he left the CES. His reasons included suspicions of financial mismanagement and their disapproval of his dressing, eating, and living like the Chinese he worked among.

Taylor married Maria Dyer, the orphaned daughter of missionary parents, in 1858. She was fluent in the Ningpo dialect and helped in the first school for Chinese girls. Suffering from poor health, the Taylors returned to England in 1860. Taylor completed his medical studies at the London Hospital in 1862, finished a Ningpo dialect New Testament, and produced a Chinese hymnbook.

The thought that a million Chinese were dying every month without God constantly challenged Taylor. What should he do? The answer was obvious—recruit workers for inland China. This work would be dangerous, but one Sunday in June of 1865 he realized that if God called men and women, then "the responsibility rests with Him and not with us." Taylor began to pray for twenty-four workers for China. He opened a bank account in the name of the China Inland Mission (CIM), and published a booklet entitled "China's Spiritual Needs and Claims." He wrote of the task and policies of the CIM: It would be nondenominational, workers must hold to the full inspiration of God's Word, and workers didn't need formal education. They would have no fixed salary but trust God to supply their needs. There would be no appeals for money, as all needs would be brought before God in prayer. They would wear Chinese dress in homes in inland China, and the work would be directed from within China rather than from England.

In May of 1866 the Taylor family, plus sixteen adult workers, went to China to join the nine workers already there. They settled in the coastal town of Hangchow. After some months of language study, they began to move inland. A major goal was to spread the gospel throughout China as rapidly as possible. They made journeys of exploration before placing teams in prefectural cities in areas with no workers. By 1870 they had 33 workers in 13 teams in 4 provinces. There were also 462 Chinese co-workers in 260 teams in all 14 provinces. One key discovery Taylor made was the value of single women as workers. Wearing Chinese dress, these women gained entrance into homes that would have been closed to men.

Taylor often battled poor health and pain from a spinal injury. His wife, Maria, and two of his children died. He had to send three of his children to relatives in England. Perhaps the greatest crisis was political unrest fuelled by hostility toward missionary activity, resulting in attacks on foreigners by a group called *I Ho Ch'uan*—the "boxers." Hundreds of Chinese Christians were killed, and Protestant missions lost 135 adults and 53 children. Of these, 91 adults and 21 children belonged to the CIM. Following the Boxer Rebellion, China experienced a mass movement toward Christianity.

In 1902 Taylor handed over leadership of the CIM. He had been recruiting workers for China from England and the United States, and lived for a time in Switzerland due to health issues. When his second wife, Jennie, died in 1904, he returned to China. By now CIM had more than 800 workers. A month after his arrival in China, James Hudson Taylor died. By 1914 the CIM was the largest missionary agency in the world, reaching its peak in 1934 with 1,368 adult workers in China.

Mary Slessor (1848–1915).[11] Mary Slessor was born into a poor family in Aberdeen, Scotland, in 1848. At age eleven she began working in the cotton mills of Dundee while still in school. By age fourteen she

---

[11]Material in this section drawn from W. P. Livingstone, *Mary Slessor of Calabar: Pioneer Missionary* (London: Hodder and Stoughton, 1918).

was working ten hours a day in the mills. Slessor was converted as a youngster through the friendship of an elderly widow. She was active in her church and eventually taught Sunday school. She began to work in a street mission, where she often had to stand up to drunken thugs and street gangs—excellent faith-building preparation for her later work in Nigeria. And the cotton mills of her youth were hot and humid, the best environment to acclimatize her for tropical Africa.

In response to the growing need for missionaries in West Africa, on August 5, 1876, Slessor boarded the steamer *Ethiopia*, bound for Nigeria. Sometime in September she arrived along the deltas where the Calabar and Niger Rivers empty into the Gulf of Guinea.[12] This part of Nigeria was renowned for slavery and its unhealthy environment due to tropical diseases such as malaria. Slessor began her work in the colonial town of Calabar, teaching in a mission school. She picked up the language quickly. But she felt uncomfortable with the ample lifestyle of the expatriate community, and her heart was for pioneering into the interior.

After three years in Calabar, Slessor was weakened by malaria and sent to Scotland to recover. On her return she moved upriver: working alone, living in a mud hut, eating local food, and dressing like the local women. She supervised a small mission school, dispensed medicines, cared for unwanted children, and was asked to mediate in local disputes. On Sundays she was an evangelist, walking through the jungle from village to village and preaching the gospel to whoever would listen.

Reaching the people was slow. Tribal customs and superstitions were deeply ingrained. Many practices were cruel; for example, twins were murdered at birth and the mother was thrown out of the tribe. Slessor courageously intervened in tribal matters and eventually gained great respect from tribal leaders.

After three years Slessor became ill and returned to Scotland again, this time with Janie—a six-month-old African girl she had rescued from death. Slessor and Janie were a sensation. There were many opportunities to speak about Africa and its needs.

She returned to Calabar in 1885 and went upcountry to the Okoyong,

---

[12]J. Theodore Mueller, Missionary Biographies, "Mary Slessor," posted on Worldwide Missions website, www.wholesomewords.org/missions/islessor.html.

even though others had gone there and been killed. A single woman going there was considered insane, but Slessor was determined to go. She believed a woman would be accepted, whereas men were a threat. For the next twenty-five years Slessor pioneered into areas where no white person had survived. For fifteen years she stayed with the Okoyong people—teaching, nursing, and arbitrating in their disputes. Her reputation as a peacemaker spread, so she was soon acting as chief judge. The British authorities recognized her role and appointed her to be the first vice-consul to the Okoyong.

Slessor was highly respected and saw a decline in witchcraft, but only a few turned to Christ. In 1903 the first baptisms took place and a church started. Other female workers tried to join her, but complained that her mud hut was infested with rats, ants, and cockroaches. Clothing was of little concern to Slessor. She wore a simple wrap-around cloth. Others found this difficult and accused her of "going native."

In 1904 Slessor, at age fifty-five, moved upriver to the Ibo people, while others replaced her among the Okoyong. After a decade of pioneering among the Ibo, she died at age sixty-six—forty years after coming to Africa—in a mud hut. When she died, there were more than ten thousand baptized believers among the Okoyong and Ibo. Slessor demonstrated that single women could indeed pioneer where men couldn't go.

When she died, there were more than ten thousand baptized believers among the Okoyong and Ibo. Slessor demonstrated that single women could indeed pioneer where men couldn't go.

Samuel Zwemer and the Student Volunteer Missionary Movement (1867–1952).[13] Kenneth Scott Latourette described Samuel Zwemer as "one of the most famous Christian missionaries to Muslims, travelling over most of the Islamic world, arousing in Europe and America interest in bringing the faith to Muslims, and recruiting and training missionaries."[14] In the early twentieth century

[13]Material in this section drawn from J. Christy Wilson, *Flaming Prophet: The Story of Samuel Zwemer*, Bold Believers Series (New York: Friendship Press, 1970).
[14]Kenneth Scott Latourette, *The Great Century in Northern Africa and Asia, A.D. 1800–A.D. 1914*, vol. 6 of *A History of the Expansion of Christianity* (New York and London: Harper and Brothers Publishers, 1944), 61.

Zwemer was acknowledged as the foremost authority on Christian witness to Islam. This brief sketch details his connection with the Student Volunteer Missionary Movement (SVMM).

Zwemer was born in Michigan in 1867 and attended Hope College in Holland, Michigan. During his senior year, Robert Wilder, a pioneer of the SVMM, visited the campus. As Wilder spoke, he displayed a map of India with a metronome set so that each tick represented another person in the Indian subcontinent dying without hearing the gospel of Jesus Christ. This so affected Zwemer that he rushed to sign the decision card that stated, "God helping me I propose to be a foreign missionary."

Zwemer and James Cantine started "The Arabian Mission," since Arabia—the cradle of Islam—was the most difficult field they could find. Zwemer traveled in Arabia and then lived for nine years (1896–1905) in Bahrain, where his ministry to Muslims was largely polemic. Later Zwemer developed a gentler apologetic and a basic way to evangelize Muslims. The books he wrote regarding these methods are still used today.

Between 1905 and 1911 Zwemer traveled for the SVMM in the United States and Canada. During presentations he would sweep his hand across a map, indicating the great crescent of the Muslim world from West Africa to Indonesia, and say, "Thou O Christ art all I want and Thou O Christ art all they want. What Christ can do for any man He can do for every man." Zwemer may have influenced more workers to go to the Muslim world than anyone else in history. God used him to mobilize workers through his books and conferences and, finally, as a professor at Princeton Theological Seminary. His legacy is that of an incisive theological critique of Islam combined with a deep compassion for individual Muslims. Zwemer and the SVMM made a huge impact on Muslim evangelism—both in numbers and in more effective ways of seeing Muslims come to faith in the Lord Jesus.

Conclusion

What have we learned from this glimpse of the dynamics and key players of the Great Century of the mission of God?

The movement of God's mission is like the tides of the ocean, having both ebbs and flows. Spiritual decline in churches leads to a decline in missionary passion for the unevangelized. But the Holy Spirit revives the church, lighting a fire in people's hearts, and this precedes the swell of kingdom expansion. God calls normal people, often tentmakers, to rise up and take the gospel of Christ to those who have never heard it. He inspires a passion—a willingness to suffer—for the sake of his mission. This personal encounter with Christ, and the call of God to service, pervades the stories of Great Century missionaries.

The power and presence of the Word of God is primary. The first task of Great Century pioneer missionaries was to translate and transfer God's Scriptures to the peoples. As twenty-first-century disciples, we must remember this prerequisite of God's mission. We also see that the message of the gospel must be communicated in a way that connects with the culture. This is the unique task of cross-cultural missions.

Finally, we understand how important it is to tell the story of God's mission. The writings of Brainerd and others from the fields inspired generations of Christ-followers to become involved in the mission of God. To that end we offer this chapter, indeed this volume. God uses the experiences and passion of those who have gone before us to inspire and mobilize us for his mission.

Discussion Points

1. What patterns do you see in the lives and work of the missionaries in this chapter?

2. Where do you see evidence of the power of the Holy Spirit in the Great Century of God's mission?

3. How important was God's written Word in this era of world missions? How important is it in our churches and mission agencies today? Can you give some examples?

4. What do you think about the concept of the "ebb and flow" of God's mission described in this chapter? Where are we in the mission of God today?

5. Do you ever read biographies of missionaries? Can you list a few good ones and share them with a friend or colleague?

Further Reading

George, Timothy. *Faithful Witness: The Life and Mission of William Carey*. Birmingham, AL: New Hope, 1991.

Neill, Stephen. *A History of Christian Missions*. New York: Penguin, 1964.

Tucker, Ruth. *From Jerusalem to Irian Jaya: A Biographical History of Christian Missions*. Grand Rapids: Baker, 1983.

17

THE GLOBAL CENTURY

Mike Barnett

In 1936, almost a decade before his classic seven-volume *History of the Expansion of Christianity*, Kenneth Scott Latourette wrote a forward-looking book titled *Missions Tomorrow*.[1] In this book the rising historian celebrated what he later described as the "Great Century" of missions—the nineteenth century. He lauded its contributions to the advancement of Christianity and society at large. He nostalgically lamented "the day which is closing." Though the Great Century of Protestant missions to the far corners of the earth had ended, looking back we might say the "Global Century" of missions was dawning.

In this chapter we will discover some of the missionaries and movements that fueled this global century of God's mission. The highlights will prepare us for part three of this book: "The Mission of God Today."

Changing Times

The world of the mid-1900s witnessed a series of dizzying and interrelated social, political, economic, technological, and religious changes that thoroughly impacted the mission of God. Before we attempt an overview of twentieth-century missions, we must remember the missiological context of the nineteenth century.

In *Missions Tomorrow*, Latourette identified fourteen "forces and movements" that would influence the future mission of God. The first thirteen concerned socioeconomic, political, and cultural changes. The

---

[1]Kenneth Scott Latourette, *Missions Tomorrow* (New York and London: Harper & Brothers Publishers, 1936).

fourteenth and final force was "the stationary character or actual decline of missionary giving and enthusiasm in much of the Occident [West], especially in Protestant circles."[2] Latourette summarized the pulse of the missions community: "The new day is one of confusion. Many have lost a sense of direction and purpose. They are terrified by the passing of the old and familiar and by specters of disaster in the path ahead."[3] This was the context of the new day. How would the church respond? Indeed, how would God respond? What would happen to God's mission to all nations in the twentieth century?

Political retreat. The "retreat of the West," or end of colonialism, hand-in-hand with the rise of nationalism, signaled the passing of an era. Ralph D. Winter illustrated the amazing turn of political events in just twenty-five unbelievable years. He claimed that in 1945, "99.5 percent of the Non-Western world was under Western domination. 99.5 percent of the Non-Western world was independent by the end of 1969."[4] This political reversal transformed the world of cross-cultural missions.

Protestant retrenchment. In the wake of the Great Century, "modern" challenges emerged. Like biblical Israel and every Christian movement, the pendulum swung from a generation focused on outward expansion of the gospel to an inward, self-interested preoccupation. In the early 1900s the church wanted to be globally minded but couldn't escape theological and sociological distractions. Nineteenth-century optimism ran full-faced into the ugly realities of a modern world gone wrong. The human condition woefully revealed itself. Ethnocentrism of entire societies manifested itself in local and regional exploitations, wars, and genocides. Dreams of social and theological utopias drowned in the backwaters of industrial waste—both material and human.

The most poignant illustration of this modern clashing of worldviews was World War I. It began in 1914 as a mobilization of honorable soldiers to fight and win "the war to end all wars." Four years later its

---

[2]Ibid., 99–100.
[3]Ibid., 213.
[4]Ralph D. Winter, *The 25 Unbelievable Years, 1945–1969* (Pasadena, CA: William Carey Library, 1970), 12.

legacy was staggering: 8.5 million dead, 21 million wounded, 7.7 million missing or imprisoned.[5] Soldiers suffered some of the most inhumane living conditions and uncivilized deaths recorded in the histories of warfare. Both sides employed chemical warfare, an innovation of the "enlightened" scientific world. And this was supposed to be a modern, civilized, just, and Great War! No wonder the state of the evangelical world was in turmoil.

By the middle of the century, mainline Protestant denominational missions—the driving force of the previous century of missions—experienced a drastic decline. Toward the end of this cycle (1971–1979), the US Protestant missionary count serving overseas decreased more than 37 percent, from 3,160 to only 1,985.[6] What caused such a decline in missions involvement? Historian J. Herbert Kane cited five factors:

1. The maturity and independence of national churches (as colonies became nations) created a sense that outside missionaries were no longer needed.

2. New nations closed doors of access to foreign missionaries.

3. Declining enrollments in liberal seminaries reduced the pool of missionary candidates.

4. A decline in funding for missions.

5. Theological liberalism (especially neo-universalism) was "cutting the nerve of the Christian mission."[7]

Kane noted exceptions to this retrenchment. "Conservative" denominations and new movements were growing in their missions commitments. But the old days of colonial missions were gone. A new day had dawned.

Mission marginalization. Along with retrenchment, a parallel insidious marginalization of the mission of God surfaced. Patrick Johnstone reflected on this marginalization and its pesky persistence. Regarding the definition of the mission of God, he surmised: "To many today, mission means little more than the general work of the

---

[5]U.S. Department of Justice data posted by PBS, www.pbs.org/greatwar/resources/casdeath_pop.html.
[6]J. Herbert Kane, *A Concise History of the Christian World Mission* (Grand Rapids: Baker, 1978), 105.
[7]Ibid.

Church in the world to alleviate social ills but with the evangelistic or missionary sending component ignored or despised."[8]

Johnstone attributed this to our misunderstanding of the concept of the kingdom of God. We lost the biblical connection between mission (sending) and evangelism (proclaiming the gospel to those who haven't heard). We abandoned the biblical pattern of discipling new believers through new churches or faith communities. We lost sight of the pioneering theme of God's mission. Johnstone blamed this on our loss of biblical terminology. We replaced the word *apostle* with the nonbiblical term *missionary*. We removed the missionary from the "growing edge of the Church"—church planting—so that "anyone going overseas with church support is therefore called a missionary."[9]

Today we hear and read much about the church growth movement. Unfortunately, when we say "church growth" many think of attracting larger numbers of people to existing event-driven meetings among those who already know the Savior. Part of the church growth movement has resulted in attractional megachurches that backed away from that "growing edge." The founder of the Institute of Church Growth, Donald McGavran (a third-generation missionary to India), would not be pleased. As Kane, a contemporary of McGavran, pointed out, "Growth with McGavran is always spiritual growth. He is not interested in more and bigger budgets, buildings, or bureaucracies. Growth to him is gaining converts, discipling the nations, multiplying churches—in a word, *church* growth."[10]

God's mission is about more than the existing church. Indeed, the existing church is the vehicle, the means not the end. As we lost a biblical understanding of the mission of God, we marginalized missions. And as new nations gained independence from their colonial parents, some closed their doors to foreign missionaries from the West. Other

---

[8]Patrick Johnstone, *The Church Is Bigger Than You Think* (Fearn, UK: Christian Focus Publications/WEC, 1998), 35.

[9]Ibid., 50.

[10]Kane, *Concise History*, 108. It is ironic that Donald McGavran's Institute of Church Growth and the movement it spawned taught against this marginalization of the biblical evangelistic mission through the church. What was co-opted by some followers of McGavran as an attractional megachurch movement among the evangelized was in its pure form a call to apostolic evangelism and church multiplication among the unevangelized.

national churches were able to keep the doors open, but the terms of partnership shifted. Often the end became the growth and development of existing church ministries more than planting new churches. So *missions* became *ministry*. And *missionaries* became *ministers*.

Missiological warnings. In retrospect, we should have heard the warnings of several frontier missiologists. By the mid-1800s, missions strategists were calling for a change in paradigm, a new emphasis on starting indigenous or "homegrown" churches rather than transplanting Western churches to the rest of the world. Henry Venn and Rufus Anderson, British and American missions leaders, respectively, adapted the method of John Nevius, Presbyterian missionary to China, and led the call for self-dependent churches. Their "three-self" methodology focused on starting churches that were self-supporting, self-governing, and self-propagating.[11]

Pioneer missionary Hudson Taylor started an Asian mission (China Inland Mission, today's OMF) as the first "faith mission" organization established outside of the West. China Inland Mission practiced a highly contextualized approach to reaching all Chinese with the gospel.[12]

Into the twentieth century we heard the voice of Roland Allen, Anglican missionary to China from 1895 to 1903, who, upon experiencing firsthand the failures of colonial missions, returned to Scotland as an advocate for indigenous missions practices. His two books, *Missionary Methods: St. Paul's or Ours?* (1912) and *The Spontaneous Expansion of the Church—and the Causes Which Hinder It* (1927), remain required reading for many missionary candidates.[13]

Cameron Townsend, who founded Wycliffe Bible Translators in 1942, sent a wake-up call for communicating God's Word in indigenous or "heart" languages—one more warning for a change in paradigm. Donald McGavran challenged Western thinkers in his groundbreaking

---

[11]Today's registered or "Three-Self Church of China" reflects the influence of Venn, Anderson, and Nevius. Thanks to the three-self principle and the Communist government, today the church in China is no longer considered foreign.

[12]For more on these early missions pioneers, see Howard Norrish's previous chapter, "The Great Century."

[13]For a concise summary of Allen's ministry, see J. D. Payne, "The Legacy of Roland Allen," www.northamericanmissions.org/files/The-Legacy-of-Roland-Allen-Article.pdf.

book, *The Bridges of God* (1955). McGavran bid farewell to the Great Century of missions and challenged readers to think in terms of "people movements" rather than individual converts and "gathered churches." His experiences with the caste system of India led him to rediscover a more biblical model for preaching, teaching, and multiplying the gospel among least-reached peoples.

These trailblazing missiologists prepared the way for a new global missions movement that would define twentieth-century missions.

A standstill? On the eve of the 1960s, what was the state of God's mission among all peoples? The powerful Protestant missions movement of the 1800s had passed. Remarkably, some even claimed the mission had been accomplished. In 1942, Anglican archbishop William Temple heralded that the "great new fact of our time was the existence of the Christian Church in nearly every nation on earth."[14] Others recognized barriers against further progress, which included the closing doors of colonialism and increasing restrictions of new nations in the wake of revolution and nationalism. Communism loomed with its walls of isolation. In 1964, *Time* magazine featured the tragic story of the martyrdom of missionary Paul Carlson in the Congo. The secular press hailed "the end of the missionary movement."[15]

The cause of missions had been marginalized. After all, wasn't everyone a missionary? Wasn't it time to bring home the foreign missionaries and take care of our own communities? Shouldn't the church cease its proselytizing and focus on meeting the social, economic, and political needs of others?

Others saw a different future. Wasn't now the time to push ahead with the Great Commission task? Hadn't the atrocities of two world wars revealed the dire need for proclamation of the good news of Jesus? Hadn't our soldiers returned with stories of great spiritual poverty around the world? Wasn't it time to stop transplanting Western faith and practice and start planting indigenous ("homegrown") churches among all nations—to the ends of the earth? These questions and more

---

[14]Paul E. Pierson, *The Dynamics of Christian Mission* (Pasadena, CA: William Carey Library, 2009), 317.
[15]Ibid.

persisted. It seemed the global mission of God was at a standstill. It was time for a new movement.

The Lausanne Movement

God raised up a prophet to catalyze a new missions movement. With help and support from respected evangelicals like Carl Henry, Jack Dain, John Stott, Donald McGavran, René Padilla, and others, American evangelist Billy Graham called Christian leaders from around the world to gather for ten days in Lausanne, Switzerland to focus on global evangelization. In July of 1974, 2,300 evangelical leaders from 150 nations convened the first International Congress on World Evangelization.[16]

The most tangible product of the congress was the Lausanne Covenant, a 3,140-word document outlining the basis and mandate for global evangelization. Lausanne I, as this first gathering would come to be known, asserted that the goal of world evangelism "should be, by all available means and at the earliest possible time, that every person will have the opportunity to hear, understand, and receive the good news."[17] The congress confessed the neglect of the evangelical church regarding the urgency of this task: "More than 2,700 million people, which is more than two-thirds of all humanity, have yet to be evangelized. We are ashamed that so many have been neglected; it is a standing rebuke to us and the whole Church."[18]

Three themes emerged: "World evangelization requires the whole Church to take the whole gospel to the whole world."[19]

The whole church. First, the whole church, not just Western churches, must engage the Great Commission of Jesus Christ. Papers presented in Switzerland reinforced biblical teachings about the cultural diversity of the church. The challenge to evangelize the world was not limited to

---

[16]"About the Lausanne Movement," Lausanne Movement website, www.lausanne.org/about.html.

[17]J. D. Douglas, ed., *Let the Earth Hear His Voice: International Congress on World Evangelization, Lausanne, Switzerland* (Minneapolis: World Wide Publications, 1975), "The Lausanne Covenant," 6. The covenant is downloadable from the Lausanne Movement website: www.lausanne.org/covenant.

[18]Ibid.

[19]Ibid., 5.

those from a certain culture, economy, or political persuasion. "The church is the community of God's people rather than an institution, and

> *"The church is the community of God's people rather than an institution, and must not be identified with any particular culture, social or political system, or human ideology."*

must not be identified with any particular culture, social or political system, or human ideology."[20] To twenty-first century believers this statement may sound trite, but after "twenty-five unbelievable years" and in the midst a global cold war, it was a powerful and necessary caveat. The whole church was about to take on the task of global evangelization.

The whole gospel. This theme recalled the old debate about proclamation versus social ministry. René Padilla wrote and spoke eloquently on the subject. He reinforced biblical teachings of Christ that place a priority on proclaiming the gospel through both word and deed. He left no room for extreme or exclusive positions. He indicted those who ignored the hereafter dynamics of the kingdom of God and claimed the only thing that mattered was this world age (e.g., liberation theology). Yet, he also challenged those who assimilated history into their futurist eschatology and withdrew from society in the name of separation from the world.[21]

Perhaps the best summary of Padilla's (and ultimately Lausanne's) position is an excerpt from his response letter to the many questions and comments from congress participants: "I maintain that both of these views are incomplete gospels and that the greatest need of the church today is the recovery of the full Gospel of our Lord Jesus Christ—the whole Gospel for the whole man for the whole world."[22]

The final covenant affirms the priority of proclaiming the gospel and the requirement for social action:

> Here too we express penitence both for our neglect and for having sometimes regarded evangelism and social concern as mutually exclusive. Although reconciliation with other people is not reconciliation

---

[20]Ibid.
[21]Ibid., 129.
[22]Ibid., 144.

with God, nor is social action evangelism, nor is political liberation salvation, nevertheless we affirm that evangelism and socio-political involvement are both part of our Christian duty. . . .

In the Church's mission of sacrificial service evangelism is primary. World evangelization requires the whole Church to take the whole gospel to the whole world.[23]

So evangelism is the primary goal of the Lausanne movement, but not without accompanying Christlike deeds or actions.[24]

The whole world. The third theme of Lausanne I provided the greatest impetus for a new global movement. Once again, God intervened. He used Ralph Winter, a professor and missions entrepreneur to stir the congress. Winter, then Professor of the History of the Christian Movement at Fuller Seminary, presented a plenary paper titled "The Highest Priority: Cross-Cultural Evangelism." He exhorted the congress to make evangelization of those without access to the gospel their top priority.

Winter shook some of the congress out of their self-focused optimism and reminded everyone that "the master pattern of the expansion of the Christian movement" was to cross cultural barriers with the gospel. He insisted we must reach those without access to Jesus and disciple them to reach their own culture with the good news of the kingdom of God.[25] Now was definitely not the time for retrenchment. As

> As the theme of Lausanne I stated, now was the time to "Let the earth hear his voice!" Winter was, in effect, adding "all peoples of the earth" to the rally cry.

the theme of Lausanne I stated, now was the time to "Let the earth hear his voice!" Winter was, in effect, adding "all peoples of the earth" to the rally cry.

In his now familiar style, Winter presented a taxonomy for evangelism (the "E-scale") and demographics to demonstrate the urgency of

---

[23]Ibid., 4–5.

[24]For recent dialogues about this and other critical missiological issues, see David J. Hesselgrave and Ed Stetzer, eds., *MissionShift: Global Mission Issues in the Third Millennium* (Nashville: B&H Academic, 2010).

[25]Douglas, *Let the Earth Hear His Voice*, 220.

this cross-cultural priority. Ever the historian and missionary trainer, his paper and follow-up letter made a lasting impact.

Almost in passing, Winter exposed the Achilles heel of the evangelical missions community—"people blindness." Why wasn't the missions community more aware of the masses of humans who had no access to Jesus? Why wasn't cross-cultural evangelism our highest priority? Winter explained:

> I'm afraid that all our exultation about the fact that every *country* of the world has been penetrated has allowed many to suppose that every *culture* has by now been penetrated. This misunderstanding is a malady so widespread that it deserves a special name. Let us call it "people blindness" that is, blindness to the existence of separate *peoples* within *countries*. . . . The "nations" to which Jesus often referred were mainly ethnic groups. . . . The various nations represented on the day of Pentecost were for the most part not *countries* but *peoples*. In the Great Commission . . . the phrase "make disciples of all *ethne* (peoples)" does not let us off the hook once we have a church in every country—God wants a strong church within every people![26]

In his published letter of response, Winter guessed that 95 percent of all missionaries deployed outside the West worked among Christians or established churches. His indictment stung: "That leaves only a tiny percentage of cross-cultural workers to deal with the three major blocs [Hindu, Muslim, Chinese] of non-Western non-Christians. Brothers and sisters, this is a grim picture."[27]

Winter's purpose was to raise cross-cultural evangelism to the highest priority. But his greatest contribution at Lausanne I, and perhaps the greatest breakthrough of the entire congress, was the exposure of this malady of people blindness. The mission of God would never be the same.[28]

---

[26]Ibid., 221.

[27]Ibid., 233.

[28]In later writings Winter acknowledged building upon the work of senior colleagues such as Cameron Townsend and Paul Hiebert. He claimed that Donald McGavran's "active efforts and writings spawned both the church growth movement and the frontier missions movement." Ralph Winter, ed., *Perspectives on the World Christian Movement* (Pasadena, CA: William Carey Library, 1981), 175. If they were the catalysts, then Winter was truly the pioneer. His emphasis and impact on frontier missions cannot be overemphasized.

AD 2000 and Beyond

The last quarter of the twentieth century saw a global movement of evangelical Christians obsessed with engaging the least-reached peoples on earth with the gospel. This became the overarching theme of the global century of God's mission. The search for hidden peoples manifested itself in numerous ways.

> *The last quarter of the twentieth century saw a global movement of evangelical Christians obsessed with engaging the least-reached peoples on earth with the gospel.*

New prayer. Thousands of missions leaders left Lausanne I committed to pray for the hidden peoples of the world. Several global prayer networks responded to the call. For example, Brother Andrew's Open Doors prayer network expanded its vision beyond the closed borders of the Soviet Union. Their emphasis on Bible distribution and prayer provided strategic outlets for other networks.

Patrick Johnstone, a British missionary to South Africa, began a remarkable journey of prayer mobilization in the 1960s. He published his first edition of *Operation World: The Definitive Prayer Guide to Every Nation* in 1974.[29] This prayer resource included demographics on every country in the world, with a breakdown of major people groups and related prayer requests. *Operation World* became the unofficial prayer handbook for missionary candidates. Many a missionary testified how God called and inspired them to go to unreached peoples through daily readings and prayers in *Operation World*.

New research. Even before Lausanne I adjourned, the unspoken question on the minds of many was "Who *are* these thousands of *ethne* who have no access to the gospel?" Missions research and demography became a priority for the evangelical missions world. Four major databases developed over the next twenty-five years.

The Ethnologue database of world languages served as a foundational resource for the other three people group databases. Predating Lausanne I, SIL International, the research and teaching arm of

---

[29]From a video posted on the Operation World website: www.operationworld.org. The seventh edition of *Operation World*, edited by Jason Mandryk, was published by Biblica in 2010.

Wycliffe Bible Translators, started publishing a snapshot of languages of the world with accompanying maps. It served as a starting point for many researchers and practitioners who were looking for Winter's hidden peoples. The current *Ethnologue* is in its sixteenth edition.[30]

The global prayer movement spawned by Operation World required an unprecedented database of the peoples on earth. How could we pray for them if we didn't know who and where they were? Johnstone's database morphed into what is today known as the Joshua Project, "a research initiative seeking to highlight the ethnic people groups with the least followers of Jesus Christ."[31]

The World Christian Database was a byproduct of the *World Christian Encyclopedia* (1982, 2001). David Barrett, Anglican missionary to Kenya, was the founder and first editor of this vast encyclopedia of missionary data published by Oxford University Press. Currently housed in the Center for the Study of Global Christianity, it remains a primary source of data for tracking the broad progress of Christianity around the world.[32]

During the years of the encyclopedia's first revision, Barrett partnered with the International Mission Board of the Southern Baptist Convention and based his research team in Richmond, Virginia. The fact that an Anglican missionary researcher could work alongside a Southern Baptist missions agency speaks volumes about the whole church working together to engage Winter's hidden peoples with the gospel.

After a few years of productive partnering, the two groups parted ways and the IMB launched its own Church Planting Progress Indicators (CPPI) database. CPPI identifies peoples without access to an "evangelical" witness and provides a dynamic field-driven reporting instrument. It focuses on levels of engagement for the purpose of evangelization resulting in church-planting movements.[33]

---

[30]Paul M. Lewis, ed., *Ethnologue: Languages of the World*, 16th edition (Dallas: SIL International, 2009), available at www.ethnologue.com.

[31]Self-definition posted on the Joshua Project website: www.joshuaproject.net.

[32]See the Center for the Study of Global Christianity website: www.gordonconwell.edu/resources/Center-for-the-Study-of-Global-Christianity.cfm.

[33]For public access to IMB database reports, see IMB's Global Research website: http://public.imb.org/globalresearch/Pages/default.aspx.

These four databases complement each other to this day and provide a valuable collection of research data for the evangelical missions community.[34] Indicative of the spirit of the global century of missions, eight representatives from these four database organizations meet monthly via Skype to update each other and collaborate on the continuing task of finding and engaging the "hidden peoples" with the gospel of Jesus.[35]

A new window. As the search for hidden peoples began, a pattern emerged. The unreached peoples on earth lived in the same global neighborhood. They lived in countries perceived as resistant to the gospel. And in this global neighborhood, government authorities restrict travel and residence. Different names for this region evolved, including "resistant belt," "unoccupied fields," "restricted-access countries," and "World A."

At the 1989 Lausanne II congress in Manila, Luis Bush, a well-known Ibero-American pastor and missions advocate, spoke on the meeting theme, "The Challenge Before Us." Bush noticed most of the world's hidden peoples lived in a band extending from West Africa across Asia, between 10 and 40 degrees north of the equator. This is where we must concentrate our mission efforts, Bush concluded. He called it the "10/40 box" until some months later when his wife, Doris, reasoned, "Rather than a 10/40 box, why not think of it as the 10/40 Window? A window is a picture of hope, light, life, and vision."[36] The term stuck and for the next fifteen years the 10/40 Window became the priority field of missions service among evangelicals.

New paradigms. As evangelical missions agencies opened the new window to unreached peoples, they began the arduous task of recreating themselves. For many, this meant revising vision and mission statements to reflect the new focus on least-reached peoples. Agencies with strong traditional fields began to think about redeployments of

---

[34]For an excellent overview of databases and people lists, see Patrick Johnstone, "Affinity Blocs and People Clusters: An Approach Toward Strategic Insight and Mission Partnership," *Mission Frontiers* (March–April 2007), www.missionfrontiers.org/issue/article/affinity-blocs-and-people-clusters.

[35]Jim Haney, Director of Global Research, IMB, e-mail message to author.

[36]Luis Bush and Beverly Pegues, *The Move of the Holy Spirit in the 10/40 Window* (Seattle: YWAM Publishing, 1999), 226. For an excellent summary of the development of the term "10/40 Window," see 225–27.

personnel into the 10/40 Window. This was tough stuff! It called for radical change of the status quo and threatened existing ministries in traditional fields. The 1990s witnessed numerous old agency name changes and mergers, along with the advent of new agencies.

In 1982, Greg Livingstone launched a sister agency of Arab World Ministries called Frontiers, one example of a new agency. Frontiers was the first mission exclusively focused on reaching "all and only" Muslims of the world. Livingstone recalls, "It was a quantitative problem. Less than 1 percent of all the missionaries in the world were in residence among Muslims, even though they are one out of every five in the world."[37] Today Frontiers has twenty-one national offices, with workers based where Muslims live throughout the world. Their slogan is "With love and respect, inviting all Muslim peoples to follow Jesus."

New missionaries. A prominent challenge to entering the 10/40 Window was the fact that professional missionaries were not granted visas for residence in restricted-access regions. So a new kind of missionary was needed, one who added value to a host society other than as a professional Christian.

Evangelicals rediscovered the biblical model of the "tentmaker" (Acts 18:3). By using the apostle Paul's approach, previous "restricted-access countries" became "creative-access countries." Tentmaker trailblazers like J. Christy Wilson and Ruth Siemens mobilized scores of twentieth-century tentmakers. Wilson taught and wrote about *Today's Tentmakers* (Tyndale, 1979), and Siemens started a tentmaking advocacy agency, Global Opportunities, in 1976. By the end of the century, a thriving network of tentmaker and BAM (Business as Mission) advocates and practitioners existed, with a substantial body of literature and numerous advocate agencies.

A short-term missions (STM) movement accompanied the push to the least-reached.[38] The shrinking global village and a renewed emphasis on cross-cultural missions resulted in a new wave of short–term volun-

---

[37]Greg Livingstone, "Where We've Been," video posted on the Frontiers website: www.frontiers usa.org/site/PageNavigator/about/about_where_we_have_been.

[38]For a survey of the STM movement, see Robert J. Priest, *Effective Engagement in Short-Term Missions* (Pasadena, CA: William Carey Library, 2008).

teers, missions trips, and projects. A radical approach by IMB's 10/40 Window team used two-year workers to open new fields without any existing support from long-term personnel. Individual church planting or "strategy coordinator" churches were also enlisted to lead missions strategies previously reserved for long-term residential missionaries.

To say the least, the role of the missionary expanded and extended itself in ways not seen since the first century. It was a new day.

New partners and networks. In this new day of global missions regular international congresses and consultations were held. Lausanne II convened in Manila in 1989, and a series of Global Consultations on World Evangelization (GCOWE) were held regularly around the world.[39]

Riding the momentum of Lausanne II in Manila, Luis Bush founded the AD2000 & Beyond Movement, which Ralph Winter later characterized as "the largest, most pervasive global evangelical network ever to exist."[40] The emphasis on AD 2000 resulted in the development and implementation of hundreds of world evangelization strategies.[41]

Smaller regional partnerships on the field were formed. In the 1990s an organization called Interdev, directed by Phil Butler, focused on assisting missions agencies and workers around the world to create and effectively manage strategic partnerships. There was unprecedented cooperation among "Great Commission Christians" at a variety of strategic levels. Most regional partnerships met annually in an "outside," secure location to share their "best and worst practices."

New strategies. New field strategies developed in concert with the other new aspects of the movement. Mission teams replaced church-style field missions. The role of the apostle or missionary shifted

---

[39]"Global gatherings include the Consultation on World Evangelization (Pattaya 1980), the Conference of Young Leaders (Singapore 1987), the Forum for World Evangelization (Pattaya 2004) and the Younger Leaders' Gathering (Malaysia 2006). Lausanne has inspired many regional networks and issue-based conferences such as the Asia Lausanne Committee on Evangelism (ALCOE), Chinese Co-ordination Centre for World Evangelization (CC-COWE), a series of Nigerian congresses on world evangelization, and several international consultations on Jewish evangelism." "About the Lausanne Movement," Lausanne Movement website, www.lausanne.org/about.html.

[40]"AD2000 and Beyond Movement Overview," AD2000 & Beyond Movement website, www .ad2000.org/ad2kbroc.htm.

[41]Stan Guthrie, *Missions in the Third Millennium: 21 Key Trends for the 21st Century* (Milton Keynes, UK: Paternoster Press, 2000), 67.

from a directive to a facilitative role. As previously noted, short-term workers and marketplacers found themselves in trailblazing roles. The role of women in missions became increasingly strategic, especially in cultures that isolated women. Humanitarian work through NGOs (nongovernmental organizations) opened previously shut doors. Bible translators created innovative tactics that reduced the timeline for translations from twenty-five to five years. New priorities and resources were allocated for radio and TV broadcasts. Satellite television became a key player in reaching through the 10/40 Window. Sixty million JESUS film products have been distributed in 1,129 different languages since 1979.[42] Chronological Bible Storying (CBS) and "orality" strategies were developed to communicate Christ and his teachings more effectively to those from oral learning (illiterate) cultures.

Space does not allow a comprehensive survey of the numerous new strategies that developed in the wake of Lausanne I in pursuit of unreached peoples.

One of the remarkable strategic developments of the last decades of the twentieth century of God's mission was the recognition and expectation of "church-planting movements." Undergirded by McGavran's people-movement observations of a half-century earlier, the dynamics of church-planting movements were overtly revealed by God himself. Missions workers noticed that if the gospel of Jesus was introduced to least-reached peoples with little or no previous knowledge of Christ, then God created movements of Christ-followers extending the kingdom through the church.

Missions workers noticed that if the gospel of Jesus was introduced to least-reached peoples with little or no previous knowledge of Christ, then God created movements of Christ-followers extending the kingdom through the church.

To clarify, this was not so much a realized plan or missionary-initiated strategy as it was a surprise from God! In a sense, once the

---

[42]"The Official Ministry Statistics of The JESUS Film Project," The Jesus Film Project website, www.jesusfilm.org/film-and-media/statistics/quarterly-statistics.

church returned to the real purpose of the mission of God—to reach the unreached with the gospel of Jesus Christ—the Holy Spirit returned to his business of extending his kingdom through church-multiplication movements. Today's missions researchers track and verify dozens of church-planting movements in process.

An online perusal of missions agencies' vision, purpose, and mission statements reveals a consistent pattern. Whether they are called "church-planting movements," "rapidly reproducing churches," "church-multiplication movements," or "discipleship-multiplication movements," evangelical missions today are generally intent on catalyzing movements of followers of Christ throughout their peoples and beyond.

Conclusion

The twentieth century of the mission of God was truly a global century. World social, political, economic, technological, and religious events challenged missions practices of the past. Mid-century, the church's commitment to God's mission came to a standstill. Was the mission accomplished? Was it time for retrenchment?

Once again, God used a few individuals to stir up thousands of missions leaders from around the world. At Lausanne I, we reframed our biblical and practical understanding of God's mission. No, the mission was not accomplished. Indeed, we had marginalized the purpose of God's mission. He was waiting for us to rediscover his mission to all peoples.

Missions pioneer Ralph Winter exposed a lethal malady—"people blindness." Of the three themes of the congress—"whole church, whole gospel, whole world," the "whole world" idea created the most traction. Winter's picture of millions of "hidden peoples" stuck in the minds and hearts of many. The call of Lausanne I went out: "Let the earth hear his voice!"

What followed was twenty-five years of global missions progress. A new wave of extraordinary strategic prayer was mobilized. New windows opened and old barriers fell. Missions researchers developed an entire industry of identifying and tracking the progress of God's mission among all peoples. New missions agencies were created; older ones were recreated. New and age-old methods of engaging peoples with the good news of Jesus Christ were discovered and implemented. Paradigms and directions turned on their heads. The scope of the mission and the range of its participants became global in scope.

Remember, it is God's mission, and the twentieth century left us with much good news regarding his expansion of the kingdom among all peoples. Let us learn lessons for tomorrow from the history of the global century of missions—so that "throughout the whole world" the gospel will bear fruit and grow (Colossians 1:6).

Discussion Points

1. How did the end of colonialism and the rise of nationalism affect God's mission in the twentieth century?

2. What warnings did we hear from late nineteenth- and early twentieth-century missiologists? Was this the first time you've heard of these missiological concepts? Read part three of this book to learn more about them.

3. Who called for a world congress of Christian leaders to meet in Lausanne? What goal in regard to world evangelism emerged from Lausanne I? What three themes emerged? Which theme does Barnett think had the greatest impact on the last twenty-five years of the twentieth century?

4. Do you pray for a specific unreached people group to receive the gospel of Jesus? Perhaps you can commit yourself to research a specific unreached people and pray regularly for them until you complete this book or your course of study.

Further Reading

Bush, Luis, and Beverly Pegues. *The Move of the Holy Spirit in the 10/40 Window*. Seattle: YWAM Publishing, 1999.

Garrison, David. *Church Planting Movements: How God Is Redeeming a Lost World*. Midlothian, VA: WIGTake Resources, 2004.

Hesselgrave, David J., and Ed Stetzer, eds. *MissionShift: Global Mission Issues in the Third Millennium.* Nashville: B&H Academic, 2010.

Johnstone, Patrick. *The Church Is Bigger Than You Think: The Unfinished Work of World Evangelism.* Fearn, UK: Christian Focus Publications/ WEC, 1998.

Steffen, Tom, and Mike Barnett, eds. *Business as Mission: From Impoverished to Empowered.* Evangelical Missiological Society Series, Number 14. Pasadena, CA: William Carey Library, 2006.

PART THREE

THE MISSION OF GOD TODAY

We have discovered the mission of God through a review of Scripture and a survey of historical eras, missionaries, and movements. The rest of this book focuses on critical issues, principles, and practices in God's mission to the nations today. These chapters are fresh from the fields of cross-cultural missions. Most of the authors are younger practitioners from a variety of fields around the world.

How much of God's mission is unfinished? What is the task before us? How do we take the good news of Jesus Christ across cultural barriers? Where does the church fit into the mission of God? How will we work together as we participate in God's mission to all peoples on earth? Where do we ourselves fit?

These and other questions concerning the mission of God will be discovered in this final part of our journey. Finish well!

See also the following e-chapters in the *Discovering the Mission of God Supplement* **e-book:**

- The Business of Building Bridges—Patrick Lai
- God's Mission Today Through Prayer—Natalie Shepherd and Peter Hawkins
- Equippers for God's Mission—Marty Glickman
- Jesus Christ: The Way, the Truth, and the Life?—Brad Roderick
- The Left Side of the Graph—Clyde Meador
- Breaking Old Habits—Rebekah A. Naylor
- Principles and Practices—Mike Barnett
- Measuring Church Planting Progress at Avant—Scott Harris
- Human Needs Ministries for God's Mission—J. Jeffrey Palmer

- Preach and Heal—Charles Fielding
- Church and Agency Co-Laboring—Jerry Rankin and Mike Edens
- Eleven Implications for the North American Church—J. D. Payne

18

THE STATE OF
THE SPREAD OF THE GOSPEL

Jim Haney

*For I am not ashamed of the gospel, because it is the power
of God that brings salvation to everyone who believes:
first to the Jew, then to the Gentile. For in the gospel
the righteousness of God is revealed—a righteousness
that is by faith from first to last, just as it is written:
"The righteous will live by faith."*

(ROMANS 1:16–17)

For centuries, the gospel of Jesus Christ resounded as a trumpet above the noise of each generation. It echoed through fortresses of spiritual darkness as unnumbered witnesses testified to the penetrating melody of God's love-message for their day. Sometimes, opportunities for sharing the gospel brought unspeakable hardships upon believers where only the surpassing comfort of Christ carried them through. Some labored without any results known to them; others saw great response and experienced the joy of a great harvest.

Those who shared were stewards of an offering—an offering of Christ to them and an offering of Christ through them to others. They rested in the depth of God's love and embraced the eternal remedy to sin. Men and women of every generation spent their lives seeking pathways through the rubble of a fallen world. Loving and passionate followers of Christ, following his example, reached out in word and deed to rescue the perishing.

As we think of how the good news of salvation has come to us and begin to understand the importance of it beyond us, we realize that God desires to use you and me in his eternal plan to share his gospel with those deprived of their opportunity to hear and believe.

What is the state of the gospel in the world today? This chapter attempts to provide a progress report to help us answer this question.

A Word About Statistics[1]

The world is a big place, and understanding the progress of the gospel in the world today is a huge undertaking. We attempt this undertaking because we are stewards of God's great mandate to make disciples of all nations. To the best of our ability, we must assure that no one is left without the opportunity of hearing and responding to the gospel. The Word of God, the Bible, provides a preview of where believers in Christ will stand one day: "After this I looked, and there before me was a great multitude that no one could count, from every nation, tribe, people and language, standing before the throne and before the Lamb. They were wearing white robes and were holding palm branches in their hands" (Revelation 7:9).

If no one could count this number in heaven, how are we able to discern today the number who will be in heaven in the future? We can't. We can't see into peoples' hearts, and we can't know for certain how many in the world today have a personal relationship with Jesus Christ. Because of this, we must be diligent to witness boldly so that every person in every generation has the opportunity to know our loving Lord, and we must humbly report statistics from multiple sources to see traces of what God is showing us.

The focus of this chapter is on the spread of the gospel as it pertains to the extent to which global ethnicities or people groups[2] are "engaged"—

---

[1]The general data, unpublished reports, and graphics in this chapter come from the Global Research Department of the International Mission Board. The author currently serves as director.
[2]"People groups" refers to ethnolinguistically related peoples.

i.e., where an evangelical[3] church-planting strategy is under way.[4] As part of this process, I will provide a global summary of the status of the gospel among all people groups. Because the global status of evangelical Christianity is dynamic, readers should keep abreast of updates, such as are found monthly at Peoplegroups.org. Periodic updates may be also found at JoshuaProject.net and, by subscription, at World Christian Database (www.worldchristiandatabase.org/wcd).

Global Studies

For the last century or so, the percentage of adherents to Christianity has remained relatively stable at about 33 percent of the global population. Compared to other major world religions, Christianity remains the largest.[5]

Within the general population of Christians, it is estimated that there are anywhere from 190 million[6] to 420 million[7] evangelicals, depending on the source. Some higher estimates may include those who affiliate with evangelical congregations but attend only occasionally, are marginal members, or were counted twice. In addition, the aspect of syncretism must be considered when seriously assessing

---

[3] In response to the question "What do you mean by 'Evangelical' Christians and churches?" the Global Research Department of IMB answers, "An Evangelical Christian is a person who believes that Jesus Christ is the sole source of salvation through faith in him, has personal faith and conversion with regeneration by the Holy Spirit, recognizes the inspired Word of God as the only basis for faith and Christian living, and is committed to Biblical preaching and evangelism that brings others to faith in Jesus Christ. Therefore, an Evangelical church is a church that is characterized by these same beliefs and principles. Some churches that are not considered Evangelical in faith and practice, may contain members who are Evangelical." "FAQs," Peoplegroups.org website, www.peoplegroups.org/faqs.aspx.

[4] Jeff Liverman, of Frontiers, suggests four essential elements of engagement: (1) Apostolic effort in residence; (2) Commitment to work in the local language and culture; (3) Commitment to long-term ministry; and (4) Sowing in a manner consistent with the goal of seeing a church-planting movement (CPM) emerge. Jeff Liverman, "What Does It Mean to Effectively 'Engage' a People?" *Mission Frontiers* (November–December 2006): 10, www.missionfrontiers.com/pdf/2006/06/200606.htm.

[5] David B. Barrett, George Thomas Kurian, and Todd M. Johnson, *World Christian Encyclopedia: A Comparative Survey of Churches and Religions in the Modern World*, vol. 1 (Oxford: Oxford University Press, 2001), 4; and Patrick Johnstone, *Operation World* (Carlisle, UK: Paternoster, 2001), 2.

[6] "Complete List of People Groups Excel Spreadsheet Confidential," unpublished, Global Research Department, International Mission Board, June 2008.

[7] Johnstone, *Operation World*, 3.

if someone is evangelical from the standpoint of faith in Jesus Christ being his or her *sole source* of salvation. Why do we distinguish between nominal Christians and evangelicals? To put it plainly, we can't afford to neglect those within our churches who continue to live their lives looking beyond the sufficiency of Christ for matters both eternal and temporal.

Table 18.1. State of the Gospel (Haney)

World Religion	World Christian Encyclopedia	Operation World	Adherents (Adjusted Indexed [2008])
Christians	33.00%	32.54%	2,234,914,000
Muslims	19.60%	21.09%	1,387,529,000
Hindus	13.40%	13.52%	917,972,000
Nonreligious	12.70%	15.46%	960,256,000
Buddhists	5.90%	6.60%	426,250,000
Sikhs	0.40%	0.34%	25,234,000
Jews	0.40%	0.24%	21,824,000
Others	14.60%	10.21%	846,021,000
Total	100.00%	100.00%	6,820,000,000

In 2007 a preliminary survey was conducted to assess the degree to which four urban centers in Brazil were evangelical. The survey concluded that although estimates showed the country to be as high as 30 percent evangelical, the four urban centers ranged from 0.6 to 4.1 percent evangelical. These percentages excluded from evangelical faith and practice those who held to any syncretistic beliefs and practices as measured in the survey.[8] There is obviously much to be done, even where strong churches exist. I use this example, and there are many others, to warn against being overly optimistic when counting evangelicals in the world today. With this in mind, let's move on to characterizing people groups and assessing priority needs.

---

[8]Alan Myatt and Nolen Pridemore, "Evangelicals in Brazil: A Preliminary Survey," unpublished, 2008. This was adapted from an original survey designed by Jim Haney, "Measuring Religious Beliefs: A Model for Assessing Evangelical Beliefs," unpublished, 2002.

Counting the Nations

Patrick Johnstone credits many with seeking to understand and list the ethnolinguistic people groups in our world. Among those who have worked to produce and maintain global lists are Wycliffe Bible Translators (*Ethnologue*); David Barrett, Todd Johnson, and others (*World Christian Encyclopedia*); Dan Scribner, Bill Morrison, and others (Joshua Project); and International Mission Board (IMB) field personnel and partners (Church Planting Progress Indicators, or CPPI).[9] In addition to the global lists, there are very good local lists of people groups focusing on individual affinity blocs, people clusters, countries, provinces, or other subsets of the global population.

Affinity blocs, people clusters, people groups, and people group segments. Just as many endeavors look toward a taxonomy for understanding their world and constructing a model for it, some missionary organizations group peoples into a hierarchical model to assist them in understanding the world of people groups. One model for doing this recognizes 15 major affinity blocs. Within these 15 affinity blocs, there are more than 250 people clusters. Within these people clusters, there are more than 10,000 specific people groups sharing nearly 7,000 living languages, not to mention dialects and new speech varieties. Within people groups, there may be a number of common sociological population segments: teachers, middle-class neighborhoods, carpenters, taxi drivers, etc. The diagram at <www.joshuaproject.net/peoples-tree.php> shows 15 affinity blocs and a breakout of the East Asian Peoples affinity bloc, including a color-coded progress scale to show the state of the gospel at each subdivision.[10]

Thinking about this approach opens a number of strategic possibilities. For example, various people group lists may disagree as to how many Chinese-Hui people groups there are. Backing up one level allows the missionary team to think strategically about the Chinese-Hui people cluster as a whole. As the team begins to network with

---

[9]Patrick Johnstone. "Affinity Blocs and People Clusters: An Approach Toward Strategic Insight and Mission Partnership," *Mission Frontiers* (March–April 2007), www.missionfrontiers.org/issue/article/affinity-blocs-and-people-clusters.

[10]"Ethnic Peoples Tree," Joshua Project website, www.joshuaproject.net/peoples-tree.php.

other partners similarly burdened for the Hui peoples, they begin to understand, along with these partners, more about worldviews, languages, and the way people identify themselves (self-ascription). As the cluster network confirms ethnicities, they further determine which groups need priority attention.

Urban centers. There is at least one other natural grouping that is calling for our attention: urban centers. Just as there were many peoples in Jerusalem at Pentecost, each hearing God's message in their own language, God may be bringing people out of the forests, villages, and mountains so that we can know them and reach them in cities. So let me ask you, "What are you doing to reach people groups in your city?" Consider these statistics:

- In China, 200 million people migrated from the countryside to cities during the past ten years.

- Every second, two people move from rural areas to cities.

- Half of all Asians and Africans will live in cities by 2030.

- In the years 2000–2030, 88 percent of human population growth will occur in cities in developing countries.

Missionary strategists in urban cities around the world need a grand vision for seeing multiplying churches among people groups flooding into cities. Our focus on people groups should lead us to see cities as collections of people groups.

Dickie Nelson, former regional leader for the IMB in South America, has an eye on both people groups and cities. He observes that the vast majority of unreached and unengaged people groups in South America live in cities. When we think of South America, we think of the vast Amazon basin, unrelenting rain forests, and high mountain peaks, but it escapes the attention of most that there are forty-one cities in ten different countries in South America with over one million inhabitants each. In fact, nearly eight out of ten people in South America live in cities.[11] We cannot neglect these cities and other cities around the world, nor assume that the churches within them are engaging the people groups coming to them.

---

[11]Dickie Nelson, e-mail message to author, June 23, 2008.

The Progress of the Gospel Today

What can be said about the progress of the gospel among the people groups in the world today? To answer this question, we will consider the monthly overview of the "Global Status of Evangelical Christianity."[12] This overview, drawing from observations of missionary church planters on many fields, provides firsthand information about what God is doing. This information is valuable to mission strategists and decision makers and helps them determine the extent to which each people group (1) consists of evangelical Christians; (2) has access to the gospel; and (3) has experienced localized or widespread evangelical church planting within the last two years.

Table 18.2. Global Status of Evangelical Christianity Model (Haney)

	Status	Description
Last Frontier	0	No evangelical Christians or churches. No access to major evangelical print, audio, visual, or human resources.
	1	Less than 2% evangelical. Some evangelical resources available, but no active church planting within past 2 years.
Unreached	2	Less than 2% evangelical. Initial (localized) church planting within past 2 years.
	3	Less than 2% evangelical. Widespread church planting within past 2 years.
	4	Greater than or equal to 2% evangelical
	5	Greater than or equal to 5% evangelical
	6	Greater than or equal to 10% evangelical
	7	Unknown

These factors contribute to a GSEC (Global Status of Evangelical Christianity) status code from zero to seven, as described in The Global Status of Evangelical Christianity Model, being given to every known people group.

In addition to the status codes and descriptions, two additional terms help us focus on those people groups most needy of gospel engagement:

---

[12]"Global Status of Evangelical Christianity Full Set," Global Research Department, International Mission Board, Peoplegroups.org website, www.peoplegroups.org/Downloads.aspx.

- Last Frontier people group—A people group that is less than 2 percent evangelical Christian, has limited evangelical resources, and has experienced no church planting activity in the past two years. (Status 0 or 1)
- Unreached people group —A people group that is less than 2 percent evangelical Christian. (Status 0 to 3)[13]

Last Frontier people groups, because they are less than 2 percent evangelical Christian, are also considered to be unreached people groups. Obviously, there is much to be done among these people groups as well; but as any particular people group surpasses 2 percent evangelical, most strategists feel there is likely to be an established core of believers who can continue the task of evangelism with minimal outside assistance. It is exciting to see that an increasing number of people groups, once part of the harvest field, have come to Christ, matured, and joined the ranks of the harvest force.

Now that we have established some common language for considering the status of people groups, we will summarize what we can see in the field report for January 2009.[14]

Table 18.3.

Status Level	People Groups		Population	
0	124	1.1%	3,457,293	0.0%
1	5,726	49.2%	1,656,377,149	24.0%
2	583	5.0%	1,960,177,658	28.3%
3	30	0.3%	380,932,208	5.5%
4	991	8.5%	1,826,425,596	26.4%
5	1,221	10.5%	438,374,308	6.3%
6	1,915	16.4%	311,329,192	4.5%
7	1,056	9.1%	338,649,093	4.9%
Totals	11,646		6,915,722,497	

---

[13]The IMB and other organizations often use 2 percent as the benchmark for determining whether a people group is unreached. That is, if a people group is at least 2 percent evangelical Christian it is no longer considered unreached. It is recognized that this percentage is only a guideline—the goal is to engage unreached people groups until such time that they have within them a sufficient core of evangelical believers who are capable and committed to finishing the task of evangelizing their people group without further engagement from the outside.
[14]To see the current month, refer to www.peoplegroups.org/Downloads.aspx.

At the time of this writing, the Church Planting Progress Indicators (CPPI) database included 11,646 people groups around the world. Note the status codes in the left column. Referring to the numbers and descriptions, as previously discussed, the data shows that of the 11,646 people groups in the world:

- 6,615 people groups (status levels 0–3), or 55.5 percent of the total number of people groups, are unreached people groups (UPGs). The global population of people living within these UPGs is 4,096,392,034, or 57.9 percent of the global population.

- 4,127 people groups (status levels 4–6), or 35.4 percent of the total number of people groups, are no longer unreached people groups. The global population of people living within these people groups is 2,576,129,096, or 37.2 percent of the global population

- 1,056 people groups (status level 7) have a status indicating that we are not able to assess if they are unreached. Many of these groups are relatively small, comprising only 4.9 percent of the global population.

Now let's investigate the relative sizes of people groups that remain unreached (status levels 0–3). The following table shows unreached people groups by population bands.

Table 18.4.

Status	Under 10K	10K - 50K	50K - 100K	100K - 1 million	1 million - 10 million	10 million & up	Population Unknown	Total
Last Frontier	2,084	1,621	577	1,269	278	21	0	**5,850**
Level 2	34	45	25	233	204	42	0	**583**
Level 3	0	0	0	7	13	10	0	**30**
Total Unreached	**2,118**	**1,666**	**602**	**1,509**	**495**	**73**	**0**	**6,463**

Currently, many organizations focus on implementing church planting strategies (engaging) within unreached people groups with a population of at least 100,000. By adding the number of people groups in the population bands of 100,000 and greater (1,509 + 495 + 73), we get 2,077 unreached people groups equal to or greater than 100,000 (UPGs ≥ 100,000). As these people groups are reached, they become partners in the missionary task.

What Is Being Done About These UPGs Now?

Today, believers in Jesus Christ are praying for unreached people groups. Prayer recognizes and claims God's promises, and those promises are many. Since God's Word promises that he will gather the nations around his throne in glory one day, prayer allows us to thank God for providing for the nations and for using us to announce this great news. Prayer also convicts us of our lack of faith that he can accomplish his purpose within unreached people groups. Prayer brings about many things, one of which is confession. It's easy to question why those who followed Moses didn't enter the promised land when God led them there—but they didn't believe God was up to the task. Prayer helps us understand that if the task is unfinished, it is God's unfinished task, and he is able to accomplish it and able to take care of us on the journey if we follow him.

The task of reaching unreached people groups is to proclaim the message of salvation to all people groups in the world in such a way that each receives a legitimate opportunity to hear the gospel, understand it, and accept it. To do this, missionaries respond to the call of God to engage unreached people groups through church planting. The goal is to tell the story of Jesus Christ and gather seekers and believers into churches so that they may enjoy fellowship with God and with each other.

The heart of the missionary church planter is to see a given people group respond to the gospel and mature to the point that they are able to continue the task of sharing the good news with the rest of their people group. When this threshold is reached, the missionary may move to another people group and sow the seed of the gospel in another field.

International Mission Board report. As of this writing, the IMB recognizes 6,615 unreached people groups in the world.[15] Of these, 2,077 are at least 100,000 in size. Of these UPGs numbering at least 100,000 in population,

---

[15]In addition to the 6,615 unreached people groups globally, there are a probable 582 UPGs in the United States and Canada.

- 1,583 (76.2 percent) are engaged by the IMB and/or Great Commission Christian (GCC)[16] partners of evangelical faith and practice. (Engaged UPGs ≥ 100,000)

- 491 (23.7 percent) are not engaged and remain a high priority. (Unengaged UPGs ≥ 100,000)

- 3 (0.1 percent) are of unknown engagement status.

Since August 1, 2005, 285 unengaged UPGs ≥ 100,000 have been removed from the unengaged list—they are no longer unengaged UPGs ≥ 100,000. Of these, some have been engaged by the IMB; some have been engaged by GCC partners; some have been engaged by both the IMB and GCC partners, and some are no longer unreached—the number of evangelicals within them now exceeds the 2 percent mark.

Finishing the Task report. Finishing the Task (FTT) was launched November 14–17, 2005, at The Cove in Asheville, North Carolina. At this meeting a number of agency leaders and pastors met and decided to engage the remaining unengaged UPGs (or UUPGs) ≥ 100,000. At that time, there were 639 people groups on the list.[17] As of December 2007, FTT partners reported that 300 of the 639 had been engaged.[18] FTT partners bring a strong commitment to training local church planters to engage unreached people groups. FTT has recently launched the Call2All initiative so that additional workers around the world can join the effort to evangelize, plant churches, engage unreached unengaged people groups, employ oral strategies, share Christ around the world, and engage in global prayer.

Unnamed report. Of the 702 Muslim unreached people groups numbering at least 100,000 in population, 481 are now reported as engaged by partners working to give Muslim people groups the opportunity to

---

[16]The term Great Commission Christians (GCC) generally refers to church, parachurch organizations, or individuals committed to and engaged in fulfilling the Great Commission—taking the gospel to all nations.

[17]Marcus Vegh with Becky Hill, "Churches and Agencies Focus on 'Finishing the Task,'" *Mission Frontiers* (January–February 2006), www.missionfrontiers.com/pdf/2006/01/200601.htm.

[18]Finishing the Task website, "Statistics," www.finishingthetask.com, accessed December 10, 2008.

hear the gospel of Jesus Christ and respond. GCC partners have confirmed these engagements through research networks. As of this writing, 221 remain unengaged and are included in the priority listing of the IMB and Finishing the Task initiatives.

Critical Issues Moving Forward

Syncretism. Phil Templin, former regional leader of Middle America and Caribbean for the IMB, sees syncretism as a critical issue in establishing the gospel among the nations of Latin America. Phil says that "a significant portion of Evangelical beliefs are simply a veneer over older beliefs such as animism, voodoo and spiritism. Evangelical Christians find it easy to revert to the older beliefs when the Evangelical practices do not satisfy heartfelt needs. . . . Evangelical beliefs only require lip service."[19]

Contextualization. How do we avoid syncretism? We must allow the uncompromised Word of God to confront each people group in such a way that the authority of the Bible is maintained while communicating in a way that people can understand it and own it for themselves. Jerry Rankin, IMB president, suggests that "contextualization is not implied compromise of the gospel message or the authority of God's Word; it is simply communicating it in a way that will be understandable in a local language and cultural worldview."[20] The engagement of a people group through their local heart language provides the possibility of engaging them deeply enough that they are able to interact with the gospel, understand it, and be confronted with its relevancy.

The Majority World.[21] Not long ago, I attended an event during which missionaries gathered around a listing of 36 priority people groups from the country in which they now serve, or may serve in the future. They prayed over the list, and each of them came away with a new appreciation of the unfinished task; some prayed to lead their own

---

[19]Phil Templin, e-mail message to author, June 21, 2008.

[20]Don Graham, "IMB Trustees Define Contextualization," *Baptist Press*, November 16, 2007, www.baptistpress.org/bpnews.asp?id=26854.

[21]The "Majority World" is used here in place of the "Global South," a term popularized by Philip Jenkins in *The Next Christendom*. It refers to the non-Western church and missions world.

stateside church to engage one of the people groups on the list. I also attended a meeting in South Asia not long after this and witnessed as many as 300 Muslim-background believers sharing testimonies of engaging 93 unreached people groups in their country. More and more, I am finding that there is a great cloud of witnesses, full

> *More and more, I am finding that there is a great cloud of witnesses, full of joy and boldness, in places once thought to be resistant to the gospel.*

of joy and boldness, in places once thought to be resistant to the gospel. The songs of these witnesses will surely reach the nations, because their songs are those of wonderful redemption:

> For we are your children
> And let us carry your cross and follow after you
> Let us be like Simon, the man of Cyrene, who went with you to
> The place of the skull.[22]

> It was the time when they locked him up for a thousand years
> That real devil and Satan who so tricks people on earth today
> Now, my brother/sister, frustrate his tricks today
> Truly that snake has no power over us again.[23]

Conclusion

Currently people groups with a combined population of more than 4 billion remain unreached, or are less than 2 percent evangelical Christian. Sadly, many remain deprived of the opportunity to hear a single presentation of the gospel message or to have even one opportunity to accept Jesus Christ as Savior in their lifetime. Statistics cannot reveal how many in the world today are saved; we cannot read the hearts of men and women. To encourage ourselves, we are tempted to look at our

---

[22]"The Dinka people of the Sudan—long victims of that nation's bloody wars and persecutions—have a rich tradition of such hymns, unsurprisingly focused on the cross." Philip Jenkins, *The New Faces of Christianity: Believing the Bible in the Global South* (Oxford: Oxford University Press, 2006), 33.

[23]"A Tanzanian song putting to verse Revelation 20:1–2. The reader should understand from this example and that of the Dinka that the state of the gospel is powerfully moving forward in boldness among many believers, witnesses and churches around the world." Jenkins, *New Faces of Christianity*, 34.

successes and breakthroughs, our strengths, the size of our missionary forces, and the number of people group engagements as the measurement of the state of the gospel. In our reporting of progress, it's easy to pat ourselves on the back, take credit for what is happening, and assume the glory that is God's alone. However, the state of the gospel is strong because it is the power of God for salvation; and you and I, privileged to be believers, are at our best when we share the Christ of the cross. He is the power of God for the mission of God.

Discussion Points

1. What is an unreached people group? What is an unengaged unreached people group?

2. Do you think that some people groups deserve priority attention in today's missionary endeavor?

3. In the beginning of this chapter, Haney writes that "for centuries, the gospel of Jesus Christ resounded as a trumpet above the noise of each generation." Do you think this is true for our generation? What practical change could you, your church, or your organization do to sound the trumpet once again?

Further Reading

Bauckham, Richard. *Bible and Mission: Christian Witness in a Postmodern World*. Grand Rapids: Baker Academic; Carlisle, UK: Paternoster, 2003.

Holste, Scott, and Jim Haney. "The Global Status of Evangelical Christianity." *Mission Frontiers* (January–February 2006), www.missionfrontiers.com/pdf/2006/01/200601.htm.

Long, Justin. "Which Peoples Need Priority Attention?" *Mission Frontiers* (January–February 2007), www.missionfrontiers.com/pdf/2007/01/200701.htm.

19

Finishing the Task

J. Scott Holste

We are a people captured by a vision—a vision of that which God wants to do and will do among the nations. We hear it as a promise in God's call of Abraham: "I will bless those who bless you, and whoever curses you I will curse; and all peoples on earth will be blessed through you" (Genesis 12:3).

We hear it again—this time as a command—in the words of Jesus: "Therefore go and make disciples of all nations, baptizing them in the name of the Father and of the Son and of the Holy Spirit, and teaching them to obey everything I have commanded you. And surely I am with you always, to the very end of the age" (Matthew 28:19–20).

We sense it in the longing of the Father, "who wants all people to be saved" (1 Timothy 2:4). And, finally, we see the vision's culmination vividly portrayed in God's revelation to the apostle John: "After this I looked, and there before me was a great multitude that no one could count, from every nation, tribe, people and language, standing before the throne and before the Lamb. They were wearing white robes and were holding palm branches in their hands. And they cried out in a loud voice: 'Salvation belongs to our God, who sits on the throne, and to the Lamb'" (Revelation 7:9–10).

Obviously, we are neither at the beginning nor at the end of God's work to bless all the peoples of the earth, to make disciples of all the nations, and to inhabit the praises of the redeemed from every language, people, and tribe. Rather, we live somewhere in the middle—in the creative tension of the "not yet"—knowing things are not yet how they should be, and will be. We live knowing that the task of blessing and making disciples of all nations has been entrusted to and demanded of each of us. Yet, at the same time, we know that the task's fulfillment is not dependent on us, for, ultimately, it is God's task.

In the previous chapter, Jim Haney summarized the state of the gospel as of the time of his writing: 6,615 unreached people groups with a combined population of more than 4 billion. Roughly half of these groups (3,233) have no known evangelical believers. While another 1,673 groups have one or more believers, they lack even one evangelical church to advance the gospel among the predominantly lost population. Clearly, the task is far from complete.

What are some of the major challenges we face in finishing the task? What unexpected breakthroughs and new initiatives are accelerating fulfillment of the vision? What are some of the important strategic issues?

Rapid, but Uneven, Population Growth

At the time of Jesus' birth, the world's population probably numbered no more than 300 million. It took another 1,800 years for the population to reach 1 billion, but only 123 years more to double that number. In 1960 the global population was 3 billion, and by 1974 it had surpassed 4 billion. Another billion people by 1987, and then in October of 1999 the population topped 6 billion.[1] Now there are nearly 6.8 billion people. Every minute, 253 people are born and 105 people die, resulting in a net increase of 148. That's 8,880 additional people per hour, 213,120 additional people a day, and 77,788,800 additional people every year. Demographers project that the world's population will continue to grow—although, at a gradually slowing pace—until the year 2050, and then plateau at a historical high of 9.2 billion. The following chart illustrates this recent and explosive growth:

---

[1]"The World at Six Billion," United Nations, www.un.org/esa/population/publications/sixbillion/sixbilpart1.pdf.

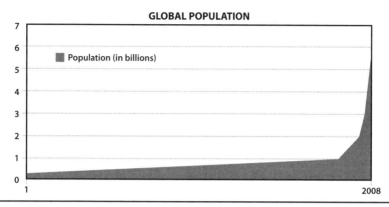

Figure 19.1.

So why is rapid population growth a significant issue for those committed to finishing the task? It is significant because our task is principally one of reaching people. A rapidly growing population means there are more and more people to reach. In this sense, the task is more than 22 times larger today than it was in the early days of the church.

But the size of the population is not the only consideration. The size of the church is also important. On the day of Pentecost (Acts 2) there were approximately 3,000 Christians in a world of 300 million—a ratio of 1 to 100,000. Today there are approximately 680 million evangelical believers[2] in a world of 6.8 billion—a ratio of 1 to 10. Thus, while the overall task is significantly larger, the relative burden on each Christian is significantly lighter—assuming, of course, that all of us are carrying our share of the load.

A rapidly growing population is significant for another reason. Population growth is uneven, as some countries are growing much faster than others. Unfortunately, many of these countries with higher population growth rates are also those with fewer missionaries and fewer Christians. For example, Yemen is one of the least reached countries in

---

[2]The Center for the Global Study of Christianity (www.gordonconwell.edu/resources/Center-for-the-Study-of-Global-Christianity.cfm) estimates that there are approximately 2.2 billion Christian adherents. It calculates the number of self-identified evangelicals at just over 250 million and the number of active church members who take the Great Commission seriously at 689 million. While no one knows exactly how many true believers there are, no matter which of these numbers you use, the ratio of believers to the lost is much better today than it was two millennia ago.

the world, having a relatively small number of missionaries and Christians among a predominately Muslim population. Yemen has a significant growth rate of 3.46 percent[3]—a rate approximately three times the global average. If this continues, Yemen's mostly lost population of 23 million will double in 20 years.

Rapid, but uneven, population growth is an issue because it means that increasing millions of individuals face an eternity without Christ unless something quickly changes. We must find additional ways to channel more personnel and resources to engage more effectively these unreached people groups with rapidly growing populations.

People Groups and the Flow of the Gospel

A population that is growing rapidly, but unevenly, is not the only challenge to finishing the task. There is the matter of people groups. From a strategic perspective, we often define a "people group" as the largest group through which the gospel can flow without encountering a significant barrier of understanding or acceptance. Those barriers are typically linguistic or cultural. People group researcher Orville Boyd Jenkins writes,

> A "people group" is an *ethnolinguistic group* with a common self-identity that is shared by the various members. There are two parts to that word: *ethno*, and *linguistic*. Language is a primary and dominant identifying factor of a people group. But there are other factors that determine or are associated with ethnicity.
>
> Usually there is a common self-name and a *sense of common identity* of individuals identified with the group. A *common history, customs, family and clan identities*, as well as marriage rules and practices, age-grades and other obligation covenants, and inheritance patterns and rules are some of the common ethnic factors defining or distinguishing a people.[4]

Significant differences in language and culture impede the flow of the gospel from one group to another. Thus, the introduction of the gospel

---

[3]See the Central Intelligence Agency's "The World Factbook," www.cia.gov/library/publications/the-world-factbook/.

[4]Orville Boyd Jenkins, "What Is a People Group?" International Mission Board website, http://imb.org/globalresearch/peoplegroups.asp.

to the Javanese of Indonesia will most likely not result in the evangelization of Madurese, Bugis, Minagkabau, Sasak, and hundreds of other Indonesian people groups. A people-group perspective reflects cognizance of this reality and demands strategic initiatives aimed toward the introduction of the gospel and planting of churches within each of these distinct groups.

Several years ago I was in Africa with a group of missionaries discussing, rather heatedly at times, whether or not a people-group approach was appropriate in their particular context. Veteran missionaries argued that this particular country's government had made great strides in eliminating ethnic diversity within the country. Nationals spoke one language and considered themselves one people. Consequently, missionaries had no desire to learn any language other than the national language and felt no need to shape their evangelism, discipleship, church planting, and leadership training efforts to address different worldviews.

An interesting dynamic at this meeting involved the presence of six national Baptist leaders. For two days these men said nothing as the missionaries debated. On the third day the head of the national Baptist convention stood and spoke to the group. "For many years, our leaders have told us that we are one people. Yet my wife knows that when I die I am to be buried in the north with *my* people." You could have heard a pin drop as he continued. "I listen to my brother," pointing to one of the other nationals, "and I know immediately that he is of another people. I watch this brother," pointing to another national, "and how he interacts with others, and I know immediately that he is from yet another people. Our leaders have told us we are one, but in reality we are *many*."

A people-group perspective is important because language and culture remain significant barriers to the free flow of the gospel around the world. We often say that the world is not a pancake, such that the syrup of the gospel flows freely over the whole. Rather, the world is a waffle: gospel syrup fills some segments, while other segments remain dry. For years we thought we could approach the world as a pancake, using national languages with the belief that these would cover the whole. But it didn't happen. Many certainly heard and responded to the gospel as it was presented in national languages around the world. Millions more, however, did not hear and did not respond because the gospel never penetrated their unique languages and cultures.

The Persistence of Unengaged, Unreached People Groups

An *unreached* people group is one in which evangelical Christians comprise less than 2 percent of the population. There are 6,615 of these groups, with a combined population of more than 4 billion. Of these unreached people groups, 571 groups have populations exceeding 1 million and 72 groups have populations in excess of 10 million. While evangelicals are implementing church-planting strategies among many of these unreached people groups, we calculate that 3,513 groups are currently unengaged. No one at all is working to start a church among these nearly 475 million lost individuals.

How could such a dire situation exist nearly 2,000 years after Jesus commanded us to make disciples of all nations? There are a variety of reasons. First, there is the problem of access. Many of these groups reside in places that are difficult for missionaries to access: deep in dangerous jungles, high on rugged mountains, and scattered across vast deserts. There are certainly those who go to such places. Still, such habitats can challenge, discourage, and sometimes deter even the most dedicated individuals.

Second, many of these groups live in political and/or social environments unfriendly to the gospel. The government may limit the activities of missionaries or prohibit their presence altogether. It may be illegal in such places for one to share the gospel with another. Facing reprisals ranging from social ostracism to imprisonment to death, those who do hear the gospel may not feel free to respond. In its 2007 survey, Freedom House[5] classifies 45 countries as "Not Free" where governments have significantly curtailed political rights and civil liberties. It classifies another 59 countries as only "Partly Free."

Third, one must consider the physical hardship of living and working among these groups. We use the United Nations Human Suffering Index as a proxy for estimating how difficult it would be for a Western

---

[5]See www.freedomhouse.org.

missionary to serve in a given location. On a scale of one to five—with one representing easier places to live, such as the United States, France, and Japan, and five representing the most difficult places to live, such as Afghanistan, Chad, and Bangladesh—we classify 727 of the unengaged unreached people groups as fours and fives. Of course, there are many missionaries who make great sacrifices to live in very difficult places. This may explain, however, why there are not more missionaries, and why so many unreached people groups remain unengaged.

A number of evangelical mission organizations are now focused on engagement of the unengaged, unreached people groups of the world. One cooperative effort involving several of these groups is the Finishing the Task partnership.[6] Its aim is to help existing churches in the United States and elsewhere plant reproducing churches among every people group in the world. The initial priority is the unengaged, unreached people groups with populations of 100,000 or more. Other organizations and networks have adopted similar goals. One of these organizations focuses on India, home to nearly half of these groups. Another network of organizations focuses on the unengaged Muslim people groups.

The Challenge of the Cities

Demographers estimate that the world's urban population surpassed that of its rural population for the first time in history on May 23, 2007.[7] This event, though widely heralded, is simply one milepost in an accelerating trend of global urbanization that began in the twentieth century and will continue unabated into the foreseeable future. According to researchers with the United Nations, urban dwellers comprised only 13 percent of the world's population in 1900. By 1950 that percentage had increased to 29 percent.[8] By 2030 the global population will approach 8 billion, 61 percent (some 4.9 billion people) of which will live in urban settings.

---

[6] See www.finishingthetask.com.

[7] "Mayday 23: World Population Becomes More Urban Than Rural," *ScienceDaily*, May 25, 2007, www.sciencedaily.com/releases/2007/05/070525000642.htm.

[8] "World Urbanization Prospects: The 2005 Revision," United Nations, Department of Economic and Social Affairs, Population Division, www.un.org/esa/population/publications/WUP2005/2005wup.htm.

While many of these urban centers are rather small, researchers estimate there may be more than 450 cities that have populations exceeding 1 million. Field personnel report that these large urban centers are frequently less reached than rural areas where many missionaries have tended to work in the past.

The following summarizes highlights of the United Nation's "World Urbanization Prospect: The 2005 Revision":

- Currently, urbanization is most pronounced in *more developed regions* of the world, where approximately 75 percent of the population live in urban settings—although, numerically, these regions account for less than one-third of the world's urban population. By 2030, this is expected to increase to 81 percent.

- However, urban growth is most dramatic in *less developed regions* of the world, where such growth will average 2.2 percent annually through 2030. Currently, there are approximately 2.3 billion urban dwellers in less developed countries. By 2030, that number will rise to 3.9 billion.

- Africa and Asia are the two least urbanized areas of the world, with 38.3 and 39.9 percent of their populations, respectively, residing in urban centers. By 2030, 54 percent of Asia's population and 51 percent of Africa's population will live in urban centers.

- Currently, 77 percent of the population of Latin American and the Caribbean is living in cities. This will increase to 84 percent by 2030.

- By 2030, Europe's urban population will rise from 72 percent to 78 percent, while North America's urban population will increase from 81 percent to 87 percent.

- In 1950, there were two cities in the world with populations exceeding 10 million.[9] By 2005, that number had risen to 20. Nine percent of the world's urban population lives in these 20 cities.

- Metropolitan Tokyo, with its 35 million inhabitants, is the largest urban center in the world. Tokyo is followed by Mexico City, New York-Newark, Sao Paulo, and Mumbai.

---

[9]The United Nations defines a "megacity" as an urban center with a population of 10 million or more.

- 6.5 percent of the world's urban dwellers live in cities 5 to 10 million in size.

- 22.6 percent of the world's urban population live in cities of fewer than 5 million people but of more than 1 million.

- The majority of urban dwellers (61.6 percent) live in cities of fewer than 1 million inhabitants.

While the Bible speaks frequently about the peoples of the world, it also speaks of its cities: Ur, Jericho, Nineveh, Babylon, Jerusalem, Antioch, Damascus, Corinth, Rome—to name only a few. God calls people out of cities, and he calls people to cities. He judges cities, and he saves cities. Cities are both the instrument and object of God's redemptive action.

Like its people-group oriented counterpart, an urban perspective is also strategically sound. Cities, by definition, are concentrations of people; and, ultimately, the gospel has as its aim the salvation of individuals. Missionaries leave home and cross cultures to go to the lost with the gospel. It makes sense that they would go to places with the largest concentrations of lost people and focus strategically on reaching those urban centers.

This is not often the case, however. While missionaries may live in large cities for a variety of legitimate reasons, their ministries are often directed outside of the cities. Why? First, because we have not adequately shown how a people-group focus and urban focus can strategically coexist. For example, while International Mission Board (IMB) field personnel do engage a number of cities as cities,[10] most of the work does not focus on the city as a whole but on specific people groups within the city. Thus, it is possible for multiple teams to be working with different people groups in the same city with virtually no interaction between them. Furthermore, because each team is focused on its own people group, no one has a comprehensive view of the whole city or a strategy for the whole city.

Second, missionaries often ignore the cities for cultural reasons. In-

---

[10]According to the most recent annual statistical report, IMB personnel and Baptist partners are engaging 170 urban centers of various sizes, 78 percent of which are classified as *unreached*.

ternational Mission Board personnel reflect the composition of Southern Baptist churches, most of which are located in rural and small town settings. The IMB's overseas leadership team regularly conducts an informal survey at field personnel orientation, asking how many participants grew up in a city of larger than 1 million. Generally this is true of fewer than 4 percent of these new missionaries. One also wonders how many of these new missionaries gained their ministry work experience with a view toward the urban center? Our guess—not very many. We must develop a better appreciation for the strategic importance of the cities, and we must find ways to address more effectively the spiritual needs of those who live there.

The Promise of Church-Planting Movements

It is through the church—in and through the fellowship, worship, discipleship, ministry, and mission of congregations of baptized believers—that God's glory is manifested within a community, people group, and nation. Though we may decry the condition of many churches today, we do not waver in our conviction that the local church and its multiplication around the world are integral to God's plan to redeem people from every language, people, tribe, and nation.

Consequently, the International Mission Board has emphasized church planting for many years. It became a particular focus in the 1980s and has continued to this day. In the late 1990s we began receiving reports of extraordinary church growth among various people groups that challenged much of what we thought possible. In the fall of 2000, I joined fellow researchers Jim Slack and J. O. Terry in traveling to northern India to probe more deeply into one of the greatest of these.

The Bhojpuri-speaking peoples of India number more than 30 million. These are mostly Hindu peoples, along with much smaller numbers of Muslims, Buddhists, and animists. When the IMB placed its first strategy coordinator among these peoples in 1989, there were only 28 churches, planted by Swedish Baptists. These churches were small and their growth was stagnant. The youngest of these churches was more than 25 years old.

As our assessment team interacted with more than a thousand pastors and laypeople attending a training conference in Uttar Pradesh, we verified the remarkable growth reported by the strategy coordinator. In fact, we found that the strategy coordinator had actually under-reported the situation. We learned that:

- The average church started two new churches per year.

- The average church started four new outreach groups per year. An outreach group is a group among which the gospel is regularly proclaimed, with the intention that the group will eventually become a church.

- Bhojpuri churches baptized 20 new believers annually for every 100 members. In contrast, the global average for all Baptist churches at that time was 9 baptisms for every 100 members. Among Southern Baptists in the United States the average was 2.5 per 100 members.

- Ten years after the strategy coordinator started with 28 churches in 1989, there were more than 4,300 Bhojpuri congregations, with approximately 300,000 members. The following chart portrays the explosive growth of the movement:

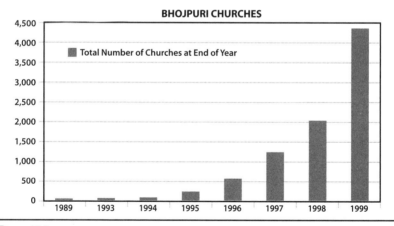

Figure 19.2.

We have assessed more than a dozen church-planting movements since then in Latin America, Africa, and Asia. We are currently tracking more than a hundred other situations in which field personnel are reporting multiplicative increases in the numbers of churches and believers—perhaps church-planting movements in the making. We rigorously examine the expansion of the movements, the health of the churches, and the strategies of those working with them. David Garrison summarized many of these early assessments and findings in his influential book *Church Planting Movements: How God Is Redeeming a Lost World* (2004).

Clearly, God is using church-planting movements to accelerate fulfillment of the vision. Because of these movements, thousands of churches and millions of believers among scores of unreached people groups around the world now bear faithful witness to the transforming power of the gospel.

Orality: The Gospel and Nonliterates

Evangelical Christians often pride themselves in being "people of the book." The expression basically means that the Bible—the book—is very important to read, study, and believe. The Bible is the supreme authority for our faith and practice. Because it is so important to Christians, we translate, print, and distribute millions of copies of it every year.[11]

But what do we do when the people to whom we go—not simply a few individuals here and there, but entire tribes—cannot read? What do we do when many of these people groups lack any written language into which the Bible can be translated? At the 2004 gathering of the Lausanne Movement in Thailand, one group of participants focused specifically on this issue. The group noted, "Current estimates indicate that around two-thirds of the world's population are oral communicators either by necessity or by choice. To effectively communicate with them, we must defer to their oral communication style. Our presentations must match their oral learning styles and preferences. Instead of using outlines, lists, steps and principles we need to use culturally relevant approaches they would understand. Are we willing to seek God to become better stewards of the Great Commission and address these issues in serving Him in these last days?"[12]

More than 4 billion people today are primarily oral learners. The

---

[11]In 2007, the United Bible Society distributed more than 306 million Scripture portions—including 26.9 million complete Bibles and 13.1 million New Testaments. See www.United BibleSocieties.org.

[12]"Making Disciples of Oral Learners," Lausanne Occasional Paper No. 54, 2004, 11, www .lausanne.org/documents/2004forum/LOP54_IG25.pdf.

majority of these people are also unreached. Several evangelical initiatives are addressing these vast populations of unreached oral communicators. OneStory is a partnership involving Campus Crusade for Christ, YWAM (Youth With A Mission), Trans World Radio, Wycliffe Bible Translators, and the Southern Baptist International Mission Board.[13] OneStory deploys two-year teams to unreached people groups, many of which have no written language. These groups have no Bible. Even if they did, they wouldn't be able to read it. OneStory teams work with native speakers to develop chronological sets of Bible stories spanning from God's creation of the world to God's redemption through Jesus Christ. Native speakers memorize and tell these stories to others who, in turn, share with others. Missionaries and national believers use these "oral Bibles" for evangelism, discipleship, and facilitating church-planting movements.

Of course, approaches like that of OneStory don't eliminate the need for a written Bible. Bible translation and literacy training are still important. But such an approach does mean that hundreds of nonliterate people groups are decades closer to the gospel than they would be if we were to rely solely on methods requiring Scripture in print.[14]

Recovering a Holistic Understanding of the Gospel

In a recent strategy meeting of leaders from across the evangelical world, the principal topic of discussion was the challenge of recovering a holistic understanding of the gospel. For much of the past forty years, the commitment of evangelicals to the gospel primarily has revolved around proclamation. We have directed considerable resources and efforts to the task of telling the world about Jesus. While giving an occasional nod to those who are feeding the hungry and ministering to the needs of the poor, we seem mainly concerned with the quantity (and sometimes quality) of our verbal witness.

Gospel proclamation and gospel demonstration, however, belong together. It's not a matter of finding the right balance between word and

---

[13]See www.onestory.org.

[14]For more information regarding strategies for working with oral communicators, visit Orality Strategies (www.oralstrategies.com) and the International Orality Network (www.oralbible.com).

deed, but rather finding appropriate ways to unite them. Proclamation and demonstration are not in competition with one another. Proclamation clarifies demonstration. Demonstration validates proclamation. We must explain why we do what we do, how we have experienced love, forgiveness, and rebirth in Christ. But we must also show that what we say is real and that it makes a difference—in us and in the lives of those around us.

According to a recent United Nations report,[15] nearly 20 percent of the population of the world's developing regions survive on less than one dollar each per day. That is true of nearly 30 percent of the population of south Asia and of more than 40 percent of the population of sub-Saharan Africa. Global estimates in 2005 suggest that more than 10 million children died before their fifth birthday in that year alone: one child every three seconds, more than 27,000 every day. Most of these deaths were preventable or treatable—the result of disease, polluted water, and hunger. Today, 900 million people lack access to safe drinking water and 2.6 billion people lack proper sanitation.[16] While the situation is gradually improving, chronic hunger persists in many places around the world. The following map portrays the relative prevalence of undernourishment.

FOOD INSECURITY IN THE WORLD

Prevalance of Undernourishment
<5% of population undernourished
5% to 15% of population undernourished
15% to 30% of population undernourished
30% to 50% of population undernourished
>50% of population undernourished

*More than 850 million people
suffer chronic undernourishment
due to food insecurity.*

Global Research   imb

Figure 19.3.

[15]"The Millennium Development Goals Report, 2007," United Nations, www.un.org/millennium goals/pdf/mdg2007.pdf.
[16]"Clean Water Campaign," UNICEF website, www.unicefusa.org/work/water/.

Fortunately, we are beginning to recapture a more holistic understanding of the gospel. In the first half of 2008 the International Mission Board appropriated more than 7 million dollars to fund more than 260 human-needs projects around the world. These projects unite word and deed, proclamation and demonstration. One of these projects addresses the country of Zimbabwe. One of our veteran missionaries there writes:

> Baptists have provided over 100 tons of food to be purchased and delivered in the form of food boxes to destitute families in Zimbabwe. The boxes include staple items which could be purchased for about $25 US, but it would take more than a year's salary for most Zimbabweans to purchase these items, if they were available in the grocery stores! One lady wept as she opened her box. "I was praying this morning to God and asking him what to do because I have no food to eat. Then you came and brought this food to me. I know God really does care about me."
>
> An elderly man, not a Baptist, who has been surviving on one bowl of porridge a day was overcome and could not speak for quite some time after getting his box. Everywhere people are saying that Baptists don't just talk about God's love, they give it away!

Conclusion

In this chapter we surveyed seven current and significant issues affecting fulfillment of the vision. We saw how rapid, but uneven, population growth complicates the task. We learned why a people-group perspective is strategically important and noted the various challenges of engaging these groups. We recognized that, while focusing on people groups, we cannot ignore the cities, as millions of lost people move there in hope of improving their lives. We rejoiced over church-planting movements and their promise for advancing the gospel. We wrestled with the challenge of reaching oral learners. And, finally, we explored the value of uniting word and deed in our understanding of the task.

Of course, there are many other strategic issues we could have discussed—the decline of Western Christianity, the growth of Islam, the resurgence of atheism, the shifting of evangelical fervor to the Global South, business as mission, the impact of the energy crisis on current mission paradigms, and more. One could very easily become overwhelmed; so it is helpful to remind ourselves that while our mission task is an awesome responsibility, we proceed in the confidence that God will accomplish it. The task, then, is not something that God has delegated to us. Rather, it is one in which he invites us to participate alongside him.

Discussion Points

1. Why is rapid population growth a significant issue for those committed to finishing the task?

2. How do we define a "people group" strategically? What are the pros and cons of focusing on individual people groups? What are your thoughts about the concept that the world is like a waffle, not a pancake?

3. How does Holste define "unengaged"? Why are there so many unengaged people groups today?

4. Holste cites two reasons why effective citywide church-planting strategies and teams are not always evident. What are these two reasons? Did you grow up in an urban setting? Do you know someone who did? How must we change our thinking and planning to reach the world's urban centers with the gospel?

5. Holste says gospel proclamation and gospel demonstration belong together. Explain what he means by this. See Christopher Little's chapter regarding the tension between the priority of proclamation and holistic ministry.

Further Reading

Haney, Jim. "First Fruits and Future Harvests." In *From Seed to Fruit: Global Trends, Fruitful Practices, and Emerging Issues Among Muslims*, edited by J. Dudley Woodberry. Pasadena, CA: William Carey Library, 2008.

Holste, Scott, and Jim Haney. "The Global Status of Evangelical Christianity." *Mission Frontiers* (January–February 2006), www.missionfrontiers.com/pdf/2006/01/200601.htm.

Johnstone, Patrick. *The Church Is Bigger Than You Think.* Fearn, UK: Christian Focus Publications and WEC, 1998.

Long, Justin. "Which Peoples Need Priority Attention?" *Mission Frontiers* (January–February 2007), www.missionfrontiers.com/pdf/2007/01/200701 .htm.

20

SPIRITUAL WARFARE AND THE MISSION OF GOD

Jerry Rankin[1]

When my family and I arrived in Indonesia to begin our church-planting ministry, we were deeply committed to our call and had no doubts about the power of the gospel to draw people to saving faith in Jesus Christ. I envisioned arriving on the shores of this populous Southeast Asian archipelago and the pages of Acts unfolding once again, with multitudes being saved every day. The peoples of the largest Muslim country in the world, like lost people everywhere, according to my perception, were just waiting for us to get there with the good news of the gospel. Obviously, that is not what we encountered upon arrival.

We had amazing opportunities to witness and to preach openly at that time, yet the people were largely indifferent and even antagonistic to our message. My language skills were not exceptional, but the people would respond with blank stares on their faces as if what I was saying did not relate to them. I came to understand that to expect a Muslim in Indonesia, or elsewhere, to respond to the gospel was not unlike asking a blind man to read a newspaper. For the Scripture says that the god of this world has blinded their eyes lest they should see and hear and be saved (2 Corinthians 4:4).

---

[1] Jerry Rankin served as president of the International Mission Board from 1993 to 2010. He and his family served for twenty-three years as missionaries in Southeast Asia. His insights into spiritual warfare grow out of personal experience and a sensitivity to the teachings of God's Word. For many years he has led training sessions on the topic with new missionaries preparing to go to the field. This chapter is adapted from the author's book *Spiritual Warfare: The Battle for God's Glory* (Nashville: Broadman & Holman, 2009).

The word "devil" comes from the Greek *diabolos*, which means "to oppose." Satan exists as an adversary, opposed to God's plan and desire to be exalted among the nations. The nations and peoples of the world outside the kingdom of God are lost. They cannot see and understand the truth of the gospel in spite of frequent and clear communication. That doesn't just happen. Satan, the god of this world, is blinding their understanding, distorting their perception of God's truth by his lies and deception. This is how Paul described the essence of his calling and our mission task in Acts 26:18. He said the Lord had called him "to open their eyes and turn them from darkness to light, and from the power of Satan to God." The task of witnessing to the lost is a matter of opening eyes that are blind to truth and turning the lost from the darkness of sin to the light of the Savior, from the power of Satan to God.

Missionaries are very aware of manifestations of Satan and demonic activity. Believers in the West also encounter Satan's activity in their lives and society every day. But we seldom recognize it, because it is cleverly disguised and is discounted by our rational worldview. Yet Satan is diametrically opposed to Christ, to the church, to the extension of God's kingdom, and to individual Christians experiencing the God-glorifying power, blessings, victory, and fullness of God's Spirit that God intends. Satan is behind spiritual failure, discord, dissension, carnal living, and worldliness. He seeks to deprive God of being glorified in our lives by tempting us to sin, defeating us, and robbing us of everything that God has given us. The Scripture warns us, "Be alert and of sober mind. Your enemy the devil prowls around like a roaring lion looking for someone to devour. Resist him, standing firm in the faith" (1 Peter 5:8–9).

We are alerted to the pervasive nature of Satan's opposition, manifested as the spiritual forces of evil, powers of darkness, and a dominion of authority ruling over the world where God is not known and worshiped.

Finally, be strong in the Lord and in his mighty power. Put on the full armor of God, so that you can take your stand against the devil's schemes. For our struggle is not against flesh and blood, but against the rulers, against the authorities, against the powers of this dark world and against the spiritual forces of evil in the heavenly realms. Therefore put on the full armor of God, so that when the day of evil comes, you may be able to stand your ground, and after you have done everything, to stand. (Ephesians 6:10–13)

In our task of global evangelism, the primary opposition is not demon possession, territorial spirits, generational bondage, or other outward manifestations of Satan's power and dominion in a world without Christ. It is the lies, deception, and attacks of the enemy to which we are subjected daily. The reality of missions needs to be seen in the context of a battle. We readily accept the barriers of religious opposition and government restrictions. We succumb to discouragement with meager results to our evangelistic efforts. We concede to obstacles raised by a postmodern world that resists and rejects our Christian message. But this is not what our Lord has told us. His Word reveals a vision of the kingdoms of the world becoming the kingdoms of our Lord. He has assured us of victory.

Satan Is Antagonistic to God's Mission

Satan is antagonistic to God's plans and purposes. He wages continual warfare, seeking to counter everything that would glorify God. But he can't win; he has already been defeated on the cross. "The reason the Son of God appeared was to destroy the devil's work" (1 John 3:8). But if Satan has been defeated, what is the explanation of his power and influence being so pervasive in our world and in our lives? Why does he seem so successful in countering our mission efforts to disciple the nations? Why do we continue to be susceptible to his lies and deception?

Basically, it's a case of vengefulness. Satan was thrown out of heaven; he was defeated on the cross. One day he will be cast into outer darkness, and all his wickedness and deceit will be finished forever. Revelation 20:1–3 tells of this future judgment, as the apostle John saw an angel descending from heaven: "He seized the dragon, that ancient serpent, who is the devil, or Satan, and bound him for a thousand years. He threw him into the Abyss, and locked and sealed it over him, to keep him from deceiving the nations . . .”

But in the meantime, Satan is trying to thwart God's purpose—to be exalted among the nations—and to delay the extension of God's kingdom to the ends of the earth. The devil finds delight in getting us to choose sin and self-centered gratifications of the flesh instead of glorifying God by submitting to his will and living a righteous and holy life. Satan is gratified when he can deceive those in the world so that they embrace the shallow, false riches of worldly values. But he is also the one who deceives the nations to keep them from knowing and exalting our Lord Jesus Christ. In vengefulness he seeks to deprive God of his glory among the nations.

We need to realize that the real battle is Satan's opposition to God. He is jealous of God's power and glory. In the account of Satan's fall in Isaiah 14:11–14, the Scripture quotes Satan as saying, “I will raise my throne above the stars of God. . . . I will ascend above the tops of the clouds; I will make myself like the Most High.” He continues to seek the glory and dominion that belong only to God, and he appears to be rather successful both in places where the gospel has been proclaimed as well as among the unevangelized fields of the world. In vengefulness he seeks to embarrass God through our failure and carnal living. We are constantly under attack. Satan does want to defeat us through temptation to sin and carnal living, but we are only pawns he uses in the conflict against God.

Ultimate Victory Is Assured

We have been given assurance of victory in our task to proclaim the gospel to the nations. We are told in Habakkuk 2:14, “For the earth will be filled with the knowledge of the glory of the LORD as the waters cover the sea.” Psalm 22:27–28 says, “All the ends of the earth will remember and turn to the LORD, and all the families of the nations will bow down before him, for dominion belongs to the LORD and he rules over the nations.” This is what God is in the process of doing in the world. The ultimate outcome appears in Revelation when a multitude from every tribe, people, language, and nation will be gathered around the throne of God, worshiping the Lamb. Obviously Satan doesn't want that to happen.

When I see the progress being made to fulfill the Great Commission in the twenty-first century, I invariably think of the words of Jesus in Matthew 24:14: "And this gospel of the kingdom will be preached in the whole world as a testimony to all nations, and then the end will come." Satan must be totally obsessed with that verse; Jesus said that the end will come, and Satan knows exactly what that implies. All of his wickedness and deceit will be finished. He and all of his demons will be cast into the lake of fire and outer darkness, and God will reign over the nations. But Jesus said that won't happen until the gospel has been proclaimed in the whole world to the *panta ta ethnē* (Matthew 28:19), all the peoples of the world.

Could Satan have had anything to do with totalitarian governments keeping nations closed to missionary witness? For seventy years he thought this strategy was working in the Soviet Union and Eastern Europe, as he kept many of the peoples of the world from having access to the gospel. But those barriers have crumbled in God's providence and sovereignty over the nations. That strategy is no longer working, and the gospel has penetrated every country on the face of the earth.

Another strategy of the enemy has been to obscure the nature of our Great Commission task. It is amazing that only in the last twenty years or so we have come to understand the mission of God in terms of the people groups of the world. Our task is not just implementing a missionary witness to nations, the geo-political entities on our map. Jesus has sent us to disciple all the people groups of the world—all of the more than 11,000 language, ethnic, racial, and cultural groups. That was not understood previously, as we saw our mission task in terms of sending missionaries to plant the gospel in each country throughout the world. Could Satan's deception have had anything to do with distorting and diverting our mission strategy so that vast people groups would remain hidden from our awareness, neglected in our witness, and still unreached? Perhaps. But obviously that strategy, successful for centuries, is now failing, as research reveals the identity and location of the *ethnē*, the peoples in the world, and those groups are systematically being reached with the gospel.

A third strategy of the enemy throughout history has been to bring persecution upon believers, presuming this would hinder the advancement of God's kingdom. But just as persecution fed the courage of New Testament believers and the growth of the early church, the blood of martyrs continues to lay the foundation for the church in cultures antagonistic to the gospel.

We alert new missionaries to expect adversity, because it is inherent in their role, just as it is for believers who, as a minority in hostile cultures, step out in faith to become followers of Jesus. Our Lord alerted his disciples to this in John 16:33. He said, "In this world you will have trouble." Just before this, as he was preparing his disciples to carry on his mission, Jesus said that they would be hated and persecuted just as he was hated and persecuted, because "a servant is not greater that his master" (John 15:20). So seeking to fulfill the mission of God is not a matter of being exempt from suffering and avoiding adversity, thinking God should put a hedge of protection around his emissaries. Persecution doesn't mean being forsaken by God and defeated in our Christian life. That is what Satan wants us to believe. In spite of persecution, harassment, and threats, a harvest unprecedented since the New Testament era continues to sweep across places such as China and parts of the Muslim world.

> *We alert new missionaries to expect adversity, because it is inherent in their role, just as it is for believers who, as a minority in hostile cultures, step out in faith to become followers of Jesus.*

Twice in Romans 15 the apostle Paul declares his intent to go to Rome to share the gospel, and on beyond to Spain. Apparently Paul never made it to Spain but found himself in a prison in Caesarea; he eventually made it to Rome, but in chains as a prisoner. He wrote from prison, "Now I want you to know, brothers and sisters, that what has happened to me has actually served to advance the gospel. As a result, it has become clear throughout the whole palace guard and to everyone else that I am in chains for Christ. And because of my chains, most of the brothers and sisters have become confident in the Lord and dare all the more to proclaim the gospel without fear" (Philippians 1:12–14). Rather than squelching the growth of the kingdom, persecution serves to embolden believers to share their faith. It gives witness that the truth of the gospel is not only something one chooses to live by, it is something worth dying for.

Satan's opposition to God's kingdom purpose was evident in the temptations of Jesus. Luke 4:5–7 reveals a portion of this encounter. "The devil led him up to a high place and showed him in an instant all the kingdoms of the world. And he said to him, 'I will give you all their authority and splendor; it has been given to me, and I can give it to anyone I want to. If you worship me, it will all be yours.'" Of course, Jesus did not succumb to that temptation. But it is intriguing that he never contradicted Satan's right to make the claim that "all the kingdoms of the world" belong to him. First John 5:19 says, "We know that we are children of God, and that the whole world is under the control of the evil one." Where Christ is not known—where he is not acknowledged as Lord—the cultures and nations and peoples of the world are the kingdoms of Satan, under dominion to the powers of darkness. He is opposed to the kingdoms of the world becoming the kingdom of our Lord.

Satan Deceives the Nations

In the parable of the sower, Jesus tells about the seed of the gospel that falls on the hardened, beaten down pathway, where it does not take root. Many missionaries go to resistant cultures that do not readily receive the gospel. Those places are like that hardened soil. Jesus says that the birds come and take away the seed, even as it is sown, and then he explains that the birds are the devil (Luke 8:12). Even when we are faithful to witness and share our faith with the lost, there is an adversary actively taking away the truth of the gospel from their hearts and understanding, lest they should understand and repent. Satan would not want us to recognize his role in those who reject the gospel, but we must not discount his involvement among those who resist a Christian witness.

Attempting to share the gospel in most Muslim countries is difficult; the seed of the gospel falls on hard soil and does not readily take root. Even though the gospel may be clearly proclaimed, Satan is there, taking away the truth of the gospel with his deception and lies. He tells them that Christians believe in three Gods, which is blasphemous to their way of thinking, or that it was an imposter, not Christ, who died on the cross. Muslims are fatalistic, and Satan convinces them they are not responsible for their sin. They are convinced Christianity is a foreign religion characterized by the immorality seen in Western movies and American lifestyles. Satan sees to it that they are deluded in their perception and understanding. He influences them through their cultural worldview and religious traditions to believe his lies, taking away the seeds of the gospel from their understanding even when the message is communicated to them.

Such deception is especially prominent in Hindu and Buddhist cultures. Satan tells people, in their pluralistic societies, that all religions are the same and one can follow any or all of them. There is nothing unique or exclusive about Jesus. One's eternal destiny is determined by accumulating karma through their own works. And once again the "birds" take away the truth of the gospel through Satan's deception and lies.

For years missionaries in Thailand and other Buddhist countries have felt that they have been on the verge of a breakthrough, an evangelistic harvest, because the people seem so interested and receptive. But few step across the line and embrace faith in Jesus Christ. As in many places around the world, it is not so much a religious barrier as it is a cultural barrier that Satan uses. He uses his lies and persuasion to tell them that to become a Christian means to cease to be a Thai. Turning to Christ is to reject one's family, culture, and ethnic identity in most societies.

Among many cultural Catholics throughout the world, Satan takes away the seed of the gospel by convincing them they are already Christians, though they have never been born again through a personal experience of trusting Jesus. He allows them to concede that they must believe in Jesus, but deceives them into believing that the sacraments of the church are also necessary. They accept the lie of a salvation of works and merit because it is cleverly disguised as the gospel, successfully enabling the adversary to keep them from a personal relationship with God.

Certainly the gospel is the power of God to draw all people to Jesus Christ. But we make a mistake in thinking that it is just a matter of gaining access, building relationships, and communicating the gospel. We must realize we have an adversary that is actively taking away the truth we are proclaiming and distorting the thinking and understanding of those to whom we witness. We must not be oblivious to the fact that we have an enemy who is opposed to the gospel and the extension of God's kingdom. Satan easily uses distorted worldviews and the cultural traditions of society to filter and distort the truth of the gospel.

We must realize we have an adversary that is actively taking away the truth we are proclaiming and distorting the thinking and understanding of those to whom we witness.

Satan's strategies that have been so successful in the past to obstruct the mission of God are beginning to fail. He can no longer keep the gospel from penetrating every nation as creative-access strategies take the gospel to previously restricted locations. He can no longer keep unreached people groups hidden from our awareness, as they are systematically being engaged with the gospel. His efforts to inhibit the growth of God's kingdom through persecution only feed the power of one's witness and the growth of the church.

Satan's Most Effective Strategy

Satan has another strategy to oppose the advancement of God's kingdom and the fulfillment of God's mission to be glorified among the nations. This may be the most effective among all his tactics: convincing Christians that missions is optional. One can choose whether or not to be involved in the mission of God. My own denomination takes pride in sending and supporting

Satan has another strategy to oppose the advancement of God's kingdom and the fulfillment of God's mission to be glorified among the nations. This may be the most effective among all his tactics: convincing Christians that missions is optional.

more than 5,000 missionaries through the International Mission Board, but that represents only .03 percent of Southern Baptists who take the Great Commission seriously and personally by going in response to God's call. Our 43,000 Southern Baptist churches channel only 2.5 percent of their financial resources to international missions.

Satan's strategies are apparently quite effective in keeping the words of Jesus in Matthew 24:14 from being fulfilled, as he subtly influences Christians to give a low priority to the mission of God and the proclamation of the good news to all nations and peoples. He does deceive the nations by his lies and distortion of the truth of the gospel. But just as he opposes individuals coming to faith in Jesus Christ, he also does everything he can among those who confess Christ to keep them from witnessing to the lost and allowing God to be glorified in their lives.

If Satan cannot get us to sin and yield to temptation, to indulge our carnal nature and live according to the flesh, he simply seeks to influence us in ways that hinder us from doing what God wants us to do. We may not indulge in an immoral lifestyle, and we may resist selfish gratifications that are contrary to the holy life to which Christ calls us; but he diverts us from God's will and distracts us from doing what God would have us do.

Often the things that hinder us from fulfilling the mission of God seem to be circumstances that are natural human obstacles. But remember, Satan is the god of this world. It is not just a matter of vocational choice and lack of willingness to go as a missionary. We allow things to hinder us from witnessing to our neighbors, from accepting responsibility at church, or simply from faithful and sincere worship. We know God wants us to minister to someone in need, but we get sidetracked by our own busy schedules and commitments. We know we should give more generously and be better stewards. In many other ways, as well, we sin by failing to be obedient to that which would fulfill the mission of God and glorify him.

First Thessalonians 2:18 says, "We wanted to come to you—certainly I, Paul, did, again and again—but Satan blocked our way." Paul wanted to come to Thessalonica and was obviously convinced this was God's will. But Satan hindered him from coming.

Putting on the Armor of God

One of the most familiar passages of Scripture that highlights the key to gaining victory in spiritual warfare is Paul's commentary on the armor of God in Ephesians 6:10–18.

> Finally, be strong in the Lord and in his mighty power. Put on the full armor of God, so that you can take your stand against the devil's schemes. For our struggle is not against flesh and blood, but against the rulers, against the authorities, against the powers of this dark world and against the spiritual forces of evil in the heavenly realms. Therefore put on the full armor of God, so that when the day of evil comes, you may be able to stand your ground, and after you have done everything, to stand. (Ephesians 6:10–13)

The nature of our enemy is clearly described as being in the spiritual realm. The scope of his influence is extensive, but God has provided the elements of protection against his attacks. I never found this especially helpful, however, because it was back to my own efforts, my own struggle—the struggle to keep the armor on and to consciously put on each implement every day.

The "armor of God" is in the genitive case, which is commonly used for the possessive form of a noun. We understand this as saying we are to put on the armor that belongs to God. It is God's armor, something that he possesses but has made available to us. Grammatically, however, there is one other use of the genitive case; it is also used in apposition. For example, if this verse had said, "Put on the armor of steel," it would also be in the genitive construct; steel doesn't possess the armor, but steel and armor are in apposition. They are one and the same.

Could the Scriptures imply that God himself is the armor? Throughout the New Testament we are told to "put on the Lord Jesus Christ," "to be clothed in Christ." Time and time again the Bible refers to Christians as "being in Christ." There are those who would disagree with this perspective but acknowledge there is nothing remiss grammatically nor theologically to understand God and the armor as synonymous. Certainly God does make available the implements of the armor we need for standing firm against Satan's tactics, but ability to put on the full armor of God is contingent on our position in Christ. The only victory and security against a devious, unseen enemy is being in Christ. He was the one who defeated Satan on the cross and rendered him powerless. We can appropriate the victory, not in our own strength and efforts, but because we are in him.

When we are in Christ and have put on the armor which is God, we have the belt of truth that quenches all the lies of Satan. We have the breastplate of righteousness; that's not righteousness that comes through our own efforts, but his righteousness. Our feet are shod, equipped, to proclaim the gospel of peace. It is the power of God's Spirit that compels us to be his witnesses, proclaiming the gospel even to the ends of the earth. We have a shield of faith when we put on God. He's the one who gives the faith to extinguish Satan's darts. As Ephesians 2:8 tells us, this faith "is not from yourselves, it is the gift of God." Only in God do we have the helmet of salvation, which is our security. We cannot put on salvation and be saved apart from him. When we are in God, he is feeding our mind with his Word—the sword of the Spirit—that builds faith to claim the victory.

The ultimate victory in spiritual warfare is our position of being in Christ. He is the one who conquered Satan and has given us all authority over him and his wickedness. Christ is our armor and protection; he is our security against Satan's temptation and deceit. It's not what we do to resist temptation, to walk in obedience, to be empowered by the Holy Spirit, and to overcome Satan. I cannot be expected to stand firm against an unseen enemy who works in darkness and anonymity, but in Christ I can claim the victory.

Fulfillment of the Mission of God

We are told the final outcome of the battle with the one who deceives us, and the whole world, in Revelation. "Then war broke out in heaven. Michael and his angels fought against the dragon, and the dragon and his angels fought back. But he was not strong enough, and they lost their place in heaven. The great dragon was hurled down—the ancient serpent called the devil, or Satan, who leads the whole world astray" (Revelation 12:7–9). The victory is assured, for this passage goes on to say, "Now have come the salvation and the power and the kingdom of our God, and the authority of his Messiah. For the accuser of our brothers and sisters, who accuses them before our God day and night, has been hurled down" (Revelation 12:10).

Revelation 13:14 tells us about a beast who "deceived the inhabitants of the earth." We are not to believe Satan's lies, but the truth of God's Word. Faith is the victory, and we should not allow the enemy to put us on a guilt trip, accusing us of our failure and defeating us in our Christian life when Christ has given us the victory. The victory comes when we believe the truth of God's Word and act upon it.

In describing that future day when Satan, the accuser, will be finally defeated, Revelation 12:11 identifies the ultimate weapon in spiritual warfare: "They triumphed over him by the blood of the Lamb and by the word of their testimony; they did not love their lives so much as to shrink from death."

In the last days, those who claimed the victory did not do so by their struggle and efforts but by the blood of the Lamb. The victory was provided when Jesus Christ died on the cross, defeated Satan, and gave us all authority over the evil one. But it also came by the word of their testimony—the confession of their faith, believing God and his Word. They did not waver even in the midst of persecution, trials, and adversity, but staked their life on what God had said. The word of their testimony proved that faith was the victory. But finally, they did not love their life, even unto death. There was no way for Satan to get to them. How could he tempt them? How could he distract them and create doubt when they were not living for self? How could the things of the world have any attraction to them when they were willing to sacrifice everything, even their lives?

It is only God's love in Christ that makes that possible. Loving God with all our heart, soul, mind, and strength enables us to love others—a lost world—and give ourselves completely. Only love makes possible the phenomenon of sacrifice. It is the ultimate victory because our enemy is self-serving, appealing to our fleshly nature. Satan does not understand love and cannot comprehend selfless commitment. He is totally disarmed by sacrifice and was disillusioned by the cross. Thinking he had won, the death and resurrection of our Lord Jesus Christ sealed his defeat. We have been called to take up that cross and walk in the assured victory it provided, knowing that one day every knee will bow and every tongue will confess that Jesus is Lord to the glory of God the Father.

Discussion Points

1. What evidences have you encountered that you recognize may be an effort of Satan to deter a witness or inhibit the advancement of God's kingdom?

2. How has Satan used subtle strategies to erode the effectiveness of mission efforts in ways that discourage, divert, and defeat us?

3. How do we reconcile God's testimony of the eventual global success of his mission with the barriers and limitations that are so evident today?

4. What is the role of faith in claiming the victory over the enemy and in fulfilling the mission of God?

Further Reading

Anderson, Neil. *The Bondage Breaker.* Eugene, OR: Harvest House, 2000.

Boyd, Gregory. *God at War: The Bible and Spiritual Conflict.* Downers Grove, IL: InterVarsity, 1997.

Bubeck, Mark. *Overcoming the Adversary.* Chicago: Moody, 1984.

Ingram, Chip. *The Invisible War.* Grand Rapids: Baker, 2006.

Lewis, C. S. *The Screwtape Letters.* San Francisco: Harper, 2001.

Mallone, George. *Arming for Spiritual Warfare.* Downers Grove, IL: InterVarsity, 1991.

Rankin, Jerry. *Spiritual Warfare: The Battle for God's Glory.* Nashville: Broadman & Holman, 2009.

Rogers, Adrian. *The Incredible Power of Kingdom Authority.* Nashville: Broadman & Holman, 2002.

Wiersbe, Warren. *The Strategy of Satan: How to Detect and Defeat Him.* Wheaton: Tyndale, 1979.

21

APOSTLES EVEN NOW

Don Dent

For more than ten years I have had the privilege to help mobilize, encourage, train, and advise hundreds of missionaries who are taking the gospel to unreached people groups. This includes veterans with decades of experience as well as "twenty-something" apprentices. In many ways, they all are regular, ordinary people who face real human problems such as loneliness, discouragement, and confusion. In other ways, however, they are extraordinary. It is hard to describe the depth of their desire to serve Christ, their perseverance in difficulties, their set-apart lives, and their faith that God can use them to reach unreached peoples. Some serve in spite of bothersome medical conditions. More than a few face intense threats. Many work for years for a breakthrough among their adopted people group. Others refuse lucrative and higher profile opportunities back home. Judging from the perspective that they have left behind loved ones and a more comfortable life, they appear to be fools.

I often ask myself: Where in the world do these missionaries come from? The answer is that they do not come from the world at all—they are sent by God. When you listen to them, it is clear that they have a deep sense of God's leading in their lives. What sets them apart is their conviction that God has called them to be missionaries and their willingness to commit their lives to fulfill that calling.

Many missions-minded Christians do

> *What sets them apart is their conviction that God has called them to be missionaries and their willingness to commit their lives to fulfill that calling.*

not search the Bible for directions on how to "do" missions today. For instance, we fail to make a connection between the work of the apostles and the ministry of missionaries today. The term "missionary" comes from Latin and "apostle" comes from Greek, but both words refer to one who was sent with authority to accomplish an assignment. The New Testament teaches that God sends apostles to spread the faith and gives us descriptions of how they carried out their mission. We should be following their examples in missions today.

GLIMPSES OF APOSTLES

Because of his religious training and zeal, he hated Christians even more than most of his contemporaries. When he heard the voice of Christ calling to him, he was confronted with the unexpected decision to follow him who called. Almost simultaneously he also sensed God's call to share this good news with many others. His newfound faith caused some concern and suspicion on the part of the Christians who learned of it. In spite of this, he began to speak openly about Jesus with his family, friends, and acquaintances. Because of his credentials as a teacher, he was sometimes invited to teach at social and religious gatherings, and he used these opportunities to introduce the Messiah. In the face of persecution he continued to tell the good news. Eventually, he began to gather new believers into small, informal congregations for worship and teaching. His ministry resulted in dozens of new groups of believers.

Although his story is similar to Paul's, Agus lives in the twenty-first century rather than the first century. God is raising up such followers today where we see gospel breakthroughs among unreached people groups.

Apostolos in the New Testament

The term *apostolos* is the noun form of the more commonly used verb *apostellō*, which has the connotation of sending for a particular purpose.

The verb was often used in business, political, and military spheres. The noun *apostolos* was rarely used in secular writings, but its frequent use in the New Testament points to the high value the early church gave to those sent by God on a mission.

The Twelve. *Apostolos* was the designation used for the twelve closest disciples of Jesus. "When morning came, he called his disciples to him and chose twelve of them, whom he also designated apostles" (Luke 6:13). After the crucifixion and resurrection, the apostles felt a need to replace Judas. This story in Acts 1:15–26 gives us insight into their self-perception. They looked for someone who had been with Jesus the whole time of his ministry and was an eyewitness of the resurrection. This was necessary because their role was to protect and proclaim the story of Jesus. It is clear from this story that there had to be twelve apostles and that only God could choose them. Although Matthias was chosen to replace Judas, there is no biblical hint of succession once they had accomplished their task. Theirs was a unique and historic role in the establishment of Christianity, but this role only lasted for their lifetimes. Many Christians today are hesitant to identify missionaries as apostles because they think that the term "apostle" is limited to the Twelve.

Other eyewitness apostles. Although the twelve apostles were a distinct group, the New Testament called other eyewitnesses apostles. Paul, the persecutor of Jesus, and James, the half-brother of Jesus, are two striking examples. Neither was included in the Twelve, but Jesus appeared to both after the resurrection (1 Corinthians 15:7). Paul affirmed that his apostleship was based on his eyewitness experience as well as his successful ministry of fulfilling the Great Commission. "Am I not free? Am I not an apostle? Have I not seen Jesus our Lord? Are you not the result of my work in the Lord? Even though I may not be an apostle to others, surely I am to you! For you are the seal of my apostleship in the Lord" (1 Corinthians 9:1–2).

Paul considered James to be an apostle: "I saw none of the other apostles—only James, the Lord's brother" (Galatians 1:19). It is interesting to note that these two "added" apostles rose to prominence in their spheres of ministry, Paul as the pioneer to the nations and James as leader of the church in Jerusalem. Many scholars believe that 1 Corinthians 15:7 refers to even more eyewitness apostles besides the Twelve and Paul and James. We can see that the term *apostolos* was used for a wider group than the Twelve.

Missionary apostles. It is of particular interest that *apostolos* is also used to describe some who were not eyewitnesses of the resurrection. If being an eyewitness is a qualification for all apostles, then there would be none today. Although Luke usually limits the title of apostle to the Twelve, in Acts 14, verses 4 and 14, he identifies Barnabas and Paul as apostles. That this takes place during the first missionary journey is important. Barnabas was mentioned in Acts 4:36 as an acquaintance of the Twelve, but he was not considered an apostle at that time. When Luke called Barnabas an apostle, Barnabas was fulfilling the calling God gave him to carry out what we now call missions. We can consider him a missionary apostle, because he was carrying out "the work" God gave him.[1]

It is a mistake to consider Barnabas's apostleship as subordinate to Paul's. For instance, though Paul's name is usually mentioned first in Acts, sometimes Barnabas is mentioned first. Later, when Barnabas and Paul part ways in Acts 15:39, Barnabas does not hesitate to continue his missionary ministry. Although Paul became more prominent, Barnabas did not view his calling or ministry as dependent on Paul's presence or blessing. Barnabas was an apostle because he was called by God to fulfill the Great Commission.

Similarly, it is inaccurate to acknowledge Barnabas as an apostle primarily because he was commissioned by the church in Antioch. Luke made it clear that God had already called Barnabas before the church knew about it: "While they were worshiping the Lord and fasting, the Holy Spirit said, 'Set apart for me Barnabas and Saul for the work to which I have called them'" (Acts 13:2). Certainly the Antioch church played a part in setting them apart for this task. The church, however, only released Barnabas and Paul to obey the Holy Spirit who sent them. In that sense it is inaccurate to consider Antioch a sending church. Barnabas was sent by God and therefore worked with his authority to accomplish the task. Barnabas was a missionary apostle of Christ be-

---

[1]See Acts 13:2 and 14:26. The "work" was proclaiming the gospel and planting churches in pioneer settings.

cause his ministry of proclaiming the gospel and planting churches ful-filled the Great Commission.

Others who appear to have been missionary apostles like Barnabas are Andronicus and Junia, as well as Apollos.[2] Since New Testament times God has called individuals to take his gospel and establish his church in pioneer settings. Missionaries who do that today are ful-filling the same role as missionary apostles.

Paul's second missionary journey started quite differently than the first. After Barnabas went his separate way, Paul recruited Silas and Timothy to join him in his work as an apostle.[3] In fact, beginning with his first missionary journey, Paul always worked with a team of co-workers. Led by a vision, they entered Macedonia and ministered in Philippi and Thessalonica. A few months after being forced to leave Thessalonica, they wrote the church a letter. First Thessalonians may be Paul's earliest canonical epistle, but it was actually written by the team of Paul, Silas, and Timothy. This apostolic team recounts how they shared the gospel boldly and poured out their lives so that the Thessalonians might believe. They also state that they did not demand all their rights as envoys of Christ: "We were not looking for praise from people, not from you or anyone else, even though as apostles of Christ we could have asserted our authority" (1 Thessalonians 2:6).

For Silas and Timothy to claim to be Christ's apostles is striking be-cause Paul does not use this designation for them elsewhere. Consid-ering the context of their ministry alongside Paul, this is not difficult to explain. Although they were gifted co-workers, they lacked the ma-turity or status that Paul and Barnabas had earned. They did not have an independent call from God, but were recruited to join Paul's apostolic team. Thus, they were apostles because they were associated with Paul's apostolic ministry. As associate apostles they were fulfilling the Great Commission of Christ and ministering in his authority. In the same way today, God may open the door for a mature Christian to join an apos-tolic team as an associate apostle. My purpose here is not to identify a hierarchy among apostles, but to point out that God calls people with a

---

[2] See Romans 16:7 and 1 Corinthians 3:4–6,22; 4:6–9.
[3] Acts 15:40 and 16:1–3.

variety of gifts who can contribute significantly to the ministry of a team that is led by an apostle. Such associate apostles are apostles of Christ.

Apostles of the churches. There is one other usage of the term *apostolos* in the New Testament that has application for missions today. On two occasions Paul refers to "apostles of the church." Since an apostle carries the authority of the one sending him, it is important for us to note the distinction between apostles of Christ and apostles of the churches. In 2 Corinthians 8:23 Paul mentions prominent brothers sent by the churches in Macedonia to assist in administering the collection that Paul was gathering to relieve the church in Jerusalem. In Philippians 2:25 Paul calls Epaphroditus his fellow worker and also a messenger (literally, "apostle") of the church in Philippi, because the church had sent him to bring news and financial support to Paul in prison. Since Paul used this designation twice in different contexts, it is instructive to see what characterized these apostles of the churches. For instance, they were both gifted workers and recognized leaders before they were sent as envoys of their churches. They were sent to work alongside the apostles of Christ and to assist them in practical ways. Their task was defined and time-specific, although travel was slow by modern standards. In both cases, Paul makes a distinction between these who were sent by the church and those who were serving long-term on Paul's team. However, Paul affirms their ministry when he declares, "As for Titus, he is my partner and co-worker among you; as for our brothers, they are representatives of the churches and an honor to Christ" (2 Corinthians 8:23).

Such a positive biblical model for short-term missions is especially relevant today since thousands of believers are going overseas on short-term mission trips. In addition to the apostles of the churches, there are two other biblical examples of short-term missions. One is the Hellenistic Jews who shared their faith courageously as they fled persecution, but focused their ministry on those who were similarly bicultural. They did not cross a big cultural gap, but limited their witness to those who were culturally close or already seekers of God.[4]

---

[4]For example, see Acts 8:27 and 11:19–20. The Greek word used in Acts 11:20 to describe the audience to whom the believers from Cyprus and Cyrene spoke is "Hellenists," not "Greeks."

The second example of believers who went on mission trips are those Paul called Judaizers. They were well-intentioned, but misguided, Jewish believers who traveled to insist that Greek believers follow the law of Moses.[5] Although their mistake could be viewed as simple cultural ethnocentrism, Paul recognized that their mix of cultural expectations with the gospel was deadly for the young churches he was planting. Those who don't have a calling as an apostle, or cross-cultural skills, may find themselves undermining the work of planting indigenous churches, no matter how well-intentioned they are.

So there is a biblical model to guide short-term missions involvement. Only strong believers with ministry experience should be sent into the crucible of a cross-cultural setting. Short-term projects are best done in partnership with apostolic missionaries, as was the case with both examples of the apostles of the churches. When done in this way, those sent out by the church bring glory to God.

The Gift of Apostles

Apostles have a special place in Paul's teaching about God's gifts to the church.

- "God has placed in the church first of all apostles, second prophets, third teachers . . ." (1 Corinthians 12:28).
- "So Christ himself gave the apostles, the prophets, the evangelists, the pastors and teachers" (Ephesians 4:11).

From these two passages we can summarize several truths about apostles. First, it is God who calls apostles and gives them as a gift to the church. Second, apostles are the first gift, although this is a priority of sequence rather than status. Apostles are not more important than other gifts; they simply come first so they can plant the church. Third, apostles are "person" gifts given to the church, not spiritual gifts given to an individual. Fourth, although everyone is called to be a witness, not everyone is called to be an apostle. Fifth, apostles, like the other gifts, are given to establish the church according to God's plan. Finally,

---

The word usually refers to Hellenized Jews, but may here refer to Greeks who were God-fearers.
[5]See Acts 15:5 and Galatians 2:4.

the context of both passages seems to imply that the gifts listed, including apostles, are ongoing.[6]

Foundation Builders

Paul ties the concept of foundation to the role of apostle. The apostles are listed as the first gift because they lay the foundation of the church. In one sense, the apostles laid the foundation of the universal church when they brought the story of Jesus to the world. This is what Paul means in Ephesians 2:20 when he describes the church as "built on the foundation of the apostles and prophets, with Christ Jesus himself as the chief cornerstone." The first-generation apostles did lay a foundation for the universal church by providing the true story of Jesus.

However, Paul also uses the foundation analogy in specifically local terms. He told the church in Corinth, "We are co-workers in God's service; you are God's field, God's building. By the grace God has given me, I laid a foundation as a wise builder, and someone else is building on it. But each one should build with care" (1 Corinthians 3:9–10). Paul was the architect who laid the foundation of the church in Corinth. In Romans 15:20 he states, "It has always been my ambition to preach the gospel where Christ was not known, so that I would not be building on someone else's foundation." The twelve apostles laid the foundation of the universal church; missionary apostles lay the foundation of the church in pioneer areas.

The twelve apostles laid the foundation of the universal church; missionary apostles lay the foundation of the church in pioneer areas.

Once again this speaks to an ongoing role for apostles, because there are many people groups where the foundation of the church has not been laid.

Apostles are the forgotten foundation in missions today. Many are trying to extend their established church into places where a foundation needs to be laid. Apostles are concerned about laying a foundation that

---

[6]First Corinthians 12 emphasizes that there is a diversity of gifts and that the body of Christ is not complete without them. It seems unlikely that Paul would have included the apostles as a gift if he did not expect the gift to continue. The five "person" gifts listed in Ephesians 4:11 are given for the purpose of equipping the saints to build up the church until we all attain the fullness of Christ. The passage assumes that the five "person" gifts will continue until Christ returns.

is strong enough to build on in the future, but they know they are not the ones to build the second or third story. Foundation building is limited to the first phase of the life of the church in a location or among a people group (although Paul had ongoing relationships for a decade or longer with the churches he established). A ministry that focuses on strengthening long-established churches may be worthy, but it is not apostolic in nature. As important as the foundation is, those who come later rarely remember or acknowledge this early stage of the church. For instance, few church members in America know the vision and sacrifice it took to plant the church they attend.

The Character of an Apostle

Holiness. Holiness and moral purity are unpopular themes in today's world. American culture emphasizes skills and abilities, to the exclusion of character. Apostles represent Jesus Christ to those who have little previous knowledge, so their character must reflect Christ. Paul said, "Now this is our boast: Our conscience testifies that we have conducted ourselves in the world, and especially in our relations with you, with integrity and godly sincerity. We have done so, relying not on worldly wisdom but on God's grace" (2 Corinthians 1:12). Paul knew that his life was at least as loud as his words, so his purity of life was an essential part of the message. Without hesitation, he could direct believers to follow his example of what it meant to follow Christ.[7] Like Paul, apostles today are overwhelmed by God's grace in their lives and live to please Christ. Those whom God is using to plant his church in pioneer situations exemplify a godly life.

Faith. Great faith is one of the most important characteristics of apostles. They must see what God can do before it happens. They must believe God is at work in difficulties. They need strong faith that the gospel has power to transform lives and cultures. Apostles have great confidence that God is working ahead, around, and behind them. This faith gives them the confidence to share Christ where he is not known and to trust the Holy Spirit to raise up the church in a short time. This

---

[7]See 1 Corinthians 4:16; Philippians 3:17; 4:9; 2 Thessalonians 3:9.

attitude comes through in Paul's words to the believers in Rome, whom he had not yet met: "I myself am convinced, my brothers and sisters, that you yourselves are full of goodness, filled with knowledge and competent to instruct one another" (Romans 15:14). Paul knew their lives were changed, they had understanding of spiritual things, and they were empowered to minister to one another—not from personal encounter, but from conviction that God was at work.

Sacrifice. A third quality of apostles is a willingness to sacrifice and take risks for the glory of God. How could they do less when Christ sacrificed himself for them? Apostles expect opposition and discomforts, but are not thwarted by them. Paul was willing to work night and day and to risk even his life in order to proclaim Christ.[8] I will never forget the words of a local apostle whom God used to lead a large

GLIMPSES OF APOSTLES

"Mark" has the biceps of a weightlifter, but gentleness fills his eyes. When asked about the great response among the Muslim people he works with, he tears up and can hardly speak. It is evident that God is using Mark, because he knows that God is the one at work, and his heart is tender to the things of God.

"Frank" works among Buddhists and is one of the most passionate evangelists I know. At a meeting I noticed he was poring over note cards instead of relaxing during the tea break. When I asked Frank what he was doing, he said, "If you guys are going to make me sit for several days in a meeting in a country where I don't speak the language, I am going to memorize a gospel presentation in this new language." Sure enough, he led a Buddhist man to Christ before the week was over.

"Shelly" prays about every decision she faces. When violence worsened in her area, she prayed about where God wanted her to serve. Instead of moving to a safer zone, she sensed God telling

---

[8]See, for instance, 1 Thessalonians 2:2,9.

her to move into one of the most dangerous places in the world. Shelly serves the people there in spite of weekly bombings and murders. Her deep faith and purity of life have recently convicted a local Islamic leader.

During his first term of service overseas, at least once a month "Tom" was ready to give up the work and take his family home to America. His first child was constantly sick, at times with a life-threatening illness. Confused and discouraged, Tom and his wife kept praying. Only by God's grace did they persevere and their child live. Today they are working among a forgotten Muslim people group that is responding to the gospel.

Another missionary family miraculously survived a terrorist attack in the country in which they were serving. In the following few years they trained local believers to evangelize almost two dozen unreached tribal groups. After seeing churches planted among all of them, they left their beloved adopted country to start over in a new country and language because they are dedicated to working on the frontier.

movement to Christ. Reflecting on the times when he was left for dead by his persecutors, he said, "A man may often say goodbye to his wife when he leaves the house, but for several years now my wife and I know that every goodbye could be our last." Yet there was absolutely no hesitation to do whatever it would take for his people to come to Christ.

Focus. A fourth characteristic is an overwhelming focus on proclaiming the gospel and planting reproducing churches. Apostles are often men and women with families and other interests. However, they are gripped by a vision to accomplish the task to make disciples of the nations. There has been so much emphasis in Christian circles on living a balanced life that apostles may seem fixated or unhealthily passionate about the work to which God has called them. They have difficulty having a conversation for five minutes without talking about the power of the gospel or the multiplication of disciples. In that sense, they seem to be on the job "24/7/365"—always mindful of the task before them. It is true that they need time with family and time to recuperate. Perhaps the need for some rest was the reason that God allowed Paul to spend six or seven periods in jail.

For those called to be missionary or associate apostles, these are qualities to pray for and to seek to emulate for the glory of Christ.

Mission Methods of Apostles

It is exciting that so many churches, volunteers, and new organizations are taking up the challenge to take the gospel to the nations. One consequence, however, is a lack of awareness regarding apostles and their mission methodology. Many mission projects look very much like ministry in the established churches that support them. Nevertheless, we have seen that God has a plan for how to launch the church where Christ is not known. Apostles pioneer new work, proclaim the good news, and plant reproducing churches.

Apostles pioneer new work. This is a corollary to apostles being foundation builders. Laying the foundation is the first phase of ministry in a particular location. Apostles carefully lay that foundation and then move to another location. We know that Paul ministered in Ephesus for about three years. During that time, though, the church was not only established in that large city, but the gospel spread through a large province. It is inaccurate to think of Paul preaching each week in a single, growing church for three years. Following his ministry pattern elsewhere, he was likely establishing dozens of house churches and training new leaders.

When circumstances moved Paul more quickly, it appears that he laid the foundation for the church in a new city within a couple of months. He didn't walk away and forget these churches. Rather, he sometimes went back for further visits, sent teammates to visit, and wrote letters of instruction to the churches for a period of years. Yet, compared to those of us from an established church background, Paul moved a lot. As he stated to the church in Rome, he was driven by a passion to work where Christ was not known: "From Jerusalem all the way around to Illyricum, I have fully proclaimed the gospel of Christ. It has always been my ambition to preach the gospel where Christ was not known, so that I would not be building on someone else's foundation" (Romans 15:19–20).

Apostles who are called from places where the gospel is well-known and the church is well-established will have a ministry that is cross-cultural. Paul and many of his co-workers worked primarily outside their home environment. Apostles often exhibit unusual, God-given abilities to adapt themselves and the gospel to other cultures. Some members of Paul's team, however, ministered in situations that were culturally similar to their own. I believe God works today to call out apostles from unreached peoples in order to evangelize their own people. In fact, in several places one of the very first believers from a people group has become the primary leader of a church-planting team reaching his or her own people.

Apostles proclaim the gospel. Paul said he was "set apart for the gospel of God" and that he was "not ashamed of the gospel" (Romans 1:1,16). Missionaries may be involved in community development, education, or other practical ministries to meet human needs, but they must focus on sharing the gospel if they want to be apostolic. This emphasis was evident in the testimonies of several local apostles I have spoken with recently. One said that when he committed his life to Christ, he knew he needed to win someone else to the Lord before he went home that afternoon. In his first year of faith, several hundred others believed because of his witness. Another local apostle living in a fairly hostile Muslim environment told me he tries to share Jesus with five new people every day. He started dozens of small groups of new Christians in less than two years. Apostles seek the filling of the Holy Spirit so they are able to share the story of Jesus powerfully.

Jesus is the core of the message. Apostles are not apologetic or confused about who the Savior is. Both foreign and local apostles, however, find new ways to communicate Christ clearly in this new setting. This makes sense, since apostles work in new areas and languages where the gospel has not been worked out for generations, as it has been in places where the church is long-established. The goal of their contextualization is to confront people bound in darkness with the scandal of God come in the flesh, crucified for our sins, and risen as Lord of lords.

Apostles plant reproducing churches. In locations geographically, economically, and culturally close to established churches, finding leaders to plant new churches where they will remain and serve as pastor is a logical strategy. In unreached areas with large populations and little awareness of the gospel, apostles spread the gospel broadly, disciple those who believe, and raise up leaders from the new believers.[9] Hiring a pastor to plant one church in an unreached people group will almost always result in one isolated, foreign, and dependent church with little chance of reproducing.

Churches planted by apostles are structurally simple and exhibit simple faith in God. Apostles know that establishing a pattern of obedience is more important than how long people have believed. New believers who face persecution, who know firsthand the power of the gospel to radically alter a life, and who start out with a pattern of obedience to the teachings of Jesus can quickly show fruit in their lives that surprises those who grew up in Christian environments.

The appropriate use of finances is one of the most critical issues in planting indigenous churches. Paul never brought outside funds into any church he planted. He accepted hospitality from those to whom he ministered, and he accepted financial support from established churches elsewhere, but he never accepted compensation from a church he was planting. Apostles know that financial subsidies will almost always result in a weaker church. New churches that trust the Lord and their own stewardship to meet their needs will not only be stronger but will reproduce many times more rapidly than a church receiving support.

Conclusion

In conclusion, we have seen that God chose to use apostles to lay the foundation of the church in pioneer areas. Today we call these foundation builders missionaries, though not all missionaries function as apostles. Churches established by those of apostolic character who use the missionary method of the apostles have the base from which to grow into churches that bring God great glory among any people group.

---

[9]See Acts 14:21–23.

Yes, there are apostles today—and we should pray for God to raise up many more. For those of us who are missionaries, we can pray that God would raise up an apostle in us!

Discussion Points

1. Do we still have apostles today? Who are they?

2. What is the difference between a missionary apostle and one of the twelve apostles?

3. What four "character" traits does Dent highlight? Why are these important? Can you think of others?

4. Are you an apostle? Is God or the church calling you to be one? Share your story.

Further Reading

Caldwell, Larry W. *Sent Out: Reclaiming the Spiritual Gift of Apostleship for Missionaries and Churches Today.* Pasadena, CA: William Carey Library, 1992.

Dent, Don. *The Ongoing Role of Apostles in Missions.* Bloomington, IN: CrossBooks, 2011.

Miley, George. *Loving the Church . . . Blessing the Nations: Pursuing the Role of Local Churches in Global Mission.* Waynesboro, GA: Authentic, 2003.

Sinclair, Daniel. *A Vision of the Possible.* Waynesboro, GA: Authentic, 2006.

Yount, William R., and Mike Barnett. *Called to Reach: Equipping Cross-Cultural Disciplers.* Nashville: Broadman & Holman, 2007.

22

STRATEGIC PRAYER
FOR GOD'S MISSION

Mike Barnett

It was more than twenty-five years ago at Kingsland Baptist Church in Katy, Texas, that I first learned to pray for "the missionaries."[1] We sat in small groups and prayed from a list, by name, for every missionary who had a birthday that week. Occasionally someone mentioned a specific prayer need of an individual missionary, but usually it was a more generic, somewhat ritualistic recognition before God of those serving him on foreign fields. "God bless the missionaries." It was a beginning.

Churches have progressed in their prayers for God's mission and his missionaries. Some churches still pray for missionaries on their birthdays; but increasingly, our prayers are better informed and infinitely more strategic. Surely this is a factor in reports from around the world about the progress of the gospel. What is behind these strategic prayers? Why should we pray for missions and missionaries in the first place? Whom should we pray for? How should we pray? And what happens when we pray?

Why Pray for God's Mission and His Missionaries?

We pray because God answers prayer. Throughout the Old and New Testaments, time after time God responds to the prayers of his people.

---

[1]This chapter is adapted from *Giving Ourselves to Prayer: An Acts 6:4 Primer for Ministry*, compiled by Dan Crawford (Terre Haute, IN: Prayer Shop Publishing, 2008). Used by permission.

On the evening after the dedication of the temple, God reminded Solomon that when God's people humbly pray and seek his will, he hears from heaven and answers their prayers (2 Chronicles 7:14). God's mission plan for Israel was to be a "light for the Gentiles," a witness among all peoples on earth (Isaiah 49:6). God's temple was to be a "house of prayer for all nations" (Isaiah 56:7). Prayer was a vital link between God's people and his mission.

Almost one thousand years later Jesus condemned the temple managers for turning God's temple from a house of prayer for the nations into a "den of robbers" (Mark 11:17). The next day he debriefed his disciples on the importance of prayer for the kingdom: "Therefore I tell you, whatever you ask for in prayer, believe that you have received it, and it will be yours" (Mark 11:24). In other words, do not forget that God answers the prayers of his faithful followers. After his resurrection, Jesus reinstated God's mission to "make disciples of all nations, baptizing them in the name of the Father and of the Son and of the Holy Spirit, and teaching them to obey everything I have commanded you" (Matthew 28:18–20).

The disciples of the early church understood the power of prayer. "They all joined together constantly in prayer" (Acts 1:14). In times of crisis they prayed (Mark 9:29; Acts 6:4; 12:1–5; 13:2–3). In the middle of the mission, they prayed (Acts 4:23–31; Colossians 4:2–4). And God answered. No wonder the gospel of Jesus Christ swept throughout the Roman Empire in such a short time. God's people prayed for his mission and his missionaries. Why? Because they knew that God answers prayer. He did then and he does now.

For Whom Should We Pray?

For the "nations" and the missionaries. Before we pray for the missionaries, we need to pray for those they serve. Paul prayed that his fellow Israelites would be saved (Romans 10:1). As part of his prayer in John 17, Jesus said, "My prayer is not for [the disciples] alone. I pray also for those who will believe in me through their message" (v. 20). As followers of Jesus, committed to his Great Commission, we must pray for all peoples on earth—especially for those who have yet to hear of Jesus.

In recent years we have become more effective in praying for the lost peoples on earth. Whereas our traditional prayers for missionaries seldom connected us with these "nations," today we have access to information about the people groups who have yet to hear the gospel. In the past we received missionary letters full of personal requests related to the well-being of the missionary family. Today we read e-letters from missions teams focused on strategic prayer needs of the local peoples.

- "Pray for Ahmed and Mohammed, that God would open their hearts and spirits to the gospel."

- "Pray for local tribal leaders and their willingness to meet with believers."

- "Pray for Fatima and her sister as they approach their mother with the truths of the gospel."

- "Pray for a specific megacity and for opportunities for humanitarian projects to provide access to the gospel."

- "Pray for local translators working with Bible societies on Bible translation projects."

Today we are able to pray more strategically for the unreached.

Should we forget the former "God bless the missionaries" prayer? Absolutely not. We must continue to pray for the missionaries. But what should we pray for the missionaries? Our Western worldview of success and individualism has unduly influenced our church culture. We seem preoccupied with personal comfort and success. Often our view of God is that his main mission is to take care of us and to make us happy. This is twisted and dangerous theology.

What do we mean when we ask God to bless the missionaries? Jesus did not pray that God would rescue the disciples from the hardships of the world. He asked the Father to "protect them from the evil one" (John 17:15). After Saul's Damascus Road experience, Christ said he would show Paul "how much he must suffer for my name" (Acts 9:16). God's call upon the life of a missionary, or any believer for that matter, does not remove the reality of pain, suffering, sickness, and persecution.

This theme of serving Christ through persecution and suffering is both a biblical and historical reality. How many of us have heard the testimonies and requests of persecuted house church leaders in China? They plead with us not to pray for the suffering and persecution to end, but rather for God to be glorified through the persecution. With persecution comes kingdom growth. It has always been so. Tertullian said that "the blood of the Christians is holy seed." Jesus said, "Whoever wants to be my disciple must deny themselves and take up their cross and follow me" (Matthew 16:24).

So perhaps we should pray less for the happiness and comfort of the missionaries and more for their endurance and character as cross-cultural disciplers. In our book *Called to Reach: Equipping Cross-Cultural Disciplers*, Rick Yount and I identify seven characteristics of effective missionaries.[2] When we pray for the missionaries (expatriates and locals), perhaps we should pray that they would:

1. Depend on the Holy Spirit in all they do (spiritual character)

2. Live according to the teachings of the Bible (biblical character)

3. Be good thinkers and teachers across cultural barriers (rational character)

4. Be willing to *suffer with* those they witness to (compassionate character)

5. Endure as they *suffer for* the sake of the gospel (impassioned character)

6. Build lasting, witnessing relationships (relational character)

7. Stay focused on God's mission, not their own (maturational character)

Whom should we pray for? Pray for the nations. Pray for the lost of this world, the unreached peoples who receive the witness of our missionaries. Intercede on behalf of the local peoples whom God will use to establish his kingdom in their lands and beyond. And pray for the missionaries—that they would endure and be of Christlike character.

---

[2]William R. Yount and Mike Barnett, *Called to Reach: Equipping Cross-Cultural Disciplers* (Nashville: Broadman & Holman, 2007).

How Should We Pray?

The disciples must have asked Jesus how to pray. After coaching them on their motives for prayer, Jesus told them to pray like this: "Father, *your* name be praised and honored. *Your* kingdom come and *your* will— your mission—be done" (Matthew 6:9–10, italics and paraphrase mine). Jesus, the Son of God, tells us to pray for God—for *his* glory, *his* name, *his* fame, *his* kingdom, and *his* mission. God desires our praise. He wants us to participate in *his* mission of a blessing for all peoples (Genesis 12:3) as he establishes *his* kingdom today on earth and forever in heaven.

So, pray for God to call out *his* laborers into *his* harvest fields more than ours. Pray for the establishment of *his* church more than individual mission organizations or denominations. Pray for the reputation of *his* name more than our recognition. It is no accident that the most effective missionaries are often standing in the background, not up front in the spotlight. Pray for the Holy Spirit to convince unbelievers through *his* teachings more than our clever arguments. Pray for new believers to obey *his* commandments more than our traditions. Pray for the new church to find answers from *his* Word more than our words. When we pray like this, he inevitably will surprise us. After all, it is *his* mission, and *he* will accomplish it.

What Happens When We Pray?

God's mission proceeds from our prayers, and he expands his kingdom.
When we pray for God's mission it is as if we are praying the gospel to ourselves. And God answers our prayers. He expands the influence of his gospel. Where there are movements of believers planting churches on earth today, they were preceded by movements of prayer for God to accomplish his mission among those peoples.[3] When we stop praying, when we relegate prayer to the fringes of our church practice like the temple managers of old, God's mission is diminished. More than eighty years ago, Helen Barrett Montgomery said it well:

---

[3]David Garrison, *Church Planting Movements: How God Is Redeeming a Lost World* (Midlothian, VA: WIGTake Resources, 2004), 172–77.

Now the Bible, which is the vehicle of the gospel, brings to light an inner message of prayer which is dynamic. The Bible may bring the knowledge of Christ to a nation or individual, but if there is no appropriation of prayer-power there is no life, no movement. It is important that men should know the gospel, it is more important that they should pray the gospel. If they pray, the gospel proceeds; if they do not pray the gospel halts. Its victories are wholly wrought by prayer; its defeats proceed from prayerlessness.[4]

Praying for God's mission and his missionaries is the most strategic endeavor of the church.

Conclusion

Why pray for God's mission and his missionaries? Because God always has and always will answer prayer. Whom should we pray for? The nations and the missionaries. Pray for the nations to hear and understand the good news of Jesus Christ. Pray for missionaries to endure and develop Christlike character as they serve. How should we pray? For *God's* mission to be accomplished. Don't focus so much on our plans, strategies, means, and methods, but for *God's* will to be done—*his* kingdom to come. And what happens when we pray? God expands his kingdom. These are the basics of praying strategically for God's mission and his missionaries.

The congregation my wife and I are part of today doesn't have a churchwide Wednesday evening Bible study and prayer meeting. We no longer pray for the missionaries on their birthdays. But we do pray for God's mission and his missionaries. God bless the missionaries! Thy kingdom come!

Discussion Points

1. Why should we pray for the mission of God?

2. Whom do you pray for? Make a list of peoples, missionaries, missions, etc., that you pray for regularly.

3. Using the model prayer of Matthew 6:9–13, take some time now to pray for the mission of God.

---

[4]Helen Barrett Montgomery, *Prayer and Missions* (West Medford, MA: The Central Committee of the United Study of Foreign Missions, 1924), 11.

Further Reading

Garrison, David. *Church Planting Movements: How God Is Redeeming a Lost World*. Midlothian, VA: WIGTake Resources, 2004.

Montgomery, Helen Barrett. *Prayer and Missions*. West Medford, MA: The Central Committee of the United Study of Foreign Missions, 1924.

Yount, William R., and Mike Barnett. *Called to Reach: Equipping Cross-Cultural Disciplers*. Nashville: Broadman & Holman, 2007.

23

CULTURES AND WORLDVIEWS

Stan May

My family had the joy of going to Africa to serve as missionaries in 1989. As we interacted with the AmaNdebele people of southern Zimbabwe, we immediately noticed certain outward traits that revealed cultural differences: women dressed in bright clothing and carried babies on their backs and bundles on their heads; buses were piled high with luggage and live animals; and instead of potato chips, dried caterpillars substituted as an everyday snack food.

Only over time, however, did we see true cultural differences. We learned, for example, that the Bantu peoples, to which the AmaNdebele belong, manifested the three "Rs" of culture: they were respectful, relational, and religious. These traits accentuated the vast difference between our Western culture and their culture. Their respect orientation contrasted greatly with our egalitarianism. Their relational bent seemed so foreign to our vocational, task-oriented outlook on life. And their religious viewpoint (though many did not have the true gospel) caused them to see life far differently from those of us raised in the secular environment of the West. These shared characteristics of their lives and tribes impressed indelibly upon us the need to learn their different, yet incredibly rich, culture.

Why Study Culture?

When missionaries and mission organizations used to talk of going to the nations, they assumed that the political boundaries and borders of the various nation-states were the "nations" of the Bible. Ralph Winter's bombshell at the Lausanne Congress on World Evangelization, however, changed that thinking forever: "All our exultation about the fact that every *country* of the world has been penetrated has allowed many to suppose that every *culture* has by now been penetrated. This misunderstanding is a malady so widespread that it deserves a special name. Let us call it 'people blindness.'"[1] Donald McGavran commented on this challenge, "Nothing said at Lausanne had more meaning for the Expansion of Christianity."[2]

As missions organizations and missionaries responded to Winter's challenge, they began to focus on differing ethnolinguistic people groups—cultures—rather than simply going to countries. The task of reaching these cultures effectively required learning languages and cultures in order to communicate the gospel in the people's heart language. Such communication is essential to ensure that people hear with understanding.[3]

What Is Culture?

Describing culture to most people is like trying to describe water to a fish. People know and function effectively in cultures. But, like the fish, they cannot describe their cultures because they are immersed in them. Unlike fish, however, humans on every part of the planet create and live in culture. As Stephen A. Grunlan and Marvin K. Mayers note, "Of all God's creatures, only humans are culture bearing."[4]

Globally, human cultures reflect incredible diversity, but major definitions demonstrate that culture itself has several shared characteristics. Grunlan and Mayers define culture as "learned and shared attitudes, values, and ways of behaving . . . [including] the material artifacts created by the members of a cultural group."[5]

[1]Ralph Winter, "The New Macedonia: A Revolutionary New Era in Mission Begins," in *Perspectives on the World Christian Movement: A Reader*, 3rd ed., ed. Ralph D. Winter and Steven C. Hawthorne (Pasadena, CA: William Carey Library, 1999), 346 (emphasis in original).
[2]Donald McGavran, introduction to Winter, "The New Macedonia," 339.
[3]In the parable of the soils, Jesus differentiated between the good soil and the path on the basis of hearing with or without understanding (Matthew 13:19,23).
[4]Stephen A. Grunlan and Marvin K. Mayers, *Cultural Anthropology: A Christian Perspective*, 2nd ed., with a foreword by Eugene H. Nida (Grand Rapids: Zondervan, 1988), 39.
[5]Ibid.

They summarize culture as "the integrated system of learned behavior characteristic of members of a society."[6] Charles Kraft defines culture as "a society's complex, integrated coping mechanism, consisting of learned, patterned concepts and behavior, plus their underlying perspectives (worldview) and resulting artifacts (material culture)."[7] Paul Hiebert defines culture as "the integrated system of learned patterns of behavior, ideas, and products characteristic of a society."[8] Ebbie C. Smith notes, "Culture then, by definition, is the learned design or pattern of living for a particular group of people."[9]

> *Charles Kraft defines culture as "a society's complex, integrated coping mechanism, consisting of learned, patterned concepts and behavior, plus their underlying perspectives (worldview) and resulting artifacts (material culture)."*

The commonalities of all these definitions (and hence of culture) are clear:

- Cultures are learned: From earliest childhood, all persons capable of learning are enculturated by immediate family members, extended family, and even society in general as to the "proper" way of doing everything. Children are not given options; cultural values are inculcated from birth as the only right way.

- Cultures are patterns: Cultures are not random events but rather systematized patterns of ideas and actions that make sense, give meaning to life, and organize life for the perpetuation of the society, the welfare of the smallest decision-making unit, and the socialization of the individual.

- Cultures are observable: They include behaviors, ideas, values, and artifacts (including tools, houses, art, and anything produced by design) that differentiate societies and identify those in any particular culture.

---

[6]Ibid., 54.
[7]Charles Kraft, *Anthropology for Christian Witness* (Maryknoll, NY: Orbis, 1996), 38.
[8]Paul Hiebert, *Cultural Anthropology* (Grand Rapids: Baker, 1983), 25.
[9]Ebbie C. Smith, "Defining Culture," in *Missiology: An Introduction to the Foundations, History, and Strategies of World Missions*, ed. John Mark Terry, Ebbie Smith, and Justice Anderson (Nashville: Broadman & Holman, 1998), 261.

- Cultures are communicative: All cultures express themselves verbally and nonverbally in languages capable of conveying the totality of the culture. Language and culture are inseparable, and the person seeking to understand the culture must invest serious effort and energy in language and culture acquisition.

Culture is any people group's learned patterns encapsulated in its shared ideas, behaviors, and artifacts, and expressed by its unique verbal and nonverbal communication. Each distinct people group has its own language and culture. In fact, these groups are identified as differing *ethnolinguistic* entities (*ethnos* is the Greek word for "people group" or "culture group"). Culture so identifies peoples that it essentially defines their lives; even when they "drop out" of culture, they drop out in culturally acceptable ways.[10]

Kraft likens culture to the script of a play.[11] All the participants learn their lines, know the cultural cues, and dress the part (though most do so without any conscious awareness of this drama). Missionaries who enter other cultures may be compared to actors who have spent their entire lives learning the script for a Shakespearean play only to find that the stage they're on is presenting *The Phantom of the Opera*. The costumes are wrong, the lines are confusing, all the props are out of place, and every memorized cue is changed. Effective missionaries determine to learn the culture, and this acculturation (learning culture as an outsider) entails learning the plot underlying the culture as well. The plot that drives the culture is that most basic nexus of allegiances and assumptions called worldview.

> *Missionaries who enter other cultures may be compared to actors who have spent their entire lives learning the script for a Shakespearean play only to find that the stage they're on is presenting The Phantom of the Opera. The costumes are wrong, the lines are confusing, all the props are out of place, and every memorized cue is changed.*

---

[10]For example, "Goths" who drop out in Western culture all dress similarly and even adopt similar patterns of thinking. On a deeper level, methods of suicide in the West differ from those in Japan.

[11]Kraft, *Anthropology for Christian Witness*, 38.

The book of Acts tells the story of Paul's first attempts at preaching in Athens (Acts 17:16–34). As was his practice, Paul seeks out the areas of the city where people gather and begins to share the gospel message with them. As he evangelizes in Athens, however, something happens that changes his outlook:

> While Paul was . . . in Athens, he was greatly distressed to see that the city was full of idols. So he reasoned in the synagogue with both Jews and God-fearing Greeks, as well as in the marketplace day by day with those who happened to be there. A group of Epicurean and Stoic philosophers began to dispute with him. Some of them asked, "What is this babbler trying to say?" Others remarked, "He seems to be advocating foreign gods." They said this because Paul was preaching the good news about Jesus and the resurrection. (Acts 17:16–18)

Paul the Jew preaches the truth of the gospel of God—"Jesus and the resurrection." What the Athenians hear, however, is something entirely different. In Greek, *Jesus* is masculine, while the word for *resurrection* (*anastasis*) is feminine. The Athenians, who live in a world inhabited by numerous deities, hear him preaching about a pair of deities whom they assume to be a new "couple." What causes this incredible distortion of Paul's message? In a word—worldview. Paul preaches from the worldview of a monotheistic (believer in one God) Jew who has embraced Jesus as the Messiah on the basis of his resurrection from the dead, while the Athenians, whose polytheistic worldview accepts a plethora of gods, entertain an entirely different idea.

What Is Worldview?

As a set of underlying assumptions and allegiances that interpret existence, worldview binds people together and provides the basic mental and cultural framework by which individuals and groups understand and respond to reality. James Sire noted, "Our ground-floor assumptions—ones that are so basic that none more basic can be conceived—compose our world view."[12] Worldview is a full-orbed grasp of life

---

[12]James W. Sire, *How to Read Slowly: Reading for Comprehension* (Wheaton: Harold Shaw Publishers, 1978), 39.

expressing the basic assumptions of every community, "a coherent thought-system that helps make sense of [shared] experiences and maintain the values developed over the history of that group."[13] This holistic worldview interprets and maps all aspects of existence.

Worldview is the mental atlas that guides people in any culture through every life situation. David Burnett referred to the specific cultural maps used to navigate each facet of life as "paradigms" or "recurrent models of reality." He juxtaposed them to worldview: "The term *paradigm* is generally used as a label for some specific model, while *worldview* is a term used for an extensive model that may include many paradigms."[14]

If each *mental map* guides us through one area of reality, then the worldview emerges as an *atlas of the mind*. This atlas aids us as we navigate each cultural setting, just as a physical atlas aids us when we travel. Driving in the United States, when we enter Tennessee we turn to the Tennessee map. When we enter the cultural setting for greetings, we innately turn to the worldview map page for greetings, and our mental map guides us through the ritual of greetings appropriate to our culture. This wonderful gift of worldview interprets the proper, learned behavior for every area of life and allows us to function effectively in our culture. This worldview has its drawbacks, however; just as an atlas of the United States is useful for traveling in the US but useless for traveling in Africa, so the mental atlas of worldview must undergo adjustments to function in other regions of the world.

What Are the Functions of Worldview?

Worldview harbors our most basic allegiances and assumptions. Worldview shapes our values, identifies our aspirations, expresses our longings, and even classifies our failures. One revealing event occurred on a segment of a video in the Disappearing World series. Anthropologist Marian Ferme interviewed a group of Mende women in Sierra Leone about the question "What is beautiful hair?" The women began

---

[13]Orville Boyd Jenkins, *Dealing with Differences: Contrasting African and European World Views* (Nairobi: Communication Press, 1991), 13.

[14]David Burnett, *Clash of Worlds* (Nashville: Thomas Nelson, 1992), 18–20.

to laugh nervously (Bantu peoples often laugh when embarrassed), for they realized that Ferme did not know that black, curly hair is beautiful. They also knew that the answer that they gave to this blond-haired, white woman would reveal that her hair was not beautiful. Their laughter surfaced in response to a worldview assumption of beauty.[15]

Worldviews serve several functions: they identify what is real, assign importance to values, underlie beliefs, and shape behaviors. The secular American worldview values education over experience, youth over age, and egalitarianism over stratification. The three "Rs" of Africa reverse each of these values. Secular assumptions insist that matter is all there is, so religious beliefs are marginalized or at least compartmentalized. Americans—even American Christians—embrace a sacred/secular dichotomy that relegates religious expression to certain times and certain places, while other cultures exude a holism that intertwines the sacred and secular into every facet of existence.

Worldview Universals

Charles Kraft noted, "Though there may be more, at least the five following categories of assumptions seem to be found in every worldview. Thus we refer to them as 'worldview universals.'"[16] These include categorization, person-group, causality, time-event, and space-material.[17] Each of these universals merits discussion.

Categorization. All peoples classify, categorize, and think according to the logic of their worldview. These categories show up in the logic itself, in the language, and in the mental structures of life. For example, the English language uses the masculine and feminine genders, and most words are gender-neutral. Greek, on the other hand, has three genders (masculine, feminine, and neuter), and every word has a gender. The pastoral AmaNdebele people have dozens of words for "cow," but their word for "blue" (*luhlaza*) means both green and blue.

Person-group. Each culture determines the size of its smallest

---

[15]*The Mende*, Disappearing World video series (Chicago: Films Incorporated Video, 1991).

[16]Charles Kraft, with Christie Varney and Ellen Kearney, *Christianity with Power: Your Worldview and Your Experience of the Supernatural* (Ann Arbor, MI: Vine Books, 1989), 195.

[17]Ibid., 183–84.

decision-making unit based on worldview assumptions. Americans prize individualism to such an extreme that neither family nor friends may interfere in serious decisions unless asked. Other cultures see the extended family as the smallest unit for decisions. Thus, the individual's desires regarding any matter that affects the family—even matters as serious as marriage—are weighed by the scales of that matter's effect on the entire family.

Causality. All peoples explain and relate various life events to immediate and ultimate causes on the basis of their worldview assumptions. Americans may believe in luck or chance, while Muslims may refer to *kismet*, the will of Allah. Animists see spirits at work behind every event. Many cultures of the world believe that all misfortune results from some offense to the ancestors.

Time-event. Worldview assumptions determine whether people structure their lives around times or events. Westerners are time-oriented—the clock directs all of life. Events start and stop at prearranged times. Church services, for example, are planned to end at noon. Many cultures, however, value events. In our experience, Africans in Zimbabwe regularly showed up late for meetings, but they would stay until the event ended. On one occasion we arrived, because of travel difficulties, two hours later than the time the people were told. They waited patiently until we came, rejoiced with us over our arrival, listened to all the speakers who accompanied us, and even insisted that someone speak again when one of their people arrived after walking several miles.

Space-material. All peoples arrange their relation to space and material objects on the basis of their worldview assumptions. Americans need a great deal of space. Every person has his or her own room, people keep their distance from one another, and buses are full when every seat is taken. In contrast, many houses in Bulawayo's western suburbs held at least three families. Each family used one of the four rooms of the house (the owners kept two rooms) for eating, sleeping, and living. Buses were crowded, and emergency taxis regularly drove the streets with legs hanging out and people hanging on the sides.

All worldviews fulfill these universal functions. The overt behaviors and patterns reflect underlying patterns, which in turn reflect worldview assumptions. Effective missionaries must determine to learn the worldview of their target people.

Why Learn Worldview?

Duane Elmer tells the story of a kindhearted monkey who sought to help without learning the worldview of the one he rescued:

> A typhoon had temporarily stranded a monkey on an island. In a secure, protected place, while waiting for the raging waters to recede, he spotted a fish swimming against the current. It seemed obvious to the monkey that the fish was struggling and in need of assistance. Being of kind heart, the monkey resolved to help the fish.
>
> A tree precariously dangled over the very spot where the fish seemed to be struggling. At considerable risk to himself, the monkey moved far out on a limb, reached down and snatched the fish from the threatening waters. Immediately scurrying back to the safety of his shelter, he carefully laid the fish on dry ground. For a few moments the fish showed some excitement, but soon settled into a peaceful rest. Joy and satisfaction swelled inside the monkey. He had successfully helped another creature.[18]

Many volunteers and some missionaries travel to other cultures with similar good intentions. Without understanding the target people's culture and worldview, however, they act from their own worldview assumptions—as the monkey did—and end up doing harm rather than good.

Worldview demands understanding because cross-cultural agents already have a worldview that they learned unconsciously from childhood, and this worldview dictates the interpretation of all events and facts. The worldview that they carry unconsciously to the field acts as the glasses they never know they've donned and causes them to "see" others in a skewed fashion.[19] David Burnett correctly observed, "He who knows but one worldview knows no worldview!"[20]

Paul recognizes the need to understand the Athenians so as to communicate God's gospel correctly. After the fiasco of misunderstanding

---

[18]Duane Elmer, *Cross-Cultural Connections: Stepping Out and Fitting In Around the World* (Downers Grove, IL: InterVarsity, 2002), 14.

[19]Norman L. Geisler, quoted in David J. Hesselgrave, "Fitting Third-World Believers with Christian Worldview Glasses," *JETS* 30:2 (June 1987): 215.

[20]Burnett, *Clash of Worlds*, 36.

(Acts 17:18), he employs their feedback to encode the gospel message more effectively. When asked to preach at the Areopagus, Paul builds bridges of understanding by acknowledging their religiosity (Acts 17:22), quoting lines from Athenian poetry to communicate truth (Acts 17:28), using their logic to present his arguments, and employing one of their altars to point them to Christ. Don Richardson says that Paul understood the story of the altar to the Unknown God and used this tool to proclaim what they worshiped as unknown.[21]

When missionaries do not develop an understanding of the culture and worldview of their target people group, they naturally tend to view their own culture as superior to the cultures of others. This tendency to judge the behaviors and objects of other cultures by the values and assumptions of our own culture is identified as *ethnocentrism*. The solution to ethnocentrism is to try to understand another culture in terms of its own values and assumptions and its members as fellow humans. God breaks us of ethnocentrism when we recognize that many values of our host culture are superior to those of our home culture, and we begin to be the learners.

Missionaries who free themselves of ethnocentrism develop the three basic attitudes necessary to be effective for the kingdom: learner, servant, and purpose. Learners come to the culture not as the great hope for the new culture, but as respectful inquirers. Since all true ministry flows out of relationships, they know that they must learn the culture and language in order to build lasting relationships and present Jesus Christ in a culturally relevant, relational manner. They determine to attain the twin goals of *bilingualism* and *biculturalism*.

The attitude of a servant reflects both the heart of Christ (Mark 10:45) and the mind of Paul (2 Corinthians 4:5). The missionary, though perhaps financially better off than his national partners, never uses his money or his position as leverage. His servant's heart shows God's love for the people and opens their hearts to the truth he speaks.

The missionary must temper the attitudes of learner and servant with the attitude of purpose. When the disciples urged Jesus to take a break and eat something, Jesus said, "My food is to do the will of him who sent

---

[21]Don Richardson, *Eternity in Their Hearts*, 3rd ed. (Ventura, CA: Regal, 2005), 20. Richardson describes the genesis of the altar on pages 9–20.

me and to finish his work" (John 4:34). Jesus and Paul lived on purpose (Colossians 1:28–29). Purpose prevents the learner from becoming a cultural tour guide and the servant from becoming a doormat.

Just as Paul adapted his presentation to reach the worldview of the Athenians, so missionaries today must change to reach the cultures to which God calls them. They never change the core message. Scripture defines the message, but it must be shaped by culture so that the hearers receive the message as strangely familiar. The diagram below rightfully depicts worldview as the deepest level of culture and of each individual life. Much contemporary American preaching targets the shallowest level—behavior. It assumes that changing behavior will produce lasting change. The Lord Jesus never taught or acted that way, however. He believed that the heart (the seat of basic assumptions and allegiances, thus worldview) was the fount of life and the seat of all true change, thus his insistence to Nicodemus on the "new birth" (John 3:3,5,7). He knew that all lasting change begins at the core and radiates outward, affecting behavior.

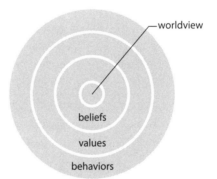

Figure 23.1.

Garth Dal Congdon further illustrated the need for worldview understanding: "'Christopagan' peoples come to a vital faith only when Christ is encountered as Lord at the core of their worldview. The promotion of this encounter by relating Christ effectually to the respondents' worldview must be a controlling objective of missionary work, if it aims to establish a truly Christian church."[22] If missionaries wish to produce lasting

---

[22]Garth D. Congdon, "An Investigation into the Current Zulu Worldview and Its Relevance to

change, they must focus on worldview transformation. Worldview transformation occurs when the gospel impacts the worldview universals that define the heart allegiance of a people. This heart allegiance must experience a fundamental shift to Jesus Christ as Lord.

How Can Missionaries Learn Worldview?

Missionaries have several tools for learning worldview. These tools include observation, engagement, interviews, and research. Good missionaries research the people before they ever set foot in their host country. They read about the people and research their lives, habits, and hearts. Effective researchers interview nationals and other cross-cultural workers, read books and journal articles about the country, and surf the Internet to build a base of knowledge about the target people. While research alone is insufficient without actual engagement, it is an essential first step. Missionaries can also find trusted cultural helpers and cultural coaches to guide them in language and culture acquisition. These cultural coaches have the insiders' emic perspective but know how to communicate their culture because they have studied their own world from an etic perspective.[23]

Paul employed the tools of observation and engagement as he interacted with the people of Athens. Luke tells us that he "was observing" (my translation of a verb in Acts 17:16) the city and its people. His observations included the peoples' religious behavior, their poetry, their altars, and their regular places of gathering. He engaged the people by going out to places where they habitually gathered and by preaching the gospel to them. Missionaries today need to be out among the people, dialoguing with them and evangelizing so that they can discover what and how people think.

How Can Worldviews Change?

Language and culture acquisition is not an end in itself; worldview change is the heart of missionary work. Just as Jesus targeted the human

---

Missionary Work," *Evangelical Missions Quarterly* 21 (July 1985): 299. The term "Christopagan" refers to those who combine pagan and Christian religious faith and practices due to their historically combined worldviews. It is a more specific denotation of the concept of folk religion.
[23]"Emic" and "etic" are anthropological terms used respectively to describe the insider's and outsider's views of culture.

heart, so the missionary who longs to make a difference targets the worldview of the people. Significant worldview change comes about through invention from within, instability from within, intervention from without, and intervention from above. When the worldview no longer answers the questions the culture asks for any of the above reasons, the fissures in the old worldview prepare the people group to hear and embrace change.

The American worldview changed considerably in the twentieth century. Inventions such as assembly lines, satellites, birth control pills, vaccines, and television reshaped society profoundly. The resulting fault lines destabilized the worldview and opened the door for competing alternatives to answer life's central assumptions. The century also witnessed cultures whose internal instability led to the throwing off of regimes and the embracing of new ways of living. Some cultures experienced intervention from without as the world shrank and their long-held traditions fell before the rush of new technologies and ideas.

Lasting change comes, however, when God intervenes from above. Missionaries introduce worldview change through a Trinitarian theology that rests in the Father's providence, the Son's presence, and the Spirit's power.[24] As missionaries learn worldviews that differ markedly from their own, they see the limitations of their own secular worldview and present a biblical Jesus who actually works in the lives of the people. As they learn the language and culture of the target people, they demonstrate the love of Christ tangibly. Through faithful prayer and contextualized evangelism, they share the gospel wrapped in cultural expressions that make the message strangely familiar. In the end, language and culture acquisition, allows them to establish churches that may look nothing like those of their home culture, but that reflect a true response to God and his gospel.

Discussion Points

1. In what ways is culture like the script of a play? In what ways is worldview like an atlas of maps?

---

[24]Paul Hiebert, "Healing and the Kingdom," *Anthropological Reflections on Missiological Issues* (Grand Rapids: Baker, 1995), 228–32.

2. What is ethnocentrism and why is it a problem for missionaries?

3. What are some practical ways to identify a specific worldview?

4. What three attitudes do missionaries develop once they free themselves from ethnocentrism?

5. Applying the illustration of the monkey and the fish, in what ways could well-meaning volunteers or missionaries do harm when they attempt to help?

Further Reading

Grunlan, Stephen A., and Marvin K. Mayers. *Cultural Anthropology: A Christian Perspective.* 2nd ed. With a foreword by Eugene H. Nida. Grand Rapids: Zondervan, 1988.

Hesselgrave, David J. "Fitting Third-world Believers with Christian Worldview Glasses." *JETS* 30:2 (June 1987): 215–22.

Hiebert, Paul. *Anthropological Reflections on Missiological Issues.* Grand Rapids: Baker, 1995.

Kraft, Charles. *Anthropology for Christian Witness.* Maryknoll, NY: Orbis, 1996.

Kraft, Charles, with Christie Varney and Ellen Kearney. *Christianity with Power: Your Worldview and Your Experience of the Supernatural.* Ann Arbor, MI: Vine Books, 1989.

24

TELL HIS STORY SO THAT
ALL MIGHT WORSHIP

LaNette W. Thompson

Jesus walks on water, and his disciples worship him. The Samaritan woman meets Jesus, and she rushes to tell the townspeople about the encounter. A paralyzed man walks, and his friends glorify God when they see him take his first steps. Worship, testimony, and praise are natural reactions to an encounter with the living God.

In more recent times, Sadio, a Muslim-background believer in Africa whose husband left her when she became a Christian, shuts herself in her bedroom to pray. There is no food left in her home, and she has no money. After hearing a knock at her door, she goes out to find two dishes of food on the table, brought by a neighbor. Four times in the next eighteen hours different people bring food, or money to buy food. When the last one appears, she is totally overcome and falls to her knees in praise.

That afternoon she hurries to the women's meeting at church to share her story. Later I hear her share the story again with believers in a village we are visiting. As the stars shine overhead, they too share their stories. "Before I knew Jesus," a nonliterate man says, "I was angry all the time. Since I have known him, no one has had to tell me to calm down."

The following day, we meet with the village women. With the Bible in her lap, Sadio tells the story of Mary and Martha. The women want to be like Mary. They want to spend time with

When people know Jesus and his story, there is worship, there is testimony, and there is praise.

Jesus. They know the passionate love story of the perfect Hero, who endured death for the salvation of his bride.[1]

Chronological Bible Storying

For more than twenty years we have used Chronological Bible Storying to introduce unbelievers to God's story. Chronological Bible Storying (CBS), a term coined by Jim Slack and J. O. Terry of the International Mission Board of the Southern Baptist Convention, describes a process of sharing biblical truths by telling Bible stories in the order in which they occurred. The person using the method presents the Bible story, then leads hearers to discover the truths inherent in the stories.[2] A desire to better communicate the gospel message to those who can't read or don't have Scripture in their language inspired these men and others to introduce a generation of missionaries to the concept and practices of orality. Approximately two-thirds of the world's population either prefers or is only able to learn by oral methods. This oral world includes secondary oral learners, who exist today in a technological world where reading books is eschewed in favor of television and the Internet.

With the 1982 publication of Walter Ong's *Orality and Literacy*,[3] an historical analysis of orality, highly literate academicians began to dip their toes into the uncharted waters of a world we literates had long forgotten. We wrote books, developed resources, and launched websites. We held training events to introduce the topic of orality to a primarily literate missionary force sent to reach primarily oral people.

We taught that in Chronological Bible Storying, "storyers" create a list of core Bible stories, identifying basic biblical truths necessary to understand salvation. These stories are supplemented with other Bible stories that speak to a people's worldview, either affirming it or questioning it. The entire process is bathed in prayer: prayer for group selection, prayer for direction as to which stories to share, prayer for the

---

[1]For more information about the concept of Jesus as Hero, see Kurt Bruner's book, *The Divine Drama* (Wheaton: Tyndale, 2001).
[2]Lausanne Committee for World Evangelization and International Orality Network, *Making Disciples of Oral Learners* (Lima, NY: Elim Publishing, 2005), 108–9.
[3]Walter J. Ong, *Orality and Literacy: The Technologizing of the Word* (London and New York: Routledge, 1982).

crafting of the story, prayer for the storyer, and prayer for the hearers.

Three tracks. The series of stories is compiled chronologically into lists called tracks. The purpose of the first track, the *evangelism track*, is to give unbelievers the chance to hear and understand Bible truths by starting in Genesis and storying through the coming of the Holy Spirit at Pentecost. The truths brought out in this track show the hearers that they are lost and introduce them to God's plan for their salvation. A track's length depends upon the amount of available time to share the stories, as well as the number of stories necessary to crack worldview barriers and present gospel truths. Evangelism CBS tracks vary from more than a hundred stories to as few as four. At the end of this track, the hearers are invited to trust in Christ.

Once the evangelism track is finished, the *discipleship track* begins. New stories are added and some stories from the evangelism track are repeated, but this time truths related to growing in discipleship are shared. The discipleship track is followed by a *church planting track*, which focuses on the Acts stories as well as the Epistles. Once the hearers know most of the stories of the Bible, the storyer does not have to retell each story in order to bring out the truths about a particular topic.

Worldview transformation. We train storyers to spend considerable time examining their people's worldview and crafting the stories that will become, for many hearers, their first exposure to Scripture. Rather than teachers of God's Word, storyers are facilitators, first in presenting the story and then by leading discussions that help the hearers discover the truths for themselves.

For example, after telling the story of Jacob's dream in Genesis 28, I asked a young Muslim man, "How can we be made right with God?" He immediately replied, "By our good actions." Then I asked, "Name Jacob's good actions that caused God to come to him and promise to be his God." The man had previously heard the stories of Jacob and Esau, and his countenance showed his confusion. The stories revealed Jacob as a trickster. According to his Islamic beliefs, God should have nothing to do with Jacob. Yet God had come to Jacob. As I continued to ask questions, he finally concluded that humankind can come to God only according to God's plan, not because a person's good works make him or her worthy. A crack appeared in his belief system that with successive stories widened until his former beliefs crumbled. He came to understand new truth and eventually accepted Christ as his Savior.

Jesus used stories in his teaching. Why? As the author of our cognitive processes, he certainly was aware of how humans think. One of the most basic units of thought is the ability to assign a name. Having learned the concept of a lion, a young child can accurately identify a lion—whether it be growling in a zoo, a caricature on the pages of a book, a character in an animated movie, or a beloved stuffed animal. One of the first assignments given to Adam after he was created was to name the animals. It's almost as if God had created this human and now wanted to see if he could think. The ability to assign different names to all the furry four-legged animals demonstrated that Adam's cognitive processes were in good shape.

Names, categories, concepts, and experiences are stored in people's minds as cognitive schemata, similar to stories or scripts. For example, we have a particular Christmas schema. Every Christmas is compared to this mental representation of what Christmas should be. We hear remarks such as, "It just didn't seem like Christmas this year." Why? The experience did not compare favorably with one's story of the holiday—one's Christmas schema. Interestingly enough, this perfect Christmas schema may never have been personally experienced, but rather is a compilation of expectations derived from others' stories.

One's worldview includes a complex of learned schemata, schemata that process information as it is perceived and stored in memory for future retrieval.[4] When people experience life together—sharing life stories—their worldviews are similar. Schemata are created through personal experience, by hearing others' stories, and by fantasizing. One's personal definition of truth depends upon how closely a given experience fits one's schema.

Personal truth and biblical truth, however, are not the same thing. Jesus is the way, the truth, and the life. Part of the work of the Holy Spirit is to lead humankind into real truth, to reshape schemata to correspond

---

[4]LaNette W. Thompson, "The Nonliterate and the Transfer of Knowledge in West Africa" (master's thesis, The University of Texas at Arlington, 1998).

with God's truth. The apostle Paul needed a total schematic change, one he received on the road to Damascus. If hearers today have cognitive schemata that are contrary to biblical truth, they must experience a miraculous encounter like Paul, hear an adequate number of Bible stories, or have experiences that will challenge their current schemata.

When asked to describe a Christian, a Muslim man told me, "They drink alcohol, worship idols, and never pray. If they do pray, they have to go into a building, and it is only once a week." For this person, because of his schemata, this is truth. I may challenge his belief, but my words alone have little effect. To him, I am expressing my opinion. Therefore I cannot ask such a person to "become a Christian" with his current schema regarding Christians. The man must have adequate exposure to Christians who don't drink or worship idols and who pray without ceasing before he will have a schematic change. In the same way, when one believes that sin is anything that causes disharmony in the community, the person must hear enough Bible stories that show how God defines sin before schematic change will occur.

One of the major advantages of storying is that it confronts the hearer's worldview without being confrontational. "I'll never use anything else," an African missionary said after being taught how to use stories. "I told a Bible story to a Muslim man the other day, and he didn't even know I was witnessing to him!"

If hearers today have cognitive schemata that are contrary to biblical truth, they must experience a miraculous encounter like Paul, hear an adequate number of Bible stories, or have experiences that will challenge their current schemata.

Those who must depend upon relationships to survive are unlikely to endanger a relationship by speaking frankly. Stories and proverbs communicate effectively without anyone losing face.

Oral cultures are relational cultures. An oral learner learns from other people, not from books.

Nathan could have exposed David's sin by addressing the issue directly. Instead, he told a simple story of a poor man, a rich man, and a little lamb. The story incensed King David. He saw the act from a different perspective. When Nathan pointed out that the story applied to the king, David was convicted.

Biblical foundation. Another key benefit of CBS is that it provides a biblical foundation, allowing the hearers to experience and know the God of the universe as he seeks those he created. The hearers see themselves in the story, as God provides for his people over and over only to be rejected by them as they continually fall into sin. One evangelist who had been preaching for more than fifteen years told me, "I never truly understood the depths of God's love until I began doing CBS."

Proponents of CBS argue that the long process of worldview study, story crafting, and presenting the stories is time well spent, because in the holistic world of orality, discipleship occurs as evangelism occurs. The hearers are being given a biblical foundation as their worldview stories are replaced with biblical alternatives, even before they are saved. Others argue, though, that the slow nature of the process doesn't adequately instill in the new believers a sense of urgency to share the gospel.[5]

This sense of urgency to reach the unreached has resulted in some practitioners streamlining the CBS process, expecting more and more results with fewer and fewer stories. The panorama of Bible stories has been condensed into one story, from five to thirty minutes in length, called the "Creation to the Cross (C2C)" story, which traces the story of God's redemptive plan from his creation of a perfect world to Jesus' death on the cross as the sacrifice for humankind's sin. Following this presentation, hearers are invited to accept Christ. In areas where the Holy Spirit is moving miraculously, many people are coming to Christ after hearing this condensed story. This single story, however, often is not enough to crack the worldview barriers that prevent a people from coming to Christ. In areas where people are not responding, it is sometimes used as a filtering tool to gauge interest to see if the hearer is ready to learn more. To understand the gospel adequately, the hearers need a CBS follow-up.

One goal of CBS is to help people develop an abridged oral Bible,

---

[5]Daniel R. Sanchez, J. O. Terry, and LaNette W. Thompson, *Bible Storying for Church Planting* (Fort Worth: Church Starting Network, 2008), 84.

a series of stories that are always available for instruction and admonition. While the idea of an oral Bible makes literate Christians uncomfortable, the simple truth is that, as Christians, we all have oral Bibles, whether or not we can read. We all have Bible stories and verses in our memories. Unfortunately, for many the Bible has become a book of isolated, fragmented stories rather than a unified storybook.[6] If our oral Bibles could somehow be printed, what would we see? For oral learners who have been schooled using CBS, their manuscripts would likely resemble the Bible much more than those of their literate counterparts.

Unfortunately, for many the Bible has become a book of isolated, fragmented stories rather than a unified storybook. If our oral Bibles could somehow be printed, what would we see?

While oral Bibles may not be as critical for literates, an oral learner—apart from having the complete Scriptures in an audio recording format—has no option but to have an oral Bible. Currently, over two thousand languages have no translated Scripture.[7] Those who speak these languages must have an oral Bible since a written one doesn't exist. Their oral Bibles will be either an untidy conglomeration of verses, propositional truths, modern stories, and sermons they have heard, or an organized, chronological series of Bible stories that the Holy Spirit uses to reveal truth.

Having an accurate oral Bible means we are never without a spiritual sword, never unarmed. Just as Jesus was able to make use of his and his companions' oral Scriptures on the road to Emmaus, so the author of Hebrews was able to draw on his readers' oral Scriptures when he described faith in Hebrews 11. For most of Acts, the disciples alluded to the stories in their Jewish audiences' oral Scriptures to help bring the crowds to an understanding of salvation. In Acts 14, problems arose for Paul and Barnabas in Lystra when they encountered a crowd that didn't

---

[6]Tom A. Steffen, *Reconnecting God's Story to Ministry: Crosscultural Storytelling at Home and Abroad* (La Habra, CA: Center for Organizational and Ministry Development, 1996), 41.
[7]For the worldwide status of Bible translation, see the Wycliffe Bible Translators' website: www.wycliffe.org/About/Statistics.aspx.

DISCOVERING THE MISSION OF GOD

have oral Scriptures. The people automatically put Paul and Barnabas into their own worldview stories, calling them Hermes and Zeus. Paul and Barnabas questioned their actions and then told them the good news of the living God, beginning with creation (Acts 14:15).

Orality and CBS Best Practices

One of the greatest uses of CBS today is in the area of discipleship. Calvin Morris, IMB training leader for South America, says, "In my discipleship of new believers, I give them the assignment of learning Bible stories, usually a series of stories from a Gospel. I believe that in learning these stories, they will discover the heart of God."[8] Many who come to faith quickly through a Creation to the Cross presentation are discipled with the longer version of CBS.

Avery Willis, developer of the MasterLife discipleship process and former IMB leader, teamed with eight specialists to produce an audio CD series entitled *Following Jesus: Making Disciples of Primary Oral Learners.* This series guides storyers through the process of using CBS with oral-preference learners, from leading the people to Christ to leading them to develop a vision for cross-cultural witness.[9] Because an adequate understanding of orality is crucial to forming effective disciples among two-thirds of the world's population, the Lausanne Committee for World Evangelism formed an issues group at the 2004 Forum for World Evangelization in Pattaya, Thailand, to discuss the topic of making disciples of oral learners. The issues group consisted of twenty-eight experts and interested parties from around the world who are determined to make literate evangelical sending organizations aware of orality issues. The findings were published as Lausanne Occasional Paper No. 54 and have since been published as *Making Disciples of Oral Learners,* an excellent resource for those wanting to know more about orality and CBS.[10] The International Orality Network continues this effort.

Personal faith stories. CBS is often the catalyst for seeing the first con-

---

[8]Calvin Morris, personal communication, July 27, 2008.
[9]Avery Willis, *Following Jesus: Making Disciples of Primary Oral Learners*, Progressive Vision, 2003, audio CDs.
[10]Lausanne Committee for World Evangelization and International Orality Network, *Making Disciples of Oral Learners* (Lima, NY: Elim Publishing, 2005).

verts among unreached people groups. As the hearers' worldviews are challenged by biblical truth inherent in the stories, they become convicted of their sin and embrace the truth of the gospel. The storyer is going to be more successful in planting a church, however, if the new believers are also taught to recognize and communicate their own faith stories—stories that relate their personal encounters with the living God of today, stories that glorify him and relate how he guides, provides, and protects.

As the new believers experience worship and grow in their relationship with God as his children, their changed lives tell their own story. Family members and friends begin to come to Christ, not because of the biblical stories but because of the new believers' faith stories. It is imperative that the church planter continue to use oral teaching methods and that those who come to Christ through someone else's faith story be given the opportunity to learn the biblical stories as well.[11]

Point-of-ministry stories. Missionaries often use Bible stories to address particular situations. Situational or point-of-ministry storying is the interjection of a Bible story into a ministry opportunity with the purpose of introducing God's Word to the hearer in the hope that the hearer will want to know more.[12] Volunteers traveling overseas to prayerwalk are encouraged to memorize certain stories that respond to typical needs. When they encounter someone who needs prayer for healing, for example, they tell the story of Jesus healing the paralyzed man. Following the story and prayer, the hearers are asked if they would like to hear more of such stories, and the prayerwalkers make follow-up arrangements. A new missionary shadowing a veteran missionary, an expert in situational storying, remarked, "She sees a hole in a conversation and out comes a story. It is amazing!"

Situational storying is different from CBS in that stories are not told in chronological order but are chosen for the particular situation involved. Following the initial situational story, a storyer may then tell a receptive audience a filtering story such as the healing of the demoniac, asking questions about the hearer's view of Jesus to discover whether the

---

[11]Sanchez, Terry, and Thompson, *Bible Storying for Church Planting*, 48–50.
[12]Lausanne Committee for World Evangelization and International Orality Network, *Making Disciples of Oral Learners*, 121.

hearer is ready for the Creation to the Cross story or traditional CBS.

One pastor had been trying to witness to a Muslim young man who sold soft drinks on the corner of a busy street. The pastor would buy a soft drink and engage the vendor in conversation, eventually sharing a gospel presentation. The response was always the same—not interested. During a CBS conference, I encouraged the pastor to try situational storying. They had already learned the story of the tower of Babel in class. During a break the pastor went to the vendor, bought a soft drink, and began the conversation as I had instructed.

"I'm in a conference and the lady teaching is an American. She is teaching in French and it isn't always easy to understand her. Wouldn't it be great if we all spoke the same language?" The vendor readily agreed. "You know, there's a story in God's Word that tells us how at one time we all spoke the same language," the pastor continued. "Would you like to hear the story?"

"Sure," the vendor replied. The pastor told the story and the Muslim young man was entranced. "There are a lot of other stories like that in God's Word," the pastor said. "Would you like to hear them?"

"Certainly," the vendor agreed. The pastor asked the young man to gather a group of his friends to hear these stories. The pastor returned to the conference excited and in awe at the power of God's Word applied in this way. He was also sobered by the fact that he would have to do considerable study to be able to tell the stories effectively.

Storying skills. When pastors who use storying are asked which is more difficult, preparing a story or preparing a sermon, the vast majority respond that preparing a story is more difficult. No longer are they sharing their own experience, knowledge, or insights. They are, instead, facilitators of God's Word and responsible for telling the story accurately from memory without exposition. A young seminary student voiced it this way: "Our assignment was to learn the creation story. I was up all night. The first half of the night I was trying to memorize the story. I kept having to go back to Scripture to get it right. The second half of the night I was calling out in repentance before God. Here I am—I've just finished my first year of seminary. I know all kinds of things *about* God's Word, but I do not really *know* God's Word."

Grant Lovejoy, former professor of preaching at Southwestern Baptist Theological Seminary and currently Director of Orality Strategies with the IMB, describes how orality has impacted his ministry:

> My exposure to orality awakened me to the fact that my approaches to teaching and preaching, such as using propositional outlines, lists of teaching points, and fill-in-the-blanks worksheets, presupposed that my audience was literate. Most textbooks on preaching assume the preacher will be addressing educated people. But once I actually took to heart the extent of orality and its impact on how people listen, understand, and process truth, I had to develop ways of preaching that were better suited to the oral learners in the audience. My study of orality reinforced the fact that preaching is the connecting of truth to listeners and that each component is indispensible.
>
> Without biblical truth to proclaim, we have nothing of eternal value to say. But if we do not communicate in ways that our listeners understand, we have failed to follow the example of Jesus. He came to earth, took human form, and deliberately chose to teach as the ordinary people were able to understand (Mark 4:33). The common people heard him gladly because he spoke truth from the Father and he spoke it in ways that they could grasp. Without diminishing our commitment to being biblical, we need to elevate our ability to speak as oral cultures can understand.[13]

In the world of orality, it is the literates who are handicapped. Literate Americans struggle with learning Bible stories and telling them accurately and interestingly. Yet more and more literate Christians, especially those who have been exposed to CBS, are practicing the spiritual discipline of learning Bible stories. Learning a story forces the storyer to enter the story and decide on connotations. When telling the story of Jesus walking on the water and recounting Jesus' words to Peter, the storyer can say, "*Why* did you doubt?" or "Why

One African church leader told me, "What I like about this method is that I get so much out of it myself. It is much harder to learn a story than to prepare a sermon. When I'm learning a story, I spend a lot more time in God's Word, trying to get it right."

[13]Grant Lovejoy, personal communication, July 15, 2008.

did *you* doubt?" Nuances that are easily skipped when read become critical to interpretation when one is storying. One African church leader told me, "What I like about this method is that I get so much out of it myself. It is much harder to learn a story than to prepare a sermon. When I'm learning a story, I spend a lot more time in God's Word, trying to get it right."

New believers who are used to navigating the oral waters are eager to help those whose oral skills have been dimmed by literacy. Local language speakers, many of whom cannot read, are assisting our personnel in translating Bible stories that are biblically sound yet expressed in language their people understand. In the OneStory partnership, vibrant teams of mostly young people, with the help of local language speakers, coach mother-tongue speakers of the language to craft a series of stories in their language and cultural storytelling style.[14] OneStory teams work with local people to test the stories for accuracy, naturalness, understandability, and acceptability. Experienced storycrafting consultants review the stories, which are then digitally recorded to preserve an accurate version.[15]

Reproducible results. When taught to use stories, Christians in oral societies quickly see results. "I had been to Bible school, and I thought I knew everything about reaching my people," an African pastor's wife said. "Our assignment was to tell the tower of Babel story to someone. I told the story to an old Fulani man who sits outside on our street. Yesterday, as I was walking home, I saw he had three people sitting beside him, and he was telling them the story. I've never seen anything like it."

Storying for literates? Case studies illustrating the efficacy of CBS and faith stories in oral cultures are documented and unarguable. What is not as well-known is their effectiveness among literates, especially literates in relational societies. A worldview shift is occurring in American culture, as younger generations are exhibiting characteristics heretofore seen in oral, relational societies. This generation quotes television and movies, loving wordplay, much as oral learners throw out proverbs and pithy sayings for entertainment. "Group hangs," casually socializing in a group,

[14]For more information on OneStory, see www.onestory.org.
[15]Grant Lovejoy, personal communication, July 23, 2008.

is preferable to individual dating. They enjoy all-night gab sessions or movie fests. Saving face, guarding the relationship, and acceptance of everyone "for who they are" in spite of their behavior are all values. The worth of the message is not necessarily intrinsic in the message itself, but is validated by the messenger. Decisions are made after group discussion. Ostracism is the ultimate evil. These young people, reared on television and movies, are influenced by stories, especially stories of personal experience. They like to be with older people who have weathered life's storms. They don't have time to read, but they will listen to a person's stories if that person is considered worthy to share.

Christian young people with this worldview are a natural bridge to unreached people groups composed mostly of oral learners. These young people embrace CBS as a natural methodology and are willing to "live on the edge" in difficult conditions, because that is where the unreached are found.

Campus Crusade for Christ is experimenting in one American city with a group of college students who are being taught to disciple using Bible stories, their personal faith stories, and other people's faith stories. New converts are encouraged to share their own faith stories as they experience their new life.[16] In another part of the United States, a youth minister used CBS for a year with the youth in his church because he realized the importance of giving the previously unchurched young people a good biblical foundation. Another seminary student seeking to reach a community of artists used CBS extensively. He admitted that the most difficult thing for him was staying up all night, because as the artists became new believers they wanted to exchange their all-night parties for all-night discussions of the stories and ethical issues.

When asked what advice he would give ministerial students just discovering orality, Grant Lovejoy replied:

> A big part of education is putting names on things we have experienced but have not thought about carefully. Just having language to describe what is happening is a big step in improving our understanding of orality.

---

[16]Lausanne Committee for World Evangelization and International Orality Network, *Making Disciples of Oral Learners*, 59.

So students need to learn the basic terms and concepts related to orality. Many students will discover how important oral means of communication are to them personally, their extended families, and the communities of which they are a part. I encourage them to rejoice in this, cultivate their skills in oral methods of communication, and cherish them alongside the literate forms of communication that seminaries cultivate.

Both oral and literate communication skills are important; students need to value both of them, recognizing the advantages and disadvantages of each. They need to keep in mind that seminaries, as institutions of higher education, have a natural emphasis on literate forms of communication. But as servants of the churches who serve the world, seminary professors and students need to understand the world and communicate effectively in it. If students sometimes feel like the rope in a tug-of-war, that's not surprising. But they need to be thinking how they can equip church members who do not have that level of education or interest in literate ways of engaging truth.[17]

Conclusion

Chronological Bible Storying, whether used with literates or oral learners, is an effective method of sharing Bible truths. Literates do have other options. For oral learners, oral methods, of which stories are a major part, are the only option. Avery Willis observes, "For the missionary, mastering oral methods is as essential as mastering the mother tongue."

Jesus commanded us to make disciples. A thirty-minute analytical lesson with limited audience participation is entertaining for oral learners, especially if it is a foreigner trying to use their language. It has limited lasting effect, however. Navigating the sea of orality can be daunting, but it is a necessary adventure if we are to follow Christ's Great Commission command.

Since the worth of the message is validated by the messenger, the hearers must have access to our lives. We must steer them through the chronological Bible stories as well as situational Bible stories as they learn to tell and use these stories themselves. We must share our faith stories and help them to convey theirs. All these stories flow together to buoy us with truth,

---

[17]Grant Lovejoy, personal communication, July 15, 2008.

the inerrant truth of Scripture and the dynamic truth of a living God working in the lives of his children. As we share these stories and live them daily, God is glorified and our response is worship, testimony, and praise.

Discussion Points

1. How have stories, both biblical stories and faith stories, influenced your life?

2. What are the differences between "preaching" and "storying," and how can the two methods effectively work together to further God's kingdom?

3. To what extent does your church or ministry reflect a literate bias? To what extent does it meet the needs of oral learners in your community? How is church growth impacted?

4. If someone could take a picture of your "oral Bible," what would they find?

5. How could storying be implemented in your ministry situation?

Further Reading

Bruner, Kurt. *The Divine Drama.* Wheaton: Tyndale, 2001.

Lausanne Committee for World Evangelization and International Orality Network. *Making Disciples of Oral Learners.* Lima, NY: Elim, 2005.

Ong, Walter J. *Orality and Literacy: The Technologizing of the Word.* London and New York: Routledge, 1982.

Sanchez, Daniel R., J. O. Terry, and LaNette W. Thompson. *Bible Storying for Church Planting.* Fort Worth: Church Starting Network, 2008.

Steffen, Tom A. *Reconnecting God's Story to Ministry: Crosscultural Storytelling at Home and Abroad.* La Habra, CA: Center for Organizational and Ministry Development, 1996.

Thompson, LaNette W. "The Nonliterate and the Transfer of Knowledge in West Africa." Master's thesis, The University of Texas at Arlington, 1998.

Willis, Avery. *Following Jesus: Making Disciples of Primary Oral Learners.* Progressive Vision, 2003. Audio CDs.

Wright, N. T. *The New Testament and the People of God.* Minneapolis: Fortress, 1992.

25

COMPREHENSIVE
CONTEXTUALIZATION

A. Scott Moreau

Since its first use in 1972 in a presentation by Shoki Coe at a World Council of Churches consultation,[1] contextualization has garnered attention and controversy among evangelicals. Today it is used widely in academic circles, but the average person in the pew has either never heard of contextualization or is confused as to just what it means. This is true today despite the fact that there has been more writing and teaching on contextualization in the past several decades in mission studies than in the preceding several centuries.[2] It is critical to missionaries and missiologists, and to anyone who intends to engage in God's mission, to be introduced to the concept as one that is central to missionary life and practice.

What, then, is contextualization? At the risk of oversimplification, it is to plant the universal gospel in local soil. It is not to change the gospel, but to plant it in such a way that what grows in local soil can be seen as a local plant. In other words, contextualization is what it takes to plant the gospel message and the life of the church into a particular setting (or context), whether it is in Barcelona or Beijing. Should a rural church in Indonesia look and feel exactly like a suburban church in Fort Worth, or an urban church in London? Contextualized thinking an-

---

[1]Ray Wheeler, "The Legacy of Shoki Coe," *International Bulletin of Missionary Research* 26:2 (April 2002): 77–80.
[2]For a searchable bibliography of more than two thousand articles and books published from 1972 to 1999, browse MisLinks.org, www.mislinks.org/index.php?cID=1.

swers with a resounding "No!"—though there will certainly be constants that span across every context.

This can sound frightening to Christians who have never lived in new cultural settings, because we are committed to the universality and the consistency of the gospel for all people. God himself does not change, so why do we "change" the gospel? The basic answer is that it is not the gospel itself we change; it's how the gospel is presented and embedded in a culture that will change. It is helpful to keep in mind that Jesus himself, through the incarnation, became a "contextual" Middle Eastern Jew in first-century culture. He did not come as a twentieth-century Russian to live in a first-century culture. He became one with the culture where he lived, and lived a life in tune (and at times with antagonism!) with the culture that was his human home. In his incarnation he shows us what the fullest extent of contextualization should be. This helps us see that contextualizing is more than a fad or a buzzword. It is God's way of communicating with people, and thus deserves to be at the heart of our agenda as we participate in God's mission.

To use another metaphor, contextualization stands at an intersection of three "streets": (1) the street of the unchanging Word of God, (2) the street of the culture of the person who brings the message of Christ into new settings, and (3) the street of the new cultural setting in which the Word of God is being planted. Contextualization as practiced by cross-cultural missionaries is the process of people moving from their own cultural street, taking the unchanging Word of God and "intersecting" it into the third street of the new culture and worldview.

We must maintain fidelity to the text of Scripture without losing sight of the fact that people can only respond to Christ when he is understandable to them. Our goal in contextualization is not to make the gospel message palatable—that is the job of the Holy Spirit. Rather, our goal is to ensure that we do not add unnecessary cultural layers onto the gospel which confuse people who are not of our culture. Rather, we find ways to plant the unchanging gospel in local cultural soil. To help you better understand what this means in practice, we will turn our attention to an approach to contextualization that encompasses all that the church is to do under God's empowerment and leading.

Comprehensive Contextualization[3]

Most of the recent writing on contextualization has focused on theology. While theology is a central concern of the church, it is not everything that the church is. If we are to help people in other cultures understand all of the implications of the Bible for their contexts, we must not only include theology but also add every other dimension of church life and Christian practice. This makes contextualization more difficult, but more enriching. It is worth the extra effort, as it enables people to come to Christ and live out their commitment to Christ in ways that are faithful to the Scriptures but still "at home" in their own culture.

To help us keep all aspects of faith in process, it is helpful to follow the outline of Ninian Smart, a comparative religions scholar who developed a seven-dimensional model for understanding the world's religions.[4] According to Smart, all seven dimensions are found in every religion. For our purposes, each dimension offers an important area of church life that needs contextualized thinking and practice. In brief, the seven dimensions are (1) doctrinal, (2) mythic, (3) ethical, (4) social, (5) ritual, (6) (supernatural) experiential, and (7) artistic (or material).

These dimensions are not to be seen as boxed off and separate from each other, but intermingled together. For example, church rules on how to discipline an erring believer (the ethical dimension) are built on doctrine and put into practice in the social setting of the church. Likewise, the ritual of baptism takes place in a social setting, is built upon doctrine, and utilizes the artistic expression (such as baptismal robes or a font) and engages the participant in religious experience. It should be clear that while we will discuss each dimension separately, all are interlinked in the life of the church.

The doctrinal dimension. The doctrinal (or theological or philosophical) dimension encompasses the significant *beliefs* that are ex-

---

[3]Adapted in part from A. Scott Moreau, "Contextualization that is Comprehensive," *Missiology* 34 (2006): 325–35. See also "Contextualization: From an Adapted Message to an Adapted Life," in *The Changing Face of World Missions*, ed. Michael Pocock, Gailyn Van Rheenen, and Douglas McConnell (Grand Rapids: Baker, 2005), 321–48.

[4]Ninian Smart, *Dimensions of the Sacred: An Anatomy of the World's Beliefs* (Berkeley: University of California Press, 1996).

pressed as religious truths.[5] Christian doctrines range from teachings about God, Christ, the Holy Spirit, the church, mission, justice, discipleship, and so on. They may be clearly stated, most often in creeds or doctrinal statements. They are also preached, studied in Bible studies, and talked about over coffee.

This includes, for example, what people believe about God. Is he a stern disciplinarian? A doting grandfather? A distant, unknowing being? Views about God vary widely even within the church, and contextualizing in the doctrinal dimension means that we find ways to help people understand who God is based on scriptural truth.

In terms of contextualization, doctrine is not just the actual truths themselves, but how they are expressed and explained within the context. Evangelical contextualizers have tended to give the bulk of their attention and energy to this dimension, and the development of African, Latin American, and Asian theologies reflects this—together with the realization that systematic theologies have been products of Western culture and are not as universal as once thought.

Contextualizing the doctrinal dimension is a two-way process. The first is the bringing of the constants of biblical truth into the new context. Our job as contextualizers is to introduce the unchanging biblical truths into ever-changing settings. We are not changing those truths, but digging them out from Scripture and communicating them in ways that local audiences can understand. Creeds, confessions, and doctrinal statements have been developed throughout the church's history in an attempt to explain doctrinal truth. Some of them, like the Apostles' Creed, are still used in churches around the world today. Even so, none of them ever replaces biblical teaching. They were written to better explain biblical truths in situations where churches needed clarity of thinking on issues they were facing. Thus every creed, confession, and statement of faith is a type of doctrinal contextualization and is to be judged first on the basis of its fidelity with Scripture and second on the basis of its clarity in communicating to the people for whom it was intended.

---

[5]Smart, *Dimensions*, 10.

The reverse side of doctrinal contextualization is the way in which bringing truth into a new setting can help the contextualizers themselves see truth in fresh ways and even discover truths they had previously overlooked. The Bible is so rich and multifaceted that we *need* insights from people who are different than us if we are to see truths more fully. A decade of serving in Africa helped me understand the biblical teaching on community and body life in a whole new way. Travel throughout Asia helped me better understand how much respect God deserves as the holy Creator. Listening to my Latin American colleagues and friends introduced me more clearly to God's view of the poor and marginalized. All of these truths are already in God's Word—I had been blinded by my own cultural constraints. I learned about them as I lived alongside sisters and brothers who were sharing what God was teaching them from the Bible.

The mythic dimension. The mythic (or narrative) dimension refers to the stories people tell and retell each other. The events in the lives of the main characters of the stories illustrate and teach important values, ideals, and aspirations about such things as sacrifice, heroism, goodness, love, and obligation. This process of passing down important stories acts as a type of cement, gluing the generation telling the stories to the generation hearing them. They bind the hearers emotionally to the narratives and to each other through the community participation in narration (from the fireplace to the movie theater).[6]

The types of stories included in myth vary widely. Classic myths explain such things as the creation of the universe (including spiritual powers), humanity's fall and potential for redemption, and the drama of interaction between the divine and the human. Folklore and fairy tales portray fantastical beings or wild adventures in mystical lands. Popular stories of historical figures exemplify values considered important for the culture. Even proverbs, riddles, and other pithy sayings embody the wisdom and rules for living wisely needed by people in every society.

Many evangelicals are rightly concerned to know just where the Bible fits in this mythic dimension. In popular use, myths are simply

---

[6]Ibid., 130–31.

understood as untrue stories. This is obviously not our view of the Bible, and there is concern when anyone treats the Bible as this type of myth. It is not in this sense that we use the term "myth" in relation to the Bible. Rather, the Bible is the ultimate Myth of which all other myths are but shadows; their value is in their congruence to the biblical story of God's work in Christ on behalf of humankind and the kingdom values as expressed in the Bible.

It is important to keep in mind that the way myth is used here is on the stories (whether in books, movies, or told around a campfire) found in a society and the *impact* of these stories on the people and their society. This is the sense in which we look at the myths of other cultures. What values do they embody, and how do those values compare to biblical ones? How might they be used as bridges for the development of local expressions of the Christian faith? In what ways do the values they promote raise barriers to the gospel that must be overcome? Ultimately, then, our task is not as much to confirm or deny the truth of local myths but to check them for congruence with the biblical text and utilize them—or deny them—in our efforts to contextualize the Christian faith in local idiom.

There are two ways in which myth is contextualized in local settings. The first is learning how to tell the biblical story in a way that local people understand it and see God's values clearly displayed in it. Efforts of this type can be seen in Bible translation, showing translated versions of the JESUS film (www.jesusfilm.org), and Chronological Bible Storying (see the previous chapter, "Tell His Story So That All Might Worship," by LaNette Thompson).

The second way myth is contextualized is through the appropriation of local myth to provide bridges to the gospel or to highlight biblical truths in ways that the local people can understand. Don Richardson's *Peace Child* is a classic example of this.[7] Other creative examples range from adapting traditional stories that teach biblical truths about God[8] to learning and using proverbs in ministry.[9] *The Lord of the Rings*, The

---

[7]Don Richardson, *Peace Child* (Glendale, CA: G/L Regal Books, 1974).
[8]Eudene Keidel, *African Fables That Teach About God* (Scottdale, PA: Herald Press, 1978).
[9]Jay Moon, "Sweet Talk in Africa, Using Proverbs in Ministry," *Evangelical Missions Quarterly* 40 (2004): 162–69.

Chronicles of Narnia, and the Left Behind series are all attempts to bring Christian truths to life through story. They engage the imagination of the audience to make biblical ideas come alive. While highly successful in terms of sales and distribution among American audiences, the ultimate success in the mythic dimension is not measured simply by popularity or sales but by faithfulness to biblical ideals and by the ability of the stories to point people to Christ.

The ethical dimension. If doctrine is concerned with what is true, ethics is concerned with the *application* of truth in our lives. For example, if it is true that God created the universe, then we should live our lives by honoring our Creator. Ethics are often expressed in English through modals: words such as *should*, *must*, or *ought*. How are we expected to behave in relation to God and the spiritual realm, to the created order, and to people? Societies often regulate ethical ideals through their laws, the way they enforce those laws, and the sanctions they impose on people who violate those laws.

In order to contextualize the ethical dimension, we must first understand how those among whom we live try to live wisely as responsible people.[10] What is their understanding of the ideal wise person? Who are heroes in the culture that exemplify wisdom? What does this mean for ordinary people in their daily lives? Once we understand these ethical contexts,[11] we can, together with the local community of believers, see how their own ideals match or do not match biblical ideals and use this as a means for interaction with the gospel.

For example, in China the term that has traditionally been translated as "sin" is related more to being caught as a criminal than to the biblical idea of violating God's standards.[12] Traditional attempts to convey the fact that all people are "sinners" in this sense do not communicate well because the vast majority of Chinese are not criminals, so rightly do not see themselves as "sinners." Almost all of them, however, realize they do not live up to the ideals of the righteous person.

---

[10]Bernard T. Adeney, *Strange Virtues: Ethics in a Multicultural World* (Downers Grove, IL: Inter-Varsity, 1995).

[11]Robert J. Priest, "Missionary Elenctics: Conscience and Culture," *Missiology* 22 (1994): 291–315.

[12]Mark Strand, "Explaining Sin in a Chinese Context," *Missiology* 28 (2000): 427–41.

Addressing sin from the universal experience of failing to live up to those ideals communicates more clearly to the Chinese the concept of sin and enables them to better see their need for a savior.[13]

Evangelicals typically have been very good at seeing the personal component of ethics. We tend to focus on personal conduct and develop rules or regulations (e.g., don't drink alcohol) as a result. We have been less effective, however, at seeing the *social* nature of sin and dealing with ethics in a systemic way. When living in places where social systems dehumanize people (e.g., tyranny, slavery, sex trade, bonded labor), contemporary evangelicals have been accused of attending so much to their freedom to preach the gospel that they fail to address systemic issues. This is an extremely delicate area, as cross-cultural workers are guests in their places of service and must act as good guests. Further, if cross-cultural workers rile local leaders, they can often escape; but that is not true for local Christians who must face the backlash. It is clear that this area deserves extensive thought and application if we are to truly contextualize as Christ would have us.

The social dimension. Smart saw the formal organization and leadership in a religion as the social dimension.[14] I have modified this approach by focusing on *social institutions* that are integrated into every society and into the religions (and churches) that are part of that society.

Sociologists and anthropologists have identified several social institutions that appear universally. I have found it helpful to follow the lead of missionary anthropologist Paul Hiebert and sociologist Eloise Hiebert Meneses, who narrowed the list to the five social institutions most central to contextualization: association, kinship, education, economics, and legal.[15]

Association. In every culture, people associate with one another in a variety of ways. This can be done voluntarily (e.g., social clubs) or involuntarily (e.g., castes). These associations give people connections with each other as well as distinguish them from others; they both connect

---

[13]Chuang Tsu-kung, "Communicating the Concept of Sin in the Chinese Context," *Taiwan Mission Quarterly* 6, no. 2 (July 1996): 49–55.

[14]Smart, *Dimensions*, 215.

[15]Paul Hiebert and Eloise Hiebert Meneses, *Incarnational Ministry: Planting Churches in Band, Tribal, Peasant and Urban Societies* (Grand Rapids: Baker, 1995).

and separate. Many of these associations are easily integrated within contextualized churches (e.g., mothers' guilds), but others are more problematic (e.g., secret societies). They can range in size from small group Bible studies to entire branches of Christendom (such as Protestants).

Contextualization for this social institution includes understanding local associations and enabling contextualized churches to take advantage of the positive means of associating already at home in the culture. Ultimately, local associations should *feel* local rather than foreign in how they are organized, how decisions are made, and how they are led. At the same time, contextualization also includes the transformation of local ways that are opposed to kingdom principles (e.g., classifying people so as to reject or marginalize them).

Kinship. Kinship is one type of association. It is so important, however, that anthropologists treat it separately. It includes such things as marriage, kinship rules and regulations, the understanding of what comprises a family, and kin obligations (including the unborn as well as the ancestors).

Kinship issues that need contextualized responses include such things as marriages of multiple spouses, ancestral beliefs and obligations, child marriages, widow burning, abortion, and honor killings. Contextualized responses to these kinship practices will range from whether to allow them within the church to how or whether the church should address them as found in the larger culture.

Education. By education, we refer to the processes that socialize people into roles they are to play in their society. Educational processes, whether non-formal, informal, or formal, provide people with the knowledge, values, and skills needed to adequately perform the roles they are expected to play by their society. They include formal schooling, apprenticing, mentoring, games, play, and all forms of child-rearing practices.

Contextualizing the educational institution involves discovering how people in the local setting prefer to teach and learn and finding means to incorporate those practices into the life of the church. Sunday school, for example, is not actually found in the Bible and yet is an integral part of many churches of Western inheritance. What might be a local equivalent to Sunday school that can be incorporated into church settings where that tradition is not found? The least we can do in contextualizing the educational institutions is to gain a solid understanding of local educational values, methods, and expectations, and utilize them as appropriate to develop methods for discipling people that will feel natural, rather than foreign, to them.

Agricultural evangelists/church planters teach farming best practices around a midday campfire during mealtime. The trainer coaches farmers on how to improve their yields and resources for sustainable produce as they discuss their morning activities. Using this same familiar training method, the same farmers gather around an evening campfire after dinner and listen to stories and compare spiritual notes regarding their relationship with Jesus Christ and best practices for church planting. This is educational contextualization of the gospel at its best.

Economics. By economics, we refer to the exchange of goods and services, including monetary as well as social capital, and how they are produced and exchanged. In the church, this monetary dynamic includes such things as giving practices, clergy salaries, loans for building churches, and expectations about the distribution of wealth among believers.

One area that has been receiving increased attention today has been that of the financial dependence of Majority World (non-Western) churches and the practices of missionaries that have fostered that dependence.[16] This is certainly something that needs ongoing awareness, but we should be careful not to simply impose our own categories (such as the American ideal of independent individual financial control) when the society in which we work has different ideals (such as patron-client relationships).[17] The debate over these issues is far from settled. Our hope is that in the future we will see deeper contextualized thinking and practices in this regard.

---

[16]See, for example, Mary Mallon Lederleitner, "The Devil Is in the Details: Avoiding Common Pitfalls When Funding New Partnership Endeavors," *Evangelical Missions Quarterly* 43 (2007): 160–65; and Robert Reese, "Discovering the Joy of Tithing in Zimbabwe," *Evangelical Missions Quarterly* 43 (2007): 504–6.

[17]See Frampton Fox, "Foreign Money and Indigenous Ministry: To Give or Not to Give?" *Evangelical Missions Quarterly* 43 (2007): 150–56.

The economic institution also includes what is called "social capital" or "social wealth." For example, people who are held in high regard have more social capital than those who are on the fringes of society. Even if they are not wealthy themselves, they have access to important people and resources that the marginalized do not share. What does the gospel have to say about this? What are rules of fairness and reciprocity in cultures that value patron-client relationships rather than individual autonomy, and how does the gospel commend or condemn these rules? How might this play out in local fellowships when the pastor is seen as a patron and the congregational members as clients?[18] What type of social capital do religious leaders have, and how should it be properly used? Attending to these and related questions is an important part of contextualizing the economic values and systems found within our churches.

Law/Legal. The legal institutions of a society are directly related to the ethical dimension. Ethics inform us regarding how to live, and the legal institutions are used to enforce the ethical values. In churches, this is seen in such things as the form of government of the local church, the rules governing church life, and the disciplining of those who violate the rules. Each of these areas need contextualized thinking.

Missionaries who represent particular denominations from their home country can have a greater struggle to contextualize in this area, since they are expected to follow their denomination's own polity (form of church government), rules, and disciplinary measures. This can make contextualization awkward at times, especially when the denominational practices go against the grain of local cultural values.

The ritual dimension. Ritual refers to symbolic actions that are used to affirm or intensify identity, change status, and deal with crises. In religious settings these include such activities as worship, pilgrimage, meditation, initiation, ordination, and consecration;[19] and they involve embedded actions, symbols, and expressions.[20]

---

[18]See Del Chinchen, "The Patron-Client System: A Model of Indigenous Discipleship," *Evangelical Missions Quarterly* 31 (1995): 446–51.

[19]Smart, *Dimensions*, 10.

[20]See A. H. Mathias Zahniser, *Symbol and Ceremony* (Monrovia, CA: MARC, 1997).

Ritual plays a crucial role in the Christian faith, but because of historical factors many evangelicals think of ritual as dead and meaningless. This is in spite of the fact that we participate in ritual every day (e.g., praying for meals, having devotional times, and reading the Bible). As a first step in contextualizing this dimension, it is important for us to recognize the rich ways in which ritual plays a role in our lives, even when we may think of ourselves as non-ritual people.

While rituals in societies that have a long church history often lose important parts of their original and intended meaning, this does not mean that we should discard them. Rather, we must find ways to revitalize them or remake them so that the meaning they once conveyed will be communicated to a new generation of participants.

When people who have disconnected ritual from their thinking go as missionaries to cultures that remain steeped in ritual, a danger will be that the missionaries will not realize how rituals can be used to invest new meanings in old practices and terms, or that they will try to develop "ritual-free" forms of faith that will have no anchor in the local setting.[21]

The (supernatural) experiential dimension. The supernatural experience dimension is concerned with our experiences of the supernatural, whether through encountering God, the demonic, dreams and visions, signs and wonders, or the like. For the purposes of contextualization, it also includes our understanding (or doctrine) of these experiences and the power(s) behind them.

In contextualizing this dimension we are not to work to discover ways to "manufacture" such experiences, but to create an atmosphere in our churches in which God can speak. We must also enable people to understand such events[22] and know how to react to them[23] in ways that are congruent with God's Word.

I would suggest that contextualization in this dimension includes the following three components: First, local churches need to explore

---

[21]Moreau, "Contextualization that is Comprehensive," 333.

[22]Paul G. Hiebert, "The Flaw of the Excluded Middle," *Missiology* 10 (1982): 35–47.

[23]See, for example, Scott Breslin, *Understanding Dreams from God* (Pasadena, CA: William Carey Library, 2004), and Randal Scott, "Evangelism and Dreams: Foundational Presuppositions to Interpret God-given Dreams of the Unreached," *Evangelical Missions Quarterly* 44 (2008): 176–84.

and develop biblical perspectives of such phenomena. Second, local churches need to develop rituals that will facilitate positive religious experiences (e.g., waiting on God) and rituals that will prevent or stop negative ones (e.g., demonic expulsion). Third, local believers need to have the freedom to talk about their experiences and find scripturally honoring, indigenous ways to handle them.[24]

The artistic (or material) dimension. This final dimension, like ritual, deals with the symbolic. It is seen, however, both in symbolic performances as well as in artifactual and artistic expressions that have symbolic values. Church steeples in Europe, for example, used to be the tallest structures in a village to give a centering point for the people who lived there.

The types of *artifacts* that comprise this dimension include such things as clothing, sculpture, drawings and paintings, architecture (from building design to the use of pews or chairs), jewelry, cemeteries, and gravesites.[25] Artistic *expressions* are seen in symbolic performances through drama, dance, song, poetry, and so on.

Some components of this dimension will be seen differently in different cultures. Many white, suburban Americans are comfortable with symbolic jewelry or clothing while less so with religious scarring. Many rural African Christians, on the other hand, are more comfortable with symbolic scarring (which is part of their heritage) than with women wearing trousers—especially in church.

At the very least, contextualizing this dimension will involve utilizing local artistic expressions to express universal Christian truths. Because of the deep connections with emotions and imagination made through the arts, our hope is that this area will be given increasing attention by evangelical missionaries in the future. (See, for example, the resources listed in the "Communicating" section of www.MisLinks.org.)

Conclusion

We live in a day in which Christians around the world are living out their relationship with Christ through culturally understood practices

---

[24]Moreau, "Contextualization that is Comprehensive," 333.
[25]Smart, *Dimensions*, 277.

that honor him and reflect the true diversity of the body of Christ. It is our hope that as we continue to await his return this will ever more be a characteristic of God's churches wherever they are found; and as we see him at work through the world's Christians, we will get a glimpse of what it will be like when those from every nation, tribe, people, and language (Revelation 7:9) gather before the throne of God to worship our eternal Creator.

Discussion Points

1. What do we mean by contextualization?

2. What do we risk if we do not contextualize? What are the risks of going too far?

3. What is the difference between "comprehensive contextualization" and the traditional approach to contextualization?

4. Can you give an example of how Western Christianity has been contextualized?

Further Reading

Adeney, Bernard T. *Strange Virtues: Ethics in a Multicultural World.* Downers Grove, IL: InterVarsity, 1995.

Breslin, Scott. *Understanding Dreams from God.* Pasadena, CA: William Carey Library, 2004.

Flemming, Dean. *Contextualization in the New Testament.* Downers Grove, IL: InterVarsity, 2005.

Hiebert, Paul. *Transforming Worldviews: An Anthropological Understanding of How People Change.* Grand Rapids: Baker, 2008.

Moreau, A. Scott. "Contextualization that is Comprehensive." *Missiology* 34 (2006): 325–35.

Tsu-kung, Chuang. "Communicating the Concept of Sin in the Chinese Context." *Taiwan Mission Quarterly* 6, no. 2 (July 1996): 49–55.

Zahniser, A. H. Mathias. *Symbol and Ceremony.* Monrovia, CA: MARC, 1997.

26

EFFECTIVE BRIDGING AND CONTEXTUALIZATION

"FISHING WITH FOOD THE FISH LIKE"

Kevin Greeson

A former Muslim traveled with me seventeen hours on a bus to a training event in the mountains of northern Pakistan. At the event I was speaking on contextualization and the use of bridges for reaching Muslims with the gospel. En route he continually mentioned his dislike for contextualization practices used by missionaries and national evangelists. But during the training event he experienced a transformation. Afterward, he excitedly expressed his new revelation. He exclaimed, "I now understand what you are talking about. When I go fishing, I don't put food items that I like on the hook; rather, I give the fish food that they like." He came to understand that as a "fisher of men" he would catch more lost people for the gospel by using communication vehicles that are friendly and meaningful to them.

Bridges aren't only used in physical transportation; they are also used in verbal communication to transport messages effectively from person to person. On the mission field, communicating a foreign message through a foreign messenger can often require a high degree of communicative skill. Missionaries therefore depend on communicative bridges, contextualizing the message, and sometimes contextualizing the messenger to help ensure that the gospel is transferred in a way that the lost can better absorb and understand. This chapter deals with the science of contextualization, its value, the controversies surrounding contextualization, and how to avoid crossing the line of contextualization and compromising the integrity of your witness and the gospel message itself.

Foreign Message by a Foreign Messenger to a Foreign Audience

Contextualization or "bridging" is a communication method that transmits a foreign thought to a willing listener. To be a missionary is to be a communicator who strives to "contextualize" his or her message by making it natural and comprehensible to people of a different culture. Ongoing research is an essential practice of missionaries committed to ensuring that the gospel message is communicated with effectiveness. To ignore the science of contextualization is risky business. You may feel good that you are obedient in sharing the gospel with a lost community, but if no one understands your message the lost remain lost.

To ignore the science of contextualization is risky business. You may feel good that you are obedient in sharing the gospel with a lost community, but if no one understands your message the lost remain lost.

Whether by their own choice or by heritage, the lost are ensnared in lies, misunderstandings, prejudices, and preprogrammed views, and are often surrounded by committed enemies of the truth. The Holy Spirit works against these forces, convicting individuals of sin, righteousness, and judgment (John 16:8). The Spirit encounters fewer communication barriers in impacting a heart than we do. So why not simply allow the Spirit to do his effective work, and we get out of the way? The New Testament does not support relying exclusively on the Holy Spirit to be the sole transporter of the gospel to a lost person. Instead, we receive encouragement from the Bible to be creative and use every communicative tool available—short of compromising the gospel—to break through to the lost. Whether they know it now or not, the lost are counting on us to do our best in this regard.

When discussing religion or a relationship with God with a Muslim, Hindu, or Buddhist, the conversation has the potential of becoming emotional or even heated. When emotions run high in conversations, the likelihood of miscommunication increases. Veteran missionary Clint High explains the communication process in emotionally charged situations:

When a hearer first receives an auditory message, the electrical sound impulse moves through the ear and enters the limbic system of the brain. This is the part of the brain that controls emotions, instincts, and preconscious action. If the emotions are heightened or the hearer feels threatened, the electrical impulse that contains the message is not allowed to pass into the cerebrum (the logical and conscious part of the mind). In other words, the message is handled with an emotional action but is not really processed logically in the cerebrum. So good communicators learn to put the hearer's emotions at ease before delivering the content of the message. This ensures that the message reaches the cerebrum where it can stay and be considered.[1]

The New Testament and Contextualization

Jesus was a master communicator. He used the accepted Jewish Scriptures to open the eyes of the Jews to the prophecies he was fulfilling. By using their revered Scripture, he started where they were and then brought them, or at least some of them, to where they needed to be. His parables had a way of calming heightened emotions, while at the same time effectively bridging his message into the minds and hearts of the people. He dressed like the common people and identified himself with his target audience to the extent that the Pharisees accused him of crossing the acceptable status line of a religious teacher by eating with tax collectors and other sinners (Luke 5:27–30). In doing so, Jesus modeled for us how to contextualize both the message and the messenger.

The apostle Paul quickly caught on to the secrets of bridging foreign or unfamiliar information to new audiences. He knew that strangers or outsiders are always treated with suspicion. To remedy this, three times in Acts 17 Paul used bridges to make his message more acceptable to those unfamiliar with the gospel. For a Jewish audience, he used the Old Testament as a bridge to the New Testament (17:2–3). Later, at the Areopagus, an audience of Stoic and Epicurean philosophers said to Paul, "May we know what this new teaching is that you are presenting? You are bringing some strange ideas to our ears, and we would like to

---

[1]Clint High (a pseudonym) provided analysis of the communication process to Kevin Greeson in an interview in June of 2009.

know what they mean" (17:19–20). Paul used the assistance of one of their familiar objects of worship to bridge his foreign message to them (17:23). Finally, Paul used a saying from some of their own poets (17:28) in an attempt to bring home his point that they should not worship images of gold or silver or stone "made by human design and skill" (17:29), but rather repent and believe in the one who was raised from the dead (17:30–31).

Often it is not the message that is rejected by a foreign audience, but rather the appearance of the messenger. Imagine your feelings when two young men wearing white dress shirts, black ties, and name tags approach your front door. For most solid evangelicals, this sight heightens the emotions, and each word from their mouth is treated with suspicion. In similar fashion, when most Muslims see Western missionaries approach them with the gospel in hand, their emotions rise and the missionary's message is handled with doubt and mistrust. For this reason, both Jesus and Paul taught us to make our appearance friendlier to strangers of the truth. In Matthew 10:9–10 and Luke 10:4, Jesus altered the disciples' appearance before sending them out. By leaving behind a change of shoes, shirt, or purse, Jesus altered his disciples' normal appearance to make them appear vulnerable and in need of help. By sending them into the harvest field as persons in need, Jesus minimized potential distractions by the messengers for the sake of the message.

Paul was particularly explicit on this topic when he said, "To the Jews I became like a Jew. . . . To those under the law I became like one under the law. . . . To those not having the law I became like one not having the law. . . . To the weak I became weak. . . . I have become all things to all people so that by all possible means I might save some" (1 Corinthians 9:20–22). Both Jesus and Paul modeled for us the power of contextualizing the messenger, not as an act of deception but as a means of making the message more acceptable to a foreigner of the gospel.

Critics and Criticism of Contextualization

Contextualization or bridging is not for the faint of heart, seeing how there are numerous critics of contextualization methods. Their disapproval is most often based on a concern that the contextualizing missionary may cross the line and compromise the integrity of the gospel. These critics accuse missionaries of altering the gospel message to make it more palatable to a foreign audience. They claim that contextualizing the gospel has the potential of removing or sidestepping the *scandalon* (the Greek word referring to the stumbling block that all must deal with when embracing Christ) of the gospel. No doubt contextualization strategies should be carefully crafted and monitored so that they do not cross the line of compromising the gospel. Missionaries should always be open to "fruit inspectors," while at the same time contextualization critics should "measure twice, saw once" before judging a missionary's contextualization method.

Contextualization critics typically use hypothetical arguments built upon "If . . . then" extreme scenarios. For example, in regard to the apostle Paul's use of the object of worship to an unknown god as a bridge in Acts 17:23, contextualization critics of Paul's day might have commented, "If you use this kind of bridge each time with pagans, where you elevate their idols, then it is likely we will see syncretism. The pagans will accept Jesus as Savior and at the same time continue their idol worship. Because of this possible threat, this contextualization bridge should not be used." This same kind of argument is widely used against missionaries who use contextualized bridges today. Missionaries have the advantage over the critics because they are not bound in "If . . . then" extreme scenarios. They have the convenience and availability to inspect immediately the use of each contextualized bridge to see if it does indeed lead to syncretism. If syncretism becomes evident from the use of a contextualized bridge, the missionary can then alter or cease using that particular bridge.

Paul's principle—"I have become all things to all people so that by all possible means I might save some"—practiced by missionaries today would not be acceptable to most critics of contextualization. They would label this as deceptive and pitch the phrase, "The end does not justify the means." There is a difference between "deception" and gradually revealing information in a timely, strategic, and acceptable manner. In addition, we must keep in mind that contextualization practices are meant to serve the target audience and not the messenger. It is an act of selflessness to adjust oneself for better acceptance and understandability. Critics must be careful not to place more emphasis on their perceived purity of the message than on clarity in its communication.

Effective communicators will always strive to connect with the target audience where they are mentally and spiritually, and bring them on a journey to the desired point of understanding. A canned, "one size fits all" gospel presentation serves the presenter more than the receiver. Most often, starting where a lost person is can make the presenter feel uncomfortable.

For example, no missionary feels comfortable inside the pages of the Koran. Nevertheless, this book is authoritative to Muslims worldwide, and many missionaries find "Koranic-bridging" to be highly effective. Critics, on the other hand, see this approach as giving credence to the Koran, and so would never use this bridge to start a conversation with a Muslim. They would prefer to start at a point that is more comfortable to them. Critics of this bridging approach are essentially saying to Muslims, "I know that your authority is the Koran, but it makes me feel uncomfortable to start my evangelism with you where you are (in the Koran). So instead, I need you to come completely out of the Koran and allow me to begin my evangelism with you at a point where I feel comfortable." The unwillingness to start where a lost person is may demonstrate not only poor communication skills but also a lack of sensitivity to the lost.

Missionaries using contextualized approaches to reaching the lost must maintain an attitude of gratitude for challenges from critics. Constructive criticism is the "breakfast of champions" that keeps us sharp. Since contextualization is risky business that dances on the edge of gospel contamination, missionaries should invite all eyes and ears to examine their contextualization practices. Yet, without compromising the integrity of the gospel message, the lost cannot afford for missionaries to sell them short in sharing the gospel in ways that are intelligible simply because of contextualization critics' cries of "extremes" and the approaches that make them feel uncomfortable.

Critics of contextualization must add practical experience to their critique and not be so quick to declare a contextualized approach in reaching the lost as heretical. It would be wonderful if the lost were more accepting of the gospel and would not require us to be innovative in presenting the gospel to them. Nevertheless, people are complex and respond best to approaches that connect with them where they are. We deeply appreciate teachers who start on a level where we are, rather than expecting us to climb to a higher level of understanding before the lesson starts. Critics should give constructive suggestions, sound guidance, and, above all, better models of working.

A woman once told evangelist Dwight L. Moody that she didn't like his method of sharing his faith. He replied, "I don't much like it either. What method do you use?" She answered, "I don't have one," to which Moody replied, "Then I prefer my method."

Three Camps of Contextualization

When it comes to the various degrees or levels of contextualization among cross-cultural communication practitioners, missionary approaches can be grouped into three basic camps or schools of thought: traditional, extreme, or moderate. This is not an exact science, as numerous missionary approaches fall between these three camps. Nor is this an attempt to categorize missionaries themselves. Rather, it is an attempt to explain and describe the various strategies or approaches for intercultural communication of the gospel and provide an evaluation of their effectiveness.

In similar fashion, John Travis provides for missionaries working among Muslims a contextualization scale sometimes referred to as the "C-scale."[2] He describes six levels of contextualized expressions and practices held by missionaries. Even though Travis developed his "C-scale" for those working among Muslims, this type of categorizing can be used in describing approaches to other religions and cults.

According to Harold Taylor, the traditional approach has been the most popular in the Western church for the past 150 years.[3] Paul Hiebert calls this a "non-contextual" approach.[4] In practice, the ap-

---

[2]For an explanation of C1 to C6, see John Travis, "The C1 to C6 Spectrum," *Evangelical Missions Quarterly* 34/4 (1998), 407–8.

[3]Harold Taylor, "Contextualized Mission in Church History," in *Encountering New Religious Movements: A Holistic Evangelical Approach*, ed. Irving Hexham, Stephen Rost, and John Morehead II (Grand Rapids: Kregel, 2004), 45.

[4]Paul Hiebert, "Critical Contextualization," *International Bulletin of Missionary Research* 2 (July 1981): 104.

pearance of the traditional approach might be described as being un-comfortable with identifying too closely with the lost. For example, using Christian rock music in order to convey the gospel to youth ad-dicted to secular rock music would not be considered under the tradi-tional approach. The fear and threat of compromising the gospel is the traditionalist's foremost concern. Not having cross-cultural skills could be another aspect of the traditional approach.

Adoniram Judson's first years in Burma working among the Burmese Buddhists is an example of the traditional approach. After months of preaching from a Western-style chapel with few results, "His first breakthrough came when he decided to build a *Zayat*—a Buddhist-style meditation room on a main street where he could hold meetings and teach passersby in a way that was not foreign to the people."[5] This adjustment produced his first convert.

Under the traditional approach, the burden of recognizing and un-derstanding the missionary's message relies more on the lost person than on the missionary. When witnessing to a Muslim, a missionary using a traditional approach might present the plan of salvation in this way: "You can be saved if you believe that Jesus is the Son of God and that when he died on the cross he paid the price for your sins."

A typical Muslim would process this gospel presentation in this way: "To become a 'Western Christian' I must go against the Koran and my forefathers' teaching by believing that the Christian God (one of their three gods, along with Jesus and the Holy Spirit) stepped out of heaven, took on sinful human characteristics, had relations with the virgin Mary outside of wedlock, and produced a baby named Jesus. Even though I was taught that no one can pay the price of sin for another, I must simply accept this. Finally, I must forsake the authority of my life, the Koran, which teaches that Jesus did not die, and accept the Chris-tians' corrupted book, the Bible, which teaches that Jesus died on a cross and paid the price of my guilt."

Needless to say, the traditional approach has seen significantly fewer results in impacting lostness than the moderate or extreme approaches.

---

[5]Courtney Anderson, *To The Golden Shore: The Life of Adoniram Judson* (Valley Forge, PA: Jud-son Press, 1987) 203, 220–21.

At the opposite end of the spectrum stands the extreme approach. Just because this approach carries the title "extreme" doesn't necessarily mean that the gospel is compromised. Nevertheless, when examining this approach, mainstream Christians ponder if this approach has gone too far (excesses in contextualism will be addressed later). Missionaries adhering to this school of thought expend much time and effort in defending their contextualized practices since most of their strategies liken to "the end justifies the means." Their reported fruit is their greatest defense.

This camp is all about igniting a movement through the means of missionaries themselves or national partners who become "insiders" (someone from outside the community who is eventually accepted into the local community). It takes a lot of time and skilled effort to convince a community that you are one of them and can be trusted. The "outsider" must go through a metamorphosis in order to be accepted, trusted, and heard. This pushes the limits of contextualization. A key difference between the moderate group and the extreme group is that, for the latter camp, new believers remain hidden or underground for longer periods of time. When witnessing to a Muslim, an evangelist from the extreme camp might say, "Over the next several months let's sit and study the Koran and the Bible together."

Like the extreme camp, the moderate camp allows a foreign culture to assimilate the uncompromised gospel. The key difference is the amount of time spent communicating the gospel message. The moderate camp relies strongly upon communicative bridges that are recognizable to the target audience, but does not go to the extent of becoming an "insider." The question is asked, "How do I craft my gospel presentation in a contextualized manner that moves the conversation from head to heart and can be shared within the initial meeting with a lost person?" Or in regard to how to dress, "How can I be myself and yet in sincerity and honesty adapt my appearance in a way that demonstrates respect to my audience?" If a lost person detects that you possess humility and sincerity, two powerful communicative bridges, it is more likely that you can effectively deliver the gospel message as early as the first encounter. These two qualities cover a multitude of cross-cultural communicative mistakes or blunders.

Sharing the plan of salvation with a Muslim who trusts in a works-based plan of salvation might be expressed in this way: "There are two ways of getting to heaven: either become holy yourself or accept Allah's plan where he provides forgiveness and solves your punishment problem. Glimpses of Allah's plan can be found in the Koran in Surah 3:54–55, but it is thoroughly and fully explained in what the Koran calls 'the Before Book,' or the *Injil* (the gospel), which means 'good news.' The 'good news' is for anyone who cannot become holy by his or her own effort. The *Injil* makes it clear that Allah loves us so much that he performed *korban* (sacrifice) using *Isa* (Jesus), and if you will believe this, you will receive eternal life. Do you think you can become holy? If not, then you should consider accepting Allah's free gift of salvation."

Moderate practitioners follow church-planting movement principles,[6] while extreme practitioners have their sights set more on "insider movements" that have a determined target of getting people saved, falling short of intentionally establishing churches inside the movement.[7] They encourage new believers to bring as many appropriate forms of worship from their culture as possible into their emerging churches.

Persecution is experienced most by new believers drawn through the moderate approach, since this approach penetrates deeper into lost communities than the traditional approach and is aggressive in establishing visible churches even within hostile environments. The traditional approach alleviates much of the persecution, as this approach tends to extract new believers from their religion and culture. Persecution in the extreme camp is more rare, as evangelists are more undercover and thoroughly trained in blending in with the lost.

In regard to effectiveness in baptisms and church planting, the moderate approach is experiencing more fruit than the other two. It is more aligned with New Testament principles of evangelism and church planting than the extreme and traditional approaches. The extreme

---

[6]See David Garrison's book, *Church Planting Movements: How God Is Redeeming a Lost World* (Midlothian, VA: WIGTake Resources, 2004).

[7]You can read about the debate between "church-planting movements" and "insider movements" in "Church Planting Movements vs. Insider Movements: Missiological Realities vs. Mythiological Speculations," *International Journal of Frontier Missions* 21:4 (Winter 2004): 151–54, www.ijfm.org/PDFs_IJFM/21_4_PDFs/Insider_Garrison.pdf.

camp may claim to have greater numbers of baptized or unbaptized believers, but because of its underground nature a significant degree of reporting is subjective. The verdict is still out on the extreme approach, as missiologists wait for a clearer picture of what lies beneath the veil of mystery that covers the extreme camp.

Establishing Your Level of Contextualization

Before developing a contextualized approach for ministry on the mission field, it is essential first to establish the nonnegotiables. A front-line evangelist must lay down an anchor of sound doctrine and faith. The line connected to the anchor can be stretched, but the anchor itself must remain unmoved. For many evangelicals, the Lausanne Covenant is a document that guards the integrity of the gospel in ministry.[8] Likewise, The Baptist Faith and Message 2000 serves as an anchor to hold Southern Baptist missionaries firmly in the harbor of sound doctrine.[9] The gospel is never to be compromised or stretched into heresy.

A front-line evangelist must lay down an anchor of sound doctrine and faith. The line connected to the anchor can be stretched, but the anchor itself must remain unmoved.

Once again, bridging the gospel to lost individuals or communities does not have a "one size fits all" presentation. The apostle Paul's servant attitude toward the lost comes out in his "I have become all things to all people" statement. This indicates that we should closely evaluate our audience and develop a contextualization level according to each lost person's needs. Missionaries need to see themselves as servants to their "clients"—the lost.

The gospel is never to be compromised or stretched into heresy.

Contextualization itself is not the goal. Connecting redemptively with the lost is the goal. When asked about your personal level of contextualizing the gospel message or your appearance for evangelism purposes, your response should be, "Whatever degree of contextualization each individual lost person needs from me, without compromising the

[8]See www.lausanne.org/covenant.
[9]See www.sbc.net/bfm/bfm2000.asp.

integrity of the gospel, is the degree to which I am willing to go." This approach to establishing a level of contextualization breaks down when evangelizing larger groups of lost people. Typically, the larger the group, the higher the degree of contextualization that is used.

Two questions that can further help a missionary decide on the degree of contextualization are "How deep into a hostile community do I want to go?" and "If I'm not seeing fruit, should I adjust my current contextualization level?" Environments hostile to the gospel or to foreign evangelists are good indicators of the need to raise the degree of contextualization and the need to use more effective bridges. Missionaries using the Koran as a bridge, for example, find themselves penetrating deeper inside hostile Muslim communities. Continue to adjust your contextualization levels until you begin to see a positive response from the lost.

> *Environments hostile to the gospel or to foreign evangelists are good indicators of the need to raise the degree of contextualization and the need to use more effective bridges.*

Upon meeting with a lost person for the first time, you can rest assured that you have not crossed the contextualization line if you share the gospel with them before parting ways. This appears to be the New Testament model. Jesus delayed disclosing the full identity of who he was and what he could do for the woman at the well until the end of their encounter. He used three bridges at the beginning of the conversation: living water, adultery, and true worship. As their conversation turned to the Messiah, Jesus finally identified himself: "I, the one speaking to you—I am he" (John 4:26).

Missionaries use different strategies in regard to the timing of when they share their true identity and/or purpose of evangelism with a lost person. Not revealing yourself and your intentions before the end of the first encounter can later become problematic for the missionary and result in a missed opportunity. There are numerous culturally sensitive ways of revealing who you are and what you desire as an outcome from meeting with the person. When Jesus sent out his disciples, he instructed them, "When you enter a house, first say, 'Peace to this house'" (Luke 10:5). Jesus then directed them to stay in a house where the people were open to hearing and not to leave for another house until they had shared their message. "Friendship evangelism" or a highly contextualized approach of convincing lost people that you are one of them—both of which can span over days, months, or even years—are not strategies provided by Jesus to his disciples in the missionary training exercises mentioned in Matthew 10, Luke 9:1–6, and Luke 10:1–24.

Finally, craft your contextualization level with the intent of finding a "person of peace," an interested person who is bent on establishing a church-planting movement among the lost in their community. Some call this "precision harvesting," in which the missionary has the mindset of "looking for a movement" rather than "making or creating a movement." The idea is to find the person who will start a church-planting movement in a community, rather than the missionary starting the movement. With tremendous effort, the missionary may be able to win one or two to Christ in the span of a year. But the person of peace, as a known member of the community, is capable of winning hundreds in a shorter period of time.

Craft your contextualization level with the intent of finding a "person of peace," an interested person who is bent on establishing a church-planting movement among the lost in their community.

In summary, allow the lost to determine your contextualization level rather than you deciding for them. Cultural research and sensitivity to the guidance of the Holy Spirit will serve as a voice for the lost in telling you the contextualization level they need. Don't assume all lost people will respond to the same contextualization levels. Constantly evaluate your approaches to ensure that you don't compromise the gospel message and that you are communicating effectively. The mission is about the lost, not about you or your comfort level.

Avoid Going Too Far

The greatest threat of crossing the line in regard to contextualization is to water down the gospel message. Extremism, by definition, involves practices that go beyond what is necessary. When I first began working with Muslims, I erred on the side of extreme contextualization and security paranoia. Soon I began to realize that my ministry had become more about the science of contextualization and the obsession of creating and even manipulating the "perfect movement" as I thought it should happen. I alienated my fellow missionaries, became exhausted as I struggled to protect my identity, and missed multiple opportunities in sharing.

Don Dent, a veteran missionary in Asia, provides missionaries who push the contextualization envelope with four foundational stones that keep extremism in check. Look for these four elements among new believers: (1) conversion: signs of lifestyle adjustments that are more pleasing to God; (2) conviction: changes in their thought processes reflected in a new sense of right and wrong; (3) confession: a longing to share their new faith with others; and (4) congregation: a desire to fellowship with like-minded believers or seekers of truth. An emerging movement void of these four foundational stones should be a signal for missionaries to revisit their contextualization approaches.

Conclusion

We are not in the "come and get it" business. We are administering medicine to fatally sick people who do not grasp the reality and seriousness of their disease. We who have the truth are forever grateful for the person(s) who stepped out of their comfort zone and into our world and shared the gospel with us, not demanding that we grow to a higher level of understanding or adjust our lifestyle before sharing the good news with us.

Discussion Points

1. Cite examples of effective bridging and contextualization practices by Jesus and the apostle Paul.

2. Describe the three camps of contextualization on the mission field.

3. Why does Greeson recommend that evangelists share the gospel in the initial meeting with a lost person?

4. Discuss the four tests for knowing if your contextualization practices have gone too far.

5. Do you agree or disagree with Greeson when he states, "The unwillingness to start where a lost person is may demonstrate not only poor communication skills but also a lack of sensitivity to the lost." Explain your answer.

Further Reading

Garrison, David. *Church Planting Movements: How God Is Redeeming a Lost World*. Midlothian, VA: WIGTake Resources, 2004.

Garrison, David, ed. *The Camel Rider's Journal*. Arkadelphia, AR: WIGTake Resources, 2009.

Greeson, Kevin. *The Camel: How Muslims Are Coming to Faith in Christ!* Arkadelphia, AR: WIGTake Resources, 2007.

Gregory, John Milton. *The Seven Laws of Teaching*. First published in 1884. Available at www.bibleteacher.org/7lot1.htm.

Musk, Bill A. *The Unseen Face of Islam: Sharing the Gospel with Ordinary Muslims at Street Level*. Grand Rapids: Monarch Books, 2003.

Parshall, Phil. *Muslim Evangelism: Contemporary Approaches to Contextualization*. Grand Rapids: Baker, 1980.

Strong, Cynthia A., and Meg Page. *A Worldview Approach to Ministry Among Muslim Women*. Pasadena, CA: William Carey Library, 2006.

Woodberry, J. Dudley, ed. *From Seed to Fruit: Global Trends, Fruitful Practices, and Emerging Issues Among Muslims*. Pasadena, CA: William Carey Library, 2008.

27

BACK TO BASICS

William R. Yount

Our people have difficulty understanding that their job is to equip others for ministry." I was listening intently to my companion, International Mission Board Strategy Coordinator Shannon Ford, as we walked along a busy street in Kiev, Ukraine. "They think the front-line work is theirs to do, as if, 'If I train someone else to do what I'm doing, then what will I do?' It's a major problem because it hinders us from doing the main thing, which is, of course, equipping leaders here to do the work themselves."

I was intrigued, because equipping others has been central to my own teaching ministry for thirty-five years. I was also puzzled. Why is equipping (Ephesians 4:11–16) such a difficult concept? Educators spend their lives organizing solutions, expanding programs, building teams, and training leaders to coordinate a variety of ministries. I assumed all ministers, and especially missionaries, understood Paul's philosophy of exponential growth through equipping leaders.

"Well, that's just it," Ford continued. "Most of us were trained as pastors. The unspoken assumption is that ministry revolves around 'me.' Worse, 'ministry' usually means 'preaching.' But we need missionaries who can equip others for a wide variety of ministries, to help others shoulder the work for themselves, in various locales, in various ways. This requires a lot more than preaching a sermon."[1]

There it was yet again. Ford was saying, as clearly as it can be said,

---

[1]Shannon Ford, Strategy Coordinator, IMB, discussion with author in Ukraine, May 26, 2008. Used by permission.

DISCOVERING THE MISSION OF GOD

that missionaries need an energized, ongoing discipleship perspective which lives itself out in practical skills and heartfelt conviction. As long as we train missionaries to be preacher-proclaimers[2] rather than minister-equippers, the problem will continue.

My first smug solution was this: engage Christian educators in missions. Yet I had to admit that seminary training for educators tends to emphasize American evangelical methods of discipleship. Unless there has been an intentional engagement of our own cultural distinctiveness, as well as how it differs from others, few can translate biblical discipleship into other cultures.[3] James Plueddemann, chair of the Missions and Evangelism department at Trinity Evangelical Divinity School and former International Director of SIM (Serving in Missions), is one such example. Reflecting on his experience as a Christian education missionary in Nigeria, he wrote:

> I soon realized that many of the things I studied as a Christian Education major were quite inappropriate for a cross-cultural missionary. . . . I tried to find people who could help me or books I could read. I found none. Missiologists seemed to be myopically focused on evangelism and church planting, while Christian Educators had yet to discover culture. . . .
>
> While it is important to reach and evangelize [the world], neither of these is the ultimate goal of missions. World-wide disciple-making is a much better definition of missions.[4]

The words of Ford and Plueddemann capture the heart of this chapter: in spite of all the resources, scientific tools, and models of contemporary missiology, being on mission with God comes down to basic biblical and relational discipling.

Two Participles Supporting One Imperative

In the Great Commission (Matthew 28:19-20), the imperative "make disciples" embraces two participles: "baptizing" and "teaching." The

---

[2]Or, perhaps more correctly, fail to train them away from such a perspective.

[3]Especially since most professors of Christian Education are experienced in American evangelical perspectives.

[4]James Plueddemann, preface to William R. Yount and Mike Barnett, *Called to Reach: Equipping Cross-Cultural Disciplers* (Nashville: Broadman & Holman, 2007).

first is what we generally think of as evangelism—that is, witnessing to and "winning" the lost, then sealing that conversion with the symbol and witness of baptism. The second is teaching. But this is more than teaching truth. It is teaching to obey truth by nurturing the saved to grow as citizens of the kingdom. The entire process is what we call discipling (or discipleship). So discipling requires more than preaching's verbal exhortations or teaching's verbal explanations. Discipling requires heart-to-heart relationships, walking together over time, and discovering the things of God's Word and kingdom together. The missions enterprise extends the equipping mandate "to all nations."

Making disciples, therefore, is process more than event. This distinction is critical. I've met more than a few who traveled to some remote part of the world, preached a sermon, exulted in seeing hundreds "saved" (well, "raised their hands"), and returned home committed to becoming missionaries. Visions of personal fields "white unto harvest" danced in their heads. Theirs was an event perspective. But the realities of living day by day submerged in a different language, culture, and worldview soon replaced high expectations with frustration, depression, and, for some, despair. They failed to see the relevance of culture shock and language mastery to the process of discipling those of other cultures and languages. Most are home now and, according to their own testimonies, have little to show for their commitment to missions than scars.

A commitment to missions? Perhaps that was their root problem. They were committed to missions more than to people.[5] Commitment to any program or task—rather than to the people for whom programs and tasks are designed—can easily degrade into scalp hunting. We see it in churches at home: goals of ten more next Sunday, regardless of who they are. The "missions mandate" is sometimes misunderstood as a mere translation of this scalp-hunting mentality worldwide. But Jesus isn't buying scalps. He gave his life so that those who believe in him—and now walk with him, live in him, obey him, and grow in him—will participate with him in the kingdom, all around the world.

---

[5]My assumption, in either case, is that they were first committed to the Lord.

The commitment that sustains us over the long-term is a commitment to people, one person at a time.

In May of 2008, God blessed me with a cross-cultural encounter in Ukraine that I'll never forget. I taught a forty-hour course based on "Created to Learn," a Christian view of educational psychology, and led a professional development seminar for the faculty at Kiev Theological Seminary. Prior to the trip, I asked Mick Stockwell if he would recommend a Russian tutor for me. Mick, a member of the regional leadership team of the Central and Eastern European region of the IMB, is based in Kiev, Ukraine. He suggested his landlord, Vladimir, who is also the chairman of one of the English departments at one of the largest universities in Ukraine. This well-educated, well-traveled man, and his elegant wife, Ludmila, a chemist, were reared under Communism and have little knowledge of the Bible. The story of our friendship is not finished, but it certainly had a heavenly beginning and provides a tangible frame for the principles discussed in this chapter.[6]

The following principles are suggestive, certainly not exhaustive, of approaches to missions that build bridges upon which the gospel can be shared. Our work is to plant and water; the results belong to the Lord (1 Corinthians 3:6–7). How, then, do we plant and water most effectively?

Principle One: Focusing on the Learner Rather Than the Task

When IMB missionary Joel Ragains first arrived in Kiev to begin his work as director of the church planting program at Kiev Theological Seminary, he asked Anatoli Prokopchuk, president of the seminary, how he could most effectively build relationships with Ukrainians. Without hesitation, Prokopchuk responded, "Be willing to waste time with them."

I've certainly seen the power of a quiet conversation—one not rushed, one without an agenda. I've experienced the importance of drinking steaming cups of tea with feet under the kitchen table, or the incredible power of sharing a meal in which "business" is never mentioned. Now Prokopchuk had fused these isolated events into a potent seven-word

---

[6]Recounted experiences with Vladimir, May–June, 2008, are used with his permission.

prescription: "Be willing to waste time with them." To task-oriented and time-driven Americans—and I certainly fit that description—"superficial" conversations over tea or supper are lulls between important events: conferences, classes, meetings, and strategic-planning sessions. In reality, such occasions are not "wastes of time" but rather emphasize that persons are more important than agendas, and relationships are more important than "the work." Must we explicitly declare such a view as biblical?

"But these are written that you . . . may have life in his name" (John 20:31). John's purpose in writing his Gospel was the life of the believer—which is much more than agendas, techniques, or programs. The obvious implication in our context is that the life of the learner takes priority over the machinery of our ministry. In the mission of God, we focus on the lives of national learners.

Before rushing on to the remaining how-to principles, let's linger a moment to underscore an essential truth. The remaining principles are nothing but marketing techniques unless we anchor them with an unshakable, God-quickened, self-giving *agape* love toward those we teach and equip. Such love cannot be worked up by our own efforts, nor developed by some educational program or orientation class. Such love bubbles up from within, energized by the Spirit of God himself, the natural fruit of a Spirit-surrendered life. "The fruit of the Spirit is love . . ." (Galatians 5:22).

Principle Two: Coming Alongside

"You'll never be like me, but we can walk together." For many years I was involved in ministry to the deaf, realizing that, because I could hear, I would never be fully accepted by the deaf community. Likewise, I'll never be Ukrainian. But despite these culture gaps I can come alongside others in a common purpose. That common purpose closes the distance between cultures. Amos condemned the sinful ways of the people of Israel, their overt rejection of God, by raising the question, "Do two walk together unless they have agreed to do so?" (Amos 3:3). The obvious answer is no. Discipleship sails on the river of mutual agreement.

Lawyers come alongside their clients, as advocates under the law, in order to defend them. Both lawyer and client agree at the point of the client's defense. In the same way, we come alongside those we engage as advocates across cultural divides. My initial agreement with Vladimir was that I would come alongside him, pay for his instruction, and be a willing student. He agreed to come alongside me with his experience in teaching language and his expertise in Russian. This mutual agreement gave us a basis for walking together. Other shared experiences followed.

What connection points can we find with others? Do we have expertise they need? Are we willing to give that expertise freely, without hidden agendas? Do they have expertise we need? Are we willing to learn from them, allow them to lead us, and even to correct us? It is here that we find initial connection points for discipleship.

Principle Three: Listening

"I will listen to what you bring, if you will listen to who I am." We are more effective in building relationships when we listen before we speak. Unfortunately, some of us are hard-wired in "telling" mode. Even God refuses to respond when we violate this principle. "'When I called, they did not listen; so when they called, I would not listen,' says the LORD Almighty" (Zechariah 7:13). Refusing to listen to others prevents relationships from forming, and breaks relationships that already exist: "Everyone should be quick to listen, slow to speak" (James 1:19).

Vladimir invited me to meet informally with the dozen teachers in his department. I was happy to accept. The day after our first language session, he mentioned his plan to his dean. She suggested that I address the division faculty, nearly a hundred teachers. The next day, she requested a list of topics I might address from educational psychology. I sketched out three. The following day, she formally invited me, through Vladimir, to speak on all three topics. One informal meeting with a dozen became three formal lectures to scores of professors. One hour of presentation became six.

The day before the first session, Vladimir and I inspected the lecture hall where we were to meet. Vladimir asked me to take a seat, and then sat down at a desk across from me. Carefully, he said, "I am not giving you advice. But many Americans offer to come and help us, and then—

when they come, they force God on us. Unfortunately, we do not believe in God. And many of the teachers resent being [he paused] . . . misled. So I am not giving you advice. You may do as you have planned."

Vladimir was asking me not to "bait and switch," offering help and delivering condemnation. I listened to him. More than that, I heard him. And I heeded what he said. My goal would be to help the teachers learn clear, fundamental principles of how students learn. I understood that God designed these principles, of course; but I prayerfully decided that, for this seminar, I would emphasize the psychology that had discovered them.

During the sessions, I mentioned the seminary where I teach and shared a few brief teaching experiences in churches. I also referenced the Bible. But I did not force God on them. Listening is important, but we need to hear what is said and then act on what we hear. Otherwise we have not really listened.

Now some of you dear readers may chide me for missing an evangelistic opportunity. Were you listening? Did you hear what I said? Vladimir told me about the tangible results produced by others who had forced an evangelistic opportunity where none existed. That tangible result was resentment. It was surprising they invited me to speak at all, given this history.

And what resulted from respecting Vladimir's suggestion? At the end of the three-day seminar, I was invited to return at any time to teach again. A second conference is being planned and other members of the missionary team are being enlisted to participate. Officials at the university are looking for ways to expand the conference to other schools. Vladimir and his dean are compiling a list of questions they want to have addressed. More contacts have been made. Relationships have been strengthened.

After our language session following the seminar, Vladimir invited me to have tea at his apartment. In this case, "tea" meant three kinds of ham, two kinds of cheese, two kinds of bread, and Austrian chocolates. Oh, and tea *or* coffee—and an hour of quiet conversation with him and his family.

Our learners plead with us: "Tell me what you think I need to know, and I may resent both you and your advice. Listen to me, and I'll be more inclined to listen to you." Look for ways to listen. Ask for advice—sincerely. Give your eyes, as well as your ears, to listening. Forget the clock. Weigh what you hear, and use offered advice when it is appropriate to do so. Be generous in gratitude for the advice you receive, but do so subtly and naturally. Doors will gradually open for you to share, appropriately, what is most important.

Principle Four: Trusting

"Can I depend on you? Will you depend on me?" We build stable human relationships on a foundation of mutual trust. Trusting others wisely[7] and establishing our own trustworthiness by the way we behave are both essential to mission success. Paul and Barnabas reflected this mutual trust in the way they planted churches. Paul established his own trustworthiness by returning to Lystra—the same day a mob stoned him and dragged him outside the city, thinking he was dead, and again after a time of ministry in other cities—to encourage the new believers (Acts 14:19–22).

Paul and Barnabas also demonstrated trust in new leaders. "Paul and Barnabas appointed elders for them in each church and, with prayer and fasting, committed them to the Lord, in whom they had put their trust" (Acts 14:23). They appointed leaders, prayed for them, and departed—trusting the leaders to carry on the ministry.

When I emphasized scientific principles in human learning and teaching (and didn't force God on the participants), Vladimir learned in a tangible way that he could trust me to do what I agreed to do. He learned I would not use the opportunity he provided for my own agenda. He learned he could depend on me to do what I said I would do.

Furthermore, Vladimir met other missionaries over the three days of the conference. He found he could trust them in tangible ways, as well, each one seeking ways to work with him in mutually beneficial ways. One missionary invited him to become more involved in teaching Russian to newly arriving missionaries. Vladimir agreed. He engaged

---

[7]That is, trust—but not too much! Trust without caution produces naiveté. Caution without trust produces suspicion.

another missionary who visited one session, a specialist in training high school teachers in public schools outside of Kiev, by asking why she wasn't working in Kiev.[8] When she told him she had never been invited to work in the high schools of Kiev, Vladimir offered to help her begin. "Why go to the ends of Ukraine when there are hundreds of teachers who need your help right here?"

Active listening led to mutual trust. Mutual trust opened more doors for service and, eventually, for opportunities to share the gospel in appropriate, Spirit-led ways.

Keep your word, every time. Do not over-promise.[9] Be on time. Keep confidences.[10] Show yourself trustworthy in every way. On the other hand, trust others. Ask for their advice, and take it. Invite them to plan activities, and depend on them to carry out those plans. Be gracious in your analysis of results: emphasize the positive and suggest correctives on less effective elements. Learn from these interactions so that you give better instructions next time. Be patient in the process. Mutual trust cannot be forced. But when it blooms and matures, it produces delicious fruit.

Principle Five: Demonstrating

"Show me how to minister here." Verbal explanations only go so far. Demonstrations, in cultural context, are necessary if we expect learners to retain what they learn. Students all over the former Soviet Union have a saying about exam preparation. My Ukrainian students always smile and nod knowingly to each other whenever I mention it—and I always mention it because it is a false system of learning. The saying

---

[8]This missionary and her small team provide educational training to interested groups of Ukrainian public school teachers. As the team provides training, team members often have opportunities to share their faith. They also begin a Bible study for those who are interested. Several have been led to faith in Christ through these efforts.

[9]Americans have a tendency to say, "We *could* do this, and we *could* do that." Americans make such statements as *possibilities* that may or may not work out (i.e., no harm done). People in other cultures usually take these words as promises that will be fulfilled. If we fail to fulfill the promise, for whatever reason, great harm is done. Instead, it's better to under-promise and over-fulfill.

[10]Before submitting this chapter I sent it to Vladimir for his approval. I wanted to make it absolutely clear to him that my experiences with him were genuine, not simply fodder for a writing assignment.

consists of three words: *zubrioshka, zdal, zabil*, which mean, "Cram (the night before an exam), pass (the exam and earn the grade), and forget (everything you memorized, and move on)."

Such a false view of learning is human, not Russian per se. I have American students who live by this same rule, though, as far as I know, it has not yet been reduced to a proverb. In a Christian education context, however, we teach to change lives. Such long-term changes are not only spiritual, but also cognitive (what learners think), and affective (what learners value), and behavioral (what skills learners master). These changes are prompted and reinforced by teachers and leaders who go beyond words to demonstrate clearheaded reasoning, warm-hearted priorities, and consistently sharp competencies.

Demonstration is time intensive, since skills in a proper cultural context differ from the way things are done back home. Our ultimate goal is for nationals to learn skills (thinking, valuing, doing) in their own context, and then to become the demonstrators for others.

Jesus demonstrated the importance of prayer by praying. "One day Jesus was praying in a certain place. When he finished, one of his disciples said to him, 'Lord, teach us to pray, just as John taught his disciples'" (Luke 11:1). Paul emphasized the importance of good demonstration, of being a good model. "Encourage the young men to be self controlled. In everything set them an example by doing what is good. In your teaching show integrity, seriousness and soundness of speech that cannot be condemned, so that those who oppose you may be ashamed because they have nothing bad to say about us" (Titus 2:6–8).

Vladimir noticed from the very first session that I actually used the principles I was discussing in the seminar itself. "We are accustomed to gathering in a large hall and listening to someone tell us, in great detail, about things they do not practice even as they speak," he remarked. This is a common problem. I remember attending an associational teachers' conference on "the use of discussion." After a two-hour speech, punctuated occasionally with rhetorical questions, we left with information about discussions but without one directed exercise of actually conducting one, or without even participating in one.

Learners will "do as we do" long before they will "do as we say," so give attention to what you do. Develop skills in the appropriate cultural context so that what you demonstrate is appropriate for those you teach. How? Observe others who are already effective. Learn cultural applications from your national learners. Encourage feedback from learners by accepting it, and being grateful for it.

Engage your learners in activities other than listening. Strengthen skillful thinking in learners by engaging them with problems to solve, questions to answer, and situations to analyze. Strengthen skillful valuing by personally sharing yourself and engaging learners to share their testimonies, relating material to personal situations in ministry. Strengthen skillful doing by hands-on practice, feedback, and repetition until learners achieve success.

Principle Six: Stretching

"Now give me this hill country." Satan, who leads the whole world astray (Revelation 12:9), will not give up his territory easily. Comfort zones will not win the battle. Moses promised faithful Caleb the hill country when Caleb was forty years old (Deuteronomy 1:36). Forty-five years later, at age eighty-five, Caleb claims his promise and succeeds in winning the battle (Joshua 14:6–14). We stretch ourselves by trusting the Lord and moving into unfamiliar territory. We accept others as they are, and then help them stretch their faith to accomplish all God intends.

Vladimir stretched me in our language lessons. For twelve years I've studied books, listened to cassette tapes, and poured over dictionaries and grammars in my attempt to learn to speak Russian. But my conversational skills remain weak. Our sessions were conducted in Russian alone, stretching me. Vladimir and Ludmila invited me to their country house, or dacha, for a weekend. For two days I was immersed in language, culture, interaction, cooking, eating, drinking,[11] fishing, and storytelling. It was an experience of a lifetime—a stretching for which I will always be grateful.

---

[11]With Vladimir's help, I was able to avoid the ever-present vodka, wine, and beer. He protected me by joining me in drinking mineral water or juice when another guest insisted I join him in a "real" toast.

Perhaps I stretched Vladimir some as well. During our weekend at the dacha, I met a woman and her four-year-old daughter. The mother corrected the little girl with shouts, which were at times quite caustic. Vladimir commented on this, but said he seldom interfered. Yet from time to time Vladimir did attempt to muffle the mother's sharper outbursts. He himself spoke kindly, yet directly, to the little girl when she needed correction. Perhaps he had been stretched some, testing some of the principles he had heard in our lectures.

By pushing ourselves into new situations, by trying new approaches, we not only grow in our own abilities but provide a model for learners to stretch themselves as well. By setting high standards and exhorting learners to move out of their comfort zones and into unfamiliar situations, we equip them to face future challenges with more confidence and determination.

Principle Seven: Delegating-Supervising

"I can do it myself! Do you care enough to watch?" In principle four, we emphasized trust. Here we emphasize letting go. We hold what we build loosely and work ourselves out of a job. Too much supervision, without delegation, can leave learners feeling oppressed, demoralized, and, eventually, ineffective. Paul delegated ministry to Timothy, who, in turn, was to delegate the work to others. "The things you have heard me say in the presence of many witnesses entrust to reliable people who will also be qualified to teach others" (2 Timothy 2:2).

On the other hand, too much delegation, without supervision, can leave learners feeling abandoned, frustrated, and, eventually, ineffective. Paul warned us to supervise those under our charge. "Keep watch over yourselves and all the flock of which the Holy Spirit has made you overseers. Be shepherds of the church of God, which he bought with his own blood" (Acts 20:28).

The delegation-supervision continuum exists where supervisor-subordinate relationships exist. Supervisors are more effective as they delegate ministry tasks to subordinates, multiplying their effectiveness through others. Delegated tasks are done more effectively as supervisors watch, and correct as needed, how their subordinates function.

Subordinates receive such oversight enthusiastically, if done with love and encouragement.

A graduate of the church planting program at Kiev Theological Seminary reinforced this principle for me. He told me with great pride that Joel Ragains, the director of the program, spent hours on a train in order to visit him and his church. "He did not have to do that. But it proved to me he really cared about me and my ministry." Ragains took the time to stand beside his student and observe his ministry. By doing so, he made a powerful and lasting impression.

Principle Eight: Supporting

"How can you strengthen the work I do for the Lord?" They were well-meaning professors, this trio who traveled to Russia from the American Midwest to present distance-learning technology to Christian school administrators. For two hours they displayed the latest in hardware and software that would allow schools to engage learners across eleven time zones. Through the "magic of the Internet," there was "no longer a need for residential schools," with related support, housing, and food costs.

At the end of the seminar, I asked one of the Ukrainian administrators for his opinion on the presentation. He was gracious to these presenters. "The information was very interesting for me. It could be a worthy dream for us." So how helpful was the presentation for his school? "Well, the problem is our antiquated phone system. There is so much noise on our phone lines that data is easily scrambled. There is no way we could employ such a system for, perhaps, twenty years. And by that time the technology will have totally changed. But the idea was very interesting." And useless in the present context, he might have added.

We would do better in meaningful discipleship to support what the Lord is already doing "there" rather than to impose what we are doing "here." Vladimir had already studied educational psychology, as had his dean. But most of the teachers in the division had not. Therefore, what I brought was added value to the secular work they are already doing in the classroom.

Joel Ragains developed a church planting program at Kiev Theological Seminary, not to import a commitment to planting churches from the United States but to support the commitment Ukrainian Baptists made ten years ago to plant ten thousand churches and become the missionary-sending hub of the former Soviet Union. It was such a blessing to sit in a recent meeting and observe key American evangelical leaders sketch out ways to support efforts already underway to train Ukrainians to be missionaries to other former Soviet republics.

The greatest support we have for discipling ministry is the Lord God himself. When King Saul pursued David, David found little support but from the Lord, who proved to be all David needed. "You are my Lord; apart from you I have no good thing" (Psalm 16:2). ". . . the Lord was my support" (Psalm 18:18). "Surely God is my help; the Lord is the one who sustains me" (Psalm 54:4).

As Vladimir and I continued to meet together, spiritual issues began to dawn. "You cite many statements from the Bible in your books, which I cannot comment on because I have never studied the Bible and know very little about it." I told him I had studied the Bible all my life, and could explain its structure and clarify its central message. His reaction was immediate: "I need this! My students ask me questions and I cannot answer them." The next day, when I suggested he begin reading the Gospel of John, Vladimir told me he had already been reading that Gospel in a Bible given him by a missionary.

Later still, I suggested he could ask God for help in understanding the Bible. He said, "I asked him once for help. After Chernobyl, my wife became ill. She required surgery, and it was very serious. I had no one I could go to for help, so I asked God to help her. She came through the surgery well, and she is well now. Perhaps he helped us in some way."

Support for what he was already doing in the classroom, support for his efforts at the university, support for future opportunities in language study and teacher training—all these opened doors into Vladimir's heart, a heart that had already sought God, and pleaded with God, and received blessings from God's hands. His support for my desire to teach teachers opened my heart to him.

By this time it was late, so after a few last words to Vladimir, encouraging him to continue to pray to Jesus, read the Bible, and ask questions, I took my leave. Vladimir and his son, Anton, walked me back to my borrowed apartment. He talked about "our future lessons," and "another conference," and "more tea."

Vladimir now knows that the Bible says each of us must decide what we will do with Jesus Christ: invite him into our lives to help us live triumphantly in his power, or reject him and live by our own strength and cunning. I will be praying for Vladimir and his family, eager to see where he is in his walk toward the Lord when we meet again.

Conclusion

We began the chapter with a problem, the need for a discipling perspective in missions. We end with a message of hope. Reinforcing the call for an equipping focus of missions, Mick Stockwell observes:

> The heart of missions is discipleship. It is the core of the Great Commission that calls us, sustains us, guides our strategies, and assures us of Jesus' presence throughout the entire process. One thing that I stress with new personnel is the fact that the most important thing is not the strategy, the work, or even the results of the missionary's personal ministry that make the biggest impact. . . . What is critical is that they are able to model, mentor, train, and entrust what they can do to many who can pass that on to other faithful followers of Christ. I challenge them to look throughout the book of Acts for words like: *added to, grew, expanded, multiplied*—words that show that the process of true discipleship is occurring. This is the model that the followers of Jesus left us as they radically changed their world.[12]

We have presented ways to equip others across cultural divides. It is essential that these discipling principles—learner focused, coming alongside, listening, trusting, demonstrating, stretching, delegating-supervising, and supporting—are not seen as techniques to be worn like some new fashion. They are the fruit of a life rooted in Jesus' greatest commandments: "Love the Lord your God with all your heart and with all your soul and with all your mind. . . . Love your neighbor as yourself" (Matthew 22:37–39). Who can argue a better foundation for practical, lifelong, missions-focused discipling than this?

---

[12]Mick Stockwell, e-mail message to author, June 26, 2008.

Discussion Points

1. What does Jesus' command to "make disciples of all nations" really mean?

2. Can you think of examples in your own journey with God in which you saw one of the eight principles of discipling lived out?

3. What does Yount mean when he says our problem might be that we are committed to missions more than people?

4. What does Yount say about strategy? What was/is his end goal regarding his relationship with Vladimir?

Further Reading

Yount, William R., and Mike Barnett. *Called to Reach: Equipping Cross-Cultural Disciplers*. Nashville: Broadman & Holman, 2007.

28

CHURCH-PLANTING
MOVEMENTS

David Garrison

Why Churches?

Over the past two decades a growing number of evangelical mission agencies have shifted their organizational focus from assorted evangelism and ministry programs to a focus on planting churches. Many of these agencies have set their sites even higher—to church-planting movements, the planting of reproducing churches.[1] Why is this? What in the mission of God is so important about churches and their reproduction? A Christian from the central Indian state of Madhya Pradesh shared this testimony:

> I came to Jesus in the late 1980s. Not long afterwards, I experienced a large evangelistic crusade in a city. Impressed, I returned to my village and organized similar crusades there and in the surrounding villages for years. Thousands came, and everyone liked it. The crusades were so successful that even the lame could walk again—and walked away, never to return; the blind could see—and they never looked back.[2]

---

[1]The paradigm shift to an emphasis on church planting is evidenced by a simple, random perusal of agency websites: "church multiplication movements" (World Team), "rapidly reproducing churches" (Greater Europe Missions), "church-planting movements" (International Mission Board, Pioneers), "reproducing churches [or communities/groups of believers]" (The Evangelical Alliance Mission, Frontiers, Operation Mobilization), "indigenous, biblical, church movements" (OMF International).

[2]In Victor Choudhrie, "India: 3,000 House Churches Planted in Madhya Pradesh Since 1994," reported in the author's *Church Planting Movements: How God Is Redeeming a Lost World* (Midlothian, VA: WIGTake Resources, 2004), 38.

Frustrated with the evaporating fruit of mass evangelism, the Indian believer sought a better way.

> In 1994, I attended a seminar about house church planting which completely changed my thinking. I gave up the costs and difficulties of organizing crusades and started to plant house churches with fiery evangelistic zeal, with the result that almost 500 house churches have been started in neighboring districts. We don't plant only one house church per village, because there are a number of people groups which require their own house churches. I hope that the number of house churches will double in the next 12 months.[3]

What this South Asian brother learned is a lesson we can all share. The joy of our salvation in Christ naturally compels us to spread the good news (John 15:8). But if new fruit doesn't remain on the vine long enough to exhibit the fruit of the Spirit (Galatians 5:22–23), then the harvest is tragically lost.

The quest for fruit that lasts is what led our Indian friend to shift his energies from mass evangelistic crusades to planting new churches. He reasoned that churches uniquely possess the ability to turn these new believers into true disciples of Christ who would grow in Christlikeness as they mature in their new faith. Growth in Christ requires a discipleship community, a church. So, like so many of us, this brother gave a new priority to the task of planting multiplying churches.

What Is a Church?

A church is a corporate or communal expression of an individual's allegiance to the sovereignty of Christ in his or her life. The value of church can be expressed in a simple syllogism: (A) If salvation is preferable to lostness, and (B) growth in Christlikeness is preferable to simple salvation, then (C) churches, which foster and nurture growth in Christlikeness, are preferable to individual or even mass evangelism.

Church-based discipleship does not replace the imperative of individual conversion—as Jesus said, "You must be born again" (John 3:7)—but rather builds upon it. What begins with a personal surrender

---

[3]Ibid.

to Christ's redemptive love grows through a lifetime in a community dedicated to his lordship, as every dimension of life is brought under the lordship of Jesus Christ. Only in the context of a discipling community can a new believer find the full range of opportunities for growth in Christlikeness.

Churches are more than just an option. They are more than a human answer to the question of how we participate in God's saving work on earth. Though each of us has contributed to mankind's fall from grace, none of us wrote the story of man's redemption. This is God's story, and we are invited participants. The church is an integral part of that story.

The church has its prologue in the children of Israel, God's first redemptive community. Flawed though it was, Israel still represented a tangible expression of God's desire for a community of witness to his glory. Jesus took the redemptive community to a new level of realization in his first official act of messianic ministry, in which he forged a community of twelve disciples. The choice of twelve disciples echoed the twelve tribes of Israel, and the mandate was the same: to be a tangible expression of God's glory on earth. In choosing the twelve disciples, Christ affirmed the value of community-based discipleship and inaugurated a *new* Israel, one that would find its identity in its association with him.

Two thousand years later there are more than 3.6 million congregations worshiping in nearly 40,000 distinct denominations.[4] Each one is different, yet each one can be measured by the same standard of identity in Christ which established and shaped the first Christian community. This rudimentary standard precedes every creed, every canon, and every ecclesiological definition the church has established in its lengthy history.

The most prolific New Testament writer was the physician Luke, the apostle Paul's traveling companion, who wrote both the Gospel that bears his name and the book of Acts. Luke's orderly account of Jesus' life and work gives us piercing insight into the symbiotic relation between the life of Jesus and the life of his church. Luke begins Acts with a reference to the Gospel narrative which preceded it: "In my former book, Theophilus, I wrote about all that Jesus began to do and to teach . . . "

---

[4]David B. Barrett, "Missiometrics 2008: Reality Checks for Christian World Communions, Table C," in *International Bulletin of Missionary Research* (January 2008): 30.

(Acts 1:1). The implication was clear: if volume one was about what Jesus *began* to do and to teach, then volume two would be about what Jesus was continuing to do and to teach through his body, the church.

Though the first Pentecost after Jesus' crucifixion and resurrection opened a new chapter in salvation history, it was still one in which he would continue to play the central, leading role. The story begins as Christ delayed his ascension long enough to bless and commission his community of disciples. It is no coincidence that our modern English word for church derives from *kuria-kon* ("the Lord's fellowship"). Our community is rooted in identity with him, even as our future prospects depend upon our continued relationship with him.

As an early persecutor of the church, Saul of Tarsus learned firsthand how intimately Christ associated himself with his community of disciples. Struck down by a blinding light on the road to Damascus, Saul heard for himself the words of association, as Jesus thundered, "Saul, Saul, why do you persecute me?" (Acts 9:4). So deep was the impression that this identification made upon Saul that from this point forward he routinely refers to the church as the "body of Christ" (Romans 12:5; 1 Corinthians 12:12,27; Ephesians 3:6; 4:12; 5:23; Colossians 1:24; 3:15).

The inseparable standard by which every Christian community is weighed and measured is this: How intimately is it related to Christ? How faithfully does it continue his life and ministry?

As it was in the beginning, so it is to this day. The inseparable standard by which every Christian community is weighed and measured is this: How intimately is it related to Christ? How faithfully does it continue his life and ministry?

What Is Better Than a Church?

We can now press our syllogism a little further. If, as stated earlier, (A) salvation is preferable to lostness, and (B) growth in Christlikeness is preferable to simple salvation, then (C) churches, which foster and nurture growth in Christlikeness, are preferable to individual or even mass evangelism. On this basis alone we have justified the planting of churches as a *summum bonum*, highest good, of Christian values.

Is it possible that something could be even more desirable than church planting? If church planting is highly desirable, then the planting of multiplying churches would seem to be higher still. While few Christians would contest the value of multiplying communities of disciples, fewer still have seen this value realized. Those who have seen it call this reality a church-planting movement.

Church-Planting Movements

A church-planting movement is *a rapid multiplication of indigenous churches planting churches that sweeps through a people group or population segment.* There is more we could add to this definition, but this one captures its essence.

Church-planting movements are not new; they have flourished periodically throughout church history, but they have recently gained new attention. A few examples are enough to show us why. Through the decade of the 1990s, Christians in one Latin American country overcame relentless government persecution to grow from 235 churches to more than 4,000 churches. In Southeast Asia, a missionary saw three small house churches of 85 members in 1993 swell to more than 90,000 baptized believers worshiping in 920 new churches only seven years later. A missionary to a North Indian people began his ministry among just 28 churches in 1989. By the year 2000, a church-planting movement had swept through the population, leaving more than 4,500 churches with an estimated 300,000 baptized believers in them. An East Asian missionary reported, "I launched my three-year master plan in November, 2000. My vision was to see 200 new churches started among my people group over the next three years. But four months later, we had already reached that goal! After only six months, we had already seen 360 churches planted and more than 10,000 new believers baptized! Now I'm asking God to enlarge my vision."[5]

Our definition of church-planting movements emerges from the movements themselves. As such, it is a descriptive rather than a prescriptive definition, describing what *is* happening in the movements rather than prescribing what could or should happen.

---

[5]Adapted from Garrison, *Church Planting Movements*, 16–17.

To take a descriptive point of view is to humbly admit that the real work of multiplying churches is a divine accomplishment. As we stated earlier, it is God's work and we are invited participants. Granted, there are vital roles for humans to play, and we should never minimize these roles, but ultimately the power behind the movement rests in him and not in us. This is why, rather than trying to squeeze him into our flawed predictions or prescriptions, we recognize him as the God of the movement who requires us to alter our understanding and our behavior to be on mission with him.

It's not easy to remain descriptive when we talk about God or his activity in the world. Each of us comes to the table with preconceived notions about how God must work. An analysis of church-planting movements is not immune to this tendency. Therefore, it may be helpful to carefully unpack this descriptive definition, examining each of its five parts.

Rapid. First, a church-planting movement reproduces rapidly. Within a very short time, newly planted churches are already starting new churches that follow the same pattern of rapid reproduction. "How rapid is rapid?" you might ask. Perhaps the best answer is, "Faster than you think possible." Though the rate varies from place to place, church-planting movements always outstrip the population growth rate as they race toward reaching the entire people group.

No part of the definition of church-planting movements has garnered as much controversy as the word *rapid*. "How can rapidly reproducing churches be real or authentic churches?" the skeptical ask. Initially, I contented myself with the accuracy of the definition. Asking whether or not these churches could rapidly multiply was like asking whether or not a bumblebee could fly. By our current knowledge of physics, a bumblebee's flight seems impossible, and yet it flies. In the same way, arguing whether or not these churches could or should multiply rapidly seemed dwarfed by the fact that they simply did multiply rapidly.

In the years that followed the publication of this descriptive definition, we noticed that those who do not believe churches should reproduce rapidly were working, either consciously or subconsciously, to subvert their rapid reproduction. These speed critics argue that they oppose rapidity in the name of biblical faithfulness, even though the New Testament era was witness to some of the fastest church multiplication in history.

Rapid reproduction accurately describes church-planting movements, but more interesting are the reasons for it. Why do these churches reproduce rapidly? There are two reasons: (1) because they can, and (2) because they must.

Churches in church-planting movements reproduce rapidly because they *can*. The churches themselves are highly reproducible. With no land to purchase or facilities to construct, no professional staff to hire or salary to raise, these churches lack many of the brakes that slow and even halt traditional church-planting efforts. The large and growing number of church planters in the movements also contributes to rapid reproduction. When primary church planters are church members themselves, it takes little imagination to see how they can accelerate reproduction.

Simple church structures and growing numbers of church planters explain how movements reproduce so rapidly, but not why they *must*. In church-planting movements, new Christians earnestly believe their family members and friends are lost without Jesus Christ. The strength of this belief overwhelms their fear of ostracism, persecution, and even death. As they win their friends and family to Christ, they gather them into new communities of discipleship, fellowship, ministry, and worship. Since these new communities typically meet in homes, space is limited. This limitation, this seeming weakness, is a final factor that propels the movement to multiply rapidly into more and more homes. It is the reason why their churches must reproduce rapidly.

Multiplication. The second key word in our definition of church-planting movements is *multiplication*. Church-planting movements do not simply add new churches. They multiply. Surveys of church-planting movements indicate that most churches in the movement are engaged in starting multiple new churches. Church-planting movements multiply churches and believers like Jesus multiplied the loaves and fish.

In church-planting movements, we rarely detect modest goals of ten or twenty additional churches in a country or city. Instead, these churches and their members are satisfied with nothing less than reaching their entire people group or city for Christ. As each church realizes that it has the capacity and responsibility to reproduce itself, the numbers start to compound.

Indigenous. *Indigenous* literally means "generated from within" as opposed to started by outsiders. In church-planting movements, the first church or churches may be started by outsiders, but very quickly momentum shifts from outsiders to insiders. Consequently, within a short time the new believers coming to Christ in church-planting movements may not even know that a foreigner was ever involved in the work. For the growing number of believers, the movement looks, acts, and feels like their own.

Churches planting churches. Though missionaries or church planters may plant the first churches, at some point the churches or their members themselves get into the act. When these churches begin planting churches, a tipping point is reached, resulting in a movement of church multiplication. It is difficult to say when the actual tipping point occurs, but at some point a critical number of new churches and new church plants is reached and, like falling dominoes, the movement cascades forward of its own momentum. Many situations have fallen short of becoming church-planting movements at just this critical juncture, as outsiders sought to gain or regain control of the rapidly reproducing churches. But once the momentum of reproducing churches outstrips the ability of anyone to control it, the movement is well underway.

Sweeps through a people group or population segment. Finally, church-planting movements occur within people groups or interrelated population segments. Because church-planting movements involve communication of the gospel message, they are naturally bound within the limits of those who share a common language and ethnicity. The story doesn't end there, however. As the gospel transforms the lives of these new believers, it compels them to take the message of hope to other people groups.

What Church-Planting Movements Are Not

Now that we have established our descriptive definition of church-planting movements, we can eliminate some of the other acts of God that are sometimes confused with church-planting movements.

Not revivals or spiritual awakenings. Church-planting movements are not the same as revivals or spiritual awakenings. Unlike great revivals or spiritual awakenings that periodically occur among Christians, church-planting movements occur within unreached people groups or concentrations of lostness. The lost aren't merely dozing in Christ, needing a revival; they are dead in their sins and trespasses until Christ gives them life.

Not mass evangelism. Church-planting movements are more than mass evangelism. We have all seen the work of dynamic evangelists whose gospel proclamations draw thousands to salvation. But what happens after the stadium empties and the evangelist moves on to a new city? Too often, the commitment to Christ ends with the mass meeting. The same cannot be said of church-planting movements. Church-planting movements multiply churches, communities of disciples.

While it is true that church-planting movements include massive evangelistic proclamation, they go the second mile—leaving in their wake hundreds of new churches where discipleship, worship, and spiritual development continue. In church-planting movements, mass evangelism is diffused through rapidly multiplying new churches.

> *In church-planting movements, mass evangelism is diffused through rapidly multiplying new churches.*

Not people movements. Beyond mass evangelism is mass conversion, in which great numbers of lost people respond to the gospel. These are sometimes called "people movements." Church-planting movements are not just people movements. People movements are occurring in several locations around the world today, but they do not always lead to multiplying churches. Thousands of Muslims coming to Christ in Azerbaijan, Algeria, and other places show us that the Holy Spirit is at work in people movements. What distinguishes these people movements from church-planting movements is the troubling absence of new churches. For a variety of reasons, many of these mass conversions aren't producing the pool of new churches needed to assimilate the converts. When this disparity occurs, these mass conversions run the risk of being a miraculous flash in the pan, like a quick burst of light that dissipates into nothing. People movements are a part of church-planting movements, but in church-planting movements the new believers gather into new churches.

Not the church growth movement. Church-planting movements are not the church growth movement. The church growth movement pertains to a school of missions and church growth begun in the mid-1960s by Donald McGavran at Fuller Theological Seminary in Pasadena, California. At the risk of losing nonmissionary readers, let's take a moment to draw some significant distinctions between the church growth movement and church-planting movements.

There are at least three areas where the church growth movement differs significantly from church-planting movements. First, the church growth movement has come to associate bigger churches with better churches. Growing megachurches has become an increasingly common part of the evangelical landscape. Church-planting movements, on the other hand, exhibit the principle that smaller is better. Intimate house churches are at the heart of every church-planting movement.

Second, the church growth movement has directed many missionaries to focus on perceived "harvest fields" or "responsive fields" at the expense of unreached—and what may appear to be unresponsive—fields. By contrast, a descriptive analysis reveals that God has chosen to launch most church-planting movements among the least likely candidates: unreached people groups, which have often been dismissed by those looking for more responsive harvest fields.

Third, the church growth movement advocates pouring resources, particularly foreign missionaries, into responsive harvest fields—the rationale being that there are limited harvesters, so we should conserve them from difficult areas and invest them instead into people groups that have already proven to be responsive to the gospel.

Despite reasoned arguments to the contrary, descriptive analysis has revealed that pouring more and more foreign resources into the harvest is actually contrary to the way God is at work in church-planting movements. In church-planting movements, the role of the foreign missionary is vital at the beginning. Once the people group begins responding, it is equally important for outsiders to become less and less prominent while the new believers themselves become the primary harvesters and leaders of the movement.

Keeping these distinctions in mind will help us avoid seeing church-planting movements through the lens of the church growth movement and free us to see what God is doing and how he is at work.

Not just a divine miracle. Church-planting movements are not just a divine miracle. Church-planting movement practitioners have been quick to give glory for the movement to God, so much so, in fact, that some have described the movements as purely an act of God. Reducing a church-planting movement to a purely divine miracle has the effect of dismissing the role of human responsibility in the mission of God. If God alone is producing church-planting movements, then God alone is to blame when there are no church-planting movements. The truth is that God has given Christians vital roles to play in the successes or failures of these movements.

If God alone is producing church-planting movements, then God alone is to blame when there are no church-planting movements. The truth is that God has given Christians vital roles to play in the successes or failures of these movements.

Over the past few years, we have learned that there are many ways we can obstruct and even stop church-planting movements. In many instances, well-intentioned activities are out of step with the ways of God and may slow or even kill a movement. Church-planting movements are miraculous in the way they transform lives, but they are also vulnerable to human tampering.

Not a Western invention. Church-planting movements are not a Western invention. Some years ago I addressed a gathering of North African church leaders on the subject of church-planting movements. Just before the session began, someone warned me, "These brothers and sisters aren't looking for the latest church-planting methods from the United States. If that's what you've brought from America, you're wasting your time and theirs." With this admonition in mind, I began with an honest confession: "Church-planting movements are not an American phenomenon. In fact, growing up in the United States I almost missed seeing this amazing thing that God was unfolding among the lost all over the world."

Church-planting movements did not originate in the West, though they have occurred in the Western world, along with other parts of our globe. Church-planting movements are a description of what God is doing in many countries, but they are not limited to one type of culture or another. As for the North African church leaders, all they really wanted to know was that it was something God was doing. From that point on they enthusiastically embraced this powerful instrument of God's salvation.

Not an end in itself. Finally, a church-planting movement is a means to an end, not an end in itself. Those who pursue church-planting movements sometimes err on the side of exuberance. They get so excited about church-planting movements that they virtually sell their souls for the sake of the movement. When this happens, they have allowed the movement to slip into a role that only God should occupy in our life. The results are disastrous both for the movement and for the individual.

Church-planting movements are simply a way that God is drawing massive numbers of lost persons into saving community with himself. That saving relationship—rather than any movement or method—is what touches the end vision, the glory of God that we so desire.[6]

Why Church-Planting Movements Are So Important

This brings us to a final important question as we examine church-planting movements. Why are they so important? Why do you need to study and understand them?

First, church-planting movements are important because God is mightily at work in them. Every church-planting movement practitioner comes to the same humble awareness that God is doing something awesome in their midst. We can scheme and dream, but only

---

[6]Adapted from Garrison, *Church Planting Movements,* 21–26.

God can turn the hearts of unbelievers to himself. If there were no other reasons than this, it would be enough. If we want to be on mission with God and not simply pursuing our own agenda, then we must turn our attention to how he is using church-planting movements to bring entire people groups to himself.

Second, we need to learn all we can about church-planting movements because of the critical role God has reserved for us to play. The difference between church-planting movements and near-church-planting movements is often the difference between God's people properly aligning themselves with what God is doing versus failing to align themselves with what he is doing.

Some aspects of church-planting movements are logical and intuitive, but many are not. Those who miss this point may well find themselves like the apostle Paul before his conversion—"kick[ing] against the goads" (Acts 26:14). A goad was a first-century cattle prod used by the herder to prod the livestock where he wanted them to go. When we act out of our own reasoning rather than aligning ourselves with God's ways, we are like an obstinate goat that puts itself at cross purposes with the Master's will. If we want to be on mission with God, we must pause long enough to understand the ways of God and then choose to go his way. Only then can we know with some degree of certainty that we are aligned as his instruments and not misaligned as his obstacles.

The third reason church-planting movements are so important is because of what they accomplish. Without exaggeration we can say that church-planting movements are the most effective means in the world today for drawing lost millions into saving, disciple-building relationships with Jesus Christ. That may appear to be an ambitious claim, but it is an accurate one, and an honest description of how God is winning a lost world.

> *Church-planting movements are the most effective means in the world today for drawing lost millions into saving, disciple-building relationships with Jesus Christ.*

Christian researchers tell us that every day more than 100,000 men, women, and children pass from this life without ever knowing the blessing of a saving relationship with God through Jesus Christ.[7] For whatever flaws an individual church may have, churches are a part of God's plan—his exclusive plan for rescuing the perishing from an eternity of separation from the Father's saving love. A Christian who can see 100,000 lost souls pass into eternity each day and not grasp the urgency of church multiplication is a Christian who has lost his faith in the truth of the gospel. If salvation is real, and hell is real, then church multiplication is more than just an option; it is an imperative.

Finally, and arguably most significant of all, church-planting movements are important because they exponentially multiply the glory of God. The prophet Habakkuk set a benchmark for us with a vision of a time when "the earth will be filled with the knowledge of the glory of the LORD as the waters cover the sea" (Habakkuk 2:14). The glory of the Lord is nothing less than the clear revelation of God himself. This is why Jesus came: to reveal to us God's glory.

The ultimate end for all Christians must be to glorify God. We glorify God when we reveal him in all of his fullness. Christians find the fullness of God in his Son and experience that fullness as his Son comes to dwell in our hearts and through our lives. "We have seen his glory, the glory of the one and only Son, who came from the Father, full of grace and truth" (John 1:14).

In his grace, Christ conveys this same glory to all who invite him into their lives as Savior and Lord. For those who submit to his reign in their lives, Christ fills them with his glory, the very glory of God. This is why Paul could say with confidence, "Christ in you, [is] the hope of glory" (Colossians 1:27). This is also why Jesus told his disciples, "This is to my Father's glory, that you bear much fruit, showing yourselves to be my disciples" (John 15:8).

Mankind without Jesus Christ may bear God's image, but not his glory. In church-planting movements, the glory of the Lord is spreading from person to person, people group to people group, like a swelling

---

[7]Extrapolated from the global mortality of approximately 170,000 persons dying each day, based on 2008 global population of about 6.7 billion. The most generous figures (David Barrett's *World Christian Encyclopedia*) allow for 33 percent of those to be Christians, leaving approximately 114,000 to perish each day into a Christless eternity.

river as it begins to spill out over its banks until it covers the earth as the waters cover the sea. No other mode of redemption has so quickly and effectively multiplied the glory of God in the hearts of so many. No other means has drawn so many new believers into ongoing communities of faith where they have continued to grow in Christlikeness. This is why church-planting movements merit our attention, why we must learn all we can about them, and why they are so very important.

Discussion Points

1. What are church-planting movements, and how do they differ from traditional church plants?

2. What are five universal elements found in all church-planting movements?

3. What role do we play in church-planting movements?

4. Why are church-planting movements so important?

Further Reading

Allen, Roland. *Missionary Methods: St. Paul's or Ours?* London: World Dominion Press, 1962.

————. *Spontaneous Expansion of the Church—and the Causes Which Hinder It.* Reprint. Eugene, OR: Wipf and Stock Publishers, 1997.

Garrison, David. *Church Planting Movements: How God Is Redeeming a Lost World.* Midlothian, VA: WIGTake Resources, 2004.

Greeson, Kevin. *The Camel: How Muslims Are Coming to Faith in Christ!* Arkadelphia, AR: WIGTake Resources, 2007.

McGavran, Donald. *Bridges of God: A Study in the Strategy of Missions.* New York: Friendship Press, 1981.

Simson, Wolfgang. *Houses That Change the World.* Emmelsbull, Germany: OM Publishing, 1999.

29

MEASURING PROGRESS
IN THE MISSION OF GOD

Gary R. Corwin

God is on a mission and he is not answerable to us for how he goes about it or for his timetable for accomplishing it. He has commanded and ordained that his people, the church globally, are to be his agents to carry out major portions of his mission in the world. This is a high privilege and calling, but both its end—God's glory—and its accomplishment are in his hands, not ours. God will accomplish his mission, but oh the loss to us if we fail to fulfill the part he has assigned to us.

> *God will accomplish his mission, but oh the loss to us if we fail to fulfill the part he has assigned to us.*

It is imperative, therefore, that God's people both understand the task they have been assigned and put their lives on a footing that declares the priority of seeing his purposes accomplished in the world. This chapter surveys the approaches that have been employed to enable strategic planning, implementation, and evaluation of the human side of the mission of God. The plans and strategies related to God's mission are as old as the church and can be numbered in the hundreds or more. In the same vein, evaluation and progress measurement efforts are far more detailed and creative than most people would imagine.[1]

---

[1]David B. Barrett and James W. Reapsome, *Seven Hundred Plans to Evangelize the World: The Rise of a Global Evangelization Movement* (Birmingham, AL: New Hope, 1988). See also David B. Barrett, Todd M. Johnson, and Peter F. Crossing, "Missiometrics 2008: Reality Checks for Christian World Communions," *International Bulletin of Missionary Research* 32 (January

Because of this expansive scope, we will merely sample a few approaches to God's mission that have been undertaken in two broad categories: the global macro picture, and the agency and church micro pictures.

Global Macro Picture

Let us start by looking at approaches to the global macro picture. The best way to do that is to begin with a brief sketch of the historical background that led us to where we are today.

People group thinking. It is no exaggeration to say that it would be impossible to do justice to the global macro picture in the last half-century without addressing the concept of people groups, and that one cannot speak meaningfully on that subject without reference to the names of Donald McGavran and Ralph Winter. McGavran, a long-time missionary to India, founder of the church growth movement, and founding dean of the School of World Mission of Fuller Theological Seminary, was a pioneer of people group thinking.

Ken Mulholland observes, "In his writings, McGavran sought to identify the factors that facilitate and those that impede church growth. Investigating various people movements within society, he used his findings to identify principles for church growth. McGavran also emphasized the importance of allowing persons to become Christian without forcing them to cross cultural barriers [homogeneous unit principle]. He was committed to the establishment of a church movement within every segment of the human mosaic."[2]

Winter, who had been a colleague of McGavran's at Fuller, had also been a missionary in Guatemala, where he and others had launched the theological education by extension movement. He later was instrumental in founding the U.S. Center for World Mission and related ministries, such as the William Carey Library and William Carey University. His most important contribution related to people groups, however, was in convincing others of their importance to the mission of

---

2008): 29, where point 42 states, "Over 20 centuries Christians have announced 1,870 global plans to evangelize the world; 250 plans focused on AD 2000 fell short of goals."
[2]Ken Mulholland, "McGavran, Donald A.," *Evangelical Dictionary of World Missions*, ed. A. Scott Moreau (Grand Rapids: Baker, 2000), 607.

God. He accomplished this with a great deal of his speaking and writing, but none more significantly than in his 1974 address to the First International Congress on World Evangelization in Lausanne, Switzerland. As part of *Missiology and the Social Sciences*, published by the William Carey Library in 1996, I wrote:

> When in 1974 Dr. Ralph Winter gave his famous speech, "The Highest Priority: Cross-Cultural Evangelism" . . . a new era in mission history was begun. It was not really so much that a new vision was born, but that a new way of looking at an old vision was provided. This focus breathed new life and a new sense of imperative into the very old biblical task of taking the gospel to the unreached where they are least reached. . . .
>
> Over the last two decades since that speech an astounding shift has taken place. The concept of unreached peoples (in contrast to unreached people) is on the lips of virtually everyone concerned with the mission of Christ's church. The 1991 encyclical *Redemptoris Missio*, issued by John Paul II, is elegant testimony to just how far the concept has come. This has been a remarkable boon to world evangelization, reflected in the strategic outreach planning of agencies and churches, and in the mobilization of new resources to see the task completed.[3]

Looking back on this seminal address, Donald McGavran commented, "Ralph Winter proved beyond any reasonable doubt that in the world today 2,700,000,000 men and women cannot hear the gospel by 'near neighbor evangelism.' They can hear it only by evangelists who cross cultural, linguistic and geographical barriers, patiently learn that other culture and language, preach the gospel by word and deed across the decades, and multiply reproductive and responsible Christian churches."[4]

The evangelism scale. The E-scale measures the linguistic and cultural distance missionaries must cross for effective evangelism to take place. E-1 evangelism involves evangelists going to their own people.

---

[3]Gary R. Corwin, "Sociology and Missiology: Reflections on Mission Research," in *Missiology and the Social Sciences*, Evangelical Missiological Society Series Number 4, ed. Edward Rommen and Gary Corwin (Pasadena, CA: William Carey Library, 1996), 21–22.
[4]Ralph D. Winter, "The New Macedonia: A Revolutionary New Era in Mission Begins," in *Perspectives on the World Christian Movement: A Reader*, rev. ed., ed. Ralph D. Winter and Steven C. Hawthorne (Pasadena, CA: William Carey Library, 1981, 1992), B-157.

This "near neighbor evangelism" involves the same language and culture, and the only barrier to be crossed is between the Christian community and the immediate culture in which it resides. E-2 evangelism involves crossing barriers into a near but not identical language and cultural situation that would be characterized by significant but not overwhelming differences. E-3 evangelism involves people who "live, work, talk, and think in languages and cultural patterns utterly different" from those of the evangelists who come to them.[5]

The import of the E-scale for strategic planning and implementation in the mission of God, and even as a basis for evaluation, is summarized well by Winter:

> The master pattern of the expansion of the Christian movement is first for special E-2 and E-3 efforts to cross cultural barriers into new communities and to establish strong, ongoing, vigorously evangelizing denominations, and then for that national church to carry the work forward on the really high-powered E-1 level. We are thus forced to believe that until every tribe and tongue has a strong, powerfully evangelizing church in it, and thus an E-1 witness with it, E-2 and E-3 efforts coming from the outside are still essential and highly urgent.[6]

The people group scale. The flip side of the E-scale is to look at the same linguistic and cultural distance from the point of view of the people group involved rather than that of the evangelist. Logically enough, this is called the P-scale and measures a people group's cultural distance from the nearest evangelizing church. A P-1 situation is one in which culturally relevant gospel-witnessing churches, capable of evangelizing that people, can be found within the people group itself. A P-2 situation is one in which a strong gospel witness can be found in a culturally and linguistically near, but not identical, people group. "To follow Christ the potential convert would have to cross both a cultural barrier as well as the 'stained-glass' barrier by adopting the social and cultural values of a local church within a people other than their own."[7] A P-3 situation is

---

[5]Ibid., B-162 and B-163.
[6]Ibid., B-165.
[7]Winter, "The New Macedonia," in *Perspectives on the World Christian Movement: A Study Guide*, 1999 edition, 194.

one in which people live in a culture without a culturally relevant gospel-witnessing church among them. There are also no nearby cultures similar to their own that have churches. To follow Christ will require crossing very significant cultural and social barriers.[8]

Unreached people groups (UPGs). In the decade immediately following Lausanne I in 1974, some important work was done in clarifying definitions. Of special importance was a meeting in March of 1982, sponsored by the Lausanne Strategy Working Group, that focused specifically on that task and managed to agree on two very basic definitions that would have great significance in the following decades:

A People Group is "a significantly large grouping of individuals who perceive themselves to have a common affinity for one another because of their shared language, religion, ethnicity, residence, occupation, class or caste, situation, etc. or combination of these." For evangelistic purposes it is "the largest group within which the Gospel can spread as a church planting movement without encountering barriers of understanding or acceptance."

An Unreached People Group is "a people group within which there is no indigenous community of believing Christians able to evangelize this people group."[9]

> An Unreached People Group is "a people group within which there is no indigenous community of believing Christians able to evangelize this people group."

It was upon these definitions that the overwhelming majority of the subsequent strategic planning, implementation, and progress measurement efforts were built, especially in the global macro picture but also in so many of the micro-picture tasks in which agencies and churches were directly engaged.

The year 2000 was the focal point of many of the goals that were set, including seeing all the unreached people groups "engaged"[10] by that

[8] Ibid.
[9] Ralph Winter, "Unreached Peoples: Recent Developments in the Concept," *Mission Frontiers* (August–September 1989), www.missionfrontiers.org/issue/article/unreached-peoples.
[10] "Engaged" means that "work has begun on-site or in specific 'non-residential' endeavor." Ralph D. Winter, "Momentum Building in Global Missions: Basic Concepts in Frontier Missiology," in *Perspectives on the World Christian Movement: A Study Guide*, 1992 edition, E-2.

year.[11] While an even more ambitious goal of seeing all unreached people groups "reached"[12] by the year 2000 was held up by many, in the end neither goal was achieved, though considerable progress was made and commitment to the task was redoubled.

UPG research and advocacy. Undoubtedly the largest endeavor (at least in terms of data processed and pages published) to employ the people group concept to describe the global state of the church and of those without the church is the work of David Barrett, Todd Johnson, and others, published most prominently in two editions of the *World Christian Encyclopedia* (1982, 2001), one volume of *World Christian Trends AD 30– AD 2200* (2001), and annual reports dating from 1985 and published each January in the *International Bulletin of Missionary Research*.

The latest annual report available at the time of this writing is "Missiometrics 2008: Reality Checks for Christian World Communions."[13] This brief article, which builds on the extensive work in the earlier volumes, makes clear that the breadth of content monitored by this team truly is remarkable. This edition includes three tables (together with commentary): (a) "World population, evangelization, and Christianity: global status and daily change"; (b) "An AD 2008 reality check: 50 new facts and figures about trends and issues concerning empirical global Christianity"; and (c) "Status of global mission, presence, and activities, AD 1800–2025." While it is not possible, for reasons of space, to provide examples from each of these tables, it is possible to give some idea of the specificity involved by repeating just the pull-out quote: "Out of the global increase of 77,000 affiliated Christians every day, 70,000 (or 91 percent) can be found in Africa, Asia, or Latin America."[14]

---

[11]Gary R. Corwin, "Just Where Are the Frontiers?" in *Evangelical Missions Quarterly* 28 (April 1992): 123; and Patrick Johnstone, "The Church Is Bigger Than You Think," in *Perspectives on the World Christian Movement: A Study Guide*, 1999 edition, 202.

[12]"Reached" refers to "a people group in which there is an indigenous community of believing Christians able to evangelize this people group." Winter, "Momentum Building in Global Missions," in *Perspectives on the World Christian Movement: A Study Guide*, 1992 edition, E-2.

[13]David B. Barrett, Todd M. Johnson, and Peter F. Crossing, "Missiometrics 2008: Reality Checks for Christian World Communions," in *International Bulletin of Missionary Research* 32 (January 2008): 27–30.

[14]Ibid., 28.

Two other global-focus entities that for years have sought to connect and engage God's people to the statistical realities concerning gospel penetration of the world's people groups are *Operation World* and the related endeavors of Patrick Johnstone and the Joshua Project. Dave Guiles, in an article entitled "Understanding People Groups," has done a good job of succinctly describing the emphasis of each:

Operation World. Having gone through at least twenty-one editions, *Operation World* is a user-friendly tool designed to "inform for prayer" and "mobilize for witness" for the salvation of the nations (Johnstone 2001, xv). They do not maintain a unique database, but rather draw heavily upon the information contained in *The World Christian Encyclopedia* and Wycliffe Bible Translators' *Ethnologue.* They also claim to have contributed significantly to the information in these sources. *Operation World* provides statistical data on people groups, answers and challenges for prayer, descriptions of the state of the church and evangelization, and much more.

The Joshua Project. The Joshua Project states its purpose as [follows]: "The mission and passion of Joshua Project is to identify and highlight the people groups of the world that have the least exposure to the Gospel and the least Christian presence in their midst. Joshua Project shares this information to encourage pioneer church-planting movements among every ethnic people group."

The Project maintains a massive online database, which allows easy access to *people group* and *unreached people group* information by country, region, affinity bloc, people, religion and more. Unreached people groups are defined as less than 5 percent adherent and 2 percent evangelical. They are constantly seeking new information from mission agencies and field staff to update their database. They currently identify 16,072 *people groups*, 6,918 *unreached people groups* and 6,800 *living languages*. The Project follows the definitions of the Lausanne Strategy Working Group of 1982.[15]

Agency and the Church Micro Picture

Much more could be said about any of these global-focus entities,

---

[15]Dave Guiles, "Understanding People Groups," unpublished paper, July 2005.

but instead we'll look at the more narrowly focused approaches some agencies and churches pursue.

Transitional influencers. Two highly effective transitional entities that have their feet planted firmly on both sides of the global/narrow (macro/micro) focus divide are Wycliffe Bible Translators and the International Mission Board of the Southern Baptist Convention.

Wycliffe Bible Translators. The *Ethnologue*, a Wycliffe product, is self-described as "an encyclopedic reference work cataloging all of the world's 6,909 known living languages." This body of work, now more than fifty years old, plays a huge role in the ongoing global assessment of gospel penetration among the peoples of the world, as well as in the more agency-specific goal, for which Wycliffe is famous, of seeing the Bible translated into the heart languages of all the world's peoples. The *Ethnologue* website provides a useful glimpse of the massive scope of this research effort. Its purpose is "to provide a comprehensive listing of the known living languages of the world." The book is divided into six major sections:

1. *Statistical Summaries* offer numerical tabulations of living languages and number of speakers by world area, by language size, by language family, and by country.

2. *Languages of the World* provide detailed information on all known living languages of the world organized by area and by country.

3. *Language Maps* detail country, continent, and world maps of languages spoken in specific regions.

4. *Language Name Index* lists the 41,186 distinct names that are associated with the 7,413 languages in this edition.

5. *Language Code Index* lists the 7,413 three-letter language identification codes used throughout the volume.

6. *Country Index* lists country names, sections referenced in the book, and the page on which its maps begin, if there are any.[16]

International Mission Board. Like Wycliffe, the International Mission Board has employed its research and assessment capabilities to make a

---

[16]"Introduction to the Printed Volume," Ethnologue website, www.ethnologue.com/ethno_docs/introduction.asp.

huge contribution both to defining reality on a global basis and to ensuring that its own efforts as an agency have been as effective in church planting and gospel ministry as possible. The byline for the Global Research Department is "We gather, analyze, systematize, preserve and disseminate strategic information for the multiplying of churches among all peoples." They do it well; and many, both within and outside of the Southern Baptist Convention, have benefited from their labors. As an agency representative to a consortium of agencies working among Muslims, I have experienced this firsthand in recent years.

Their website further describes the sections of the department this way:

Analysis—Analyzes strategic information for communicating mission-critical findings to missions strategists.

Field Services and Assessments—Identifies, develops, and communicates approaches that promote evangelism, church growth, and church-planting movements within people groups and people-group segments. Leads in field assessments in order to provide objective reports measuring the vitality of overseas work. Communicates lessons learned to other missions strategists.

Jenkins Research Library—Provides expertise in research services and assistance for field personnel, IMB staff, trustees, SBC constituents, and the general public, as well as country and people-group materials and reference services for missionaries and missionary candidates.

International Learning Center Libraries—Provides research services and assistance for IMB field personnel, children of field personnel, and IMB staff. An important function of the libraries is to design and conduct age-appropriate research training and library orientations for adults and children.

Archives and Records Management—Serves as the corporate memory of the International Mission Board by identifying, organizing and preserving information that reflects the Southern Baptist international missions experience. This information is available through appropriate applications and formats to assist in decision making.

Research Data and Delivery Services—Gathers strategic information from field personnel, national believers, mission agencies, and researchers. Develops, maintains, and promotes systems for linking mission-critical information. Reports strategic information to internal and external missions strategists.[17]

One project that captures the spirit of the department particularly well is called the Global Analysis Project—"Closing the GAP." The website succinctly summarizes it this way:

> We have been captured by a vision of what God intends to do among the peoples of the world. It is clear, however, that there exists a wide gulf between our current situation and that day when "every nation, tribe, people, and tongue" will worship before the throne. The Global Analysis Project is an ongoing study of the nature of this gap and its implications for our mission task. The Global Analysis Project explores demographic trends, political dynamics, economic themes, religious affiliations, human needs and more. The project also identifies barriers that hinder the spread of the gospel as well as bridges that may facilitate it.[18]

Again, much more could be said about the work of the International Mission Board with regard to measuring progress in the mission of God. Other chapters and writers tackle significant parts of that.

Progress assessment measurement. A slightly different but absolutely crucial aspect of the progress assessment question is "How do we measure progress in the central task of church planting, not just in a global sense but in the nuts-and-bolts realities of a particular local effort?"

The eight phases of church planting. One of the tools mostly widely employed to this end is a methodology as old as the one employed by the apostle Paul. It has been described with slight variation in the writings of notable missiologists like David Hesselgrave,[19] and has evolved into what is commonly known today as the eight phases of pioneer church

---

[17]"About Us," IMB Global Research Department website, http://public.imb.org/globalresearch/Pages/AboutUs.aspx.

[18]"Closing the 'GAP,'" IMB Global Research Department website, http://public.imb.org/globalresearch/Pages/GAP.aspx.

[19]See, for example, David J. Hesselgrave, *Planting Churches Cross-Culturally: North America and Beyond*, 2nd ed. (Grand Rapids: Baker, 2000); or George Patterson and Richard Scoggins, *Church Multiplication Guide*, rev. ed. (Pasadena, CA: William Carey Library, 2001).

planting. Many agencies, including large ones such as Frontiers and the International Mission Board, make extensive use of these phases in their strategic planning for, and ongoing evaluation of, the efforts of their many church-planting teams.

The name most closely associated with these eight phases is Dick Scoggins. In addition to being an experienced church planter, for decades Scoggins has trained other church planters. His website offers a free download of the *Church Planting Manual*, of which he is the primary author.[20] The website also offers a brief description of the eight phases of church planting, paraphrased here:

> Phase 1: Visioning—When someone, usually the team leader, gets a vision for a team in a particular country or people group. This leader or others may write a vision/strategy paper, develop a Covenant of Team Understandings (COTU), devise entrance strategies, and recruit a team.
>
> Phase 2: Landing—The team arrives, though often not all at the same time. Team members begin language and culture acquisition and learn team dynamics as they survive in a new culture. Their entrance strategy often has to be modified. Often team member character flaws are exposed at this point. Experience "tests" the team as they work through trials and conflicts.
>
> Phase 3: Evangelizing—Team member language acquisition has reached a level enabling members to give testimonies to locals. They devise and discern ways to contextualize the gospel message, which is being shared regularly. They develop understanding of how groups function in the culture and how to recognize a man or woman of peace and share the gospel within their group.
>
> Phase 4: Gathering (Discipling)—Locals have made professions of faith. Type of "soil" is discerned. Missionaries attempt to get groups to study Jesus in the Word so a cohesive social group can decide to follow Jesus as a group.
>
> Phase 5: Covenanting—A number from a cohesive social group have converted and are ready to commit to becoming a kingdom family (home church). Often peacemaking becomes crucial here. Group de-

---

[20]"Church Planting Manual," Dick Scoggins website, www.dickscoggins.com/page136.html.

cision dynamics are tested. Leaders (influencers) emerge. This phase culminates with the believers covenanting to be a church.

Phase 6: Leadership development—Church planter's focus shifts almost exclusively from the group to the leaders. The group begins to "own" areas of evangelism, shepherding, and mutual care expressed in the covenant. Discipleship chains are set up. This phase culminates with ordination of elders or appointment of deacons.

Phase 7: Reproducing—The church focuses on penetrating other cohesive social networks and starting new Bible studies that could develop into kingdom families. Usually leaders write a vision statement to this effect, which the congregation adopts. This phase culminates when a new group covenants to be a church, and a network of cooperating home communities is established with a shared eldership.

Phase 8: Exiting—A second generation of elders emerges, trained in discipleship chains, either from a new church plant or in the original church. (The elders are reproducing themselves.) This phase culminates when the new elders are ordained, some kind of a presbytery is formed, and the church planter leaves. Ephesians 4 ministries are functioning under the authority of the elders.[21]

Once again, there is much more that could be said than space allows. A worthy description of the essential nature and implications of the church-planting phases by veteran missionary and field director James Rockford, however, may suffice to round out the subject:

The Church Planting Phases are a combination of two tools in one:

1. A MEASURE or *yardstick*. Seven [now eight, according to Scoggins] clear phases, with definitions that endeavor to make as clear as possible what phase a team is at, and precisely when they will pass into the next phase.

2. A GUIDEBOOK. This is mainly the specific, numbered activities under each phase. While this is certainly not meant to be a cookbook, nor a list of mandatory steps that all teams must do, it does seek to comprehensively identify most of the activities teams should be focused on in

---

[21]"Eight Phases of Church Planting," Dick Scoggins website, www.dickscoggins.com/page190.html.

each phase, and it encourages teams to think ahead into the next phase. Regardless of what phase you are in as a team, the priorities for you at that time ought to be clear, and the CP phases try to make that possible. We have found having a large number of possible activities under each phase especially helpful for teams in resistant soils who tend to try a few activities over and over again, often losing hope and creativity.[22]

Mission agency metrics. Scott Harris's e-chapter "Measuring Church Planting Progress at Avant" in the *Discovering the Mission of God Supplement* describes Avant Ministries' system of metrics. It represents a successful attempt to take the church-planting phases approach to an even more specific and quantifiable level of accountability. The "evaluative elements" in this case are based on Avant's ends—i.e., how the agency understands its mandate of "biblically irreducible minimum" outcomes.[23]

As helpful as the church-planting phases and Avant metrics approaches have been to strategic planning and accountability for many churches and agencies, they are not the only effective means that have been undertaken. Arab World Ministries, for example, has developed a rolling, strategic five-year plan of specific ministry goals that a plan overseer closely monitors. Additionally, annual corporate leadership meetings include strategic reviews during which success is measured and new goals are agreed upon and incorporated. Progress is also reported to members and constituents a number of times each year through a series of report "Snapshots."

In a similar way, during the last decade Serving in Mission (SIM) has employed major peer review processes to assess reality, determine strategic next steps, and allocate human and other resources on a priority basis. This was first done through a year-long corporate review called "Seize the Day," in which significant feedback was gained from all the agency's stakeholders (especially including all the churches that have grown out of SIM's work), as well as from half a dozen missiologists from across the globe. This was then followed by an agency reorganization

---

[22]James Rockford, "Introducing the Pioneer Church Planting Phases," unpublished article, 2005, www.churchplantingphases.com/stuff/contentmgr/files/93521342e548c98722f90795 5bf51724/doc1/introducing_the_cp_phases.pdf, 2–3.

[23]See Scott Harris' e-chapter, "Measuring Church Planting Progress at Avant," in the *Discovering the Mission of God Supplement* e-book.

called "Faith Effects," which established specific priorities, assigned "champions," and deployed resources. This has more recently evolved to include "Country Reviews." These utilize the same basic approaches on a more local level and look not only at all the church-planting, mercy-ministry, and partnership efforts being undertaken to fulfill the agency purpose statement, but also at the country context to determine other ministry efforts needs. Review teams are established that include six or eight individuals with relevant expertise from elsewhere within or outside the agency, and within the country but not related to SIM.[24] So far, the record of these review teams has been noteworthy.

A Cautious Conclusion

Important voices during the last couple of decades have raised genuine concerns with regard to the macro picture associated with the year 2000, the unreached people "listing frenzy" of an earlier period, and about the many efforts to measure progress as being over-hyped and too simplistic. Many of these concerns are valid. Perhaps no one has been more outspoken than Samuel Escobar, a leading Latin American theologian and missiologist. We will give him the last word about what he calls "managerial missiology":

> Its basic tenet is that Christian mission can be reduced to a "manageable enterprise" thanks to the use of information technology, marketing techniques and managerial leadership. [Missiologists' efforts] to visualize the missionary task with "scientific" precision has led to the formulation of concepts such as "unreached peoples," "homogeneous units," the "10-40 window" or "adopt-a-people." These concepts and techniques need the correction that comes from a biblical view of people. What I am seeing in the application of these concepts in the mission field is that missionaries "depersonalize" people into "unreached targets," making them objects of hit-and-run efforts to get decisions that may be reported.[25]

---

[24]Information on both Arab World Ministries and Serving in Mission is based on this writer's personal experience as a twenty-seven-year member of SIM and long-time International Board member, and later as a part-time staff officer with AWM on loan from SIM.
[25]Samuel Escobar, *The New Global Mission: The Gospel from Everywhere to Everyone* (Downers Grove, IL: InterVarsity, 2003), 167.

Escobar has offered an important cautionary note. In our quest for being responsible stewards of our thinking, planning, and accountability, it is crucial that we not lose sight of the importance of our humanity and relationships as we focus on the task that the Lord Jesus Christ has left his people. May God give us the grace to be faithful in both callings.

Discussion Points

1. Why do you think "unreached" and "least-reached peoples" thinking has become so significant in the mission of God today?

2. What has history and/or personal experience taught us about the importance of good progress measurement related to good strategy?

3. What are the strengths and limitations in current approaches to measuring the global progress of the gospel? What about church-planting team progress?

4. How detailed does church-planting team progress measurement need to be? Does the particular context make a difference? How so?

Further Reading

Barrett, David B., Todd M. Johnson, and Peter F. Crossing. "Missiometrics 2008: Reality Checks for Christian World Communions." *International Bulletin of Missionary Research* 32 (January 2008): 27–30.

Johnstone, Patrick. *The Church Is Bigger Than You Think: The Unfinished Work of World Evangelisation.* Fearn, UK: Christian Focus, 2000.

Rommen, Edward, and Gary Corwin, eds. *Missiology and the Social Sciences.* Evangelical Missiological Society Series Number 4. Pasadena, CA: William Carey Library, 1996. See Gary Corwin, "Sociology and Missiology: Reflections on Mission Research," 19–29.

Winter, Ralph D., and Steven C. Hawthorne, eds. *Perspectives on the World Christian Movement.* Pasadena, CA: William Carey Library, 1999.

30

Breaking Bad
Missiological Habits

Christopher R. Little

If the father of the church growth movement, Donald A. McGavran (1897–1991), were among us today he would be quick to point out that several unnecessary obstacles have been placed in the path of discipling the nations. In fact, these obstacles appear to be "missionary made"— the result of bad missiological habits. Since it would be difficult to find a person more acquainted with factors that either facilitate or impede church growth, all those dedicated to reaching the lost should seriously consider his insights. Given the present context at the outset of the third millennium of Christian missions, he would surely argue for (1) the local sustainability of national workers, (2) the contextualization of the Christian faith, and (3) prioritism over holism.

Local Sustainability

In his magnum opus, *Understanding Church Growth*, McGavran, while interacting with the views of John Nevius, opined:

> The old or traditional method of mission is to hire paid agents from among the converts. To those chosen this is very welcome. They need the money. They speak the language fluently. They can go anywhere. They know the region. They live on small wages. When trained and tested, they do well as evangelists and village pastors. The method appears to be sound and advantageous to both missions and converts.
>
> But the old method has grave defects hidden under the surface. It

harms the convert who becomes an evangelist, for now he witnesses for money. Sincere though he doubtless is, he has become a paid agent. This method renders it impossible to distinguish true believers, because noting that some believers are put on salary, each inquirer—specially the more able—is tempted to become Christian in the expectation that in due time he will qualify for a job. Thus the method stirs a mercenary interest in all believers.[1]

For whatever reason, McGavran's view is being largely ignored today. Recent statistics show that national workers supported with Western funds has risen from 59,843 in 2001 to 80,834 in 2005. During the same period, the number of American missionaries sent overseas has declined from 42,787 to 41,329. What this means is that in 2005 the division of resources going for personnel overseas was 67.6 percent for foreign workers to 32.4 percent for homegrown ones.[2] This is roughly a two-to-one ratio.

Chief among those leading the charge to support nationals is K. P. Yohannan. His organization, Gospel for Asia, has experienced a 154 percent growth rate from 6,439 individuals in 1996 to 16,377 in 2005.[3] Moreover, Joseph D'Souza, director of Operation Mobilization in India, has argued that supporting nationals is "the way forward in many nations. To ignore it, attack it or play it down is to miss what God is doing in our world."[4]

Apparently these non-Western leaders have prevailed upon some of their Western counterparts. For example, George Verwer previously stood against more and more funds flowing from the West to the non-West,[5] but now seems to have embraced the idea.[6] In addition, Bob

---

[1]Donald McGavran, *Understanding Church Growth*, rev. ed. (Grand Rapids: Eerdmans, 1970), 337.

[2]This data was presented by A. Scott Moreau during his overview of the *Mission Handbook* at the Evangelical Missiological Society annual meeting in Minneapolis, 2007, pages 4–6 of handout.

[3]Michael Jaffarian, "The Statistical State of the North American Protestant Missions Movement," from the *Mission Handbook*, 20th ed. Cited in *International Bulletin of Missionary Research* 32/1(2008): 35–38.

[4]Joseph D'Souza, *Supporting Nationals Is the Way Forward (an analysis of the bogey of dependency)* (Secunderabad, India: 1999), 16.

[5]George Verwer, *Out of the Comfort Zone* (Waynesboro, GA: OM Publishing, 2000), 100ff.

[6]John Rowell, *To Give or Not to Give? Rethinking Dependency, Restoring Generosity, and Redefining Sustainability* (Tyrone, GA: Authentic, 2007), i.

Finley, founder of Christian Aid, in what can only be considered the inevitable end game of the movement to subsidize national workers, believes, "We must no longer misdirect the young people of our churches by trying to motivate them to go live and work in foreign cultures. Rather, we must challenge them to take up the cause of our Saviour NOW by living simply and sacrificially, and using their awesome power to earn money as a means to supply the needs of some of the thousands of God's servants who are out on all the mission fields of the world with little or no support."[7]

Some might take issue with the assertion that the Western evangelical missionary movement is in the midst of a crisis, but Wade Coggins, executive director of Evangelical Foreign Missions Association from 1975 to 1990, saw it coming: "If our churches give only their money, and not their sons and daughters, our missionary vision will be dead in a generation or less. We can't substitute money for flesh and blood. . . . On the surface, it appears cheaper to send our money for less expensive workers from Asia, Latin America, and Africa, but in the long run this strategy will be far more costly, because it will destroy missionary vision and there will be no support for either foreign or local missionaries."[8]

It is entirely possible, of course, that those who oppose the support of nationals can be disparaged for appearing self-serving and self-preserving. However, there is substantial evidence to show that such an agenda harms not only the Western church but the non-Western church as well. As a case in point, Ralph Winter relates the following:

> [A] mission executive called me asking my advice about 4,000 congregations in a certain country that had been planted without depending on foreign support, and were constantly in the process of planting still more congregations. However, an "Indigenous Ministries" type of agency began to "assist" some of the pastors financially. After a few years, 400 congregations had been taught to depend on foreign funds, and wanted to pull away from the other 3,600. The executive who called me was not worried about losing congregations to another group—"they

---

[7]Bob Finley, *Reformation in Foreign Missions* (Longwood, FL: Xulon Press, 2005), 245.
[8]Wade Coggins, "The Risks of Sending Our Dollars Only," *Evangelical Missions Quarterly* 24, no. 3 (1988): 204–5.

belong to God not to our denomination." He was sorry that these churches were being withdrawn from a dynamic movement in which churches did not need to wait for foreign funds in order to plant more congregations. Another executive commented that these 400 churches, instead of being truly helped, had been "reduced to beggars."[9]

Furthermore, Glenn Schwartz, executive director of World Mission Associates, reports that in one particular Asian country,

> People [are] coming . . . with money and literally 'buying' church leaders. They ask a church leader how much those other overseas people are paying them. "Oh, they give you only $35 a month. We pay $50!" In one congregation of 300 members, there were 262 members in foreign pay. One house church movement had 80 percent of their pastors on foreign support. And what was even more disturbing is that following the [turnover of the government], the church grew rapidly. That growth slowed considerably when foreign people and foreign money [later] poured in.[10]

This substantiates McGavran's observation a half-century ago: "Evidence shows that greatly aided churches do not grow greatly. There is seldom positive correlation between degree of aid and amount of growth."[11]

> *"Evidence shows that greatly aided churches do not grow greatly. There is seldom positive correlation between degree of aid and amount of growth."*

Those who persist in raising funds for national workers in the majority world could quickly dismiss McGavran's claim on the basis that his information is dated. Yet further research has only confirmed it. Wayne Allen, who investigated the consequences of paying national church workers among the Dayak people in Indonesia in the 1990s, compared the growth rates in four districts of national churches where the conditions were the same. One district received no subsidy for national workers, while the other three did. After analyzing the data, he concluded, "My findings reveal that

---

[9]Ralph Winter, "Six Spheres of Mission Overseas," *Mission Frontiers* 20, nos. 3–4 (1998): 41–42.

[10]Glenn Schwartz, *WMA Perspectives Special Edition* (Lancaster, PA: World Mission Associates, 2002), 2.

[11]Donald McGavran, *How Churches Grow: The New Frontiers of Mission* (London: World Dominion Press, 1959), 117.

the growth of the national church plateaued or halted when the mission began to subsidize the national church workers. . . . The use of subsidy in this instance did not further the cause of Christ. In all three districts where it was used, church growth ceased. In the district where it was not used, growth continued. Clearly, there is something wrong with providing foreign money for national pastors."[12]

For those who remain unconvinced about the disastrous effects of supporting national workers (especially pastors) with foreign funds, just imagine what would happen if well-meaning people from overseas came to an American church and started offering millions of dollars to those present. In relative terms, this is precisely what is happening in the reverse and why no one should be surprised that "non-Christians . . . say a new colonialism has dawned: 'First the Christians came with the Bible in one hand and the sword in the other. Now they come with the Bible in one hand and dollars in the other.'"[13]

> *"First the Christians came with the Bible in one hand and the sword in the other. Now they come with the Bible in one hand and dollars in the other."*

In the midst of this chaos, the church engaged in mission needs clarity. There is no better person to illuminate the path ahead than the best church planter the world has ever witnessed—the apostle Paul. With regard to how he sparked the successful expansion of the Christian faith in the first century, three facts are obvious: (1) he gave no inducements to either convert to or serve Christ (1 Corinthians 9:15–18; 2 Corinthians 2:17; 4:2); (2) he never transferred funds from churches in one area to pay for the ministries of churches in another (the Antiochene church offering along with the Gentile church offering to the Jerusalem church was for famine relief, not to subsidize local ministries—Acts 11:27–30; Romans 15:25–27); and (3) he expected churches to step out in mission using local resources (Acts

---

[12]Wayne Allen, "When the Mission Pays the Pastor," *Evangelical Missions Quarterly* 34, no. 2 (1998): 176, 181. See also Jim Lo, "I Tried Paying National Workers," *Evangelical Missions Quarterly* 35, no. 1 (1999): 14–16.

[13]Ajith Fernando, "Some Thoughts on Missionary Burnout," *Evangelical Missions Quarterly* 35, no. 4 (1999): 442.

19:9–10; 20:33–35; Romans 1:8; 16:19; 1 Thessalonians 1:6–8). May all those interested in the healthy advance of the global church today resolve to follow in his footsteps.[14]

Contextualization of Christianity

Being a third-generation missionary in India, McGavran was keenly aware of the ethnocentric tendencies of those who attempt to transmit the Christian faith from one culture to another. He referred to this phenomenon as "cultural overhang," and believed it was most damaging in the area of theological training. In his opinion, a "seminary which takes its curriculum and its standards from the famous seminaries of the West is in grave danger. . . . Hence we should discover and include in the curricula of the younger seminaries subjects that will help students to multiply the churches they serve."[15]

Of course, every culture reserves the right and duty to contextualize the gospel for its own people. This applies to the Western world as much as to the non-Western world. But as any particular community indigenizes Christianity for itself, there is an ever-present possibility to over-contextualize and unknowingly adopt cultural beliefs, values, and practices that are incongruent with Christianity. Commenting on the American scene, Andrew Walls observes:

> We may still recognize a specifically American Christianity . . . [characterized by] vigorous expansionism; readiness of invention; a willingness to make the fullest use of contemporary technology; finance, organization, and business methods; a mental separation of the spiritual and the political realms combined with a conviction of the superlative excellence, if not the universal relevance, of the historic constitution and values of the nation; and an approach to theology, evangelism, and church life in terms of addressing problems and finding solutions.[16]

In light of this, it is fairly obvious that "American missions are . . . both

---

[14]For more on this subject, see the author's *Mission in the Way of Paul: Biblical Mission for the Church in the Twenty-First Century* (Berne, Switzerland: Peter Lang, 2005).

[15]McGavran, *How Churches Grow*, 142.

[16]Andrew Walls, *The Missionary Movement in Christian History: Studies in the Transmission of Faith* (Maryknoll, NY: Orbis, 1996), 234–35.

products and purveyors of American culture."[17] A prime example is found in those who advocate the use of technology as a means to speed up world evangelization.[18] Yet technology is a profoundly dehumanizing force. Charles Taber notes:

"American missions are . . . both products and purveyors of American culture."

> Our affluence has led us to develop the ecclesiastical analog of capital-intensive methods of work. In our economy, the most expensive thing is human time, and any procedure or equipment which saves human time is an improvement. We have thus developed methods and techniques which require the large amounts of money we have at our disposal, and we unthinkingly give others the impression that is the way to do Christian work. In most of the rest of the world, equipment is prohibitively expensive, and the cheapest and most abundant resource is human time and strength. But we bypass the resource in which nationals are rich and major on the ones which we have in abundance. In such a "partnership" it is inevitable that the partner with the most highly valued resource will dominate.[19]

This domination directly points to the inherent danger of inadvertently imposing a Western formulation of Christianity upon the global church, and nowhere is this more evident, as McGavran contended, than in the area of theological education. Theological education in the non-Western world is regrettably still captive to Western philosophical constructs. Through its systematized methodology, God is not only approached as an idea to be examined but also forced into very arbitrary categories. These categories are oftentimes culturally derived and bound. For instance, the preoccupation with eschatology comes from a crisis-oriented culture that is obsessed with the future. Most of the rest of the world abides in a noncrisis environment contented with the present. But where, then, is a theology of the present in systematics? It's

---

[17]Andrew Walls, "The American Dimension in the History of the Missionary Movement," in *Earthen Vessels: American Evangelicals and Foreign Missions, 1880–1980*, ed. Joel Carpenter and Wilbert Shenk (Grand Rapids: Eerdmans, 1990), 8.

[18]Louis Bush and Lorry Lutz, *Partnering in Ministry: The Direction of World Evangelism* (Downers Grove, IL: InterVarsity, 1990), 63.

[19]Charles Taber, "Structures and Strategies for Interdependence in World Mission," in *Supporting Indigenous Ministries*, ed. Daniel Rickett and Dotsey Welliver (Wheaton: Billy Graham Center, 1997), 68.

absent, along with many other vital subjects, thereby indicating that the theologization process is riddled with human imperfections and cultural biases. One should therefore not be alarmed by impassioned calls for de-Westernization from the four corners of the earth.

- From India, Ebenezer Raj states: "Indian Christianity, partly, is contained in an alien crucible, with its Western patterns, rituals, festivals, music, architecture, unintelligible names and terms and sacerdotal paraphernalia, which according to close study have little relation to Indian cultures or the Bible. . . . The Lord Jesus who incarnated in the Asian soil can more naturally be recognised by the East, if stripped of this Western camouflage. . . . Some Christians in India, in their life style, have not sufficiently discerned the difference between Christian life and a pseudo-Western culture. This cultural alienation, especially in some parts of our country, does not help authenticate the Christian to his fellowmen."[20]

- From China, Jonathan Chao says: "Any attempt to 'improve' the present form of theological education is not enough. What we need is not renovation, but innovation. The whole philosophy and structure of theological education has to be completely reshaped."[21]

- From Korea, David Cho declares: "We must boldly remove the obstacles hindering Christian mission. We must remove all remnants of Western culture, Western colonialism, Western methodology, and Western thought from Asian theology, doctrine, churches, structures, and methods."[22]

- From the Commonwealth of Independent States, national leaders concerned with the state of theological education for their churches insist: "We do not want ready-made Western Christianity dumped on us." [23]

"We do not want ready-made Western Christianity dumped on us."

[20]Ebenezer Raj, *The Confusion Called Conversion* (Chennai, India: Bharat Jyoti, 1998), 38.

[21]Jonathan Chao, "Education and Leadership," in *The New Face of Evangelicalism: An International Symposium on the Lausanne Covenant*, ed. René Padilla (Downers Grove, IL: InterVarsity, 1976), 202.

[22]Jonathan Lewis, *World Mission: An Analysis of the World Christian Movement* (Pasadena, CA: William Carey Library, 1994), 15–24.

[23]Deyneka, Peter, and Anita Deyneka, "Evangelical Foreign Missionaries in Russia," *International Bulletin of Missionary Research* 22/2 (1998): 58.

- And from Africa, George Kinoti writes: "Theologies and church agendas developed in the West for Western Christians may not only distort Christianity in our circumstances but they may also make it peripheral to the needs of the African people. Therefore, I appeal to African theologians and pastors to make Christianity at once truly biblical and truly African—truly African in expression and relevance. For example, worship services, and especially music, need to become genuinely African, not mere copies or adaptations of Western forms, if they are to be truly meaningful to the worshippers and, I believe, to God."[24]

Accordingly, the Western church must now confer to the non-Western church the "first freedom," which "is the right to be different."[25] It can do this by renouncing the view that "the West is best" and by steadfastly working toward "the contextualization of theological education in all its dimensions" around the globe.[26]

Not to move in this direction and maintain the status quo amounts to resisting what Walls refers to as the "Ephesian moment," whereby the Christian faith successfully passes from one culture to another. The truth is, the "Christian story is serial; its center moves from place to place. No one church or place or culture owns it. At different times, different peoples and places have become its heartlands, its chief representatives. Then the baton passes on to others. . . . In other words, cross-cultural diffusion has been necessary to Christianity. It has been its life's blood, and without it the faith could not have survived."[27] As such, Christianity through its cross-cultural diffusion has become "a progressively richer entity."[28] May God grant this richness to grow today for his glory and for the benefit of his church.

---

[24]George Kinoti, *Hope for Africa and What the Christian Can Do* (Nairobi: AISRED, 1994), 95.

[25]Tite Tienou, "Which Way for African Christianity: Westernization or Indigenous Authenticity?" *Evangelical Missions Quarterly* 28, no. 3 (1992): 261.

[26]Tite Tienou, "Indigenous African Christian Theologies: The Uphill Road," *International Bulletin of Missionary Research* 14, no. 2 (1990): 76.

[27]Andrew Walls, *The Cross-Cultural Process in Christian History* (Maryknoll, NY: Orbis, 2002), 79, 66–67.

[28]Ibid., 10.

Prioritism vs. Holism

In McGavran's day, ecumenists clashed with evangelicals over the church's missionary obligation to the world. Ecumenists, fueled by an over-realized eschatology regarding the kingdom of God, embraced and implemented mission in terms of a socioeconomic program. McGavran opposed this trend toward horizontalization by articulating a mission theology in which reconciliation between God and humanity was primary:

> We realize that Christian mission must certainly engage in many labors. A multitude of excellent enterprises lie around us. So great is the number and so urgent the calls, that Christians can easily lose their way among them, seeing them all equally as mission. But in doing the good, they can fail of the best. In winning the preliminaries, they can lose the main game. They can be treating a troublesome itch, while the patient dies of cholera. The question of priorities cannot be avoided. . . .
>
> Most cordially admitting that God has other purposes, we should remember that we serve a God *Who Finds Persons*. He has an overriding concern that men should be redeemed. However we understand the word, biblical witness is clear that men are "lost." The Finding God wants them *found*—that is, brought into a redemptive relationship to Jesus Christ where, baptized in His Name, they become part of His Household. . . .
>
> Among other characteristics of mission, therefore, a chief and irreplaceable one must be this: that mission is a divine finding, vast and continuous.[29]

In a disturbing historical repeat, evangelicals are now battling other evangelicals over the same issue: What is the church supposed to do on behalf of the world? A dividing line has been drawn between two camps: holism and prioritism.[30]

---

[29]McGavran, *Understanding Church Growth*, 32.

[30]It is not a simple matter to differentiate between holism and prioritism, as mission theologians and practitioners are defining these terms differently. As such, in some cases they are actually talking past each other. So who has the right to define these terms? In addition to what is presented in this chapter, the following criteria are offered as a starting place: (1) prioritism is more committed to the lost than the poor whereas holism is either equally committed to both or even more committed to the poor; (2) prioritism maintains that the gospel pertains to what Jesus has done for us whereas holism contends that what humans do for others also comprises the gospel; and (3) prioritism understands social work as a means to the end of disciple-making, but holism sees social work as valid in and of itself apart from such a goal.

Holistic mission, which in some circles is now being referred to as "integral mission," views proclamation and social work "as inseparable aspects of Christian mission."[31] That is, holism understands evangelism and social action as equal partners, "like the two blades of a pair of scissors or the two wings of a bird. . . . The partnership is, in reality, a marriage."[32] Since God is concerned about all dimensions of life—political, social, economic, as well as spiritual—mission that is oriented toward just making disciples and planting the church is considered biblically indefensible.

Prioritism, on the other hand, asserts, in line with the Lausanne Covenant (paragraph 6), that the priority of the church in mission should be the proclamation of the gospel, whereby genuine disciples of Jesus Christ are made. While prioritists would place varying emphases on the role of social work in mission, all would grant that word should take precedent over deed, or proclamation over social action, while pursuing mission to the world. Thus, prioritism seeks to maintain the "distinction between the primary *mission* of the church and secondary or supporting ministries. With reference to spiritual transformation and social transformation, it gives priority to spiritual transformation. With reference to spirit, mind, and body, it gives priority to the spirit or soul. With reference to social action and evangelism, it gives priority to evangelism."[33]

While prioritists would place varying emphases on the role of social work in mission, all would grant that word should take precedent over deed, or proclamation over social action, while pursuing mission to the world.

The debate is more significant than the average person may realize. Recent statistics on missions giving in the American evangelical church show a stark decrease in the support of evangelism/discipleship minis-

---

[31]C. R. Padilla, "Holistic Mission," in *Dictionary of Mission Theology: Evangelical Foundations*, ed. John Corrie (Downers Grove, IL: InterVarsity, 2007), 158.

[32]John Stott, ed., *Making Christ Known: Historic Mission Documents from the Lausanne Movement, 1974–1989* (Grand Rapids: Eerdmans, 1996), 182.

[33]David Hesselgrave, *Paradigms in Conflict: 10 Key Questions in Christian Missions Today* (Grand Rapids: Kregel, 2005), 121.

tries and a surprising increase in the support of relief/development ministries from 2001 to 2005. In 2001, agencies reporting evangelism/discipleship as their primary activity accounted for 58.7 percent of the total amount spent on overseas ministries, whereas agencies involved in relief/development accounted for 35.1 percent.[34] In 2005, the figures were 47.5 percent for evangelism/discipleship and 46.1 percent for relief/development. In addition, the increase in income from 2001 to 2005 for relief/development was 73.4 percent, while for evangelism/discipleship it was only 2.7 percent.[35]

Assuming the continuation of this trend, we can be fairly certain that the missions community in the United States is presently spending more on alleviating human suffering than on addressing the eternal destiny of the lost. In fact, this is already a reality in Canada. In 2005, agencies reporting evangelism/discipleship as their primary activity comprised only 24.9 percent of the total amount spent on overseas ministries, whereas agencies involved in relief/development accounted for 73.6 percent.[36] This data shows that the greatest problems in missions today are not financial, strategic, or methodological, but theological.

Given this predicament, it is incumbent upon all those committed to God's mission to interact more deeply with his Word to discern what the church has actually been commanded to do. In this connection, although holistic mission appears to rest on solid biblical foundations, upon further investigation, in my opinion this turns out not to be the case.

Perhaps the best-known verse in support of holism is Matthew 5:16: "Let your light shine before others, that they may see your good deeds and glorify your Father in heaven." This statement by Jesus is often taken to justify any number of humanitarian or philanthropic causes around the world in his name. Yet by following the hermeneutical principle of interpreting Scripture with Scripture, a noteworthy truth emerges. The apostle Peter, who was there when Jesus said these words

---

[34]Dotsey Welliver and Minnette Northcutt, *Mission Handbook U.S. and Canadian Protestant Ministries Overseas 2004–2006* (Wheaton: Evangelical and Missions Information Service, 2004), 26.

[35]Linda Weber and Dotsey Welliver, *Mission Handbook U.S. and Canadian Protestant Ministries Overseas 2007–2009* (Wheaton: Evangelical and Missions Information Service, 2007), 44–45.

[36]Ibid., 73.

in the Sermon on the Mount, writes in 1 Peter 2:12: "Live such good lives among the pagans that, though they accuse you of doing wrong, they may see your good deeds and glorify God on the day he visits us." The careful exegete will notice that the same two Greek words here for "good deeds" are also used in Matthew 5:16, signifying that the apostolic interpretation of Jesus' message concerning being light had to do with living morally in the midst of unbelievers. What this means is that it is clearly an anachronistic reading to equate what Jesus was talking about with the multitudinous relief and development projects taking place around the world today.[37]

There also is the famous Matthew 25 passage, in which Jesus responds to the righteous, "Truly, I say to you, as you did it to one of the least of these my brothers, you did it to me" (v. 40 ESV). Holistic advocates assume that when Jesus mentioned "these my brothers," he was referring to the poor masses around the globe. This passage cannot be properly understood, however, apart from Matthew 10, where Jesus sends out his disciples and informs them that they will face persecution along the way. He concludes by stating, in verses 40–42: "Anyone who welcomes you welcomes me, and anyone who welcomes me welcomes the one who sent me. Whoever welcomes a prophet as a prophet will receive a prophet's reward, and whoever welcomes a righteous person as a righteous person will receive a righteous person's reward. And if anyone gives even a cup of cold water to one of these little ones who is my disciple, truly I tell you, that person will certainly not lose their reward."

The phrase "little ones" can also be translated "least ones" and carries the same meaning as "one of the least of these my brothers" in Matthew 25:40.[38] In identifying "these my brothers," D. A. Carson surmises, "By far the best interpretation is that Jesus' 'brothers' are his disciples (12:48–49; 28:10; cf. 23:8). The fate of the nations will be determined by how they respond to Jesus' followers, who . . . are charged with spreading the gospel and do so in the face of hunger,

---

[37]For more on the subject of compassion ministries dilemmas, see the author's "What Makes Mission Christian?" *Evangelical Missions Quarterly* 42, no. 1 (2006): 78–87.

[38]Hesselgrave, *Paradigms in Conflict*, 304.

thirst, illness, and imprisonment."[39] Accordingly, this passage is teaching that the nations are judged on the basis of how they respond to and treat Christ's emissaries who are sent out by him, not that Christians will be judged by how they minister to the less fortunate portion of humanity throughout church history.

Then there is the messianic mission of Luke 4:18–19, where Jesus quotes Isaiah 61. Holistic theologians James Engel and William Dyrness, in their book *Changing the Mind of Missions*, maintain that since this passage defines Jesus' agenda, "it also must define ours."[40] So what was Jesus' agenda? Bill Larkin points out: "Of the four infinitives from Isaiah that show the purpose of the Spirit's anointing and sending of Jesus, three involve preaching. . . . The other purpose is to send the oppressed away in freedom. Luke, then, regards the primary activity of Jesus' ministry as preaching. Other tasks are present, such as Jesus' healing and exorcism ministry or his sacrificial death and mighty resurrection, but these either validate or become the content of the gospel message."[41] Consequently, if anyone wishes to follow Jesus in mission, he or she will have to place a priority on preaching.

And last, John 17:18 and 20:21 often arise in discussions about holistic mission, as the idea is advanced that just like the Father sent Jesus into the world, so he sends his disciples. Yet after a very extensive analysis of semantic clusters in the Gospel of John, Andreas Köstenberger deduces that the disciples of Jesus are not to "model their own mission" after his.[42] This is confirmed by the Greek terms employed both in John 17:18 and 20:21, in which the Father's sending of Jesus is specifically differentiated from the sending of Jesus' disciples.[43] And, in reality, it can be no other way, since among other things: (1) Jesus was God incarnate sent into the world, and no other human being can claim

[39]D. A. Carson, "Matthew," in *Expositor's Bible Commentary, Volume 8*, Frank Gaebelein, gen. ed. (Grand Rapids: Zondervan, 1984), 520.

[40]James Engel and William Dyrness, *Changing the Mind of Missions* (Downers Grove, IL: InterVarsity, 2000), 223.

[41]William Larkin Jr. and Joel Williams, eds., *Mission in the New Testament: An Evangelical Approach* (Maryknoll, NY: Orbis, 1998), 158.

[42]Andreas Köstenberger, *The Missions of Jesus and the Disciples According to the Fourth Gospel* (Grand Rapids: Eerdmans, 1998), 220.

[43]Ibid., 186ff.

that designation (John 1:14); (2) Jesus was born to die for the sins of the world (Matthew 20:28; Mark 10:45; Luke 19:10); (3) Jesus essentially confined his mission to the Jewish people (Matthew 10:6; 15:24); and (4) Jesus' signs and miracles were meant to separate him and his mission from all others (John 2:11; 4:54; 7:31; 20:30).[44]

A simple but clear way of explaining the difference in mission between Jesus and his disciples is to recognize that Jesus pointed to himself whereas his disciples point to him. Therefore, any missiological paradigm which does not distinguish Jesus from his disciples in any age is not credible, because his mission to the world was wholly unique and unrepeatable.

So where does all this lead? Surely it leads away from holism and toward prioritism as the theological basis upon which Christian mission must be pursued in the world. There are at least two reasons for this. First of all, given the fact that the greatest problem fallen humanity faces is alienation from God, the greatest demonstration of compassion toward humanity can only be the solution to this problem—and that is the message of reconciliation through Christ. In other words, because eternal needs outweigh temporal ones, the priority in Christian mission must be proclamation. As C. S. Lewis wisely observed, "There are a good many things which would not be worth bothering about if I were going to live only seventy years, but which I had better bother about very seriously if I am going to live forever."[45]

And what should people be concerned about if they are going to exist forever? Jesus answers: "I tell you, my friends, do not be afraid of those who kill the body and after that can do no more. But I will show you whom you should fear: Fear him who, after your body has been killed, has authority to throw you into hell. Yes, I tell you, fear him" (Luke 12:4–5). Yes, hell is eternally worse than any temporal disease (Matthew 25:46; Hebrews 10:31; Revelation 20:11–15), and only the church has been entrusted with its remedy.

Second, the church cannot sacrifice what is best on the altar of what is good. Of course, it is good to teach people to read and write, to feed the hungry, to provide water for the thirsty, and to care for God's green

---

[44]Ibid., 169ff.
[45]C. S. Lewis, *Mere Christianity* (New York: Macmillan, 1952), 59.

earth. But the fact is that the world can also do all of these good things, and actually is doing them. Yet only the church has been commissioned by God to do what is best for the world: proclaim the gospel. As such, the church must restrain itself from duplicating what the world can do and concentrate on what the world cannot do in and of itself. Too much is at stake—indeed, the very eternal destiny of the lost.

Conclusion

These three obstacles or bad habits—creation of outside dependencies, lack of effective contextualization, and loss of priority of proclamation—are not new or unique to our times, but they have taken on renewed urgency today. As we attempt to take the gospel across cultural boundaries, we unnecessarily create dependencies. We unwittingly impose our way of doing things on the global church. And we unfortunately drift away from the priority of proclamation by substituting other less important tasks. Perhaps this reminder will empower us to break these bad habits. May it be so, for the sake of God's mission.

Discussion Points

1. How have you seen the Western church create dependencies overseas? What can be done to motivate people to work toward the local sustainability of the church worldwide?

2. Have you ever experienced the Western way of doing Christianity being imposed on others? Cite examples. What can be done to work for the de-Westernization of Christianity in these contexts?

3. Have you witnessed the drift away from evangelism toward social action in missions in your circles of influence? What steps need to be implemented to reverse this trend?

Further Reading

Allen, Roland. *Missionary Methods: St. Paul's or Ours?* Grand Rapids: Eerdmans, 1962.

Garrison, David. *Church Planting Movements: How God Is Redeeming a Lost World.* Midlothian, VA: WIGTake Resources, 2004.

Hesselgrave, David. *Planting Churches Cross-Culturally: North America and Beyond.* 2nd ed. Grand Rapids: Baker, 2000.

Hiebert, Paul. *Anthropological Insights for Missionaries.* Grand Rapids: Baker, 1986.

Piper, John. *Let the Nations Be Glad! The Supremacy of God in Missions.* 2nd ed. Grand Rapids: Baker, 2003.

Steffen, Tom. *Passing the Baton: Church Planting That Empowers.* Rev. ed. La Habra, CA: Center for Organizational and Ministry Development, 1997.

31

Multiplying Leaders on Mission with God

R. Bruce Carlton

At the beginning of the twenty-first century, Hollywood released the movie *Pay It Forward*. In this film a teacher gave his twelve-year-old students a challenge: think of a project to change the world and then put it into action. One student developed a plan to change the world through the simplest of ideas: an act of human kindness for three people. The genius of this student's idea was that he would challenge the person for whom he performed this act of kindness not to pay him back, but instead to "pay it forward." That is, he asked the person on the receiving end of the good deed to respond with a good deed for another person, and so forth. The intent was to change the world through the multiplication of acts of kindness continually paid forward.

In the twenty-first century, missions history is witnessing a significant change. We are seeing the spontaneous expansion of the church through the intentional, intense equipping and empowering of leaders who "pay it forward." Leaders are being equipped and empowered to train leaders, who in turn train leaders, who in turn train leaders. This has generated leadership chains of multiple generations. In one church-planting movement[1] in Asia, a local strategy coordinator[2] gathered around him a

---

[1] A church-planting movement is "a rapid multiplication of indigenous churches planting churches that sweeps through a people group or population segment." David Garrison, *Church Planting Movements: How God Is Redeeming a Lost World* (Midlothian, VA: WIGTake Resources, 2004), 21.

[2] A strategy coordinator is a missions strategist responsible for coordinating efforts to catalyze a church-planting movement among a specific population segment or people group.

handful of faithful men whom he trained, mentored, and empowered to pay it forward. Within the first two years, two of these men had leadership-training chains of sixteen and twenty-one generations, respectively.

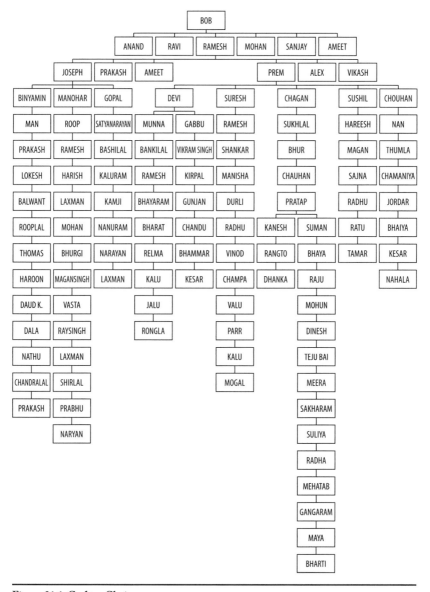

Figure 31.1. Carlton Chain

"Pay it forward" is not a Hollywood-inspired idea. Rather, it is a biblical principle. While in prison in Rome, Paul wrote these words to young Timothy, whom he had mentored: "The things you have heard me say in the presence of many witnesses entrust to reliable people who will also be qualified to teach others" (2 Timothy 2:2). In his prayer for his disciples, Jesus reveals how he invested his life into them so that they might carry forth the message (John 17:6–19). Jesus prayed not only for that inner circle of twelve, but also for those who would come to follow him as a result of their ministry. Jesus expected his initial band of disciples to pay it forward (John 17:20).

Paying it forward through multiplying leaders to be on mission with God is changing missions history. In one Asian country, believers planted more than 44,000 new churches in a four-year period, resulting in more than 480,000 new followers of Christ.[3] In another Asian country, during a seven-year period, more than 6,000 new churches emerged with more than 150,000 new followers of Christ.[4] How did this happen? While there are various reasons, all contributing in some form or fashion to this great harvest, a common thread runs through the majority of these movements: intentional and intensive training aimed at multiplying leaders empowered by the Holy Spirit to be on mission with God.

Another analogy for this concept of multiplying leaders is provided by parenting. I remember the birth of our first daughter, Elizabeth. As young parents, Gloria and I were overwhelmed with the responsibility entrusted to us to rear her to become a responsible human being and dedicated follower of Jesus Christ who would one day rear her own children to be the same. Less than two years later, Gloria gave birth to our second daughter, Mary. As our girls grew and matured into their teenage years and then into young adulthood, Gloria and I were amazed at how much they reflected our personalities. Today our daughters tell people that Elizabeth thinks like her father but acts like her mother, while Mary, on the other hand, thinks like her mother but acts like her father! Clearly,

---

[3]"Executive Overview for an Asian Church Planting Movement" (Richmond, VA: Southern Baptist International Mission Board, 2005).
[4]*Tribal Church Planting Movement in Middle India* (Midlothian, VA: WIGTake Resources, 2005). Based also on reports received by the author from the national strategy coordinator in this field.

Gloria and I have passed on a large part of ourselves to our children.

Twenty years after Elizabeth was born, we had the privilege of "giving her away" in marriage to an outstanding young Christian man. At the time of this writing we are awaiting the birth of our first grandchild, thus fulfilling God's plan: parents who rear children who will one day become parents themselves. Multiplying leaders is a process of spiritual parenting. Leaders take on the role of spiritual parents who parent believers with leadership potential to lead their own spiritual families, and the process is passed on from generation to generation.

Biblical Foundations

This concept of paying it forward through spiritual parenting has become a hallmark of mission efforts in recent years, especially within church-planting movements that have emerged around the world. This concept is not new, however. God's Word reminds us, "What has been will be again, what has been done will be done again; there is nothing new under the sun" (Ecclesiastes 1:9). The biblical record demonstrates that God's intention has always been to multiply leaders among his people. God's plan has never been one of appointing a single person to bear the burden of leading his people alone.

After the exodus, Moses' father-in-law, a Midianite, heard about everything God had done for Moses and the people of Israel. So Jethro went to visit Moses and the Israelites as they camped in the wilderness. There Jethro observed the people standing before Moses day and night in order for Moses to judge the cases brought before him. Jethro advised Moses:

> What you are doing is not good. You and these people who come to you will only wear yourselves out. The work is too heavy for you; you cannot handle it alone. Listen now to me and I will give you some advice, and may God be with you. You must be the people's representative before God and bring their disputes to him. Teach them his decrees and instructions, and show them the way they are to live and how they are to behave. But select capable men from all the people— men who fear God, trustworthy men who hate dishonest gain—and appoint them as officials over thousands, hundreds, fifties and tens. (Exodus 18:17–21)

Moses heeded Jethro's advice, and the men Moses appointed served alongside him in judging the people of Israel.

The appointing of the seventy elders in Numbers 11 is yet another example of God's intention to multiply leadership among his people. The people of Israel were complaining against God, and Moses was distraught. Overwhelmed with the burden of having to lead God's people alone, Moses cried out to God. God responded to Moses' plea:

Moses obeyed God and gathered the seventy elders. God took some of the power of the Spirit that he had poured out on Moses and put it on these men. Upon receiving God's Spirit, they began to prophesy. Two elders, Eldad and Medad, had remained in the camp, yet God's Spirit came upon them and caused them to prophesy like the others. Joshua pleaded with Moses to forbid Eldad and Medad from prophesying. Moses, realizing that God's plan was to appoint and anoint leaders who would shoulder the burden of leading God's people with him, replied to Joshua, "Are you jealous for my sake? I wish that all the Lord's people were prophets and that the Lord would put his Spirit on them!" (Numbers 11:29)

No better model of multiplying leaders exists than that employed by our Lord Jesus Christ. His coming ushered in the kingdom of God, and he spent his earthly ministry primarily in preparing faithful followers who, through their ministry, would faithfully carry God's message of hope, redemption, and reconciliation beyond the nation of Israel to the ends of the earth (Matthew 28:18–20; Acts 1:8).

Robert Coleman notes, "These early converts of the Lord were destined to become the leaders of his church that was to go with the gospel to the whole world, and from the standpoint of his ultimate purpose, the significance of their lives would be felt throughout eternity."[5] Jesus called those initial twelve disciples early in his ministry, and Scripture records that the purpose for doing so was that they might be with him and that he might send them forth to preach (Mark 3:14). This verse succinctly reveals the primary intent of Jesus' earthly ministry as well as his simple methodology. Coleman asserts that Jesus' "concern was not with programs to

---

[5]Robert E. Coleman, *The Master Plan of Evangelism* (Grand Rapids: Revell, 1993), 22.

reach the multitudes, but with men whom the multitudes would follow."[6]

Again, Jesus called these initial disciples to be *with* him. They traveled together, lived together, ate together. And through this process, Jesus was able to impart those things necessary for the future ministry that he would entrust to them. Jesus taught them privately, and they were with him as he taught and ministered to the multitudes. Jesus sent them out to preach, and he sent them with his authority—even over demons (Mark 3:15). Jesus empowered those whom he equipped. Jesus expected his disciples to reproduce and multiply, as this would be the key to the expansion of his church throughout the world. These men needed practical experience, seeing that they were destined to become the leaders of the church whom he would entrust with the responsibility to multiply themselves in the lives of others.

David Garrison suggests an intriguing scenario. In Luke 6, Jesus chose twelve disciples. In Luke 9, he sent them out. And we learn from the next chapter, Luke 10, that Jesus' pattern was to send them out two by two. In Luke 10, Jesus sent out seventy-two disciples. Where did these seventy-two come from? If we understand the principle of multiplication, it's easy to imagine that the original six pairs of disciples did just what their Master had modeled: they discipled twelve others, resulting in seventy-two (six times twelve) disciples.

Garrison observes, "If multiplication was truly at the core of Jesus' discipleship model, then we might expect these seventy-two disciples to have multiplied themselves as well. If they closely followed Jesus' example, then the seventy-two (comprising thirty-six pairs of disciples) would have produced four hundred forty-four disciples (thirty-six times twelve equals four hundred forty-four). Adding these four hundred forty-four to their seventy-two mentors would produce an early church of more than five hundred disciples of Jesus."[7]

The biblical record tells us that Jesus, after he rose from the dead, did indeed appear to more than five hundred followers (1 Corinthians 15:6). Whether Garrison's scenario corresponds to what actually transpired is beyond our capacity to know, but I do believe that Jesus intended his

---

[6]Ibid., 21.
[7]Garrison, *Church Planting Movements*, 206.

disciples to multiply—and this expectation remains valid for church leaders, missionaries, and all believers today.

Barnabas and Paul stand out as excellent models regarding this concept of multiplying leaders to be on mission with God. Most in the church have grown up hearing of the relationship between Paul and Timothy, and many herald this relationship as a model for discipleship. Yet we must not overlook how Barnabas paid it forward to Paul. After Paul's conversion on the road to Damascus, he began to preach about Jesus in the synagogues. To hear this persecutor of the followers of Jesus proclaim Jesus as the Son of God astounded those in Damascus. So astounded were the Jews that they plotted to kill Paul, forcing him to flee the city by night. Arriving in Jerusalem, Paul attempted to meet the followers of Christ, but they were afraid of him. At this point, Barnabas brought Paul to meet the apostles and spoke on his behalf. Barnabas was able to convince the apostles and the church in Jerusalem that Paul's conversion was genuine (Acts 9:19–30). Thus began the relationship between Barnabas and Paul.

Later, the apostles in Jerusalem heard about great numbers of people in Antioch who believed in Jesus through the preaching of those scattered by persecution. Upon hearing the reports, the apostles sent Barnabas to Antioch to confirm the news. There Barnabas witnessed firsthand this newly formed church. Barnabas immediately went to Tarsus to find Paul and bring him to Antioch. For an entire year, Barnabas and Paul taught this young church (Acts 11:19–26).

Realizing Paul's potential, Barnabas included Paul in the teaching and leadership of the church. Before long, the Holy Spirit would call Barnabas and Paul out of the church at Antioch to preach the gospel and plant churches in new places (Acts 13:1–3). One fact often overlooked in the calling out of Barnabas and Paul from Antioch is that these two men, during the course of their year ministering to this young church, had paid it forward by preparing others in the church to lead. By the time Barnabas and Paul set out on that first missionary journey there were at least three other leaders in this church: Simeon, Lucius, and Manaen (Acts 13:1).

From the time Barnabas and Paul set out on that mission until the end of Acts, Paul's ministry takes center stage. Paul must have been thankful that Barnabas had spoken on his behalf in Jerusalem and had given him the opportunity to develop as a leader by bringing him to Antioch.[8] Paul, in turn, paid it forward in the lives of others that God brought into his life. We witness Paul paying it forward in the lives of people such as Timothy, Titus, Epaphroditus, and Aquila and Priscilla. We should not forget all the elders Paul appointed in the churches he planted. Neither should we forget that all of this started with Barnabas and his willingness to defend Paul and provide him the opportunity to develop into a leader in the church at Antioch.

Multiplying leaders has always been God's plan for his people and his church. From Moses to Paul, the biblical record bears witness to this reality. While this process of multiplying leaders has become a recent hallmark of missionary practice, it is really nothing new. After all, "What has been will be again."

Present-Day Models

It is one thing to understand the biblical teaching about models of multiplying leaders; it is another thing to understand how to apply this practically to one's missionary work. Yet if we cannot make the transition from principle to practice, our learning is in vain. Numerous examples abound on the mission field of those who have successfully demonstrated how to multiply leaders effectively. Furthermore, through this process of multiplying leaders, churches have multiplied, leading to thousands upon thousands of people coming into God's kingdom.

Training for Trainers (T4T)

Most of the missionaries within the International Mission Board (IMB) of the Southern Baptist Convention are aware of "Training for Trainers" (T4T). This process for multiplying disciples, multiplying leaders, and multiplying churches was the brainchild of "Mark" (not

---

[8]It must have pained Barnabas deeply when Paul opted to separate from him concerning the dispute over John Mark (Acts 15:36–40). After all, Barnabas had defended Paul in Jerusalem when many doubted his conversion. When Paul refused to allow John Mark to accompany them on the second journey, it must have seemed, from Barnabas's perspective, that Paul had forgotten the grace extended to him. This separation should serve as a reminder that the task of spiritual parenting, at times, brings pain and disappointment. Although the two separated, Barnabas continued to pay it forward through the grace extended to John Mark, the future author of the second book in the New Testament.

his real name, which is withheld for security reasons), a strategy coordinator who had a Holy Spirit–inspired vision for reaching a densely populated region, comprised of 30 million people, in an Asian country. In the year 2000 it was estimated that approximately .3 percent of the population, about 100,000, people, were Christians. After four years of implementing T4T, Mark witnessed the birth of more than 44,000 new churches consisting of nearly 480,000 new followers of Christ—more than quadrupling the number of believers. The vision of T4T was that every person in the region would receive a witness about Christ, and that every person who responded in repentance and faith would be trained to witness and become a leader capable of training others.[9]

Those who know this strategy coordinator well will assert that the key to T4T is not the program but the person. Mark exemplifies and models all that he teaches. He is a devout man of prayer, spending several hours each morning on his knees talking to and hearing from God. He is a constant witness to those around him, so when he trains others to be a constant witness he does so with credibility. Mark invests his time prudently, spending the majority of his time witnessing and training people who come to faith in how to witness, how to train others to witness, and how to gather believers into churches. Through this process, Mark serves as a trainer of multiplying generations of trainers. Mark is paying it forward through multiple generations.

The training sessions Mark conducts typically consist of three parts. The initial time focuses on prayer, discussing the participants' spiritual lives, and reviewing the previous week's session. In training others to be trainers and spiritual leaders, holding a high standard of accountability is essential. Obedience is key and is measured at two levels. First, there is the expectation of obedience to the truth of God's Word. Second, there is the expectation of obedience by imitating the model that is set before them. Mark sets the example of applying the lessons learned in the training sessions, and he expects the same from those he is leading.

The second component of the time together is spent on learning a new lesson that the trainee is expected to teach in the church being

---

[9]IMB, "Executive Overview," 2005.

planted. The final part of Mark's time together with his developing leaders has them practicing in small groups what they have just learned. Those being equipped must demonstrate the ability to pass along what they have learned.

A simple principle is employed at this point: the discipler or trainer needs to know only one more thing than the student being discipled or trained. Further, the new material each week is simple and easily reproducible by those receiving it. Obedience is measured one step at a time, or, in the case of Mark's T4T, one lesson at a time. Such a process seems foreign to those who come from the knowledge-oriented, program-based discipleship systems of the West, in which students are loaded with a lot of information over a period of time with little or no expectation to pass it along to others. In Mark's process of multiplying leaders, he gives those he equips a little at a time, expects them to obey it, and expects them to pass it on to others before he gives them any further instruction.

Mark utilizes the training process of "Model, Assist, Watch, and Leave" (MAWL). Mark is an exemplary model to all he trains. He untiringly assists and watches them as they reproduce. The objective is to train, equip, empower, and hold accountable new believers to witness to their family and friends. He communicates this expectation to them from the beginning. These believers are then equipped to train those they lead to Christ; it is their responsibility to train and disciple these people rather than pass that responsibility on to someone else. These groups, which the believers train, are encouraged to form into new churches. In the same way, others that these believers train should do the same, leading to extensive leadership chains and multiple church plants. Mark typically assists and watches until such chains reach three or four generations before beginning to phase out of his intense involvement with those he is training. He is consistently initiating new leadership training chains.[10]

In reading this description of T4T, one might assume that everyone Mark trains becomes a leader who reproduces other leaders. Such is not

---

[10]Ibid.

the case. Mark has found, however, that nearly 20 percent of those who were already established believers begin, in turn, to train others; and the percentage is even higher among new believers.[11] Mark focuses his energy and efforts on those who demonstrate a willingness and a passion to be obedient in their spiritual life, sharing their faith, discipling and training others, and forming new churches.

There is another important component to Mark's work. A number of those he trains have demonstrated giftedness in training and a steadfast obedience. Mark nurtures and equips these gifted believers to become master trainers, or "Big Trainers."[12] These Big Trainers continue to train those they have led to Christ, while at the same time serving as overseers for leaders "who are in their stream of churches."[13]

> *The process captivates many in the West, so we are tempted to believe that replicating the process will yield the same results. We must learn from the process as it exemplifies the practical application of sound biblical principles. At the same time, we must not fall into the trap of turning the T4T process into another training program.*

Mark often spends additional time and energy nurturing and equipping these Big Trainers. Thus there are multiple training levels to equip and sustain the movement by constantly growing and preparing new leaders.

While Mark's training process is exceptional, we must not overlook the fact that the key to success is the disciplined model of the one driving the process. The *process* captivates many in the West, so we are tempted to believe that replicating the process will yield the same results. We must learn from the process as it exemplifies the practical application of sound biblical principles. At the same time, we must not fall into the trap of turning the T4T process into another training program. As Mark demonstrates, multiplying leaders involves investing one's life into the lives of others and possessing a passionate desire to help others become effective leaders and trainers of others.

---

[11]Ibid.
[12]Ibid.
[13]Ibid.

Acts 29: Finding Faithful Followers

The year is 2000, and the setting is a training center in a southern city of a populous Asian country. For the previous three years, a Rapid Advance team had sought to respond to the challenge of rapidly deploying church planters and strategy coordinators to engage the neglected harvest fields in this area of the world. After three years of training Western missionaries and engaging in extensive research, the results were dismal. Sitting on the carpeted floor of a room, I challenged the team (as their strategy leader) to rethink their vision and mission. After a time of prayer and dialogue, the team envisioned every people group and every city in this area of Asia engaged with a church-planting movement strategy within ten years. They believed they would fulfill this vision by mobilizing and equipping indigenous missionaries, church planters, and church leaders to serve as strategy coordinators. This vision gave birth to the Acts 29 training, which over the next five years would unfold throughout the region and subsequently expand to other places around the globe. (There is no Acts 29 in the Bible, of course; this term is used for the work of God that continues today beyond the time frame of the biblical narrative.)

The intent of the Acts 29 training is to mobilize and equip indigenous leaders to plant reproducing house churches and to multiply leaders for these churches among the neglected harvest fields of their country. Built upon biblical principles and focusing on the areas of research, prayer, partnership, platforms, evangelism, discipleship, and church planting, the training is practical and experiential. One key component of the training is learning how to find faithful followers and implementing an obedience-based discipleship and leadership development process. The model, or ecclesiology, of church taught in the training is simple, which provides a more appropriate environment for rapid church reproduction as well as rapid leadership development. Central to the entire training process is the belief that God does not desire that anyone should perish, but that all come to repentance (Ezekiel 18:23,32; 1 Timothy 2:4; 2 Peter 3:9). Therefore, the most effective way to begin to see this fulfilled is through planting simple, reproducing churches and multiplying leaders to be on mission with God.

I began to conduct Acts 29 training whenever and wherever local partners invited me. The basic idea was to train as many people as possible while using the training as a filtering mechanism to find faithful disciples. Believing that Jesus filtered out of the multitudes faithful men into whom he could pour out his life, the core message that the Acts 29 training sought to communicate was this:

> If each of us can gather a few faithful men around us, pour our lives into theirs, and teach them how to reproduce, then the kingdom of God will expand beyond our imaginations. The legacy we leave behind in our ministries is not the work we do but the work that our disciples accomplish! We may plant a few churches in our ministries. However, if we gather a small group of faithful disciples around us and equip them to the fullest, they will plant more churches than we ever could. The result will be that more people are brought into the kingdom of God.[14]

Although, we expect everyone to benefit from the Acts 29 training, the reality is that not everyone will catch the vision and reproduce leaders. In each training event, therefore, we seek to identify potential faithful followers who have a passion for the lost, catch the vision for planting reproducing churches, are willing to pay it forward by training others, and are teachable. Once we have identified such believers, we seek to bring them into a mentoring relationship or a follow-up process in order to encourage and empower them. This mentoring relationship may be with a mature missionary or with the key local person with whom we cooperated to conduct the training in his area. The belief is that if we can find one faithful follower, pour our lives into his, and teach him to reproduce himself in the lives of others, the results will far surpass anything we could have imagined (see sidebar, "Finding Faithful Followers: A Living Example").

Within the first four years of conducting the training across this region of Asia, local believers were working with approximately one hundred different people groups and fourteen cities. During that same time, the Rapid Advance team trained more than a dozen different men who had faithfully implemented the training in their respective areas to become trainers of trainers. In one area where we led several

---

[14]R. Bruce Carlton, *Acts 29: Practical Training in Facilitating Church-Planting Movements Among the Neglected Harvest Fields* (Singapore: Radical Obedience, 2003), 160.

Acts 29 trainings and where we equipped two faithful followers to be trainers of trainers, men whom these two men trained engaged forty-five of the one hundred unreached people groups in that area.

In another area, an IMB strategy coordinator was targeting a cluster of Buddhist people groups scattered in three adjoining countries. While conducting several Acts 29 trainings in this area, the worker was able to find a few faithful disciples. He began to invest his life into theirs: mentoring, encouraging, and training them. Training expanded, and churches began to appear among Buddhist people groups that, for the most part, had no previous access to the gospel. In the year 2007, one man whom this strategy coordinator and others trained and mentored planted thirty-six house churches among seven different people groups in one state.

Most recently, while conducting Acts 29 training in a former Soviet Union country, I met a pastor who attended the first training I led in his country in January of 2007. I had the privilege of spending time with Alexander[15] and the seven key men he is equipping to become leaders of seven new house churches they plan to start in a heavily populated area of their city. It was a joy to witness Alexander's intent to pay it forward in the lives of these seven men. I also spent time with two other men who had attended that first training in 2007. These two brought with them two young men into whom they are seeking to pay it forward. I fully expect that within the next year or two, I will receive reports of reproducing churches being planted and more leaders being equipped in this country that has otherwise witnessed little evangelical church growth during the past century.

The T4T and Acts 29 training, along with variations and innovations of these two training processes, continue today throughout the world. As a result, there are thousands of leaders on mission with God around the globe: planting new churches, discipling new followers of Christ, and paying it forward by equipping others to be leaders on mission with God. Multiplying leaders to be on mission with God is changing missions history.

---

[15]Not his real name, which is withheld for security reasons.

FINDING FAITHFUL FOLLOWERS: A LIVING EXAMPLE

After more than a hundred men and women completed an intensive ten-day Acts 29 training session on a rural farm in India, Ramesh approached Bob (not their real names, which are withheld due to security concerns) with a question. "Will you mentor me?"

Bob wasn't sure how to respond because he lived in another country and knew he wouldn't be able to devote much face-to-face time with Ramesh. So he said, "I would be happy to assist you in any way I can, but you need to know that most of our contact will have to be through telephone calls and e-mail."

Ramesh warmly smiled and replied, "I understand, and I am willing to have you mentor me in this way."

Thus began their relationship. Some time later Ramesh planted the first house church in his community. More than four years after Bob began mentoring Ramesh, nearly 6,000 house churches with approximately 150,000 believers had been planted, spanning two states and at least three different people groups.[16] How did it all happen?

After Bob and Ramesh agreed to work together, Ramesh began to train other men. He trained more than a hundred believers in house-church planting and church-planting movement principles. He was seeing very little fruit, however. In addition, the funds he had available for training were running dry. Ramesh was frustrated. Bob advised Ramesh to model what he learned through the Acts 29 training: find a few faithful followers into whom he could invest the majority of his time and energy. Ramesh began searching for faithful men. He found six.[17]

---

[16]The International Mission Board of the Southern Baptist Convention assessed this work and verified the movement's existence. Further, an internal assessment revealed similar findings as the IMB assessment.

[17]If you follow the flow of the Discipleship Chain chart presented in this chapter, under

As Ramesh began investing in these six men, he taught them to do the same with others. At first Ramesh would visit the men once each week. He would either travel to where they lived and worked or he would ask them to come to his home in the city.[18] These men began to plant house churches. Ramesh's discipleship method was simple: having learned a Bible-storying curriculum during his Acts 29 training, he used that as his primary teaching method. He expected those he trained to strive to live like Christ, guard their character, plant churches that reproduce, raise up leaders for those churches, and train those leaders to do the same.

Ramesh and Bob also began training other groups, as Acts 29 training opportunities expanded throughout South Asia. What began as a long-distance relationship took on a new dynamic. Now Ramesh and Bob were able to spend ten days with each other three or four times a year, which provided for more personal interaction. Most of their time together was spent discussing personal and specific ministry issues. Over time, Bob and Ramesh moved from having a mentor/mentoree relationship to more of a peer-to-peer relationship. Many now recognize Ramesh as a well-qualified trainer in a church-planting movement, and the fact that he is a practitioner as well as a trainer enhances his effectiveness and credibility as a trainer.

Bob eventually had the opportunity to meet with the six men whom Ramesh had mentored/discipled for the past several years. Two of the men had participated in training that Bob and Ramesh had conducted a few years before. Bob had no ongoing relationship with any of these men, however, so this was the first time he had the opportunity to sit down and have a heart-to-heart talk with them.

Bob's name you will see Ramesh's name, and under Ramesh's name you will see the names of six other men. These are the six men Ramesh mentors.

[18]Ramesh and these men live and work in a state known for the persecution of Christians. Thus Ramesh was often unable to visit those he mentored in their home villages or towns.

Bob's role was to invest in Ramesh's life and work. Ramesh's role was to invest in the lives of those six men, who in turn invested in the lives of others. Bob and Ramesh are living examples that the biblical principle of 2 Timothy 2:2 can be effectively implemented.

Conclusion

On the campus of Southern Baptist Seminary in Louisville, Kentucky, resides the Legacy Center. This facility's name reminds students, faculty, staff, and visitors of the great legacy left to the school by its founders and subsequent leaders over these many years. Many of us are concerned about our legacy—what we will pass on to our children and our children's children. As followers of Christ, we should be concerned about our legacy. Robert Coleman reminds us, "We must decide where we want our ministry to count—in the momentary applause of popular recognition or in the reproduction of our lives in a few chosen people who will carry on our work after we have gone."[19]

In 2 Timothy 2:2, Paul reminded Timothy of the necessity and responsibility to develop leaders who could, in turn, do the same. A key word in this verse is *faithful*, or *reliable*. Paul urged Timothy to find faithful followers. Faithfulness involves much more than just passing along the content of what one has learned. Faithful men and women are people who have learned what it means to be obedient in their journey with Christ, who strive to imitate Christ in their lives, and who then take up the mantle of responsibility to pass that along to others.

Later in his letter to Timothy, Paul wrote, "You, however, know all about my teaching, my way of life, my purpose, faith, patience, love, endurance, persecutions, sufferings—what kinds of things happened to me in Antioch, Iconium and Lystra, the persecutions I endured. Yet the Lord rescued me from them all. . . . But as for you, continue in what you have learned and have become convinced of, because you know

---

19Coleman, *Master Plan*, 32.

those from whom you learned it" (2 Timothy 3:10–11,14). These words echo Paul's words to the Corinthian Christians: "Follow my example, as I follow the example of Christ" (1 Corinthians 11:1).

May our legacy be multiple generations of leaders of God's church among every nation and tribe. When we come to the end of our lives, our desire should be that we can pray as our Lord Jesus: "I have brought you glory on earth by finishing the work you gave me to do. . . . I have revealed you to those whom you gave me out of the world. They were yours; you gave them to me and they have obeyed your word" (John 17:4,6).

Discussion Points

1. Explain the strengths of the T4T model. Why are relationships and character issues key in this process?

2. Carlton makes the statement, "The legacy we leave behind in our ministries is not the work that we do but the work that our disciples accomplish." What implications does this have for your present and future life and ministry?

3. What filtering mechanisms do you employ in your life and ministry to find faithful men and women? How do you disciple and equip them after you have found them? As a result of reading this chapter, what changes do you anticipate making in order to see disciples, leaders, and churches reproduce and multiply?

Further Reading

Allen, Roland. *Missionary Methods: St. Paul's or Ours?* Grand Rapids: Eerdmans, 1962.

———. *The Spontaneous Expansion of the Church.* Eugene, OR: Wipf and Stock, 1962.

Carlton, R. Bruce. *Acts 29: Practical Training in Facilitating Church-Planting Movements Among the Neglected Harvest Fields.* Singapore: Radical Obedience, 2003.

———. *Amazing Grace: Lessons on Church-Planting Movements from Cambodia.* 2nd ed. Singapore: Radical Obedience, 2004.

Coleman, Robert E., *The Master Plan of Evangelism.* Grand Rapids: Revell, 1993.

Garrison, David. *Church Planting Movements: How God Is Redeeming a Lost World*. Midlothian, VA: WIGTake Resources, 2004.

Hodges, Herb. *Tally Ho The Fox! The Foundation for Building World-Visionary, World-Impacting, Reproducing Disciples*. Memphis: Spiritual Life Ministries, 1999.

Patterson, George. "The Spontaneous Multiplication of Churches," in *Perspectives on the World Christian Movement: A Reader*. 3rd ed. Edited by Ralph D. Winter and Steven C. Hawthorne. Pasadena, CA: William Carey Library, 1999.

32

CREATIVE-ACCESS PLATFORMS

Tom Steffen

Dave and Donna were anxious to begin ministry in a country long closed to the gospel of Jesus Christ. After years of preparatory study at college and seminary they finally received their degrees and were ready to head overseas. Knowing they couldn't enter their host country on a traditional missionary visa, they applied for a business visa. They planned to start a tour business to gain and maintain entrance into the host country. As they anxiously awaited their visas, they Googled "tour business" to glean all the information they could about starting such a business. After six long months, lots of prayers and tears, more paperwork, and a roller-coaster ride, the host government granted Dave and Donna a business visa for their tour business.

Upon arrival in the host country they rented a small office, added some office furniture, had a phone installed, made up some business cards, and put a sign on the door. They were open for business. Well, kind of. Once the office was completed, they rarely visited it. Nor did they conduct many tours. Rather, Dave and Donna found themselves busily meeting and befriending people in various parts of the city. Out of these new relationships they hoped to start house churches that could multiply under the radar of the government. The "tour business" platform provided them opportunity to be involved full time in "real" ministry.

This fictional scenario raises a number of issues relevant to the use of platforms as a means to gain and maintain entrance into countries hostile to Christ. This chapter will begin with a brief definition of platforms before interacting with related foundational matters, such as legal and ethical issues, work and worship, profit, and educational preparation. From there a broader background will be painted, shedding light on the legitimate use of platforms. Consideration will be given to key players, gatherings, publications, institutions, and global influences that have helped shape the definition of viable platforms, concluding with types, goals, and concerns that surround the use of platforms.

Definition

Approximately seventy countries in the world are considered hostile to the gospel.[1] These nations, therefore, require creative ways for kingdom workers to gain entrance for expansion that addresses people's social and spiritual needs.[2] Since the 1990s, mission strategists have used the term "platform" as one such means to accomplish this goal. Platforms include people's skills, services, and occupations that serve as a legitimate means to gain entrance, make a living, help others make a living, convey the good news of Jesus Christ through word and deed, and facilitate church multiplication. This is particularly true when such gifts and skills are desired by the host country. Possible platforms include business, education (including teaching English as a second language), consultant, trainer, student, community development, medicine, and technology.[3] While all of these areas of expertise are needed, useful, creative, and legitimate platforms, this chapter will concentrate heavily on the business world.

While the use of the term "platform" is relatively new, the concept certainly is not. Priscilla and Aquila pioneered in this area during New Testament times (Acts 18:1–3), using business as a legitimate means to multiply new churches. From the efforts of this entrepreneur couple, three house churches emerged in three different cities: Corinth (Acts 18:26), Ephesus (1 Corinthians 16:19), and Rome (Romans 16:5). One wonders if this was by intentional design.

---

[1] David Barrett and Todd Johnson, *World Christian Trends AD 30–AD 2000: Interpreting the Annual Christian Megacensus* (Pasadena, CA: William Carey Library, 2001), 60.

[2] Formerly, countries that did not allow missionaries entrance were called "restricted-access countries." As missionaries became successful in penetrating the so-called resistant countries through alternative ways, the term was changed to "creative-access countries."

[3] See Mike Barnett's chapter, "Innovation in Mission Operation: Creative-Access Platforms," in *The Changing Face of World Missions*, ed. Michael Pocock, Gailyn Van Rheenen, and Douglas McConnell (Grand Rapids: Baker, 2005), 209–44. This chapter draws heavily upon his work.

> **Platforms** *are a legitimate means for expatriate kingdom workers to gain entrance into countries open to, or hostile to, the gospel, as they serve their constituents in various integrative ways that wed work and worship, the secular and the sacred.*

This couple's business-as-missions model adds another element to the definition of platform—the context. While "platform" today usually refers to entry into countries with high resistance to the gospel, it can also be used in contexts open to the gospel. Platforms are a legitimate means for expatriate kingdom workers to gain entrance into countries open to, or hostile to, the gospel, as they serve their constituents in various integrative ways that wed work and worship, the secular and the sacred. This can be accomplished through individual efforts or by working through existing institutions such as churches, missionary agencies, schools, businesses, or governments. The possibilities for the types of platforms are limited only by one's imagination.

Foundational Issues

This section will address foundational issues related to the use of creative-access platforms, seeking to bring clarity and comprehensiveness to the definition. Ethical questions are addressed first before considering various views about work and worship, profit, and educational preparation.

Legal and ethical issues. Some of the first questions that arise out of the fictional scenario at the beginning of this chapter include: Is it really ethical to use platforms to enter a country hostile to Christianity? Doesn't this strategy promote entry under false pretences? Why do Dave and Donna feel it is OK to have a tour business yet spend most of their working hours doing what they consider as "real" ministry (i.e., starting new house churches)? Isn't this illegal?

The Bible is clear—someday all peoples of all nations will bow at Jesus' feet (Philippians 2:10). For this to become a reality, the good news of a risen Savior must be heralded by his followers to all peoples as they traverse the globe (Genesis 12:1–3; Psalm 67; Matthew 28:19–20). Yes, entering countries that restrict Christian proselytizing is a matter of legality. But there is a higher law than those of human governments (i.e., the law of God). When the Sanhedrin commanded Peter and James not to speak or teach in the name of Jesus, the reply and example of these first-century apostles instructs twenty-first century marketplace kingdom workers: "Which is right in God's eyes: to listen to you, or to him? You be the judges! As for us, we cannot help speaking about what we have seen and heard" (Acts 4:19–20). Paul followed Peter and James' example, sometimes resulting in harsh days and nights in filthy prisons, as well as brutal beatings (2 Corinthians 11:23–25). Paul's passion to reach the nations for Christ made him a frequent target of painful persecution.

While God's law always trumps human law (legality), a number of ethical considerations must be asked by marketplace kingdom workers who choose to enter restricted countries to expand his kingdom legitimately or illegitimately. Will their actions needlessly endanger nationals who associate with them or work for them? National Christians? Other missionaries in the area? The expatriate's government? Themselves?

All marketplace kingdom workers should give prayerful attention to these questions no matter what their platform of entry. This would be particularly true for those like Dave and Donna who wish to focus more on reaching people for Christ than the tour business under which they were allowed to enter the host country. Should the couple be discovered for who they really are—clandestine religious proselytizers— who will be endangered? What will be the long-term impact for Christianity within the country, or outside the country—for example, in new recruitment?

This raises other questions. Should work and worship be bifurcated? Should work be considered ministry? Should kingdom workers in the marketplace be as skilled in their work as they are in theology?

Work and worship issues. Some people see work—in Dave and Donna's case, their tour business—as a deterrent and delay to ministry. They see real ministry as being out on the streets, in the cafés, shops, and parks; building relationships; communicating the gospel; and facilitating the maturation and multiplication of churches. Taking tourists on tours is a distraction, robbing time from real ministry. That's why Dave and Donna would consider studying theology alone as sufficient for ministry preparation. Ken Eldred identifies some possible reasons for this perspective:

> Those who devalue economic or spiritual results, consider work in the marketplace as second rate, see business as ignoble, view profit as dirty, or consider wealth as the enemy may have difficulty accepting Kingdom business as a laudable part of the missions movement. Kingdom business rests on notions that God cares about people's spiritual, social and economic transformation, that work in the business world is both a ministry and a calling, that profit is both necessary and a sign of useful service, and that poverty is a social disease to be addressed.[4]

Eugene Peterson takes the conversation back a step further. "Our work is derivative from God the worker. . . . Work is the primary context. . . . Work is our Spirit-anointed participation in God's work."[5] The Moravians regarded "the working day as just as holy as Sunday; work is never meaningless, because Jesus works for us."[6] Work *is* ministry, just as evangelism, discipleship, and church multiplication are ministry. The tour business and church multiplication are both genuine ministry, because each is an expression of worship.

Preparatory education should therefore include not only theology but also business.[7] Otherwise, the chosen entry platform can easily become a "cover" for covert activities endangering the total missions enterprise for decades. Each marketplace kingdom worker should select a viable means to enter a country, for the goal is business *as* mission, not business *and* mission—not business alone, or mission alone.

Profit issues. Dave and Donna's goal is to see a sustainable movement for Christ established. What becomes of the tour business in the future is of little consequence to the couple. Even if they had hired employees, they believe, like John Wesley, that "as riches increase, so will pride,

---

[4]Kenneth A. Eldred, *God Is at Work: Transforming People and Nations Through Business* (Ventura, CA: Regal Books, 2005), 69.
[5]Eugene H. Peterson, *Leap Over a Wall: Earthy Spirituality for Everyday Christians* (San Francisco: HarperCollins, 1997), 27.
[6]William J. Danker, *Profit for the Lord: Economic Activities in Moravian Missions and the Basel Mission Trading Company* (Grand Rapids: Eerdmans, 1971), 71.
[7]Heinz Suter and Marco Gmur, *Business Power for God's Purpose* (Greng, Switzerland: VKG, 1997), 32–33. Blumhardt calls these workers "'the craftsman-theologian,' an integrated model of human life in all its aspects."

anger, and love of the world in all its branches."[8] So they focus their attention on the eternal—souls.

Others, particularly in developing countries, however, desire to see three sustainable movements in place: (1) apostolic (church multiplication), (2) deaconal (social), and (3) business (profit). They recognize that strong tensions exist between each point of the triad as each vies for dominance. This drives marketplace kingdom workers back to the Holy Spirit and the Word so that balance prevails and *shalom*, or peace, rules in their lives, the lives of employees, and all others associated with the business. People who love to share what they have with others will find it much more difficult for riches to rule their lives.[9]

Educational preparation issues. At least four camps of marketplace kingdom workers exist today in relation to educational preparation: (1) those who train theologically, (2) those who train as marketplace professionals, (3) those who train theologically and professionally in business, and (4) those who train theologically, professionally in business, and missiologically.

Those who go the first route and only train theologically often believe that knowing the Word and living its universal principles is sufficient in any cross-cultural context. Like Dave and Donna, these individuals often bifurcate work and worship, tending to assume that cultural differences are minimal.

Those who train only for business run into a similar challenge, but from a different perspective. These entrepreneurs often assume they know how to plant theologically solid churches in cross-cultural contexts, not to mention start a new business.

A global economy and world demands that marketplace kingdom workers should be astute theologically, professionally, and missiologically. While this preparation will take longer, it will help avoid what Ralph Winter calls the "amateurization of missions." Lois McKinney Douglas and I attempted to capture the ongoing generational concern:

---

[8]Danker, *Profit for the Lord*, 30.
[9]Tom Steffen, "Making God the Hero-King of the Great Commission Company," *Mission Frontiers* 29, no. 6 (November–December 2007): 14–16.

The Moravians and the Basel Mission preferred qualified professional recruits because "Such work calls for specialists and professionals rather than for clerical amateurs. When the latter [amateurs] dabble in it, they often bring harm to both the mission and economic activities" (Danker, 1971, 136–37). J. I. Packer raised a similar concern: "The blunderings of sanctified amateurism, impervious to the need to get qualified in the area where one hopes to function, are neither good Christianity nor good business" (1990, 24). Genuine dedication, availability, or brief training does not necessarily translate into missionary astuteness.[10]

Patrick Lai may provide the reason for extended interdisciplinary education. He contends that "the majority of *effective tentmakers* (emphasis mine) have received training in either missions, Bible school, or seminary. A solid majority (78 percent) had training in missiology. . . . All workers, especially tentmakers going into business, should seriously consider investing the time to get some cross-cultural training before moving abroad."[11]

Pioneer Players

This section will highlight three pioneers who used creative-access platforms to promote the gospel in parts of the world hostile to Jesus Christ. Heaven will provide opportunity to hear the many other stories of fearless, faith-filled heroes who attempted to use creative-access platforms to present Christ. Many of these dedicated pioneers died in their youth, giving their lives so that others could hear the good news that drove them to the frontiers of mission.

> *"Those two pioneers of civilization—Christianity and commerce—should ever be inseparable."*—David Livingstone, *lecture at Cambridge University in 1857*

---

[10]Tom Steffen and Lois McKinney Douglas, *Encountering Missionary Life and Work: Preparing for Intercultural Ministry* (Grand Rapids: Baker, 2008), 353. The quotation cites William J. Danker, *Profit for the Lord: Economic Activities in Moravian Missions and the Basel Mission Trading Company* (Grand Rapids: Eerdmans, 1971), 136–37; and J. I. Packer, "The Christian's Purpose in Business," in *Biblical Principles and Business: The Practice*, ed. Richard C. Chewning (Colorado Springs: NavPress, 1990), 24.

[11]Patrick Lai, *Tentmaking: Business as Missions* (Waynesboro, GA: Authentic, 2005), 96.

John Leonard Dober. One of the most unique platforms ever proposed was by the first two Moravian missionaries sent to St. Thomas in the West Indies in 1732. John Leonard Dober, a potter, and David Nitschman, a carpenter, left secure jobs in Copenhagen to become indentured slaves on sugar plantations in an effort to reach slaves. Shortly after they arrived, Nitschman returned home, leaving Dober on his own. Dober worked for the governor; but this communicated the wrong message to the slaves he desired to reach, so he rented a small hut close to them. His job as a potter provided few funds, forcing him to live in abject poverty, even as it provided opportunity to communicate the good news to slaves after long hours of daily toil.

From the start of the mission work until 1766, sixty-six Moravian men and women died in service, mostly from illnesses. Even so, new volunteer replacements arrived to replace the fallen heroes of faith. Their collective effort saw hundreds of slaves find freedom in Christ.[12]

J. Christy Wilson. In 1951, a little more than two hundred years after Dober left for St. Thomas, J. Christy Wilson and his wife, Betty, packed their possessions for a very different part of the world, Afghanistan—the "forbidden harvest"—where they served for twenty-two years. They became self-supporting when Wilson contracted to serve as the principal of a government high school. He also taught English to the crown prince and diplomats. As a couple, the Wilsons started a school for the blind in Kabul. Wilson later served eleven years as pastor of Community Christian Church in Kabul.

Eventually the Afghan government expelled the Wilsons, closed the school for the blind, and demolished the church building. In 1975, at the age of fifty-three, Wilson joined the faculty of Gordon-Conwell Theological Seminary, where he taught and promoted missions for seventeen years before his death in 2001. Of his numerous books, *Today's Tentmakers: Self-Support: An Alternative Model for Worldwide Witness* captures his challenge for the mission enterprise of his day. Wilson helped bring the role of self-supported tentmakers mainstream, no matter what the platform, in that age of missions—something that did

---

[12]Miron Winslow, *Sketch of Missions; or History of the Principal Attempts to Propagate Christianity Among the Heathen* (Andover, MA: Flagg and Gould, 1819), 148–51.

not go unnoticed by John Cox, who credited this pioneer with being "the father of the modern-day tentmaking movement."[13]

Ruth E. Siemens. Male missionaries weren't the only gender involved in using creative-access platforms to reach the world. Ruth Siemens left her footprint in tentmaking, with twenty-one years of ministry in Peru, Brazil, Portugal, Spain, and Austria, followed by some twenty-five years more as she helped other potential tentmakers find salaried, secular jobs around the globe.

But tentmaking was never in Siemens' initial plans, since she only knew the donor-supported model for those going out as full-time missionaries. Growing up in an immigrant family who was actively involved in a small Mennonite Brethren church, she learned about missions through those sent out from the church and by reading and rereading the ten or so missionary biographies in the church library. After learning the Bible, how to walk with the Lord, and signing a card promising to serve abroad during her days as a student at Biola University, Siemens enrolled in Wycliffe's Summer Institute of Linguistics at the University of Oklahoma.

Then serious illness struck and Siemens lost the function of one lung. Assuming her opportunities for missionary service were over, she studied education and English at California State University, Chico, where she also learned inductive Bible study from InterVarsity Christian Fellowship staff.

God surprised Siemens (again) in 1954 with a salaried, secular teaching position (platform) in Peru. This began a journey in tentmaking. She practiced her trade on various continents, and from around 1975 she helped potential tentmakers locate secular job opportunities around the globe. She founded Global Opportunities (www.globalopps .org), which remains an active tentmaker mobilization organization. In 2005, at the age of eighty, the former tentmaker and missions mobilizer entered the presence of the Lord.[14]

---

[13]John Cox, "The Tentmaking Movement in Historical Perspective," *International Journal of Frontier Missions* 14:3 (1997): 116.

[14]For a detailed account of Ruth Siemens' autobiography, see "Ruth's Story: The Story Behind GO," Global Opportunities website, www.globalopps.org/ruths_story.htm.

Foundational Publications and Gatherings

Nothing happens in a vacuum. Political, economic, social, and even theological trends impact what happens in the world. The same is true for the development and use of platforms in missions, whether in the eighteenth, twentieth, or twenty-first centuries. For example, Moravians Dober and Nitschman followed the expansion of colonialism and commerce of their day. Moving to the twentieth century, both Wilson and Siemens were able to ride a post–World War II wave, all directed by the sovereign God of history. Siemens astutely noted that when World War II ended, "The U.S. was giving massive reconstruction aid to Europe, and decolonization was in full swing. Soon 120 newly independent countries would need development help of every kind. An international job market began to grow. Americans were considered very provincial, but ten million men had been recruited by the military, and many Christians came home with firsthand experience of the mission field. A new wave of missions interest began to grow."[15] And part of that new wave would be full-time missionaries, often lay people, who supported themselves, seeing no distinction between their job and ministry. They considered secular work as spiritual ministry, whether as a businessperson, educator, or any other legitimate platform.

By the mid-1980s, globalization made its impact on the world—flattening it, to use Thomas Freidman's terminology.[16] Former economic, political, and social barriers broke down, making the global exchange of products, technology, services, culture, and information not only possible but, more importantly, multidirectional.[17] Tentmaking, and the coming business-as-mission movement, would benefit from this new era, which of course did not catch God by surprise. The following are some of the groundbreaking writings and gatherings of the twentieth and twenty-first centuries, influenced to a great extent—intentionally or unintentionally—by globalization.

---

[15]Ibid.

[16]Thomas Friedman, *The World Is Flat: A Brief History of the Twenty-First Century* (New York: Farrar, Straus, and Giroux, 2005).

[17]Steve Rundle and Tom Steffen, *Great Commission Companies: The Emerging Role of Business in Missions* (Downers Grove, IL: InterVarsity, 2003), 46–62.

Don Hamilton's TMQ Research, established in 1985,[18] followed shortly after Siemens' Global Opportunities. TMQ Research serves as a network for tentmakers to provide best traits and practices, sources, and training contacts. In 1987, Hamilton's *Tentmakers Speak: Practical Advice from Over Four Hundred Missionary Tentmakers* demonstrated the maturing of a young movement by providing practical advice by those serving in the trenches.[19]

Also in 1987, Tetsunao Yamamori, former president of Food for the Hungry, called for a new breed of missionaries who would move beyond tentmakers in training and strategy. His seminal book referred to this new breed as "God's new envoys."[20] Many of these new envoys would wed the social—relief and development platforms—to the spiritual. He calls such integration "symbiotic ministries."

The 1989 Lausanne II Congress that met in Manila provided a forum to network all the individual ideas floating in the tentmaking world. John Cox highlights something often overlooked in the "Tentmaker Declarative Appeal" produced by the Tentmaker Track of that meeting. The appeal called for lay involvement and recognized the role of the local church in mobilizing and equipping, producing training materials, assisting in placement and orientation, nurturing tentmakers, and assisting in reentry.[21]

As the third millennium approached, tentmaking continued to enjoy growth and notoriety. One example of this is the *International Journal of Frontier Missions*, which dedicated two complete issues to tentmaking (14, no. 3 [1997] and 15, no. 1 [1998]). Consultations, partnerships, databases now possible through developing technology, formal and informal training, and member care continued to be tested and honed.

The Global Consultation on World Evangelization (GCOWE 1997), held in Pretoria, South Africa, drew approximately five thousand attendees from around the world. Through the Business Executive

---

[18]For information on this network, see www.missionresources.com/tentmakers.html.
[19]Don Hamilton, *Tentmakers Speak: Practical Advice from Over Four Hundred Missionary Tentmakers* (Ventura, CA: Regal Books, 1987).
[20]Tetsunao Yamamori, *God's New Envoys: A Bold Strategy for Penetrating "Closed Countries"* (Portland, OR: Multnomah Press, 1987).
[21]Cox, "Tentmaking Movement," 114.

Track, some five hundred committed businessmen and businesswomen called for cooperation between churches, agencies, and marketplace ministries to complete the Great Commission.

In 2000, seventy-nine books were published about the broader topic of faith and work. The International Coalition of Workplace Ministries (ICWM) counted two thousand new titles in just a two-year span.[22] Interest in integrating work and faith in the marketplace continues to grow. Following are a few of the noteworthy books that address another camp[23] of tentmaking, business as mission (BAM), as well as related formative gatherings.

David Befus, president of Latin American Mission (LAM), published *Kingdom Business: The Ministry of Promoting Economic Activity* in 2001.[24] The author promotes commercial ventures to fund ministries.

A consultation on kingdom business was held in 2002 at Virginia Beach. From this came *On Kingdom Business: Transforming Missions through Entrepreneurial Strategies,* edited by Tetsunao Yamamori and Ken Eldred.[25] The contributors answer the question of how to reach a globalized world more interested in lucrative jobs than in the gospel. The answer moves beyond the traditional tentmaker role to kingdom business. Kingdom business does not take jobs, but rather creates jobs.

In 2003, Steve Rundle, an economist, and I, a missiologist, collaborated to write *Great Commission Companies: The Emerging Role of Business in Missions.* We defined a Great Commission Company (GCC) as "a socially responsible, income-producing business, managed by kingdom professionals, created for the specific purpose of glorifying God and promoting the growth and multiplication of local churches in the least developed and least-evangelized parts of the world."[26] GCCs

[22]Brad A. Greenberg, "A Spiritual Growth Industry," *Christianity Today,* March 2007, 62.

[23]For a description of four business camps (Tentmaking, Market Place Ministries, Enterprise Development, and Business as Mission) in this modern movement, see Neal Johnson and Steve Rundle, "Distinctives and Challenges of Business as Mission," in *Business as Mission: From Impoverished to Empowered,* ed. Tom Steffen and Mike Barnett (Pasadena, CA: William Carey Library, 2005), 21–26.

[24]David R. Befus, *Kingdom Business: The Ministry of Promoting Economic Activity* (Miami: Latin America Mission, 2001).

[25]Tetsunao Yamamori and Ken Eldred, eds., *On Kingdom Business: Transforming Missions through Entrepreneurial Strategies* (Wheaton: Crossway, 2003).

[26]Rundle and Steffen, *Great Commission Companies,* 41.

establish legitimate macro-enterprise businesses that employ local workers, thereby contributing to the economic and spiritual health of the workers, their families, their community, and their nation. The book categorizes types of GCC models used around the world (from which we learned God is too creative for this to be accomplished). We also identified the helpful and harmful principles and practices used within these models.

In 2004, an issue group produced Lausanne Occasional Paper No. 59, entitled "Business as Mission: A New Vision, a New Heart, a Renewed Call."[27] This document does an excellent job of providing a sweeping overview of BAM.

The Evangelical Missiological Society's (EMS) theme for 2005 focused on BAM. Doug Pennoyer set the tone for the IFMA (Interdenominational Foreign Mission Association)/EMS annual meeting in 2006 when he stated, "To put it bluntly . . . business as mission (BAM) is a work in progress. It is a field that needs definition, theological clarity, and missiological focus. . . . Our call for papers . . . puts us in a place to make a pivotal contribution in a sea of some confusion and even controversy.[28] *Business as Mission: From Impoverishment to Empowerment* (2006), which I coedited with Mike Barnett, resulted from the papers presented. The various authors contributed to the literature by bringing some clarity to the "sea of some confusion and even controversy" within the BAM movement.

Ken Eldred's *God Is at Work: Transforming People and Nations through Business* was published in 2005. Borrowing some content from *On Kingdom Business*, which he coedited, Eldred provided one of the broadest (including micro, small, medium, and large privately owned companies) and clearest baseline definitions and visions of the BAM movement to date. Based on his personal experience with two successful companies and his wide grasp of BAM literature and practice, Eldred believes that "the overall objective of kingdom business is *sus-*

---

[27]Available at the Lausanne Movement website: www.lausanne.org/documents/2004forum/LOP59_IG30.pdf.
[28]Steffen and Barnett, *Business as Mission*, 15–16.

tainable spiritual and economic transformation."[29] For this to become a reality he calls for a triple bottom line: "(1) profitability and sustainability, (2) local job and wealth creation, and (3) advancing the local church and building spiritual capital."[30] Eldred believes that the church is more than ready to join the BAM movement.

In 2006, Michael Baer's *Business as Mission: The Power of Business in the Kingdom of God* was released.[31] As a founder of several businesses and as one who has launched "a small business incubation process" in some seventeen nations, Baer believes that corporations are presently replacing the role of nation states. This affords businesspeople an opportunity unprecedented in history to transform society and communicate the gospel. For this to happen, however, biblical thinking will have to challenge several areas: the bifurcation perception of work and ministry; the belief that Christian principles do not work in the real world; the role of God's kingdom today; and God's plans for the world tomorrow. Baer outlines ways for businesspeople to develop kingdom businesses that can transform the world.

So where do we go from here? What types of platforms exist? What should the ultimate goal of platforms be? What are the concerns that surround platforms? Let's consider these questions now.

Types, Goals and Concerns of Platforms

Platforms in missions tend to present themselves in one of two categories: individual or corporate.[32] Each category comes with its own strengths and weaknesses, but both are necessary to reach the 10/40 Window, and beyond. The category descriptions found in Table 1 should be understood as soft rather than hard, as there will always be exceptions.

One of the most common categories is an individual hired by a foreign institution. Teachers of English often fall into this category. A second category, the corporate, calls for setting up a platform, such as a

---

[29]Eldred, *God Is at Work*, 154 (italics in original).
[30]Ibid., 8.
[31]Michael R. Baer, *Business as Mission: The Power of Business in the Kingdom of God* (Seattle: YWAM Publishing, 2006).
[32]Barnett, "Innovation in Mission Operation," 221. See also Mike Barnett, "Creative Access Platforms," *Evangelical Missions Quarterly* 41, no. 1 (January 2005).

business. The first type tends to be short-term while the latter tends to be long-term. One reason for this is that it requires significant finances to start up a business as opposed to signing a teaching contract overseas, which usually requires little out-of-pocket expenses. The English teacher saves time and finances by taking advantage of existing infrastructure, while those in the business world usually have to build an infrastructure, which requires time, networks, and significant funding.

Due to its long-term vision and potential to create wealth, the business platform, unlike the teacher platform, has the potential to aggressively address holistic concerns beyond income-producing jobs.[33] It also has the potential to start new businesses, thus multiplying itself.

Table 32.1. Platform Distinctives

Categories	Individual	Corporate
Duration	Short-term	Long-term
Infrastructure	Provided	Required
Financial investment	Minimal	Significant
Holistic	Minimal	Strong
Multiplication	Minimal	Strong
Abuse potential	Philosophy	Philosophy

Effective platforms don't just evolve. Rather, they require careful planning, goal setting, and implementation, all of which should find their foundations in biblical principles. Either platform category can be abused, depending on one's philosophy and perspective. Dave and Donna, as you will recall, believed that business was a distraction from "real" ministry. Others see business *as* missions, not *for* missions. The same could be true of teachers in the classroom.

Platform participants should ask themselves a number of questions before arriving on the scene. What are the time requirements of the job? How much governmental or institutional restriction is placed on the expatriate on and off the job? What is the biblical view of work? Is work ministry or business? Platforms work best when seen not as a

---

[33]See case studies in Rundle and Steffen's *Great Commission Companies* for holistic involvement.

means to an end but as an end in itself, just as Christianity is best perceived as a total way of life.

Regarding business platforms specifically, I wish I could share Eldred's optimism that the church is more than ready to join the BAM movement and give business the rightful platform it deserves at home and abroad. Unfortunately, I find myself to be more pessimistic. Consider these two comments in regard to the clergy:

> "For people in the pews, business can be both a calling and a ministry," Neil Johnson says, "but for people in the pulpit, business is often a mystery, and for some, even an anathema."[34]

> Unfortunately, clergy don't know how to help those parishioners and they often show benign neglect, or even outright hostility, toward the marketplace.[35]

David Miller, who made this second observation, goes on to offer pastors some practical ways to improve the situation, one being commissioning services for those entering the workforce. But we must backtrack and go deeper in order for marketplace ministry to become a reality in churches. We must backtrack to the seminaries and training institutions from which pastors graduate. Rare is the seminary or training institution that addresses the business world, even though 39 of the 40 miracles done in Acts were conducted in the workplace, where 122 of 132 of Jesus' public appearances occurred in the workplace, where Jesus spent the major portion of his 33 years on earth before beginning his preaching ministry, and where the majority of people spend the majority of their time interacting with the majority of unsaved people.[36]

When theologians and pastors discern from Scripture that business is a divine calling, a legitimate ministry, and much more than philanthropy, things will begin to change. This may require the development of a "theology of work" in general and a "theology of business" in particular.[37]

---

[34]Joe Maxwell, "The Business of Business," *Christianity Today*, November 2007, 27.
[35]David Miller, "Scripture and *The Wall Street Journal*," *Christianity Today*, November 2007, 33.
[36]"Faith and Work Factsheet, 2004," Marketplace Leaders Ministries website, www.market placeleaders.org/faith-work-factsheet.
[37]On its website, the Business as Mission Network lists the top twenty-five Business as Mission

When this happens, business, missions, and the church will intersect, giving businesspeople the rightful status they deserve in the church while making legitimate business platforms commonplace.

Figure 32.1.

The future of the BAM movement is closely tied to how the educational arm of the church, and the church itself, will respond. I agree with Eldred when he says, "Seminary education should include validation of kingdom business as a legitimate calling for full-time Christian workers, not as an inferior alternative to the ministry. Seminarians should leave with a vision for mobilizing the laity—and especially business people—for the Kingdom, understanding the tremendous untapped potential of business professionals in the pews."[38]

My prayer is for legitimate business platforms endorsed by the church throughout the 10/40 Window, and every other nation, so that funding and qualified lay and professional business personnel may help complete the Great Commission.

Conclusion

Does the proposed platform bring respect to Jesus Christ and his teachings? Does it bless families and the nations? Does it demonstrate God's "worthship"? Those establishing legitimate business platforms will answer yes to all three questions. Not only do such platforms provide marketplace kingdom workers a legal means to enter and remain in host countries, particularly those hostile to the gospel, they also offer opportunities to serve others, pointing them toward Christ. More importantly, they offer kingdom workers the opportunity to

---

books, www.businessasmissionnetwork.com/2007/07/top-25-business-as-mission-books.html.
[38]Eldred, *God Is at Work*, 8.

worship the Creator. Why? Because work done through the power of
the Holy Spirit is worship. "Without exception the most secure business
'platform' is the profitable, job-creating, tax-paying, worshiping
company."[39] Are you listening, Dave and Donna?

Discussion Points

1. Define the word *platforms*. Are platforms good or bad?

2. Are platforms and BAM ventures legal? Ethical? Why or why not?

3. What does Steffen mean by the deaconal movement in a platform?
   How should it relate to the apostolic and business aspects of a platform?

4. Do you have a platform for your work in the mission of God? Explain.

Further Reading

Eldred, Ken. *God Is at Work: Transforming People and Nations Through Business.*
   Ventura, CA: Regal Books, 2005.

Prahalad, C. K., *The Fortune at the Bottom of the Pyramid: Eradicating Poverty
   through Profits.* Upper Saddle River, NJ: Wharton School Publishing, 2005.

Rundle, Steve, and Tom Steffen, *Great Commission Companies: The Emerging
   Role of Business in Missions.* Downers Grove, IL: InterVarsity, 2003.

Steffen, Tom, and Mike Barnett, eds. *Business as Mission: From Impoverishment to Empowerment.* Pasadena, CA: William Carey Library, 2006.

---

[39]Rundle and Steffen, *Great Commission Companies*, 23.

33

BIBLICAL LESSONS FROM THE PERSECUTED CHURCH

Nik Ripken and Kurt Nelson

So do not be ashamed of the testimony about our Lord
or of me his prisoner. Rather, join with me in suffering
for the gospel, by the power of God.

2 TIMOTHY 1:8

Christians who live in nations where persecution is not a normal occurrence often cringe in horror when they hear reports that their brothers and sisters around the globe are experiencing atrocities of suffering and death for their faith in Jesus Christ. Our natural inclination is to cry out to God and governments to stop these tragedies. But we must pause to ask ourselves, "Are our responses biblically informed and missiologically sound?" A biblical theology of persecution creates the framework within which we can develop a proper missiology of suffering, which, in turn, enables us to have "ears to hear" essential lessons on persecution from the persecuted church worldwide.

Definitions

For the purpose of this chapter, we define persecution as "the negative reactions by governments, ideologies, societies, and families to the presence of Christ, incarnated through a positive witness by believing individuals and communities for the purpose of silencing witness."[1]

The most extreme form of Christian persecution is that in which a believer in Jesus Christ is killed for the practice or profession of their faith. The term "martyr" has been used for Jesus' own death at the hands of Jewish and Roman authorities, as well as for the persecution and related deaths of his followers for more than two thousand years. Church history is replete with examples of Christian martyrs, most notably recorded by John Foxe in his book *Foxe's Book of Martyrs*.[2] The church has consistently celebrated the heroic faith of those who have died for their witness for Christ. As Dietrich Bonhoeffer noted, "A few, but only a few, of [Christ's] followers are accounted worthy of the closest fellowship with [Christ's] sufferings—the blessed martyrs. No other Christian is so closely identified with the form of Christ crucified."[3]

Recent publicity on persecution and martyrdom during the twentieth century has brought renewed attention to the usage and definition of the term "martyr" by Protestant believers, among others. Susan Bergman, in her book *Martyrs*, offers what she calls "the simplest understanding of martyrdom" as occurring when a person "is required to deny Christ and live, or confess [Christ] and die. Under such duress the martyr freely chooses death over life—death seals a life's belief—in order to act as a witness to the truth of Christ's claims and to his or her own faith."[4]

Moody Bible Institute, which has produced twenty-one graduates who have been martyred for their faith and witness, adopted the definition of a martyr as "those who were killed because they refused to renounce their faith or because of active opposition to their witness for Christ."[5] Missiologists note that while it is inaccurate to state that "Christian martyrs always die strictly for their testimony

---

[1]Nik Ripken, "A Missiology of Suffering: Witness and Church Planting in the Midst of Persecution" (paper presented during doctoral studies class at Columbia International University, 2006).

[2]John Foxe, *Foxe's Book of Martyrs*, rewritten and updated by Harold J. Chadwick (Gainesville, FL: Bridge-Logos, 2001).

[3]Dietrich Bonhoeffer, *The Cost of Discipleship* (New York: Touchstone, 1995), 302.

[4]Susan Bergman, ed., *Martyrs: Contemporary Writers on Modern Lives of Faith* (Maryknoll, NY: Orbis, 1998), 3.

[5]Marvin J. Newell, *A Martyr's Grace* (Chicago: Moody, 2006), 12.

for Christ . . . it is apparent that most Christian martyrs die in circumstances *related* to their witness for Christ."[6]

Christian Persecution: Past and Present

When examined from a historical perspective, it is universally agreed that the early persecutors of the church and of Christians were the Jewish leaders (AD 32–64), followed by the Roman state (AD 64–313). Following the persecutions led by the Roman state, the Catholic Church then became the principle persecutor of various "heretical" sects of Christians for the next 1,500 years (AD 385–1870).[7] The papacy waged persecutions against "heretics" and "heathens" across Europe and South America well into the nineteenth century. It was not until 1870 that the Roman Catholic Church officially renounced papal persecutions.[8]

The twentieth and twenty-first centuries have seen the most dramatic upsurge in worldwide persecution, beginning with the Soviet Communist empire (1917 to 1991) and the Communist regime in China (1949 to present). Other significant persecutions of Christians have occurred, including those in North Korea (1945 to present), Japan (1941 to 1945), and Latin America, where the Communist dictatorship of Cuba continues to persecute Christians to the present day.[9] Persecutors of Christians in this era have included, among others, Hindus in India; Buddhists in Sri Lanka; the Orthodox in Eastern Europe; Catholics in Eastern Europe and Latin America; Muslims in Africa, the Middle East, and Asia; and a few remaining Communist and totalitarian regimes. Paul Marshall describes the magnitude of this persecution as a "spiritual plague" affecting "over two hundred million people, with an additional four hundred million suffering from discrimination and legal impediments."[10]

---

[6]James C. Hefley and Marti Hefley, *By Their Blood: Christian Martyrs of the Twentieth Century* (Grand Rapids: Baker, 1996), 9.

[7]John McClintock and James Strong, *Cyclopaedia of Biblical, Theological, and Ecclesiastical Literature*, vol. 7–8 (New York: Arno Press, 1969), 963.

[8]Charles S. Carter and G. E. A. Weeks, eds., *The Protestant Dictionary: Containing the Articles on the History, Doctrines, and Practices of the Christian Church* (London: The Harrison Trust, 1933), 503.

[9]John Bowden, ed., *Encyclopedia of Christianity* (New York: Oxford University Press, 2005), 917.

[10]Paul Marshall, *Their Blood Cries Out* (Nashville: W Publishing Group, 1997), 4.

Those who monitor the persecution of Christians worldwide have observed that the worst perpetrators today tend to be the Islamic states (more than fifty nations), where persecution is currently at a significant level.[11] Marshall cited a 1997 State Department report noting that there were more than sixty countries where "Christians face the reality of massacre, rape, torture, mutilation, family division, harassment, imprisonment, slavery, discrimination in education and employment, and even death, simply for what they believe."[12]

In the 2001 updated version of *Foxe's Book of Martyrs*, Harold Chadwick noted that in the twentieth century "more Christians have been killed for their faith than in all the previous centuries combined."[13] Current trends include a "wave of persecution [across] the Islamic belt from Morocco on the Atlantic eastward through to the southern Philippines."[14] Other trends include the continuing threat of Communism, rising religious and ethnic nationalism, the persecution of Christians by other Christians, and widespread, worldwide religious discrimination.[15]

Biblical Perspectives

An objective look at the Bible reveals a different perspective on how we view and respond to persecution.

Anticipated and necessary in God's plan. Jesus foretold the necessity of his own persecution and death in fulfilling the mission that God the Father ordained for him (Mark 8:31; 9:31; 10:32–34). Jesus was destined to encounter and endure violent persecution and ultimately death in order to effect God's plan for the salvation of the world. The Bible repeatedly reveals that Christ's disciples will also encounter the same

[11]Paul Strand, "Why the West Won't Hear about Persecution," CBN.com, original broadcast, January 8, 2011, www.cbn.com/cbnnews/world/2011/January/Why-the-West-Wont-Hear-about-Christian-Persecution; Christian Examiner staff report, "Islamic Countries Dominate Christian Persecution List" Christian Examiner Online, January 2011, www.christianexaminer.com/Articles/Articles%20Jan11/Art_Jan11_19.html#.TurTfz0xiBk.email.

[12]Paul Marshall, "Present Day Persecution of Christians," *Evangelical Review of Theology* 24, no. 1 (2000): 19–30.

[13]Foxe, *Book of Martyrs*, 425.

[14]Paul Marshall, ed., *Religious Freedom in the World: A Global Report on Freedom and Persecution* (Nashville: Broadman & Holman, 2000), 27.

[15]Ibid., 28–29.

hostile responses from the world that he experienced, simply because they bear witness to him (Matthew 10:22; Mark 13:9–13; Luke 11:49; 21:12–19; 2 Timothy 3:12; 1 Peter 4:14; Revelation 1:9). The sufferings of Christ naturally overflow into the lives of those who bear his name (2 Corinthians 1:5). Persecution is a necessary corollary of our identification with Christ. In his book intended to guide the twenty-first century church through the fires of persecution, Ronald Boyd-Mac-Millan observes that "persecution is the default standard of the Christian life because the world hates Christ, and we bear in our own lives the marks of that enmity."[16]

Essential to establishing the church. Persecution is not only a necessary axiom of identifying with and following Christ, but it is also is a necessary force in the extension of Christ's kingdom. As Hilaire Valiquette concludes, "Persecution and rejection are necessary steps in the process of the coming of God's kingdom; they are not unfortunate and temporary setbacks."[17] Jesus understood that the expansion of the church and God's kingdom upon the earth would only be achieved in the context of a cosmic battle against the kingdom of darkness. Following Peter's confession that Jesus is Messiah-God, Jesus promised to build his church upon *that* reality, stating, "On this rock I will build my church, and the gates of Hades will not overcome it" (Matthew 16:18). Jesus thus affirmed that his church would be birthed in the midst of spiritual warfare in which the church would ultimately prevail.

The apostle Paul warned the church in Philippi, "It has been granted to you on behalf of Christ not only to believe in him, but also to suffer for him" (Philippians 1:29). Both saving faith and suffering for that faith are essential aspects of God's plan for establishing the church. Thus Paul invites his young disciple, Timothy, to join him in preaching the gospel and in suffering for the gospel of Christ (2 Timothy 1:8). Persecution is "biblically and historically normative for the emerging church; it cannot be avoided or eliminated."[18] Paul told the church of

---

[16]Ronald Boyd-MacMillan, *Faith That Endures: The Essential Guide to the Persecuted Church* (Grand Rapids: Revell, 2006), 109.

[17]Hilaire Valiquette, "Handed Over to the Gentiles: The Centrality of Persecution for Missiology," *Missiology: An International Review* 26, no. 4 (1998): 431–43.

[18]Mohit Gupta, "Servants in the Crucible: Findings from a Global Study on Persecution and the

Thessalonica that persecution was, in fact, a part of his destiny as a servant of God's church (1 Thessalonians 3:3–4).

Evil and temporal. Persecution, at its core, is essentially a form of spiritual warfare that is completely evil in its origin and power. As Paul describes spiritual warfare, he notes that the ultimate source of persecution of God's people is Satan: "Our struggle is not against flesh and blood, but against the rulers, against the authorities, against the powers of this dark world and against the spiritual forces of evil in the heavenly realms" (Ephesians 6:12).

The New Testament record clearly affirms the central role that Satan played in afflicting and tempting Jesus to stray from his God-ordained mission (Matthew 4:10; 16:23; Mark 1:13; 8:33; Luke 4:1–13; 22:3). Similarly, Satan opposes the faith of believers from its inception, seeking to destroy it (Mark 4:15). Satan sought to destroy the faith and ministry of Simon Peter (Luke 22:31) and entered into Judas, causing him to betray Jesus (Luke 22:3; John 13:2,27). Satan filled the heart of Ananias and caused him to lie to the Holy Spirit about a gift to the church (Acts 5:3). Satan is the source of temptation and of apostasy for the Christian believer (1 Corinthians 7:5; 1 Timothy 5:15), and he hinders the work and mission of God (1 Thessalonians 2:18). Satan is the adversary of the Christian, whom he seeks to devour and to destroy (John 10:10; 1 Peter 5:8); and he is the deceiver of the whole world (Revelation 12:9).

Intermediate sources of persecution of Christians include the fallen "world system" (John 15:18–21) as well as people who oppose the work of God (Matthew 5:11,44). Notable in the New Testament record is the identification of religious and political systems and authorities as persecutors of Christian believers and, therefore, of Christ's church (Matthew 10:17–23; 23:34; Luke 11:49; 21:12; Acts 8:1; 9:4–5, 13:50; 22:7–8; 26:14–15). If persecution is evil, then it is also, by necessity, temporal and ultimately destined to cease. This will occur at the second coming of Christ when Satan will be forever vanquished and God's kingdom will eternally destroy the forces of evil and darkness.

Implications for Sending Agencies and Sending Churches" (paper presented during doctoral studies class at Columbia International University, 2006).

The Bible repeatedly offers a perspective that juxtaposes the present suffering of believers, which is referred to as "light and momentary," in contrast to the future of Christians, which is described as being filled with "eternal glory" (Romans 8:18; 2 Corinthians 4:17–18; Colossians 3:1–4). Christians are urged to keep this eternal perspective in mind in order to help them endure evil (but temporal) persecutions.

The Purposes of Persecution

Though there are not extensive biblical texts related to the goal or motive of the persecutors, the apostle Paul's testimony of his own preconversion motives as a religious persecutor of Christians provides significant insight.

Satan's purpose. Paul states that his personal goal in persecuting Christians was to force them to blaspheme against Christ (Acts 26:11). He acknowledges that he sought to destroy the church (Galatians 1:13) and the Christian faith (Galatians 1:23). Jesus, furthermore, acknowledged that the purpose of the persecutors was to cause his followers to "turn away" or "fall away" from their faith (Matthew 11:6; 24:9–10, 26:31) and to hate and betray each other (Matthew 24:10).

Believers living in the midst of persecution suggest strongly that the goal of Satan is not to beat, torture, or kill believers. Suffering believers remind us that the goal of Satan and his persecutors is to silence believers, to make believers lose (or give up) their voice, and to diminish witness. Persecutors strive to silence witness as covertly as possible. The most successful persecution happens when an immediate family member, a boss, a spouse, or the culture in general pressures the convert into remaining quiet, keeping faith "personal." The persecutors want to relegate faith to the environs of the Western world. Or they desire that faith be practiced only within the walls of a few church buildings that are closely monitored by the state or the local religious authorities. Such are the clandestine purposes of the persecutors.

God's purpose. We cannot fully comprehend all of God's purposes in allowing the persecution of Christ's followers. We can only understand those purposes articulated in Scripture, though they are few in number. The book of Acts records the fact that the early believers left Jerusalem and scattered to other key cities as a result of intense persecution (Acts 8:1–4; 11:19). One may conclude that God purposed to use persecution to spread and multiply the church. Persecution serves to test and strengthen a believer's faith (Romans 5:3–4; James 1:3, 1 Peter 1:6–7; 4:12). There is a mysterious purpose in persecution and suffering related to bringing about the kingdom of God (2 Thessalonians 1:4–5).

Scripture tells us that Jesus was "perfected" as the author of salvation and in his obedience through suffering (Hebrews 2:10; 5:8–10). This principle has limited but valid application to God's purposes for suffering in the lives of Christian leaders. And, finally, one of God's purposes in affliction and suffering is to equip his servants with the ability to comfort and sustain others who endure similar afflictions (2 Corinthians 1:3–11).

Responding Wisely

In response to persecution, the protocol for many well-meaning advocacy groups often reflects a four-fold agenda:

1. Stop the persecution.

2. Punish the persecutors.

3. Promote Western forms of government and democracy.

4. Raise money to aid in assisting in the rescue or resourcing of persecuted believers.

A biblical missiology of persecution might lead us to respond differently, however. Understanding that persecution and martyrdom are predicted and necessary (though temporal) evils that are allowed in God's plan to establish his church and inaugurate his kingdom on earth might argue for different responses. Understanding that Satan's goal is to silence witness, either by the intimidation or elimination of believers, might further motivate other ways and objectives in responding to persecution. And finally, understanding that God has allowed the evil of persecution to serve his sovereign purposes to expand, purify, strengthen, and multiply his kingdom on earth leads us to respond differently to persecution as followers of Jesus' example.

What follows are some helpful do's and don'ts that we have gleaned from the persecuted church to better inform our responses to the present reality of persecution.

Things not to do:

1. *Do not model fear for those who suffer persecution.* When believers who live and minister in the midst of persecution are asked, "What have you learned from the Western missionaries?" too often their replies have been sobering. "Western missionaries teach us to be afraid." This is not a missiological mistake; it is a sin.

2. *Do not continue unwise mission tactics or practices that expose those under persecution to greater and unnecessary risks.* In spite of all we have been taught in our literate seminaries about how the Bible progressed from its oral forms to written forms, in the New Testament era it didn't take God twenty to sixty years to become literate. God could have had his writers pen the words as they happened, but he was too wise to do that. He kept his word in oral forms until the days when those in the stories had joined him in heaven or were no longer at risk. Putting the stories of believers suffering persecution (even motivated by advocacy on their behalf) in literate forms, in real time, often increases their persecution. The church and its workers need to learn how to advocate and share their stories orally, writing this generation's stories for the succeeding generation.

Persecuted believers are often harmed for their relationships with outsiders. They are targeted because of those with whom they work and worship. When local believers are observed regularly worshiping with Westerners or having outsiders frequent their homes (to the exception of the broader lost community), persecution is heightened. Missionaries should avoid taking the place of the local church when it comes to caring for local believers financially or providing a place or culture for worship.

Even in settings where the majority of the populations are oral communicators, Western workers have a practice of handing out the written Word of God in a wholesale fashion. Too often these oral communicators are persecuted for being found with a Bible that they can't read, but they couldn't refuse such a lavish gift from a visiting outsider. The least that Western workers should do in these settings is to tell the recipient that their gift is indeed a Bible, and ask them if they desire the gift. And would they be able to read it, or would they prefer to have someone read it to them?

The goal is not to make people afraid from the first witness but to model wisdom for them. This may also serve to give greater perceived value to God's Word. In environments framed by severe persecution, paying local believers to evangelize (often using Western methods of sharing one's faith) can be extremely dangerous. This writer has experienced such practices where there was 90 percent unemployment. Muslims came to the evangelist asking for a job with "those Christians who are paying for salvations," then adding, "I need to feed my family."

3. *Do not extract persecuted believers out of their country or people group context to safety.* After conducting hundreds of interviews among those living in persecution, it can be noted that, once persecution becomes serious, approximately 50 percent of local believers are extracted to a place or country of safety by Western missionaries. Among believers from within Islam, this percentage is as high as 70 percent. It would be difficult to plant churches in the United States, the United Kingdom, or anywhere in the Western Christian world if 70 percent of those baptized were extracted to other countries. This also models fear and a nonbiblical missiology of suffering.

Jesus didn't command his followers to stay within persecution, placing children and others at risk no matter the cost. His advice was to flee to the next city, the next village, or the next location inhabited by extended family. The goal, as much as possible, must be to stay within one's people group, not forsaking a bold witness continually within their midst. God did direct Joseph to take Jesus and

Mary to Egypt because Herod wanted to kill Jesus, but the intention was always to return (Matthew 2:13–20). Those we extract almost never return.

Reflecting on Joseph's experience in Genesis, we might ask: *How do we know when it is within the will of God for our "Joseph" to spend a season in "Pharaoh's prison"?* It is always easier when it is someone else's "Joseph." No matter how good the intentions, if Joseph had been rescued prematurely it would have led to the starvation of both the Egyptians and Joseph's family (the people of Israel).

4. *Do not flee as missionaries or ministers of the gospel.* As faith is shared among the nations, the Bible is clear: both those who give witness and those who receive witness will often be called upon to pay a price for their godliness. What risks are foreign missionaries willing to assume in regard to their children? This is not a call for an absence of common sense. There have always been places in the world where a missionary would perhaps be unwise to minister, at least initially, with a spouse and children. Where violence reigns and there is the barest opportunity for witness, it may be wise to consider sending only one spouse and/or single adults into traumatic environments. As civil war and violence ease, couples may be able to minister together fruitfully. It may take another season of the fledgling mission before it becomes prudent for families with children to incarnate a biblical witness more fully within the matrix of their host society. Yet should the Western missionary be the last in and first out? Never!

Globally, those serving in the military, the United Nations, and the building and engineering trades are taking great risks for the cause of humanity, nationality, or financial gain. In the worst environments, people serve for various reasons and ideologies. Shouldn't Christ trump any other reason for going to places defined as high risk?

5. *Do not withhold your witness, but do the work of an evangelist.* The number one cause of persecution is people coming to Jesus. We cannot change that. What we must do is pray to be found worthy of sharing in Christ's sufferings. In areas rife with persecution, it is often problematic when God gives new missionaries fruit early in

their ministries. The new workers might then spend 90 percent of their time "pastoring" the ten to fifteen new believers, relegating evangelism to a secondary ministry.

Can it be suggested that the role of a missionary is different, while complementary to, the role of a pastor? Pastors gather and minister to those who are within the kingdom. Missionaries intentionally strive to remain among the lost.

6. *Do not run from persecution, and do not seek it.* If you or a team member fears and always flees from persecution, you have a serious problem. Conversely, if you or a team member seeks persecution and suffering, then you need to look for a counselor who can help bring restoration of emotional and spiritual health.

When it comes to giving a consistent and bold witness, the issue is not one of living in a particular political, social, or religious environment that is defined by freedom or persecution. Individuals are equally free to share Jesus in Saudi Arabia as they are in the United States. At all times and in all places we are equally free to share Christ with those outside of the kingdom of God. The commandment to be a witness was never predicated upon political freedom. Witness is not tied to governments or to one's social setting; it is firmly aligned with obedience. Individuals are free to share Christ in every environment if they are willing to suffer the consequences of their obedient witness. God determines our political and social setting. We determine if we will be obedient within that setting.

7. *Do not regret when those who come to saving faith in Christ are persecuted.* The Bible is clear: it is an honor to share in the sufferings of Christ and to be found worthy of his cross. But experiencing persecution and suffering for any reason, even for Jesus, is never fun and should never be sought. Persecution is truly blood, sweat, and tears, involving things like separation from loved ones, incarceration, abuse, humiliation, and having one's children grow up without a father or a mother. And yet it was the early church's willingness to remain faithful witnesses—to suffer and die—that authenticated their faith in Christ.

When brothers and sisters are paying big prices for their faith, it is the church's task to intercede for them. This provides a God-given opportunity for the local church to care for their families, and they should never forget them. We should constantly remind them, and ourselves, that their suffering is for Jesus.

Things to do:

1. *Do accept the hard truth that persecution is normal, and prepare yourself and others for that reality.* Pastors in the former USSR describe persecution as being as normal as the sun coming up in the east. When asked why they didn't write down the impressive and heartbreaking stories of their sufferings, persecution, and martyrdom under Communism so that we in the West would have a record of their stories, they reply, "When did you chaps in the West stop reading the Bible? From Genesis to Revelation the Word is filled with the accounts of those choosing to follow God and consequently paying a big price for doing so."

2. *Do pray.* Believers living in the midst of persecution call us to intervention through prayer. They call Western Christians who are not themselves in the midst of overt suffering to pray: not that persecution for other believers might end, but that the persecuted would be obedient in the midst of their suffering—obedient to endure and to share, especially with their persecutors, the forgiveness and love that is found through the resurrection of Jesus Christ.

   Ronald Boyd-MacMillan states, "Ask the persecuted, 'How can we help you?' and you will invariably find that their first answer is 'Pray for us!' Usually their second answer is 'Pray for us!' And their third answer is 'Pray for us!' There is absolutely no question that when it comes to tactical assistance, it is prayer that the persecuted crave more than anything else from their less persecuted brothers and sisters."[19]

3. *Do focus on "lostness," taking risks for the gospel.* Believers suffering persecution ask Western missionaries to model for them how to take risks among those who still remain outside the kingdom of God.

---

[19]Boyd-MacMillan, *Faith That Endures*, 255–56.

They define a missionary as one who was made for lostness. Conversely, they note that most Western missionaries take the bulk of their risks among those already saved, those within the kingdom of God. Where, they ask, are missionaries getting into trouble or coming to the attention of the authorities—the persecutors? Many times missionaries get into trouble because of their associations with emerging or existing churches: in corporate worship with locals, at baptisms, and at the Lord's Supper. Local believers ask the Western workers, however, to model taking risks by associating with their neighbors, the corrupt policeman, the customs officer, the shop owner, and those they meet at tea and coffee shops. "Model for us," they say, "how to do the task of a missionary. Will you risk a bold witness, allowing us to gather and minister to the sheep?"

4. *Do be tough in the face of suffering.* It requires physical, emotional, psychological, and spiritual toughness to stay the course in the face of suffering and persecution, especially when Satan attacks one's fruit (new disciples). Few things are more devastating to Western missionaries than when the fruit of their witness suffers for their newfound faith, often while the outsider goes unscathed. Recognize this as spiritual warfare that needs to be resisted and rebuked. Satan loves to persecute one's fruit and then make the one who gave a bold, faithful witness feel guilty for being obedient.

5. *Do be bold in your personal witness—starting now.* Missionaries often answer a call to overseas missions, anticipating sharing Christ with the nations, while they have been lukewarm in their witness within their own culture and to their own families. We are to be bold witnesses as we go from Jerusalem, Judea, Samaria, and among the nations. Set goals for how often you will share your faith. Covenant with God regarding how many people you desire to see come to him and be gathered into house churches. Answer four questions for yourself that lead to effective witness: (1) What will I say? (2) Who will I say it to? (3) Who will hold me accountable as to whether I witness or remain silent? (4) What will I do when someone responds to my witness?

6. *Do prepare missionaries and national workers to suffer in the midst of persecution.* Slowly, but thankfully, Western workers are moving ever deeper among those who are dangerously unreached. It is becoming more common for Western missionaries to suffer individually and as families. Martyrdom of Western workers becomes more common as obedience deepens. The time and place to prepare followers of Christ for the cost of "cross-bearing" is within the confines of their local churches. If the task is delayed until cross-cultural workers arrive at their respective missionary training centers—or worse, after they arrive on their respective mission fields—it is too late. Much of the Western church has a nonbiblical missiology of suffering, persecution, and martyrdom. The Western church must return to its biblical roots and embrace a bold witness to the nations, whatever the cost.

7. *Do become culturally astute in order to minimize unnecessary persecution.* The number one way to reduce persecution for secondary reasons is to learn the local language and culture. As missionaries become competent in sharing Christ as much as possible as an insider, persecution is significantly reduced. The converse is sadly true. The more one operates as a "missionary tourist," then the more persecution related to the outsider escalates.

   Those that came to Christ in the New Testament era came to him through a local or regional language. When God reveals himself through dreams and visions he always appears to the lost in their heart language. Short-term missions trips are valuable, but the goal must always be to retain a long-term commitment by someone who is astute in the local language and culture.

8. *Do continue to deploy workers, especially to areas of greatest "lostness."* Depending upon which figures are used, 70 to 80 percent of all Western missionaries are deployed within the reached, Christian world. It takes intentionality for churches, mission agencies, and missionaries to stay deliberately among the "wolves." Missionaries are very accomplished at recognizing open doors and developing entry strategies. Generally, though, we do a very poor job of developing exit strategies. We stay too long and thereby deny millions outside of Christ their

opportunity to hear, to understand, and to believe the gospel, and to establish indigenous churches in their midst.

9. *Do persevere in work and witness for the extension of Christ's kingdom.* The apostles were shrewd regarding this aspect of the missionary journey. Some workers sowed the gospel seed while others watered the emerging faith, yet God makes it grow and brings the harvest (1 Corinthians 3:6). Hebrews 12:1 speaks of the "cloud of witnesses" that the sovereign God uses to bring faith into fruition. Historically, accounts abound of those who serve sacrificially their whole lives with little fruit as a result, but then missionaries generations later, standing on the shoulders of the saints that went before them, witness a great harvest.

Perseverance and the Glory of God

As believers share in experiencing Christ's sufferings and persevere in their faith, God is glorified in the end. The apostle Paul writes to the church in Rome to tell the believers there, "Now if we are children, then we are heirs—heirs of God and co-heirs with Christ, if indeed we share in his sufferings in order that we may also share in his glory" (Romans 8:17). Paul exhorts the church in Colossae to set their hearts and minds on "things above" where Christ is and where their eternal life is, so that when Jesus appears, "then you also will appear with him in glory" (Colossians 3:1–4).

The singular strategy promoted in the New Testament for persevering in the face of persecution is found in the exhortation to remain focused upon Jesus' person and presence as "the pioneer and perfecter of faith" (Hebrews 12:2), and to consider his personal example of persevering through persecution (Hebrews 12:3). The apostle John also recognized that the source of our perseverance is to be found "in Jesus" (Revelation 1:9). Therefore, it is not surprising that the first martyr, Stephen, who was stoned to death for his faith, gazed into heaven and saw Jesus, and cried out to him to receive his spirit (Acts 7:54–60). Focusing on Jesus' example, his person, and his presence is the unique strategy offered in the New Testament to

Christians who would successfully endure persecution.

Jesus taught his followers that those who hold to his teaching "will know the truth, and the truth will set you free" (John 8:31–32). A number of key passages in God's Word are extremely motivating in encouraging believers to persevere in the face of persecution. These New Testament perspectives greatly encourage and inspire perseverance through tribulation and persecution:

1. It is a great honor to be persecuted (Matthew 5:10–11; 2 Thessalonians 1:5; Hebrews 11:26).

2. Persecution results in our good and our growth (Romans 5:3; James 1:2–4).

3. The persecuted will receive a heavenly reward (Matthew 5:12; 2 Thessalonians 1:7–10; James 1:12).

4. Persecution can never separate us from the love of God (Romans 8:35–39).

5. Persecution cannot conquer our faith (Romans 8:33–39).

6. God limits our persecution according to his will (2 Corinthians 4:8–9).

7. God is our sole deliverer (2 Timothy 3:11).

8. God will ultimately avenge the persecuted (2 Thessalonians 1:6).

9. Persecution "rightly endured" reveals Jesus to the world (2 Corinthians 4:8–11).

10. Persecution is spiritual (not human or physical) warfare; therefore the battle must be fought spiritually (2 Corinthians 10:3–5; Ephesians 6:10–20).

Conclusion

Understanding and embracing these New Testament perspectives on persecution in the context of a comprehensive New Testament theology of persecution and appropriate Christian response can effectively prepare, equip, and galvanize the follower of Christ to endure persecution victoriously. Such endurance and perseverance will glorify God and further the gospel witness of our Lord Jesus Christ, for whom we suffer.

In closing, the response of the apostles, after having been flogged and ordered by the high priest and the Sanhedrin to cease speaking further in the name of Jesus, is a great pattern for believers to follow today: "The apostles left the Sanhedrin, rejoicing because they had been counted worthy of suffering disgrace for the Name. Day after day, in the temple courts and from house to house, they never stopped teaching and proclaiming the good news that Jesus is the Messiah" (Acts 5:41–42).

Their two-fold response was to *rejoice* that they had been persecuted for the name of Christ and to continue both publicly and privately *proclaiming the good news* of Jesus the Messiah. Joy and a bold witness in the face of opposition and persecution should mark every disciple of Jesus until he returns to fully establish God's kingdom and to receive his church as his perfect bride for all eternity.

Discussion Points

1. If the number one cause of persecution is people turning to Jesus, then how should the believing church pray?

2. Since the satanic foundation/goal of persecution is denying others access to Jesus, what has the evil one used to silence the witness of Western believers?

3. Do you consider persecution today (as it is in Scripture) to be "normal"?

4. How does your personal perspective on persecution need to be re-aligned with New Testament perspectives on persecution?

5. In responding to the present reality of worldwide persecution, which "Do nots" and which "Dos" do you need to incorporate into your personal life and witness?

Further Reading

Alcorn, Randy. *Safely Home.* Carol Stream, IL: Tyndale, 2003.

Bridges, Eric, and Jerry Rankin. *Lives Given, Not Taken.* Richmond, VA: International Mission Board, 2005.

Estabrooks, Paul, and Jim Cunningham, eds. *Standing Strong Through the Storm.* Santa Ana, CA: Open Doors International, 2004.

Fernando, Ajith. *The Call to Joy and Pain.* Wheaton: Crossway, 2007.

Foxe, John. *Foxe's Book of Martyrs.* Rewritten and updated by Harold J. Chadwick. Gainesville, FL: Bridge-Logos, 2001.

Hefley, James C., and Marti Hefley. *By Their Blood: Christian Martyrs of the Twentieth Century.* Grand Rapids: Baker, 1996.

Marshall, Paul. *Their Blood Cries Out.* Nashville: W Publishing Group, 1997.

Muller, Roland. *Honor and Shame: Unlocking the Door.* Bloomington, IN: Xlibris Corporation, 2001.

Newell, Marvin J. *A Martyr's Grace.* Chicago: Moody, 2006.

Swartley, Keith. *Encountering the World of Islam.* Colorado Springs: Authentic, 2005.

34

WOMEN ON MISSION
WITH GOD

Meg Page

The two young women had just experienced an emotional day saying goodbye to neighbors in a West African village. It was a sad time, but also an encouraging and affirming time. Two years earlier they had come to live as Christ's followers among this unreached West African people group. They learned their language and culture by sharing their daily life—living and working with the villagers twenty-four hours a day, seven days a week. This involved living in a simple hut without electricity or running water, working in the fields with the women, eating whatever was placed before them—total submersion.

They were a OneStory team.[1] Based on what they learned of the language and culture, they chose a basic set of stories from the Bible that effectively communicated God's redemptive work for the human race to this unreached people. They began with creation and ended with Christ's promised return. They included stories that effectively overcame cultural barriers that prevented belief among their people, while at the same time using God-ordained cultural bridges that enabled individuals to believe. Then they carefully selected a native speaker to help them translate and craft their stories. They also back-translated, tested, and corrected the set of stories by telling them to

---

[1] OneStory is a partnership of the International Mission Board, Wycliffe Bible Translators, Campus Crusade for Christ, Trans World Radio, and YWAM to provide a beginning set of Bible stories for oral unreached people groups who do not have Scripture in their own language.

native speakers in order to make sure the gospel message was accurately communicated and understood.

This particular OneStory team had a rocky start. Other than the normal challenges of crossing cultural and language barriers, missionaries and national believers had told them that no Western person could learn the language of their people group—and certainly not in one year. In addition, though arrangements had been made with village elders before their arrival, they were not initially welcomed into the village. The villagers didn't know what to do with them, and at first seemed to resent their presence. But they persevered, and God was faithful. Problems were ironed out; they learned the very difficult language, grew comfortable in the culture, and became valued members of the village. They chose, translated, and tested their set of stories and were almost finished with their corrections. That day, as they said goodbye, everyone in the village cried—a very un-African thing to do, especially for the chief and his sons.

The women would spend the next couple of weeks working with their story crafter (being trained in another country) to finalize their set of stories and then record them. Soon the recordings would be widely distributed among their unreached people group. Yes, they were sad to leave, but they were also very excited about what God had done in their lives and in the lives of their people. Because they had obeyed God's call and persevered through difficulties, the gospel would be available for the first time to this largely illiterate unreached Muslim people group. They were also excited about the future and ready to be involved in God's mission to reach a lost world—wherever he sent them, whatever he asked them to do.

God Entrusted Women

In biblical times. God, "who works out everything in conformity with the purpose of his will" (Ephesians 1:11), chose to entrust women, in particular Mary Magdalene and "the other Mary" (Matthew 28:1)—probably Mary the mother of James and Joseph (Matthew 27:56,61)—with the wonderful news of the resurrection. The risen Christ's words to them were, "Do not be afraid. Go and tell . . ." (Matthew 28:10). They were the first women to be entrusted with this life- and world-transforming news, but they certainly were not the last.

In the Gospels we read of many women who brought to Jesus their grief, their illnesses, and their burdens and found in him a strong refuge and source of help. Many women listened intently to his words and believed that he was the anointed Messiah (John 11:27). Many of those believing women supported the ministry of Jesus, some with their money and others through their gift of hospitality (Luke 8:1–3; 10:38).

After Christ's ascension, believing women played an important role in the spread of the gospel. Women like Lydia, Euodia, and Syntyche shared their resources with Paul and the other missionaries who were making disciples in the uttermost parts of the world (Acts 16:14–15; Philippians 4:2–3). Women fervently interceded for the ministry of those God was sending out. Local bodies of believers met in the homes of women like Phoebe and Nympha (Romans 16:1–2; Colossians 4:15). Women like Priscilla and Peter's wife joined their husbands as they took the gospel to unreached cities and provinces (Acts 18:1–4,24–26; 1 Corinthians 9:5). Paul commended Mary, Tryphena, Tryphosa, and Persis for their hard work in the Lord (Romans 16:6,12). He praised Priscilla and her husband Aquila because they risked their lives for him (Romans 16:3–4).

Throughout history. In the period of the early church, women like Felicitas (along with her seven sons), Perpetua, Cecilia, Donatila, Theodota, and many more were martyred because they would not deny their Lord. They were not afraid to go and tell. They refused to stop sharing their testimony.[2]

From the late Middle Ages through the sixteenth, seventeenth, and eighteenth centuries, Christianity was refreshed, revitalized, and awakened by what Kenneth Scott Latourette termed the "greatest revivals which it had yet known."[3] As believers read the Bible in their heart language, they listened to the voice of the Holy Spirit and became more aware of the Great Commission of Christ to go and tell

---

[2]Mark Water, comp., *The New Encyclopedia of Christian Martyrs* (Grand Rapids: Baker, 2001), 76–77, 176–82, 432–37.
[3]Kenneth Scott Latourette, *Three Centuries of Advance, A.D. 1500 to A.D. 1800* (New York: Harper & Row, 1939; Grand Rapids: Zondervan, 1970), 451.

the peoples who walked in darkness that there is a light.

As the age of exploration began, followers of Christ sailed with the explorers and entrepreneurs on a spiritual quest. They were committed to obeying Jesus' commission to make disciples, baptizing and teaching those who had never heard to live according to God's revealed will. While most of the initial wave of missions-minded believers were men, women soon joined their husbands on journeys to the New World. Their mission was to establish colonies where God was worshiped and to start churches in places where the gospel had not been proclaimed previously.

In the world today. Women across the globe continue to obey Jesus' command, "Do not be afraid. Go and tell." In 1999, records showed that women comprised two-thirds of the international missions force.[4] In obedience to Jesus' commission, they are following him to villages, small towns, urban centers, and megacities around the world. They are telling the good news to people from other languages and cultures who have never heard that God loves them.

God's Call to Women

We commonly speak of these women as being "called" or as having "a missions call." Most mission agencies require that candidates who apply to work for them provide solid evidence that they are called to international missions.

What is this call? What does it look like? Why is it important? Could you be called? Are you called?

Before Jesus spoke the words "Go and tell" to Mary Magdalene and the other Mary, he called them to follow him. At least ten different times in the New Testament Jesus commanded people, "Follow me." The most comprehensive command was repeated in each of the Synoptic Gospels: "Whoever wants to be my disciple must deny themselves and take up their cross and follow me" (Mark 8:34). Obedience to Christ is primary. When we decide to follow Christ, to say yes to whatever he asks us to do, then and only then are we ready to hear his call to international missions.

---

[4]Marguerite Kraft and Meg Crossman, "Women in Mission," *Mission Frontiers* (August 1999): 16.

A tragic case study. In 1793 William Carey and his wife, Dorothy, sailed to India, and the era of evangelical foreign missions began. It was an inauspicious beginning for women. Dorothy was shocked when her husband announced that he had offered himself as a missionary. She had three sons and was pregnant with their sixth child, having already lost two girls in their infancy. She adamantly refused to go with him until her baby was delivered. But Carey was determined to go, even if it meant going without her. Dorothy agreed to let him leave her and even allowed their oldest son, Felix, to accompany him. Then Carey's departure was unexpectedly delayed, so he was still in England when their baby was born. Yielding to pressure from her husband and his partner, John Thomas, Dorothy finally agreed to leave immediately for India if her younger sister, Kitty, went with her to help.

The voyage was difficult, as were their early months in India. Sickness plagued the family; and one year after their arrival, their five-year-old son Peter died. After his death, Dorothy was never the same. Eleven years later she died, ending eleven years of mental and emotional anguish.[5]

It is sad and ironic that William Carey, who through his writing and persistent advocacy ushered in a new global missions era among English Baptists and eventually among almost all Protestant groups in both Europe and America, was not able to inspire a similar vision and passion in his wife. One problem may have been his refusal to watch and pray and wait for God to speak to Dorothy's heart. She felt no call to missions, and that fact may have left her without an anchor as their family went through frightful and, for her, overwhelming storms.

Married women missionaries. The earliest American international missionary women were Ann (Nancy) Hasseltine Judson and Harriet Atwood Newton. Both were young brides of young aspiring missionary men. Before their marriage each had carefully considered the outcome of their decision to say "I do."

One month after meeting Ann Hasseltine, Adoniram Judson wrote her a proposal letter. Though usually an impetuous person, she didn't

---

[5]Ruth A. Tucker, *Guardians of the Great Commission: The Story of Women in Modern Missions* (Grand Rapids: Zondervan, 1988), 15–17.

answer immediately. Instead she prayed and carefully considered the implications of this marriage. Rosalie Hunt writes, "In her personal journal that August, Ann speculated as to whether she would truly commit herself 'entirely to God to be disposed of according to his pleasure.' After asking herself several questions, she concluded that, 'Yes, I feel I am willing to be placed in that situation, in which I can do most good, though it were to carry the gospel to the distant benighted heathen.'"[6]

In a similar way, after receiving her proposal letter from Samuel Newell, Harriet Newton consulted with her widowed mother. After much anguish and many prayers, her mother finally agreed, "If a conviction of duty and love to the souls of the perishing heathen lead you to India, as much as I love you, Harriet, I can only say go." Harriet continued to hesitate for another month, mainly concerned about whether she had the strength to endure the physical and spiritual trials she would face. In the end she said yes.[7]

Harriet's fears were realized as she died shortly after the couple's arrival in Asia. Their only child was born aboard ship, and the next day both she and the baby girl were drenched in a storm at sea and caught pneumonia. The baby died four days later and Harriet died seven weeks later, confident that she was on her way to a better world. Courtney Anderson writes, "She looked forward to it, all but gloried in the prospect, and expressed no fears and no regrets except that of being parted temporarily from her husband."[8]

Ann and Adoniram Judson had eighteen years of life and ministry together in Burma. During that time Ann experienced loneliness and life-threatening illnesses, gave birth to three children and buried two of them (the third died not long after her own death), and managed a household, which was often filled with guests and fellow missionaries. She learned a complex language; began a school for Burmese children; translated the books of Jonah, Daniel, and Matthew into Burmese; wrote numerous letters to supporters and family; made a voyage for

[6]Rosalie Hall Hunt, *Bless God and Take Courage: The Judson History and Legacy* (Valley Forge, PA: Judson Press, 2005), 25.
[7]Courtney Anderson, *To the Golden Shore: The Life of Adoniram Judson* (Boston: Little, Brown & Company, 1956; Dolphin edition, 1961), 106.
[8]Ibid., 161–62.

health reasons to England and America; and inspired many Baptists to be more committed to missions. Her most challenging work may have been keeping her husband alive during his two years of unimaginable suffering in Burma's death prison.

Would Ann have persevered with her husband and seen the first Burmese converts and the planting of the first churches among the Burmese without a deep conviction that she was in the very center of God's will? Only God knows, but many modern missionary friends and colleagues of mine have testified that their confidence in God's call on their lives has enabled them to persevere in the midst of similar challenges.

In her book *Beyond Surrender: One Family's Quest to Bring Light to a Dark and Desperate World*, Barbara Singerman, a missionary to Benin, writes of her call to missions:

> That Thursday night, alone on a pine-scented balcony, I fell on my knees before the Lord. I sensed that a great wall existed between me and a call to missions: a thick, impenetrable wall that consisted of all the plans Pride and I had made. There, weeping, I died to the ministry ambitions I had fashioned for us. I surrendered my dreams of building a house with a large front porch. Drenched with my tears, I placed at the feet of Jesus my private desires and future hopes which didn't seem to fit a missionary call. In those moments the wall crashed into dusty ruins around me and blew off the porch in the breeze. The Call came.

Years later, Singerman wrote, "God's calling—God's will isn't directing you into personal disaster but personal wholeness. God has designed your heart's desires to be incredibly granted, but only as you daily commit to His Lordship. Resistance brings emptiness, surrender brings immeasurable depths of fulfillment."[9]

Single women missionaries. While some married women have followed their husbands to the field without hearing God's call, this would not be true for the vast majority of single women missionaries, some of whom have persistently followed their call in spite of discouraging responses from family, churches, and missionary societies. Lilias Trotter,

---

[9]Barbara J. Singerman, *Beyond Surrender* (Garland, TX: Hannibal Books, 2003), 22–23.

pioneer missionary to Muslims in North Africa, was turned down by the North Africa Mission in 1887 because of a weak heart; but certain of her call, she decided to go independently.[10]

Cynthia Farrar was the first single female Western missionary to India. She arrived on December 28, 1827, and spent the next thirty-five years supervising schools for girls and taking every opportunity to share the gospel with her students and their families. The next year Mary Wallace arrived in Malacca where she supervised several schools for Malay, Tamil, and Chinese girls. Similarly, Eliza Agnew taught Buddhist girls in Sri Lanka for forty years.

After a slow start, the number of single women missionaries dramatically increased. By 1900 there were two missionary women (some married, many single) in China for every man. Valerie Griffiths explains the need: "For over a thousand years the custom of foot-binding (to produce 'lily' feet, three or four inches long) had crippled millions of women, and made walking painful, if not impossible. The first missionaries to China soon realized that unless Christian women could visit them in their homes—a massive task—they would never hear the message of God's love."[11]

Like Chinese women, Buddhist, Muslim, and upper caste Hindu women also stayed at home. They didn't go out in public, and male missionaries had very few if any opportunities to share the gospel with them. It was this need, their commitment to the Lord, and their obedience to his call that multiplied the female missionary force. Women in the churches at home caught the vision and, through a quickly multiplying number of women's missionary societies, supported the growing force of single women missionaries with their money and their prayers.

The ministry of missionary women—both single and married—made a tremendous difference especially in Korea and China, where large numbers of women served and where they focused their energies on winning and training national women. Rebecca Lewis researched the rapid growth of the church in Korea in the late nineteenth century

---

[10]Patricia St. John, *Until the Day Breaks: The Life and Work of Lilias Trotter* (Leicestershire, UK: Arab World Ministries, 1990), 20.

[11]Valerie Griffiths, *Not Less Than Everything* (Oxford: Monarch Books, 2004), 10.

and in China in the early twentieth century. Significantly, she found that strategies to reach and train women were emphasized and implemented in both cases.

Indigenous women missionaries. In the early days of the church in Korea there was an intentional, organized effort to train Korean women, enabling them to effectively distribute Christian literature and give biblical instruction. Women in Korea were excluded from the all-important rituals of ancestor worship. Lewis notes, "They were surprised and grateful that they were encouraged to attend Christian worship gatherings. . . . Women missionaries—Methodist and Presbyterian alike—specifically trained Korean women in their forties and fifties to be 'Bible Women,' preferring widows who could travel as itinerant teachers."[12] The Bible women of Korea played a key role in the growth of the church in South Korea from a small minority in 1900 to more than 30 percent of the population today.

Bible women were also trained and employed in China. While the female foreign missionaries themselves did not convert large numbers of Chinese women, "Their example of independent female evangelism, coupled with their training of native Bible women (who were very well received and were effective evangelists), all proved invaluable."[13]

As a result of her research on the key role of women in these and other church movements, Lewis strongly encourages missionaries, missionary teams, and missionary agencies to emphasize and develop strategies for reaching and training the Muslim women of today, whose role and position in their culture is much like that of Chinese and Korean women in the twentieth century. Lewis maintains that believing women who come from a Muslim background can be effective forces for evangelism and church multiplication among their people, both through teaching their children and through reaching and training the women in their circle of influence.[14]

Today many missionary women—both single and married—are fo-

---

[12]Rebecca Lewis, "Underground Church Movements: The Surprising Role of Women's Networks," *International Journal of Frontier Missions* (Winter 2004): 147.
[13]Ibid., 148.
[14]Ibid., 150.

cused on reaching women and training them in evangelism and discipleship. This is happening among Muslim women, but also among lost women from every belief system: Hindu, Buddhist, Catholic, and animist. I personally know of such focused efforts in Central Asia, North Africa, Southeast Asia, South Asia, and West Africa. The fields are ready for harvest, but the laborers are few!

Which Women Does God Call?

Women missionaries come in all shapes and sizes, with a wide variety of God-given gifts and abilities, strikingly different backgrounds and experiences, married and unmarried, with empty nests and nests filled with children of varying ages. When God looks for a missionary to call to work in his fields, he isn't looking on the outside but at the heart. He is looking for women who love him and are completely surrendered to his will. God uses all kinds of women in all kinds of ways.

Working women. What are missionary women doing today to share the gospel with the lost? The list is long and varied. They work in areas of agriculture, dentistry, humanitarian aid, leadership training, public health, medicine, veterinary medicine, social work, sports ministry, student or university ministry, children's ministry, women's ministry, teaching English as a second language, teaching in schools for nationals, teaching the children of missionaries either in institutions or home-based classes, developing indigenous worship music, theological education, strategy coordination, chronological Bible storying, vocational training, financial and logistical support of other missionary personnel, writing, graphic design, Scripture translation, and much more.

No matter what type of ministry God gives a missionary woman, the ministry is a tool, a door through which she enters into the lives of lost women. The goal of every ministry is the same: to build redemptive relationships through which we can share the love and truth of Christ, call people to faith, and gather them into communities of believers whom we disciple and equip to do what we have done.

Learners of language and culture. Understanding the language and culture of the women God has called you to serve is foundational to building redemptive relationships. That is why the two young women on the OneStory team spent a year immersed in the life of their village. What they learned in that year enabled them to choose Bible stories and, with the help of their translator/story crafter, to tell those stories in a way that opened closed hearts and spirits to listen, to believe, and to be changed. It isn't easy—in fact, humanly speaking, it is impossible. We can't do it, but God can through us by his Spirit, if we trust and obey.

Why were our young women choosing, translating, and recording Bible stories? The Central Intelligence Agency Fact Book reports the literacy rate of women in the country where they were living at nearly 40 percent, and most of the women included in that percentage live in the cities, not the villages. In short, the women and probably at least half of the men in their people group could not read God's Word even if it were available in their language.

Worldwide, the female literacy rate is estimated at 77 percent. It is estimated that about half of the women in South Asia, West Asia, sub-Saharan Africa, and the Arab states are illiterate. Literacy rates are based on the number of women who have completed primary school. However, many women who have learned to read don't actually read. Their preferred way of learning is not through reading but through hearing, watching, and doing. Understanding the preferred learning style of the women among whom you are ministering is an important factor in developing effective evangelism strategies.

Wives and mothers. The way God uses any woman at any particular moment in time may be very different. For example, many means of service may seem out of reach for the missionary wife who has young children at home. The presence, age, and number of children in her home greatly influence the focus of the daily ministry God gives to married missionary women.

My husband and I often laugh with new missionary parents about a question most of them have heard from at least one of their family members or friends: "You aren't taking the children with you, are you?" It is strange that believers can think that God's plan for the parents of a family would not include the children he has entrusted to their care. God doesn't just call parents to missions; he calls families.

Elizabeth Edwardson emphasizes that families have their greatest impact when they see beyond themselves and determine to live as kingdom people committed to declaring the glory of God's name wherever he has sent them. She shares three implications or results of this kingdom-focused paradigm: (1) God calls entire families—not just individuals—to his "work": to follow him, to share, to hurt, to look outward; (2) our job as parents is to empower our children to live as kingdom people in our neighborhoods and communities; (3) our children can thrive and have a significant impact in the setting where God places our family.[15]

Young mothers with small children may sometimes feel frustrated that they aren't able to spend as much time as they want or feel they should in evangelistic or church-planting activities. At the same time, however, the presence of a baby or young child can provide an instant link with mothers and grandmothers in most communities around the world. Placing your children in a local preschool or elementary school also opens up a network of relationships and opportunities to impact the lives of the people you have come to reach, as well as enabling your children to learn the language and make friends with whom they can share the gospel.

In an international setting, an important part of being what Edwardson has called a kingdom family is adapting your family's lifestyle, as much as possible, to the cultural schedule and the accepted social activities of your community. If everyone in your community is out in the neighborhood every evening, your family shouldn't choose to stay inside because the baby must be in bed by 7:30 p.m. and you have a set of nighttime rituals that must be followed before you put him to bed. Maintaining a Western lifestyle can isolate your family and severely diminish your opportunities for redemptive relationships.

In many cultures, birthdays are the most acceptable occasion for celebrating with people outside the family. If that is true in your new culture, it follows that your family needs to take advantage of that

---

[15]Elizabeth Edwardson, "Signs and Symbols in the Land," in *A Worldview Approach to Ministry Among Muslim Women*, ed. Cynthia A. Strong and Meg Page (Pasadena, CA: William Carey Library, 2006), 225–36.

custom by entertaining your neighbors and acquaintances on your child's birthday instead of, or in addition to, having a traditional Western-style party with your child's Western friends. On such occasions, you have the opportunity to creatively combine culturally accepted activities with special activities that demonstrate your Christian values and beliefs in a positive way.

The key to successfully living as a kingdom family lies in the heart—your heart and the heart you shape and nurture in your children through your prayers, conversations, attitudes, and example. Among the group of about fifty families with whom my husband and I served for our first fifteen years on the mission field, at least twenty-six children from these families have served or are serving as missionaries, most as long-term missionaries. I believe this is in large part due to the heart for missions their parents nurtured in them as valued members of a kingdom family.

I encourage missionary moms to look at their lives in terms of seasons. In the season of family-building when there are often multiple babies and young children in our nest, a mother's time and energy can be almost totally consumed by caring for their needs. The season of homeschooling can also take up enormous amounts of the teacher mom's time and energy. These seasons will end and there will be more time for ministry. Mothers shouldn't feel guilty when they realize that they can't be full-time moms *and* full-time evangelists. However, missionary mothers in partnership with their husbands must ensure that when the season of full-time evangelism comes, the mother will be prepared and effective. How? There are at least three main ways: (1) daily time with the Lord, which keeps her in the Word and filled with the Spirit; (2) successful language and cultural acquisition and consistent, daily practice; (3) at least one intentional time of ministry among her unreached people each week.

It is almost impossible for a busy wife and mother to do these three things week in and week out unless her husband, as her spiritual leader, helps her. He must encourage her and guard her time so that she has uninterrupted opportunity each day to meet with the Lord. He must also encourage and enable her to focus adequate time and energy on language learning and ministry involvement. This might be achieved by coordinating his schedule with hers so that he can teach a home-school subject or take care of the children one or two mornings or afternoons each week. The plans won't always work out or run smoothly, of course. Nevertheless, when a husband and wife work together under the leadership of the Lord, they can enable each other to be and do all that the Lord desires.

Conclusion

God is looking for women—married and single—to join him in his work. He will shape, empower, and enable those who are willing to be his instruments of grace to go wherever he sends and to do whatever he asks. Our responsibility, our privilege, is to say, "Yes, Lord!"

Jessie Payne, a twentieth-century missionary who served with her husband in China, wrote, "I am sure of this forever, that whether we in our wisdom do missionary work or not, God does it, and will do it. If we care about Him and His desires . . . it must be done. No, say not it must be done! Infinite and eternal honor and glory it is to us that we are permitted to do it."[16]

Discussion Points

1. How important is it for a female missionary to experience a personal call from God? Why?

2. In the early history of modern missions in China, how did agencies respond to the tremendous spiritual needs and isolation of Chinese women? Who did they mobilize?

3. The role of Chinese women in Chinese families and society has greatly changed, but there are other populations of women who are similarly isolated from the gospel in this century. Who are they and why is it important for women to take the gospel to these groups?

4. Why is it critical for the women of any society—not just the men—to believe and to be discipled and trained?

---

[16]Lavinia Byrne, *The Hidden Journey: Missionary Heroines in Many Lands* (London: Society for Promoting Christian Knowledge, Holy Trinity Church, 1993), 121.

5. What things should shape the strategies and methods female missionaries use to reach a particular group of lost women?

6. What impact can missionary children have on their mother's ministry? How can any negative influences be minimized? How can the positive benefits be optimized?

Further Reading

Benge, Janet, and Geoff Benge. *Lottie Moon: Giving Her All for China.* Seattle: YWAM Publishing, 2001.

Byrne, Lavinia. *The Hidden Journey: Missionary Heroines in Many Lands.* London: Society for Promoting Christian Knowledge, Holy Trinity Church, 1993.

Clarkson, Sally. *The Ministry of Motherhood: Following Christ's Example in Reaching the Hearts of our Children.* Colorado Springs: WaterBrook Press, 2004.

Griffiths, Valerie. *Not Less Than Everything.* Oxford: Monarch Books, 2004.

Kraft, Marguerite, and Meg Crossman. "Women in Mission." *Mission Frontiers* (August 1999): 13–16.

Lewis, Rebecca. "Underground Church Movements: The Surprising Role of Women's Networks." *International Journal of Frontier Missions* (Winter 2004): 145–50.

Singerman, Barbara J. *Beyond Surrender.* Garland, TX: Hannibal Books, 2003.

St. John, Patricia. *Until the Day Breaks: The Life and Work of Lilias Trotter.* Leicestershire, UK: Arab World Ministries, 1990.

Strong, Cynthia A., and Meg Page, eds. *A Worldview Approach to Ministry Among Muslim Women.* Pasadena, CA: William Carey Library, 2006.

Stuart, Arabella. *The Three Mrs. Judsons.* Springfield, MO: Particular Baptist Press, 1999.

Tucker, Ruth A. *Guardians of the Great Commission: The Story of Women in Modern Missions.* Grand Rapids: Zondervan, 1988.

35

Caring for God's Missionaries

Robert Edwards and Nathan Evans

True to the "one-another" teachings of the New Testament, missionaries care for each other on their fields of service. For many, their call is to provide God-centered care for colleagues while being witnesses to the nations among whom they serve. It is a high calling. We sometimes call these missionaries "Stephens."

Welcome to the Field! (Robert Edwards)

The Smith family landed in a North African capital city for a brief stay before they would continue to their new home and place of service in another city about 250 miles away. They were new to the mission field. Fortunately, another couple from a different mission group met the family at the airport. The young Joneses had worked in the capital for three years. Before arriving on the field, the Smiths contacted the Joneses several times but only received brief responses. Yet now they were looking forward to sitting with the Joneses in the capital for a few hours to get as much information as possible before they took the five-hour train ride with their three children, ten pieces of luggage, and five carry-ons.

Arriving at the hotel that hot summer afternoon, the Smiths asked the Joneses if they could visit, hoping for some answers. At the Smiths' final destination, there would be no one else there from their organization or any other mission organization that they could rely on. The Joneses were busy, but promised to meet with them for a few minutes the following day before driving them to the train station. The Smiths were pleased. The offer of taking them to the train station along with their mountain of luggage was appreciated too.

The first night for the Smiths was rough. The air conditioning in their primitive hotel room didn't work properly. Noise from the street traffic outside was almost unbearable, with drivers tooting their horns long past midnight and the crowded streets looking like noon in downtown New York. A sidewalk café attached to the hotel was busy late into the night. Fortunately the children slept, but soon they would be up and ready to go. Sure enough, the children were awake by six.

At breakfast downstairs, the waiter greeted them with *"Bonjour."* Maureen was the first to try her fledgling French in a real-life situation. After the waiter left, the five recited to each other, *"bonjour, bonjour, bonjour . . . "* They ate and returned to their room. Parents Seth Sr. and Maureen were already exhausted and wanted to go back to sleep. The children, however, were climbing the walls. Seth Sr. thought it would be good to explore the old part of the capital. Maureen was not up to walking or exploring. She suggested they go to the beach so the children could play, though all she really wanted was to rest.

Most of the bags in the crowded room had to be opened to find swimsuits. They managed to do it, though, and rushed to the street to catch a taxi. Although they had studied some basic French words, they couldn't think of the word "beach" in French to tell the taxi where to go. Seth Sr. ran back to the reception desk to get help. Also, he remembered he needed local currency for the taxi ride. He left the reception desk repeating, *"plage, plage, plage."* Now all the family were saying *"plage"* in unison.

They flagged down three taxis, but none would take all five of them. Taxis in this city were small and could only accommodate three passengers. They had no choice but to take two taxis. They managed to stop two taxis, motioning for the second taxi to follow the first. The two taxi drivers chatted. This helped Seth Sr. relax—a bit. They made it to the *plage*, which at 9 o'clock in the morning was deserted. It was dirty, but private, at that time of the day.

Seth Sr. and Maureen sat down and started going over the journey of the past fourteen months from the time they responded to God's call. The missionary who originally requested more help for this North African city had since returned to the States and wouldn't respond to their e-mails. Now they had to find their own way and establish the ministry to which God had called them. Although they had researched their new city on the Internet, even marked the area where they thought they wanted to settle, they wondered how many surprises awaited them similar to the three-passengers-per-taxi surprise.

The next day the Joneses called them, apologizing profusely that their young son had a fever and needed to see a doctor. However, they had managed to arrange for a large van to pick the family up from the hotel for the drive to the train station. The Smiths managed to hide their disappointment that they wouldn't get to visit with the Joneses, and they promised to pray for their son and to stay in touch. After traveling on the train, getting to the hotel in their destination city was a major chore with three young children and their heap of luggage. But fortunately, they found a taxi-van. They had booked two rooms at a three-star hotel, which would be their home for the next two, maybe three, weeks.

Seth Sr. and Maureen had compiled a large list of things to do, from finding an apartment and furnishing it to exchanging money. They had to open a bank account, buy a mobile phone, register a company for the purpose of getting residency in that country, explore school options for their children, and find a used car for five passengers—all while using a foreign language in an unfamiliar city.

Seth Sr. had been an educational pastor at his church for several years. Before that he had served six years with the US military, including handling logistics during Operation Desert Storm for a few months. In the military, operations were organized. Senior officers handed down orders. He only wished his list of things to accomplish could be organized like that.

Without going into more detail about the Smiths' first year on the field, their story is not unique. Pioneer missionaries spend significant amounts of time meeting logistical and legal requirements for living in creative-access countries.[1] They often burn out or lose focus before they even start the task God called them to do. The list above is a small one compared to the many details that must be attended to. For example, when the Smiths were offered a used car by one of the hotel employees, after paying 1,000 D (local currency) as a deposit they discovered that they were unable to register the car before they obtained a residence permit and a local driving license. In some countries, opening a personal bank account can be an all-day chore. Living under "What surprises do we have today?" conditions exacts a toll on missionary individuals or families and often keeps them from implementing strategy and doing the "main thing": spreading the gospel and seeing lives changed.

The Role of "Stephening"

The apostles in the early church recognized early on what needed to be done. They wanted to keep the "main thing" their focus. So they summoned the congregation of the disciples and said, "It would not be right for us to neglect the ministry of the word of God in order to wait on tables" (Acts 6:2). Waiting on tables consumed the apostles' time, causing them to neglect the teaching of the Word. Overseas, similar daily tasks can overwhelm Christian workers. Many missionaries lose sleep over having to carry out administrative responsibilities they were not called to nor gifted in, in addition to teaching and preaching the Word. The apostles' solution was simple: "Brothers and sisters, choose seven men from among you who are known to be full of the Spirit and wisdom. We will turn this responsibility over to them and will give our attention to prayer and the ministry of the word" (Acts 6:3–4). The proposal pleased the church members, and they selected men who had a good reputation and were full of the Holy Spirit and wisdom.

After the seven men were selected, commissioned, and began their daily responsibilities, the results were evident almost immediately. "So the word of God spread. The number of disciples in Jerusalem increased rapidly, and a large number of priests became obedient to the faith"

---

[1]See Tom Steffen's chapter, "Creative-Access Platforms."

(Acts 6:7). Such was the outcome of a godly, strategic decision supported through the unity of the body of Christ.

One of those seven was Stephen. In addition to the three characteristics mentioned above, Stephen had more: a Christlike character with a drive (power) to carry out work with grace, charming people he worked with through kind benevolence and a helpful personality. It is part of who he was—powerfully graceful[2] as well as of good reputation, wise, and sensitive to the Spirit. This recipe is hard to beat; it is a recipe that we attempt to model and instill in the "Stephens" in our missions organization. Yet it is a recipe that always needs improvement and never attains perfection.

In his book *The Fred Factor*, Mark Sanborn "recounts the true story of Fred, the mail carrier who passionately loves his job and who genuinely cares about the people he serves. Because of that, he is constantly going the extra mile handling the mail—and sometimes watching over the houses of the people on his route, treating everyone he meets as a friend. Where others might see delivering mail as monotonous drudgery, Fred sees an opportunity to make a difference in the lives of those he serves."[3] Fred changed the way Sanborn viewed customer service. He made life easier for Sanborn and met a need Sanborn was not even aware of. It's a book worth reading to help understand how service can impact the lives of busy people—people who need to stay strategically focused.

"Stephens" defined. When I accepted the privilege of leading eight men who were called to a "Stephening" type of service in support of missionaries on the field, these men lived in various countries where our missionaries lived. They came from different business and professional backgrounds and had all lived on the field before. They all understood what it meant to stay focused on the task. We gathered for a week of training and began by looking at the Stephen model—not only

---

[2]Stephen was "full of God's grace and power" (Acts 6:8). Power is an important characteristic in our Christian "doings," and Stephen used his power in a graceful manner. "Grace-filled" or "gracious" is not the same as "powerfully graceful." Many gracious people in this world show no evidence of power in their lives.

[3]Mark Sanborn, *The Fred Factor: How Passion in Your Work and Life Can Turn the Ordinary into the Extraordinary* (Colorado Springs: WaterBrook Press, 2004), inside cover.

a powerfully graceful, service-oriented, spiritually wise person of good reputation, but a fearless witness. He exemplified to the early church the importance of standing strong until the last minute, not fearing death. It would be difficult to follow such an example. We studied the purpose to which Stephen and the six others were called. They were called to perform a much-needed role in order to help the apostles stay focused—not neglecting "the ministry of the word of God."

Before looking at the responsibilities that our Stephens needed to perform in service of the missionaries whose primary focus is sharing God's Word, we developed a list of core values that would characterize a Stephen:

1. a servant-leader committed to Stephen-type leadership

2. an entrepreneurial spirit that strives to find creative and resourceful solutions

3. a proactive approach, anticipating solutions to business services and to problems

4. a striving for excellence, recognizing that if something is worth doing, it is worth doing to the best of one's ability

5. modeling by setting the example for others in living standards and witness

6. an ethos of ongoing group-learning

These were high standards set for the Stephens: the dynamo, the engine, the motivation for each Stephen called to this task. None of these operating modes were 100 percent achievable, but we agreed that together we would strive toward these goals.

After specifying the character traits we would aim for, we proceeded to specify the services we would offer. Recalling the needs of the Smith family in our case study, we determined a few of the services the Stephens would offer: assistance with housing and travel, residence visa applications, platform management, guesthouse management, assistances with government and legal issues, research on school options, medical center options, phone and Internet services, etc. These are a sampling of issues that any missionary family would need to deal with on the field. Accordingly, we drafted a job description for the Stephens and agreed to refer to these services as member-care services. Tasks that take a few minutes or a simple phone call in the West might consume days in some third-world countries. Missionaries sometimes leave the field because of the lack of such member-care services or assistance.

The tasks of Stephens. In the past ten years, many more services have been added to these Stephens—including financial-reporting assistance, crisis management, and member-care referrals. Many missionaries find it difficult to manage their financial books or keep their business bank statements balanced. The Stephens help with such services.

Like the Smiths, who spent many days and weeks focusing on completing chores that distracted them from the main task they had come to fulfill, many missionaries lose sleep worrying whether or not they made the right decision on a house contract, visa application, or used-car purchase. They neglect the main thing they came to carry out— sharing God's Word.

As the number of Stephens in our mission organization's region has grown, representing approximately 10 percent of the total missionary task force, we often have to remind ourselves to cultivate and maintain the attitude of powerfully graceful service. The first and foremost of these reminders is that strategy drives the logistical services. The focus—the ministry of the word of God—needs to stay intact. Accordingly, Stephening type services are carried out in support of the focus.

The second most important thing is that services are never imposed, but are "offered to clients." We consider our missionaries "clients." They need to be happy and taken care of well. Some missionaries enjoy going to government offices, meeting officials, and completing ten-page applications in French or Arabic. If missionaries build relationships in this manner and are not distracted from the main thing, we support what they are doing. Stephens become so good at what they do, however, that their services become highly valued and sought after. They work hard for the team members on the ground and understand that without the apostles' ministry of the Word, they would not have a job "waiting on tables." Stephens take "work orders" from their missions colleagues and carry out these requests to the best of their ability. If the task is too great for one Stephen, he or she may solicit the help of another Stephen specialist who has expertise in one or more specific fields.

One of the Stephens I work with is a construction specialist; he is often relied upon to travel to other countries to offer his expertise on construction projects. Stephens do not control; they facilitate. It's easy for a Stephen to get sucked in to a control mode if he or she isn't careful. When grace is dropped and power alone is at play, mission work suffers. This is the philosophy of our Stephens.

The front lines for Stephens. In addition to providing equitable service to the widows, Stephen was a great orator. He knew the Scriptures well and was able to tell the story from creation to the cross. Our Stephens must be able to tell the story in the heart language of the people they live among as well. It's not an added task. It's who they are.

One of our Stephens, Sam, excels in telling the story. He and his family learned the heart language of the people they live among very well. Their children attend a local school. Before Sam went into the country where he serves, the only visa that was easy to obtain was a student visa for language learning. Sam's past experience in customer service for a major US corporation helped in this situation. He knew how to build bridges and establish relations. In a matter of a few weeks he was able to register a service company that would provide services for expatriates. His host country granted him a residence permit and he was able to help others obtain one as well. More importantly, however, Sam is proactive in sharing God's Word, especially among government officials. While he is directly involved in discipleship, he often introduces contacts to his missionary colleagues devoted to the ministry of the Word.

Consider the Smiths. With their expectations of support on the field in contrast to the realities of their arrival—needing to find their own way while wondering what other surprises awaited them as they tried to establish a home, purchase a vehicle, and enroll their children in a school—would they make it?

God-Centered Care (Nathan Evans)

Let me share with you a different story. This story describes what it looks like for a team to come around and support someone they have just met.

Josh arrived, in the middle of a bitter winter, in a country that was part of the former Soviet Union. Just out of college, Josh was ready for a robust task. He was also feeling the tension of going to a place he had never been, coupled with the weight of some understandable concerns back home. A year earlier, his only sibling had died in a terrible car accident. Josh and his brother were very close; the loss remained strong, and Josh's mother continued to grieve deeply. Josh's sending organization monitored his progress as time passed, and over time agreed he was ready. Throughout the process, his field team was kept fully informed.

The day after Josh arrived, the team leader met with him and asked if he felt comfortable telling his story to the team at a meeting the following week. Josh agreed, though internally he worked through a range of concerns about what he might say, how it might be received, and if he was setting himself up for an early departure.

As he corresponded with his mother by e-mail over the next few days, Josh knew she was trying to support him in this adventure. But she wasn't a believer and didn't really understand why he went halfway around the world when there were plenty of adventures closer to home. Josh also knew that because his mom didn't know Christ, getting through the death of her only other child was a fierce battle. She even told Josh that she felt like she was losing two sons.

The next week came. The team had prepared a great welcome meal for Josh, and during the meal they shared some funny things about his new culture that helped break the ice for Josh. But as the meal concluded, he felt the butterflies churning in his stomach. Then something unexpected happened. The meeting time began with every team member sharing, in turn, a part of their own story. Josh heard his new teammates talk about parents with Alzheimer's, grandparents who threatened a lawsuit if their grandchildren were taken overseas, a sister with terminal cancer, an only child who just started college after living the last ten years on the field. By the time everyone finished, Josh was flooded with relief. He could tell his own story knowing his teammates cared for him. This team obviously carried one another, so Josh would not be alone in bearing his burdens.

God-centered care flows out of loving relationships.

God-centered care flows out of loving relationships. Josh experienced that kind of care, which should happen wherever believers are. When biblical truth is applied in our lives, we will live out biblical care in our home, in relationship to our team or fellowship of believers, and in the world of people around us—next door, and at the ends of the earth.

Here is another story. Corey and Cammie Brown and their three children served in a developing area of Asia. They endured some rough spots during their first four years on the field, but overall they did a great job of learning the language and developing deep and dynamic relationships with their focus people. They were also a great blessing to their team. After a vibrant first term, the Browns spent six months back in the States visiting and sharing their story with family, friends, and supporting churches. The kids viewed this time as a fun adventure. They enjoyed a healthy balance of travel, sharing, rest, fun, and eating all their favorite foods.

The family returned to Asia refreshed and anticipating a deeper engagement with their focus people. The first month was full of wonderful visits with their team, reunions with local friends, and getting reestablished in their home. They began working on the plan they had developed with their leadership. Energy was high and fruitfulness was in sight. This, they felt, is what they had come to do. But then, about six months later, some strange things began to happen.

It began with their oldest daughter, age nine, having bad dreams at night. She would awaken with a very real fear that something was in the room with her. Nothing was visible; but whatever it was, it didn't go away. The family began praying. Others from their team began praying. Their local church body and their supporting churches joined in. After two nightmarish weeks that seemed like two years, the dreams suddenly stopped and the girl believed the mysterious presence had finally left her room. She began to sleep well and returned to being a happy nine-year-old. But Cammie, while grateful the dreams had stopped, worried that they would return. She was almost convinced of it, to the point of not sleeping at night. She began having anxiety attacks during the day that had her asking all kinds of "what if" questions, so much so that it began to affect her otherwise strong marriage.

Corey was trying to be strong and caring, but honestly could not understand the depth of despair his wife was experiencing. In his mind, the storm had passed and calm had returned. Their team was committed to biblical care, leading Corey and Cammie to be fully transparent about their situation. The team suggested that Corey and Cammie meet with a counselor from their sending organization to help them better understand the root of Cammie's fear. As the counselor became involved, the team lovingly gathered around Corey and Cammie, prayed for them, and stood with them as they walked through this valley that lasted about four months.

The truth is, every believer, at some point in their journey, walks through some type of difficult valley. These valleys have different shapes and sizes. They can be as deep as the grief of losing a child or as the severe depression that makes it hard to get up in the morning. Some valleys are narrow and shallow, like the constant irritation of chaotic driving in a host country or dealing with corrupt officials in a government office. Other valleys seem to vary in intensity daily or weekly, like the strain of conflict with extended family or the pain of separation from aging parents. Left in the valley alone, fruitfulness and joy can wither on the vine. Why does this happen?

The truth is, every believer, at some point in their journey, walks through some type of difficult valley.

Our adversary, Satan, is actively and continually working to thwart the purposes of God among the nations. Scripture shows us that Satan has already been defeated through the finished work of the Lord Jesus on the cross. Yet he is intent on inflicting as many wounds as possible among believers in Christ. A host of D-words clearly describe Satan's activity and purpose. He seeks to *disrupt* the home, marriage, and family of believers and to *deter* their effectiveness. He attempts to *divide* and *destroy* the fellowship and unity believers enjoy. He works to *distract* believers in turning their attention to unholy thoughts, unhelpful choices, and unwise words. He tries to *deceive* believers into thinking they are useless to God's kingdom. He aims to *distort* biblical truth to those in personal crises, hoping they will lose focus, burn out, and quit the race.

Satan was active in attacking both Josh and the Brown family in different ways. By God's grace, each of their teams came around them and loved and cared for them. But this type of care didn't just happen. Their teams were prepared and equipped for God-centered care for one another.

What does God-centered care look like, in any context? First, it is biblical; the Word of God is the authority and foundation for godly care (1 Peter 1:22–23). Second, it is intentional, as teams practice what it means to love and care for one another (Colossians 3:12–17). Third, it is replicable; because the truths of godly care are modeled by the team, local believers follow their example and teach others in their culture (1 Thessalonians 1:2–8).

God-centered care is biblical. Scripture forms the basis of godly encouragement, exhortation, and equipping. Josh and the Brown family were part of a team that was rooted in the Word of God and believed fully that the Lord would be faithful. They reminded Josh and the Browns of God's promises and truths, which encouraged their teammates to cling to them.

God-centered care is intentional. It is one thing to believe what Scripture teaches. The fruit comes to those who practice these truths daily with perseverance and joy. Josh and the Brown family belonged to teams that put into action that which they knew to be true. They lovingly formed and consistently maintained a strong support structure for one another.

God-centered care is replicable. Living out Scripture translates into a lifestyle that is undergirding to believers and is an inviting aroma to those who are attracted to Christ (2 Corinthians 2:14–16). Josh and the Brown family were on teams that trusted, practiced, and longed to see many from their focus peoples come to faith in Christ. It took time, patience, and endurance; but both of these teams were blessed to see significant numbers of new believers learn to practice God-centered care.

These principles of God-centered care are applicable to every believer in every culture. In the context of this chapter, the focus is the fields where missionaries serve, but these truths apply just as fully to any church anywhere.

When Crisis Comes

How does God-centered care apply to a crisis? Every crisis involves an abrupt change of some type, usually traumatic, and is definitely gut-wrenching. Crisis brings personal pain and hurt into intense focus. It is deep and real. It may be unique to a particular individual or involve an entire team. At its core, a crisis stretches the emotions beyond what seems humanly possible to endure. As you read this, a personal or team crisis is surely in progress somewhere in the world. We need to uphold one another continually.

During times of crisis, the team is still the first line of God-centered care. On many fields, there are also biblically trained clinical and pastoral care workers who can and do respond. When someone has experienced a personal crisis, structured debriefing is very important. Providing this debriefing a few days after the crisis allows the person, couple, or family to tell their story, guided and facilitated by a trained debriefer. The debriefing is often a major step down the path of healing and restoration. While further counseling may be needed, the beautiful part of the initial debriefing is that, once trained, anyone can facilitate it.

In normal seasons of ministry, clinical and pastoral workers visit teams and encourage them, hear their stories, pray for them, and provide biblical counsel. Frequently they bring books or other resources with them, and equip the team to spur each other on to maturity and unity as a team. A goal of God-centered care is for counselors to spend the vast majority of their time encouraging, exhorting, and equipping instead of rescuing, mediating, and containing.

When not visiting teams in person, counselors encourage individuals and teams by phone and e-mail, sometimes providing follow-up care in situations that need special attention. In many parts of the world, counselors who focus on a particular geographic region form a member-care team. They may live in different parts of the region, or they may base together in one location. A good member-care team constantly will be developing their understanding of how Scripture speaks into the life of every believer, so that all of their counsel and equipping is biblical, intentional, and replicable.

Responsible Care for Missionaries

Sending churches have an important role in providing care to the missionaries they send. Missionaries are an extension of the church, which has a biblical and loving obligation to intentionally nourish them. Today's technology provides many ways to encourage their hearts, equip them with books and music and good teaching, and send and receive prayer needs. Committed sending churches make it a priority to connect with their missionaries regularly, often sending a team to visit them each year.

Missionaries are an extension of the church, which has a biblical and loving obligation to intentionally nourish them.

Strong supporting churches love the missionaries they support as their own. Going well beyond financial support, they commit to intentional care and contact. This is a two-way street. The blessing will be wonderfully felt by the missionaries, which greatly blesses and encourages the supporting church.

Godly care is a like a wheel: a balanced and sturdy frame with many spokes. The more spokes, the better the support, and the longer and more effective the wheel will function. Tires are fitted to the wheels. Good tires with strong frames have a much better chance of making it through rocky terrain. Tires that are reinforced, contain the right amount of air, and are given good care tend to last a long time. The spokes of a balanced, sturdy wheel are given their strength by the Word of God, the body of Christ, the principles of the sending organization, the support on the field, the fellowship of local believers, and the team. The tires are maintained by loving, intentional, and consistent care.

Josh's "tire" could have deflated in the first few weeks after his arrival. With no air in the tires, an already uphill journey would have been nearly impossible to endure. Unfortunately, some have had a similar experience but with little support, and consequently have left the field discouraged and defeated. But a strong wheel and intentional, loving care kept Josh's tire full of air, pushing ahead. His tire/call was tested numerous times over the subsequent two years, yet he enjoyed a fruitful ministry. He later married and returned overseas with his wife and their child.

Though the Brown family faced punishing blows to their tire, many spokes of support were reinforced during their ordeal. After four months of struggling with anxiety attacks, Cammie began to see her joy restored. Corey committed himself to God's Word, received godly counsel, and sought to love his wife as Christ loves the church. He walked with Cammie through her valley. They continued in their journey, aware that new attacks could return like a thief in the night. Their team, weekly fellowship group, supporting churches, and counselors continued the journey with them. God also used their journey for his glory, as the Browns ministered to leaders in five local fellowships, sharing the truths they learned during their struggles. These five fellowships, all with a deep cultural understanding of how Satan deceives through fear, developed a series on biblical endurance and restoration and began teaching others.

Conclusion

What does God-centered care look like? It is biblical, intentional, and replicable. It applies to every place where believers live, not just to the ends of the earth. By God's grace, his Word, and his purposes, all believers need to experience the joy of giving and receiving godly care. Romans 12 and Ephesians 4 reveal the church as a beautiful tapestry: one body with members that belong to one another, interwoven in Christ, which equips and builds up one another into unity and maturity. The beauty of this tapestry becomes gloriously attractive to many in darkness.

Discussion Points

1. Like the "Stephens" in Acts 6, modern-day Stephens have specific tasks to perform. How can they ensure that their primary identity and self-worth are seen as witnesses for Christ and not just taskmasters?

2. According to 1 Corinthians 12:28, several gifts are given to different parts of the body. Which gifts did Fred, in *The Fred Factor*, practice? How did his "clients" respond to the extra mile he offered?

3. If you were to build a team of care providers, what components and characteristics would you most want to see represented in its members?

4. How can the principles of biblical care be developed in your context?

Further Reading

Bridges, Jerry. *Trusting God: Even When Life Hurts.* Colorado Springs: Nav-Press, 1990.

Jennings, Ken, and John Stahl-Wert. *The Serving Leader: 5 Powerful Actions That Will Transform Your Team, Your Business and Your Community.* San Francisco: Berrett-Koehler Publishers, 2004.

Powlison, David. *Speaking Truth in Love.* Greensboro, NC: New Growth Press, 2005.

Sande, Ken. *The Peacemaker: A Biblical Guide to Resolving Personal Conflict.* Grand Rapids: Baker, 2004.

Tripp, Paul David. *Instruments in the Redeemer's Hands.* Phillipsburg, NJ: P & R Publishing, 2002.

36

THE TROUBLE WITH
OUR JERUSALEMS

Ed Stetzer

We've sought in this volume to look at the mission of God from every possible angle. We have assumed throughout that you are reading this book because you are committed to responding to the world's spiritual need. We have detailed the means and the methods of mission action with the expectation that, having done all this, we Christians will each want to do all we can to fulfill our own mission—from our own Jerusalem. And there's the rub. A primary reason we need to reexamine all this material—and recommit to it—is that, since the beginning of the church, we Christians have been much more ready to respond to the problems and realities of our own Jerusalems than our Judeas—not to mention our Samarias and all the rest. From the very beginning, Christians have tended to adopt a "Jerusalem *before* Judea, Samaria, and to the ends of the earth" interpretation of Acts 1:8.

Not all churches have been so shortsighted, of course. The church at Antioch was the first to respond in earnest to the missionary call, setting aside Barnabas and Paul to fulfill the work the Holy Spirit had assigned them. But the church in Jerusalem—where Jesus gave that command to be his witnesses—remained myopic to the needs of the rest of the world. What does the example of that original Jerusalem church say to us about being missional?

The Jerusalem Pattern

Jerusalem was initially the center of the Christian movement. It was in Jerusalem where the great outpouring of Pentecost took place, where Peter preached his first dynamic sermon, where believers were added daily to the church, and where all believers held everything in common and worshiped daily in the temple. Jerusalem was the site of the golden age of the church, but it was a golden age that lasted all too briefly.

Contentious distractions. In Acts 6 we learn of a problem that grew in the Jerusalem church as a direct result of differences between people. The Hellenistic Jewish widows—more than likely, Jewish women who had spent their lives in the wide dispersion of the Jewish race but who had returned to the Holy City to die—felt they were being ignored in the daily distribution of food. The problem could have been the result of miscommunication—after all, the apostles were all Aramaic-speaking Jews—but it was a problem nevertheless, and one the apostles felt was too distracting for them to contend with. We can imagine the raised voices of debate and contention running between the lines of Acts 6: the hurt and frustration, perhaps from both sides. This conflict summoned the Jerusalem church to look beyond traditional lines of relationship to care for a larger community. You can almost hear the lament, too frequently heard in our American churches, that "These are not our kind of people!"

> A congregation in suburban San Antonio had long grown insular and stagnant. After the retirement of their longtime pastor, their new minister urged them to open their eyes to the needs in the surrounding community, pressing them gently but persistently to stop worrying about whether visitors had to wear name badges (one of their many concerns) and start worrying about whether they were actually reaching the lost. To do so meant more change than this church was comfortable with. One couple told him that lost people should learn how to like the church the way it was. If they didn't, well, "It didn't matter what they thought because they're lost." "Why should we change for them?" the wife asked. "They should change for us." "Us" versus "them." It's not only as old as the church, it's as old as time.

The Holy Spirit provided a solution to the dispute over the widows' communal fund. Seven men of good reputation and "full of the Spirit and wisdom" were chosen to handle the task. It is significant that these seven each had Greek names rather than traditional Jewish names. The church solved the argument by widening the leadership structure of the Jerusalem church to accommodate cultural differences. But these new leaders were not to remain in Jerusalem long.

Inward focus. There was no question that the Jerusalem church was missionary minded among its own type of people and within its own surroundings. Acts 6:7 says that in the days after Pentecost even many priests joined the Way. But while the energy and excitement of the early Jerusalem church was pervasive and infectious, Luke does not record the disciples and church leaders giving direct attention to the impact of this mission upon the rest of the world—despite Jesus' clear direction in the Great Commission.

> The young adult ministry of a Nashville area church recently advertised its "community service" project. The details of the notice revealed that this "community service" consisted entirely of landscaping the church grounds. Perhaps that church really needed some upkeep! But the characterization of this work as "community service," as part of the ministry's concerns to become more missional, only demonstrates how far we will go to keep missions as close to home as possible.

Maybe this is just human nature: we care most for those we know and see, and indeed the needs around us are great. There is that old cliché, "Charity begins at home," which some Christians believe is surely somewhere in the Bible (Hezekiah, perhaps?). Besides, these first Christians believed that Jesus was coming back immediately. They probably felt there wasn't time to actually *plan* for reaching the world. But surely this excuse has an expiration date. Time passed, and they still made no plan to reach beyond the walls of their city. Those who did manage to take the mission outside the city were actually driven out by the persecution of Saul, especially after the martyrdom of Stephen (Acts 7–8). Philip the evangelist, for example, began to witness in Samaria. Others who had been scattered by the attacks—men from Cyprus and Cyrene—preached the gospel to both Jews and Greeks (Acts 11:19–20). The expansion of the church had begun, *from* Jerusalem, as the Lord had said—but not as an action of that church.

Preoccupied with scrutiny, not spirituality. The Jerusalem church seemed strangely oblivious to the spreading of the gospel outside the city walls, at least until they began to hear of Philip's activities in Samaria. When they heard of Philip's exploits, they sent two representatives, Peter and John, to the city (Acts 8:14). I wonder what the spirit of that visit was? Were they surprised when the Samaritans received the Holy Spirit?

Later, after being directed to Caesarea by a vision from God and witnessing the faith of Cornelius and his household, Peter acknowledged "that God does not show favoritism but accepts from every nation the one who fears him and does what is right" (Acts 10:34–35). Yet, upon his return to Jerusalem, Peter was practically apologetic to the Jerusalem church for the fact that God had blessed Cornelius and his household with the Holy Spirit. Maybe it is reading into the embassy of Peter and John to Samaria to wonder if there was a similar Jewish elitism working in this Samaritan visit, but we do know what John's attitude toward Samaritans had previously been (Luke 9:54). In any event, the visit went well—so much so that Peter and John, perhaps inspired by Philip's example, preached the gospel all the way back to Jerusalem (Acts 8:25).

Nevertheless, the thread of Jewish elitism remained in the Jerusalem church. It showed up again when Paul and Barnabas returned from their first missionary journey. The church of Jerusalem seemed more concerned about Paul's methodology and orthodoxy than the extraordinary outpouring of the Holy Spirit among the Gentiles—clearly preferring to scrutinize the man rather than discern the work of God (Acts 15). We see this today when a church gets bogged down in nonessential matters of theology—or worse, matters of style or context—and ends up missing out on the blessings of unity and missional cooperation.

Praising in the temple, not witnessing to the world. How long did the traditional Jewish Christians remain hidden in Jerusalem because of persecution? We really don't know. We do know, however, that they eventually began praising in the temple again. But Acts 8 prompts an unpleasant conjecture. Where was the Jerusalem church when the Ethiopian eunuch came to the city looking for God? We meet him on the road south as he's returning home. He has a copy of the Isaiah scroll, which he reads aloud but doesn't understand. Philip, the evangelist and leader of the new church in Samaria, joins him. Philip has been waiting by the side of this desert camel track, led there by the Holy Spirit. Now this is interesting: Philip was leading a great movement of God in Samaria, north of Jerusalem. God calls him to wait in the desert for the Ethiopian, south of Jerusalem.

Why did the Lord have to go to Samaria to find someone to witness to the Ethiopian, when the eunuch spent days in the city of Jerusalem, which was filled with the Jerusalem church? Could it be that the Jewish Christians were too busy praising God in the temple to notice someone— an outsider—who had come to Jerusalem in search of the same God they were praising? Were they too busy to notice? Was their notion of outreach merely an invitation to those outside to come see what they were doing in their standing-room-only services? Or did they just not have a wide enough view of God to believe those outside of Judaism were worthy of him? Or was it—as I'm afraid the case may be too many times for modern Christians—that they didn't feel bold enough or trained enough to share a word of witness with someone they didn't know? If our Jerusalem is all we think about, our Jerusalem is all we will reach.

Suspicion of outsiders. Why do we hesitate or flat-out neglect to reach those outside our narrow spheres of comfort and familiarity? Our abdication of the scope of the Great Commission must surely be in part because we—like the Jewish Christians of the first century— are suspicious of outsiders. This suspicion did not extend in Jerusalem only to those they didn't know. It included some they did know but assumed God couldn't change. Saul/Paul was certainly among these. Despite the time he'd spent boldly proclaiming Christ in Damascus after his conversion—which must have been widely reported in Jerusalem, since it was such a dramatic turnaround—the Jerusalem church didn't want to have anything to do with him. It was Barnabas who introduced Paul to the rest of the "pillars," but it still doesn't appear that Paul was welcomed with open arms. He was still an outsider.

Do Christians today regard the brothers and sisters outside of our culture and experience as worthy of suspicion?

Legalism, not protection. A local pastor shared from the pulpit his struggle with temptation to lust, speaking frankly about the lures of the seedier side of the Internet. His purpose was to communicate his own transparency and frailty, with the hope of encouraging others struggling with private sins. His intention was to begin the hard work of making the church a safe place to be honest, to begin dismantling the façade built up by ages of hypocrisy. Instead, he received a critical e-mail a few hours later complaining that his message was "very uncomfortable and more than a bit unsettling . . . to remind the congregation of such worldly ugliness in a house of worship and safe haven." This person was clearly uncomfortable with the content of the pastor's message, but that discomfort seems to come from a deeper seated discomfort with the outside world. The church, in this critic's mind, exists to protect those inside—as if sin comes from without, not within. What sort of impact does this kind of thinking have on our concept of God's mission?

When Paul and Barnabas returned to Jerusalem after their first missionary journey and proclaimed the wonderful movement of God among the Gentiles, what happened in Jerusalem? The listeners argued, doubted, and expressed suspicion. Eventually they wrote a letter that welcomed the new Christians to the faith . . . so long as the newcomers observed certain practices that the Jews felt were required as a minimum for Christian fellowship (Acts 15:23–29). Paul was willing to lead the Gentile churches to follow these directions because he wanted to see Jerusalem tied into the worldwide church. But this response shows that the Jerusalem church was more legalistic than it was protective of the Christian movement.

This policy was still apparent later on when Paul returned to Jerusalem with an offering from the larger church to the Jerusalem body. Their reaction to Paul was not warm and embracing, nor was it protective of Paul. Instead, they reverted to legalism and thought only of protecting themselves. They advised Paul to make sacrifices and to pay the high price of making sacrifices for others in order to maintain the goodwill of the Jews (Acts 21:17–24). Again, legalism and self-protection go hand-in-hand. The temptation toward insular religion may initially seem pious and pure, but will ultimately get in the way of missional living.

Yet Christians today still seem more inclined to urge new Christians to follow old church practices rather than to embrace the outsiders, wherever they may be. Like the Christian Jews in Jerusalem, we continue to try forcing outsiders into the mold of our local brothers and sisters instead of urging our local brothers and sisters to question the necessity of the mold itself. We stay so busy protecting the "tried and true" formulas of our cultural Christianities that we have forgotten the great gospel call to move out of Jerusalem and introduce Jesus Christ to the ends of the earth.

Much Ado About Nothing?

Is this an uncharitable appraisal? Is this being unfair? Perhaps. Surely much of the Jerusalem-like attitude discussed here would not apply to many reading this book, nor perhaps to their churches. After all, we reckon ourselves as the ones in the Christian community who *are* committed to reaching the world. But isn't this "Jerusalem pattern" a major reason we *need* to commit ourselves to such action? Doesn't this often-automatic neglect remain the primary blind spot for Western Christians (along with a tendency to dismiss the practical, physical needs of the world's peoples)? You may be intentional about living and sharing the gospel beyond your church walls with the outsiders in your community and beyond, but are you willing to admit the reason for your intentionality is precisely because you are not naturally inclined toward outsiders? The reason Jesus tells us to love our neighbors "as ourselves" is because he knows we naturally love ourselves more than anyone else. Additionally, it is one thing to recognize (and even understand) this blind spot in the Western church, but it is entirely something else to begin the hard, selfless work of doing something about it.

Perhaps, then, this is the primary practical purpose of this volume: our task is not merely to know and understand these things, but to light a fire under our Christian brothers and sisters to return to a Pauline zeal for reaching the world—a zeal which, blessed by God, changed history and can do so again. None of this will make any difference to the witness of our local churches unless we help others get the message of what we all must do.

A Practical Call to Great Commission Witness

How do we communicate these ideas to others who need to examine them? We must begin by understanding and internalizing the ideas ourselves. We must express these ideas clearly and communicate them passionately. Most importantly, however, we must incarnate these ideas and become a living witness ourselves.

Rediscovering God's mission. This book began with a presentation of missions as reflective of the mission of *God*. If we think for a few minutes about how evangelicals often think about missions, we might conclude that missions has less to do with God than it does with our own activity. In this popular view, missions is something we do because God first loved us. That's true—he did; and we want to respond to him by showing our faithfulness and zeal. But this attitude is not only self-focused, it is also self-defeating. It fails to recognize missions as beginning within the heart and counsel of the Trinity, and thus fails to grasp the weight of its import: the significance of its originating within the community of Almighty God. Nor does this busywork-type attitude acknowledge that Christ did not dispatch the church on this mission in its own power. At one point, for instance, God told his disciples to wait in the city until they were clothed with power from on high.

Are we clothed in power from on high? Or are we only looking for ways to express our spiritual enthusiasm and obedience? How has the cosmic explosion of the missionary will of God been replaced by the popgun of our own personal experience? The witness we give is not of us, but of God. Before the Holy Spirit can address the world in power, our churches at home must be empowered by a Holy Spirit revival of new understanding and new commitment.

This is all well and good to say, but how do we go about doing it? Wait. Isn't that the point? Missions is not our doing, but the work of the Holy Spirit. Should we seek to find new ways to "inspire" our churches to do what they should have been doing for two thousand years, or should we wait on the Lord to inspire us? What new ideas are being advanced by the Holy Spirit that move far beyond the knowledge of the churches in our personal Jerusalems? Have we exhausted the practical applications of the Holy Spirit in this postmodern age? Or have we decided that in regard to missions, there is nothing new under the sun? That's unlikely, given the way the Holy Spirit pursued new methods and means of accomplishing God's mission in the book of Acts. Imagine how radical Paul's new ideas for missions seemed to readers of his letters. More than likely, we have exhausted our old ideas, even as we try to find new and different ways to restate doing the same old things only to get the same old results.

Have we set our minds upon a new world revival that goes beyond all that we have expected or imagined? Are we seeking earnestly for ways in which the Spirit's power might unite us into a mighty army of faith? Or are we attempting to limit God to the expression of ideas about missions that will not challenge our own denominational or ideological agendas? And are we mired in our certainty that *we* are doing God's mission right while other groups are not?

If we should break out of old patterns and do new things in new ways for the same, single-minded purpose—to advance the mission of God—what might the results be? Here, then, is the first principle of our response: let us wait in one accord for the coming of the Spirit; let's wait with the expectancy that the Holy Spirit is indeed capable of making himself known to more than just our own church, our own board and agency, our own denomination, our own group. It sounds simple, but in reality it is an unfathomably radical idea, and perhaps outside the realm of possibility for the evangelical sphere within Christendom. Nevertheless, wouldn't it be wonderful if each of us—as individual evangelicals and as Christian communities—would commit spiritually and practically to being a part of the whole body of Christ?

Learning from the history of missions. A radical realignment of God's people for the pursuit of God's mission has been tried many times before, and usually with the same results: Satan has used some form of the ancient religious power struggle to divide and defeat God's people from the first century on. We have to ask ourselves if it has really been God's mission that has compelled our attempts to coerce or control by political power the activities, thoughts, and methodologies of all other Christians so that they will conform to our own. The study of the history of missions should cause us to ask ourselves some hard questions: Are these religious wars of God? Have they advanced the cause of Christ? Or have they instead demonstrated the power of the evil one to divide and conquer God's own people?

When church leaders have sought to force others to submit to their own cultural understandings, the result has not been unity in Christ but division in Jesus' name. When church councils have struggled to force everyone to get on the same page and form a single organization, the result, ironically, has been a proliferation of organizations. We've witnessed within our own lifetimes attempts to unify the world church by relegating God's mission to the back burner. Reorganization is not the key. Instead, why not learn the lessons of missions history?

One readily seen lesson is how much more effectively the church has worked together, historically, when under the pressure of persecution. Today the house churches of China underscore this hard-earned lesson. But given power, prestige, position, wealth, and the potential proclivity to control others, the church in the West exchanges God's mission for its own. What could the mission of the church possibly be if it is not God's mission? A regular meeting? Following the prescribed rituals of its own denomination (and the feeling of self-satisfaction achieved thereby)? Is the mission of the church to maintain the current roll call of the backsliders, or to rail against the terrible cultural changes taking place right outside the church walls? I am amazed by how many preoccupations we can find to keep us from the occupation of God's mission, and I am astounded by our apparently limitless ability to seek them out. Maybe one of these "church purposes" is the dominating fixation on your own Jerusalem.

There has been a constant battle in the history of the church between the body of Christ, which seeks to perform the mission of God, and the "worldly" church, which has the appearance of godliness but is not interested in actually bearing fruit. This internal conflict has been evident from the beginning. It caused Tertullian to narrow down the "true" church to only himself. It caused Montanus to view himself as the Paraclete. It caused the Eastern and Western churches to split because Greek didn't translate easily to Latin, and vice versa. It caused popes, whose names will long be remembered, to kill many of the anonymous saints whose "sin" was not submitting to an apostate leadership (and presuming to tell other people about Jesus). Yet this same conflict caused Francis of Assisi to throw off all his clothes and declare himself God's alone, rather than accepting the authority of a father who wanted religion to be put in its proper place. It caused Martin Luther to tremble in shame at the behavior of Christian leaders as he got closer and closer to Rome.

The joint lesson of missions history and church history is that we can never expect to accomplish God's mission through human power plays. We cannot expect the church in any place or generation to be perfect or perfectly submitted to God. We cannot expect the most dazzling Christian leader to be free from human frailties. (Doing so only causes more damage when one of our cherished leaders falls.)

The joint lesson of missions history and church history is that we can never expect to accomplish God's mission through human power plays.

Obviously, we can't always expect God's people to agree on everything. The history of the mission of God reminds us—as does surveying the present landscape of Christendom—that we cannot hope for organizational unanimity among believers until we are joined together in heaven. But neither can we expect to "go it alone" and win the world on our own. We have seen where this sinful self-reliance has led. The results past and present issue a clarion call: the churches in our own Jerusalem must humble themselves before the Lord and seek out their unique task from the empowering Holy Spirit. And then we must faithfully and relentlessly tend to the task.

We must do so without expecting public praise and recognition. Loving our neighbors is not about getting a pat on the back from our fellow believers. Neither is missions about getting good public relations for the church. In fact, Jesus promised—and the believers who have dared to leave their Jerusalems to live and share the gospel in the uttermost parts of the earth have proved—that the church, by and large, will be hated for proclaiming and living the good news. But if we were to become single-minded about this outward work, focusing upon our own task without insisting that all others follow our instructions or our orders, imagine what the Holy Spirit could accomplish.

Centering on the gospel. As we see in Paul's missives to some seriously messed up churches, one common failing they all clearly shared was forgetting their first love, as seen in the apostle's exasperation in the opening lines of his letter to the Galatians. We see within the marvelous words of 1 Corinthians 15:3–8 this reminder to the church at Corinth: "For what I received I passed on to you as of first importance: that Christ died for our sins according to the Scriptures, that he was buried, that he was raised on the third day according to the Scriptures, and that he appeared to Cephas, and then to the Twelve. After that, he appeared to more than five hundred of the brothers and sisters at the same time, most of whom are still living, though some have fallen asleep. Then he appeared to James, then to all the apostles, and last of all he appeared to me."

This is what Paul considers "most important": the historical fact of Christ's atoning work and the historical witness and impact of that work. This is important for authentic missionalization because the gospel both unifies and empowers. It unifies all believers, regardless of culture or context or countenance, in our common faith in the Lord who has saved us all. There is no greater grounds for commonality, no more unifying quality for all Christians, than the finished work of Christ himself applied to us all equally.

Centering on the gospel empowers missionalization because it makes us humble and worshipful. There isn't a more effective witness to the gospel than believers who orbit around the incomparable goodness of the good news, because they serve their neighbors and submit to their Savior. When churches do not treat the most important thing like it's the most important thing, they lose sight of who they exist for. Instead of existing for God and neighbor, they instead revert to the self-focus they claim to have repented of in the first place. And that is when Corinthian-type licentiousness or Galatian-type legalism can take root.

Finding our place. A potential disadvantage in a book like this, written in multiple voices, is a sense of disparity. Each of us is writing independently rather than in one voice throughout. We may share solid reputations, but our styles and points of emphasis are different. The advantage of such a book, though, is that it reflects in microcosm the nature of God's mission in the world. Despite our differences and our diverse approaches (not to mention our diverse ministry contexts and mission fields), we nevertheless write "in one accord." And the cooperative effort of this volume can serve as a practical missiological mosaic, each of us shaping our own perspectives and giving shape to the larger perspective we all share.

We don't all need to know each other's names or personal histories to know God's purpose for us as individuals. We don't all have to sing in the same key for the Lord to be praised. There is unanimity in our diversity—not our diversity in content, which remains fixed in the Word itself, but in our contexts, which are, by definition, different.

This is how God decided to reveal himself and his love to the world: not through a single thunderous voice from heaven, but through our voices in our places in our languages. Finding our place in this worldwide miracle of Pentecost has less to do with marching in unison than it does with marching in a unified direction, each of us marching with our particular discipleship communities to the beat of our own spiritual drummer. The Holy Spirit works in different ways in different parts of the book of Acts. The fact that the Holy Spirit does all things in creative ways is one of the biggest causes of crisis in a church that wants everyone to think alike. The Holy Spirit doesn't want discipleship clones. You may read ideas expressed in these pages that seem absolutely contradictory. Don't be confused by that; simply realize that each of us speaks from our own missional contexts.

You need to do the same. As you seek your place in God's mission, and as you aspire to lead the church of your Jerusalem to follow, keep a sharp eye out for the ideas and methodologies that will fit your context and help you faithfully focus on incarnating God's mission. By God's grace, I'll do the same.

Let us all remember that it will help the cause of the mission of God if we put our criticisms and corrections of one another on hold, and instead work with determination on our divine assignment, like those who joined Nehemiah in rebuilding Jerusalem's wall.

Many of the ideas and approaches in this volume may seem new to you. Give them a chance. Innovation isn't a bad thing, as long as it isn't pursued simply for the sake of innovation. Apply some of these concepts in your own ministry contexts and see if they fit. Note especially Mike Barnett's chapter, "Strategic Prayer for God's Mission," and make certain that prayer is a priority among those who serve alongside you. In recent years, missiologists have conducted studies that give us marvelous new insights into how to communicate the gospel effectively to the world. Contextualization studies can free you from having to worry about "the right way" to do things. There are many right ways to apply. Understand and emphasize in your ministry that contextualization does not mean a jot or tittle of change in the content of the gospel—it is not compromise. Remember how that old dictum for young preachers, "Preach the Word and love the people," encompasses both the necessity of proclamation evangelism and the care for human needs. And be reminded once again that the essential foundation to all missionary efforts is basic biblical discipleship.

How do we find our place in God's mission? The principle is clear. We follow the Lord as disciples—we don't advise him as consultants.

Working through the church. We are all part of a worldwide web of spiritual dynamism, linked through and empowered by God himself and directed by him through the Holy Spirit. The true church is the true body of Christ in the world, and the dimensions of that church cannot be encompassed by any one of us individually. I celebrate this! While individual churches in human history may have failed miserably and repeatedly, we serve a forgiving God who already knows the ultimate outcome of our service. We share within this network the blessing and the heritage of Peter and Paul, Barnabas and Silas, Timothy and John Mark, Polycarp and Iranaeus, Tertullian and Augustine, Patrick and Boniface, Francis and Ignatius, Luther and Calvin, Spener and von Zinzendorf, Carey and Edwards, Whitfield and Wesley, and all the anonymous saints of history who have faithfully and fruitfully functioned with and through the church to pursue their understandings of their part in the mission of God. They used different approaches, and sometimes new ideas. They struggled, many with each other. Out of these various historical threads of ministry they wove their part of the patchwork quilt that is missions history. All of them had this in common: they advanced God's mission through Christ's church.

It's our turn now. We are surrounded by a great cloud of witnesses. The race set before us is the same one that Paul ran. The topography we run through has been changed by time and culture, but we can run with the same motivation. Our methodologies may be new, but our mission is not. We carry a single message, each one of us from our own Jerusalems to a radically shifting world. Each of us must ask ourselves: "How shall I run?"

Discussion Points

1. If your church's location and culture is Jerusalem, where is your Judea and Samaria? How is your church on mission to these places?

2. What are some practical ways that churches can prevent developing an inward focus in the community?

3. How central to the life of your church is (a) prayer, and (b) communicating the gospel? How central are these two elements to your own life?

4. One well-known minister remarked on the extravagant, multi-million dollar auditorium a large church decided to build within walking distance of the poorest area of town. What are some specific signs a church may have begun favoring "praising in the temple" over "witnessing to the world"?

Further Reading

Frost, Michael, and Alan Hirsch. *ReJesus: A Wild Messiah for a Missional Church.* Peabody, MA: Hendrickson, 2008.

Stetzer, Ed, and Philip Nation. *Compelled by Love: A Journey to Missional Living.* Birmingham, AL: New Hope, 2008.

Stetzer, Ed, and David Putnam. *Breaking the Missional Code.* Nashville: Broadman & Holman, 2008.

37

THE LOCAL CHURCH AND
THE MISSION OF GOD

H. Al Gilbert

What could happen if everyone in your church viewed life through the mission of God? What if the *whole church* "got it": every heart on fire, every skill and gift deployed, every relationship and circumstance submitted to the lordship of Christ, the people of God understanding and living out the mission of God?

What if every member lived the *whole gospel*: not just viewing the message of Christ as a ticket to heaven, but the whole gospel—daily depending on Christ and living out the Christ-life with grace and power. What if every member lived life consumed with the yearning, "Your kingdom come, your will be done, on earth as it is in heaven"?

What if every member lived with the *whole world* in view: not just the normal traffic patterns of life called "our world"—but the big world God created and Jesus died to save? What if everyone lived it out locally while longing for the global glory of God?

Christian leaders from around the world gathered at the first Lausanne Congress on World Evangelization in 1974, and while discussing how to share Christ with the entire world, one thing became very clear: world evangelization requires "the whole church to take the whole gospel to the whole world."[1]

Years later, this phrase reminds leaders of the challenge faced by the

---

[1]See Christopher J. H. Wright, "Whole Gospel, Whole Church, Whole World," The Global Conversation website, a collaborative partnership of the Lausanne Movement and Christianity Today, www.christianitytoday.com/globalconversation/october2009/index.html.

local church. Aware of the daily hurts and fears of God's people, leaders know they must challenge every member to look beyond circumstances and personal comfort and find their place in the big picture. And this is the big picture: the people of God and the mission of God.

What will it take to convince the members of *your church* that this mission of God should involve every member? It starts with understanding what it means to be a disciple.

Disciples and the Mission of God

For too long, discipleship has been separated from missions. Christian education and training opportunities have multiplied, and yet the assignment of missions continues to be relegated to the "professional missionary." This results in a misunderstanding of what it means to be a disciple. When disciples step into the light of God's mission, the burden of the Great Commission returns to its rightful place: every disciple and every church.

True discipleship is not measured by church attendance or activities. Disciples go beyond knowing things about God. Disciples follow. Jesus repeatedly said, "Take up your cross and follow me."

When disciples follow Jesus, they help others follow Jesus. Responding to the mission of God, disciples lay down dreams of earthly success to focus on the eternal glory of Christ. In reading this book, you have come to know more about the mission of God. What should you call this pressure, this fresh burden on your heart? How about just calling it "discipleship"?

With hearts set on Jesus, the author and finisher of their faith, disciples gladly submit to the responsibility given to his church. Willing to go anywhere—longing for the message of hope to go everywhere—disciples hear the voice of the Shepherd and follow him! For some, the mission of God demands selling everything and moving to a distant land; for everyone, it demands holding every possession in an open hand. That is what disciples do!

In Matthew 28:19, Jesus commands his followers to make disciples of all the nations (*ethnos*). Don't be afraid of the word "disciple." True discipleship is not a program; it is life-to-life, walking with God. The original text presents the words for "disciple-making" and "all nations" side by side. When Jesus says "all nations," he is not suggesting a potential extent. He is announcing his plan and intent! To be a disciple, one must understand God's mission.

Talk with your church leaders and clarify this dimension of disciple-making. Discuss how your church can teach every believer God's plan for his church. Explain what you have learned about God's plan to take the gospel to the nations (*ethnos*). The people of God (the *laos*) understand about reaching all the peoples of the world (the *ethnos*).

Mobilizing the Local Church

Is God sending you to the mission field? If not, what can you do about the mission of God? People who have seen the big picture must accept the responsibility of involving others. This has been called mobilization.

"Mobilization" is a process, and it typically includes three components: awakening, moving and growing, and strategic alignment. Although that sounds rather linear, mobilization is usually relational and often messy.

Mobilization is not a science; it's a journey. God works through his Spirit, his Word, and his people; and there are "aha moments" all along the way. Church leaders cannot cause these moments, but they can facilitate an environment and an ethos to provide opportunities and response. Identifying some of the markers along the trail will help you provide intentional leadership to the mobilization process. First, consider the possibilities and dream about what could be.

The possibilities. Is there really something for everyone to do? Can everyone "own" the Great Commission? Can you even imagine how it would look if the whole church responded to the mission of God?

Keep in mind, as you look at these possibilities, that leaders are not limited to just one. Living out the mission of God in the context of the local church, leaders have overlapping and interlocking circles of influence. Consider the following possibilities for you and your church.

Sent ones and senders. If you don't leave the homeland, that doesn't mean you only care about the homeland. Some are "sent"; the rest are to be "senders." By definition, if there are "sent ones," then someone does the "sending." Agencies may facilitate the work of missionaries, but local churches must find ways to stay connected when missionaries go out from the church.

Some are sent; all are involved in spreading the message. Some come face to face with ethnicity on foreign soil; all must arrest every opportunity to see that Jesus is worshiped by all peoples.

Hook your life to those who go. Serve them as they go. Help others see sending as more than throwing money in the offering plate during a missions emphasis. Lead your church to regularly examine life *here* in the light of their going *there*. "Sending" moves us to adjust our lives, to align with those who are sent as they go.

William Carey told his friend Andrew Fuller to "hold the ropes" as he went down into the "gold mine" of India. Do you hear the same call today? As the sent ones go, who will hold the ropes? Our children can know their children. We talk about them in our homes and church gatherings. We pray for them at the dinner table and at the Lord's Table. It is only right—they are family. They are sent; we are the senders.

Some hear God say, "Your feet will be beautiful as you take the message." Others hear him say, "Buy the shoes for those beautiful feet! Help them make the trip!" Either way, our hearts will be hooked to the message. We want all peoples to worship Christ. He desires it and he deserves it. Lordship and discipleship demand it.

It has rightly been said that there are only three choices when it comes to world evangelization: sent, sender, or disobedient. The mission of God does not expect everyone to go. But it does clearly expect those who stay to be inextricably linked to those who go. Sharing the same commitment to the gospel, senders hold the ropes for the sent ones.

Welcomers and international connectors. When your church is gripped by the mission of God, people will want to serve the international families moving into your city. You will help these new families find their way around their new hometown, serve as tutors so they can learn English, and open your homes and lives to use every possible means to love them and lead them to Christ. In the world of missions mobilization, this is the strategic ministry of "welcomer."

Teaching English as a second language (ESL) opens many doors. It not only provides the opportunity to make new international friends, but allows the interaction needed for church members to love people of ethnicity.

International business leaders begin to consider how to use their influence and networks to share Christ in places where missionaries are not allowed. Business owners find ways to facilitate new believers with jobs, strategically placing them where the gospel is not. Some business leaders go overseas on short-term trips, doing things like conducting seminars for small business owners and interacting with business executives and community leaders. Finding ways to utilize their vocational proficiencies to build relationships, businesswomen and businessmen delight in the opportunity to use their expertise as a natural platform to speak of a relationship with God. Going as teachers, trainers, and international colleagues, professionals earn the right to share. Every responsibility and relationship is focused through a lens of faith. International friends expect conversations about faith and the deep things that motivate leaders.

At home, campus ministries reach out to international students to welcome them, serve them, and share Christ with them. As internationals come to know Christ over time, they are trained to join in the mission of God to take the good news back to their homeland.

All of these possibilities and opportunities are critical if we are to take the whole gospel to the whole world.

The process. Mobilization is a process. It may take time for people in your church to discover a strategic place, but there are distinct moments of discovery along the way. They can be anticipated.

Awakening. This is the first step in the process.

Scripture: The Word of God breaks the human heart. God uses his Word to awaken his people to his plan. "He says, 'Be still, and know that I am God'" (Psalm 46:10a). When we stop and listen to God's Word, we begin to understand the rest of the verse: "I will be exalted among the nations, I will be exalted in the earth" (Psalm 46:10b). Listening to his Word, the selfish heart is challenged to more than personal comfort.

People-to-people: Missionaries stay in our homes, visit our churches, and come to our small group meetings. We hear their heart through stories, see their pictures, and look into the faces of their children. That's when we begin to realize that something is missing. They are living the gospel; we only talk about it. No, they're not perfect. It's their willingness to lay everything on the altar that challenges our comfortable lifestyle. We look at how they are following Jesus, and it causes us to reexamine our lives in the light of the lordship of Christ. Lordship always demands a willingness to go anywhere, anytime for his glory. Time with missionaries reminds us of this demand.

Face-to-face: Short-term trips can be used to awaken God's people. Eyes are opened and people begin to ask, "Why me? Why do I have so many blessings and opportunities?" These encounters with ethnicity and poverty are not limited to foreign soil. Any opportunity to cross a human barrier with the love of Christ affords the opportunity of awakening. Awakening is not the end of mobilization; it's just the first step.

Moving and growing. Mobilization is more than a feeling or idea. It is more than a moment. It requires movement. Following Jesus into the mission of God requires leaving one's comfort zone and routine. Awakening may be the initial experience, but the process of mobilization continues to move and seek direction.

Sometimes when people are moved into action, they act without considering the long-term impact. Their hearts are broken and they are overwhelmed by compassion for those in need of witness or ministry. It seems logical to empty their pockets and take the shirt off their backs. But leaders must challenge their people to grow and ask questions such as:

- Am I trying to relieve my guilt or really help?
- Is this culturally appropriate?
- Is it time to speak or time to listen?
- Will my action breed dependency or facilitate a movement of the gospel?
- What does the missionary think?

Strategic alignment. Once on the move, people begin to consider: "There's so much to do—is this the right thing to do? Is this the best use of my skills and gifts?"

Keep moving and growing until you find your place. Your role may change over time, but you will always be amazed to watch what can happen when the body of Christ works together and ministry is properly aligned. As you grow, you won't want to do it alone. Your heart will long for the opportunity to use your gift in alignment with others in your church.

Mobilizing your church. Just as people are different, churches are different. Every church has unique opportunities through the relationships and skills of its members. How do you discover this uniqueness and mobilize your church?

DNA (discernable natural affinities). Look around your church and notice the medical workers, farmers, teachers, business professionals, etc. Consider who God has placed together. What is your church's DNA?

Scientific research may refer to DNA (deoxyribonucleic acid) when trying to understand the complex code that uniquely defines an individual body. When we consider DNA and the mission of God, however, it is not technical—it is relational. We can simply ask, "How has God uniquely placed people together in our church?" If you are going to be used to mobilize them, you need to take time to understand what they do and whom they know. Then you won't have to create something new; you can simply cooperate with who you are—with who God made you to be as a fellowship.

Relationships, relationships, relationships. You can't say it too many times. God leads his people by connecting people. Most often his invitation will come through the relationships in your church.

When our church sent a team on a mission trip to Europe to work with refugees, Tim and Jodi sensed a call to missions. Within a year, they packed up their family and moved to Europe. For the next eight years they served refugees in major European cities.

John and Brooke, also members of our church, serve as Bible translators. They spent years working on the New Testament for a hidden people group in Southeast Asia. While John and Brooke were home for furlough, more than two hundred individuals from "their" people group moved to our city. Members of our church stepped up to help John and Brooke welcome these refugees.

Tim and Jodi were home on furlough and discovered that their refugee ministry was needed in our city. Now Tim and Jodi direct that ministry.

Two missionary couples, a church, and refugees met on the common ground of need and love. Our people supplied furniture, transportation, job training, English lessons for the adults, tutoring for the children, etc. This provided an incredible alternative for hundreds of church members who will never go overseas on a mission trip. Now, face to face with ethnicity and need, God is teaching his people the heartbeat of his mission.

Partnerships and people groups. It may seem easy to join others on a short-term mission trip, but it takes a lot of effort to develop a partnership. By definition, a partnership is multitiered and lasts multiple years. Someone has to organize and facilitate the partnership, but that's really not a job for the pastor. Someone else in your church needs to take this responsibility. Could this be your assignment?

What about unreached people groups? Has your church adopted a people group? If not, do you know how? Remember, God uses relationships to lead his people. Consider these questions: Have refugees relocated to your community? Do you have a relationship with a missionary who is focusing on an unreached people group? Has something you read in this book turned your heart to a certain part of the world? These are all ways that God may invite you to focus on a specific people group.

Then what happens? When you begin to focus on a group, you will be amazed at how God will provide ways to network with others whose hearts have been turned the same direction. When you discover the many places in the world where "your" people group lives—maybe Yemeni Arabs in Detroit, Libyan Arabs in Europe, or Persians in Baltimore or Los Angeles—you will start looking for ways to go there. If you can find literature already published about that group, use it to get others involved. If not, create the literature yourself and take advocacy to a new level.

Clarify permission. People often hesitate to move because they are uncertain about the assignment. When you and the leaders of your church clarify the expectations, great things can happen. Deputize these mobilizers and give them a title: team leader, advocate, champion, etc.

Caught and taught. God's Word will not allow us to set our affections on the comforts of this world. The Scriptures were not written to help us find ways to make life easy and comfortable. Instead, the Bible moves us to explain the global and eternal purposes of God to every Christ-follower, every disciple. When others in your church begin to catch a glimpse of the mission of God, they will begin to talk about suffering and sacrifice in a whole new light. Clearly lived and taught, it will be caught—in your homes, discipleship groups, and church gatherings.

Pray to the Lord of the harvest. When Jesus saw the crowds, he felt compassion for them. Then he said to his disciples, "The harvest is plentiful but the workers are few. Ask the Lord of the harvest, therefore, to send out workers into his harvest field" (Matthew 9:37–38). This is why we must teach present-day disciples to pray, "Lord, since I am part of your church, I will go anywhere anytime for your glory!"

The greatest test of this kind of praying comes when we add our children to the prayer. Are we willing to pray, "Lord, I will go anywhere anytime for your glory. And if not me, it would be a great honor if you would send my children"? We want our children to understand that the mission of God is global. The best way for them to understand our heart is to pray this kind of prayer with them, and let them know we are praying it for them.

Anywhere? Our community? The inner city? The great population centers of America? To the hidden peoples still at the ends of the earth?

Anytime? At the end of college? While the kids are young? When I retire? Right now, in the middle of my career? Yes, for God's glory.

Conclusion

These final chapters focus on how we can co-labor for the sake of the gospel. And that co-laboring begins and ends with the local church. God wants to use the whole church to equip and mobilize disciples to go to all peoples on earth. Is your church a part of the mission of God? It should be . . . until every tribe, tongue, nation, and people gather around the throne and give God the praise that he deserves. Amen!

Discussion Points

1. What could happen if everyone in your church viewed life through the mission of God?

2. What does Gilbert mean when he says we need to "clarify this dimension of disciple-making"? What does disciple-making mean at your church? Does it fit the biblical meaning and intent?

3. Gilbert writes about the DNA of churches. How does he define this DNA? How will your understanding of your church's DNA allow you to "simply cooperate with who you are"?

Further Reading

Guder, Darrell L. *Missional Church: A Vision for the Sending of the Church in North America.* Grand Rapids: Eerdmans, 1998.

Mays, David. *Becoming a World Changing Church.* ACMC, 2006.

38

WHERE DO YOU FIT IN THE MISSION OF GOD?

Clyde Meador

Bob and Marge had been long-time missionaries serving in Southeast Asia. The final assignment of their thirty-year career was an itinerant training assignment in the Indian subcontinent. Just before retirement, they made a circuit of the places where they had been training, explaining that they wouldn't be back again.

Is Anyone Else Coming?

One evening they were meeting with church leaders in the Kondh Hills of the state of Orissa in India. As Bob explained that they wouldn't be coming back again, Mr. Naik, an elderly pastor who was usually very quiet, stood up, raised his hand, and said, "I have a question: Is anybody else coming?"

All over the world, Christian pastors and other leaders who have had little opportunity for training are asking the questions, "Is anyone else coming?" "Is anyone else coming to train us?" "Is anyone else coming to walk alongside us?" "Is anyone else coming to encourage us?"

And we ask the question on behalf of lost people all over the world: "Is anyone else coming—someone who will tell us about a Savior?"

The answer to that question lies with you! Through your involvement in the mission of God—praying for missions, giving toward missions, going and participating in missions, and many other ways—you must answer that question.

As a follower of Jesus, how are you responding to that question? Perhaps your response is that you don't know or you're unsure of how God might use you in telling people about the Savior. Perhaps your response is that you are involved halfheartedly and want to know how to be more deeply involved.

You must not only celebrate what God is doing to accomplish his mission; you must also seriously consider your role and place—where and how you fit into the mission of God.

This volume is filled with information and inspiration about the ways God is bringing the peoples of the world to him. However, you must not only celebrate what God is doing to accomplish his mission; you must also seriously consider your role and place—where and how you fit into the mission of God. How will you respond to the question "Is anyone else coming?"

OUR RESPONSIBILITY, HIS TASK

As you think through this question and others, it is important to start at the beginning. God's desire is that every person on earth be involved in the accomplishment of his mission. First, each person is the object of his love, sought by him to come to saving faith in him. "The Lord . . . is patient with you, not wanting anyone to perish, but everyone to come to repentance" (2 Peter 3:9).

Once you came to faith in Christ, you became charged with the responsibility to take the good news of salvation to the rest of the world.

Once you came to faith in Christ, you became charged with the responsibility to take the good news of salvation to the rest of the world. All believers have that responsibility. We are to be his ambassadors and the sweet aroma of the knowledge of him in every place. This is not simply an option for the believer. God commands it, and we must do it.

Whether taking the gospel to your next-door neighbor or to those who are lost in the far corners of the earth, it is your responsibility to participate in God's mission. But just where do you fit? Is it to pray? Is it to give? Is it to go? Is it to mobilize others to go? Is your part primarily local, near where you live? Is your part primarily international, far from where you live now? Or is it some combination of all these expressions of obedience?

In any case, whether your involvement is to be primarily local or primarily somewhere else in the world, it is important to have all of God's world and all of God's mission in view. God reminds Israel in Isaiah 49:6 that the task is global: "It is too small a thing for you to be my servant to restore the tribes of Jacob and bring back those of Israel I have kept. I will also make you a light for the Gentiles, that my salvation may reach to the ends of the earth."

You may think that you are inadequate to take the gospel to a place you don't know, to communicate the beautiful news of salvation in Christ to people you don't know. And you are correct, for none of us is able to accomplish our part of the mission of God without complete dependence upon him. Our responsibility is to demonstrate and speak the gospel faithfully, and then leave the results to the Holy Spirit. He is the one who brings people to faith and repentance. As Paul stated to the Corinthians, "I planted the seed, Apollos watered it, but God has been making it grow. So neither the one who plants nor the one who waters is anything, but only God, who makes things grow" (1 Corinthians 3:6–7).

Frankly, a sense of inadequacy is essential to being an effective communicator of the gospel—especially in challenging circumstances. Dependence upon ourselves will only lead to disappointment. Evaluating yourself in light of other Christian workers and deciding that God could never use you to take his truth to others around the world, or even locally, is denying God's power.

In 2 Timothy, Paul talks about the gospel as something that has been entrusted to us by God. Yet he expresses the beautiful certainty that such a trust is safe, for not only do we guard the trust, but God guards it also. In wondrous confidence, Paul says, "Of this gospel I was appointed a herald and an apostle and a teacher. That is why I am suffering as I am. Yet this is no cause for shame, because I know whom I have believed, and am convinced that he is able to guard what I have entrusted to him until that day" (2 Timothy 1:11–12).

Yes, we are inadequate; but God is adequate. We are called not to be supermen and superwomen, but to be faithful and respond to his mission and task as he calls and allows us. It is essential to remember that it is *his* task. He graciously allows you to have a part in it. He has a plan for what your part is to be. He has created and developed you to serve him in the

Yes, we are inadequate; but God is adequate. We are called not to be supermen and superwomen, but to be faithful and respond to his mission and task as he calls and allows us.

ways in which you can be most useful to him. So consider the experiences and opportunities that he has brought into your life that have helped you to grow in him and have equipped you to be useful in his mission.

Where Do You Fit?

There are many factors to consider as you seek your place in God's mission. The most important input, by which all other factors must be judged, is what his Spirit is saying to you about your part in his mission. Through intentional communion with God via his Word and prayer, you must seek his direction for your involvement in the task.

However, you must also be committed to obey as he leads. God does not reveal his will to you in order that you might evaluate that direction and then decide whether or not to obey. He reveals his direction only when you have already made the commitment to obey whatever he reveals.

God's Spirit speaks to us in many ways. A principal way is through his Word. As you immerse yourself in his written Word, Scripture becomes the voice of God to you in a very personal way. As you listen to him speaking to you and as you commune with him in prayer, he reveals his direction for your life.

Another way the Lord leads us is through experiences and influences that have previously touched us. Have you met others who have been deeply involved in his mission? What have you learned from them? Have you had opportunities to learn about his mission around the world? What has most interested you and attracted you?

God often speaks to us as he piques our interest by allowing us to hear from others who are involved in his work. The world is filled with people groups who vary greatly in their settings, culture, traditions, and beliefs. One step toward finding God's place for you in his world involves seeking information about this world.

Each of us is unique. What grips my interest may not interest you. Traditions and other cultural aspects that are boring to me may be quite intriguing to you. God may use such interest and attraction to place a people group in your heart and to draw you to serve among them.

As you review what God has brought you through and how he has used you thus far, you will realize that you are indeed his instrument and that he uses you in carrying out his mission. You may have walked with the Lord for a couple of years or for many decades. Throughout your Christian walk, you have seen God change lives around you. In what ways has he allowed you to be a part of his work? Through words which you have spoken, prompted by his Spirit? Through acts of care and compassion as you have ministered to the needs of those around you? Through teaching others about God and his Word? Through working with children or youth? The ways in which you have served God and others in the past quite possibly point to ways in which he will use you in days to come.

The ways in which you have served God and others in the past quite possibly point to ways in which he will use you in days to come.

What Roles?

Another aspect to consider is your gifts and abilities. What do you find yourself able to do especially well? What gifts has God blessed you with? What interests has God placed in your heart?

Preachers and teachers. When you think of having a part in the mission of God, you may think especially about the ministry gifts and roles of preaching and teaching. Indeed, proclaiming God's Word and teaching his truths are vital aspects of carrying out his mission. If you have found that God uses you in these ways, you can be certain that in those same ways you can have a vital part in his mission.

Yet God uses believers with many kinds of abilities, gifts, training, and occupations to achieve his purposes. As you commit to God whatever you have to give and to do, he uses it to minister to others and to attract others to himself.

Marketplace workers. A couple (I'll call them Dan and Rose) who had been faithful, active members of our church for many years are now serving in a distant part of the world. In our local community, Dan worked as a veterinarian and Rose as a schoolteacher. When they were in their early fifties, the time came for Dan to retire.

Dan and Rose had been interested in missions all their lives, but they had no idea that they could be a part of missions outside of their local setting. Then someone challenged them regarding the need for their skills in an undeveloped part of the world. They responded in obedience, still not understanding what God could do with them. In the last three years Dan and Rose have freely shared their professional skills in remote South American villages, while telling others the truth of the gospel. They have seen many former animists come to faith in Christ and have seen dozens of new churches planted.

Accountants and attorneys likewise use their professional abilities and understandings to open doors to the gospel in many settings around the world. Businesspeople, engineers, and construction personnel find God using them to share his truth in places where their skills are especially needed and where using those skills gains credibility and authenticity and enables them to talk freely about the Lord.

Doctors and nurses and other medical personnel are finding more opportunities than ever to share Jesus as they serve the physical needs of people around the world. Rather than ministering in hospitals or other institutional settings, heath education and treatment are often taken to people in areas where resources are scarce and a cup of clean water in Jesus' name meets a vital need and also opens hearts to truth.

Short-term workers. Although we often focus especially on those who go to another part of the world for an extended period of time—learning the local language and culture, and impacting a people group with the gospel for many years—God often uses people even during brief periods of time. Those who give of themselves in a missions trip of only a week or two frequently see God do remarkable things in and through and around them. Many go for assignments of a year or two and see God use them in amazing ways. God may use you in a particular place for a short time or a long time, so you must be open not only to where he may lead you but also for how long he may lead you.

It is also essential to hear what others have to say about where you fit, how they have seen God using you thus far, and how he is likely to use you in days to come. Many of us tend to have an inordinate sense of inadequacy. Others see past that, and their insights are valuable. Again, of course, it is God's direction that is definitive; yet he may use all of these factors to communicate his direction to us.

In all of this it is very important to remember that it is not your gifts, abilities, experiences, or influences that enable you to carry out your part in God's mission effectively. The mission belongs to God. He is the one who makes sure it gets done. He enables you to do that which he directs you to do. He equips you when and how you need to be equipped. He makes your service effective for his purpose in his mission. The key to sensing God's direction, as well as to effective participation in his mission, is your relationship with him and your dependence upon him.

The key to sensing God's direction, as well as to effective participation in his mission, is your relationship with him and your dependence upon him.

Which People and Place?

If you sense that God is calling you to serve in some other part of the world, especially for something longer than a short-term trip, another major decision is to determine if he is calling you to work among a particular people group. All the factors listed above apply again. What people group needs the gifts and abilities you have to offer? Where does God seem to be directing your interest?

A very special factor to be considered—though always subject to what the Lord says through his Word, prayer, and the individuals he brings into your life—is the degree of availability of the gospel among various people groups. In many places in the world, the gospel is available in abundance and in various ways. In other parts of the world, however, the gospel is largely unknown. As you consider where God might be leading you to serve, it is essential to seriously consider that he might lead you to one of these places where the gospel has not yet penetrated. That emphasis was important to Paul, as he stated in Romans: "It has always been my ambition to preach the gospel where Christ was not known, so that I would not be building on someone else's foundation. Rather, as it is written: 'Those who were not told about him will see, and those who have not heard will understand'" (Romans 15:20–21).

In dealing with that possibility, it is important to realize that there are usually reasons why the gospel has not penetrated the particular people group or collection of people groups to whom God might be calling you. There is a significant likelihood that those who have been most hidden from the gospel are in a place that is physically challenging and therefore is a difficult place in which to live and serve. There is also a significant likelihood that persecution will arise when the gospel is proclaimed, and you may suffer from that persecution.

As you deal with where God may be calling you in this world, you must count the cost, remembering that the world is greatly influenced by the evil one and that a response of obedience to participate in the mission of God may mean a response of sacrifice. Yet that sacrifice is one that carries with it the gracious privilege of sharing in the mission of God—the one mission that is truly important.

Special Kinds of Servants

God doesn't call every person to go to some other part of the country or the world to carry the gospel. There are other critical, strategic ways in which you may be called to participate in his mission.

God doesn't call every person to go to some other part of the country or the world to carry the gospel. There are other critical, strategic ways in which you may be called to participate in his mission.

To pray. One way that every one of us must be involved in God's mission is through prayer. God's mission is accomplished when God acts, and God acts in response to the prayers of his people. You and I must pray. Jesus said, "The harvest is plentiful, but the workers are few. Ask the Lord of the harvest, therefore, to send out workers into his harvest field" (Luke 10:2).

Paul outlined many of the ways we must be praying for the mission of God: "Pray in the Spirit on all occasions with all kinds of prayers and requests. With this in mind, be alert and always keep on praying for all the Lord's people. Pray also for me, that whenever I speak, words may be given me so that I will fearlessly make known the mystery of the gospel. . . . Pray that I may declare it fearlessly, as I should" (Ephesians 6:18–20).

- We must pray for those who go out as missionaries: that they will be bold and effective, sharing the truth through their actions and words wherever God leads them.

- We must pray for believers in difficult situations, where persecution threatens to hinder them every day. We pray that they will remain faithful, true to the Lord in every circumstance.

- We must pray for Christian leaders and workers around the world, who often labor with little training and little worldly appreciation. We pray that they will have wisdom and love as they serve the Lord, and that they will be used effectively by him.

- We must pray for the lost, that they will have opportunities to hear, even in places and among people groups where the Word has not yet come. We pray that their hearts will be open to the Word when it does come, and that they will come to faith.

Even though all of us must be undergirding the work of missions through prayer, there are some whom the Lord has formed into great prayer warriors. People such as these do their greatest work as they pray, spending large amounts of time pleading with the Lord to do what he so wants to do.

As you examine your life and see who God has made you to be at this time, you may see that he is leading you to be a special kind of servant, devoting yourself to extensive, intensive prayer for every aspect of the mission of God.

To enable. As we have previously discussed, God calls some to be primarily ones who go and others to be primarily ones who pray. He also calls some to be enablers. As with going and telling and as with praying, we all are to be enablers; but some are called by God primarily to be enablers at certain times of their lives. There are at least three kinds of enablers: givers, mobilizers, and equippers.

Givers. You may be most aware of the enablers who are givers. We live in an expensive world, and the work of carrying out the mission of God is no exception. Sending the gospel to those who have not yet heard requires funds. It costs money to send his servants to other places. It costs money to communicate the gospel—through print, broadcasts, the Internet, or whatever means. It costs money to respond to the physical needs of people, whether medical needs, educational needs, or the basic needs of life.

People who give provide necessary funding. All of us are called to give, but some are especially blessed and divinely enabled to give. That special equipping may involve an unusual supply of resources that have been made available to a believer. It may involve a heart that is prepared to give sacrificially and meaningfully in any circumstance. Thus, God may call some to have a special responsibility in giving.

Mobilizers. The second kind of enabler is one who mobilizes others. Mobilization is communicating to others the compelling need and certain command to be involved in God's mission, helping them to see how they may be involved in the mission and encouraging them to put those pieces together. Mobilizers are essential people in the task of the mission of God.

Mobilizers are people who have a strong commitment to seeing the mission of God accomplished. They communicate that passion clearly and effectively, either publicly or, more often, in small groups. What is important is that they are able to help others see how they can have a part in God's mission and can encourage them to step out and follow God in obedience.

God may have equipped you with a personality that can connect with others in a meaningful and encouraging way. He may have implanted within you a desire to see many others take their place in his mission. He may be calling you to be involved most especially as a mobilizer of others.

Equippers. The third kind of enabler I will mention is an equipper. An equipper is primarily a trainer, a person who helps others gain knowledge, understanding, and skills to take the gospel more effectively to those who have not yet heard. The equipper probably has experience as one who has gone and effectively communicated the gospel to others, seeing people come to faith and churches started.

If you have experienced God using you as a teacher and you have experiences to share with those he is sending, God may be calling you to be an equipper of others God has called to participate in his mission.

Are You Willing?

Remember that God expects every believer to go and tell, to pray, to give, to encourage others to go, and even to equip others to serve. But there is a particular way—or a combination of these ways—through which God especially wants to use you at this time in your life. As you examine your life, be sure to seek counsel from others and, most importantly, ask God what that way is. As you ask, you must have already said, "Yes, Lord, I will gladly follow however you lead." Then God will reveal the part of his will that you need to know at that time. And as you obey, he will enable you to serve him faithfully as he leads.

It is quite likely that where and how you fit in God's mission will vary from time to time. You may serve in one way in his mission today and in very different ways in other periods of your life. It's not unusual for believers to see their current place in life simply as preparation for the future, without realizing how God wants to use them now. Your current situation, however, is never solely preparation for some other time yet to come. God has a purpose and plan for each of us at every moment. As Paul writes in his letter to the Ephesians, "We are God's handiwork, created in Christ Jesus to do good works, which God prepared in advance for us to do" (Ephesians 2:10).

Conclusion

Serving as God directs right now and being consistent with current opportunities makes it possible for God to use us in other ways in days to come. Those who are faithful in little will be faithful in much.

It is God's task. The most important task for you is whatever he calls and directs you to do. Every element, every place, every act of service, and every witness is important and is service to him. It is not his plan that you avoid being a part of his mission now, only to serve at some later time and place.

As a believer in the Lord Jesus Christ, you do have a part in carrying out his mission here and now, and he includes all of his children in his call to participate in his mission. The question is clear: "Is anyone else coming?" What are the ways in which you give a resounding affirmative answer to that question? May you clearly sense God's purpose for you in the mission of God for this season of your life!

Discussion Points

1. How are you responding to the question, "Is anyone else coming?"

2. What experiences and opportunities has God brought into your life to equip you to be used by him in his mission?

3. Of all that you know about God's mission in the world today, what most interests you?

4. Of the training, gifts, and abilities you have, what have you seen God use to express his love to others?

5. Which ways, or combination of ways, do you see God using you in days to come: going and telling, praying, giving, mobilizing, or equipping?

6. Reflect on your willingness to obey whatever God leads you to do. Share your thoughts with a faithful friend or family member.

Further Reading

Blackaby, Henry T., and Claude V. King. *Experiencing God*. Nashville: Broadman & Holman, 1994.

Blackaby, Henry T., and Avery T. Willis Jr. *On Mission with God*. Nashville: Broadman & Holman, 2002.

Piper, John. *Don't Waste Your Life*. Wheaton: Crossway, 2003.

Rankin, Jerry. *Empowering Kingdom Growth to the Ends of the Earth*. Richmond, VA: International Mission Board, 2005.

About the Contributors

Bryan Beyer is professor of Old Testament at Columbia International University Seminary and School of Missions, Columbia, South Carolina. He is the author of *Encountering the Book of Isaiah* (Baker Academic, 2007) and has co-written *Encountering the Old Testament,* 2nd edition (Baker Academic, 2008) and co-edited *Readings from the Ancient Near East: Primary Sources for Old Testament Study* (Baker Academic, 2002). He also writes regularly for LifeWay Christian Resources, and has ministered cross-culturally in Costa Rica, Germany, and Albania. He and his wife, Yvonne, have three adult children and four grandchildren.

Karen O'Dell Bullock enjoys the classroom best, having taught at the undergraduate, master, and doctoral levels for more than 25 years. She earned the M.Div. and Ph.D. degrees from Southwestern Baptist Theological Seminary, where she taught Christian history for 15 years and directed the Ph.D. program as associate dean. Since 2004, she has served the same roles at Dallas Baptist University (2004–2007) and the new B. H. Carroll Theological Institute in Arlington, Texas (2007–present). Fascinated about all areas of Christian heritage, she is especially passionate about missions, the persecuted church, Baptist history, and justice.

R. Bruce Carlton, his wife, Gloria, and two daughters, Elizabeth and Mary Margaret, lived and served in Asia for more than 20 years. They served in Hong Kong, Cambodia, India, and the subcontinent of South Asia. During his service in Asia, Bruce was involved in church planting and training church planters, focusing primarily on people groups with little or no Christian witness. Holding a D.Th. in missiology from the University of South Africa, he presently serves as an associate professor of missions at Boyce College in Louisville, Kentucky, and continues to train church planters internationally.

Gary R. Corwin currently serves as missiologist with the International Office of Serving in Mission (SIM). He is also associate editor and writes for the *Evangelical Missions Quarterly.* Gary has served since 1981 in leadership training in Ghana, in various staff roles with SIM's International Administration, and since 1994 in broader evangelical mission roles, including serving as editor of *EMQ* from 1997–2001. He has also held leadership roles with the Evangelical Missiological Society and holds graduate degrees from East Stroudsburg University, Trinity Evangelical Divinity School, and Northwestern University. He is widely published and is co-author with Scott Moreau and Gary McGee of a widely used missions text, *Introducing World Missions: A Biblical, Historical, and Practical Survey* (Baker Academic, 2004).

Don Dent has worked as an urban church planter, an unreached people group strategist, a regional leader, and an apprentice program director during almost 30 years in Asia. He earned an M.Div. from Golden Gate Baptist Theological Seminary and a D.Miss. from Malaysia Baptist Theological Seminary. Both of his adult children, Chesed and Rob, have served for two years overseas. Don and his wife, Anne, are transitioning back to the U.S. where he will direct the Kim School of Global Missions at Golden Gate.

Robert Edwards* was reared and educated in Lebanon and started in the business world early on in his career. In 1978, he relocated to Athens, Greece, where he managed a multimillion-dollar trading company. Thereafter, he and his family moved to Cyprus, where Robert managed the work of WVI for the Middle East and Southern Europe. For the past 13 years, he has provided logistical support to mission organizations in several countries. He presently acts as the CEO for a charity organization with projects and personnel in more than 20 countries.

Nathan Evans* has been a local and regional administrator for non-profit organizations in the U.S. and overseas for 25 years. He has lived and worked overseas with unreached people groups and mission agency personnel for the past 16 years. Most recently he led a group of umbrella services for 400 missionaries and their families, which included medical coordination, member care, and MK (missionary kid) education. Evans loves biblical pastoral counseling and helping disciples be the body of Christ to one another. He and his wife, K, have four children.

David Garrison is a veteran of global missions and is a pioneer in the understanding of church-planting movements. For five years Garrison served as the Southern Baptist International Mission Board's associate vice president for global strategy. He has also directed IMB work in South Asia, in Northern Africa and the Middle East, and in Central and Eastern Europe. He earned a Ph.D. in historical theology from the University of Chicago. Garrison's books include *The Nonresidential Missionary* (MARC, 1990), *Something New Under the Sun* (IMB, 1998), and more recently, *Church Planting Movements: How God Is Redeeming a Lost World* (WIGTake, 2004).

H. Al Gilbert is executive director of the Love Loud initiative at the North American Mission Board. He and his wife, KK, have four grown children and 11 grandchildren. Gilbert and KK have had the privilege of traveling and seeing God's hand at work in many places around the world. Love Loud connects mercy ministries with missional living, and connects the people of God with the people of the world.

Kevin Greeson is a native of South Texas. He received degrees from the University of Mary Hardin-Baylor and Southwestern Baptist Theological Seminary. Greeson and his family served as missionaries in Bangladesh (1994–2002).

During this time, Kevin was instrumental in establishing five church-planting movements among Muslims. Today, each of these movements claims more than 2,000 Muslim background believers and scores of churches. Kevin is the author of *The Camel: How Muslims Are Coming to Faith in Christ!* (Wigtake Resources, 2007), and continues to serve as a missionary in South Asia with the International Mission Board, SBC.

Jim Haney serves as director of the Global Research Department of the International Mission Board. From 1981 to 1995 he was a church planter in Nigeria. In 1995, Haney moved to Accra and established the Evangelism and Mission Board of the Ghana Baptist Convention. He served with his wife, Donna, and they have been married for 34 years. They have two grown children, Heather and Rachel.

Scott Holste is the International Mission Board's vice president of global strategic mobilization, an initiative that works with Christian leaders in business and marketplace professions around the world. Previously he served in the IMB's office of global strategy and oversaw global research. Holste, who holds a Ph.D. in organizational leadership, began working with the IMB in 1987. He and his wife, Janie, have three sons and three grandsons.

R. Alton James has served since 2002 as associate professor of missions at Southeastern Baptist Theological Seminary in Wake Forest, North Carolina. Previously he served with his wife, Cathy, with the International Mission Board for approximately 10 years in South Asia and Southeast Asia. He served as a strategy coordinator for an unreached people group and seminary professor before assuming the role of strategy leader for the Filipino people group. Al and Cathy have four children, Emily, Angie, Elizabeth, and Chris, as well as four grandchildren. He holds the M.Div. and Th.D. from New Orleans Baptist Theological Seminary.

William J. Larkin Jr. (Ph.D., University of Durham) is professor of New Testament and Greek at Columbia International University Seminary and School of Missions. He is author of *Culture and Biblical Hermeneutics* (1988, 2003), *Acts* (IVP New Testament Commentary, 1995), *Acts* (Cornerstone Biblical Commentary, 2006), and co-editor and contributor to *Mission in the New Testament: An Evangelical Approach* (1998). He is an ordained minister in the Presbyterian Church in America. He is married to Edna, and they have two grown children.

Jeff Lewis has been a mobilizer for 25 years through a variety of ministry positions, and served as a consultant both nationally and internationally. Jeff is currently assistant professor of intercultural studies at California Baptist University in Riverside, California. He also ministers as a church planter and teaching elder with Fortysixten Fellowships in north county San Diego, and works with the U.S.

Center for World Missions and Perspectives International. Jeff is author of *God's Heart for the Nations*. Jeff holds a B.A. from the University of Tennessee and an M.Div. from Southwestern Baptist Theological Seminary. Jeff and his wife, Elaine, live in Escondido, California, and have seven children and 10 grandchildren.

Christopher R. Little has eighteen years of cross-cultural experience in which he has sought to advance God's mission in Kenya, Europe, the Asian sub-continent, Mozambique, and Jordan. Presently, he is professor of intercultural studies at Columbia International University where he equips others for Christian mission. He is the author of *The Revelation of God Among the Unevangelized: An Evangelical Appraisal and Missiological Contribution to the Debate* and *Mission in the Way of Paul: Biblical Mission for the Church in the Twenty-First Century*, as well as numerous articles in various journals. He holds a Ph.D. from Fuller Theological Seminary.

Alex Luc has taught at Columbia International University Seminary and School of Ministry, Columbia, South Carolina, since 1982. As a linguist he draws from his understanding of intercultural issues and comparative religions. Dr. Luc has contributed to *The New International Dictionary of Old Testament Theology and Exegesis*, and has published two books and many articles on Old Testament studies. He holds a Ph.D. from the University of Wisconsin and an M.Div. from Trinity Evangelical Divinity School. He has also taught at the Theological College of Vietnam and served as a pastor of the Chinese Christian Alliance Church in Saigon.

Stan May is chairman and professor of the department of missions at Mid-America Theological Seminary. Before joining Mid-America in 1997, he served as youth minister in three Tennessee churches, as pastor of two Arkansas churches, and as a missionary with the International Mission Board to Zimbabwe in Southern Africa. He holds a degree in history from Union University, and both the M.Div. and Ph.D. from Mid-America.

Clyde Meador has served as executive vice president of the International Mission Board since 2003. He and his wife, Elaine, were appointed as career missionaries in 1974. Clyde served as general evangelist, theological teacher, and mission administrator in Indonesia until 1989. He served in leadership for Southern Asia and Pacific region, and was regional leader for Central and Southern Asia. He holds a Ph.D. of ministry from Southwestern Baptist Theological Seminary, and an M.Div. from Midwestern Baptist Theological Seminary.

A. Scott Moreau (D.Miss.) is professor of intercultural studies and missions at Wheaton College, where he has taught for 18 years after a decade of missionary service in Africa with Campus Crusade for Christ. He also is the editor of *Evangelical Missions Quarterly* and managing editor of the Network for Strategic Missions KnowledgeBase, an online collection of over 18,000 articles on mission (www.strategicnetwork.org). His academic interests include contextualization, intercultural communication, trends in missions, folk religions, and spiritual conflict.

Kurt Nelson is a graduate of the University of North Carolina, Chapel Hill, where his involvement with IVCF led him to Urbana 76 and a call to missions. A graduate of Dallas Theological Seminary (Th.M. in missions) and Columbia International University (D.Min. in missions), Kurt serves as the executive vice president of East-West Ministries International. He and his wife, Pat, have nine children, three of whom they adopted from Russia, and three grandsons.

Howard Norrish was born in India of missionary parents. He was mainly educated in England and has a doctorate in organic chemistry from Cambridge University. He has been involved in the Arab world for the last forty-plus years with Operation Mobilisation. He has been a door-to-door salesman, a student worker, a professor of biochemistry in an Arabian medical school, and, finally, a consultant advising and supporting others into an effective ministry in the Arab world and the wider Muslim world. He is married with three children and seven grandchildren.

Meg Page* and her husband went to Asia in 1975 with their two daughters, where they served in various locations and roles for twenty-seven years with the International Mission Board of the Southern Baptist Convention. Meg continues to facilitate the ministry of women missionaries through encouragement, prayer mobilization, and leadership training. She is co-editor of the book *A Worldview Approach to Ministry Among Muslim Women*.

John Piper was pastor for preaching and vision at New Bethlehem Baptist Church in the Twin Cities of Minnesota. He studied at Wheaton College, Fuller Theological Seminary and the University of Munich (D.Th.). He is the author of more than 40 books. His preaching and teaching is available at desiringGod.org. He and his wife, Noel, have four sons, one daughter, and 12 grandchildren.

Robert L. Plummer is associate professor of New Testament interpretation at The Southern Baptist Theological Seminary and an elder at Sojourn Community Church, Louisville, Kentucky. He is the author of numerous articles and two books, *Paul's Understanding of the Church's Mission* (Paternoster, 2006) and *40 Questions About Interpreting the Bible* (Kregel, 2010). Dr. Plummer is married to Chandi. They have three daughters: Sarah Beth, Chloe, and Anabelle.

Zane Pratt is dean of the Billy Graham School of Missions and Evangelism. He served as a church planter and pastor in New England and as an Army Reserve chaplain before appointment with the International Mission Board in 1991. During his service with the IMB, he and his wife, Catherine, lived and worked in Central Asia until 2011, the last 10 years in leadership. He and Catherine have two children, Charlotte and Greg. He has a B.A. in religion and history from Duke University and an M.Div. from Gordon-Conwell Theological Seminary. His is currently pursuing Ph.D. studies in missiology at Southeastern Baptist Theological Seminary.

Jerry Rankin retired in 2010 after 40 years of service with the Southern Baptist International Mission Board. Rankin and his wife, Bobbye, served in South and Southeast Asia for 23 years; they lived in Thailand, Singapore, Indonesia and India. For the last 17 years before retirement, Rankin served as president of the IMB, which sends and supports more than 5,000 missionaries in 190 countries. Rankin now provides consultation for mission agencies and conducts seminars on spiritual warfare. He is adjunct professor of missions at Mississippi College and is director of the Zwemer Center for Muslim Studies at Columbia International University. He is the author of eight books on missions, spiritual warfare and devotional topics.

Nik Ripken* and his wife, Ruth, are mission veterans, having served 28 years in Malawi, South Africa, Kenya, Somalia, Ethiopia and Germany. As mission strategists in Northern Africa and the Middle East, they have specific responsibilities for witness and church planting in the context of persecution. Ripken is the author of numerous articles on missions and, along with Ruth, has done extensive interviews and research in regard to bold witness and church planting among followers of Christ who live in environments framed by persecution. He holds a doctorate of ministry from The Southern Baptist Theological Seminary in Louisville, Kentucky. Nik and Ruth are the parents of three sons: Jeremy, Benjamin, and Jesse.

Tom Steffen served 20 years with New Tribes Mission, 15 of those in the Philippines. He is professor of intercultural studies in the School of Intercultural Studies at Biola University in La Mirada, California, where he directs the Doctor of Missiology program. He has authored *Encountering Missionary Life and Times* (with Lois McKinney Douglas), *Great Commission Companies: The Emerging Role of Business in Missions* (with Steve Rundle), *Passing the Baton: Church Planting That Empowers,* and *Reconnecting God's Story to Ministry: Crosscultural Storytelling at Home and Abroad.*

Ed Stetzer has planted churches and transitioned declining churches. He has also trained pastors and church planters internationally. He is a columnist for *Outreach Magazine* and *Catalyst Monthly,* and is frequently cited or interviewed in news outlets such as USA Today and CNN. He is visiting professor of research and missiology at Trinity Evangelical Divinity School and visiting professor at Southeastern Baptist Theological Seminary. He also serves on the Church Services Team at the International Mission Board. His primary role is president of LifeWay Research and LifeWay's Missiologist in Residence.

John Mark Terry received his master of divinity and doctor of philosophy in missions at Southwestern Baptist Seminary. He and his wife, Barbara, served with the International Mission Board in the Philippines for 14 years. He also served as academic dean of Clear Creek Baptist College and as professor of missions and associate dean of the Billy Graham School of Missions and Evangelism at The Southern Baptist Theological Seminary. He is the author of *Evangelism: A Concise History* and the editor of *Missiology: An Introduction*. He currently teaches at a seminary in the Pacific Rim. The Terrys have two grown children.

LaNette W. Thompson and her husband, Marvin, were appointed in 1985 to IMB Connecting, serving in West Africa in various positions of church planting and leadership. They pioneered the use of Chronological Bible Storying in their region and have trained numerous cross-cultural workers and African church leaders in its use. LaNette's writings include *Sharing the Message Through Storying* and her master's thesis from the University of Texas at Arlington, *The Nonliterate and the Transfer of Knowledge in West Africa*. In August 2011, LaNette began the Ph.D. program in educational psychology at Baylor University.

Preben Vang is married to Liselotte; they have two grown children. After receiving his Ph.D. from Southwestern Baptist Theological Seminary in New Testament studies, he went back to his native Denmark to pastor. He returned to the U.S. with his family in 1997 to begin a teaching career. He is presently professor and chair of the Department of Biblical and Theological Studies at Palm Beach Atlantic University. Still passionate about the church, he has focused some of his academic research on the global aspects of the Christian faith and has continued to pastor local churches in a bi-vocational capacity. He has published with Baker Books, InterVarsity Press, and B&H publishers.

Joel F. Williams received his graduate training in New Testament studies at Dallas Theological Seminary (Th.M.) and Marquette University (Ph.D.). Since 1993, he has taught in the area of biblical studies at Columbia International University, Columbia, South Carolina. Along with William J. Larkin Jr., he co-edited the volume *Mission in the New Testament: An Evangelical Approach* (Orbis, 1998). He and his wife, Becky, have three children: Anna, Matthew, and Luke.

Christopher J. H. Wright was born in Belfast, Northern Ireland. His doctorate from Cambridge is in Old Testament ethics. He taught in India 1983–1988, and then at All Nations Christian College, a mission training college in England, where he was principal from 1993–2001. He is now the international director of the Langham Partnership International, which provides literature, scholarships, and preaching training for Majority World pastors and seminaries. He is also chair of the Lausanne Theology Working Group. His books include *Old Testament Ethics for the People of God* and *The Mission of God*. Chris and his wife, Liz, have four adult children and several grandchildren, and live in London.

William "Rick" Yount is assistant dean and professor of foundations of education at Southwestern Baptist Theological Seminary, Fort Worth, Texas. Since 1981, he has taught educational psychology, principles of teaching, cross-cultural discipleship, and research and statistics. He has made annual teaching trips to the former Soviet Union since 1996: Ukraine, Kyrgyzstan, Kazakhstan, and Russia. He has authored or co-authored *Created to Learn* (1996), *Called to Teach* (1999), *Called to Reach* (2007), and *Teaching Ministry of the Church* (1st and 2nd ed.). He and Barb Parish married in 1969. They have two married children, Bonnie and Chris, and granddaughter Madilyne.

*Denotes pseudonyms used for security purposes by individuals who work in countries whose governments may be hostile to the gospel message.

Subject Index

Abraham, 11, 20-21, 25, 39, 41, 43-44, 47, 88-91, 100-102, 115-16, 132-33, 323
accommodation, 237
Acts 29 (training), 509-13
AD 2000 and Beyond, 297, 301
affinity bloc(s), 299, 313
Afghanistan, 177, 225-26, 229, 232, 329
Africa(n), 176-77, 194, 202, 277, 282-83, 327, 330, 333, 377, 382-83, 391, 401-2, 409, 410, 471, 461-62, 481, 483, 489, 537, 555
    North Africa, 174, 181, 208-11, 243, 561, 563, 569, 571
    South Africa, 297, 527
    sub-Saharan Africa, 336, 564
    West Africa, 177, 282, 284, 299, 394, 405, 554, 563
agricultural, 164, 270, 415
agriculture, 278, 563
AIDS, 246-47
Algeria, 459
allegiance, 37, 75, 222, 380, 381-82, 387-88
Allen, Roland, 291
Alopen, 226
Anabaptist(s), 254-56, 265
Anderson, Rufus, 277, 291
angels, 87, 93, 114, 124, 352
animism, 320
anthropology, 378-80, 390
apostolic, 165-66, 205-6, 214, 216, 218, 220, 226, 259, 265, 311, 359, 361, 363, 367-68, 522, 534
apostolos, 356-58
American, 155-56, 174-77, 180-83, 225, 277, 279, 291, 293, 299, 347, 363, 383-84, 387, 389, 400-403, 412, 415, 418, 436, 439-40, 444, 447-48, 462, 482, 486-87, 526, 558
    American church, 307, 485, 492, 586
    colonies, 264
    Latin American, 330, 409-10, 455, 479, 528

Native American(s), 267-68
    South American, 615
Arabic, 227, 242-43, 272, 275
Armenia, 194, 202, 208, 222, 273
Asia, 61, 173, 221, 226-34, 244, 272-73, 277, 299, 321, 330, 333, 336, 410, 433, 455, 471, 482-84, 498, 500, 509-10, 513, 537, 559, 563-64, 578, 606, 610
Asia Minor, 190-91, 196-99, 202-3, 206-7, 209, 211-12, 220, 222
Asian, 130, 279, 291, 313-14, 340, 409, 452, 455, 488, 500, 506
Assyria(n), 90, 118, 120, 124, 229
atheist, 183
audio recording, 397
Augustine, 598
Australia, 346
awakening(s), 264, 268, 271, 278-79, 459, 602, 604-5
baptism, 44, 54, 136, 138, 143, 235, 238, 255, 283, 333, 408, 429, 437, 548
behavior, 165, 171, 238 ,258, 239, 379-80, 382-84, 386-88, 403, 444, 456, 595
belief(s), 258, 312, 320, 383, 387, 393-94, 408, 414, 486, 566, 614
Benedictine, 239
Bible, 22-24, 31, 33-46, 123-27, 159-60, 334-35, 391-405, 408-11
bicultural, 360, 386
bilingual, 386
bishop, 213, 217-18
blessing for all peoples/ nations, 20, 24-25, 29, 39, 41, 43, 47, 89-90, 101-3, 374
Boniface, 239-41, 598
Bosch, David, 18, 30, 66
Brainerd, David, 265, 267-68, 271
Brazil, 33, 237, 253, 312, 525
bridges, 243, 292, 386, 411, 420, 422, 424, 428, 431, 438, 475, 554, 576

Britain, 208, 210, 213, 238, 242, 275
Buddhism, 226, 244
Buddhist, 228, 244-45, 312, 332, 347, 364, 421, 427, 511, 537, 561, 563
Burma, 427, 559, 560
Burns, William, 274-76, 280
Bush, Luis, 299, 301
business as mission (BAM), 231, 300, 518-23, 526, 528, 529-34
business professionals, 523, 538, 604, 606
Byzantine, 224
Calvin, John, 251, 253, 598
Cambridge, 33, 271, 523
Carey, William, 12, 71, 252, 264, 268-71, 279, 467-68, 558, 603
Carthage, 208, 214
caste, 260, 292, 413, 470, 561
Celtic, 213, 237-39
Central Asia, 190, 196-98, 202, 221, 226-32, 563
children of God, 53, 346, 399
China, 105, 181, 183, 226-33, 237, 243-44, 268, 274-76, 279-81, 291, 314, 345, 373, 412, 488, 537, 561-62, 567-68, 594
China Inland Mission, 280, 291
Chinese, 226, 237, 243-45, 274-76, 280-81, 291, 296, 313, 412-13, 561-62, 567
Christ-centered, 93
Christ-followers, 22-23, 103, 105, 153, 285, 302, 608
Chronological Bible Storying (CBS), 261, 302, 392-93, 396-403, 404, 411, 563
Church Planting Progress Indicators (CPPI) database, 317
church-growth movement, 144
church-planting movement, 58, 144, 256, 261, 298, 302-3, 311, 328, 332-34, 337-38, 367, 429, 432, 451, 453, 455, 465, 472, 474, 476-80, 498, 501, 509-10, 512-13, 515, 565

civil war, 545
Clement, 201, 212
cognitive, 137, 394-95, 444
colonialism, 278, 288, 292,
    485, 488, 526
Columba, 237-39
communication, 146-47, 228,
    252, 277, 334, 341, 378,
    380, 404, 420-22, 425-26,
    434, 458, 586
Communism, 292, 538, 547
compassion, 78, 180, 284,
    373, 495, 605, 608, 614
compassionate character, 373
confession, 159, 256, 318,
    352, 409, 433, 462, 539
conquered, 11, 221, 227-28,
    243, 351
Constantine, 206, 208, 211,
    224-25, 235
contextualization, 320, 406-33,
    481, 486, 489, 496, 498
Coptic, 209
covenant, 36, 39, 47, 101-2,
    117, 146-47, 263, 294, 326,
    430, 476-77, 491, 548
creative access, 300, 348, 492,
    517-19, 523, 525, 572
credibility, 139, 506, 513, 615
cross-cultural, 29, 139-41,
    172-73, 192, 243, 285, 288,
    295-96, 300, 307, 361, 373,
    385, 388, 398, 407, 413,
    426-28, 436, 438, 468, 489,
    522-23, 549
Crusades, 242, 451-52
c-scale, 426
cultural diversity, 293
culture shock, 437
Cyrene, 190, 221, 321, 588
Daniel, 92, 118, 119, 168, 559
Danish-Halle mission,
    260-61
database (research), 297-99,
    311, 317, 472, 527
David, King, 44-45, 90, 107,
    116-23, 127, 164, 395-96,
    448
demons, 93, 103, 106, 344, 503
denomination, 248-59, 265,
    277-80, 289, 348, 374, 416,
    453, 484, 593-94
dependency, 265, 279, 605
descendants, 25, 251
devotion, 60, 65, 148, 151-52,

176, 235, 242, 248, 417
Diaspora, 221
Didache, 212
Diocletian, 208, 210, 211
disciple-making, 105, 131,
    134, 141, 259, 436, 602
disciples of all nations, 11, 26,
    45, 53, 66, 94, 99, 102-5,
    131-32, 174, 177, 270,
    323-24, 328, 365, 371
discipleship chains, 477
discipline, 63, 167, 217, 248,
    276, 401, 408
discipling, 23, 25-26, 276,
    290, 415, 436-37, 448-50,
    453, 476, 481, 511
disease, 103, 106, 130, 177,
    282, 336, 433, 496, 521
Dober, John Leonard, 524,
    526
Dominicans, 252
dreams, 288, 417, 549, 560,
    578, 601
Dutch, 252-53, 269
East India Company, 260,
    271
Edessa, 196, 206, 208,
    214-15, 225
Edict of Milan, 208, 211, 235
Edwards, Jonathan, 75, 269
Egypt, 89-90, 92, 124, 142,
    190-91, 203, 209, 211, 221,
    278, 545
Elamites, 190, 221
Eliot, John, 265, 267
An Enquiry (by William
    Carey), 264
enterprise, 72, 79-80, 83, 131,
    134, 258, 437, 479, 490,
    521, 524, 529
entrepreneur, 295, 518, 522,
    528, 557, 574
equipper, 26-27, 307, 436,
    619-20
e-scale, 295, 468-69
Escobar, Samuel, 479-80
Ethiopia, 192, 194-95, 203,
    237, 282, 289
ethne, 132, 296-97, 344
ethnicity, 86, 326, 458, 470,
    603-5
ethnologue database, 297
ethnocentrism, 288, 361, 386
Europe, 173, 198, 214,
    220-21, 231-32, 237, 240,

242, 251-52, 260, 267, 277,
    283, 330, 344, 418, 526,
    537, 558, 606-7
European, 72, 155, 233, 239,
    256, 261, 268, 438
Eusebius, 189, 196, 201, 209,
    212, 214
evaluative, 478
evangelize, 209, 212-13, 230,
    238, 241, 270, 284-85, 293,
    319, 343, 365, 367, 381,
    436, 470, 528, 544
Evangelical Fellowship of
    Mission Agencies (EFMA),
    174
Evangelical Missiological
    Society (EMS), 529
evangelization, 12, 96, 213,
    231, 293-95, 301, 378, 468,
    472, 487, 527, 600, 603
evil, 24, 59, 73, 92, 103, 134,
    148, 184, 342, 350, 403,
    540-42
evil one, 346, 372, 594, 617
excluded middle, 417
exodus, 20-21, 37, 501
expansion, 190-91, 205-7,
    211, 214, 217, 251, 261, 265,
    267, 285, 287-88, 291, 304,
    334, 469, 485-86, 498, 503,
    518, 526, 539, 588
face-to-face, 512, 605
faith and culture, 345, 408,
    486, 489
felt needs, 261, 265, 320
Finney, Charles, 279
France, 202-3, 237, 253, 278,
    329
Franciscan, 252
Francke, A. H., 258, 260, 262
French, 237, 269, 400, 570,
    575
Friar John, 244
Frontiers (agency), 176, 300,
    311, 476
Gaul, 202-3, 208, 210-11
Genghis Khan, 228
genocide, 288
Gentiles, 19, 25, 36, 40, 44,
    46-47, 50, 52, 58, 81, 92,
    95, 102, 107, 162, 173, 178,
    192, 193-94, 197, 221, 371,
    539, 588, 612
Germany, 18, 239-41, 251,
    256-57, 262, 268

Ghana, 278
Global Consultations on World Evangelization (GCOWE), 301, 527
Global South, 155-57, 338
globalization, 526
God of the universe, 70, 72, 85-86, 91, 94, 114, 120, 132, 142, 396, 412
God-centered, 75-76, 81, 569, 576, 578, 580-82, 583
God-fearers, 61, 207, 361
God's call, 47, 59, 82, 88-90, 149, 164, 177-80, 248, 285, 297, 323, 331, 349, 387, 555, 557-58, 560, 563-67, 572, 589, 616, 620-21
God's plan, 11, 21, 53, 139, 144, 152, 240, 310, 332, 341, 366, 393, 501-5, 530, 538, 602
Graham, Billy, 293, 487
Great Century, 267-85
Great Commandment, 72
Great Commission, 99, 105, 140, 144, 197, 255, 296, 349, 587, 589
Great Commission Christians (GCCs), 301, 319
Gregory Thaumaturgos, 213, 215
Guatemala, 467
Halle University, 258-59, 260
Haystack Prayer Meeting, 268
healing, 52, 57, 93, 94, 117, 179, 399, 494, 581
Henry, Carl, 293
herald, 163, 519, 612
Hesselgrave, David, 475
Hiebert, Paul, 379, 413, 426
Hindu(s), 174, 269-70, 296, 312, 332, 347, 421, 537, 561, 563
holism, 383, 484, 490-95
holistic, 93, 97, 218, 335, 337-38, 382, 396, 426, 491, 493-94, 531
homogeneous, 467, 479
Hong Kong, 274-75
house church(es), 206, 214-15, 235, 250, 255-56, 259, 276, 366, 273, 452, 455, 460, 484, 509, 511-13, 517-19, 548, 594

house of prayer, 53, 371
household, 20, 43, 89, 112, 167, 192, 193, 215, 490, 559, 588
humility, 126, 135, 137, 428
hunger, 103, 158, 173, 181, 336, 494
identification, 539-40
idolatry, 150-51
Ignatius, 236, 598
illegal, 131, 207, 224, 519
illiterate, 302, 555, 564
impassionate character, 373
imperial, 194, 202
incarnational, 179, 259, 413
India, 12, 71, 192, 196, 203, 206, 212, 225-29, 237, 244-47, 260-61, 264, 268-69, 270-72, 284, 290, 292, 329, 332, 451-52, 455-57, 482, 486-88, 500, 512, 537, 558-61, 603, 610
indigenous, 27, 261, 277, 291-92, 368, 415-18, 455, 458, 470-71, 483, 487, 498, 509, 550, 562-63
individualism, 153, 372, 384
Indonesia, 183, 284, 327, 340, 406, 484
Injil, 429
insider, 388, 428, 458, 549
insider movements, 429
International Congress on World Evangelization, 293, 468
International Mission Board (IMB), 13, 15, 68, 175-76, 298, 301, 311-20, 331-32, 335, 337, 349, 392, 398, 401, 438, 473-76, 505, 511
Iran, 203, 229, 232, 272
Iraq, 176-77, 181, 184, 229, 232
Irenaeus of Lyons, 213
Islam, 225-28, 243, 272, 283-84, 337, 365, 393, 538, 544
Japan, 237, 244, 329, 537
Jerusalem pattern, 586-91
Jesuits, 236-37, 252-53
JESUS film, 302, 411
Jesus movement, 27-28
Jewish Christians, 189-91, 194-98, 206, 588-89
Jewish culture, 11, 173,

197-98
Jews, 25, 47, 52, 58, 102-3, 107-8, 127, 162-63, 165, 170, 178, 190-99, 201, 207, 209, 212, 221, 225, 242, 255, 312, 360-61, 381, 422-23, 504, 586, 588, 590-91
Johnstone, Patrick, 289, 297, 313, 472
Joshua Project, 298, 311, 313, 472
Judson, Adoniram, and Ann, 427, 558-59
Justin Martyr, 216
Kenya, 298
kingdom business, 521, 528-30, 533
Korea(n), 175, 488, 537, 561-62
Kyrgyzstan, 229
laity, 255, 266, 533
Latin America, 130, 320, 330, 333, 409, 455, 471, 483, 528, 537
Lausanne Congress, 293-303, 334, 378, 398, 430, 468-72, 491, 527, 529
Lausanne Covenant, 294, 430, 491
least reached, 292, 297, 300, 302, 468, 492
Lebanon, 175
literacy, 261, 335, 392, 402, 564
Ludwig von Zinzendorf, 262-64, 598
Lull, Raymond, 241-43
Luther, Martin, 168, 251, 254, 256-57, 262, 595, 598
Majority World, 320, 415, 484
Malaysia, 237, 278
managerial missiology, 479
marketplace, 17, 231, 382, 520-22, 528, 532, 615
marketplacer, 302
Marshman, Joshua, 270
Martyn, Henry, 271, 279
martyr(s), 154-56, 173, 176, 179-80, 211-16, 235, 255, 345, 536-38, 550
martyrdom, 194-95, 201, 216, 292, 536, 542, 547, 549, 587
McGavran, Donald, 12, 290-93, 296, 302, 378, 460, 467-68, 481-82, 484, 486-87, 490

Medes, 190, 221

merchants, 229-33

Mesopotamia, 37, 190, 194, 196, 202, 208, 210, 221-22, 225-28, 232

missiology, 17, 277, 436, 468, 479, 523, 535, 542, 544, 549

missionary societies, 216, 560-61

mobilization, 172, 219, 288, 297, 468, 482, 525, 602, 604, 605

mobilizer, 525, 619

"Model, Assist, Watch and Leave" (MAWL), 507

money, 60, 142, 253-54, 279-81, 386, 391, 481-87, 542, 556, 561, 603, 619

Mongolia(n), 228

monks, 231-32, 236-38

Montgomery, Helen Barrett, 374

Moody, D. L., 279, 426

Moravian Brethren, 262-64, 268, 279, 521-23

Morocco, 538

Mother Teresa, 245-47

mother tongue, 402, 404

multiplication, 28, 104, 303, 332, 366, 455-58, 464, 498, 503, 518, 520-21, 528, 531, 562

generation(s), 498-99, 506-7, 515

Muslim background believer, 321, 391

Muslims, 174, 241-43, 272, 283-84, 300, 312, 332, 347, 384, 420, 423, 425-26, 432, 459, 474, 537, 544, 561

mystical, 242, 410

myths, mythic, 37, 408-11

nationalism, 288, 292, 538

Nestorians, 222-23, 228-30

Netherlands, 239

networks, networking, networker, 248, 297, 300-301, 314, 320, 329, 398, 477, 527, 531, 565, 598, 604, 607

Nevius, John, 291, 481

NGO (non-governmental organization), 302,

Nigeria, 282, 436

OneStory, 335, 402, 554-55, 564

Operation Mobilization, 175, 482

Operation World (database), 297-98, 312, 472

orality, 302, 334, 392, 396-98, 401-4

Origen, 212-17

Orthodox Church, 223, 537

Padilla, René, 293-94

Pakistan, 196, 420

Parthians, 190, 221, 226

partnership(s), 15, 139, 291, 301, 329, 335, 361, 402, 479, 487, 491, 509, 527, 566, 607

passion of/for God/Christ, 28, 45, 69, 72, 75-79, 82, 112, 171, 173-74, 177-79, 183-84, 231, 245, 262, 269, 277, 285, 366, 508, 510, 520, 619

Patrick of Ireland, 598

Pentecost, 108, 146-47, 150, 155-56, 190-91, 194, 200, 209, 221, 232, 314, 325, 393, 454, 586-87, 597

people blindness, 296, 303, 378

people clusters, 313

people movements, 292, 302, 459-60, 467

people-to-people, 25, 605

Perpetua, 214, 556

persecution, 56, 173, 181, 194-95, 208, 211, 214, 216-18, 224, 226, 229-33, 235, 255, 276, 345-46, 348, 352, 356, 360, 368, 372-73, 429, 455, 457, 493, 504, 513-14, 520, 535-52, 587-88, 594, 617-18

Persian(s), 118, 221-22, 224-29, 272-73, 607

Philippines, 176, 538

Pietist, 256-58, 262

pioneers, 250, 268-69, 277, 279, 523

platforms, 509, 517-19, 523-27, 529-33

Portugal, 237, 525

poverty, 236, 292, 521, 524, 605

prioritism, 481, 490-91, 495

proclamation, 50, 107-8, 126-27, 131, 134, 148, 169, 172, 200, 260, 279, 292, 335, 336-38, 459, 491, 495-96, 598

providence, 13, 173, 181, 184, 228, 344, 389

radio, 302, 335

reconciliation, 95, 294, 490, 495, 502

relief work, 216, 485, 492-93, 527

repentance, 38, 51, 57, 64, 107-8, 135, 163, 168, 178, 215, 400, 506, 509, 611-12

Ricci, Matteo, 243-45

Roman Empire, 191, 194, 202-10, 213, 217-18, 221-22, 224, 235, 371

rural, 209-11, 213-14, 329-30, 332, 406, 418, 512

Russia, 175, 192, 407, 438, 440, 442, 444, 445, 447

sacrifice, 81, 114, 172, 176-78, 183, 208, 236, 247, 329, 352-53, 364, 396, 410, 429, 496, 590, 608, 617

Samaria, 56-57, 94, 111-12, 127, 191-92, 194-95, 548, 585, 588-89, 599

Saudi Arabia, 546

senders, 156, 602-3

sent ones 26, 603

Serampore Trio, 270-71

short-term mission(s) (STM), 52, 104, 300, 360-61, 549, 607

short-term worker, 302

Siemens, Ruth, 300, 525-27

Slessor, Mary, 281-83

sovereignty, 87-91, 251, 344, 452

Soviet Union, 175, 181, 297, 344, 443, 448, 511, 577

sowing God's Word, 160-61, 215, 239

Spain, 59-60, 173, 199, 201, 203, 206, 208, 210, 237, 242, 345, 525

Spener, Philip, 256-58, 262, 266, 598

spiritual conflict, 87, 343, 353

spiritual warfare, 87, 270, 340, 350-52, 539-40, 548, 551

statistics, 310, 314, 321, 482, 492

Stott, John, 19, 81, 293

Student Volunteer Missions Movement (SVMM), 283-84

supremacy of God, 36, 68, 72, 77, 79, 82

syncretism, 311, 320, 424

Syria, 120, 193, 194-95, 202-3, 211, 222, 225

Tamerlane, 228

Taylor, James Hudson, 275, 279, 281, 291

team(s), 105, 255, 281, 331, 335, 372, 402, 435, 476-79, 562, 580-81

10/40 Window, 299, 300, 301, 302, 479, 530, 533

tentmaker(s), 61, 264, 270, 277, 285, 300, 523-25, 527-28

terrorist, 175, 179, 181, 183, 365

Tertullian, 179, 210, 373, 594, 598

Thaddeus, 206, 214-15

Thailand, 334, 347, 398

theological education by extension (TEE), 467

three-self method, 277, 291

tower of Babel, 88, 100-101, 146, 156, 400, 402

Townsend, Cameron, 291, 296

training, 26, 31, 34, 50, 61, 166, 174-75, 177-78, 215, 235-38, 248, 257, 261, 283, 319, 327, 332, 335, 340, 356, 366, 392, 398, 415, 420, 432, 435-36, 443, 448, 474, 486, 499-500, 505-13, 523, 527, 532, 549, 561-63, 573, 601, 607, 610, 614, 618

T4T (Training for Trainers), 505-8, 511

transformation, 22, 167, 267, 268-70, 388, 393, 414, 420, 491, 521, 530

tribal, 282, 356, 372

Ukraine, 196, 203, 435, 438, 443

unengaged, 314, 319-20, 322, 328-29, 338

unengaged unreached people groups (UUPG), 319

unevangelized, 33, 241, 285, 290, 343

universal, 131, 218, 245, 278

universalism, 289

universality, 42, 407

unreached people groups (UPG), 139, 250, 297, 314-19, 321, 324, 326, 328-29, 334-35, 344, 348, 355, 365, 367, 372, 399, 511, 554, 607

urban, 206, 210, 213, 312, 314, 329-32, 338, 557

urbanization, 329-30

Uzbekistan, 225

Venn, Henry, 277, 291

vernacular, 277

Vietnam, 183

Waffle, 327, 338

Ward, William, 270

Wesley, John, 264, 269, 271, 521, 598

Whitfield, George, 269, 598

Wilder, Robert C., 284

Wilson, J. Christy, 300, 524

Winter, Ralph, 12, 277, 288, 295-96, 301, 303, 377-78, 467-68, 483, 522

women on mission, 214, 241, 280-83, 302, 524, 528

World Christian Database (Encyclopedia), 311, 472

World Council of Churches, 406

worldview, 379-90, 392-96, 398-99, 402-3, 407

Wycliffe Bible Translators, 291, 298, 313, 335, 472-73, 525

Youth With A Mission (YWAM), 335

Ziegenbalg, Bartholomäus, 260

Zinzendorf, Nicolas Ludwig von, 262-64, 598

Zoroastrianism, 226-27

Zwemer, Samuel, 283-84

Scripture Index

Genesis
1, *41*
1–11, *100*
1:1-31, *159*
1:1–2:4, *120*
1:3, *86, 159*
1:26-28, *87*
1:28, *42, 100*
2:8, *87*
2:15, *42*
3, *150*
3:15, *87, 91, 95,*
   115
4, *88*
10, *43, 100*
11:4, *100*
11:6-9, *146*
11:7, *88*
12:1-3, *20, 41, 43,*
   88, 115, 128,
   133, 519
12:2-3, *101*
12:3, *25, 116,*
   323, 374
14:23, *89*
15:1, *160*
15:1-6, *115*
15:4, *160*
17:1-22, *115*
18:1-15, *115*
18:19, *43*
21:1-5, *115*
22:15-18, *115*
26:1-5, *115*
26:18-22, *89*
26:23-24, *115*
28, *393*
28:12-15, *115*
30:27, *89*
35:11-12, *115*
39:5, *89*
45:7-8, *87*
45:9, *87*
50:20, *89*

Exodus
3, *142*
3:8, *89*
3:12, *89*
4–12, *89*
4:21, *90*
9:13, *21*
9:13-16, *21*

9:20-21, *160*
12:12, *90*
12:46, *124*
15:2, *124*
15:11, *121*
15:14-16, *21*
15:18, *90*
18:17-21, *501*
19:4-6, *44*
19:5-6, *90*
19:16-19, *146*

Leviticus
4:3, *122*
19:2, *90*

Numbers
3:16, *160*
3:51, *160*
11, *502*
11:23, *160*
11:29, *502*
15:31, *160*
24:13, *160*
36:5, *160*

Deuteronomy
1:36, *445*
4:5-8, *101*
4:6-8, *44*
4:35, *42*
4:39, *42*
5:5, *160*
6:4, *42*
9:5, *160*
18:15-19, *116*
18:22, *160*
31:21, *88*
32:8, *90*
34:5, *160*

Joshua
8:27, *160*
14:6-14, *445*

1 Samuel
3:1, *160*
8:5, *90*
8:7, *90*
10:10, *160*
12:20-22, *73*
15:10, *160*
16:1-13, *119*

2 Samuel
5:17-25, *116*
7, *116*
7:2, *116*
7:3, *116*
7:8-16, *122*
7:12-13, *116*
7:12-16, *90*
7:14, *160*
7:14-16, *116*
7:23, *73, 101*
8, *116*
24:11, *160*

1 Kings
6:11, *160*
8:41-43, *44*
13:1-9, *160*
19:11-12, *146*
19:15-16, *122*

2 Kings
2:11, *146*
18:29, *87*

1 Chronicles
17:14, *90*

2 Chronicles
7:14, *371*
26:16-21, *119*

Ezra
1:3, *87*
3:2, *116*

Job
1:8-9, *91*
26:14, *71*

Ecclesiastes
1:9, *501*

Isaiah
2:1-4, *127*
2:3, *108*
4:2, *119*
6:1-8, *92*
6:9-13, *160*
7:1-9, *120*
7:10-12, *120*
7:14, *120*
9, *120*

9:1-2, *94, 101*
9:6, *121*
9:6-7, *122*
9:7, *92*
10:21, *121*
11, *121*
11:1-10, *122, 127*
11:6-9, *92*
14:11-14, *343*
19:19-25, *44*
19:25, *92*
24:21, *92*
25:1, *121*
29:14, *121*
32:1-4, *122*
37:35-37, *124*
40–66, *117*
40:25-26, *71*
42:1, *44, 106*
42:1-4, *117, 122*
42:6, *145*
43:6-7, *73*
43:9-13, *42*
43:10-12, *45*
44:6-20, *42*
44:28, *122*
45:1, *122*
45:17, *124*
45:22, *117, 124*
45:23, *42*
48, *21*
48:9-11, *22*
49:3, *73, 92*
49:6, *45, 46, 92,*
   94, 95, 101, 371,
   612
52:13–53:12, *117,*
   122, 127
53, *92*
55:10-11, *160*
56:2-8, *44*
56:7, *371*
61, *494*
61:1, *122*
61:1-2, *93, 117,*
   118
64:4, *79*
66:19, *117*
66:19-21, *44*

Jeremiah
2:13, *75*
4:1-2, *44*

10:1-16, *42*
13:11, *73*
20:7-9, *160*
23:5, *119*
23:5-6, *118*
23:29, *160*
33:15, *119*
33:15-18, *118*

Lamentations
1:9, *121*

Ezekiel
5:5, *101*
18:23, *509*
18:32, *509*
20:14, *73*
37, *147*

Daniel
4:3, *92*
7, *118*
7:9-14, *123*
7:13, *118*
7:13-14, *118*
12:6, *121*

Amos
3:3, *439*
9:11-12, *44*
9:12, *44*

Micah
5:2, *119*

Habakkuk
2:14, *74, 133,*
   343, 464

Haggai
2:20-23, *116*

Zechariah
2:10-11, *44*
3, *119*
3:8, *119*
6:9-13, *119*
6:12-13, *119*
7:13, *440*

Malachi
1:11, *102*
1:14, *92*

Matthew
1:1, *116, 123*
1:18-23, *120*
1:22, *142*
1:23, *94, 104*
2:1-12, *52*
2:3-6, *119*
2:13-20, *545*
3:2, *103*
4:10, *540*
4:17, *93, 103, 127*
4:19, *52*
4:23, *51*
5–7, *105, 236*
5:10-11, *551*
5:11, *540*
5:12, *551*
5:13-16, *53*
5:14, *94*
5:15, *74*
5:16, *492, 493*
5:44, *540*
6:9-10, *374*
6:9-13, *375*
7:24-25, *125*
8:5-13, *52*
8:17, *117*
8:28-34, *52*
9:12-13, *51*
9:13, *79*
9:36-38, *78*
9:37-38, *608*
10, *432, 493*
10:1-42, *52*
10:5-6, *52*
10:6, *495*
10:9-10, *423*
10:16, *106*
10:17-23, *540*
10:22, *539*
10:23, *52*
10:24-25, *54*
10:25, *104*
11:2-6, *51*
11:6, *541*
11:28-30, *54, 80*
12:15-21, *53*
12:18-21, *117*
12:28, *93*
13:1-23, *161*
13:19, *93, 378*
13:23, *378*
14–28, *103*
15:21-28, *52*
15:24, *52, 495*

16:18, *539*
16:21, *51, 126*
16:23, *540*
16:24, *54, 179, 373*
16:27-28, *93*
19:23, *81*
20, *51*
20:28, *495*
22:37, *25*
22:37-39, *449*
22:39, *25*
23:34, *540*
24:9-10, *541*
24:10, *541*
24:11, *168*
24:14, *53, 93, 96, 111, 344, 349*
24:24, *168*
24:31, *53*
25, *493*
25:21, *79*
25:23, *79*
25:32, *53*
25:40, *247, 493*
25:46, *75, 495*
26:13, *53*
26:31, *541*
26:56, *127*
26:64, *119*
27:54, *52*
27:56, *555*
27:61, *555*
28, *28*
28:1, *323, 555*
28:10, *555*
28:16-20, *39*
28:18, *103, 112*
28:18-19, *94*
28:18-20, *17, 26, 45, 53, 102, 124, 127, 131, 371, 502*
28:19, *99, 259, 344, 601*
28:19-20, *54, 144, 436, 519*
28:20, *112*

Mark
1, *51*
1:13, *540*
1:14, *50*
1:15, *93*
1:17, *52*

1:38-39, *50*
2:17, *51*
3:13-19, *52*
3:14, *502*
3:15, *503*
4:1-20, *161*
4:15, *540*
4:19, *161*
4:20, *161*
4:33, *401*
5:1-20, *52*
6:7-13, *52*
7:24-30, *52*
7:31-37, *52*
8:31, *51, 538*
8:33, *540*
8:34, *557*
8:38, *125*
9:29, *371*
9:31, *538*
9:37, *81*
10:32-34, *538*
10:45, *51, 79, 155, 386, 495*
11:17, *53, 371*
11:24, *371*
13:9-13, *539*
13:10, *53*
13:27, *53*
13:31, *161*
14:9, *53*
14:28, *53*
15:39, *52*
16:9-20, *106*
16:15, *99, 105, 127*

Luke
1:32-33, *117*
1:78-79, *145*
2:11, *124*
2:29-32, *44*
3:34, *116*
4:1-13, *540*
4:5-7, *346*
4:16-21, *51*
4:16-30, *118*
4:18, *93*
4:18-19, *494*
4:22-30, *53*
4:43, *50, 93*
5:1, *125*
5:10, *52*
5:27-30, *422*
5:31-32, *51*

6, *503*
6:12-16, *52*
6:13, *357*
6:47-48, *161*
7:1-10, *52*
7:18-22, *148*
7:18-23, *51*
8:1-3, *556*
8:4-15, *161*
8:12, *346*
9, *503*
9:1-6, *52, 432*
9:22, *51*
9:54, *588*
10, *196, 503*
10:1-16, *52*
10:1-24, *432*
10:2, *617*
10:4, *423*
10:5, *431*
10:38, *556*
11:1, *444*
11:20, *93*
11:49, *539, 540*
12:4-5, *495*
13:28-30, *53*
13:33, *51*
14:26-33, *104*
17:21, *93*
17:25, *51*
19:10, *51, 495*
21:12, *540*
21:12-19, *539*
22:3, *540*
22:31, *540*
22:37, *51, 117*
22:39-44, *126*
22:42, *126*
23:47, *52*
24:6-7, *51*
24:26, *51*
24:44-46, *51*
24:45-47, *99*
24:45-48, *45*
24:45-49, *54*
24:46-47, *38*
24:46-48, *204*
24:46-49, *107, 127*
24:49, *112*

John
1:1, *31, 115*
1:1-3, *125*
1:1-18, *128*

1:14, *31, 125, 464, 495*
1:29, *124*
1:36, *124*
2:11, *495*
2:19-21, *119*
3:1-8, *93*
3:3, *387*
3:5, *387*
3:7, *387, 452*
3:16, *25*
3:17, *101*
3:34, *125*
4:9, *191*
4:26, *431*
4:34, *126, 387*
4:42, *101*
4:54, *495*
5:19, *109, 346*
5:23-24, *110*
5:24, *125*
5:30, *112, 126*
5:36, *110*
5:38, *110, 125*
6:15, *127*
6:38, *110, 112*
7:18, *74*
7:29, *110*
7:31, *495*
8:12, *94*
8:31, *104*
8:31-32, *551*
8:32, *125*
8:40, *125*
8:47, *125*
10:10, *540*
10:16, *53*
10:30, *109*
10:38, *109*
11:27, *556*
11:52, *53*
12:20-22, *52*
12:27-28, *74*
12:38, *117*
12:44-45, *110*
13:2, *540*
13:27, *540*
13:35, *104*
14:6, *178*
14:10, *109, 112*
14:24, *125*
15:5-8, *104*
15:8, *452, 464*
15:11, *79*
15:18-21, *540*

...v, 106, 345
16:2-3, 180
16:8, 421
16:14, 74
16:33, 345
17, 110, 371
17:1, 74
17:3, 128
17:4, 112, 126, 515
17:6, 515
17:6-19, 500
17:8, 125
17:13, 79
17:13-18, 102
17:14, 125
17:15, 372
17:18, 494
17:20, 500
17:26, 79
19:36, 124
20:21, 55, 94, 95, 127
20:21-22, 109
20:21-23, 94
20:30, 495
20:31, 439

Acts
1:1, 125, 454
1:3, 99, 127
1:6, 111, 127
1:7-8, 112
1:8, 26, 28, 45, 54, 94, 111, 112, 127, 192, 196, 502, 585
1:14, 371
1:15-26, 357
1:21, 163
2, 108, 151, 189, 325
2–5, 191
2:2, 146
2:5, 108, 146
2:5-11, 190
2:6-11, 222
2:9-11, 190
2:10, 191
2:10-11, 209
2:17, 146
2:21, 190
2:41, 161
2:42, 151
2:42-47, 146

2:44-45, 152
2:47, 56
3:21-24, 116
4:4, 125, 161
4:12, 178
4:19-20, 520
4:23-31, 371
4:25-26, 181
4:29, 125, 161
4:31, 125, 161
4:36, 358
5:1-10, 152
5:3, 540
5:14, 56
5:31, 124
5:41-42, 552
6, 145, 154, 162, 583, 586
6:2, 161, 572
6:3-4, 572
6:4, 161, 370, 371
6:7, 56, 161, 162, 164, 573, 587
6:8, 573
7–8, 587
7:3, 163
7:4, 163
7:7, 163
7:54-60, 550
8, 192, 589
8:1, 540
8:1-4, 542
8:4, 161, 213
8:5-12, 94
8:12, 127
8:14, 161, 588
8:14-17, 192
8:25, 159, 161, 588
8:26-40, 192
8:27, 360
8:32-33, 117
9:1-19, 193
9:4, 454
9:4-5, 540
9:16, 83, 372
9:19-30, 504
9:26-30, 193
9:31, 56
10:1–11:18, 192
10:23, 163
10:34-35, 588
10:36, 159, 161
10:37, 161
10:44, 161

11, 194
11:1, 161
11:19, 161, 194, 542
11:19-20, 588
11:19-26, 504
11:20, 360
11:24, 56
11:25, 163
11:25-26, 193
11:26, 225
11:27-30, 485
12, 162, 485
12:1-5, 371
12:17, 195
12:24, 56, 161, 162, 164
13:1, 504
13:1-3, 504
13:2, 358
13:2-3, 371
13:4, 197
13:5, 161
13:7, 161
13:44, 159, 161
13:46, 161
13:47, 46, 58, 95
13:48, 161
13:49, 59, 161
13:50, 540
14, 358, 397
14:3, 161
14:15, 398
14:19-22, 442
14:21-23, 62, 368
14:22, 95, 127
14:23, 62, 442
14:25, 161
15, 44, 195, 197, 204, 588
15:5, 361
15:7, 161
15:9, 193
15:9-11, 197
15:16-18, 44
15:23-29, 590
15:28-29, 198
15:35, 161
15:36, 161
15:36-40, 505
15:39, 358
15:40–18:22, 198
16, 215
16:1, 163
16:5, 56

16:6, 161
16:6-10, 61
16:14-15, 556
16:30, 124
16:32, 161
17, 61, 422
17:1-10, 60
17:6-7, 198
17:11, 161
17:13, 161
17:16, 388
17:16-18, 381
17:16-34, 381
17:18, 386
17:22, 386
17:23, 424
17:25, 79
17:28, 386
18:1-3, 518
18:1-4, 190, 556
18:2, 191
18:3, 264, 300
18:11, 161
18:19, 163
18:23, 199
18:24, 163, 191
18:24-26, 556
18:26, 518
19, 162
19:1, 191
19:8, 127
19:9, 145
19:10, 59, 161
19:20, 56, 161, 162, 164
19:23-40, 199, 204
20:15, 163
20:24, 58
20:25, 127
20:28, 63, 446
20:28-32, 168
20:32, 62, 161
20:33-35, 62
21–28, 200
21:7, 163
21:17-24, 591
22:7-8, 540
25:13, 163
26:11, 541
26:14, 463
26:14-15, 540
26:17-18, 58
26:18, 341
26:22-23, 40

28:23, 127
28:30-31, 112, 201
28:31, 127

Romans
1, 201
1:1, 367
1:1-5, 58
1:5, 81, 82
1:8, 486
1:11-12, 61
1:14, 173
1:15, 60
1:16, 28, 59, 61, 158, 162, 164, 367
1:16-17, 309
1:18, 75
1:23, 75
3:11, 135
3:21-26, 58
3:21-30, 58
3:21-31, 168
3:23, 75
4:17, 160
5:1, 121
5:3, 551
5:3-4, 542
6:3-7, 136
7:21, 148
8:3-4, 62
8:9, 112
8:12-14, 63
8:13, 137
8:17, 550
8:18, 541
8:18-27, 39
8:22, 146
8:28-30, 161
8:29, 163
8:30, 163
8:33-39, 551
8:35-39, 83, 551
9–11, 39
10:1, 371
10:9, 124
10:9-10, 58
10:16, 117
11:36, 74
12, 583
12:1-2, 126
12:2, 125
12:5, 454
14:17, 95

15, *345*
15:7-16, *44*
15:8-9, *77, 78*
15:14, *364*
15:15-16, *58*
15:18, *64*
15:19, *59, 200*
15:19-20, *367*
15:20, *60, 196, 362*
15:20-21, *60, 617*
15:21, *117, 173*
15:22, *60*
15:24, *201*
15:25-27, *485*
16:1-2, *556*
16:3-4, *556*
16:3-5, *58*
16:5, *518*
16:6, *556*
16:7, *359*
16:12, *556*
16:19, *486*
16:20, *95*

1 Corinthians
1:2, *165*
1:12, *170*
1:17-25, *163, 164*
1:21, *145*
1:23-25, *59*
2:2, *169*
2:4-5, *62*
3:4-6, *359*
3:5-9, *58, 60*
3:6, *550*
3:6-7, *438, 612*
3:7, *164*
3:7-9, *60*
3:9-10, *362*
3:10, *60*
3:10-15, *58, 60*
3:16, *153*
3:16-17, *119*
3:22, *359*
4:6-9, *359*
4:15, *164*
4:16, *363*
5:1-13, *63*
5:7, *124*
5:13, *153*
6:1-6, *63*
6:19-20, *132*
7:5, *540*
7:15, *163*

8:5-6, *42*
9:1-2, *357*
9:1-18, *62*
9:5, *196, 556*
9:11-12, *164*
9:12, *164*
9:15-18, *485*
9:16, *58*
9:20-22, *423*
9:22, *62*
10:31, *74*
11:1, *104, 515*
11:16, *165*
11:20-34, *145*
12, *152*
12–14, *141*
12:12, *454*
12:27, *454*
12:28, *361, 583*
14:8, *276*
14:26, *58*
14:33, *165*
14:36, *163*
15:1-2, *166*
15:1-8, *58*
15:3-4, *159*
15:3-8, *596*
15:3-11, *168*
15:6, *503*
15:7, *357, 358*
15:8, *195*
15:10, *196*
15:24, *95*
15:32, *178*
16:1-4, *63*
16:19, *58, 518*

2 Corinthians
1:3-11, *542*
1:5, *539*
1:12, *363*
1:15–2:1, *61*
2:5-11, *63*
2:14-16, *63, 580*
2:17, *60, 485*
4:1-6, *59*
4:1-7, *64*
4:2, *485*
4:4, *340*
4:5, *386*
4:8-9, *551*
4:8-11, *551*
4:17-18, *541*
5:14, *173*
5:14-21, *128*

5:17, *39*
5:19-20, *95*
8–9, *165*
8:1-15, *63*
8:18-20, *63*
8:23, *360*
9:7, *63*
10:3-5, *551*
10:14, *163*
10:16, *60, 173*
11:23-25, *520*
11:23-28, *154*
11:28, *58*
11:32-33, *193*
12:7-10, *64*
13:5, *168*

Galatians
1:8-10, *168*
1:13, *541*
1:15-16, *58*
1:17, *193*
1:19, *357*
1:23, *541*
2:4, *361*
2:11-14, *197*
2:14-21, *58*
3:1-5, *62*
3:6-8, *39*
3:8, *101*
3:14, *62*
3:16, *101, 116*
3:28, *214*
4:4, *207*
4:4-5, *115*
5:13, *198*
5:16-25, *62*
5:22, *439*
5:22-23, *137, 452*

Ephesians
1, *153*
1:4, *153*
1:4-6, *73*
1:11, *153, 555*
2:1-3, *75*
2:8, *351*
2:8-10, *58*
2:10, *620*
2:11–3:6, *44*
2:19-21, *119*
2:20, *362*
3:1-6, *58*
3:6, *454*
3:7-12, *58*

3:8, *19*
3:10, *19*
3:20-21, *28*
4, *477, 583*
4:9-13, *26*
4:11, *59, 361, 362*
4:11-16, *58, 140, 435*
4:12, *454*
4:17-32, *137*
4:18, *75*
5:18-21, *63*
5:23, *454*
6:10-13, *342, 350*
6:10-18, *350*
6:10-20, *551*
6:12, *540*
6:15, *59*
6:18-20, *618*
6:19-20, *59*

Philippians
1:3-5, *59*
1:6, *62*
1:12-14, *346*
1:12-18, *59*
1:14, *159*
1:27, *59, 62*
1:29, *539*
2:1-4, *63*
2:5-8, *120, 126*
2:7, *104*
2:7-8, *173*
2:9-11, *42*
2:10, *519*
2:10-11, *81*
2:11, *124*
2:13, *62*
2:16, *59*
2:24, *201*
2:25, *360*
3:2-11, *168*
3:17, *165, 363*
4:2-3, *556*
4:3, *59*
4:9, *363*
4:10-20, *62*

Colossians
1:3-8, *59*
1:4-7, *164*
1:6, *28, 251, 304*
1:7, *199*
1:13, *104*
1:13-18, *102*

1:16-17, *120*
1:24, *454*
1:27, *464*
1:28-29, *58, 387*
3:1-4, *541, 550*
3:5-11, *137*
3:12-14, *137*
3:12-17, *580*
3:15, *454*
3:16, *165*
4:2-4, *59, 371*
4:15, *58, 556*
4:16, *199*

1 Thessalonians
1:2-8, *580*
1:5, *163*
1:6, *159, 165*
1:6-8, *165, 486*
1:8, *59, 159, 165*
1:9-10, *199*
2:2, *60, 364*
2:6, *359*
2:9, *60, 62, 364*
2:13-14, *165*
2:13-16, *164*
2:14-16, *165*
2:18, *540*
3:3-4, *540*
5:12-13, *63*

2 Thessalonians
1:4-5, *95, 542*
1:5, *551*
1:6, *551*
1:7-10, *551*
1:9, *75*
3:1, *59, 106, 159, 165*
3:1-2, *59*
3:7-9, *165*
3:9, *363*

1 Timothy
1:3, *201*
2:4, *323, 509*
4:16, *168*
5:15, *540*

2 Timothy
1:8, *535, 539*
1:11-12, *612*
2:1-2, *202*
2:2, *446, 500, 514*
2:8-9, *164*

3:1, *106*
3:10-11, *515*
3:11, *551*
3:12, *539*
3:14, *515*
4:13, *201*
4:16, *201*
4:20, *201*

Titus
1:5, *201*
1:6-8, *167*
1:9, *167*
2:6, *444*

Philemon
2, *206*
4-6, *168*
12-14, *63*
23, *199*

Hebrews
1:1-2, *114*
1:3, *101*
1:4-14, *114*

1:10-12, *121*
2:10, *542*
3:1-6, *114*
4:14–5:10, *114*
5:8-9, *126*
5:8-10, *542*
5:11–6:2, *114*
7, *114*
7:22-25, *118*
8, *114*
9, *114*
10, *114*
10:7, *126*
10:31, *495*
11, *397*
11:26, *551*
11:38, *273*
12:1, *550*
12:2, *126, 172,*
   550
12:3, *550*

James
1:2, *183*
1:2-4, *551*

1:3, *542*
1:12, *551*
1:19, *440*
1 Peter
1:1, *196*
1:6-7, *542*
1:22-23, *580*
1:25, *159*
2:12, *74, 493*
2:21, *172*
2:22, *117*
4:11, *74*
4:12, *542*
4:14, *539*
5:1, *182*
5:3, *165*
5:8, *540*
5:8-9, *341*

2 Peter
3:9, *509, 611*

1 John
1:1-3, *125*
2:27, *122*

3:8, *342*
4:14, *101*
3 John
6-7, *81*
7, *82*

Revelation
1:2, *125*
1:9, *125, 539, 550*
1:11, *203*
4-5, *123*
5:1, *123*
5:2-4, *123*
5:5, *123*
5:9, *78, 133*
5:9-10, *20, 96,*
   123, 203
7:9, *43, 102, 310,*
   419
7:9-10, *64, 133,*
   323
7:17, *124*
11:15, *96*
12:7-9, *352*
12:9, *445, 540*

12:10, *96, 352*
12:11, *106, 124,*
   176, 352
13:14, *352*
14:1-4, *124*
14:11, *75*
15:3-4, *83*
15:4, *64*
17:14, *96*
19, *125*
19:11-16, *118*
19:13, *125*
19:16, *96*
20:1-2, *321*
20:1-3, *342*
20:4, *125*
20:6, *123*
20:10, *75, 96*
20:11-15, *495*
20:13-15, *96*
21:8, *75*
21:23, *75*
22:3-5, *96*
22:5, *87*
22:20, *96*